UMI ANNUAL COMMENTARY

PRECEPTS FOR LIVING®

MISSION STATEMENT

*W*e are called
of God to create, produce, and distribute
quality Christian education products;
to deliver exemplary customer service;
and to provide quality Christian
educational services, which will empower
God's people, especially within the Black
community, to evangelize, disciple,
and equip people for serving Christ,
His kingdom, and church.

Urban Ministries, Inc.
The African American Christian Publishing
& Communications Co.

i

UMI ANNUAL SUNDAY SCHOOL LESSON COMMENTARY
PRECEPTS FOR LIVING® 2019–2020
INTERNATIONAL SUNDAY SCHOOL LESSONS
VOLUME 22
UMI (URBAN MINISTRIES, INC.)

Melvin Banks Sr., LittD, Founder and Chairman

C. Jeffrey Wright, JD, CEO

Cheryl Price, PhD, Vice President of Content

Bible art: Fred Carter

Scripture quotations marked NLT are taken from the Holy Bible, New Living Translation, copyright © 1996, 2004, 2007, 2013, 2015 by Tyndale House Foundation. Used by permission of Tyndale House Publishers, Inc., Carol Stream, Illinois 60188.

Unless otherwise indicated, Scripture references are taken from the King James Version of the Bible.

Item No.: 1-2020. ISBN-13: 978-1-68353-344-3.

PFL Large Print Item No.: 1-2620. ISBN-13: 978-1-68353-348-1

Publisher: UMI (Urban Ministries, Inc.), Chicago, IL 60643. To place an order, call us at 1-800-860-8642,

or visit our website at www.urbanministries.com.

Get the Precepts for Living® eBook!

Are you among those reading books using a Kindle, iPad, NOOK, or other electronic reader? If so, there's good news for you! UMI (Urban Ministries, Inc.) is keeping up with the latest technology by publishing its annual Sunday School commentary, *Precepts for Living®*, in the leading eBook formats: Kindle (Amazon), NOOK (Barnes & Noble), and iBooks (Apple).

To buy an eBook copy of *Precepts for Living®*, visit our website at urbanministries.com/precepts to find download links and step-by-step instructions.

If you've purchased *Precepts for Living®*, for your e-reader, be sure to leave a rating and a review at the iTunes or Amazon store sites to tell others what you think. Also, spread the word on your favorite social networking sites, and follow *Precepts for Living®* on Facebook @ facebook.com/urbanministriesinc, @umichicago on Twitter, and @umi on Instagram.

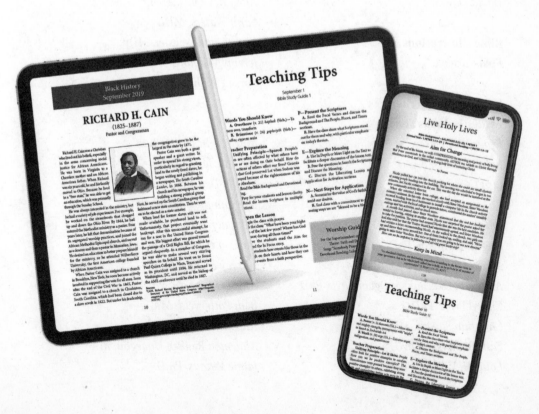

CONTRIBUTORS

Editor
Adonijah Okechukwu Ogbonnaya, PhD

Developmental Editor
Beth Potterveld, MA

Copy Editors
William McGee
Daschell Phillips
Jordan Taylor

Cover Design
David Dawkins

Bible Illustrations
Fred Carter

Contributing Writers
Essays/In Focus Stories
Evangeline Carey
Kelvin Childs, BA
Lisa Crayton
Rukeia Draw-Hood, PhD
Judith St. Clair Hull, PhD
Angela Lampkin, PhD
Marvin A. McMickle, PhD
Adonijah Okechukwu Ogbonnaya, PhD
Cheryl Price, PhD
Christian Savage, MDiv
Faith Waters, MDiv
Louis H. Wilson, PhD

Bible Study Guide Writers
Heaven Berhane, MDiv
Felicia Chinyere, PhD
Christian Savage, MDiv
Jaimie Crumley, MDiv
Malcolm Foley, MDiv
Kimberly Gillespie, MA
Harvey Kwiyani, PhD
Angela Lampkin, PhD
Beverly Moore, MS
Joshua Mitchell, DMin
Allen Reynolds, MDiv
Faith Waters, MDiv
Charmaine Webster, MDiv
Jeremy Williams, MDiv
Porsha Williams, MDiv

More Light on the Text
Melanie Jones, PhD
Cecilia Dennery, PhD
Bertram Melbourne, PhD
J. Ayodeji Adewuya, PhD
Moussa et Assita Coulibaly, PhD
Harvey Kwiyani, PhD
Angela Lampkin, PhD
Beth Potterveld, MA
Allen Reynolds, MDiv
Alajemba Reuben Unaegbu, MA
Jamie Viands, Ph.D.

Dear Precepts Customer,

It is our privilege to present the 2019–2020 *Precepts for Living*®. As you encounter God's Word through these lessons, we anticipate that you will find this resource to be indispensable. *Precepts for Living*® comes to you in four versions: the Personal Study Guide (the workbook), the eBook version, the large print edition, and the Pastor's Edition. You will also notice that the biblical text for each lesson includes the New Living Translation in addition to the King James Version. This contemporary translation will enhance your textual understanding when you compare it side by side to the classic English translation. It is very helpful in illuminating your understanding of the text.

Precepts for Living® is designed to be a witness through our learning and sharing more of the Bible. Our intent is to facilitate innovative ways of pursuing a deeper understanding and practice of God's Word. One of the ways we strive to do this is by highlighting the larger narrative of God's work in salvation as a key part of understanding each biblical passage. We believe it is important to help you understand not only the particulars of the text but also the broad extent of God's revelation to us. This panoramic approach enhances our ability to witness to others about the saving power of Jesus Christ.

This year we explore the themes of Faith, Worship, Justice, and Wisdom. Each year of Bible study offers great potential for a more intimate and transformative walk with God.

We want to continually refine *Precepts for Living*® as we endeavor to meet our customers' needs. We are always looking for ways to enhance your study of the Bible, and your comments and feedback are vital in helping us. If you have questions or suggestions, we encourage you to please email us at precepts@urbanministries.com or mail your comments to UMI, Precepts for Living®, PO Box 436987, Chicago, IL 60643-6987.

As you read and study this year's Precepts, join us in planning to celebrate, in 2020, UMI's 50th year anniversary.

May God draw you closer to the fullness of life with Him through this book.

God's blessings to you,

Adonijah Okechukwu Ogbonnaya

Adonijah Okechukwu Ogbonnaya, Advanced Teachers' Certificate, BA; Bible and Philosophy, MA Theological Studies, MA Religion, PhD Theology and Personality
Editor

Uncovering the Benefits of Precepts

It is a great privilege to participate in Christian education and play a significant role in the spiritual formation of fellow Christians in our churches. *Precepts for Living®* is a resource that is designed to help you lead others toward greater knowledge and practice of following Jesus Christ. To that end, please take full advantage of the substantive offerings provided to you in this year's commentary.

We want the liberating lesson to help you think about collective application and perspective beyond the individual level and the "Application for Activation" to help you think about personal ways to live out the lessons' themes and draw closer to God.

From the standpoint of your vocation as a teacher, it is very important to be aware of the great responsibility that goes along with your position. James 3:1 reminds us that we have such a great opportunity in front of us that we run the risk of greater judgment if we are derelict in our duties. In the Gospels, Jesus is often referred to as "Teacher." Being a teacher means participating in one of the church's greatest tasks, one that the ancient church called "*catechesis*."

This is a strong word that helps us understand the great influence we have when we help our students learn about God's Word. It carries with it the idea of imparting the entirety of the faith to Christians. While many teachers might not be familiar with this word, the truth is that every time we help others learn about God's Word and ways, we are participating in this great task of the church that has been with us from the beginning. Unfortunately, this gets lost amid other concerns. As a teacher, you have an opportunity to energize or revitalize this aspect of your church's ministry. Reflect on how you have prepared for the challenge.

What is the goal when you use *Precepts for Living®* to open up the riches of the Bible to your students? It is beyond the mere acquisition of information. We want students to receive revelation that becomes application. Certainly, we want our students to grow in knowledge, but the knowledge we seek to pass on does not solely comprise Bible facts but includes a larger sense of comprehension where the information and doctrine conveyed is oriented toward a faithful life of discipleship. That is why it is called *Precepts for Living®*, and not Precepts for Knowing.

The "People, Places, and Times," "Background," "In Depth," and "More Light on the Text" sections are there to help you provide insight and understanding of the text. But the sections include more than a simple compilation of information. In each lesson, you will also see "In Focus" stories and "Liberating Lesson" and "Application for Activation" sections serving as catalysts for applying the biblical text to life situations. It is very important that we as teachers pass on knowledge that will enable our students to deepen their devotion to God in an upward focus and encourage them to better embody that devotion in a way that makes their lives a living witness to the world. Our hope from every lesson should be to inspire students to become the best living examples of the Scriptures with the understanding that their lives may be the only Bible some people ever read.

To best take advantage of this commentary, utilize the essays to emphasize quarterly themes and enhance the classroom experience.

We believe this commentary is a great tool to help form fully devoted followers of Christ, and we invite you to wholeheartedly partake in all of the resources provided here. May God be glorified as you play your part in this great task of the church!

Creative Teaching

Updated Features
Precepts for Living® 2019-2020

Liberating Lesson Section

In each lesson, there is a "Liberating Lesson" to replace "Lesson In Our Society." This section is dedicated to highlighting parallels and/or applications to modern life that are reflected in the Bible. This section challenges us to consider how the scriptures relate to our modern society and asks us to respond individually, collectively, and as a community to God's Word. There is a special emphasis on social justice or justice implications in Christian Scripture that the Liberating Lesson brings to the forefront.

Application for Activation Section

In each lesson, there is an "Application for Activation" to replace "Make It Happen." This section provides guidance for practical application the reader or the local church could pursue in response to the lesson to take the lesson from information to living activation.

Teaching Tips Essays

Take advantage of our new Teaching Tips Essays, which give insight for engaging your class and helping your students grow each quarter. They are tailored for adult learners, but many of the concepts work for instructing other ages as well. Below are some additional tips for making your students effective disciples of Jesus.

More Tips for Teachers

• **Energizing the Class.** If the class does not seem enthusiastic or energy is low, after you open with prayer, have everyone stretch to the sky or outward. Then tell the class to shake off the low energy and open up their hands to receive the love of God that is right there. You can always have a 30-second meet and greet time. This usually helps to wake people up so you can begin class on a higher energy level.

• **Two Teachers in One Class—Bring Out the Best in Both.** Taking turns works in some classes, but in others it creates tension and favorites. Encourage teachers to study together, and then divide the segments of the lesson. Perhaps one will teach the introduction while the other teaches a section of the text. Encourage them to also become a true team with each contributing throughout the lesson.

• **Remember.** Everyone cannot read or write at the same level. Use different teaching techniques and styles when teaching. How you learn affects how you teach, so be open and willing to learn and teach through various media.

• **Avoid Study in Isolation.** People often "get it" when they are involved with more than talking about the lesson. Why not allow the class to see the connections themselves? Try using a chart to have adult students work in pairs or groups to compare and contrast Bible people such as David and Solomon or Ruth and Orpah, Naomi's daughters-in-law. To help the students get started, suggest specific categories for comparisons such as lifestyles, families, or public ministry. As class members search the Scriptures, they will learn and remember much more than if you told them about either person individually.

• **Group Studies.** Have the class form groups, and have each group read the Scripture lesson and a section of the Background for the text. Have each group create a two-minute skit about the Scripture to share with the class. Encourage the groups to use their imaginations and energy. You may want to have at least one "leader" in a group if you have more than two or three reserved people in your class.

• **Volunteers.** Many classes begin with reading the lesson. When class members have studied, this activity is more about "bringing minds" together than about the actual lesson. Still, some classes can benefit from dramatic and creative reading of Bible passages at any point in the lesson. When the passage under study lends itself, assign parts to volunteers. This need not be formal—standing up isn't even critical. This strategy works best in passages that have a story such as the conversation between Moses and his father-in-law, Jethro, or Paul confronting the merchants in Thessalonica. Assign one person to each speaking character in the Bible text. Feel free to be creative with giving the class roles as "the crowd." Make sure to assign a narrator who will read the nonspeaking parts. It is fun, it is fast, and it makes for memorable Bible reading.

• **Materials.** You may want to have large sheets of paper, markers, glue or tape, newspapers, and magazines available on a weekly basis for the various activities.

• **Additional Methods.** Write the theme on a large poster board or sheet of paper, and ask each person to write a word or draw a picture that best describes the theme. Read the themes aloud, and discuss any of the pictures before you begin your class discussion or activities. If you have a very large class or time is limited, only select a few words or pictures for discussion. You can either lead the discussion or invite members of the class to do so.

• **Websites.** Connect with us by logging onto www.urbanministries.com. Follow us on social media on Facebook at facebook.com/urbanministriesinc, @umichicago on Twitter, and @umi on Instagram.

• **Email us at precepts@urbanministries. com**, and send us some of your favorite Teaching Tips for ages 18 and older that you want to share with others. If yours is selected, we will post them under our Teaching Tips sections for Precepts. If you have ice-breaker activities, please submit them as well. Your submissions should be no longer than 125 words.

• **Closing.** At the end of the lesson, give your class the assignment of looking for scenes from films or television, advertisements, or parts of songs that either demonstrate the coming week's "In Focus" story, "Liberating Lesson" section, or "Application for Activation" section. Encourage them to be creative and to come up with an explanation of how their contribution helps make the truth of the lesson come to life.

• **Prayer.** Have a Prayer Request Board for people to write their prayer requests on each Sunday. You may want to make this a weekly activity. Have someone read the prayer request and let the class decide which prayer requests they will pray for during the week. One Sunday School teacher has his class write their prayer requests on sheets of paper and place them in the middle of the floor once a year. He then shares with the class that he will write them all down in a prayer journal that he keeps and will pray over them at least once a week. Be creative and create your own prayer journal or prayer tradition(s) within your class.

TABLE OF CONTENTS

Fall Quarter 2019

RESPONDING TO GOD'S GRACE

LESSONS
Unit 1: God Is Faithful
SEPTEMBER

Unit 2: Responses to God's Faithfulness
OCTOBER

Unit 3: Faith Leads to Holy Living
NOVEMBER

Winter Quarter 2019–2020

HONORING GOD

LESSONS
Unit 1: David Honors God
DECEMBER

Unit 2: Dedicating the Temple of God
JANUARY

Unit 3: Jesus Teaches about True Worship
FEBRUARY

2016–2022
SCOPE & SEQUENCE–CYCLE SPREAD

	FALL	WINTER	SPRING	SUMMER
1 YEAR 2016-17	**GOD: SOVEREIGNTY** **Sovereignty of God** Isaiah Matthew Hebrews Revelation	**CREATION** **Creation: A Divine Cycle** Psalms Luke Galatians	**LOVE** **God Loves Us** Psalms Joel Jonah John Romans Ephesians 1 John	**CALL** **God's Urgent Call** Exodus Judges Isaiah Jeremiah Ezekiel Amos Acts
2 YEAR 2017-18	**COVENANT** **Covenant with God** Genesis Exodus Numbers 1 & 2 Samuel Nehemiah Jeremiah Ezekiel 1 Corinthians Hebrews	**FAITH** **Faith in Action** Daniel Matthew Acts Ephesians Colossians 1 Timothy James	**WORSHIP** **Acknowledging God** Genesis Exodus Leviticus 2 Chronicles Psalms Luke John 2 Corinthians Hebrews Revelation	**JUSTICE** **Justice in the New Testament** Matthew Luke Romans 2 Corinthians Colossians
3 YEAR 2018-19	**CREATION** **God's World and God's People** Genesis	**LOVE** **Our Love for God** Exodus Deuteronomy Joshua Psalms Matthew Mark Luke Philippians 2 Thessalonians James 2 John	**CALL** **Discipleship and Mission** Matthew Luke Romans	**COVENANT** **Covenant in God** Ruth 1 Samuel Matthew Luke John Ephesians Hebrews Romans

2016–2022
SCOPE & SEQUENCE–CYCLE SPREAD

	FALL	WINTER	SPRING	SUMMER
4 YEAR 2019-20	**FAITH** **Responding to God's Grace** Genesis Exodus Numbers Deuteronomy 1 Samuel 1 Kings Luke 2 Corinthians 1 Thessalonians 1 & 2 Peter	**WORSHIP** **Honoring God** 1 & 2 Chronicles 1 Kings Ecclesiastes Matthew Luke	**JUSTICE** **Justice and the Prophets** Esther Isaiah Jeremiah Hosea Amos Micah Habakkuk Zephaniah Zachariah Malachi 1 Corinthians	**GOD–WISDOM** **Many Faces of Wisdom** Proverbs Ecclesiastes Matthew Mark Luke John James
5 YEAR 2020-21	**LOVE** **Love for One Another** Genesis 1 & 2 Samuel Luke John Acts 1 Corinthians James 1, 2, & 3 John	**CALL** **Call in the New Testament** Isaiah Matthew Mark Luke John Acts Romans 1 Corinthians Hebrews 2 Timothy	**COVENANT** **Prophets Faithful to God's Covenant** Deuteronomy Joshua 1 & 2 Kings Ezra Nehemiah Isaiah Jeremiah Lamentations Ezekiel Luke	**FAITH** **Confident Hope** Matthew Mark Luke Romans 2 Corinthians Hebrews 1 John
6 YEAR 2021-22	**WORSHIP** **Celebrating God** Exodus 2 Samuel Ecclesiastes Psalms Mark Luke Acts Revelation	**JUSTICE** **Justice, Law, History** Genesis Exodus Deuteronomy 2 Samuel 1 Kings Ezra Job Isaiah Nahum Luke	**GOD–LIBERATION** **God Frees and Redeems** Deuteronomy Ezra Matthew John Romans Galatians	**CREATION** **Partners in a News Creation** Isaiah John Revelation

Responding to God's Grace

The study this quarter focuses on God's gift of faith and how we respond to it both personally and communally. The sessions from the Old and New Testaments illuminate how God's grace impacts the lives of all believers, as demonstrated by their obedience, gratitude, and holy living.

UNIT 1 • God Is Faithful

This unit has five sessions that tell the story of God's faithfulness. In Genesis, God is faithful to Abraham by blessing his nephew Lot, and God is faithful in answering Hannah's prayer in 1 Samuel. In Exodus, God is faithful to the people of Israel by providing manna when they complain of hunger. In Numbers, Caleb and Joshua remind the Israelites of the faithfulness of God who hears their cries and forgives.

Lesson 1: September 1, 2019
Faith and Doubt
Genesis 19:1, 15–26, 29
People's lives are often affected by what others have done or are doing on their behalf. How do the actions of others affect our lives? Genesis says that God preserved Lot when Sodom was destroyed because of the righteousness of his uncle Abraham.

Lesson 2: September 8, 2019
God Answers Prayer
1 Samuel 1:9–20
People often feel that no one hears them when they express their deepest desires. Is anyone really listening? Hannah, who had no children, asked God for a son, promising to dedicate him to God's service, and soon she conceived and gave birth.

Lesson 3: September 15, 2019
Bread from Heaven
Exodus 16:1–8, 13–15
People are often unhappy with what they have in life. How can people be truly satisfied? Despite the complaining of the Israelites as they wandered in the wilderness, God provided meat and bread for them.

Lesson 4: September 22, 2019
God Hears Our Cry
Numbers 13:1–2, 17, 25–28; 14:1–2, 5–10
When life puts obstacles in our paths, we are tempted to abandon the promises the future holds. Why don't we believe the promises made to us? Caleb and Joshua believed that God would lead Israel to possession of the Promised Land and tried to persuade the people to trust God's faithfulness.

Lesson 5: September 29, 2019
God Forgives
Numbers 14:10–20
Everyone wrongs others, even those who love them and those whom they love. When we have done wrong, is forgiveness possible? According to Numbers, God forgave the rebelling people of Israel and promised to lead their descendants forward to the Promised Land.

UNIT 2 • Responses to God's Faithfulness

This unit has four sessions that explore reactions to the many benefits accrued to humans because of God's grace. Deuteronomy teaches that faith requires a response of obedience. The story of Elijah and the widow of Zarephath in 1 Kings shows that faithful obedience saves Elijah, the widow, and her son. Luke's Gospel tells about gratitude for God's faithfulness in the anointing of Jesus and the healing of the centurion's servant.

Lesson 6: October 6, 2019
Obedient Faith
Deuteronomy 4:1–8, 12–13

People desire and appreciate faithfulness in all of their relationships. How are we to respond to the faithfulness of others? Deuteronomy 4 and 5 set forth obedience as God's expectation of Israel in response to God's faithful deliverance.

Lesson 7: October 13, 2019
Blessed for Faithfulness
1 Kings 17:8–16

When people are denied the necessities of life, they may give up hope. What is the reward for faithful obedience in times of hardship? The widow of Zarephath faithfully ministered to God's prophet, and God miraculously provided for her throughout the time of famine.

Lesson 8: October 20, 2019
Faith Can Heal
Luke 7:1–10

People often have faith in others based on their good reputation. How does one demonstrate that trust? The centurion in Luke demonstrated his trust in Jesus' ability to heal by telling him just to speak a word.

Lesson 9: October 27, 2019
Faith Saves
Luke 6:37–48

People often respond to forgiveness with loving acts. What can we do to show gratitude to those who forgive us? In Luke, the sinful woman showed her gratitude to Jesus by washing his feet with her tears and anointing him with expensive oil.

UNIT 3 • Faith Leads to Holy Living

This unit has four sessions that examine letters to early churches that tell them how to live as faithful followers of Christ. 2 Corinthians tells the people to examine themselves to see if they are living in faith. 1 Thessalonians urges Christians to be positive examples of faith. 1 and 2 Peter teach that faith requires holy living and goodness.

Lesson 10: November 3, 2019
Self-Examination
2 Corinthians 13:1–11

People often set goals to achieve personal growth. What can we do to gauge our personal development? Following previous difficulties, Paul now forcibly reminds the Corinthians to examine themselves in comparison to God's standards for faithful living.

Lesson 11: November 10, 2019
Be Examples of Faith
1 Thessalonians 1:2–10

People often look for positive examples to emulate. How can we be positive examples? The Thessalonians were praised because they were positive examples to others, exhibiting strong faith and committing loving acts even in the midst of trials and persecution.

Lesson 12: November 17, 2019
Live Holy Lives
1 Peter 1:13–25

People admire and emulate those who live in accord with what they say. How can we put our beliefs into action? 1 Peter teaches believers that they must live holy lives and do good, loving deeds for others, thus demonstrating that they trust in God and have been born anew.

Lesson 13: November 24, 2019
Stick to Your Faith
2 Peter 1:1–15

People can be harmed by the corruption in the world. How can we guard against those negative influences? 2 Peter stresses the importance of supporting one's faith with goodness, knowledge, self-control, endurance, godliness, mutual affection, and love.

Effective Christianity: Avoiding Shortcuts to Maturity

by Lisa Crayton

Shortcuts work—sometimes. However, the shortest path to accomplishing a goal results in a dream deferred. Goal seekers abandon scholastic objectives, home improvement projects, and exercise programs each day because they take shortcuts that promise success but end in disaster. Similarly, spiritual shortcuts that appear to be fast tracks to growth and maturity are usually detour to destruction. These manifest as an overemphasis of works, self-confidence, personal gain, or abilities, but contrast with the Bible's teachings about grace, faith, service, and spiritual gifts. Jesus warned of spiritual shortcuts when He advised, "Enter ye in at the strait gate: for wide is the gate, and broad is the way, that leadeth to destruction, and many there be which go in thereat: Because strait is the gate, and narrow is the way, which leadeth unto life, and few there be that find it" (Matthew 7:13–14). Effective Christians seek that narrow way, embracing a covenant with God that lows to self and others.

An Enduring Covenant

A covenant is a fully enforceable, binding agreement. A form of legal contract, it affords privileges and responsibilities to each party. Knowing contract provisions makes it easier to adhere to them and avoid forfeiture of contractual promises. Ignorance, on the other hand, hinders a party's ability to fulfill contractual obligations and may result in forfeiture. Whether you're the policyholder or beneficiary, it is necessary for you to understand and adhere to the contracts to which you are a party.

Covenant with God

Christians can easily understand their rights and responsibilities by turning to a trusted source: the Bible. From it, we understand that recognizing one's sin nature is a necessary first step to making peace with God (Romans 5:1). Accepting, by faith, the atoning sacrifices of Jesus are the second step (Ephesians 2:8–9; 1 John 2:2). Conforming to biblical definitions of godly behavior is a third (Titus 2:11–12). It would be impossible to live such a life if not for the Jesus' godly example while on earth, who then sent the Holy Spirit to give us the power to do the same. Nonetheless, many try a spiritual shortcut around the third step. This attempt will be subtly encouraged by people around us who resent the effective Christian's Christlike behavior. Like the serpent that wooed Eve, those seemingly caring individuals will question, "Did God really say that?" In other words—"Who says you can't do that? Why can't you go to that place? Why must you tithe, attend church regularly, and serve others?" "You used to be more fun (caring, sharing, forgiving, etc.) before you were a Christian." That's the one that hurts the most; it questions whether we're self-righteous or spiritual. It often compels otherwise effective Christians to water down the Word of God to please others.

Covenant with Self

The cure for that ailment is to acknowledge that our covenant with God spurs self-improvement. No matter how good we think we are before coming to Christ, we're reminded that "All have sinned and come short of the glory of God ... justified freely by his grace through the redemption that that is in Christ Jesus" (Romans 3:23–24). The Apostle James warns, "But be ye doers of the word, and not hearers only, deceiving your own selves" (James 1:22). Heeding James' admonition, effective Christians actively seek to know the written and Living Word (Jesus). Thus, knowledge is gleaned and acted upon through prayer, Bible reading and study, and regular church attendance. Spiritual health is only one aspect of our self-covenant. The other is physical health. As living temples of God (1 Corinthians 3:16), effective Christians take care of their bodies by fueling them with proper nutrition, rest, and exercise. Proper medical care is also essential, especially regular annual examinations as one ages.

Covenant with Others

Serving others is also an integral right and responsibility of our covenant with God. Leading others to follow Christ, or grow up in Him, also is a great privilege. From sharing the Gospel to treating our enemies with kindness to helping those less fortunate, we become instruments of grace, peace, and hope. More so, embracing a global perspective of the term *neighbor* helps us to be more effective as we adapt to changing societal needs in times of peace and war.

Long-Term Effectiveness

Spiritual effectiveness is a worthy, long-term goal. Shortcuts compel you to focus on short-term achievement garnered by either physical, mental, or emotional power. Admonishing the Galatians' reliance on a similar shortcut, the apostle Paul queried, "Are you so foolish? After beginning by means of the Spirit, are you now trying to finish by means of the flesh?" (Galatians 3:3). The power of the Holy Spirit will infuse Christians to fulfill their covenant with God. If we live in Him, praying, reading and studying the Bible, and attending church regularly, He will mightily dwell in us.

Lisa Crayton is an award-winning, internationally published freelance writer and the editor of Spirit-Led Writer, an online magazine for Christian writers. Lisa is also an ordained, licensed minister.

Faith Faces the World

by Judith St. Clair Hull, PhD

We often think of faith as an attitude of the heart, but James gives us the other side of faith—faith that is lived out in the world. Faith is more than emotion or cognition; it is the stuff that changes what we are and what we do. For James, faith is not just cerebral. If we say we have faith, we must show it. James wrote to Jewish Christians who had been scattered due to persecution to help them keep the faith. We may not be suffering the same kind of persecution that these early Christians faced, but God is able, through our faith, to help us live out our faith. When we suffer, we should see our trials as experiences that help us grow spiritually.

James gives us a job description of the one who has faith in God. He deals with what we say and how we say it. He talks about our attitudes toward money and what we do with it. We tend to think that God has blessed those who have more money and that they deserve the greater honor, but James warns against just such an attitude. We should show no partiality to those who are richer. In his epistles, Peter gives us another perspective on faith facing the world. To Peter, faith includes the concept of hope. But just as James, he views hope as more than just religious sentiment. The life of hope equals a life of discipline and reverence to God.

Just as the recipients of James' letter were suffering persecution, so were those addressed in Peter's epistles. Peter's answer was to live holy lives in the presence of tribulation because the God who calls and saves us is Himself holy. Our style of living is based on our reverence for God. Again, the circumstances of our lives may not be precisely like those Peter addressed, but the message is relevant for whatever our situation. In Jesus Christ, we have a new life, which is significantly different from the old. Others may criticize our lifestyles, but God must be glorified if we are living for Him. Still others will ask why we live the way we do. Then we should be ready to give a testimony.

Love is the key to holy living. When we love others, we are able to look beyond a multitude of personal inadequacies in them. The power for holy living is prayer. Our prayer life must be disciplined. That means we must set aside time every day for prayer, and we must live our lives in an attitude of prayer, always looking to the Lord in everything we do. What does the holy life look like? The holy life is characterized by goodness, knowledge, self-control, endurance, godliness, mutual affection, and love (cf. 2 Peter 1:5–7). As Christians, we must be growing in these attributes as we grow in spiritual maturity. The recipients of Peter's epistles were suffering and wondering when the Lord would come back to rescue them. Peter warned that Christians must keep on living holy lives. We do not know when the Lord will return. But, be assured; He will come back. So we must continue to live for Him and be ready for Him. Faith faces the world with hope.

The epistles of John exhort believers to walk as children of God. John wrote with several objectives in mind. One objective was to combat the heresy of early Gnosticism. According to its adherents, everything consisted of either matter or spirit. The matter was bad; the spirit was good. God was a spirit, and Jesus did not truly die on the Cross as a physical human being. This belief led to wanton immorality because what the body did, did not matter. Although doctrinal heresies vary from age to age, cult to cult, and religion to religion, sticking with biblical doctrine is important—first because we dare not misunderstand who Jesus is, and second because doctrinal heresy leaves us without the necessary support for leading holy, moral lives.

John wrote of opposing forces, but not like the Gnostic opposites of matter and spirit. In every opposite named by John, we see God in opposition to the devil and evil. These opposing forces, however, are not equal. God is always superior, and He will always win. John wrote of light and darkness, truth and untruth, life and death, love and hate. God is pure light, truth, life, and love

without any adulteration. These characteristics are to be present in all believers. These are the signs that we really are born again.

In John's second and third epistles, he writes to individuals. Second John is to a woman and her children, who are followers of the Lord. This woman was obviously a woman of great hospitality, inviting visiting preachers to stay in her home. John commends her for this, at the same time warning her to refuse to lodge to false teachers, such as the Gnostics. By offering hospitality to false teachers, she would be furthering their work. One of John's favorite themes, in both his first epistle and his second, is love. He exhorts believers to love one another as Jesus loved us. Faith faces the world with love. The book of Jude echoes the same theme of living out our faith. Jude, the brother of James and half-brother of Jesus, warns believers of those who would deny Jesus Christ and Lord and Master and pervert the message of faith.

Judith St. Clair Hull, PhD, is Senior Editor at UMI. She received her MA in Inner Cities Studies from Northeastern Illinois University and her PhD in Theological Education from Trinity Evangelical Divinity School.

Becoming a Good Storyteller

by Cheryl Price, Ph.D.

Many teachers of God's Word prefer or enjoy lecturing as their style of teaching. Yet, teaching has varied styles. This is important to remember because people of all ages receive and process information differently. What is your teaching style of choice? Do you use a variety of teaching methods? As a teacher, try a new teaching technique or style that you are unfamiliar with or hesitant to try, like sharing stories. You will discover how you retell a story will refresh your teaching and encourage you to think of new and creative possibilities. Let us explore this popular and fun teaching technique for this quarter.

Storytelling is an ancient art used by all cultures throughout the world to illustrate or highlight people, events, and community history. One popular series of stories often told by storytellers is the Anansi Tales. For centuries storytellers have used these tales that originated from the Akan people, from present-day Ghana. Anansi is a spider who is a trickster and smart. Although Anansi often appears as a spider, he sometimes transforms into a man. Anansi uses his skills to deceive other animals, defeat the larger animals, or show kindness and care. The stories of Anansi remind us of the deception we have in each of us and our abilities to choose to do good and show compassion to others. When introducing biblical concepts of good and bad, you can present a character like Anansi after the biblical story to reinforce the concepts of good and bad.

Our theme for this quarter is God's faithfulness. The faithfulness of God is more than a good story. From miraculous events to everyday moments in life, the narrative of God's faithfulness is experienced again and again throughout the Bible and in our lives. How do we tell this wonderful story of God's faithfulness? What are some effective ways teachers can capture the attention, the hearts, and the minds of believers and non-Christians about the Lord's faithfulness? Becoming an effective and exciting storyteller is one way to share God's faithfulness with others.

Ready to begin your journey of storytelling? Eight storytelling tips to assist you in preparing to tell a story are listed for you:

1. Before you tell a story, practice memorizing a story. Select a story you can easily memorize and feel comfortable sharing. Begin with a short story, personal or from another source. This will boost your confidence and ability to trust you can remember a story.

2. Practice telling the story over and over and over. Look in the mirror when you are telling the story. You may feel uncomfortable at first, but seeing yourself helps you see your actions and movements.

3. If you are a mobile person, use movement when telling the story. Make the movements consistent with the characters and words in the story.

4. Select additional props you may need to bring the story to life and set the stage for the listener and the viewer.

5. Unless the character or story calls for a monotone voice, include voice inflections, accents, and laughter to enhance the story. A well-placed pause or silence adds an unexpected dimension to the story.

6. Including people from the class or event as part of the story draws people into the story. The participants do not have to speak; maybe they can tiptoe with you as you quietly share a secret.

7. Make notes about how the story begins, what events occur as the story unfolds, what the high point or the main event of the story is, what events occur after the story, and what the ending of the story is. Retell the story using what you have written and without using your notes. Practice each of these three times.

8. Practice, practice, practice, and more practice telling your story. The more you practice and tell stories to others, the better you will become. You learn new ideas and ways you can better present to various types of crowds.

Think of a personal story you want to tell the class regarding God's faithfulness in your life. Tell the story in a more animated way than you usually do or plan to act out one or two of the characters in your story. Practice, relax, and pray for God to work through you as a new or refreshed storyteller of God's Word.

Cheryl Price, PhD, is Vice President of Content at UMI. She has co-authored and edited many books.

RICHARD H. CAIN

(1825–1887)

Pastor and Congressman

Richard H. Cain was a Christian who lived out his beliefs, especially in the areas concerning social justice for African Americans. He was born in Virginia to a Cherokee mother and an African American father. When Richard was six years old, he and his family moved to Ohio. Because he lived in a "free state," he was able to get an education, which was primarily through the Sunday School.

He was always interested in the ministry, but he had a variety of job experiences. For example, he worked on the steamboats that chugged up and down the Ohio River. By 1844, he had entered the Methodist ministry as a pastor. Four years later, he left that denomination because of its segregated worship practices, and joined the African Methodist Episcopal church, and served as a deacon and then a pastor in Muscatine, Iowa. He desired an education to better prepare himself for the ministry, so he attended Wilberforce University, the first American college founded by African Americans.

When Pastor Cain was assigned to a church in Brooklyn, New York, he soon became actively involved in supporting the vote for all men. Soon after the end of the Civil War in 1865, Pastor Cain was assigned to a church in Charleston, South Carolina, which had been closed due to a slave revolt in 1822. But under his leadership, the congregation grew to be the largest in the state by 1871.

Pastor Cain was both a great speaker and a great writer. In order to spread his strong views, particularly in regard to granting land to the newly freed slaves, he began writing and publishing in a newspaper, *The South Carolina Leader*, in 1866. Between his church and his newspaper, he was building a strong political group. First, he served on the South Carolina group that fashioned a new state constitution. Then he went on to be elected as a state senator.

When land for former slaves still was not made available, he purchased land to sell. Unfortunately, that project eventually went bankrupt. After this unsuccessful attempt, he ran for a seat in the United States Congress and won. His biggest effort was geared toward the passage of a Civil Rights Bill, for which he argued eloquently. As a member of Congress, he was able to make several very stirring speeches on its behalf. He went on to found Paul Quinn College in Waco, Texas and served as its president until 1884. He returned to Washington, D.C., and served as the bishop of the AME conference until he died in 1887.

Sources:

"CAIN, Richard Harvey, Biographical Information." Biographical Directory of the United States Congress. http://bioguide. congress.gov/scripts/biodisplay.pl?index=C000022 (access 3/20/19).

Teaching Tips

Words You Should Know

A. Overthrow (v. 21) *haphak* (Heb.)—To turn over, transform

B. Brimstone (v. 24) *gophriyth* (Heb.)—Sulfur, cypress resin

Teacher Preparation

Unifying Principle—Spared! People's lives are often affected by what others have done or are doing on their behalf. How do the actions of others affect our lives? Genesis says that God preserved Lot when Sodom was destroyed because of the righteousness of his uncle Abraham.

A. Read the Bible Background and Devotional Reading.

B. Pray for your students and lesson clarity.

C. Read the lesson Scripture in multiple translations.

O—Open the Lesson

A. Begin the class with prayer.

B. Ask the class: "What have been your highs and lows of the last few years? Where has God been present during all those times?"

C. Have the students read the Aim for Change and the In Focus story.

D. Ask students how events like those in the story weigh on their hearts and how they can view these events from a faith perspective.

P—Present the Scriptures

A. Read the Focal Verses and discuss the Background and The People, Places, and Times sections.

B. Have the class share what Scriptures stand out for them and why, with particular emphasis on today's themes.

E—Explore the Meaning

A. Use In Depth or More Light on the Text to facilitate a deeper discussion of the lesson text.

B. Pose the questions in Search the Scriptures and Discuss the Meaning.

C. Discuss the Liberating Lesson and Application for Activation sections.

N—Next Steps for Application

A. Summarize the value of God's faithfulness amid our doubts.

B. End class with a commitment to pray for seeing ways we are "blessed to be a blessing."

Worship Guide

For the Superintendent or Teacher
Theme: Faith and Doubt
Song: "Somebody Prayed for Me"
Devotional Reading: Luke 17:22, 26–37

Faith and Doubt

Bible Background • GENESIS 18:16–19:29
Printed Text • GENESIS 19:1, 15–26, 29 | Devotional Reading • LUKE 17:22, 26–37

Aim for Change

By the end of the lesson, we will: EXPLORE the reasons the angels spared Lot and his family from the destruction of Sodom, IDENTIFY with Lot's fear of impending disaster, and CELEBRATE God's deliverance from seemingly hopeless situations.

In Focus

Charon and her husband Chauncey moved with their two children, Jesse and Bryan, outside of Pomona, California, into their dream home. Charon, who is an interior designer, and Chauncey, who is an independent contractor, had saved, made good investments, and worked hard to afford their custom-designed home. Although they never said it, they both knew the other was happy to have some time alone with their children in their sanctuary.

It was six months to the day when the raging fires began engulfing homes within 20 miles of their home. Fortunately, no one was killed, and there were only minor injuries. Although their home and lives were spared, it woke Chauncey and Charon up to a reality they had forgotten. They said a quick word of thanks to God for their new home and spent time praising and thanking God for their safety from the fire and the care of others. They decided that evening to pray with the children and give thanks unto the Lord. Charon and Chauncey reminded their children to always be thankful to the Lord and say, "Thank you" for protecting and caring for them and others.

God's protection comes in many ways. When have you forgotten to say, "Thank you," to God? How do you, your family, or community praise the Lord?

Keep in Mind

"And it came to pass, when God destroyed the cities of the plain, that God remembered Abraham, and sent Lot out of the midst of the overthrow, when he overthrew the cities in the which Lot dwelt" (Genesis 19:29, KJV).

"But God had listened to Abraham's request and kept Lot safe, removing him from the disaster that engulfed the cities on the plain" (Genesis 19:29, NLT).

Focal Verses

KJV **Genesis 19:1** And there came two angels to Sodom at even; and Lot sat in the gate of Sodom: and Lot seeing them rose up to meet them; and he bowed himself with his face toward the ground;

15 And when the morning arose, then the angels hastened Lot, saying, Arise, take thy wife, and thy two daughters, which are here; lest thou be consumed in the iniquity of the city.

16 And while he lingered, the men laid hold upon his hand, and upon the hand of his wife, and upon the hand of his two daughters; the LORD being merciful unto him: and they brought him forth, and set him without the city.

17 And it came to pass, when they had brought them forth abroad, that he said, Escape for thy life; look not behind thee, neither stay thou in all the plain; escape to the mountain, lest thou be consumed.

18 And Lot said unto them, Oh, not so, my LORD:

19 Behold now, thy servant hath found grace in thy sight, and thou hast magnified thy mercy, which thou hast shewed unto me in saving my life; and I cannot escape to the mountain, lest some evil take me, and I die:

20 Behold now, this city is near to flee unto, and it is a little one: Oh, let me escape thither, (is it not a little one?) and my soul shall live.

21 And he said unto him, See, I have accepted thee concerning this thing also, that I will not overthrow this city, for the which thou hast spoken.

22 Haste thee, escape thither; for I cannot do any thing till thou be come thither. Therefore the name of the city was called Zoar.

23 The sun was risen upon the earth when Lot entered into Zoar.

24 Then the LORD rained upon Sodom and upon Gomorrah brimstone and fire from the LORD out of heaven;

NLT **Genesis 19:1** That evening the two angels came to the entrance of the city of Sodom. Lot was sitting there, and when he saw them, he stood up to meet them. Then he welcomed them and bowed with his face to the ground.

15 At dawn the next morning the angels became insistent. "Hurry," they said to Lot. "Take your wife and your two daughters who are here. Get out right now, or you will be swept away in the destruction of the city!"

16 When Lot still hesitated, the angels seized his hand and the hands of his wife and two daughters and rushed them to safety outside the city, for the LORD was merciful.

17 When they were safely out of the city, one of the angels ordered, "Run for your lives! And don't look back or stop anywhere in the valley! Escape to the mountains, or you will be swept away!"

18 "Oh no, my lord!" Lot begged.

19 "You have been so gracious to me and saved my life, and you have shown such great kindness. But I cannot go to the mountains. Disaster would catch up to me there, and I would soon die.

20 See, there is a small village nearby. Please let me go there instead; don't you see how small it is? Then my life will be saved."

21 "All right," the angel said, "I will grant your request. I will not destroy the little village.

22 But hurry! Escape to it, for I can do nothing until you arrive there." (This explains why that village was known as Zoar, which means "little place.")

23 Lot reached the village just as the sun was rising over the horizon.

24 Then the LORD rained down fire and burning sulfur from the sky on Sodom and Gomorrah.

25 And he overthrew those cities, and all the plain, and all the inhabitants of the cities, and that which grew upon the ground.

26 But his wife looked back from behind him, and she became a pillar of salt.

29 And it came to pass, when God destroyed the cities of the plain, that God remembered Abraham, and sent Lot out of the midst of the overthrow, when he overthrew the cities in the which Lot dwelt.

25 He utterly destroyed them, along with the other cities and villages of the plain, wiping out all the people and every bit of vegetation.

26 But Lot's wife looked back as she was following behind him, and she turned into a pillar of salt.

29 But God had listened to Abraham's request and kept Lot safe, removing him from the disaster that engulfed the cities on the plain.

The People, Places, and Times

Sodom and Gomorrah. Sodom, Gomorrah, and Zoar belonged to the "five cities of the plain." This plain has been engulfed by the Dead Sea in modern times. However, while they stood, Sodom, Gomorrah, and the other three cities were on the southeastern shore of the Dead Sea, with the plain stretching further south of them. These cities became synonymous with the sinful behavior that infested them in Lot's day.

Brimstone. A sulfurous deposit in rock which is easily flammable. When brimstone catches fire, it melts the stone, releasing the terrible and possibly poisonous smell of sulfur into the air. Deposits of this stone are found around the world, especially around volcanoes, and famously around the Dead Sea.

Background

In Genesis 18–19, Sodom and Gomorrah are facing impending judgment and destruction as a result of their wickedness. Genesis is not explicit as to which sins of Sodom and Gomorrah caused God to want to destroy the cities, but the Lord later tells Ezekiel some reasons as part of a prophecy against Jerusalem (Read Ezekiel 16:44–50). Abraham intercedes for the city, asking that the Lord spare the cities if there are only ten righteous people there (Genesis 18:16–33). The Lord agrees, but when the angels go to visit Lot, they find the

outcries of wickedness to be true (Genesis 19:4–9). All the men of the city wanted to sexually assault the angels, and when Lot refuses to give them up, they promise to abuse him even worse. The angels blind the men of the city and protect Lot for the night and then tell him to take his family and flee the city. In contrast to Abraham's plea, there were not even ten righteous men, and the outcry of sinfulness in the city had reached God's ears. Lot tries to warn his other family members of the destruction, but they would not believe him (19:14). God's punishment and destruction was certain to happen, which is where verse 15 picks up.

At-A-Glance

1. The Place of Destruction
(Genesis 19:1, 15–17)
2. The Place of Safety (vv. 18–22)
3. Salvation from Destruction (vv. 23–26, 29)

In Depth

1. The Place of Destruction
(Genesis 19:1, 15–17)

Lot is sitting by the city gate when the angels of the Lord arrive from Abraham's house outside the city. He immediately offers them hospitality, which is customary in that culture. He not only welcomes them as all strangers should be welcomed with kindness and warmth, but he bows down to them, recognizing God has sent them. Next, the account contrasts the violence of the people of Sodom and Gomorrah with the hospitality of Lot (vv. 2–14). The angels protect Lot and tell him to take his family and leave town. From the angels' encounter with the men of the city, God has judged not even ten righteous people are in the cities, so they must be destroyed. Lot hesitates to leave, so the angels transport him and his family outside the city borders and tell them to run for their lives to safety in the mountains.

Why do we sometimes hesitate to follow God's call or instructions?

2. The Place of Safety (vv. 18–22)

Lot makes another request of the Lord. In the midst of the Lord's provision for protection, there is still space for conversation through prayer. Lot actually negotiates with the angel of the Lord. Lot first thanks the Lord for His grace and mercy in saving his life and his family. But he has an important concern. Lot felt that if he retreated to the mountains, they would not be safe very long because of the dangerous terrain that had fewer resources and people. He could be vulnerable to attack from animals, bandits, or some other sort of disaster. But instead he wants to be safe in a nearby village, which had all of the comforts and familiarity of civilization. Surprisingly, the angel of the Lord grants Lot's request. But Lot must be obedient to get there quickly and follow directions so that the destruction of Sodom and Gomorrah does not reach him. The village Zoar (which means "little") receives its name through this encounter.

Lot has already received great grace from God and yet asks for more and receives it. What does this teach us about God and our relationship with Him?

3. Salvation from Destruction (vv. 23–26, 29)

Lot travels during the night from the edge of the city of Sodom toward Zoar and reaches the village just as the sun is dawning. The Lord waits for him to arrive to the place of safety before destroying Sodom, Gomorrah, and every other city in the plain. The destruction is total as fire rains down from heaven. The destruction may have been a volcanic eruption or a special phenomenon from God; in either case, the fire and sulfur burn up people and vegetation. Yet in the midst of the fires, Lot is protected. Unfortunately, his wife looks back to the city as they are fleeing and turns into a pillar of salt. The Scripture does not indicate why she turns back or why she turns into a pillar of salt as a result. Still, Lot and his daughters miraculously make it to safety as a result of Abraham's earlier intercession (Genesis 18). The prayers of Abraham, the righteous man, availed much (cf. James 5:16), and his nephew and his great nieces are saved.

How do we feel when we survive or succeed in the face of destruction or failure all around us?

Search the Scriptures

1. How did Lot respond when he encountered the angels? What does it say about his character?

2. Why does Lot desire to go to the village instead of the mountains? What happens to the village as a result?

Discuss the Meaning

1. People often read Genesis 19 and get caught up trying to define the sins of Sodom, which happen before the institution of the Law of Moses, instead of focusing on God's desire to save Lot and those who listened. Why do we sometimes focus more on the sins of others instead of the salvation of God?

2. The angels are willing to transport and then wait for Lot to be safe before they execute judgment on the cities because Abraham

intercedes for him. What does this teach us about God's faithfulness?

Liberating Lesson

Hospitality matters to God. Perhaps Lot was spared because he welcomed God's messengers. Presently, we live in a shut-down, shut-out society that encourages keeping immigrants out and practices exclusion rather than building relationships with others. God's destruction of Sodom is a reminder that He is not pleased when we shut people out or devise schemes to abuse others. Lot stood up against the men of Sodom who desired to abuse God's messengers. We must pray for protection of those who suffer injustice. We are challenged in this moment to intercede in prayer and in action so that God's will might be accomplished in our world. His will is that none should perish and all should know Him.

Application for Activation

This is one of the most powerful stories about intercession in the book of Genesis. God is listening to those who seek Him and is willing to respond to their requests, even in the midst of turmoil. Abraham intercedes not just for himself, but for his family members who are in harm's way. Lot does not just try to save himself, but tells everyone close to him that judgment is coming. God responds to their requests with protection and salvation. Take the opportunity this week to pray for someone who may be in a destructive situation. Although God may not always answer the way we anticipate, He will answer. A person's response to God's invitation is ultimately their choice. But as the story shows us, sometimes our prayers are the vehicle God uses for the salvation of others.

Follow the Spirit

What God wants me to do:

_____

Remember Your Thoughts

Special insights I have learned:

_____

_____

_____

_____

More Light on the Text
Genesis 19:1, 15–26, 29

The "why" of Sodom and Gomorrah's destruction is debated. Yet, Ezekiel 16:44–50 highlights reasons Sodom is destroyed. Violating hospitality is a critical part of this, as Jewish scholars note. Sodom and Gomorrah's lack of caring for strangers and strange practices against those who do, only heighten their destruction. The lack of hospitality includes such offenses as lying, pride, sexual abuse, and blasphemy. Read Genesis 19:4-10 to see how the men of the town demand to have sex with God's messengers, strangers, and how the messengers and Lot respond. Our text today focuses on God's faithfulness and how Lot and his family are delivered.

1 And there came two angels to Sodom at even; and Lot sat in the gate of Sodom: and Lot seeing them rose up to meet them; and he bowed himself with his face toward the ground;

The men who were sent by God to tell Abraham of God's promise of a seed (Genesis 18:2–15) are the same who journey to Sodom during Abraham's exchange with God (Genesis 18:1–15). They are now identified as two angels (one fewer than the three men who visited Abraham earlier). Given Yahweh's intent to discern Sodom's injustice, readers may interpret He sends the men to Sodom to test the city (Genesis 18:21). Lot is present, sitting at the entrance or gateway of Sodom, which may be symbolic of Lot's leadership and authority in Sodom and also his welcoming hospitality. Upon noticing the men, Lot arises to greet them and bows to honor them.

15 And when the morning arose, then the angels hastened Lot, saying, Arise, take thy wife, and thy two daughters, which are here; lest thou be consumed in the iniquity of the city. 16 And while he lingered, the men laid hold upon his hand, and upon the hand of his wife, and upon the hand of his two daughters; the LORD being merciful unto him: and they brought him forth, and set him without the city.

The angelic messengers announce to Lot that God has heard the cries of wickedness in Sodom and they have been sent to destroy the city. Lot receives his first warning to gather his "son in law, and thy sons, and thy daughters, and whatsoever thou hast in the city" and flee (Genesis 19:12–13). Since there is no other reference to sons that Lot might have, and they certainly do not escape with him, one can assume the angels are guessing he might have sons when he did not. Only God is omniscient. Lot approaches his sons-in-law with the warning he received, but they think he is joking (Genesis 19:14–15). It can be hard to understand that Lot has sons-in-law when he just said his daughters were virgins (v. 8). It is possible the Lot has more daughters than just the two who escape with him. Some scholars suggest these men might have been future sons-in-law, engaged to marry his daughters.

Lot then hesitates and does not heed the advice of the messengers by leaving Sodom immediately. In the morning, the messengers give Lot a second urgent warning to take his wife and daughters and leave the city. Lot hesitates, and the messengers spare Lot again by grabbing Lot, his wife, and two daughters by the hand and leading them outside the city. This is to show God's mercy, not only to Lot who directly benefits from this escape but also to Abraham, who prayed that God would spare the city where his nephew lived.

17 And it came to pass, when they had brought them forth abroad, that he said, Escape for thy life; look not behind thee, neither stay thou in all the plain; escape to the mountain, lest thou be consumed. 18 And Lot said unto them, Oh, not so, my LORD: 19 Behold now, thy servant hath found grace in thy sight, and thou hast magnified thy mercy, which thou hast shewed unto me in saving my life; and I cannot escape to the mountain, lest some evil take me, and I die: 20 Behold now, this city is near to flee unto, and it is a little one: Oh, let me escape thither, (is it not a little one?) and my soul shall live. 21 And he said unto him, See, I have accepted thee concerning this thing also, that I will not overthrow this city, for the which thou hast spoken. 22 Haste thee, escape thither; for I cannot do any thing till thou be come thither. Therefore the name of the city was called Zoar.

Once outside the city, the messengers give Lot and his family a third warning to save themselves by not looking back and escape to the mountains (Genesis 19:17). Lot hesitates again by pleading with the men not to escape to the mountains, where the destruction could consume him and his family, but to a small city named Zoar. Zoar (also known as Bela) is a small city that will be spared. Though small in size, Zoar was a flourishing city because of its location beneath the mountains of Moab where it received flowing waters. It was also a place where trees blossomed and plant life flourished. The city of Zoar is spared because Lot boldly asks to seek refuge there instead of where the angels told him to go. The city is a reminder that God prepares a place for the righteous. One of the messengers instructs Lot to hurry there and that the city will be spared once Lot and his family arrive.

23 The sun was risen upon the earth when Lot entered into Zoar. 24 Then the LORD rained upon Sodom and upon Gomorrah brimstone and fire from the LORD out of heaven; 25 And he overthrew those cities, and all the plain, and all the inhabitants of the cities, and that which grew upon the ground. 26 But his wife looked back from behind him, and she became a pillar of salt.

Sodom and Gomorrah are destroyed with "brimstone and fire from the LORD out of heaven." Brimstone is a form of sulfurous, flammable rock. Both cities lay entirely in ruins with many lives lost, as well as plants and animals completely devastated. An image in the word "overthrow" (Heb. *haphak*, **haw-FACK**) is that of flipping over a hand or flat bread. Everything in Sodom and Gomorrah is turned upside down in this destruction, so much so that the word "overthrown" becomes entwined with the cities (cf. Lamentations 4:6; Amos 4:11).

We can only speculate why Lot's family is spared and other families are not. Sadly, this is not the first time that Lot and his family are caught in a bad situation and spared since they also had been taken captive by kings (Genesis 14). This is a sad story that does not have a fairy-tale ending. The first mention of Lot's wife is as she looks back and turns into a pillar of salt (v. 26). No name of Lot's wife is given. No sense of her disposition or an account of what she meant to her family is told.

29 And it came to pass, when God destroyed the cities of the plain, that God remembered Abraham, and sent Lot out of the midst of the overthrow, when he overthrew the cities in the which Lot dwelt.

Perhaps you have heard the gospel song, "Somebody Prayed for Me." For Lot that somebody is Abraham. The final verse of our passage points back to Abraham's conversation with God. It could be that Lot's life was spared, not because of his good works or fortune, but because Abraham interceded for Sodom. God spares Lot's life on several occasions because of Abraham. Though Abraham did not mention Lot's name in his exchange with God, one could interpret that Abraham's plea was on behalf of seeking justice for the righteous of Sodom and his kin. The theme of being spared because of connection emerges again later with the story of Rahab whose whole household was spared because of her hospitality to the Israelite spies (Joshua 6:25).

In some traditions, believers are taught not to question God. Abraham's exchange with God in Genesis 18 is part of what spares Lot and his family. God remembers Abraham's petitions and ensures that Lot and his family are spared from the destruction. Perhaps this is a reminder to believers to take a stand before God with all of our issues and intercessions because God is just and able to handle whatever inquiries we bring. If there is any good news in the passage, it is that God remembers (Genesis 19:29).

God destroys Sodom and Gomorrah because of their injustice. Reading Genesis 18 and 19 together, readers may interpret that Yahweh did not find enough righteous people to spare these cities, even though Abraham had persuaded Him down to only needing to find ten righteous people. Lot's hospitality to the messengers to bring them into his home separated his family from the men of the Sodom. God shows His faithfulness to His chosen people by saving Lot, both because of Lot's honest hospitality and Abraham's bold love for his kin.

Sources:
Attridge, Harold W., Wayne A. Meeks, and Jouette M. Bassler. *The HarperCollins Study Bible: New Revised Standard Version, including the Apocryphal/Deuterocanonical Books with Concordance.* San Fransico, CA: HarperOne, 2006.
Brueggemann, Walter. *Genesis: A Bible Commentary for Teaching and Preaching.* Atlanta, GA: John Knox Press, 1982.
Smith, William. *Smith's Bible Dictionary.* Peabody, MA: Hendrickson Pub, 1990.
Trible, Phyllis. *Texts of Terror: Literary-feminist Readings of Biblical Narratives.* Minneapolis, MN: Fortress Press, 1984.
Williams, Judy Fentress, ed. *The CEB Women's Bible.* Nashville, TN: Common English Bible, 2016.

Say It Correctly

Sodom. **SAW**-dohm.
Gomorrah. go-**MORE**-rah.
Zoar. **ZOH**-are.

Daily Bible Readings

MONDAY
Remember Lot's Wife
(Luke 17:22, 26–37)

TUESDAY
Abraham and Sarah - Becoming Parents
(Genesis 18:1–15)

WEDNESDAY
Concerned about the Family
(Genesis 18:16–21)

THURSDAY
Pleading Justice for the Righteous
(Genesis 18:30–33)

FRIDAY
God Rescues the Godly
(2 Peter 2:4–10)

SATURDAY
Sodom's Sin Revealed
(Genesis 19:2–14)

SUNDAY
The Family Escapes Successfully
(Genesis 19:1, 15–26, 29)

Teaching Tips

Words You Should Know

A. Belial (v. 16) *beliya'al* (Heb.)—Worthless; a demonic force

B. Handmaid (v. 16) *'amah* (Heb.)—Maidservant or female slave

Teacher Preparation

Unifying Principle—Heart's Desire. People often feel that no one hears them when they express their deepest desires. Is anyone really listening? Hannah, who had no children, asked God for a son, promising to dedicate him to God's service; and soon she conceived and gave birth.

A. Read the Bible Background and Devotional Reading.

B. Pray for your students and lesson clarity.

C. Read the lesson Scripture in multiple translations.

O—Open the Lesson

A. Begin the class with prayer.

B. As a class, discuss answers to these questions: How do you understand prayer in relation to God's promises, providence, and provision? How have your prayers changed over time as you have prayed for a particular situation and God has responded either "Yes," "Not now," or "No"?

C. Have the students read the Aim for Change and the In Focus story.

D. Ask students how events like those in the story weigh on their hearts and how they can view these events from a faith perspective.

P—Present the Scriptures

A. Read the Focal Verses and discuss the Background and The People, Places, and Times sections.

B. Have the class share what Scriptures stand out for them and why, with particular emphasis on today's context.

E—Explore the Meaning

A. Use In Depth or More Light on the Text to facilitate a deeper discussion of the lesson text.

B. Pose the questions in Search the Scriptures and Discuss the Meaning.

C. Discuss the Liberating Lesson and Application for Activation sections.

N—Next Steps for Application

A. Summarize the value of waiting for God's timing.

B. End class with a commitment to continue faithfully telling God our cares, even when we fear they are unheard.

Worship Guide

For the Superintendent or Teacher
Theme: God Answers Prayer
Song: "Standing in the Need of Prayer"
Devotional Reading: Psalm 99

God Answers Prayer

Bible Background • 1 SAMUEL 1:1–2:10
Printed Text • 1 SAMUEL 1:9–20 | Devotional Reading • PSALM 99

Aim for Change

By the end of the lesson, we will: RECALL the story of Hannah's desperate longing for a child, REFLECT on longings for God to intervene in our lives, and PRAY with confidence that God will provide what is best for us.

In Focus

One day, Kenny collapsed in a chair and just shook his head. He asked God, "Why haven't I heard from the Young Leader's Fellowship Program for grad school?" Since all of his friends were accepted, he began to wonder what was wrong with him? Every time he thought about the situation, it made him angry.

The next day, Kenny and his friends were playing a pick-up game of basketball. AJ kept blocking his shots. When AJ went to shoot, Kenny purposely tripped him. AJ jumped up, slammed the ball on the court, and told Kenny to stop acting like a big baby. Before Kenny could respond, Jamal jumped in between them to cool things down. Jamal told Kenny he needed to get it together. They asked what was wrong.

At first, Kenny sharply said, "Nothing." His friends told him he was lying. Kenny finally told them he was upset because he hadn't heard from the Fellowship Program. They assured him things were going to be okay. He just needed to relax and pray.

When Kenny got home, he saw a letter from the program in the mailbox. He hesitantly opened it, and then shouted, "Amen!" He had been accepted. Kenny quickly sent a group text to his friends.

How do you help your friends who are unable to move forward? As a believer how does your faith encourage you when you are struggling?

Keep in Mind

"Then Eli answered and said, Go in peace: and the God of Israel grant thee thy petition that thou hast asked of him" (1 Samuel 1:17, KJV).

"'In that case,' Eli said, 'go in peace! May the God of Israel grant the request you have asked of him'" (1 Samuel 1:17, NLT).

Focal Verses

KJV **1 Samuel 1:9** So Hannah rose up after they had eaten in Shiloh, and after they had drunk. Now Eli the priest sat upon a seat by a post of the temple of the LORD.

10 And she was in bitterness of soul, and prayed unto the LORD, and wept sore.

11 And she vowed a vow, and said, O LORD of hosts, if thou wilt indeed look on the affliction of thine handmaid, and remember me, and not forget thine handmaid, but wilt give unto thine handmaid a man child, then I will give him unto the LORD all the days of his life, and there shall no razor come upon his head.

12 And it came to pass, as she continued praying before the LORD, that Eli marked her mouth.

13 Now Hannah, she spake in her heart; only her lips moved, but her voice was not heard: therefore Eli thought she had been drunken.

14 And Eli said unto her, How long wilt thou be drunken? put away thy wine from thee.

15 And Hannah answered and said, No, my lord, I am a woman of a sorrowful spirit: I have drunk neither wine nor strong drink, but have poured out my soul before the LORD.

16 Count not thine handmaid for a daughter of Belial: for out of the abundance of my complaint and grief have I spoken hitherto.

17 Then Eli answered and said, Go in peace: and the God of Israel grant thee thy petition that thou hast asked of him.

18 And she said, Let thine handmaid find grace in thy sight. So the woman went her way, and did eat, and her countenance was no more sad.

19 And they rose up in the morning early, and worshipped before the LORD, and returned, and came to their house to Ramah: and Elkanah knew Hannah his wife; and the LORD remembered her.

20 Wherefore it came to pass, when the time was come about after Hannah had conceived, that she bare a son, and called his name Samuel, saying, Because I have asked him of the LORD.

NLT **1 Samuel 1:9** Once after a sacrificial meal at Shiloh, Hannah got up and went to pray. Eli the priest was sitting at his customary place beside the entrance of the Tabernacle.

10 Hannah was in deep anguish, crying bitterly as she prayed to the LORD.

11 And she made this vow: "O LORD of Heaven's Armies, if you will look upon my sorrow and answer my prayer and give me a son, then I will give him back to you. He will be yours for his entire lifetime, and as a sign that he has been dedicated to the LORD, his hair will never be cut."

12 As she was praying to the LORD, Eli watched her.

13 Seeing her lips moving but hearing no sound, he thought she had been drinking.

14 "Must you come here drunk?" he demanded. "Throw away your wine!"

15 "Oh no, sir!" she replied. "I haven't been drinking wine or anything stronger. But I am very discouraged, and I was pouring out my heart to the LORD.

16 Don't think I am a wicked woman! For I have been praying out of great anguish and sorrow."

17 "In that case," Eli said, "go in peace! May the God of Israel grant the request you have asked of him."

18 "Oh, thank you, sir!" she exclaimed. Then she went back and began to eat again, and she was no longer sad.

19 The entire family got up early the next morning and went to worship the LORD once more. Then they returned home to Ramah. When Elkanah slept with Hannah, the LORD remembered her plea,

20 and in due time she gave birth to a son. She named him Samuel, for she said, "I asked the LORD for him."

The People, Places, and Times

Hannah. She was the devoted mother of Samuel and wife of Elkanah. Hannah sought the Lord before she conceived and gave birth to Samuel (1 Samuel 1:5–11). Every year, she and her husband Elkanah went to the sanctuary at Shiloh to offer sacrifices to the Lord. She devoted her son to the service of God and offered a "prayer of thanksgiving for God's blessing" (1 Samuel 2:1–10). Hannah also gave birth to two other sons and two daughters.

Eli. He was the high priest of Israel with whom the prophet Samuel lived during his boyhood years. Eli, a devout but flawed priest, was the father of Phinehas and Hophni, who were killed by the Philistines (see 1 Samuel 2:12–25). Eli died upon learning of their deaths (1 Samuel 4:1–18).

Background

Samuel is noted as the last judge and a prophet. During his time, Israel underwent a shift in leadership from judges to kings. Samuel would anoint the first king, Saul, and would also anoint David as king. While there is much debate regarding who wrote the books of 1 and 2 Samuel and when they were written, we can be sure they were originally one book that told the story of the rising monarchy after the time of the judges. Together, these two books as one book are considered part of a collection of books called the Deuteronomic history. These books are Deuteronomy, Joshua, Judges, 1 and 2 Samuel, and 1 and 2 Kings.

In this first chapter, we are given Samuel's birth story. His father, Elkanah, was married to Hannah and to Peninnah, as polygamy was the common marital system of the time. Peninnah was able to bear children while Hannah was barren, like many other women in the biblical text (e.g., Sarah [Genesis 17:16–19], Rebekah [Genesis 25:21–26], Rachel [Genesis 29:31; 30:22–24], Samson's mother [Judges 13:2–5], and Elizabeth [Luke 1:5–17]). This opening chapter shows the persistence of Hannah's prayers for a child explicitly while God had shut her womb. Peninnah bullied and provoked Hannah to the point of tears, yet Hannah received a double portion of Elkanah's sacrifice because he loved her.

Prayer is a practice in which we all need to engage. How does Hannah teach us that we must be persistent in our prayers?

At-A-Glance

1. Pressing to Pray (1 Samuel 1:9–11)
2. Persecution to Peace (vv. 12–20)

In Depth

1. Pressing to Pray (1 Samuel 1:9–11)

At this point in the text, we know that Hannah is unable to conceive a child. After Hannah finishes eating, she goes to pray. Hannah's prayer of deep anguish shows us that bearing a child is an experience that she desires. People tend to bring the Lord their deepest desires and are willing to weep before the Lord with full passion, as Hannah does in her heart. Hannah asks the Lord to look to her misery and remember her. Hannah continues to pull on God's heartstrings and promises God that she will dedicate her son back to the Lord and will never put a razor to his head. Here, we see that Hannah is not only praying, but she is willing to commit to God well before she receives her blessing. Her promise to God is not an afterthought of receiving; rather, it is standing in the expectation that God will move.

Describe a time you prayed fervently to God. What did you pray for? How has God answered the prayer so far?

2. Persecution to Peace (1 Samuel 1:12–20)

Hannah continues to pray. Eli, who was sitting at the doorpost, sees Hannah praying. He watches her mouth closely as he sees her lips moving with no audible words coming out. Hannah prays within her heart, and only God hears her words. This reminds us that people can see us praying but still have no idea what the circumstances are behind the prayer. Not all prayers need to be spoken out loud, as some things are between God and the individual. Eli assumes that Hannah is drunk, but she tells Eli that she is praying to God out of her anguish and grief. In her loss and pain, she continues to pray with hope that she will be able to conceive a child. Now knowing this, Eli blesses her with peace and adds his prayer to hers that God would grant her prayer request. After this, Hannah is no longer downcast, eats something, and leaves the sanctuary. Already Eli's blessing of peace has calmed the anguish seen in her prayer.

When they return home, Hannah and Elkanah are able to conceive, and she later births a son. She names him Samuel, meaning "God heard me." Sometimes it takes longer than our expected timelines to receive the things we pray for, but God hears every single prayer. God provided for Hannah, and Hannah never gave up on praying and worshiping.

Describe a time you made an inaccurate assumption about someone who was worshiping. How do we avoid making those assumptions?

Search the Scriptures

1. Eli makes a hasty assumption about Hannah when he sees her praying silently. What is Eli's reaction when Hannah corrects him (v. 17)?

2. How does Elkanah try to cheer Hannah up (1 Samuel 1:8)? What eventually makes her glad (v. 18)?

Discuss the Meaning

1. We see the provision of God as a significant theme within the text. Think back over your life. How has God provided for you after seasons of unanswered prayers?

2. We also see that Hannah's faith did not go unwitnessed. Is there anyone who can give an account for your faith or prayer life? What testimony of faith could they speak on your behalf?

Liberating Lesson

Infertility among the African American community is more common than spoken of. The rates of infertility and the shame around it are topics that need to be discussed more often. This text, along with other texts in the Bible, is an example of how families struggling with infertility are not alone and can rest in hope. Today, 10 percent of couples experience infertility. It is easy to think that God has forgotten the deep desires of our hearts after years of praying. But that is not so. Even in moments when things seem impossible, God reminds us that nothing is impossible for God. No matter the prayer—be it fertility, finances, education, or collective liberation—God will provide. It may take days, months, and even years; yet, we are to remain hopeful in the Lord, no matter when it comes. Our prayers ought not to be about the blessing as much they should be about the one who provides the blessing. Even in her sorrow, Hannah remained faithful. We ought to do the same.

Application for Activation

So often we become discouraged and believe in the things we see rather than believing in the one who will provide. Hannah teaches us about the faith that is required for prayer. Hannah's prayers remind us that there is truly nothing too hard for God when we believe and have faith. Faith is the key to this narrative as Hannah had faith to continue praying, and God eventually answered her prayer. A great way to keep track of how God provides on a promise is to journal our prayers. This will allow us to trace our prayers and to track God in the process.

Follow the Spirit

What God wants me to do:

_____

_____

_____

_____

Remember Your Thoughts

Special insights I have learned:

_____

_____

_____

_____

More Light on the Text

1 Samuel 1:9–20

9 So Hannah rose up after they had eaten in Shiloh, and after they had drunk, Now Eli the priest sat upon a seat by a post of the temple of the LORD.

Although he lives in the land belonging to the tribe of Ephraim, Elkanah is a Levite, which meant he holds religious responsibilities (1 Chronicles 6:26, 34), and he is also Hannah's husband. Hannah is very sad because the Lord has closed her womb, and she is unable to conceive. Elkanah and his other wife, Peninnah, have several children. Elkanah sees Hannah sadness but thinks his kindness should console her grief. He always gives her a double portion of meat because he loves her.

They eat in Shiloh, a prominent city in Ephraim and the religious center of Israel as the home of the tabernacle at the time. Israelite men go there three times a year: for Passover, the Feast of Weeks, and the Feast of Tabernacles (Exodus 23:14). This is where God promised to meet His people, which is the house of prayer.

Hannah has not been able to eat or drink. So, she gets up. She does not know the answer to her husband's question, if he is better to her than ten sons (v. 8). She knows Elkanah can only give what he has, more meat, but God has the power to give her the desires of her heart. She goes to God with a remorseful heart and prays.

10 And she was in bitterness of soul, and prayed unto the LORD, and wept sore.

Peninnah has been teasing Hannah for something she has no control over. This makes Hannah even more sorrowful and sad. She is heartbroken. It brings her to tears, but more importantly, it brings her to prayer. She knows God is able to change her situation. She knows all power is in His control. So, she brings her concerns and issues to Him. She pours out her heart and tells the one who closed her womb how much she desires Him to open it. She cries with deep passion from her heart as it was evident from the tears coming from her eyes.

This is the place we all should go when we feel hopeless and "bitterness of soul" (Heb. *marah nefesh*, **MAW-rah NE-fesh**). We should go toward God (Psalm 62:8; Philippians 4:6–7; 1 Peter 5:7) in our deepest sorrow. This poignant phrase is also used of another kind of a fiercely sad mother: a bear robbed of her cubs (2 Samuel 17:8). Four times Job describes his misery, inflicted by Satan himself, as the bitterness of soul (Job 3:20, 7:11, 10:1, 21:25). King Hezekiah uses the phrase to describe a wasting sickness that almost killed him before he received healing from God (Isaiah 38:15).Hannah is confident in whom to confide and leave her concerns with. Although her husband would help her if he could because he loves her, he cannot do what God has not done. God closed her womb. He is the one to open it. We should be as confident with our cares and concerns. God is the one to run to. No one else can change the situation, only God.

11 And she vowed a vow, and said, O LORD of hosts, if thou wilt indeed look on the affliction of thine handmaid, and remember me, and not forget thine handmaid, but wilt give unto thine handmaid a man child, then I will give him unto the LORD all the days of his life, and there shall no razor come upon his head.

Humbling herself as a submissive servant, calling herself "handmaid" (Heb. 'amah, aw-MAW), a maidservant or female slave, Hannah makes a vow to the Lord. A vow is more intense than a promise; she pleads for Him to answer her prayer. She is very specific in her prayer asking for a child, a "man child." She does not ask for many children; she asks for just one. She wants this one to be a boy, insisting if the Lord gives her this son, she will give him back to the Lord for the rest of his life.

God did not ask her to do this; Hannah volunteers this commitment unto the Lord. Hannah is not selfish to just want this baby for herself. She wants the Lord to use him in His service. She passionately promises the Lord no razor will come upon his head ever in his life, like the Nazirite vow. This was the requirement God set for Samson (Judges 13:5).

Hannah knows that if the Lord chooses to grant her request, He will give her the ability to keep her vow to Him. She is insistent and persistent. She desperately wants this child, and she is determined to keep her word, trusting the Lord will grant her request.

12 And it came to pass, as she continued praying before the LORD, that Eli marked her mouth. 13 Now Hannah, she spake in her heart; only her lips moved, but her voice was not heard: therefore, Eli thought she had been drunken. 14 And Eli said unto her, how long wilt thou be drunken? Put away thy wine from thee.

Eli is watching Hannah as she prays very closely. He marks (Heb. (shamar, shaw-MAR), meaning to keep watch or guard, generally to protect or attend to, her mouth. Eli is there to be a watchman or overseer. He answers questions, gives direction, and keeps order. They are in a public place, but Hannah prays to the Lord as if this is just between Him and her. She is passionate in her prayer, but she prays in her heart. Her lips move, but there is no sound coming from her mouth. Hannah is not confused about the way she needs to pray for God to hear her. She understands God hears her whether she speaks out loud to Him or petitions Him in her heart. There may be instances when we cry aloud to the Lord, but it is not necessary for Him to hear us. He hears the secrets of our hearts; we do not need to be loud to be heard as those who do not know God cry out (Isaiah 58:4). Hannah realizes it was not the volume of the prayer but the sincerity of her heart that is important. Eli thinks she is drunk. He watches her pray, her mouth moving and tears flowing, but silent. He just knows she must be drunk. He has been watching her the whole time she has been in the temple. He passes judgment and concludes she must have been drinking. He feels the need to address the situation and rhetorically asks how long she will be drunk. Authoritatively, he tells her to put the wine away.

15 And Hannah answered and said, No, my lord, I am a woman of a sorrowful spirit: I have drunk neither wine nor strong drink but have poured out my soul before the LORD. 16 Count not thine handmaid for a daughter of Belial: for out of the abundance of my complaint and grief have I spoken hitherto.

As politely and respectfully as she can (addressing him as "my lord"), Hannah explains to Eli, the high priest, she has not been drinking anything. She wants him to know she has been pouring out her heart to the Lord. She informs him that she is of a sorrowful (Heb. *qasheh*, **kaw-SHEH**) spirit. The word *qasheh* could also be translated austere, so the word either reiterates her grief or refers to an avoidance of alcohol. She had previously been reprimanded by her husband for not drinking or eating. Now, she is being accused of having too much to drink. This has to add to her grief. Hannah has been in prayer, calling out to the Lord, and someone watching her from a distance assumes she must be a lowly drunk. Hannah asks him not to categorize her as a woman who has been drinking. A daughter of Belial (Heb. *beliya'al*, **beh-lee-YAH-al**), meaning one of disobedience and wickedness, is not who she is. Children of Belial was a common way during the time to refer to wicked people, those who did not worship God (1 Samuel 2:12; 1 Kings 21:10). The term *belial* means worthless, but it came to be understood as a proper name for the devil (2 Corinthians 6:15). She wants to assure Eli his assumptions are incorrect and give validity to her demeanor.

17 Then Eli answered and said, Go in peace: and the God of Israel grant thee thy petition that thou hast asked of him.

Hannah persuades Eli that her explanation of her appearance is sincere. He doesn't give her a formal apology for jumping to the wrong conclusion, but he responds with kind words. He even cosigns her prayer. He does not know what she prayed, nor does he ask to hear what he now understands to be a private, fervent prayer. Being convinced of her innocence, he agrees with her in prayer. Whatever she prays to the God of Israel, may He give her what she asks of Him. He blesses her to go knowing her request has been heard, and the high priest responds with an amen. Sometimes just knowing someone else is agreeing with us in prayer is all we need. We may often call on our pastors or other elders of the church, asking for prayer after we have already prayed. It is not that we

think God cannot hear our prayers alone, but it is to agree with one another in prayer.

Therefore, Eli is the elder for Hannah, and he agrees with her, sending her on her way in peace. She leaves in confidence and faith, recognizing the God of the universe hears her prayer. She just waits patiently for Him to answer. She knows that He would. By faith, Eli confirms it.

18 And she said, Let thine handmaid find grace in thy sight. So, the woman went her way and did eat, and her countenance was no more sad.

Hannah's attitude changes. She has prayed to the Lord God Almighty, entrusting all her concerns to Him. She poured out her heart to Him, giving Him all her passion and energy, making her request known. Eli, the high priest also prayed for her. She goes away believing one way or another, God will answer her prayer. Resting in the assurance of answered prayer, Hannah is able to eat and be happy again. She does not have to be sad; she spoke to the all-powerful God. She made her requests known; by faith, she knows she has been heard. In addition, the high priest has spoken to Him also on her behalf. She is, with good cause, extremely happy.

Attitude adjustments in the Lord show in our demeanor. Joy should be all over us—the joy we have because we live in the confidence and assurance that God, the Righteous One, hears us and works on our behalf. God already knows what He wants for us; we just need to ask (Jeremiah 29:11; Matthew 7:9–11). God wants what is best for us. He also wants us to recognize who He is. He is the giver of good gifts. He is the one who can when others cannot.

19 And they rose up in the morning early, and worshipped before the LORD, and returned, and came to their house to Ramah: and Elkanah knew Hannah his wife; and the LORD remembered her.

and Elkanah knew Hannah his wife; and the LORD remembered her.

The family understands the importance of seeking the Lord first. God requires the first of our time as well as our fruits. It is expected we adhere to God's voice and direction first. We should awake with a grateful heart and a focused mind toward the Lord. God is faithful in His ways toward His people. His people should be faithful in their focus toward Him. Elkanah's household intentionally gets up early in the morning and worships the Lord. Keep in mind, prayer is a form of worship. It is always in order to pray.

After worshiping the Lord, they go back home, and Elkanah sleeps with his wife. Elkanah and Hannah have their part to play in working out the miracle of having a child.

"The LORD remembered" means that God acted on her behalf in answer to her prayer. It does not mean to imply that God had forgotten about Hannah until this point or that He should remember her just now. The word "remember" (Heb. *zakar*, **zaw-KAR**) in this context means to think on, be mindful of, or contemplate. God is actively thinking about Hannah now in a special way and is acting to answer her prayer for a child. Just as the Bible tells of several instances when God intervenes in the lives of infertile women, allowing them to bear great heroes of the faith such as Sarah and Rachel, He also does not forget Hannah (Genesis 21:1, 30:22). He remembers what Hannah asks Him for. She wants a son. God hears and answers the prayers of His people. We may not know when, where, or how, but God answers the prayers of His people (Psalm 91:15; Mark 11:24).

20 Wherefore it came to pass, when the time was come about after Hannah had conceived, that she bare a son, and called his name Samuel, saying, Because I have asked him of the LORD.

Hannah wholeheartedly cried out to the Lord for this son and now God answers her prayer and grants her request. Her answered prayer is reflected in her name for him. Samuel means "God hears." God never forgets about His children. He is faithful; He hears and answers our prayers. What is our response to Him? Do we live in such a way that others can see our joy from a relationship with Him?

Sources:

Henry, Matthew. *Matthew Henry's Commentary on the Whole Bible.* Peabody, MA: Hendrickson Publishers, 2008.

"Infertility." U.S. Department of Health and Human Services. Office of Women's Health. https://www.womenshealth.gov/a-z-topics/infertility

1 Samuel. The Preacher's Outline & Sermon Bible. Vol 10. Chattanooga, TN: Leadership Ministries Worldwide, 1996.

Peterson, Eugene H., trans. *The Message: The Bible in Contemporary Language.* Colorado Springs, CO: NavPress, 2002.

Richards, Lawrence O. *The Teacher's Commentary.* Wheaton, IL: Victor Books, 1987.

Severance, W. Murray. *That's Easy for You to Say: Your Quick Guide to Pronouncing Bible Names.* Nashville, TN: Broadman & Holman, 1997.

Say It Correctly

Shiloh. **SHY**-lo.
Belial. be-**LEE**-al.
Ramah. raw-**MAH**.
Elkanah. el-kaw-**NAW**.
Peninnah. pen-in-**NAW**.

Daily Bible Readings

MONDAY
The Nazirite Vow
(Numbers 6:1–5, 13–15)

TUESDAY
"O LORD Our God, You Answered"
(Psalm 99)

WEDNESDAY
Hannah Is Childless and Suffering
(1 Samuel 1:1–8)

THURSDAY
Elkanah Attends the Yearly Sacrifice
(1 Samuel 1:21–23)

FRIDAY
Samuel Is Dedicated to the Lord
(1 Samuel 1:24–28)

SATURDAY
Hannah Rewarded for Her Faithfulness
(1 Samuel 2:18–21)

SUNDAY
God Answers Hannah's Prayer
(1 Samuel 1:9–20)

Notes

_____

_____

_____

_____

Teaching Tips

Words You Should Know

A. Murmur (v. 2) *lun* (Heb.)—To stubbornly complain

B. Manna (v. 15) *man* (Heb.)—Bread God provided the Israelites in the wilderness, meaning "what is it?"

Teacher Preparation

Unifying Principle—Where's the Food? People are often unhappy with what they have in life. How can people be truly satisfied? Despite the complaining of the Israelites as they wandered in the wilderness, God provided meat and bread for them.

A. Read the Bible Background and Devotional Reading.

B. Pray for your students and lesson clarity.

C. Read the lesson Scripture in multiple translations.

O—Open the Lesson

A. Begin the class with prayer.

B. Ask the class: "How can we tell the difference between a need and a desire? Why is it hard to be thankful for having the necessities of life when we do not have everything we want?"

C. Have the students read the Aim for Change and the In Focus story.

D. Ask students how events like those in the story weigh on their hearts and how they can view these events from a faith perspective.

P—Present the Scriptures

A. Read the Focal Verses and discuss the Background and The People, Places, and Times sections.

B. Have the class share what Scriptures stand out for them and why, with particular emphasis on today's context.

E—Explore the Meaning

A. Use In Depth or More Light on the Text to facilitate a deeper discussion of the lesson text.

B. Pose the questions in Search the Scriptures and Discuss the Meaning.

C. Discuss the Liberating Lesson and Application for Activation sections.

N—Next Steps for Application

A. Summarize the value of trusting in God's provision for our physical needs.

B. End class with a commitment to pray for God to give our daily bread.

Worship Guide

For the Superintendent or Teacher
Theme: Bread from Heaven
Song: "There Shall be Showers of Blessings"
Devotional Reading: 2 Corinthians 8:9–15

Bread from Heaven

Bible Background • EXODUS 16
Printed Text • EXODUS 16:1–8, 13–15 | Devotional Reading • 2 CORINTHIANS 8:9–15

—————— Aim for Change ——————

By the end of the lesson, we will: CONTRAST God's provision in the wilderness with Israel's former slave masters in Egypt, CONSIDER the times we have complained about God's provision, and EXPRESS thanks for the many ways God takes care of us.

—————————— In Focus ——————————

Hot days, warm evenings, or cool breezes were easier for outdoor living than harsh winters. Mr. and Mrs. George had lost their jobs and home, and their three children—twin girls and a boy—were in foster care. They would stay there until the Georges found jobs and a place to live. It was a terrifying and extremely tearful day when the social workers came and took the children away.

The cold winter snow and storms had begun. Mr. and Mrs. George had both found part-time jobs, but finding a place to live was hard. One evening, they decided to stay at a shelter because the bitter cold air and winds were too much to endure. The family shelter was filled with children, teens, adults, parents, and even some grandparents. This particular evening, the shelter provided light snacks and hot chocolate for an event everyone was invited to attend about job training, legal assistance, and housing opportunities. The best part was that the legal program would help them with having their children returned to them after finding them housing and jobs The Georges talked about things and prayed. They accepted the offers and were counting the days until they would hold and kiss their children again.

Why do you trust God to answer your prayers? How do you respond when God does not answer your prayers the way you want?

—————————— Keep in Mind ——————————

"And when the children of Israel saw it, they said one to another, It is manna: for they wist not what it was. And Moses said unto them, This is the bread which the LORD hath given you to eat" (Exodus 16:15, KJV).

"The Israelites were puzzled when they saw it. "What is it?" they asked each other. They had no idea what it was. And Moses told them, "It is the food the LORD has given you to eat" (Exodus 16:15, NLT).

Focal Verses

KJV **Exodus 16:1** And they took their journey from Elim, and all the congregation of the children of Israel came unto the wilderness of Sin, which is between Elim and Sinai, on the fifteenth day of the second month after their departing out of the land of Egypt.

2 And the whole congregation of the children of Israel murmured against Moses and Aaron in the wilderness:

3 And the children of Israel said unto them, Would to God we had died by the hand of the LORD in the land of Egypt, when we sat by the flesh pots, and when we did eat bread to the full; for ye have brought us forth into this wilderness, to kill this whole assembly with hunger.

4 Then said the LORD unto Moses, Behold, I will rain bread from heaven for you; and the people shall go out and gather a certain rate every day, that I may prove them, whether they will walk in my law, or no.

5 And it shall come to pass, that on the sixth day they shall prepare that which they bring in; and it shall be twice as much as they gather daily.

6 And Moses and Aaron said unto all the children of Israel, At even, then ye shall know that the LORD hath brought you out from the land of Egypt:

7 And in the morning, then ye shall see the glory of the LORD; for that he heareth your murmurings against the LORD: and what are we, that ye murmur against us?

8 And Moses said, This shall be, when the LORD shall give you in the evening flesh to eat, and in the morning bread to the full; for that the LORD heareth your murmurings which ye murmur against him: and what are we? your murmurings are not against us, but against the LORD.

13 And it came to pass, that at even the quails came up, and covered the camp: and in the morning the dew lay round about the host.

NLT **Exodus 16:1** Then the whole community of Israel set out from Elim and journeyed into the wilderness of Sin, between Elim and Mount Sinai. They arrived there on the fifteenth day of the second month, one month after leaving the land of Egypt.

2 There, too, the whole community of Israel complained about Moses and Aaron.

3 "If only the LORD had killed us back in Egypt," they moaned. "There we sat around pots filled with meat and ate all the bread we wanted. But now you have brought us into this wilderness to starve us all to death."

4 Then the LORD said to Moses, "Look, I'm going to rain down food from heaven for you. Each day the people can go out and pick up as much food as they need for that day. I will test them in this to see whether or not they will follow my instructions.

5 On the sixth day they will gather food, and when they prepare it, there will be twice as much as usual."

6 So Moses and Aaron said to all the people of Israel, "By evening you will realize it was the LORD who brought you out of the land of Egypt.

7 In the morning you will see the glory of the LORD, because he has heard your complaints, which are against him, not against us. What have we done that you should complain about us?"

8 Then Moses added, "The LORD will give you meat to eat in the evening and bread to satisfy you in the morning, for he has heard all your complaints against him. What have we done? Yes, your complaints are against the LORD, not against us."

13 That evening vast numbers of quail flew in and covered the camp. And the next morning the area around the camp was wet with dew.

35

14 And when the dew that lay was gone up, behold, upon the face of the wilderness there lay a small round thing, as small as the hoar frost on the ground.

15 And when the children of Israel saw it, they said one to another, It is manna: for they wist not what it was. And Moses said unto them, This is the bread which the LORD hath given you to eat.

14 When the dew evaporated, a flaky substance as fine as frost blanketed the ground.

15 The Israelites were puzzled when they saw it. "What is it?" they asked each other. They had no idea what it was. And Moses told them, "It is the food the LORD has given you to eat.

The People, Places, and Times

Aaron. The son of Amram and Jochebed, and brother of Moses and Miriam, Aaron was Israel's first high priest. Aaron's family was descended from the Levites, Israel's first priests. Later all Levites were subordinated to Aaron and his descendants within their tribe. God commanded Moses to set apart Aaron and his sons from among the Israelites to serve God as priests by a perpetual ordinance. Moses ordained Aaron and his sons as God had instructed to make sacrifices, offerings, and atonement at the altar in the sanctuary. Prior to being consecrated as the high priest, Aaron served as Moses' spokesman before Pharaoh in Egypt, as Moses had protested that he was not able to speak directly to Pharaoh (Exodus 4:10–14). One of Aaron's shortcomings was yielding to pressure from the Israelites to make a golden calf for worship at Mount Sinai, also called Mount Horeb (Exodus 32:1–4).

Background

The Israelites were delivered from 400 years of bondage in Egypt and escaped with great wealth because of the power of God and His judgment against the Egyptians and their false gods (Exodus 15:1–21). They sang a song of God's glory and mercy toward them and celebrated as God now traveled with them as a pillar of cloud by day and a pillar of fire by night on their way to Mount Sinai where they would worship God as free people. On the journey, they had seen God part the Red Sea to allow them to walk through on dry land while the Egyptians pursued them. Yet when the Egyptians arrived at the sea, it closed, drowning Pharaoh and his armies. On the other side of the sea, they traveled for three days without water and stopped at a place called Marah. The water there was bitter, unfit for drinking, and they complained to Moses that God is going to have them die of thirst. God set up an agreement there that if they obey Him, He will continue to provide for them and make the bitter waters drinkable. They leave there and then set camp at a huge oasis called Elim where they can get water and rest before they continue their travel.

How has God shown His provision in your life? Did any provisions feel miraculous?

At-A-Glance

1. The Complaint (Exodus 16:1–3)
2. The Response (vv. 4–8)
3. The Provision (vv. 13–15)

In Depth

1. The Complaint (Exodus 16:1–3)

It has only been a month since the Children of Israel had been miraculously delivered from Egypt. After a rest at the oasis of Elim, they begin the journey into the wilderness on their way to Mt. Sinai where God has appointed them to meet Him. Yet only a short time into the journey, they begin to complain against Moses and Aaron, their leaders. Even though their complaint against their leaders and God is ridiculous, the whole community joins in the despair. They are hungry. But rather than asking the all-powerful God who just delivered them from 400 years of slavery for provision, they complain. They cry out that God should have killed them in Egypt because while they were enslaved, at least they could eat when they wanted. Now that they are free, they are hungry, and that is a fate worse than death. Their temporary hunger makes them feel it would be better to be well fed in bondage to Egyptians than to be hungry and free in a relationship with God.

Why might some people choose bondage over freedom whether physically, mentally, or spiritually?

2. The Response (vv. 4–8)

The Lord hears the cries of the Israelites and responds with provisions. God is willing and able to provide for His people, but he will give them instructions to obey in order to receive the provision. The Lord will provide only enough food for the day, so no one can hoard or store it up and become dependent upon themselves. They will all be dependent on God alone for their daily bread. Yet they will also keep the Sabbath, so God will miraculously allow them to have enough for two days every six days, so no one has to work on the Sabbath. Moses and Aaron clarify for the Children of Israel that God will do this as a display of His power to provide. God hears their complaints and will respond; Moses and Aaron are just the messengers. The Israelites do not need to seek multiple gods as other nations do in order to have their needs met. The same Lord who is their deliverer is also their provider.

Why do we sometimes complain about our situations rather than rely on God who is able to deliver us from them?

3. The Provision (vv. 13–15)

Quail is an available source of wild poultry in the wilderness. Yet it is an act of God that so many quail show up in the camp for the Children of Israel to have meat. In addition, God sends dew that produces a flaky substance that acts as flour for the Children of Israel to make bread. They are confused by what they are seeing and call it "manna," which means "what is it?" in Hebrew. God responds to their complaint with His own word that He will provide food for them in the wilderness. God is faithful to His Word: He provides meat and bread daily for the Israelites. Moses serves again as an interpreter when the Children of Israel are confused about what they are seeing. Although they complained and God answered before, they still do not understand God's provision. Moses informs them that what they are seeing is food that the Lord had promised.

How has God intervened or provided for your life in unexpected ways?

Search the Scriptures

1. How soon do the Israelites begin complaining after being freed from slavery? Why might they make such an extreme complaint?

2. Why does the Lord make it so the food from heaven or manna only lasts for one day?

Discuss the Meaning

1. God is able to provide for those who seek His provision. What keeps us from seeking God for provision?

2. How can we shift our focus from what we don't have to be grateful for what we do have?

Liberating Lesson

Hunger is one of the greatest problems in our world today. An estimated nine million people die of starvation every year all over the world. Yet, research shows that there is more than enough food in the world for everyone to have enough to eat. The problem is not a lack of resources but the distribution of resources that leaves places like North America and Europe wasting more food in a day than other places in Africa and Asia consume in several months. God is able to provide food for all people on earth. But those who hoard it up for themselves instead of sharing it with those who have none cause their brothers and sisters to face starvation daily. We are called as followers of Jesus Christ to do what He did. Not only should we pray for daily bread for all of God's children, but we must use what we have individually and systemically to feed the multitudes. Some people feel the poor and hungry are in situations of their own making. They should work harder, so they would have more to eat and live better lives, but God recognizes the needs of all people despite their economic status. God treated even ungrateful, complaining Israel not with contempt, but with mercy, feeding them even though they were complaining. How much more so should we believe that God wants to feed all those who hunger? God is able to take what seems like enough for our own lunch and feed five thousand with more than enough left over. We are the body of Christ in the world, and the world is hungry. Will we feed them today and use our wisdom and resources that have produced abundance to help them eat for a lifetime?

Application for Activation

Take some time this week to journal or write down some things God has provided for you in the past year. How has God provided for you in ways that really impacted you? Are there any situations you are facing now where you are more focused on what you need than who

God is? Pray for God's provision and then use wisdom to manage and be thankful for what you have to do for today rather than worry about what you need for tomorrow. God will be the same providing God tomorrow that He was yesterday and is today. How can you show your gratitude to God this week instead of complaining?

Follow the Spirit

WHAT GOD WANTS ME TO DO: _____

_____

_____

_____

_____

Remember Your Thoughts

Special insights I have learned:

_____

_____

_____

More Light on the Text
Exodus 16:1–8, 13–15

The book of Exodus contains a major part of Israel's history and their relationship with God. It records God's acts of faithfulness and grace as He leads them to the Promised Land in fulfillment of His promise to their forefathers, Abraham, Isaac, and Jacob. The book presents a series of problems the people face and God's solutions. Repeatedly during their wilderness wanderings, the Children of Israel grumble against Moses and Aaron whenever they face a crisis (Exodus 15:24, 16:2, 17:3; Numbers 14:2, 29, 16:41). However, in reality, they grumble against the Lord (Exodus 16:8). Nonetheless, each time God demonstrates His sovereignty, faithfulness, and grace. God always comes to their rescue and solves their problem in spite of their unfaithfulness and lack of trust. The book is summed up as "God's faithfulness and grace in dealing with His people."

For instance, Israel witnessed God's sovereignty and the act of deliverance (Exodus 14). He miraculously parted the Red Sea (one of the greatest obstacles on their way) and made the whole multitude (about 600,000 men, besides women and children, 12:37) of Israel walk through on dry land while the whole Egyptian army drowned (14:21–31). This resulted in praise and worship (15:1–21). They then journey through the wilderness of Shur. After the three day journey, they arrived at Marah and were thirsty. They found the water there undrinkable—bitter (which is what Marah means). They complained, and God turned the undrinkable bitter water into drinkable, "sweet water" (15:25). They arrived at Elim. In contrast to Marah, in Elim were twelve sources of water and seventy palm trees, and they camped there for some time before proceeding in their journey (15:27).

1 And they took their journey from Elim, and all the congregation of the children of Israel came unto the wilderness of Sin, which is between Elim and Sinai, on the fifteenth day of the second month after their departing out of the land of Egypt. 2 And the whole congregation of the children of Israel murmured against Moses and Aaron in the wilderness:

The people leave Elim and come to the wilderness of Sin. The English phrase, "they took their journey" is the Hebrew word, *nasa'* (**naw-SAH**), which means "to pull up" and is used often when referring to pulling up tent

stakes, as in the start of a journey. That indicates that they camp in Elim for some time, perhaps several days. The word Elim (Heb. *'Eylim*, **ay-LEEM**) means "palm trees." They camp and rest there because of the presence of the oasis and trees, which provides water and shelter—a proper place for rest (Exodus 15:27). After leaving Elim, the people arrive at the "wilderness of Sin, which is between Elim and Sinai." The wilderness's name is a transliteration of the Hebrew *Sin* (**SEEN**), which means "thorn" or "clay." The area is not named "Sin" because of the people's rebellious or sinful acts, nor should it be interpreted in its English meaning, as if the people were traveling through a "sinful" place. Rather Sin is a place, a stretch of desert land along the way across the Sinai Peninsula. It is a vast expanse of sand and stone which tests the faith of the Israelites. It should be noted that sometimes God uses our "wildernesses" to test our faith and trust in Him. He often uses the crises we face to display His faithfulness and to demonstrate that He cares for and is in control of our affairs.

The people of Israel arrive at the wilderness of Sin precisely one month after their departure from Egypt (12:6). (One month more would bring them to Sinai, Exodus 19:1.) The food supply they carried along seems to have depleted. It is not out of place for the people to run out food, especially given the length of time since they left Egypt and have been wandering in the desert, a dry, sandy, stony place. There is nowhere they could replenish their food supply after leaving Elim because of the nature of the place; no life existed there. They become hungry and in need of food. They again resort to murmuring and complaining bitterly against Moses and Aaron as they did in Marah (Exodus 15:24). It is not unnatural for people to express their need. However, instead of expressing their need to Moses and Aaron, the people murmur and begin to speak evil against them. The word "murmur" (Heb. *lun*, **LOON**) means to be stubbornly against someone and complain. The whole congregation of Israel grumbles against Moses, though in reality, they are grumbling against God.

3 And the children of Israel said unto them, Would to God we had died by the hand of the LORD in the land of Egypt, when we sat by the flesh pots, and when we did eat bread to the full; for ye have brought us forth into this wilderness, to kill this whole assembly with hunger.

The lack of food causes them to forget their awful plight in Egypt. In spite of their suffering and bondage in Egypt, they at least had enough to eat, they say. They seem to prefer their bondage in Egypt to what they are going through presently and wish they had died in Egypt rather than perish in the wilderness. They charge Moses and Aaron with conspiring to murder them in the wilderness. "If only the Lord had killed us back in Egypt," they moan. Oftentimes, when faced with certain crises, we forget God's past work of deliverance, protection, and provision. There is no difference between these people. Within one month of their departure, Israel experienced God's mighty deeds. He led them through the Red Sea (Exodus 14:21–31); He turned the bitter water at Marah to drinkable, sweet water (15:25). At the desert of Elim, God also provided a place of rest, a camping ground (15:27). They forget that the God who did all of this is capable of supplying them with food. Instead, they crave all the meat (KJV: "flesh pots") and bread in Egypt. Present predicaments, crises, and discomforts often tend to becloud our memories of past victories and successes. Thus we tend to become ungrateful and unfaithful toward God. This is where we find the people of Israel at this time.

4 Then said the LORD unto Moses, Behold, I will rain bread from heaven for you; and the people shall go out and gather a certain rate every day, that I may prove them, whether they will walk in my law, or no. 5 And it shall come to pass, that on the sixth day they shall prepare that which they bring in; and it shall be twice as much as they gather daily.

In spite of our ingratitude and disbelief, God always remains faithful. As He did with the people's complaint for water at Marah, and consistent with His character, the Lord responds to the people's cry. He promises Moses that He will provide the people food in an unusual manner: "Behold I will rain bread from heaven for you" (v. 4). Often God provides for us with known resources, and other times He will provide from unexpected sources. In the present circumstance, the provision will come directly from heaven. The phrase, "I will rain bread from heaven for you," describes not only the source of the food but the quality and quantity. It is from heaven ("angels' food," Psalm 78:25), and it will fall down like rain and cover the camp ("bread to the full," Exodus 16:8).

The promise comes with a definite instruction of obedience and responsibility. The people are to go out daily and gather a certain quantity. This is to test their obedience to God as well as their ability to trust God for their daily bread. Obedience and trust are essential in any relationship; more so with God. We must believe that our God is able to supply our daily needs. Jesus taught His disciples to pray, "Give us this day our daily bread" (Matthew 6:11; cf. Luke 11:3). By the same token, obedience to the Law of the Lord is vital in our relationship with Him. The test concerns the institution of the Sabbath rest. The people are to go out daily and gather enough for the day, but on the sixth day, "it shall be twice as much as they gather daily" so that they can rest on the seventh day. This is consistent with the written Law to be given at Sinai (Exodus 20:8–11; cf. Genesis 2:2–3). This law also forces the people to trust the Lord to provide enough for them to make it through an extra day even without disciplined daily work. Equally important is the part they are responsible to perform. They are to go out daily and collect as much they can use for the day. The provision is made; it is their responsibility to go and to pick up what they need.

6 And Moses and Aaron said unto all the children of Israel, At even, then ye shall know that the LORD hath brought you out from the land of Egypt: 7 And in the morning, then ye shall see the glory of the LORD; for that he heareth your murmurings against the LORD: and what are we, that ye murmur against us?

After receiving the promise from the Lord, Moses and Aaron summon the people to break the news to them. In answer to their murmuring, Moses and Aaron assure them of God's presence and concern over their affairs. Moses guarantees them that by the evening (KJV: "at even") they "shall know that the LORD hath brought" them out of the land of Egypt. It will be doubtful to suppose that the people do not know the Lord was the one who delivered them from Egypt. Their experiences of the plagues in Egypt, the Passover, and their deliverance at the Red Sea, coupled with the provision of drinking water at Marah, are enough evidence to the fact. The truth of the matter is that they know the truth—they experienced all these extraordinary occurrences. However, it does not take much to cause an average person or group to complain when confronted with the slightest temporary shortage of life's essentials: water, food, or shelter.

The verb "know" is the Hebrew *yada'* (**yaw-DAH**). It is used in different ways and in a variety of senses, figuratively and literally, to mean "to know." So Moses says to them that in the evening they will really know and be certain that it is God who brought them out of Egypt. In other words, they will be convinced of the fact when they see what the Lord is going to do.

Then in the morning, Moses promises, they are going to see God's glory displayed. The word "see" is the Hebrew *ra'ah* (**raw-AW**) and the two verbs *yada'* and *ra'ah* are often used synonymously. "Glory" is the Hebrew word *kabod* (**kaw-BODE**, weight, heaviness). They are not going to see the glory of the Lord as in His splendor or His enthroned radiance, but in the display of His love, mercy, and grace as He miraculously provides them with food in answer to their complaint. Moses assures them that the Lord hears their murmuring. Moses and Aaron did not bring them out of Egypt, God did. Moses and Aaron are only God's servants, God's spokesmen, following His directions.

8 And Moses said, This shall be, when the LORD shall give you in the evening flesh to eat, and in the morning bread to the full; for that the LORD heareth your murmurings which ye murmur against him: and what are we? your murmurings are not against us, but against the LORD.

Moses' closing remarks emphasize his previous statement (v. 7). Here Moses reiterates the fact that their complaints are in reality not against him and Aaron but against God. To reassure them that their complaint has been heard, the Lord is not only going to rain down "bread in the morning" (vv. 4, 8), He is also going to give them "flesh [meat] to eat" that evening. What an amazing grace. Instead of raining down His fury, fire, and brimstone to consume them for their murmuring, the Lord promises to take care of their problems and rain down food from above. How often do we do wrong toward God, and yet He shows us mercy? Even while we are still sinners, Christ died for us (Romans 5:8). God's love is consistent at all times, and His faithfulness never fails. Indeed He does not treat us as our sins deserve, and He does not reward us or pay us back in full for our wrongs (Psalm 103:10).

This is an eternal truth that the people of Israel are about to experience.

13 And it came to pass, that at even the quails came up, and covered the camp: and in the morning the dew lay round about the host. 14 And when the dew that lay was gone up, behold, upon the face of the wilderness there lay a small round thing, as small as the hoar frost on the ground. 15 And when the children of Israel saw it, they said one to another, It is manna: for they wist not what it was. And Moses said unto them, This is the bread which the LORD hath given you to eat.

That very evening, faithful to His promise and in response to the people's craving for meat, God miraculously provides them with quails. The flock comes in abundance of the supply and provision: it covers the camp. The psalmist describes it thus: "He rained flesh also upon them as dust, and feathered fowls like as the sand of the sea. And he let it fall in the midst of their camp, round about their habitations. So they did eat, and were well filled: for he gave them their own desire" (Psalm 78:27–29; cf. Psalm 105:40).

Likewise and in fulfillment to His promise (Exodus 16:4, 12), the next morning the Lord rains down bread described as "round" and "small as the hoar frost" (v. 14). On seeing these strange elements, the people are puzzled. They ask one another, "What is it?" because they have no idea what it is. Since they do not understand the strange food, the Israelites name it "manna," which means "What is it?" from the Hebrew *man* (**MAWN**). It is described as white like a coriander seed, tasting like honey wafers (v. 31). Even though some try to explain away this miracle with natural phenomena, the truth remains that God is a faithful, miracle-working God who supplies our needs at all times in unique ways as He did for Israel. Jesus is the ultimate manna from heaven (John 6:32–35). In Him we have life.

Sources:
Strong, James. *New Strong's Exhaustive Concordance of the Bible with Expanded Greek-Hebrew Dictionary.* Biblesoft, 2006.
Interlinear Transliterated Bible. Biblesoft, 2006.
Zondervan NIV Study Bible. Grand Rapids, MI: Zondervan, 2008.

Say It Correctly

Manna. MAN-uh.
Jochebed. JAH-cuh-bed.
Elim. EE-lim.

Daily Bible Readings

MONDAY
Striking a Fair Balance
(2 Corinthians 8:9–15)

TUESDAY
Believers Depend on One Another
(1 Corinthians 12:18–26)

WEDNESDAY
The Lord Responds to Complaints
(Exodus 16:9–12)

THURSDAY
Conducting Daily Family Duties
(Exodus 16:16–21)

FRIDAY
Observing the Sabbath Day
(Exodus 16:22–30)

SATURDAY
Symbols of Remembrance
(Exodus 16:31–36)

SUNDAY
God Provides for the People
(Exodus 16:1–8, 13–15)

Teaching Tips

Words You Should Know

A. Spy (13:2) *tur* (Heb.)—To go before and search out

B. Glory (14:10) *kabod* (Heb.)—Majesty, honor, splendor; especially of God

Teacher Preparation

Unifying Principle—We Don't Believe You! When life puts obstacles in our paths, we are tempted to abandon the promises the future holds. Why don't we believe the promises made to us? Caleb and Joshua believed that God would lead Israel to possession of the Promised Land and tried to persuade the people to trust God's faithfulness.

A. Read the Bible Background and Devotional Reading.

B. Pray for your students and lesson clarity.

C. Read the lesson Scripture in multiple translations.

O—Open the Lesson

A. Begin the class with prayer.

B. As a class, brainstorm a list of big decisions that adults make—with marriage, children, health, and so on. Discuss specific ways God can be a part of each decision.

C. Have the students read the Aim for Change and the In Focus story.

D. Ask students how events like those in the story weigh on their hearts and how they can view these events from a faith perspective.

P—Present the Scriptures

A. Read the Focal Verses and discuss the Background and The People, Places, and Times sections.

B. Have the class share what Scriptures stand out for them and why, with particular emphasis on today's context.

E—Explore the Meaning

A. Use In Depth or More Light on the Text to facilitate a deeper discussion of the lesson text.

B. Pose the questions in Search the Scriptures and Discuss the Meaning.

C. Discuss the Liberating Lesson and Application for Activation sections.

N—Next Steps for Application

A. Summarize the value of trusting in God's promises.

B. End class with a commitment to pray for courage to cling to the truths God has revealed to us.

Worship Guide

For the Superintendent or Teacher
Theme: God Hears Our Cry
Song: "We Have Heard the Joyful Sound"
Devotional Reading: Psalm 106:1–12, 48

God Hears Our Cry

Bible Background • NUMBERS 13:1–14:10
Printed Text • NUMBERS 13:1–2, 17, 25–28; 14:1–2, 5–10
Devotional Reading • PSALM 106:1–12, 48

Aim for Change

By the end of the lesson, we will: EVALUATE the reasons for the Israelites' refusal to listen to Joshua and Caleb, DESIRE deeper trust in the promises of God, and CONFRONT the future in confidence of God's guidance and provision.

In Focus

Clara was the only one professing faith in Christ within her extended family. She had grown up learning to be kind, but when a friend at school invited her to youth group she heard the true Gospel for the first time. Clara realized just being kind was not enough; she repented of her sins and accepted salvation that night.

When she was old enough to live on her own, Clara wanted her faith to be seen in all of her life. But her family didn't understand. Often, she came up against persecution from family members because she would not join in their parties and trips to casinos to gamble. Many of the family members encouraged her to join them and have some fun. Occasionally, two of her cousins would tease her about her faith keeping her from having a good time with the family. A few even wanted to start an argument by saying things which they thought would cause Clara to respond in negative ways. Clara did not argue with them. She simply quietly lived out her faith.

However, Clara looked forward to the gatherings at church with other Christians. She found encouragement and strength from her church family to continue to work out her salvation as she walked daily with God

How is Clara witnessing to her extended family? Our behavior is often a powerful witness to others. How can she further her witness to her family?

Keep in Mind

"If the LORD delight in us, then he will bring us into this land, and give it us; a land which floweth with milk and honey" (Numbers 14:8, KJV).

"And if the LORD is pleased with us, he will bring us safely into that land and give it to us. It is a rich land flowing with milk and honey" (Numbers 14:8, NLT).

Focal Verses

KJV **Numbers 13:1** And the LORD spake unto Moses, saying,

2 Send thou men, that they may search the land of Canaan, which I give unto the children of Israel: of every tribe of their fathers shall ye send a man, every one a ruler among them.

17 And Moses sent them to spy out the land of Canaan, and said unto them, Get you up this way southward, and go up into the mountain:

25 And they returned from searching of the land after forty days.

26 And they went and came to Moses, and to Aaron, and to all the congregation of the children of Israel, unto the wilderness of Paran, to Kadesh; and brought back word unto them, and unto all the congregation, and shewed them the fruit of the land.

27 And they told him, and said, We came unto the land whither thou sentest us, and surely it floweth with milk and honey; and this is the fruit of it.

28 Nevertheless the people be strong that dwell in the land, and the cities are walled, and very great: and moreover we saw the children of Anak there.

14:1 And all the congregation lifted up their voice, and cried; and the people wept that night.

2 And all the children of Israel murmured against Moses and against Aaron: and the whole congregation said unto them, Would God that we had died in the land of Egypt! or would God we had died in this wilderness!

5 Then Moses and Aaron fell on their faces before all the assembly of the congregation of the children of Israel.

6 And Joshua the son of Nun, and Caleb the son of Jephunneh, which were of them that searched the land, rent their clothes:

7 And they spake unto all the company of the children of Israel, saying, The land, which we passed through to search it, is an exceeding good land.

NLT **Numbers 13:1** The LORD now said to Moses,

2 "Send out men to explore the land of Canaan, the land I am giving to the Israelites. Send one leader from each of the twelve ancestral tribes."

17 Moses gave the men these instructions as he sent them out to explore the land: "Go north through the Negev into the hill country."

25 After exploring the land for forty days, the men returned

26 to Moses, Aaron, and the whole community of Israel at Kadesh in the wilderness of Paran. They reported to the whole community what they had seen and showed them the fruit they had taken from the land.

27 This was their report to Moses: "We entered the land you sent us to explore, and it is indeed a bountiful country—a land flowing with milk and honey. Here is the kind of fruit it produces.

28 But the people living there are powerful, and their towns are large and fortified. We even saw giants there, the descendants of Anak!"

14:1 Then the whole community began weeping aloud, and they cried all night.

2 Their voices rose in a great chorus of protest against Moses and Aaron. "If only we had died in Egypt, or even here in the wilderness!" they complained.

5 Then Moses and Aaron fell face down on the ground before the whole community of Israel.

6 Two of the men who had explored the land, Joshua son of Nun and Caleb son of Jephunneh, tore their clothing.

7 They said to all the people of Israel, "The land we traveled through and explored is a wonderful land!

8 If the LORD delight in us, then he will bring us into this land, and give it us; a land which floweth with milk and honey.

9 Only rebel not ye against the LORD, neither fear ye the people of the land; for they are bread for us: their defence is departed from them, and the LORD is with us: fear them not.

10 But all the congregation bade stone them with stones. And the glory of the LORD appeared in the tabernacle of the congregation before all the children of Israel.

8 And if the LORD is pleased with us, he will bring us safely into that land and give it to us. It is a rich land flowing with milk and honey.

9 Do not rebel against the LORD, and don't be afraid of the people of the land. They are only helpless prey to us! They have no protection, but the LORD is with us! Don't be afraid of them!"

10 But the whole community began to talk about stoning Joshua and Caleb. Then the glorious presence of the LORD appeared to all the Israelites at the Tabernacle.

The People, Places, and Times

Promised Land. A hill country east of the Mediterranean Sea and west of the Jordan River, also called Canaan. God promised Abraham that this land would be given to his descendants (Genesis 13:14–17). The Israelites would occupy the Promised Land under the leadership of Joshua, fighting or conquering such people as the Canaanites, Hittites, Amorites, Perizzites, Hivites, and Jebusites. The land was described as "flowing with milk and honey," showing how the land could sustain not just subsistence living, but a life of abundance.

Caleb. This spy was from the tribe of Judah, the tribe that would be associated with royalty, as it produced King David as well as Jesus. Only he and Joshua stood as a voice of courage when the twelve spies returned from the Promised Land (v. 24), saying they could surely take the land. For his faithfulness, God promised to allow him to enter the land. Therefore, when it came time to take the land a generation later, Caleb led his clan to conquer the portion of land allotted to him. He defeated some of the toughest opponents of Canaan, the giant sons of Anak (Joshua 15:13-15).

Background

In Numbers 13 and 14, we find the Israelites near the beginning of their journey in the wilderness to Transjordan. God commands Moses to send one man from each ancestral tribe to spy in Canaan (Numbers 13). Shammua goes from the tribe of Reuben, Shaphat from Simeon, Caleb from Judah, Igal from Issachar, Joshua (Moses changed his name from Hoshea) from Ephraim, Palti from Benjamin, Gaddiel from Zebulun, Gaddi from Manasseh, Ammiel from Dan, Sethur from Asher, Nahbi from Naphtali, and Geuel from Gad. They were to determine the quality of the land and the strength of the people. They conclude that although Canaan is full of good things, the people could be too strong to overcome. As they listed their objections to entering the land God has given them, only Caleb and Joshua dissent (v. 30). Upon hearing the report, the Israelites lament that they had not remained in Egypt and want to choose a leader to help them return. But Joshua and Caleb trust God and encourage the assembly to trust Him, too. Just as the people are preparing to stone them, the glory of the Lord (cf. Exodus 14:10) appears.

The Israelites are tired of wandering, and they can now enter the land that God had given them. Why are they reluctant to claim what God has promised them?

In Depth

1. Spies in Canaan (Numbers 13:1–2, 17)

When God commands Moses to send spies into Canaan, the men Moses chooses have distinguished themselves as the leaders of their respective tribes. The twelve ancestral tribes are the descendants of the twelve sons of the patriarch Jacob, who was renamed Israel (Genesis 32:28). One man from each tribe is sent to the Negev, which is a generally dry waste country north of the Sinai Peninsula, south of what became Judah, and to the west and south of the Dead Sea. The hill country referenced here is part of the central spine of hills that runs north and south through Canaan.

Why did God command Moses to send one leader from each tribe to spy in Canaan?

2. Fear in the Land of Milk and Honey (vv. 25–28)

We see the phrase "forty days" often repeated in Scripture (Genesis 7:4; Matthew 4:2), so it is no surprise that the spies remained in Canaan for forty days. Here, we see the first reference to Kadesh, an oasis where much of the forty years in the wilderness will be spent (v. 26). At Kadesh, the spies show the assembly the fruit of the land. The spies tell them that the land "floweth with milk and honey" (v. 27). Although this is a common phrase used in the Torah to describe Canaan (Exodus 3:8; Leviticus 20:24), it is the first time it is used in the book of Numbers. However, the spies also report that the people in the land are strong and that some of them are constant enemies of the Israelites. The spies observe real danger in Canaan.

How might we overcome our fears and follow God?

3. Human Rebellion and God's Grace (Numbers 14:1–2, 5–10)

The people complain as soon as they hear the report from the spies. The people's complaining is a common theme we see in Numbers (Numbers 11:1; 16:41). The people often complain because of the challenges of life in the desert. They long for their settled lives in Egypt and lament having left the familiar to wander into the unknown. They wish they had died in Egypt or the wilderness before reaching Canaan.

As the people rebel against God, Moses and Aaron fall on their faces as an act of contrition. Joshua and Caleb tear their clothes, which is an act of mourning, a sign of humility before God. These men foreshadow the Lord's rejection of this generation with their words "if the LORD delight in us" and "only rebel not ye against the LORD" (vv. 8–9). They inform the people that with God, the people of Canaan will be bread to them because the Canaanites' protection is removed. The idea of lost protection is a condemnation of foreign gods who are not as strong as the God of Israel. They assure the people that God is with them. God is faithful to keep His promise. As they encourage the people and intercede on their behalf, the glory of God appears.

Like the Children of Israel, we are often afraid, and sometimes our fear leads us to rebel against God's plan for us. When we are afraid, let us remember that with God's help, we are more than overcomers. When God is with us, we can face any obstacle that stands in our way with confidence.

What are some ways you have been encouraged to trust God when facing difficult obstacles?

Search the Scriptures

1. The Israelites' experience of what happened in the past made them want to derail their future, although God already promised them the victory. Most of the assembly wanted to return to Egypt, two factors stopped them—God's presence and His chosen leadership. Describe God's presence in this Scripture. What difference does Moses' leadership make in this story?

2. The Israelites long to return to Egypt where they labored as slaves (Numbers 14:1–2). Their fear of the unknown overpowered their fear of losing their freedom. Why were they so afraid of the future even though God promised them victory?

Discuss the Meaning

When the Israelites wanted to return to Egypt, effective leadership became essential to the outcome of this story. God told Moses to choose one leader from each of the twelve ancestral tribes to spy in Canaan. Had it not been for two God-fearing spies, the people would have turned around. Effective and diverse leadership is essential to a functional congregation. How might we choose congregational leaders who represent the diversity of our membership?

Liberating Lesson

God has placed a call on the church to enter our lands and be the hands and feet of Jesus in the world. Despite that call, many churches remain silent on issues like violence against women and children, the plight of refugee and migrant families, and environmental concerns. While we often justify our silence by arguing that churches are spiritual, not political spaces, Jesus taught us that the first and greatest commandment is to love the Lord with all our heart and strength (in addition to our spirits) and that the second commandment is to love our neighbors as ourselves. God has promised never to forsake us. In the Great Commission in Matthew, Jesus promised to be with us until the end of the age.

God has already promised us the victory! So, why are we so afraid to follow God's call to love our neighbors radically?

Application for Activation

We are all leaders in some space, whether at home, at work, in our churches, or in our communities. Fear is a natural reaction to the unknown, but trust that God has not forsaken you. When we feel panic, angst, and frustration because we do not know what lies ahead, leaders are called to intercede on our behalf. Leaders are also called to encourage us to continue to follow God wherever the call might lead. Think about how you can be a leader this week, who encourages people to face their fears and overcome obstacles to see them succeed. God is faithful to us, and even when we feel alone, God is with us.

Follow the Spirit

What God wants me to do:

_____

_____

_____

_____

Remember Your Thoughts

Special insights I have learned:

_____

_____

_____

_____

More Light on the Text
Numbers 13:1–2, 17, 25–28; 14:1–2, 5-10

The Lord leads the Children of Israel systematically through the barren wilderness to their destination—Canaan. It is now about two years since they departed from Egypt. They have reached the wilderness of Paran and encamped at Kadesh, a few days' journey from the Promised Land, on the southern border of Canaan. The course of the journey changes because of Israel's rebellion and faithlessness.

13:1 And the LORD spake unto Moses, saying, 2 Send thou men, that they may search the land of Canaan, which I give unto the children of Israel: of every tribe of their fathers shall ye send a man, every one a ruler among them.

Israel followed the Lord's leading into the wilderness of Paran and camped at Kadesh. Moses speaks with confidence and trust, recognizing the Lord's great deeds of the past and what God is capable of doing, and exhorts the people to take possession of the promised inheritance. The Lord orders Moses to send out men to search the land of Canaan. The word for "search" (Heb. *tur*, **TOOR**) means to go before and explore or spy. The Lord instructs Moses to choose twelve men, one from each Israelite tribe, to go and make a preliminary survey of the land and bring back reports. Moses obeys the Lord and sends the men into the land.

The phrases "every one a ruler among them" and "all those men were heads of the Children of Israel" (Numbers 13:3) are synonymous, meaning that Moses selects the leaders of each tribe (cf. 1:4). They probably belong to the ruling class, those referred to in Exodus 18:25 as "heads over the people" or the council, which represent different groups (thousands, hundreds, and fifties). This group is, however, different from the group that conducts the census (cf. Numbers 1:5–17; 13:4–16). The number of spies is significant, both to have a representative for each tribe, but also perhaps to allow each one to spy out land for his own tribe. God directs Moses to choose the rulers or leaders, people of character, authority, and prudence who would be "credible" in their report to the people. Alas, how they failed! Numbers 13:4–16 lists the names of the spies and their tribes, and verses 17–25 narrate how the search goes and the outcome.

17 And Moses sent them to spy out the land of Canaan, and said unto them, Get you up this way southward, and go up into the mountain:

Moses sends the twelve men selected from the twelve tribes to spy out the Promised Land of Canaan. The "southward" Moses refers to here is actually north of the camp through the Negev desert which lies in the southern part of Canaan. The confusion comes from Negev being the name for that region of desert, as well as the word for "south" (Heb. *negeb*, **NEH-gev**). The "mountain" (NLT: "hill country") is where Moses instructs them to go, whichgives them an elevated position from which to survey the land.

25 And they returned from searching of the land after forty days. 26 And they went and came to Moses, and to Aaron, and to all the congregation of the children of Israel, unto the wilderness of Paran, to Kadesh; and brought back word unto them, and unto all the congregation, and shewed them the fruit of the land.

In verses 18–24, there are more instructions from Moses to determine key attributes of the land during their search, such as what the crops are like, what the soil is like, and most importantly what the people are like: strong or weak, many or few. The last question becomes the point of contention later in the account. They find during their northward journey that the land is very fruitful and bring samples back for the congregation to evaluate. But they also find out the descendants of Anak the giant live there.

Here, they show their leaders and the congregation the excellent produce they found in the land. The produce is so large it takes two people to carry a single cluster of grapes (v. 23). Showing the Children of Israel the fruit validates God's word that the land is exceedingly fruitful and plentiful. It is also evidence for them that they could have a prosperous life there and be able to farm and forage for food.

27 And they told him, and said, We came unto the land whither thou sentest us, and surely it floweth with milk and honey; and this is the fruit of it. 28 Nevertheless the people be strong that dwell in the land, and the cities are walled, and very great: and moreover we saw the children of Anak there.

The spies capture the dilemma of the Children of Israel well. They give their report in response to the questions in Moses' mission for them (vv. 18–20). God's word is true: the land "floweth with milk and honey"; that is, it was lavish with resources. God's provision is not simply for sustenance but for abundance. There is more than enough room to settle and food to eat. But the answer to Moses' other question is that, despite more than enough in the land God is calling them to, giant cities filled with giant people intimidate the Israelite spies. The children of Anak are known as giants in the Bible from this point forward (Deuteronomy 9:2). The promise of God is waiting before them, but the obstacle in the way looks too great to defeat.

Verses 29–33 tell of Caleb objecting to this general report of fear. He encourages the people to take the land through God's strength, but the other spies only reiterate their negative report.

14:1 And all the congregation lifted up their voice, and cried; and the people wept that night.

Nothing breaks a parent's heart like seeing a child cry unless those tears are the fruit of selfish desires and ingratitude. The tears of the ungrateful often get an angry response. God delivers the children of the promise to the edge of the Promised Land. Spies have been sent in and brought back a mixed report. The majority of the spies hold that the inhabitants of the land are too formidable to be conquered, and any attempt to do so would result in the destruction of the people and their children. Only two spies offer that God would be sufficient to deliver the land into the hands of the Children of Israel. The people believe the report from the majority of the spies and wept. Their loud wailing is an expression of sadness and lament. Their perspective is based on the report of the spies, not on the promises of the one true God.

2 And all the children of Israel murmured against Moses and against Aaron: and the whole congregation said unto them, Would God that we had died in the land of Egypt! or would God we had died in this wilderness!

The people forget how God delivered them from all the hardships they endured for the previous two years piled on top of each other. They embrace the report from the majority of the spies and turn on Moses and Aaron, God's appointed leaders. Nothing of the excitement and exuberance that greeted the departure from Egypt remained, and now they just want to die. They fear that they will be "prey" and envision themselves being carted off as the spoils of a losing war (v. 3). They conclude that Moses failed as a leader by bringing them to the edge of the Promised Land only to ultimately be destroyed by the giants in the land. Their earlier lust for the meat, fruit, and vegetables of Egypt help dull the memories of the harsh conditions of enslavement there (Numbers 11:4–5, 33–34). God greeted their earlier complaints with fire and holy wrath, so the people now just ask for death. If God is not going to make the task of occupying the Promised Land easy, then they will take matters into their own hands and go back to Egypt. In the following verses, they even plot to find a new leader instead of Moses who will take them back to Egypt (vv. 3–4).

5 Then Moses and Aaron fell on their faces before all the assembly of the congregation of the children of Israel.

Both Moses and Aaron know that the actions of the people will not be pleasing to God. They fall on their faces, whether in a posture of begging them to stop or in anticipation of what they felt God is about to do. Earlier complaining resulted in fire and plague from God, and now in the face of outright rejection by the assembly, Moses and Aaron do not know how God will react. They only know that it will not be pleasant.

6 And Joshua the son of Nun, and Caleb the son of Jephunneh, which were of them that searched the land, rent their clothes: 7 And they spake unto all the company of the children of Israel, saying, The land, which we passed through to search it, is an exceeding good land.

As Moses and Aaron lay prostrate on the ground, Joshua and Caleb, the two spies who came back with a message of faithful anticipation that God will give the people the land, "rent" (Heb. *qara'*, **kaw-RAH**, to tear or cut) their clothes, step up, and address the people. Though they are the two spies who returned and gave the minority report concerning the Promised Land, Joshua's name is not mentioned until this time. Now he stands in support of Caleb and tries to help persuade the masses not to reject God and His appointed leaders. Though the journey had been difficult, they had not lost faith in God or His plan for Israel's future. They remind the people that the land is truly a marvelous place.

8 If the LORD delight in us, then he will bring us into this land, and give it us; a land which floweth with milk and honey. 9 Only rebel not ye against the LORD, neither fear ye the people of the land; for they are bread for us: their defence is departed from them, and the LORD is with us: fear them not.

Torn clothes show their great sorrow. Caleb and Joshua stand before the people and try to make

their case not to abandon God. Earlier, the people seen a single branch of grapes, cut from a tree in the Promised Land, which required two men to carry back to the encampment (Numbers 13:23). Caleb and Joshua do not refute the report of the other spies but simply try to remind the people that the God who promised the land to them is sufficient to fulfill His word and deliver that land. They emphasize that if God delights in His people, the land will be theirs. Thus they encourage and warn the people not to rebel against God. They also indicated that, because God is with the people, the inhabitants of the land will be defenseless. Joshua and Caleb are reminding the people of the power of the same God who delivered them from Egypt. Yet the people already have their minds made up not to listen.

10 But all the congregation bade stone them with stones. And the glory of the LORD appeared in the tabernacle of the congregation before all the children of Israel.

As Caleb and Joshua plead with the people to remember God, the crowd becomes more and more convinced that they want nothing to do with the things they are saying. As a response, they call for them to be stoned to death. Stoning is a legitimate judicial punishment that an assembly has the authority to exact upon anyone they feel is guilty of a religious crime (e.g., witchcraft, blasphemy, or breaking the Sabbath; Leviticus 20:27, 24:16; Numbers 15:32–36). The people do not believe that Caleb and Joshua are communicating the will of God to them. Rather, they feel they are false witnesses and worthy to be stoned. The congregation allows itself to become convinced that God is in favor of their desire to return to Egypt.

The Children of Israel feel justified in their belief and actions until God's glory appears before them and speaks to Moses. The glory of the Lord is a special manifestation of His presence. The word literally means heaviness or weightiness, as we might talk about a "weighty subject"; however, it is always used in a figurative way to refer to glory, splendor, and majesty. While the word is used to refer to a nation's or a person's glory (Job 19:9; Isaiah 60:13), no human can rival God's glory. His fiery presence overwhelms His priests and prophets (2 Chronicles 7:1–3; Isaiah 6:1–5). Here in the wilderness, God's glory descends and causes the Israelites to cut themselves short of further sin against God and His messengers.

Sources:

Life Application Study Bible (New International Version). Wheaton, IL: Tyndale House Publishers, 1991.

Packer, J. I., Merrill C. Tenney, and William White. *Nelson's Illustrated Encyclopedia of Bible Facts*. Nashville, TN: Thomas Nelson Publishers, 1995.

Unger, Merrill F. *The New Unger's Bible Dictionary*. R.K. Harrison, editor. Chicago: Moody Press, 1988.

Daily Bible Readings

MONDAY
Praise the Lord!
(Psalm 106:1–12, 48)

TUESDAY
Spying Out the Land
(Numbers 13:17–24)

WEDNESDAY
Reporting Mixed Reviews
(Numbers 13:30–33)

THURSDAY
Moses Resists God's Proposal
(Exodus 32:7–14)

FRIDAY
God Decides Who Will Enter Canaan
(Deuteronomy 1:34–40)

SATURDAY
Moses Intercedes for God's People
(Numbers 14:13–20)

SUNDAY
Don't Doubt; Trust God's Promises
(Numbers 13:1–2, 17, 25–28; 14:1–2, 5–10)

Notes

_____

_____

_____

_____

Teaching Tips

Words You Should Know

A. Pestilence (v. 12) *deber* (Heb.)—A divine judgment of infestation with disease or pests

B. Pardon (v. 19) *salach* (Heb.)—Forgiveness from God

Teacher Preparation

Unifying Principle—One More Chance. Everyone wrongs others, even those who love them and those whom they love. When we have done wrong, is forgiveness possible? According to Numbers, God forgave the rebelling people of Israel and promised to lead their descendants forward to the Promised Land.

A. Read the Bible Background and Devotional Reading.

B. Pray for your students and lesson clarity.

C. Read the lesson Scripture in multiple translations.

O—Open the Lesson

A. Begin the class with prayer.

B. Discuss times of intercession on behalf of a friend or family member who was engaging in sinful action.

C. Have the students read the Aim for Change and the In Focus story.

D. Ask students how events like those in the story impact their faith walk and their reactions to family members.

P—Present the Scriptures

A. Read the Focal Verses and discuss the Background and The People, Places, and Times sections.

B. Have the class share what Scriptures stand out for them and why, with particular emphasis on today's themes.

E—Explore the Meaning

A. Use In Depth or More Light on the Text to facilitate a deeper discussion of the lesson text.

B. Pose the questions in Search the Scriptures and Discuss the Meaning.

C. Discuss the Liberating Lesson and Application for Activation sections.

N—Next Steps for Application

A. Summarize the value of God's love and forgiveness toward us.

B. End class with a commitment to pray for being faithful to God in all areas of their lives.

Worship Guide

For the Superintendent or Teacher
Theme: God Is Faithful
Song: "Faithful Is Our God"
Devotional Reading: Psalm 103:1–14

God Forgives

Bible Background • NUMBERS 14:10–23
Printed Text • NUMBERS 14:10–20 | Devotional Reading • PSALM 103:1–14

Aim for Change

By the end of the lesson, we will: COMPREHEND the significance of Moses' intercession for the people of Israel, REPENT of rebelling against God's plans and not trusting God's strength, and ASK for forgiveness for our sins.

In Focus

Even after counseling, Carla and her husband, Al, decided to divorce after twenty-three years of marriage. Their teenage children, Nikki and George, wanted their parents to work out their issues and blamed their mother. Carla felt it was time to tell them the truth about why she was divorcing their father.

As Carla began to say why they were divorcing, George interrupted her. "We already know, Mom. You are so busy working at your fancy news anchor job. You are never home. Dad always made time to attend our school activities but not you."

"George, I am so sorry that I've worked so many hours. About six years ago, I discovered your father was having an affair. They have four-year-old twin boys. I tried to work it out with him, but he wants to be with her. Plus, your father spent all the money in your college saving accounts. So I've been working extra hard to replenish that money. Please forgive me for not always being there, and try to forgive your father."

George hugged his mother. "Mom, I'm sorry. I didn't know the truth. I understand and forgive you. But it may take some time for me to forgive Dad."

Nikki shrugged her shoulders, "I don't care. I will never forgive you. I may even ask Dad if I can live with him."

How difficult do you find it to forgive others whom you love but have wronged you?

Keep in Mind

"Pardon, I beseech thee, the iniquity of this people according unto the greatness of thy mercy, and as thou hast forgiven this people, from Egypt even until now" (Numbers 14:19, KJV).

"In keeping with your magnificent, unfailing love, please pardon the sins of this people, just as you have forgiven them ever since they left Egypt" (Numbers 14:19, NLT).

Focal Verses

KJV **Numbers 14:10** But all the congregation bade stone them with stones. And the glory of the LORD appeared in the tabernacle of the congregation before all the children of Israel.

11 And the LORD said unto Moses, How long will this people provoke me? and how long will it be ere they believe me, for all the signs which I have shewed among them?

12 I will smite them with the pestilence, and disinherit them, and will make of thee a greater nation and mightier than they.

13 And Moses said unto the LORD, Then the Egyptians shall hear it, (for thou broughtest up this people in thy might from among them;)

14 And they will tell it to the inhabitants of this land: for they have heard that thou LORD art among this people, that thou LORD art seen face to face, and that thy cloud standeth over them, and that thou goest before them, by day time in a pillar of a cloud, and in a pillar of fire by night.

15 Now if thou shalt kill all this people as one man, then the nations which have heard the fame of thee will speak, saying,

16 Because the LORD was not able to bring this people into the land which he sware unto them, therefore he hath slain them in the wilderness.

17 And now, I beseech thee, let the power of my lord be great, according as thou hast spoken, saying,

18 The LORD is longsuffering, and of great mercy, forgiving iniquity and transgression, and by no means clearing the guilty, visiting the iniquity of the fathers upon the children unto the third and fourth generation.

19 Pardon, I beseech thee, the iniquity of this people according unto the greatness of thy mercy, and as thou hast forgiven this people, from Egypt even until now.

NLT **Numbers 14:10** But the whole community began to talk about stoning Joshua and Caleb. Then the glorious presence of the LORD appeared to all the Israelites at the Tabernacle.

11 And the LORD said to Moses, "How long will these people treat me with contempt? Will they never believe me, even after all the miraculous signs I have done among them?

12 I will disown them and destroy them with a plague. Then I will make you into a nation greater and mightier than they are!"

13 But Moses objected. "What will the Egyptians think when they hear about it?" he asked the LORD. "They know full well the power you displayed in rescuing your people from Egypt.

14 Now if you destroy them, the Egyptians will send a report to the inhabitants of this land, who have already heard that you live among your people. They know LORD, that you have appeared to your people face to face and that your pillar of cloud hovers over them. They know that you go before them in the pillar of cloud by day and the pillar of fire by night.

15 Now if you slaughter all these people with a single blow, the nations that have heard of your fame will say,

16 'The LORD was not able to bring them into the land he swore to give them, so he killed them in the wilderness.'

17 Please, Lord, prove that your power is as great as you have claimed. For you said,

18 'The LORD is slow to anger and filled with unfailing love, forgiving every kind of sin and rebellion. But he does not excuse the guilty. He lays the sins of the parents upon their children; the entire family is affected—even children in the third and fourth generations.'

19 In keeping with your magnificent, unfailing love, please pardon the sins of this

20 And the LORD said, I have pardoned according to thy word:

people, just as you have forgiven them ever since they left Egypt."

20 Then the LORD said, "I will pardon them as you have requested.

The People, Places, and Times

Numbers. The book of Numbers is the fourth book out of five that compose the Pentateuch. It gives us an account of Israel's journey from Mount Sinai to the plains of Moab on the border of Canaan, the Promised Land. The name of this book does not adequately communicate the book's actual theme of faithfulness of God and the faithlessness of God's people. The English name (taken from the Greek translation) refers to the fact that the book begins and ends with censuses of God's people. In Hebrew, however, Numbers is called *Bemidbar* (**beh-MEED-bar**), "in the wilderness." The Hebrew title is apt because it is actually about a familiar cast of characters (Moses, Aaron, Miriam, Caleb, and Joshua) who lead the Israelites through the wilderness for forty years.

Background

God had delivered the Israelites from slavery in Egypt (Exodus 14). He provided all their needs as they journeyed toward Canaan. But before they entered Canaan, God had to prepare the people first. God had requirements the people had to agree to follow. So while the Israelites were camped at Mount Sinai for a year, they received all the laws and requirements needed to live as a new nation in a new land. All the people agreed to fully obey all God had commanded.

Before they could depart from Mount Sinai, Moses was commanded by the Lord to take a census of all the people. They had to determine how many men were fit for military duty, as they would soon encounter enemies in Canaan (Numbers 1–4). According to God's command, Moses divided the men into various assignments

for military responsibilities and what they would carry. The Lord also wanted the people to remain pure, so strict guidelines were given to Moses (Numbers 5:1–10:10). Moreover, Moses also had to oversee the dedication and consecration of the tabernacle and all its furnishings.

The Israelites set out for the Promised Land, and that is when the people started complaining. Their complaints included: (1) their general misfortunes (11:1), (2) lack of meat (v. 4), (3) jealousy of Moses' authority (12:1–16), and (4) fear of battle against the men who inhabited the Promised Land (13:1–14:4).

How should we respond to God's gracious acts of love and forgiveness?

At-A-Glance

1. The Israelites' Rebellion (Numbers 14:10–12)
2. Moses' Intercession (vv. 13–19)
3. God's Response (v. 20)

In Depth

1. The Israelites' Rebellion (Numbers 14:10–12)

Caleb and Joshua believed the Israelites would be able to defeat all the Canaanite armies. However, unbelief and fear spread among the people. How often do we doubt God's promises? No one believed Caleb's report. Everyone desired to go back to Egypt (14:4). Even after all God had done, they still did not trust Him.

Moses and Aaron fell on their faces and interceded on behalf of the Israelites (v. 5). Caleb and Joshua tried to convince the Israelites to trust God and go possess the land. The Israelites responded with death threats (v. 10). Then suddenly, "the glory of the LORD appeared in the tabernacle of the congregation." When we pray, God responds.

God spoke to Moses about the transgressions of the Israelites (v. 11). His questions reveal He has become impatient with the Israelites' refusal to trust in His power to defeat their enemies and give them the Promised Land. They have witnessed the signs of His power in sending the plagues upon the Egyptians, parting the Red Sea, providing manna from heaven, and more, but they still doubt. So God decides to enact a final judgment against the people, then start over with Moses and create people faithful to Him. We cannot expect God to continually allow us to rebel and not change.

How does one compare and contrast God's love versus God's justice?

2. Moses' Intercession (vv. 13–19)

Moses responds to God by arguing that it is important for Him to protect His reputation, especially among the Egyptians. If they realize God has removed His protection from the Israelites, He would suffer disgrace. The other nations, who know of His love for Israel and powerful presence that dwells with them, would now say God killed the Israelites because He was not able to fulfill His promise for them to possess the Land (14:15–16).

As Moses interceded for the Israelites, he quoted God's own description of Himself back to God. Numbers 14:18 is quoted from Exodus 34:6–7, when He revealed Himself to Moses on Mt. Sinai. In spite of the Israelites' rebellion, Moses pleads for God to show patience, love, forgiveness, discipline, and mercy. Even today, we each need to ask God to do the same for us. Our sins not only affect our lives but those we love as well as others.

When people harm you, do you pray for them? Why or why not?

3. God's Response (v. 20)

God's response to the prayers of Moses and Aaron is to pardon the Israelites. But He also disciplines the people so they wander in the wilderness forty years and do not enter the Promised Land. We must recognize that God hears our prayers and is willing to forgive us. But there are consequences for our sins. God loves us enough to discipline us, so we can learn from our mistakes and strive to live holy and be faithful servants of God (cf. Hebrews 12:6).

How often do you pray, repent, and seek forgiveness from God?

Search The Scriptures

1. Why was God impatient with the Israelites (Numbers 14:11–12)? What action was God going to take against the Israelites?

2. What characteristics of God are mentioned (v. 18)?

3. What reasoning did Moses give to God for forgiving the iniquities of the Israelites (v. 19)?

Discuss The Meaning

1. Moses struggled as the leader of the rebellious people. What impact did his prayers make in the lives of the people? What impact have you seen in the lives of people you have prayed for?

2. How can your sins draw others away from God? How can you seek reconciliation with those you have harmed?

3. Often we are surprised by God's plans for our lives. How can we rely on our faith that God will accomplish His will for our lives?

Liberating Lesson

Moses believed intercession on behalf of the rebellious Israelites would make a difference in their lives. He understood that God is loving, merciful, and forgiving. God hears our prayers and will respond. So when we fail to obey God's commands, we can pray and ask Him to forgive us. We also should take the time to pray for others, including our communities and nation. Everything we do has a direct or indirect impact on someone's life. So when we are wounded by another person, we must forgive them just as God forgives us.

Forgiving those who have harmed us can prove difficult sometimes. For example, how can a young man forgive a police officer who shot him in the back due to mistaken identity? How can an innocent man forgive the justice system that gave him a life sentence in prison, only to realize twenty-five years later it was a wrongful conviction? The people's water in Flint, Michigan, was poisoned because of the actions of city officials in 2014, so many of them now have serious illnesses, and the water is still not drinkable. No matter the circumstances we must forgive and pray for those who have harmed us, even while we trust God to bring justice. God is just, so we can believe He will make sure the people responsible for harming us are held accountable. It frees us to live a life of peace and fulfill God's plans.

Application for Activation

This week take some quiet time in prayer to confess all your sins of thoughts, words, and deeds and ask God to reveal to you any other hidden sins so you can repent. Second, pray for your family and friends. Ask God to help you forgive any of them who have harmed you in any way. Pray for God to change their lives and bless them. And third, pray for your church, community, and nation. All our leaders need us to pray for them, whether we agree with their direction or not. Our communities and nation will only change when we intercede for God to convict those who are doing wrong to repent and do what is morally and spiritually right. Then the world will be a better place.

Follow the Spirit

What God wants me to do:

_____

_____

_____

_____

Remember Your Thoughts

Special insights I have learned:

_____

_____

_____

_____

More Light on the Text

Numbers 14:10–20

10 But all the congregation bade stone them with stones. And the glory of the LORD appeared in the tabernacle of the congregation before all the children of Israel.

In their journey to the Promised Land, the people of Israel reached Kadesh Barnea (Deuteronomy 1:19). Upon the Lord's instruction, Moses sent spies to explore the land and come with a report that would give them the certainty of the promises of God. These were twelve leaders from each tribe of Israel sent to survey Canaan and give a report. Upon returning from spying the land, these men did not honor the Lord with their report. Out of their unbelief, they held the view that the Israelites could not overcome their Canaanite enemies. Moses and Aaron, the leaders, were in the minority, supported only by Joshua and Caleb, the only two spies who held a dissenting view. They had seen the scene depicted by the ten other spies, but they believed God to fulfill His promises by giving them the land. But the ten spies, who were among the leaders of their tribes (13:1–3), succeeded in convincing the entire congregation to follow their views. In their rebellion against the will of God, they decided to stone the leaders God appointed and follow their own course and probably return to Egypt. At the very moment when the lives of Moses, Aaron, Joshua, and Caleb were threatened, the Lord stepped in.

The glory of the Lord describes the fire and cloud that descended on the tabernacle and is the visible manifestation of God's presence. It may have appeared at the door of the tabernacle or filled the tabernacle and surrounded it for all to see. In any case, it prevented the people from attacking Moses and Aaron and was an occasion for God to speak to Moses.

11 And the LORD said unto Moses, How long will this people provoke me? and how long will it be ere they believe me, for all the signs which I have shewed among them?

Repeatedly throughout the journey of the people in the wilderness, there was constantly a rebellious attitude. The children of Israel complain about hardships, and Aaron and Miriam oppose Moses (Numbers 11–12). The golden calf account (Exodus 32) describes to what extent the people could go in their rebellious attitude toward God.

Their attitude can hardly be understood in light of what the Lord had performed to show them who He is and assures them of His faithfulness in fulfilling His promises. All the signs He has performed in Egypt with the ten plagues, crossing the Red Sea, and later providing food and water during their wilderness journey were convincing proof of the Lord's presence with His people, which other nations heard of and were frightened. A sign is something that directs to someone or something beyond itself. The refusal to trust the Lord in spite of these

signs is unbelief, and it brings disobedience, which in turn brings dire consequences.

12 I will smite them with the pestilence, and disinherit them, and will make of thee a greater nation and mightier than they.

A pestilence is a divine judgment destroying either human or animal life. It is contrasted with the plagues of Egypt (Exodus 9:3–4). While the plague spared some lives, the pestilence was intended for utter destruction. The Lord not only suggests to Moses that He will not only destroy the people entirely but also disinherit or drive them out. The word used for disinherit (Heb. *horish*, **ho-RISH**) is the reverse of the related word *yarash* (Heb. **ya-RASH**, to inherit), and indicates that Israel will no longer be the inheritance of God. God's promise to provide an inheritance was an oath, a covenant He made with Abraham and renewed it with Isaac and Jacob. The Lord will forever cling to His covenant toward Israel, but He must also have a faithful covenant keeper.

When there is sin or rebellion calling for God's wrath, He expects people who will intercede in favor of the offenders. The Lord desires candidates who will stand in the gap and prevent Him from carrying on with His judgment of destruction (Ezekiel 22:30). God is asking Moses in this case—as in the golden calf situation—to intercede on behalf of the people. It indicates that God-directed intercession can stop divine judgment; in this case, God's desire to show mercy is greater than His desire to judge (James 2:13). The Lord proposes to Moses that He can establish a greater and mightier nation than Israel. While God offered the possession of the land to Israel through an oath, it was proposed to Moses through a question. The great destruction of the people God contemplated indicates the seriousness of rebellion.

13 And Moses said unto the LORD, Then the Egyptians shall hear it, (for thou

broughtest up this people in thy might from among them;) 14 And they will tell it to the inhabitants of this land: for they have heard that thou LORD art among this people, that thou LORD art seen face to face, and that thy cloud standeth over them, and that thou goest before them, by day time in a pillar of a cloud, and in a pillar of fire by night.

Moses responds to the challenge and stands in the gap for the Israelites, reminding God that His great reputation is at stake. The Egyptians who have witnessed the great power and might of God during the deliverance of the people of Israel will hear of it. They know the close relationship between the Lord and His people. Word will spread, and the Egyptians will inform the Canaanites. They were also aware of the visible manifestation of God by the pillar of cloud and fire over the people in the wilderness.

Unlike the idols of the nations, the God of Israel was close to His people with the visible sign of the pillar of cloud by day and the pillar of fire by night. He was a personal God for them, guiding them and protecting them against their enemies, and it resulted in creating a fear of the Israelites from other nations.

15 Now if thou shalt kill all this people as one man, then the nations which have heard the fame of thee will speak, saying, 16 Because the LORD was not able to bring this people into the land which he sware unto them, therefore he hath slain them in the wilderness.

God was suggesting the death of not only a few people that were involved in the rebellion but all the Israelites. Moses, therefore, continues his plea, asking the Lord not to destroy the people entirely. The phrase "as one man" echoes "all the congregation" and all the children of Israel (v. 10) to indicate that all the people heeded the word of the ten spies who disregarded the promises of God except four people: Moses, Aaron, Joshua, and Caleb.

Again the fame of the Lord was a concern for Moses. It is important that Christians today demonstrate the same concern about the fame and the name of God. The psalmist calls on God's people to give glory to His name (Psalm 115:1). God's fame and name are sacred and holy. We can never compare who we are with the glory of God. True intercessors are consumed with God's glory. Moses suggests the nations will not credit the destruction of the people on God's anger but on His inability to fulfill His promises by leading them to Canaan.

The perpetuity of the covenant between the Lord and His people is expressed in pointing to the sun, the moon, and the stars (Jeremiah 31:35–36). If these luminaries could stop their operation, only then Israel would cease to be a nation before the Lord.

17 And now, I beseech thee, let the power of my lord be great, according as thou hast spoken, saying, 18 The LORD is longsuffering, and of great mercy, forgiving iniquity and transgression, and by no means clearing the guilty, visiting the iniquity of the fathers upon the children unto the third and fourth generation.

After he has presented the consequences of the divine judgment of complete annihilation of the people of Israel to the Lord, Moses now pleads for the Lord to manifest His compassionate and forgiving character. The power Moses calls on here is the power to prevent the destruction, stemming out of God's faithfulness and patience. The intent of Moses, in this case, is to call on God's heart of mercy and forgiveness. The word for mercy is *chesed* (Heb. **KHEH-sed**),which in this context can contain the idea of a prior relationship and loyalty between God and humankind, which becomes the hope for Israel against destruction.

In this instance, Moses recalls God's own proclamation of His character (Exodus 34:6–7). Some scholars have noted verse 18 is probably a liturgical confession. The confession is formatted at different places making abstraction of some phrases to suit the occasion. Some scholars argue that God was not canceling the judgment but simply delaying it in His mercy with the covenant faithfulness in view. God does not consider a guilty person to be innocent, but God can choose to delay or redistribute His judgment. God's judgment includes the third and fourth generations of children who would need to be born to the fathers who created the iniquity. Therefore, God is not killing all of them right away because the future generations have not been born.

19 Pardon, I beseech thee, the iniquity of this people according unto the greatness of thy mercy, and as thou hast forgiven this people, from Egypt even until now.

Moses asks the Lord to "pardon" (Heb. *salakh*, **saw-LAKH**) the people. When this word is used elsewhere in the Old Testament, it is often in the context of presenting an offering while confessing and repenting of sin. In doing these, one invites God's great mercy (as Moses invokes here) and hopes for restoration of fellowship with God (the only one who can pardon). Since only Moses, Aaron, Joshua, and Caleb repent for a sin committed by the entire nation, God's pardon here will fully restore His relationship with them, but He will deal with the rest of Israel differently. They will experience not the absolution of sin but the suspension of anger. The Lord, because of His mercy, turns His anger away from Israel even when they rebelled (Psalm 78:38). The word for "forgiven" in Hebrew is *nasa'* (**naw-SAW**), and it carries three meanings: to lift up, to bear (up or away), or to forgive someone. Some scholars argue that Moses is not asking the Lord to forgive the Israelites, but to "put up" with them so He can continue to keep His covenant.

Moses calls for God to continue to bear with His people by His covenant faithfulness as He

was doing it since Egypt. Many times, they rebelled, and God in his mercy did not forsake them as His chosen nation. He held on to the covenant He made with Abraham. This is a reflection of the depth of God's forgiveness that covers not only the gravity of sin but also the multitude of sins.

20 And the LORD said, I have pardoned according to thy word:

The psalmist, referring to this instance, states that God would have destroyed the people if Moses did not stand for them in the breach to turn away wrath from them (Psalm 106:23). This is a call for our generation, where evil prevails in every segment of our contemporary society, to stand in the gap and plead with God to hold His anger and show once again His mercy to a rebellious and disobedient society. For even the church, like the ten spies, is afraid to tackle the giants of society, even when the Lord said He has overcome the world (John 16:33). A plea with God in favor of His people, bought by the precious blood of Jesus Christ shed on the Cross, would bring renewal and revival in the church. For the merciful God will hear and answer as He did in this case.

The fact that God pardons (Heb. *salakh*) expresses God's readiness to listen and answer those who intercede in favor of the unbelievers, the unfaithful, and the disobedient. A full pardon, however, would only follow full repentance and dedication to obedience. He will not treat the guilty as innocent. Instead of destroying them all as He first told Moses (v. 12), He will give them more years to wander in the desert until they all die without ever seeing the Promised Land. Their children, however, will receive God's abundant promises.

Sources:

Ashley, T. R. *The New International Commentary of the Old Testament: The Book of Numbers*. Grand Rapids, MI: Wm B. Eerdmans, 1993.

Life Application Study Bible, New Revised Standard Version. Wheaton, IL: Tyndale House Publishers, Inc., 1989. 226–227.

Milgrom, J. *The JPS Torah Commentary: Numbers*. (N. M. Sarna, Ed.) Philadelphia, PA: The Jewish Publication Society, 1990.

Unger, Merril F. *Unger's Bible Dictionary*. Chicago, IL: Moody Press. 1985. 799.

Unger, Merrill F. *The New Unger's Bible Handbook*. Chicago, IL: Moody Press. 1984. 100–101.

VanGemeren, W. A. *New International Dictionary of Old Testament Theology and Exegesis*. Vol. 2. Grand Rapids, Michigan: Zondervan, 1997.

Say It Correctly

Kadesh Barnea. **KAY**-desh bar-**NEH**-ah.
Pentateuch. **PEN**-tuh-took.
Aaron. **AIR**-on.

Daily Bible Readings

MONDAY
Bless the Lord Who Forgives
(Psalm 103:1–14)

TUESDAY
Jesus Forgives Our Sins
(Acts 10:34–43)

WEDNESDAY
God's Forgiveness Doesn't Allay Suffering
(Numbers 14:21–25)

THURSDAY
God's Forgiveness May Involve Harsh
Judgments (Numbers 14:26–30)

FRIDAY
Children Suffer for Adults' Sins
(Numbers 14:31–35)

SATURDAY
People Rebelled and Were Defeated
(Numbers 14:39–45)

SUNDAY
The Lord Says, "I Do Forgive"
(Numbers 14:10–20)

Notes

Teaching Tips

Words You Should Know

A. Cleave (v. 4) *dabeq* (Heb.)—To cling or adhere or to stick closer

B. Keep (v. 6) *shamar* (Heb.)—To guard, observe, protect or attend to

Teacher Preparation

Unifying Principle—Do as You're Told. People desire and appreciate faithfulness in all of their relationships. How are we to respond to the faithfulness of others? Deuteronomy 4 and 5 set forth obedience as God's expectation of Israel in response to God's faithful deliverance.

A. Read the Bible Background and Devotional Reading.

B. Pray for your students and lesson clarity.

C. Read the lesson Scripture in multiple translations.

O—Open the Lesson

A. Begin the class with prayer.

B. Have the students read the Aim for Change and the In Focus story.

C. Ask students how events like those in the story weigh on their hearts and how they can view these events from a faith perspective.

P—Present the Scriptures

A. Read the Focal Verses and discuss the Background and The People, Places, and Times sections.

B. Have the class share what Scriptures stand out for them and why, with particular emphasis on today's context.

E—Explore the Meaning

A. Use In Depth or More Light on the Text to facilitate a deeper discussion of the lesson text.

B. Pose the questions in Search the Scriptures and Discuss the Meaning.

C. Discuss the Liberating Lesson and Application for Activation sections.

N—Next Steps for Application

A. Ask participants to choose a verse from the Focal Verses that can be a reminder for faithfulness and write that verse on an index card that can be kept in a conspicuous place as a daily reminder.

B. Summarize the value of knowing and experiencing God's faithfulness.

C. End class with a commitment to pray for obedience to God's Word.

Worship Guide

For the Superintendent or Teacher
Theme: Responses to God's Faithfulness
Song: "Great is They Faithfulness"
Devotional Reading: Hebrews 8:1–12

Obedient Faith

Bible Background • DEUTERONOMY 4:1–14; 5:1–21
Printed Text • DEUTERONOMY 4:1–8, 12–13 | Devotional Reading • HEBREWS 8:1–12

—————— Aim for Change ——————

By the end of the lesson, we will: SUMMARIZE why people should obey God's commandments, EXPERIENCE awe at the majesty of God, and COMMIT to faithfulness to God through the new covenant as the Israelites were to be faithful to the Old Covenant.

—————— In Focus ——————

Danielle was a college student at Clark-Atlanta University in Georgia. She was student government president for the senior class and on the dean's list. The youth in her Bible study class admired her wisdom about the Bible and how she related it to real-life issues.

However, some of the youth began to notice Danielle's clothes smelled like marijuana, and she always was eating snacks while teaching the class. They began to talk among themselves. Was she using drugs?

One youth, Trent, decided to confront Danielle. One night before youth group, he prayed and then said, "The youth love coming to your class. You're a great teacher."

"Well, thank you, Trent."

"But we think that there is a problem. You sometimes smell like marijuana and look high when you come to class. You're not using drugs, are you?" Trent swallowed hard and waited for a response.

Danielle looked at Trent's worried face and knew she had to repent. "I am so sorry. You're right. I'm teaching you how to follow God's commands but I don't follow them myself. Using marijuana is not the best way to handle my stress. I will go talk to Pastor Hearst and maybe take some time off from teaching. Thank you, Trent, for being so concerned about me." She hugged Trent and went to find the pastor.

Why is it important for Christians to be good examples for others?

—————— Keep in Mind ——————

"Ye shall not add unto the word which I command you, neither shall ye diminish ought from it, that ye may keep the commandments of the LORD your God which I command you" (Deuteronomy 4:2, KJV).

"Do not add to or subtract from these commands I am giving you. Just obey the commands of the LORD your God that I am giving you" (Deuteronomy 4:2, NLT).

Focal Verses

KJV **Deuteronomy 4:1** Now therefore hearken, O Israel, unto the statutes and unto the judgments, which I teach you, for to do them, that ye may live, and go in and possess the land which the LORD God of your fathers giveth you.

2 Ye shall not add unto the word which I command you, neither shall ye diminish ought from it, that ye may keep the commandments of the LORD your God which I command you.

3 Your eyes have seen what the LORD did because of Baalpeor: for all the men that followed Baalpeor, the LORD thy God hath destroyed them from among you.

4 But ye that did cleave unto the LORD your God are alive every one of you this day.

5 Behold, I have taught you statutes and judgments, even as the LORD my God commanded me, that ye should do so in the land whither ye go to possess it.

6 Keep therefore and do them; for this is your wisdom and your understanding in the sight of the nations, which shall hear all these statutes, and say, Surely this great nation is a wise and understanding people.

7 For what nation is there so great, who hath God so nigh unto them, as the LORD our God is in all things that we call upon him for?

8 And what nation is there so great, that hath statutes and judgments so righteous as all this law, which I set before you this day?

12 And the LORD spake unto you out of the midst of the fire: ye heard the voice of the words, but saw no similitude; only ye heard a voice.

13 And he declared unto you his covenant, which he commanded you to perform, even ten commandments; and he wrote them upon two tables of stone.

NLT **Deuteronomy 4:1** And now, Israel, listen carefully to these decrees and regulations that I am about to teach you. Obey them so that you may live, so you may enter and occupy the land that the Lord, the God of your ancestors, is giving you.

2 Do not add to or subtract from these commands I am giving you. Just obey the commands of the LORD your God that I am giving you.

3 You saw for yourself what the LORD did to you at Baal-peor. There the LORD your God destroyed everyone who had worshiped Baal, the god of Peor.

4 But all of you who were faithful to the LORD your God are still alive today—every one of you.

5 Look, I now teach you these decrees and regulations just as the LORD my God commanded me, so that you may obey them in the land you are about to enter and occupy.

6 Obey them completely, and you will display your wisdom and intelligence among the surrounding nations. When they hear all these decrees, they will exclaim, 'How wise and prudent are the people of this great nation!'

7 For what great nation has a god as near to them as the LORD our God is near to us whenever we call on him?

8 And what great nation has decrees and regulations as righteous and fair as this body of instructions that I am giving you today?

12 And the LORD spoke to you from the heart of the fire. You heard the sound of his words but didn't see his form; there was only a voice.

13 He proclaimed his covenant—the Ten Commandments—which he commanded you to keep, and which he wrote on two stone tablets.

The People, Places, and Times

Baal-peor. Baal was worshiped in various aspects all around Canaan, taking on different names to denote a particular shrine's worship. Peor refers to a mountain in Moab, the location of this branch of Baal worship. People worshiped Baal as a god of storms, dew, and fertility. From the biblical account, it appears the worship of Baal-peor was focused on fertility since the practice involved licentiousness with Moabite women (Numbers 25:1–9). God's punishment for falling into the idolatry of Baal-peor was to send a plague, which killed 24,000 Israelites before the nation's crimes were expiated by Phineas.

Stone Tablets. Often used for recording the legal documents of that day, stone tablets were generally shaped like rounded off rectangles. God inscribed stone tablets with the Ten Commandments, which gave insight into the nature of God. There were two sets of stone tablets. In anger, Moses destroyed the first set that God inscribed, when Moses saw the Israelites worshiping a golden calf. He cut the second set that was rewritten by God.

Background

The book of Deuteronomy is the fifth book of the Pentateuch. The new generation of Israelites was standing on the banks of the Jordan River, preparing to go possess the Promised Land that their parents never got acquainted with. Moses told them about God's mighty acts in the past, including the deliverance from slavery in Egypt, as well as His provisions and protection in the Exodus and the wilderness. But this never satisfied the Israelites, so they complained and rebelled against God, provoking Him to let them wander in the wilderness forty years and then die without ever entering the Promised Land.

This book is a partial restatement and explanation of the previous laws given to the Israelites, so the new generation would not repeat the same rebellious behavior. They also renewed the covenant with God before entering the Promised Land. God requires obedience to His commands. If they obeyed His commands, God promised blessings. If they disobeyed, God promised curses.

What happens when new generations do not know their family history?

At-A-Glance

1. Hear and Obey God's Commands
(Deuteronomy 4:1–4)
2. The Benefits of Keeping the Covenant
(vv.5–12)
3. God's Covenant Keepers (v.13)

In Depth

1. Hear and Obey God's Commands (Deuteronomy 4:1–4)

Moses addresses the new generation of Israelites and first reviews God's mighty acts (1:6–3:29). It was important that they knew the history of God's faithfulness to their ancestors. Now, Moses urges the people to listen and obey God's commands. If they are obedient, everything would go well in their lives and relationships. Moreover, their obedience will lead to guaranteed possession of the Promised Land, victory over enemies, wealth, and contentment.

The people were warned not to add nor subtract anything from the commands of God (4:2). It is easy for humans to desire to add or take away something in God's Word to please themselves. This enables us to do what we please and not what God commands. And it will end up being harmful to us.

The example Moses gave as a warning was the incident at Baal-peor (4:3–4). The incident at Baal-peor referred to when 24,000 Israelites are noted to have died because of unfaithfulness (Number 25:1–9, cf. Psalm 106:28–29). If we insist on defying God, we have to be willing to accept the consequences. But those who faithfully obey God will be saved from destruction.

Moses told the people it is obeying God's commands that gives a person a reputation for wisdom (4:6). Studying and obeying God's Word makes us wise (4:8).

How does obeying the Word impact our relationship with God and others?

2. The Benefits of Keeping the Covenant (vv. 5–8, 12)

Keeping the covenant by keeping the commandments will set Israel apart and cause them to possess and display uncommon wisdom and understanding. If their ingenuity and understanding flow unhindered from the God whose covenant they keep, the unbelieving nations will observe them and call them great, wise, and understanding. This assessment and estimation may lead the nation to seek out the God of their covenant, and thus God's glory will be magnified. Israel should have such relational intimacy with Yahweh—manifested through their obedience and its resultant wisdom and understanding—to show them to be a great nation. It will also remove the Gentile notion that God is so far that objects in creation must be deified. For in the case of Israel, their obedience will show that God is imminently intimate with them and is the LORD "our God" who answers when they call upon Him as a father does with his children.

The statutes, judgments, and precepts that surround the covenant are the impetus toward righteousness, which will keep them exalted as a nation. Even for us as children of God today, following divine declarations and listening to His voice through the Word, especially as it has been spoken in the person of His son Jesus Christ, places before us the same promises here proclaimed for the nation of Israel. Moses ends this call to covenant keeping with the statement, "Ye heard the voice of the words, but saw no similitude; only ye heard a voice," suggesting that all covenant obedience is informed by faith, a kind of trust in speech offered within context of the covenant. A covenant can only be kept effectively where the words of covenant are believed.

How can faith help the keepers of the covenant? In what ways can we express obedience to the covenant of God in our lives?

3. God's Covenant Keepers (v. 13)

God's covenant with the Israelites was given at Horeb, but this generation needed to be told and reminded of its significance for their lives. It is vital that we share with our children the stories of God's faithfulness and mighty works. This can encourage them to remain faithful to God even in the midst of trials because He is always present with us. All we have to do is pray, and God hears us. God will respond because He's loving, merciful, and forgiving. The new generation would possess the Promised Land as God promised. But He required obedience to His commandments, which were inscribed on two tablets (4:13; Exodus 19–20).

Have you encountered people who believe some part of God's Word is more important to obey than others? Why or why not?

Search the Scriptures

1. Why do you think Moses reminded the new generation of Israelites of the incident relating to Baal-peor (4:3–4)?

2. What did Moses tell the people to do to gain wisdom and discernment (4:6)?

3. Why was obedience to the statues and ordinances of God vital for the Israelites to have success in the Promised Land (4:14)?

Discuss the Meaning

1. Some people argue about the interpretation of a verse to prove their sinful behavior is acceptable according to the Scripture. How can we handle those who add or take away from the Word of God for selfish reasons?

2. How can we instill into the next generations the importance of obeying God's Word?

3. When we have an encounter with God's presence during prayer or worship, how does it inspire us to be faithful to God's commands?

Liberating Lesson

People hate to obey rules because they believe it restricts their freedom. But God has given His Word to us, so we can be in right relationship with Him and others. The Ten Commandments give the people the laws of God. The Israelites promised to obey the covenant between them and God, but they continued to break the covenant over and over again. Christians are under the covenant of grace. When we violate God's Word and repent, God forgives us because the blood of Jesus Christ cleanses us from all sin. We have to make a commitment every day to demonstrate our love for Jesus by showing love for others. This includes how we treat people as individuals, as well as a community. We must advocate for laws that uphold the value of all lives and protect everyone, not just those who have power. God holds all of His people accountable to obey Him, and in our obedience, we are blessed and bring a better world to everyone around us.

Application for Activation

This week think about the covenant of grace we are now under. First, pray and ask God how to reflect His love and grace in all relationships. Second, make an effort to love others in the same way Jesus loves you. And third, remember to study Scripture to discover how God wants you to live as a Christian. How can your knowledge of God's faithfulness in keeping His Word impact your response to God?

Follow the Spirit

What God wants me to do:

_____

_____

_____

_____

Remember Your Thoughts

Special insights I have learned:

_____

_____

_____

_____

More Light on the Text

Deuteronomy 4:1–8, 12–13

It has been 40 years since the children of Israel left Egypt for the Promised Land. They have reached the oasis of Kadesh Barnea, an eleven-day journey from Mount Horeb (Mount Sinai) where the Law was given. The land of Canaan is now in sight, only a few days' journey and within reach. As a result of their unbelief and rebellion, the Lord had vowed that none of the older generations that left Egypt would enter the Promised Land except Joshua and Caleb. Therefore the Lord turns a few days' journey into 38 years of wilderness wandering (Numbers 13–14). Moses and Aaron were also forbidden to enter the Promised Land (Numbers 20:12), Moses is instructed to commission Joshua in his place to lead the people (Number 27:12–14, 18–23; cf. Deuteronomy 3:27–28). Therefore, Deuteronomy is Moses' farewell message to prepare the new generation to enter Canaan. In his farewell speech to the new generation, Moses reviews Israel's past and reminds them who they are and how they got where they are (Deuteronomy 1–5). Knowing their past, the new generation of Israelites could avoid repeating the sins of their fathers as they settle in the land, which they are about to possess.

Moses narrates to them all that the Lord has done for Israel and how graciously He has dealt with them and led them. He now exhorts them to observe the law and the ordinances, which the Lord has given them so that they would continue to enjoy the blessing of the covenant.

1 Now therefore hearken, O Israel, unto the statutes and unto the judgments, which I teach you, for to do them, that ye may live, and go in and possess the land which the LORD God of your fathers giveth you.

Using the Hebrew conjunction *'attah* (**at-TAW**), translated "Now therefore," referring to what he has been telling them (chapters 1–3), Moses calls on the people to diligently pay attention to the "statutes and the judgments" he is teaching them. The word to "hearken" is the Hebrew, *shama'* (**shaw-MAH**), which means "to hear intelligently" with the implication of paying attention and obedience. "Hearkening" involves laying it in the heart and changing your behavior to match what you just heard. The phrase "Hear … O Israel" or *Shema Yisrael* is a common theme in Deuteronomy, calling on God's people to hear and obey (5:1; 6:3–4; 9:1; 20:3). It is also found in other places in the Old Testament. This phrase is also found in Deuteronomy 6:4–9 where it is referred to as the Shema; there it is recognized as the Jewish confession of faith. The Shema is central in the Jewish morning and evening prayer services. It is recited daily by devout Jews and on every Sabbath day in the synagogue. It is quoted by Jesus (Mark 12:29-30; Matthew 22:37–38, etc.).

So, Moses says to the people, based on all that the Lord had done for you, listen and obey all the statutes and judgments that I am about to expound to you. Obedience to this law has its reward: they would live for a long time and enjoy the land, which the Lord of their fathers is giving them. The word translated "statutes" is the Hebrew *choq* (**KHOKE**), while "judgments" is *mishpat* (**mish-POT**). The two often appear synonymously together in the Bible and are often translated as "decrees and regulations" or "ordinances." The combined use of the words denotes the sum total of the Law or the covenant (see Leviticus 19:37).

2 Ye shall not add unto the word which I command you, neither shall ye diminish ought from it, that ye may keep the commandments of the LORD your God which I command you.

Moses tells them that the whole law should be kept as it was given. Nothing is to be added or taken from it, but men should submit to it as to the unbreakable Word of God. In other words, they should not make new laws of their own and join them to God's set laws. This precept was repeated later in Deuteronomy (13:1–3) and is proclaimed by the prophets (Jeremiah 26:2). They were not to abolish or diminish the law of God or make void any part of it. However, the Scribes and Pharisees in Jesus' day were guilty of this offense. They treated the Word of God as less important than their traditions (Matthew 15:1–9; Mark 7:1–13). Jesus says that He did not come to destroy or nullify the law but to fulfill it and that not even the smallest detail of God's law would fade away until its purpose is achieved. He then warns, "Whosoever therefore shall break one of these least commandments, and shall teach men so, he shall be called the least in the kingdom of heaven: but whosoever shall do and teach them, the same shall be called great in the kingdom of heaven" (Matthew 5:19). The

Apostle John warns about the consequences for anyone who adds or takes away anything from "this book" (Revelation 22:18–19). Obedience to the law of God is a mark of faith and has its rewards, but disobedience to the law is a mark of unbelief and has its consequences. This truth is made apparent in the immediate history of the people of Israel.

3 Your eyes have seen what the LORD did because of Baal-peor: for all the men that followed Baal-peor, the LORD thy God hath destroyed them from among you. 4 But ye that did cleave unto the LORD your God are alive every one of you this day.

To reinforce his point and stress the importance of keeping the law, Moses calls the attention of the people to a recent event that took place along the way, as a reminder of God's consistency and faithfulness to His words. The Israelites had just witnessed how a faithful observance of the law could mean life, while disobedience could result in death. The people had been enticed into the sin of adultery and idol worship at Baal-peor by the daughters of Moab and Median (Numbers 25:1–9; cf. Psalm 106:28–29, Hosea 9:10). All those who participated in this evil were either put to death by the sword or died in a plague (about 24,000 died in the plague). It was not made known the type of plague that killed these people. The Lord probably allowed it because of the people's unbelief and disobedience to the Law. Apart from safeguarding the moral principles, the Law can be seen as rules for our own and others' physical safety and health. In this context, the Seventh Commandment reads: "Thou shalt not commit adultery" (Exodus 20:14). Paul warned the Corinthian church, "Flee fornication. Every sin that a man doeth is without the body; but he that committeth fornication sinneth against his own body" (1 Corinthians 6:18). In contrast, all those who held fast to the Lord were spared.

This incident was still fresh in the minds of the people Moses was presently addressing. He says to them, "You saw for yourself what the Lord did to you at Baal-peor" (NLT). The Lord spared their lives because they remained faithful and did not follow the rest of the people to sin; neither did they fall into the trap of the Moabite women in their adultery and idolatry. Moses uses the Hebrew word *dabeq* (**daw-BAKE**), meaning to cleave, to cling or adhere, or to stick closer to describe the people's faithfulness to the Lord. Because of their obedient faith and close relationship with the Lord by obeying the law, they all lived and were still alive at the present time. It is therefore undeniable because they were not only eyewitnesses, but they were beneficiaries of God's grace and reward of faithfulness. God spared them from being killed in battle or by the plague.

5 Behold, I have taught you statutes and judgments, even as the LORD my God commanded me that ye should do so in the land whither ye go to possess it.

Moses now tells them that he has taught them the Law (i.e., "statutes and judgments") as the Lord directed him. In other words, he has fulfilled his part, and it is now their part to obey and follow his teachings. Here Moses applies the Hebrew word *ra'ah* (**raw-AW**), translated "see or look" (or to see with attention). It is sometimes used as an interjection to stress an important point in the discourse. With the clause "even as the Lord my God commanded me," Moses seems to say, "I have taught you the whole law, I have not added or subtracted (withheld) anything" (cf. v. 2). It is now left for them to totally follow God's order as they go into the land. Moses tells them that these decrees and ordinances should guide them once they take possession of the land. Obedience to the commandments should be part of their lifestyle in the new Promised Land.

6 Keep therefore and do them; for this is your wisdom and your understanding in the sight of the nations, which shall hear all these statutes, and say, Surely this great nation is a wise and understanding people.

Moses now appeals to them to "Keep therefore and do them," referring to what he has been teaching them, the whole commandment of God. He employs two Hebrew verbs to emphasize the importance of this teaching. The first is *shamar* (**shaw-MAR**), translated "keep." It means "to guard, observe, protect, or attend to." The second verb is *'asah* (**AW-saw**), which means to "do." Here keeping or guarding the word of God is tantamount to doing it. In other words, they are to practice or live it out in their daily living and worship. As they keep and practice the law, they will become wise and filled with understanding. When other nations hear of or see them, they would acknowledge them as a great and distinctive nation among other nations because of their wisdom. Therefore, through Israel's faithful obedience to the covenant, God's intention was to exalt them among their neighboring nations so that foreign nations would recognize that their God was indeed God (cf. 1 Kings 10:1–13). Therefore, by knowing God's wisdom, the people would not only succeed, but they would also be an influence and witnesses to other nations dwelling among them in the land they are about to possess. Their life would shine as light in the midst of a dark world. Jesus says, "Let your light so shine before men, that they may see your good works and glorify your Father in heaven" (Matthew 5:16).

7 For what nation is there so great, who hath God so nigh unto them, as the LORD our God is in all things that we call upon him for? 8 And what nation is there so great, that hath statutes and judgments so righteous as all this law, which I set before you this day?

Moses reminds the people how privileged they are to have the Lord as their God and to have a righteous Law for guidance. This relationship has put them so close to God that He does whatever they ask of Him. Rhetorically, Moses questions what other nation has a God like the Lord who gives a Law like this. Of course, the answer is obvious: "None!" There is no nation so privileged as Israel. Later in this discourse, Moses would remind them that God chose them and set them apart as His special possession. He did this not because of what they have accomplished, but because of His love for them and because of His covenant with their forefathers. Moses says, "The LORD did not set His love on you nor choose you because you were more in number than any other people, for you were the least of all peoples; but because the LORD loves you, and because He would keep the oath which He swore to your fathers" (from Deuteronomy 7:6–8; 14:2). Moses emphasized God's great favor toward Israel. Having such knowledge ought to encourage them to obey the law faithfully. They do not have to work to be worthy; God has already chosen them and will not change His mind.

12 And the LORD spake unto you out of the midst of the fire: ye heard the voice of the words, but saw no similitude; only ye heard a voice. 13 And he declared unto you his covenant, which he commanded you to perform, even Ten Commandments; and he wrote them upon two tables of stone.

Moses encourages them to be diligent in keeping the commandment the Lord gave to them (vv. 9–11). They should never forget their experience as long as they lived; they should teach them to their children and grandchildren. He narrates to them of their awesome experience when they were gathered at the foot of Mount Sinai. There they witnessed an amazing sight. The mountain blazed with fire up to heaven; black clouds and thick darkness covered the whole place; the place was filled with thunder and lightning. The people were utterly frightened by this sight.

Then the Lord spoke to them out of the fire. Moses reminds them that while they heard the voice of God speak to them, they "saw no similitude; only ye heard a voice" (v. 12). The word "similitude" comes from the Hebrew, *temunah* (**te-moo-NAW**), and means "something fashioned out, as a shape, or an embodiment, or (figuratively) manifestation." It also means an image, likeness, or representation. The people heard the voice of God, but they didn't see any form of God or how He looks. With this, the Lord made it known His people would be guided by His Word rather than His face. They can hear their God speak but could never see any image of Him that could be copied and worshiped (Deuteronomy 4:12, 15). With this, God forbids His people from worshiping any visible representations of Him or anything created, whether humans, animals, birds, fish, or the sun, moon, and stars. To worship the creation instead of the creator is a form of idolatry (Romans 1:22–25). Since God has no visible form or similitude, any image intended to look like Him is a sinful misrepresentation of Him. Jesus told the woman at the well that God is Spirit (He has no form, and He is invisible); therefore, He is to be worshiped in spirit and in truth (John 4:24).

Verse 13 continues Moses' narrative reminding them of the Mount Sinai phenomenon. Although they could not see a form of God, they heard Him speak, proclaiming to them His covenant, which they are to keep and observe. That covenant is the "Ten Commandments," which God Himself had written on two tablets of stone and given to Moses (Exodus 20:1–14, 24:12; cf. 31:18). "Covenant" is translated from a Hebrew noun, *berith* (**ber-EETH**); it is derived from the verb *bara'* (**baw-RAW**), which means "to cut down" or "to create." It is common to use the word "cut" when making a covenant so that the phrase is "to cut a covenant." In business even today, people sometimes use the phrase "Let's cut a deal." The "Ten Commandments" here are shorthand for the entire Law of the covenant. Referring to a large concept by only mentioning part of it is a common literary device called a synecdoche.

Moses wants the Israelites to remember that obeying the law does not save them; rather they ought to obey the law because they are saved. From verses 7–8 on, Moses couches his exhortations to follow the law not as a "have to" but as a "get to." This awesome God revealed Himself to the people at Mt. Sinai, not as any form they could understand, but as a voice and a fire. This awesome God gave His people a law that makes its adherents wise and understanding, a law that is far better than any other country's laws. This awesome God is the one who loves us, and whom we get to worship.

Sources:

Biblesoft's New Exhaustive Strong's Numbers and Concordance with Expanded Greek-Hebrew Dictionary. Biblesoft, Inc. and International Bible Translators, Inc., 2006.

Interlinear Transliterated Bible. Biblesoft, Inc., 2006.

Zondervan NIV Study Bible. Grand Rapids, MI: Zondervan, 2008

Life Application Study Bible, New Revised Standard Version. Wheaton, IL: Tyndale House Publishers, Inc., 1989. 273 – 277.

The NIV Study Bible (Tenth Anniversary Edition). Grand Rapids, MI: Zondervan Publishing House 1995. 247–248.

Unger, Merrill F. *The New Unger's Bible Handbook.* Chicago, IL: Moody Press. 1984. 110.

King, L. W. *The Code of Hammurabi.* The Avalon Project. Yale Law School. http://avalon.law.yale.edu/ancient/hamframe.asp Accessed November 12, 2018.

Mark, Joshua J. "Ancient Egyptian Law." *Ancient History Encyclopedia.* https://www.ancient.eu/Egyptian_Law/ Accessed November 12, 2018.

Say It Correctly

Synecdoche. sih-**NECK**-doe-key
Baal-peor. **BALE**-pee-**OR**.
Kadesh Barnea. **KAH**-desh bar-**NAY**-uh.

Daily Bible Readings

MONDAY
Praise God's Works
(Psalm 111)

TUESDAY
Mediator of the New Covenant
(Hebrews 8:1–12)

WEDNESDAY
God Made a Covenant with Us
(Numbers 13:30–33)

THURSDAY
Remember That You Were There
(Deuteronomy 4:9–11)

FRIDAY
Make No Heavenly or Earthly Idols
(Deuteronomy 1:34–40)

SATURDAY
God Will Not Abandon You
(Deuteronomy 4:25–31)

SUNDAY
Commit to Covenant Obedience
(Deuteronomy 4:1–8, 12–13)

Notes

Teaching Tips

Words You Should Know

A. Zidon (v. 9) *Tsidon* (Heb.)—A major city of Phoenicia on the eastern coast of the Mediterranean Sea

B. Cruse (v. 12) *tsappachath* (Heb.)—A small jar for liquids as water or oil

Teacher Preparation

Unifying Principle—Doing Right Pays Off. When people are denied the necessities of life, they may give up hope. What is the reward for faithful obedience in times of hardship? The widow of Zarephath faithfully ministered to God's prophet, and she was miraculously provided for throughout the time of famine.

A. Read the Bible Background and Devotional Reading.

B. Pray for your students and lesson clarity.

C. Read the lesson Scripture in multiple translations.

O—Open the Lesson

A. Begin the class with prayer.

B. Ask the class to reflect on feelings of emptiness or hopelessness.

C. Have the students read the Aim for Change and the In Focus story.

D. Ask students how events like those in the story weigh on their hearts and how they can view these events from a faith perspective.

P—Present the Scriptures

A. Read the Focal Verses and discuss the Background and The People, Places and Times sections.

B. Have the class share what Scriptures stand out for them and why, with particular emphasis on today's context.

E—Explore the Meaning

A. Use In Depth or More Light on the Text to facilitate a deeper discussion of the lesson text.

B. Pose the questions in Search the Scriptures and Discuss the Meaning.

C. Discuss the Liberating Lesson and Application for Activation sections.

N—Next Steps for Application

A. Summarize the value of faithfulness and obedience during hardships.

B. End class with a commitment to pray for obeying God regardless of the circumstances.

Worship Guide

For the Superintendent or Teacher
Theme: Blessed for Faithfulness
Song: "Elijah Rock"
Devotional Reading: Proverbs 3:1–10

Blessed for Faithfulness

Bible Background • 1 KINGS 17:1–24
Printed Text • 1 KINGS 17:8–16 | Devotional Reading • PROVERBS 3:1–10

Aim for Change

By the end of the lesson, we will: TELL how the widow of Zarephath was blessed for her faithfulness to do as the prophet instructed her, FEEL confident that God can reward sacrificial faithfulness, and PLAN ways to support people and causes as acts of faithfulness to God.

In Focus

Bertha had agreed to drive Mother Mason, one of the elderly women at the church, to a town a couple hours away. Mother Mason wanted to go to her sister's house to help prepare for an upcoming family reunion.

On the way over to pick up Mother Mason, Bertha tuned in to the local weather and traffic radio station. "There's been a major accident on Highway 30," the radio announcer reported. "Traffic is backed up, and it may take hours to clear the road. Avoid this area, if at all possible." Bertha sighed to herself. Highway 30 was the only way to travel to Mother Mason's sister's home.

"Sorry, Mother Mason," Bertha said when she arrived at the house. "I'll have to take you later this afternoon or tomorrow. But no way are we going to get into all that traffic."

Mother Mason agreed. "I'll just go ahead and make some dishes and desserts here at home and wrap them up and take them tomorrow."

God uses circumstances, the prompting of the Holy Spirit, the Bible, and wise counsel from godly people to guide His children. When we follow what God has said, we find that everything works together for good. Identify how you can learn to listen to and follow the Holy Spirit's direction, even if it means giving up something you cherish.

Keep in Mind

"There was always enough flour and olive oil left in the containers, just as the Lord had promised through Elijah" (1 Kings 17:16, NLT).

"And the barrel of meal wasted not, neither did the cruse of oil fail, according to the word of the LORD, which he spake by Elijah" (1 Kings 17:16, KJV).

Focal Verses

KJV **1 Kings 17:8** And the word of the LORD came unto him, saying,

9 Arise, get thee to Zarephath, which belongeth to Zidon, and dwell there: behold, I have commanded a widow woman there to sustain thee.

10 So he arose and went to Zarephath. And when he came to the gate of the city, behold, the widow woman was there gathering of sticks: and he called to her, and said, Fetch me, I pray thee, a little water in a vessel, that I may drink.

11 And as she was going to fetch it, he called to her, and said, Bring me, I pray thee, a morsel of bread in thine hand.

12 And she said, As the LORD thy God liveth, I have not a cake, but an handful of meal in a barrel, and a little oil in a cruse: and, behold, I am gathering two sticks, that I may go in and dress it for me and my son, that we may eat it, and die.

13 And Elijah said unto her, Fear not; go and do as thou hast said: but make me thereof a little cake first, and bring it unto me, and after make for thee and for thy son.

14 For thus saith the LORD God of Israel, The barrel of meal shall not waste, neither shall the cruse of oil fail, until the day that the LORD sendeth rain upon the earth.

15 And she went and did according to the saying of Elijah: and she, and he, and her house, did eat many days.

16 And the barrel of meal wasted not, neither did the cruse of oil fail, according to the word of the LORD, which he spake by Elijah.

NLT **1 Kings 17:8** Then the LORD said to Elijah,

9 "Go and live in the village of Zarephath, near the city of Sidon. I have instructed a widow there to feed you."

10 So he went to Zarephath. As he arrived at the gates of the village, he saw a widow gathering sticks, and he asked her, "Would you please bring me a little water in a cup?"

11 As she was going to get it, he called to her, "Bring me a bite of bread, too."

12 But she said, "I swear by the LORD your God that I don't have a single piece of bread in the house. And I have only a handful of flour left in the jar and a little cooking oil in the bottom of the jug. I was just gathering a few sticks to cook this last meal, and then my son and I will die."

13 But Elijah said to her, "Don't be afraid! Go ahead and do just what you've said, but make a little bread for me first. Then use what's left to prepare a meal for yourself and your son.

14 For this is what the LORD, the God of Israel, says: There will always be flour and olive oil left in your containers until the time when the LORD sends rain and the crops grow again!"

15 So she did as Elijah said, and she and Elijah and her family continued to eat for many days.

16 There was always enough flour and olive oil left in the containers, just as the LORD had promised through Elijah.

The People, Places, and Times

Famine. A famine is an extreme shortage of food. God often used famines in response to Israel's continued disobedience. One of the common forms of famine was a drought, which is the excessive dryness of the land. Famines and droughts are recorded throughout the Bible during the time of Abraham (Genesis 12:10), Isaac (Genesis 26:1), Joseph (Genesis 41:27), the Judges (Ruth 1:1), and the Israelites in the days of David (2 Samuel 21:1), Elijah (1 Kings 18:2), Elisha (2 Kings 4:38), Haggai

(Haggai 1:11), and Nehemiah (Nehemiah 5:3). In an agrarian society like Israel, the failure of a single season's crop could mean the starvation and death of many during the resulting famine.

Background

In their first iteration, the books of 1 and 2 Kings were a single literary work meant to provide a continuous account of Israel's history after the death of David, the second king of Israel. God blessed David and his descendants, and Jesus was part of his lineage. In Hebrew texts, 1 and 2 Kings were divided into separate books during the Middle Ages under the influence of earlier Greek and Latin translations, which saw them as the continuation of the history of Israelite kingship beginning in 1 Samuel. In Jewish tradition, they are part of the division of the Bible called the Former Prophets which includes Joshua, Judges, 1 and 2 Samuel, and 1 and 2 Kings. Together the books of the Former Prophets recount the history of Israel from the conquest of Canaan to the end of the monarchy and the beginning of exile.

The theological concern of these books is worship that was meant to happen at the temple in Jerusalem. In 1 and 2 Kings, the rulers are assessed based on their adherence to regular worship in Jerusalem and their commitment to worshiping only the God of Israel. For example, Ahab became king of Israel and did more evil things than all the kings before him (1 Kings 16:29–30). Ahab and his wife Jezebel angered God by worshiping Baal. In an abrupt introduction to the prophet, Elijah tells Ahab that there would be a drought in Israel (1 Kings 17:1). The three-year drought proved the efficacy of God over Baal. (Baal was a storm god who was believed to bring rain and fertility to the land.) God then commands Elijah to go live in Zarephath, which was in the heartland of the Baal cult (1 Kings 17:8–16). God told Elijah that a widow there would feed him. The story focuses on Elijah's ability to perform miracles, but it also demonstrates the way God cares for those who love and serve Him.

At-A-Glance

1. Encounter at the Gate (1 Kings 17:8–10)
2. Confronting the Fear (vv. 11–13)
3. God Provides Enough (vv. 14–16)

In Depth

1. Encounter at the Gate (1 Kings 17:8–10)

Although there was a drought in Israel, God had always provided Elijah with meat, bread, and water. God tells Elijah to go to Zarephath on the Phoenician coast south of Sidon (1 Kings 17:8-9). It is a highly charged location for Elijah to visit because it is in the heartland of the Baal cult. While there, Elijah learns God had commanded a widow to feed him. Although in the ancient world hospitality would have demanded that the widow open her door to a stranger, she had no means to care for herself because she lacked the economic support her husband had provided. Since the king did not provide for her, the widow was soon to become impoverished. In the midst of a drought, here is a woman who had so little and could not acquire resources for herself or her household because she was a widow, and she is the one Elijah asks to bring him some water to drink. Elijah faithfully traveled into enemy territory and asks for resources from a woman who had very little to give.

What does Elijah's commitment to following God and their shared commitment to caring for each other teach us about hospitality?

2. Confronting the Fear (vv. 11–13)

Just as the hospitable widow went to get water for Elijah to drink, he asked her to bring him some bread as well. At this, she refuses his request. She tells the prophet that she only has a handful of meal in a jar and a bit of oil. Before his arrival, she had planned to cook her remaining meal in the rest of her oil for herself and her son. After they ate it, they planned to die. In the face of such dire conditions, it seems that the prophet would have left her alone. She only had a bit of food left, and as a widow, she lacked the means to gain additional resources in the future. The social expectations of the ancient world made women depend on the men in their lives to gain the resources they needed. Even though Elijah was a man, he could not provide for her, but Elijah knew that the God of Israel was a provider. He assuaged her fear, promising that after she had made something for him, she and her son would still have enough.

What does this story reveal about the way God can provide for us even when we believe we have nothing left to give?

3. God Provides Enough (vv. 14–16)

Although the widow had so little meal left in her jar, Elijah assured her that the jar would not be emptied and that the jug of oil would not fail until the drought was over. She did as Elijah commanded her, and she and her household had food to eat for many days as the Lord had promised them. The widow lived in Baal territory, and the Scripture does not reveal whether she believed in Israel's God, but her wording to Elijah "the LORD your God" (v. 12) would imply the Lord was not also her God. In this case, though, she listened to a prophet of the Lord, and she was never without. When Jesus taught His disciples to pray, he taught them to ask for their daily bread, and the story of a widow who had so little yet received daily provision for herself and her household challenges us to be faithful to God, believing that God will provide what we need for each day.

What happens to the widow when she releases her fear of not having enough and surrenders to the will of God? What might her witness have revealed to those who encountered her during the drought?

Search the Scriptures

1. What compelled Elijah to move to a new location, and how does he forge a new relationship when he arrives?

2. When the widow is most desperate, God commands her to care for a stranger. What does this Scripture reveal about the connection between serving others and self-care?

Discuss the Meaning

1. What evidence in the Scripture demonstrates the extreme situation the woman is facing?

2. Why did the widow do what this stranger, Elijah, instructed?

Liberating Lesson

Many of us can relate to the feeling that we do not have enough to provide for ourselves and the people we love. Many of us have encountered financial hardships. Most of us have survived large and small natural disasters that impacted our quality of life. In those moments, it feels like it is all we can do to take care of our own needs. Some of us even feel like the widow in our Scripture for today, ready to use the scant resources we have left and then accept death, and yet God provides. The challenge this Scripture presents is to choose not to turn inward and to care only for our immediate needs in times of difficulty. The Scripture indicates that even in the midst of our struggles, there are people we are called to serve. If you are enduring hardship right now, know that if you are faithful to God, God will bring you through every challenge; pray that you will be a source of hope, joy, and encouragement to others even amid your personal storm.

Application for Activation

In times of hardship, "fear not" (v. 13); you are not alone. Obey God's voice because He will direct you toward the resources you need to not only survive but also to thrive. Even in times of famine, we can care for each other. In all seasons of our lives, we can lean into opportunities to serve others. We all have something we can give to spread the love of God to others. You can choose not to give in to your fear and desperation. Even on your darkest days, God is with you. Choose life, compassion, and hope.

Follow the Spirit

What God wants me to do:

_____

_____

_____

_____

Remember Your Thoughts

Special insights I have learned:

_____

_____

_____

_____

More Light on the Text

1 Kings 17:8–16

17:8 And the word of the Lord came unto him, saying, 9 Arise, get thee to Zarephath, which belongeth to Zidon, and dwell there: behold I have commanded a widow woman there to sustain thee.

Elijah receives instructions directly from God. It was time to leave the first place of hiding beside the brook Cherith, being fed by ravens (1 Kings 17:3). The Lord had made other arrangements for Elijah's survival. This time God's instructions take Elijah right into the midst of Baal worshipers. Zarephath was a coastal Phoenician city south of Zidon (or Sidon), the principal city of Baal worship. This was out of Ahab's territory. The time for another confrontation had not yet arrived. Elijah was to live there and be sustained by the poorest of the poor, a widow. Widows fell quickly into poverty without a husband to provide for them, being reduced to begging. In Israel, the commandments urged the local priesthood or palace to include widows and orphans under their care. This may not have been the case in Phoenicia.

10 So he arose and went to Zarephath. And when he came to the gate of the city, behold, the widow woman was there gathering sticks: and he called to her, and said, Fetch me, I pray thee, a little water in a vessel, that I may drink.

As he had when delivering his first message and then retreating to the brook, once again Elijah obeys the Lord's instructions. When he arrives at the entrance to the city, immediately he sees a widow gathering sticks for a fire. But how would he be sure whether she was the one God commanded to sustain him? Surely she is not the only widow in the city. He calls to her and politely asks her to get him a drink of water in a vessel. The expression "I pray thee" turns the simple understanding of the verb as a command ("Fetch me") into a request. After all, he is the stranger. She would have had to draw this water from a deep well, supplied by underground springs because there had been no rain.

The whole encounter raises questions about hospitality. Usually, men and women did not address one another in public places. It is even more unusual for Elijah, a stranger to the city, to approach a local citizen. Normally, rulers stationed men near the gate of the city. It was their job to check out strangers to determine whether they were friend or foe. Friends would be welcomed into the city and shown the utmost hospitality. Foes would be escorted out. This unusual behavior was likely Elijah's way of testing to see if she was the one whom Yahweh commanded. Abraham's servant uses a similar test to ask God to reveal the woman who should marry Isaac (Genesis 24:10–20).

11 And as she was going to fetch it, he called to her, and said, Bring me, I pray thee, a morsel of bread in thine hand.

Instead of fleeing from this stranger, the widow goes to get him the water he had requested. She has no way to know how far he had come without water. Perhaps her instinct for caring coupled with the norms of hospitality took over her sense of fear. When she responds in this way, Elijah is more confident that she is indeed the one. Before she can fulfill his first request, he calls to her with a second request. Again very politely, he asks her for a small portion of bread. Again he is very humble in his request as he does not ask for much, just a morsel.

12 And she said, As the LORD thy God liveth, I have not a cake, but a handful of meal in a barrel, and a little oil in a cruse: and, behold, I am gathering two sticks, that I may go in and dress it for me and my son, that we may eat it, and die.

Somehow, the widow recognizes that Elijah is a worshiper of the Lord, Yahweh, and not of Baal. She is even familiar with the name of Yahweh ("LORD" v. 12). The phrase "as ... God liveth" is a common way

to affirm the truth of your statement (Judges 8:19; 1 Samuel 19:6; Jeremiah 38:16), as we might say today "I swear to God." Despite her knowledge of Jews and their God, however, the woman distances herself from them in speaking to Elijah of the Lord "thy" God. Even though the woman is willing to be kind to Elijah and bring him water during a drought, she still affirms that she is separate from him in culture and deity.

Then she confesses to Elijah that she is at the end of her supplies and cannot see how she will provide for herself and her son. Ideally, a widow's family would take care of her after her father died. However, usually, a woman's children were grown before her husband died and were physically and financially able to care for the widow. This widow's son must have been very young if she was still taking care of him even in such desperate poverty. She had planned to prepare this last meal for herself and for her son; then they would die of starvation in a few days.

13 And Elijah said unto her, Fear not; go and do as thou hast said: but make me thereof a little cake first, and bring it unto me, and after make for thee and for thy son.

Elijah gives her assurance, "Fear not." He tells the widow to go ahead as she had planned, only make a small cake for him first and bring it to him. Then she should prepare for herself and her son. Elijah is asking her to put her trust in him and his God. If she is willing to do this act of kindness first, demonstrating obedience and trust in Yahweh, then she could go on with her plan. But Elijah has more to offer her than words of assurance. He also has a promise from God!

14 For thus saith the LORD God of Israel, The barrel of meal shall not waste, neither shall the cruse of oil fail, until the day that the LORD sendeth rain upon the earth.

Elijah tells the widow of Yahweh's promise to sustain them throughout the drought. The barrel of meal, which contains only a handful, will never spoil or run out. Even the container of oil, which has only a few drops, will never fail to supply their need until the time that Yahweh causes the rain to return to the earth. She will be sustained better during this drought than she had been before if she only trusts in the man of God and obeys what Yahweh had commanded her.

15 And she went and did according to the saying of Elijah: and she, and he, and her house did eat many days.

The widow decides to trust and obey Yahweh, a God foreign to her. Her faith in Baal had not kept her from the brink of starvation, but she experiences the power of Yahweh for herself. And thus, she and Elijah and her son eat for a long time from the food Yahweh supplies. Surely others must have noticed how well fed she and her household looked, while others looked malnourished.

16 And the barrel of meal wasted not, neither did the cruse of oil fail, according to the word of the LORD, which he spake by Elijah.

Because of her obedience, Yahweh fulfills His promise. This is the very lesson that Yahweh wants Israel to learn, but they are too busy putting their trust in Baal.

Elijah's successor, Elisha, will help another widow in a similar way. That widow receives an abundance of oil that she can sell to liberate her family from the threat of starvation (2 Kings 4:1–7). God provided for the Zarephath widow daily but provided for the other widow in one grand gesture. Our God does both. Be careful not to overlook God's small daily provision hoping for a bigger blessing.

Say It Correctly

Zarephath. **ZAIR**-uh-fath
Sidon. **SIE**-don
Phoenecia(n). foe-**NEE**-shuh(n)

Daily Bible Readings

MONDAY
Keep God's Commandments
(Proverbs 3:1–10)

TUESDAY
On the Mountain with Jesus
(Matthew 17:1–7)

WEDNESDAY
Prophetic Examples of Faithfulness
(Luke 4:24–30)

THURSDAY
Paul in Faithfulness Restores Life
(Acts 20:7–12)

FRIDAY
God-sent Raven Feeds Elijah
(1 Kings 17:1–7)

SATURDAY
Elijah Restores Life to Widow's Son
(1 Kings 17:17–24)

SUNDAY
Widow's Faithfulness Rewarded
(1 Kings 17:8–16)

Teaching Tips

Words You Should Know

A. Dear (v. 2) *entimos* (Gk.)—Honored, esteemed

B. Besought (v. 4) *parakaleo* (Gk.)—To beg, entreat

Teacher Preparation

Unifying Principle—Just Say the Word. People often have faith in others based on their good reputation. How does one demonstrate that trust? The centurion in Luke demonstrated his trust in Jesus' ability to heal by telling Him just to speak a word.

A. Read the Bible Background and Devotional Reading.

B. Pray for your students and lesson clarity.

C. Read the lesson Scripture in multiple translations.

O—Open the Lesson

A. Begin the class with prayer.

B. Ask the class to write two words which describe how they felt when healing or deliverance took place in their lives.

C. Have the students read the Aim for Change and the In Focus story.

D. Ask students how events like those in the story weigh on their hearts and how they can view these events from a faith perspective.

P—Present the Scriptures

A. Read the Focal Verses and discuss the Background and The People, Places, and Times sections.

B. Have the class share what Scriptures stand out for them and why, with particular emphasis on today's context.

E—Explore the Meaning

A. Use In Depth or More Light on the Text to facilitate a deeper discussion of the lesson text.

B. Pose the questions in Search the Scriptures and Discuss the Meaning.

C. Discuss the Liberating Lesson and Application for Activation sections.

N—Next Steps for Application

A. Summarize the value of having faith to believe in healing for others.

B. End class with a commitment to pray for trusting that Jesus will heal.

Worship Guide

For the Superintendent or Teacher
Theme: Faith Can Heal
Song: "Jesus, You Are My Healer"
Devotional Reading: James 5:13–18

Faith Can Heal

Bible Background • LUKE 7:1–10
Printed Text • LUKE 7:1–10 | Devotional Reading • JAMES 5:13–18

—————— Aim for Change ——————

By the end of the lesson, we will: EXPLORE the faith of the centurion who sought healing for his servant, ENDEAVOR to demonstrate the same kind of faith in Jesus as the centurion when we experience trouble, and REJOICE in the power of God to reward the faithfulness of God's people.

————————— In Focus —————————

Melissa was the primary caregiver for her mother, who suffered from Parkinson's disease. Just as Melissa felt she had begun to find her footing in her post-college life, she found herself shaping her work, church schedule, and personal life around her mother's increasing physical needs. At her doctor's insistence, Melissa sought counseling to manage both her mother's needs and her own as a caregiver.

While filling out the registration form at the therapist's office, Melissa checked off a list of things she wanted to discuss. She hadn't realized how many stressful concerns she was holding inside. Melissa knew therapy would help; she just hoped she had followed God to the right therapist. She prayed silently as the therapist approached her.

Melissa followed Dr. Shelley into her office. Dr. Shelley skimmed the information Melissa had written down on her chart and began the conversation. "I see you you're experiencing some losses and dealing with caregiving issues. I'd like to help you find constructive ways to deal with these losses and guide you toward the experience of new life," she said. "It won't be the same life you had before you began to deal with these stresses, but your life will move forward and can still be a very joyful experience."

Melissa let out a heavy sigh and quietly said, "Thank you, God." Relief was on the way.

How did Melissa's faith reassure her? In what ways is therapy helpful? God provides care, wisdom, prayer, and resources to assist us and others in times of trouble.

—————— Keep in Mind ——————

"Wherefore neither thought I myself worthy to come unto thee: but say in a word, and my servant shall be healed" (Luke 7:7, KJV).

"I am not even worthy to come and meet you. Just say the word from where you are, and my servant will be healed" (Luke 7:7, NLT).

Focal Verses

KJV **Luke 7:1** Now when he had ended all his sayings in the audience of the people, he entered into Capernaum.

2 And a certain centurion's servant, who was dear unto him, was sick, and ready to die.

3 And when he heard of Jesus, he sent unto him the elders of the Jews, beseeching him that he would come and heal his servant.

4 And when they came to Jesus, they besought him instantly, saying, That he was worthy for whom he should do this:

5 For he loveth our nation, and he hath built us a synagogue.

6 Then Jesus went with them. And when he was now not far from the house, the centurion sent friends to him, saying unto him, Lord, trouble not thyself: for I am not worthy that thou shouldest enter under my roof:

7 Wherefore neither thought I myself worthy to come unto thee: but say in a word, and my servant shall be healed.

8 For I also am a man set under authority, having under me soldiers, and I say unto one, Go, and he goeth; and to another, Come, and he cometh; and to my servant, Do this, and he doeth it.

9 When Jesus heard these things, he marvelled at him, and turned him about, and said unto the people that followed him, I say unto you, I have not found so great faith, no, not in Israel.

10 And they that were sent, returning to the house, found the servant whole that had been sick.

NLT **Luke 7:1** When Jesus had finished saying all this to the people, he returned to Capernaum.

2 At that time the highly valued slave of a Roman officer was sick and near death.

3 When the officer heard about Jesus, he sent some respected Jewish elders to ask him to come and heal his slave.

4 So they earnestly begged Jesus to help the man. "If anyone deserves your help, he does," they said,

5 "for he loves the Jewish people and even built a synagogue for us."

6 So Jesus went with them. But just before they arrived at the house, the officer sent some friends to say, "Lord, don't trouble yourself by coming to my home, for I am not worthy of such an honor.

7 I am not even worthy to come and meet you. Just say the word from where you are, and my servant will be healed.

8 I know this because I am under the authority of my superior officers, and I have authority over my soldiers. I only need to say, 'Go,' and they go, or 'Come,' and they come. And if I say to my slaves, 'Do this,' they do it."

9 When Jesus heard this, he was amazed. Turning to the crowd that was following him, he said, "I tell you, I haven't seen faith like this in all Israel!"

10 And when the officer's friends returned to his house, they found the slave completely healed.

The People, Places, and Times

Capernaum. Capernaum, meaning "a village of Nahum [comfort]," was a city on the western shore of the Sea of Galilee in the region of Gennesaret. The city was on the road from Damascus to Acco and Tyre, in a heavily populated and commercially prosperous district of Galilee. It is considered the home base of Jesus' ministry and was the home of Matthew, Peter, Andrew, James, and John. Many important events in the Gospel narrative took place in the city of Capernaum where Jesus healed the nobleman's son (John 4:46), Peter's mother-in-law (Mark 1:31), and the paralytic (Matthew 9:6). Jesus prophesied the downfall of Capernaum due to the people's lack of repentance, even though so many mighty works were done there (Matthew 11:23, Luke 10:15).

Synagogue. A synagogue was a building that housed gatherings of Jews for prayers and the worship services. These buildings began to be constructed during the time of the Babylonian exile in the absence of the temple. Ten Jewish males were required to form a synagogue, as they served as a Jewish meeting place throughout the Diaspora. In New Testament times, synagogue services were held on feast days and every Sabbath day. As an observing Jew, Jesus frequented the synagogue, which became the site for healing and miracles. Paul also frequented the synagogue in an effort to convince the attendees that Jesus was the Messiah.

Background

Jesus' public ministry brought Him fame as word spread about His doing miracles, healing those who were diseased and afflicted. People sought to touch Jesus and to hear Him teach. Luke gives an account of Jesus teaching a crowd of people following Him what would be known as the Beatitudes (Matthew 5). Christ shared instruction on how people were to relate to God and to each other. He called people to love and forgive. He taught the principle of reaping what we sow. He further teaches that He would know people who do the will of the Father intimately. People who performed outwardly but did not bear His fruit inwardly gained no special favor. Jesus shared how a person is known by what comes from the heart (Luke 6:45), which leads to an interesting transition to Jesus' next display of power.

At-A-Glance

1. Jesus' Reputation Precedes Him (Luke 7:1–3)
2. Jesus Shows Mercy and Moves (vv. 4–8)
3. Jesus Is Moved by Faith (vv. 9–10)

In Depth

1. Jesus' Reputation Precedes Him (Luke 7:1–3)

Jesus concludes His teaching time with the crowd and makes His way into Capernaum, where He frequently returns. Luke introduces readers to a centurion, a Roman soldier assigned to police occupied territory. This centurion did more than his duty to become a part of the community. The centurion had a servant who was ill to the point of death, and the officer was very concerned for his wellbeing. It is noteworthy that Luke would share how this centurion valued his servant. The centurion heard of Jesus' reputation for healing the sick and sent Jewish elders to ask for Jesus to come heal his servant. The text does not tell us if his servant was Jewish or Gentile.

How does your life help promote Jesus' reputation?

2. Jesus Shows Mercy and Moves (vv. 4–8)

The Jewish elders reach Jesus and, with a sense of urgency, ask Him to come with them to heal the centurion's servant. They plead with Jesus, giving Him reasons He should follow them and comply with their request. The centurion loved their nation, he was good to their community, he built their synagogue, and he was not like soldiers who were brutal and oppressive. The elders were seeking to use their cultural influence to persuade Jesus to come. Jesus with a heart of compassion agrees to come with them. He was not far off from the centurion's house when the centurion sent friends out to stop Him. Speaking on the centurion's behalf, they express his heart in receiving Jesus into his home. In humility, the centurion acknowledges that he is not worthy to have someone who has such power to enter his home. He further states that he did not presume or ask Jesus to come personally to lay hands on his servant but that Jesus could speak the word and he would be healed. The centurion (through his friends) shared how he understood authority, as a person who was under the authority of higher power (Caesar) as well as being a man in authority (as representative of Caesar) to Roman occupied territory.

When did you seek Jesus' mercy?

3. Jesus Moved by Faith (vv. 9–10)

Jesus admires the faith of this centurion—a Gentile. With his actions, the centurion acknowledges Jesus' power and authority based on what he heard about Him, and he humbles himself before Jesus. Jesus turns to the crowd following Him and says in short that He has not seen anyone express this level of faith in all of Israel. Even though the Jews had the Torah (the Old Testament Law) with stories that were passed down to them of God's salvation, power, and the promise of the Messiah, it is a Gentile Roman soldier who says to Him, "If You just speak the word, I know it is done." When those who were sent by the centurion return inside the house, they find the servant healed. Jesus did exactly what the centurion soldier believed He would do.

How would Jesus assess your level of faith?

Search the Scriptures

1. Why did the centurion call for Jesus? (Luke 7:1–2)

2. What did the Jewish elders say to Jesus about the centurion? (vv. 3–5)

3. Why did the centurion send friends to halt Jesus' arrival to his home? (vv. 6–8)

Discuss the Meaning

The centurion stepped out on faith and believed that Jesus could heal his servant by asking for help. From the moment the Jewish elders approached and shared the story of the centurion's love and service, Jesus already determined He was going to intervene. He displayed even greater faith when he sent friends to let Jesus know that he was not expecting special privileges because of his position but he respected Jesus' power. Jesus marveled at his faith, and all who were around him were witnesses of the power of His spoken word. How can we be effective witnesses in our sphere of influence to the power of faith in Jesus? Why was it so significant to Jesus that this centurion showed such great faith?

Liberating Lesson

The world needs to see Christians who are faithful in their beliefs. As we trust in God through adversity and trials, our steadfastness ought to provoke unbelievers to ask the source of our strength. We have only to respond that while we have this treasure in earthen vessels, the surpassing greatness of power is of God and not us (2 Corinthians 4:7). Our faith in God's ability to use us changes situations. Whether we face oppressive laws, unscrupulous politicians, or injustice in the workplace, we have the assurance that God can deliver and has given us the power to stand for Him in the midst of our situations. If we believe and speak the word He has given us, we realize that faith is not for our personal piety alone but is the avenue through which God will transform broken systems. God's way of doing and being in the earth enables us to have a positive impact on the culture and communities.

Application for Activation

Is there an area in your life where you sense God calling you to radical faith to go on His Word? Seek God's purpose in your situation as you reflect on what He would have you to do to effectively translate His truth to draw others to Him. Brainstorm ideas on how the church (local and universal) can be more effective at using the available tools of this age to love people. Emphasize reaching across generational, social, and ethnic barriers.

Follow the Spirit

What God wants me to do:

_____

_____

_____

_____

Remember Your Thoughts

Special insights I have learned:

_____

_____

_____

_____

More Light on the Text

Luke 7:1–10

In Luke 7, Jesus ministers to a centurion, a widow with one child, and a sinful woman. On the whole, the chapter shows that Jesus cares for those who are deemed as outsiders. In this lesson, Luke narrates the miracle of the healing of a centurion's servant. The narrative is not so much concerned with the miracle itself as with the faith of the centurion who recognized the authority Jesus has to heal in the name of God. The passage illustrates Gentile involvement in Jesus' ministry, as well as Gentile responsiveness to Jesus' reputation. It also shows that racial or ethnic differences should not be an obstacle to seeking the Lord's favor. In this text, Jews intercede for a Gentile, and Jesus responds to the request. The centurion's story is an example that God is willing to accept all people (2 Peter 3:9). It also demonstrates that commendable faith is faith that reaches out in trust to Jesus.

1 Now when he had ended all his sayings in the audience of the people, he entered into Capernaum.

Luke transitions into the account of the centurion by explaining that Jesus enters Capernaum after speaking to the people. The reference to the "people" is important because it refers back to the audience of Jesus' message and forward to the people accompanying Jesus during His encounter with the centurion's household (7:9).

2 And a certain centurion's servant, who was dear unto him, was sick, and ready to die.

This verse reveals the central figure of the narrative: a centurion who had a slave. A centurion was the term used for a man who commanded roughly a hundred soldiers. The story shows this man to have been humane, wealthy, and pious. Although Luke does not provide the details of the servant's illness, its seriousness is clear; the life of the servant could be described as hanging by a thread, near death. The centurion was concerned, for the slave was dear to him (Gk. *entimos*, **EN-tee-moce**, honored, esteemed). The centurion's love and high estimation of his servant shows that he considers him not only in his function but also as a person. Here we see faith and love mingled together. It is important that, like the centurion, we esteem people based on who they are as people rather than the functions they perform or their social status. Jesus' love, which reaches both the nearest and the farthest, responds to this double affection.

3 And when he heard of Jesus, he sent unto him the elders of the Jews, beseeching him that he would come and heal his servant.

Because the servant's situation is a serious one, the centurion decides to take action. The centurion has heard about Jesus and His ministry as a miracle worker (Luke 4:37). His faith leads him to action. However, he appeared to be hesitant to ask Jesus directly for help. This may be because he is a Gentile and Jesus is a Jewish teacher. Sensitive to Jewish sentiment, he does not himself approach Jesus. The centurion feels his unworthiness in the presence of the great Jewish teacher and worker of miracles and thus requests his Jewish friends, who are important people in the community, to intercede for him, which they do most readily. Army officers, as a rule, bear themselves proudly and feel their dignity, yet this commander shows the deepest and most honest humility.

The emissaries are described as "elders of the Jews." It may be implied that the centurion being a benefactor (v. 4), the Jewish elders were not ordered but went as grateful recipients of his patronage. The Greek word *presbuteros* (**pres-BOO-te-roce**) may refer either to elders of the synagogue or civic leaders. Each synagogue had its board of elders that administered the affairs of the community. These leaders came with a simple request: they wish Jesus to come and heal the servant. The Gentile soldier believes that Jesus can heal his servant, and so he appeals for his aid.

4 And when they came to Jesus, they besought him instantly, saying, That he was worthy for whom he should do this:

In verse 3 we learn what the centurion wanted the Jewish elders to ask, but verse 4 records what they really said. They did more than present the centurion's request. They went on beseeching Jesus earnestly for this man who was their benefactor. The emissaries brought the centurion's request and lobbied vigorously

on his behalf. The adverb, *spoudaios* (**spoo-DIE-oce**) "quickly" (KJV: instantly) indicates an eagerness in their efforts, and the word *parakaleo* (Gk. **pa-ra-ka-LEH-oh**) "besought," or beg and entreat, indicates emphatically the length to which these Jews labored on behalf of this Gentile. They implore Jesus by offering a commendation. They describe the centurion as worthy of benefiting from Jesus' power. It is also important to note that the elders' confidence contrasts with the centurion's own evaluation of himself since he sent others to speak for him.

5 For he loveth our nation, and he hath built us a synagogue.

The elders give the reason they think this man is worthy of Jesus' attention; this was no ordinary centurion. They specify two things: the centurion had goodwill for the conquered people ("he loveth our nation"), and he had given expression to that goodwill by aiding local worship ("he hath built us a synagogue"). Here is a Gentile who respects Jewish worship and has affection for the people. In addition to showing his heart for the Jewish people, this detail also gives insight into the centurion's economic status. The centurion clearly is a man of means and generosity.

6 Then Jesus went with them. And when he was now not far from the house, the centurion sent friends to him, saying unto him, Lord, trouble not thyself: for I am not worthy that thou shouldest enter under my roof:

Jesus accepted the invitation of the elders to go with them. In so doing, He demonstrates that His compassion transcends all racial boundaries and that all are worthy of His mercy regardless of status or ethnicity. Now, when the centurion believes that Jesus is on His way to his dwelling, he holds himself bound not only to await the Lord, but also to receive Him (v. 7). Yet he sends in his place intimate friends of his family, who can in some measure take his place in greeting the highly honored guest. For those who wielded power in Hellenistic society, which was the dominant culture in the time of Jesus, friends were usually political allies or associates. The centurion declares his unworthiness. As such, the centurion sent friends to stop Him and implores Jesus not to trouble Himself to enter the house. In addition to showing his humility, this also shows the centurion's awareness of Jewish culture. As Jews would be considered unclean if they ate together with Gentiles, most Jews would not even enter a Gentile's house to avoid becoming unclean. The centurion's humility stops Jesus from having to confront this social expectation.

7 Wherefore neither thought I myself worthy to come unto thee: but say in a word, and my servant shall be healed.

The messengers' report of the centurion's humility continues. He is not worthy to have Jesus come into his home, but neither is he worthy to go to Jesus. However, the centurion has not given up asking for Jesus' help. He trusts in Jesus' authority. He recognizes that Jesus has access to God and that this powerful figure simply needed to speak, and healing would occur. He has faith that Jesus' command is all that is needed. He trusts Jesus to such an extent that he believes His mere word will suffice to heal his servant. It is important to remember that, in antiquity, miraculous healings were expected to involve direct contact (cf. 6:19). The centurion, however, believes in the divine efficacy of Jesus' word, a conception of language not impossible in antiquity. It is not so much the difference in the transmission of divine power (language instead of action) that amazes Jesus, but the fundamental trust in the power of Jesus' word. In the faith of the centurion, the word of Jesus, given unseen and from a distance, can deliver the precious

servant from his illness. It is a profound insight that the centurion possesses and expresses: even though physically absent, Jesus can show His presence effectively. The lesson is a key one for us today who do not have Jesus' physical, visible presence with us.

8 For I also am a man set under authority, having under me soldiers, and I say unto one, Go, and he goeth; and to another, Come, and he cometh; and to my servant, Do this, and he doeth it.

The centurion explains through his messengers why he knows the servant will be healed by the power and authority of Jesus' word. The centurion makes a minor-to-major comparison. Surely if he, as a member of the government's army, is obeyed, so also the spiritual forces subject to Jesus will obey Him. The centurion is under another's authority, but nonetheless is in charge of his own forces. The picture parallels Jesus, who ministers for God, serving Him with a clear sphere of authority. Just as the soldiers and servant obey the centurion, so will those forces afflicting the centurion's slave obey Jesus. In his reference to his place in a graded hierarchy and subordination to others when he might well have spoken only of his superiority to those beneath him, the centurion demonstrates his humility.

9 When Jesus heard these things, he marvelled at him, and turned him about, and said unto the people that followed him, I say unto you, I have not found so great faith, no, not in Israel.

Jesus' response to the request is one of admiration and commendation, especially for the centurion's confident declaration of Jesus' authority. Jesus' reaction is emotional: He is amazed at the soldier. Jesus takes note of the quality of a Gentile's response to him. This unique faith recognizes Jesus' authority and the power of his word, not only over the illness but also in the face of his physical absence and distance. Neither His presence nor His touch is required for healing, only the power of Jesus' command and will. The centurion recognizes that God's power works through Jesus without spatial limitations. Jesus is entrusted with great authority. In addition, there is a resultant recognition of personal unworthiness. Jesus praises the centurion's humility mixed with deep faith. The soldier approaches the man of God on the proper terms. Through His commendation, Jesus calls us to trust him in a similar way. The question is, "Will you trust as the centurion has?" Such faith brings Jesus' approval.

10 And they that were sent, returning to the house, found the servant whole that had been sick.

Luke's report simply notes that when the messengers returned, they found the sick servant "whole"; that is, they found him well. Notably, the slave's healing is reported without any indication of Jesus' command to be healed. This lack of command is probably to accentuate the focus on the centurion's faith rather than the healing. The faith of the centurion and the power of Jesus exercised from a distance saved the slave from the jaws of death.

Sources:
Bock, Darrell L. *Luke: 1:1–9:50*, vol. 1, Baker Exegetical Commentary on the New Testament. Grand Rapids, MI: Baker Academic, 1994.
Bovon, François and Helmut Koester. *Luke 1: A Commentary on the Gospel of Luke 1:1–9:50*, Hermeneia—a Critical and Historical Commentary on the Bible. Minneapolis, MN: Fortress Press, 2002.
Carroll, John T. *Luke: A Commentary*. New Testament Library. Louisville, KY: Wesminster John Knox Press, 2012.
Johnson, Luke Timothy. *The Gospel of Luke*. Sacra Pagina, vol. 3. Collegeville, MN: The Liturgical Press, 1991.
Keener, Craig S. *The IVP Bible Background Commentary: New Testament*. Downers Grove, IL: InterVarsity Press, 1993.
Lenski, R. C. H. *The Interpretation of St. Luke's Gospel*. Minneapolis, MN: Augsburg Publishing House, 1961.
John A. Martin, "Luke," in *The Bible Knowledge Commentary: An Exposition of the Scriptures*, ed. J. F. Walvoord and R. B. Zuck, vol. 2. Wheaton, IL: Victor Books, 1985.
Morris, Leon. *Luke: An Introduction and Commentary*, vol. 3, Tyndale New Testament Commentaries. Downers Grove, IL: InterVarsity Press, 1988.
Noland, John. *Luke 1:1–9:20*, vol. 35A, Word Biblical Commentary. Dallas, TX: Word, Incorporated, 2002.
Stein, Robert H. *Luke*, vol. 24, The New American Commentary. Nashville, TN: Broadman & Holman Publishers, 1992.

Say It Correctly

Capernaum. kuh-**PERR**-nay-uhm
Centurion. sehn-**TOOR**-ee-uhn
Gentile. **JIN**-tile
Hellenisitic. hel-lin-**ISS**-tik
Synagogue. **SIN**-uh-gog

Daily Bible Readings

MONDAY
The Prayer of Faith Is Powerful
(James 5:13–18)

TUESDAY
Your Faith Has Made You Well
(Mark 5:25–34)

WEDNESDAY
Believers Are Blessed
(Galatians 3:6–9)

THURSDAY
Bartimaeus Healed by Faith
(Mark 10:46–52)

FRIDAY
Faith Is Expressed Through Actions
(Luke 6:46–49)

SATURDAY
Jesus Raises Widow's Son
(Luke 7:11–17)

SUNDAY
Jesus Heralds the Centurion's Healing Faith
(Luke 7:1–10)

Teaching Tips

Words You Should Know

A. Ointment (v. 37) *muron* (Gk.)—An expensive, aromatic perfume

B. Alabaster (v. 37) *alabastros* (Gk.)—An expensive stone, originally from Egypt, used to store costly perfumes

Teacher Preparation

Unifying Principle—Extravagant love. People often respond to forgiveness with loving acts. What can we do to show gratitude to those who forgive us? In Luke, the sinful woman showed her gratitude to Jesus by washing his feet with her tears and anointing him with expensive oil.

A. Read the Bible Background and Devotional Reading.

B. Pray for your students and lesson clarity.

C. Read the lesson Scripture in multiple translations.

O—Open the Lesson

A. Begin the class with prayer.

B. Have the class identify and briefly discuss two barriers that keep people from forgiving others.

C. Have the students read the Aim for Change and the In Focus story.

D. Ask students how events like those in the story weigh on their hearts and how they can view these events from a faith perspective.

P—Present the Scriptures

A. Read the Focal Verses.

B. Have the class share what Scriptures stand out for them and why, with particular emphasis on today's context.

C. Discuss the Background and The People, Places, and Times sections.

E—Explore the Meaning

A. Use In Depth or More Light on the Text to facilitate a deeper discussion of the lesson text.

B. Pose the questions in Search the Scriptures and Discuss the Meaning.

C. Discuss the Liberating Lesson and Application for Activation sections.

N—Next Steps for Application

A. Summarize the value of showing gratitude for those who forgive.

B. End class with a commitment to pray for the capacity to forgive others and show gratefulness with kind acts.

Worship Guide

For the Superintendent or Teacher
Theme: Faith Saves
Song: "Your Love is Extravagant"
Devotional Reading: John 13:3–11

Faith Saves

Bible Background • LUKE 7:36–50
Printed Text • LUKE 7:37–48 | Devotional Reading • JOHN 13:3–11

———————————— **Aim for Change** ————————————

By the end of the lesson, we will: EXAMINE how the sinful woman demonstrated her love and gratitude to Jesus, REFLECT on how the woman's love and devotion led her to cross social barriers to anoint Jesus, and BECOME emboldened to resist social pressures that would prevent expressions of love and gratitude for our salvation.

———————————— **In Focus** ————————————

Gary steadied himself as he stood to walk to the podium above the casket where his sister peacefully lay. He told himself that he could deliver the speech he had rehearsed a million times in his head without breaking down. "Y'all know if Gabby were up here, she'd throw up two fingers and yell, 'Hollaaaah!'" When everyone laughed, Gary relaxed. "Gabby was known for being the life of the party, even though sometimes she tried to be the life of the wrong kind of party. She had us worried before she knew Jesus."

He cleared his throat again and said, "You know, Gabby died way too young. It's hard for me to believe that just a few hours after our family had Sunday dinner together, she was killed in a car accident. Our family is heartbroken."

"One of the things bringing us comfort right now is knowing that Gabby belongs to God," Gary said. "She accepted Him as her Savior. She became a new person, with a new life. She lived her last years thankful every day to the Lord for saving her from the destructive life she saw in some of her friends. Gabby always lived as a joyful hope for them to find the better way she had found. And we know that she's experiencing new life now in heaven with the Lord." After Gary spoke, the people rose from their seats, clapping in celebration for Gabby's life and the new life she had gained in Christ.

Identify ways Gabby affected people's lives. What was the main point of Gary's message about his sister Gabby? Share how others may testify to the goodness of Christ in your life.

———————————— **Keep in Mind** ————————————

"And stood at his feet behind him weeping, and began to wash his feet with tears, and did wipe them with the hairs of her head, and kissed his feet, and anointed them with the ointment" (Luke 7:38, KJV).

"Then she knelt behind him at his feet, weeping. Her tears fell on his feet, and she wiped them off with her hair. Then she kept kissing his feet and putting perfume on them" (Luke 7:38, NLT).

Focal Verses

KJV Luke 7:37 And, behold, a woman in the city, which was a sinner, when she knew that Jesus sat at meat in the Pharisee's house, brought an alabaster box of ointment,

38 And stood at his feet behind him weeping, and began to wash his feet with tears, and did wipe them with the hairs of her head, and kissed his feet, and anointed them with the ointment.

39 Now when the Pharisee which had bidden him saw it, he spake within himself, saying, This man, if he were a prophet, would have known who and what manner of woman this is that toucheth him: for she is a sinner.

40 And Jesus answering said unto him, Simon, I have somewhat to say unto thee. And he saith, Master, say on.

41 There was a certain creditor which had two debtors: the one owed five hundred pence, and the other fifty.

42 And when they had nothing to pay, he frankly forgave them both. Tell me therefore, which of them will love him most?

43 Simon answered and said, I suppose that he, to whom he forgave most. And he said unto him, Thou hast rightly judged.

44 And he turned to the woman, and said unto Simon, Seest thou this woman? I entered into thine house, thou gavest me no water for my feet: but she hath washed my feet with tears, and wiped them with the hairs of her head.

45 Thou gavest me no kiss: but this woman since the time I came in hath not ceased to kiss my feet.

46 My head with oil thou didst not anoint: but this woman hath anointed my feet with ointment.

47 Wherefore I say unto thee, Her sins, which are many, are forgiven; for she loved much: but to whom little is forgiven, the same loveth little.

48 And he said unto her, Thy sins are forgiven.

NLT Luke 7:37 When a certain immoral woman from that city heard he was eating there, she brought a beautiful alabaster jar filled with expensive perfume.

38 Then she knelt behind him at his feet, weeping. Her tears fell on his feet, and she wiped them off with her hair. Then she kept kissing his feet and putting perfume on them.

39 When the Pharisee who had invited him saw this, he said to himself, "If this man were a prophet, he would know what kind of woman is touching him. She's a sinner!"

40 Then Jesus answered his thoughts. "Simon," he said to the Pharisee, "I have something to say to you." "Go ahead, Teacher," Simon replied.

41 Then Jesus told him this story: "A man loaned money to two people—500 pieces of silver to one and 50 pieces to the other.

42 But neither of them could repay him, so he kindly forgave them both, canceling their debts. Who do you suppose loved him more after that?"

43 Simon answered, "I suppose the one for whom he canceled the larger debt." "That's right," Jesus said.

44 Then he turned to the woman and said to Simon, "Look at this woman kneeling here. When I entered your home, you didn't offer me water to wash the dust from my feet, but she has washed them with her tears and wiped them with her hair.

45 You didn't greet me with a kiss, but from the time I first came in, she has not stopped kissing my feet.

46 You neglected the courtesy of olive oil to anoint my head, but she has anointed my feet with rare perfume.

47 I tell you, her sins—and they are many—have been forgiven, so she has shown me much love. But a person who is forgiven little shows only little love."

48 Then Jesus said to the woman, "Your sins are forgiven."

The People, Places, and Times

Alabaster. The term "alabaster box" actually refers to a flask or jar made of special white or yellow translucent limestone named after Alabaster, the town in Egypt where it is chiefly found. The material was often used to carve vases in which to store perfume. The vases are usually made without handles and can be easily broken to remove their contents.

Pharisee. A religious party or school among the Jews at the time of Christ, called "the separated ones." They were founded in the second century BC, as a protest against the Hellenistic influence that was threatening to undermine the sacred religion of their fathers. They were known for their zealous obedience to God's law. They also became major opponents of Jesus. They believed in a twofold law: the written and the oral Torah, or tradition. This tradition is what usually brought them into arguments with Jesus.

Background

The Gospel writer Luke inserts an editorial comment in his account of Jesus' ministry: "But the Pharisees and lawyers rejected the counsel of God against themselves, being not baptized of him" (Luke 7:30). Jesus was a controversial figure who attracted crowds and generated much interest. Some people in the crowd were excited about His presence and received Him as a prophet; some looked for Him to be the king who would free them from Roman occupation; some were onlookers who followed the reports of miracles, signs, and wonders. All of this chatter was disturbing to those who were Jewish leaders: the Pharisees, Sadducees, and scribes (or lawyers). Jesus disrupted the balance of communal power by declaring God accessible to all no matter their social status. Jesus was known for calling out the religious leaders for contradictions in their public appearance and treatment of people while, in contrast,

showing compassion and acceptance to those who were marginalized. He would be classified as one who would associate with tax collectors and sinners, which made encounters with the Pharisees strained (Luke 7:34).

At-A-Glance

1. Faith That Shows Hospitality
(Luke 7:37-38)
2. Faith That Receives Forgiveness
(vv. 39–43)
3. Faith That Results in Salvation
(vv. 44–48)

In Depth

1. Faith That Shows Hospitality (Luke 7:37-38)

Jesus was invited to dinner at the home of a Pharisee named Simon. Pharisees often used meal invitations to question and challenge Jesus and to trap Him publicly. Although held at a home, the gathering was more like a public banquet where others were able to look on as guests were feasting. This unnamed woman approached Jesus while He was reclining at the table. She had with her an alabaster box containing expensive, fragrant oil. She stood behind Him and washed Jesus' feet with her tears, wiped His feet with her hair, and kissed His feet. Like the woman caught in the act of adultery (John 8:2–11) or the woman at the well (John 4:7–30), this woman had what was considered an unsavory reputation. The woman mentioned in Luke is not believed to be the same person as Mary Magdalene or Mary of Bethany. As the woman was engaged in this loving act of worship, Simon smugly commented to himself that if Jesus were really a prophet He would know what kind of woman was touching Him. Simon looked down on her as a sinful woman. From his perception, this woman's display was another example of Jesus' connection with those deemed less than respectable. It was cause enough for him to internally dismiss Jesus' ministry.

Why are people so quick to dismiss and judge people who are different?

2. Faith That Receives Forgiveness (vv. 39–43)

Jesus in His wisdom and omniscience addresses Simon with a parable. He uses this illustration to prove why this unnamed woman's act of love was acceptable to Him. In the story, two people owed a debt that they could not repay. The lender forgave both debtors, but one of the borrowers had a substantially greater amount of debt he could not repay. Jesus then asked Simon a pointed question: Which one of these debtors would love the lender more and prove to be more grateful? Simon supposed that the one with the larger sum would love the most, which was the correct answer.

What should be our response to the full payment of our sin debt?

3. Faith That Results in Salvation (vv. 44–48)

Jesus expands His message by replying to Simon about his ungracious behavior and commending the woman for her hospitality. It was a custom in Jesus' time for the host to warmly greet guests upon arrival. If they were people of means, the host would have a servant wash their feet of the filth from the dusty roads. Jesus in His response also reveals that He knew Simon's thoughts about Him and the woman. He lets it be known that He is aware of what she is doing and why. We don't know what her sins are. We don't know how she came to know that Jesus could forgive her sins, but she takes a risk as a woman and a known sinner to approach Jesus in this manner. Although her sins are many,

she is forgiven, and He received her love. This unnamed woman in humility worships Jesus and is able to express her gratitude and receive redemption for her soul as well as her reputation.

How we can show hospitality that leads others to Christ?

Search the Scriptures

1. Who was the uninvited guest who approached Jesus during dinner? (Luke 7:37)

2. What did this uninvited guest do for Jesus at the dinner table? (v. 38)

3. How did Jesus respond to the uninvited guest? (v. 48)

Discuss the Meaning

This unnamed woman gave life to the point of Jesus' illustration to Simon not only for her situation but also for all who receive the gift of salvation. One who recognizes the priceless gift of salvation loves much (Luke 7:47). How can we demonstrate our gratitude to Jesus for salvation? How should Christians carry out Jesus' ministry of love and acceptance across the lines that separate us?

Liberating Lesson

We live in a world obsessed with celebrity and fame. People are quick to lift to icon status those who possess extraordinary talent, power, or money. At the same time, there is too often no regard for those who are considered everyday working people. There is dignity in all work, and no matter the labels, all people have extraordinary value. In Christ we all have received forgiveness of sins and are made equal before Him. Therefore, His church should be reflective of people who love much because they have been forgiven much. The church should be a community of equity where God's people carry the spirit of reconciliation to influence the world. They will know we are Christians by our love (cf. John 13:35).

Application for Activation

What a radical idea: The church should lead the way in showing love, forgiveness, and the ministry of reconciliation! How can we be used by God this week to reflect His love to others and lead them into relationship with Him (cf. Romans 2:4)? Jesus receives us; how can we be intentional about receiving others?

Follow the Spirit

What God wants me to do:

_____

_____

_____

_____

Remember Your Thoughts

Special insights I have learned:

_____

_____

_____

_____

More Light on the Text

Luke 7:37–48

This passage illustrates the different reactions Jesus and the Pharisees have toward sinners. In a complex, yet vivid account, Luke narrates the anointing of Jesus' feet by a sinful woman. In the face of differing reactions, Jesus offers comfort to the woman and also manages to rebuke the Pharisees who complain of his openness to her. The passage illustrates the previous comment that Jesus openly associates with sinners (7:34). Jesus' parable clearly explains why He does so (7:41–43). In addition, Jesus declares the woman's sin forgiven. Thus, the passage has two points of confrontation: association with sinners and the right to forgive sin. The passage is a picture of forgiveness and faith that is offered to everyone. It shows that God's call is nondiscriminatory, transcending both social and gender barriers.

37 And, behold, a woman in the city, which was a sinner, when she knew that Jesus sat at meat in the Pharisee's house, brought an alabaster box of ointment,

A woman in the city described as a sinner comes to know of the presence of Jesus at a meal in a Pharisee's house. There have been attempts to identify this woman. Early scholars identify this nameless woman as Mary Magdalene, but there is no biblical evidence for this identification. Furthermore, "a sinner" simply states her character. It is too severe to make the usual judgment of the woman as a prostitute or harlot who is known the town over as such. Charity demands that we do not think worse of a person than indicated by the available evidence. As such, "a sinner" may not necessarily imply more than that this woman had at some time done wrong and that her fall became publicly known and damaged her reputation ever after. Simply stated, we do not know the nature of her sinfulness. As the phrase "in the city" suggests, her sinfulness is sufficiently public to be known to the people at large. It does not warrant her label as a common prostitute.

A meal, such as the one that Jesus attended, was not private. People could come in and watch what went on. At the same time, a woman of questionable character would not have been very welcome in Simon's house, so it took courage for her to come. The woman brings an alabaster flask of ointment. The word *alabastros* (Gk.) describes an expensive container for costly perfumes.

The significance of Christ's acceptance of an invitation to a dinner in a Pharisee's house must not be lost. He has dined with Pharisees at other times, too (Luke 11:37, 14:1). However, here he is depicted as treating them in the same way he would treat tax collectors and sinners (7:34). He was neither contemptuous of the religious and wealthy nor prone to give them undue respect. He accepted invitations across the board. He was neither aloof nor class-discriminatory. Ultimately, Jesus was more concerned with the quality of relationships than arbitrary classifications due to the accident of birth, social history, or status.

38 And stood at his feet behind him weeping, and began to wash his feet with tears, and did wipe them with the hairs of her head, and kissed his feet, and anointed them with the ointment.

The narrative has to be understood against the backdrop of dinner settings. People reclined on low couches at meals, leaning on the left arm with the head toward the table and the body stretched away from it. The sandals were removed before reclining. The woman was thus able to approach Jesus' feet without difficulty. She may have intended to anoint them (or the head), but her emotions got the better of her, and her tears fell on his feet.

She promptly wiped them with her hair, a significant action, for Jewish ladies did not unbind their hair in public. In fact, Jewish women would have their heads covered at all times outside their own houses. Any woman with her hair exposed to public view would be considered promiscuous. This is likely where historical commentators have surmised the woman was a prostitute, but again, this is not necessarily so. While this woman's ethnicity is never revealed, it is worth noting that Greek and Roman women had fewer restrictions concerning women covering their hair. While Roman women were more likely than Greek women to cover their heads in public, it was socially acceptable for a respectable woman to leave her house without covering her hair at all. Even with that allowance, however, any physical contact between a man and woman in public would have been shocking. Whether this woman had her hair loose in public because she was a Jew used to sexual licentiousness or because she was a Gentile, she would not have usually been welcomed into such an intimate setting with a respectable Jewish man. That this woman wiping Jesus' feet with her hair would thus indicate not only her humility but also her marginal social status.

Clearly the woman was oblivious to public opinion in the grip of her deep emotion. This will explain also her kissing of the feet. Finally, she anointed Jesus' feet with the perfume. Normally this would have been poured on the head. To use it on the feet is probably a mark of humility. To attend to the feet was a menial task, one assigned to a slave. The passage does not state why she was weeping. It may have been because she was seeking forgiveness. Or she may have been weeping for joy at the opportunity to be near the One she obviously considered to be the Messiah.

39 Now when the Pharisee which had bidden him saw it, he spake within himself, saying, This man, if he were a prophet, would have known who and what manner of woman this is that toucheth him: for she is a sinner.

The whole scene must have appeared shameful to Simon the Pharisee. Jesus' failure to rebuke this sinful woman is proof to Simon that Jesus has no idea of what kind of woman she is. The irony here is that while Simon is inwardly musing about the limitation of Jesus' prophetic insight regarding the true character of the woman, Jesus is reading Simon's thoughts. Simon's thoughts reveal a common belief: A prophet ought to be able to perceive the character of persons with whom he associates. Jesus shows that He not only has perfect insight into the character of the woman but knows Simon's as well. In the preceding section, Jesus portrays Himself as one who "ate and drank" and who is a friend of sinners (v. 34). This passage is a perfect illustration for Jesus' description of Himself. Here we find Jesus dining with sinners.

40 And Jesus answering said unto him, Simon, I have somewhat to say unto thee. And he saith, Master, say on. 41 There was a certain creditor which had two debtors: the one owed five hundred pence, and the other fifty. 42 And when they had nothing to pay, he frankly forgave them both. Tell me therefore, which of them will love him most? 43 Simon answered and said, I suppose that he, to whom he forgave most. And he said unto him, Thou hast rightly judged.

Here Jesus gives His parable of the two debtors. Jesus seeks to disarm Simon's prejudice by drawing him into the parable. This parable, both in its substance and application, reveals an excellent example of the overwhelming force and persuasiveness in Christ's arguments. The parable is straightforward and intelligible, serving the purpose of clarifying a real-life situation. Jesus succeeds in maintaining the conversation and affecting conviction, where direct speech would have failed this objective. The link between the analogy and life is provided by the concept of "forgiveness" applied respectively to debt and sin (v. 42). Jesus is not merely trying to convince Simon that He knows and understands him; He wants to help Simon understand himself. The story, as a parable, opens a new reality to Simon, but the tragic fact is that this reality has already been revealed to him in the relationship between Jesus and the sinful woman, and he remains blind to it. The

Pharisee admits that the greatest debtor would feel the greatest gratitude (v. 43).

The implicit Christological teachings in this incident should be noted: (1) Jesus knows Simon's thoughts; (2) He knows that the woman is a sinner as the parable shows and thus refutes Simon's second presupposition; (3) Jesus is able to forgive sins—something God alone can do [7:49]; and (4) Simon's and the woman's standing before God is revealed and determined by their attitude toward Jesus. Jesus' subsequent explanation of the miracle shows that each part of the parable has a parallel: The creditor represents God; the debt is sin. From His parable, we can conclude that the debtor who owes less depicts the Pharisee, while the one who owes more represents the woman.

The important feature in the account is the forgiveness of the debt. God is ready and willing to forgive the debts of people and to act graciously beyond expectation. This picture of God's grace motivates Jesus' acceptance of those in dire need, regardless of who they are, and His openness toward sinners. It is this very point that Simon needs to realize, as the following verses make clear. The sinner who realizes the nature of the forgiveness received freely will be in a position to love God greatly. Jesus is not concerned with what the sin is, but who the sinner could be through God's love. Jesus' awareness of how God can transform people makes Him look forward to what God can make of them rather than dwell on their past (cf. Hebrews 12:2).

44 And he turned to the woman, and said unto Simon, Seest thou this woman? I entered into thine house, thou gavest me no water for my feet: but she hath washed my feet with tears, and wiped them with the hairs of her head. 45 Thou gavest me no kiss: but this woman since the time I came in hath not ceased to kiss my feet. 46 My head with

oil thou didst not anoint: but this woman hath anointed my feet with ointment.

Simon has neglected all of the customary courtesies accorded to guests and fails to act as a hospitable host. The phrase "thou gavest me no" is repeated for each of the ways Simon fails in hospitality: water for cleansing (v. 44), a kiss of greeting (v. 45), and oil for anointing (v. 46). The heat and dust of Palestine and the fact that sandals were merely soles bound to the feet with leather tongs made the washing of feet on entering the home both a courtesy and a necessity. Simon fails in this. In contrast to Simon, it is the "sinner" woman, an unwelcome guest for that matter, who provides the hospitality that Simon should have provided. By the logic of the parable, the woman's actions show her state of forgiveness. Simon has proven by his own treatment of his Guest that he is thoughtless and almost, if not quite, loveless.

The woman makes up for Simon's thoughtlessness by washing Jesus' feet with her tears. Furthermore, Simon does not kiss the master, but the woman, with purity and true humility, has more than made up for the lack by repeatedly kissing the feet of Jesus. Finally, Simon does not supply simple "oil" (Gk. *elaion*, **EH-lye-own**) to anoint Jesus' head, as was the customary hygiene of the day. A different word for anoint would have been used for religious connotations. Jesus is not blaming Simon for not recognizing Him as the anointed Messiah, only for not helping Him wash up for dinner. Simon's lack of common hospitality is highlighted more by the woman as she anoints the dirtiest part of Jesus' body with expensive, aromatic perfume (Gk. *muron*, **MOO-ron**, "ointment").

47 Wherefore I say unto thee, Her sins, which are many, are forgiven; for she loved much: but to whom little is forgiven, the same loveth little.

Jesus' pronouncement concludes the parable. Curiously, Jesus repeats His declaration of the woman's forgiveness, first by addressing Simon, then the woman. Simon sees a "woman sinner," but Jesus sees a "forgiven woman." In order to properly convey the point that Jesus wants to make from the parable, He has to argue in reverse from the "love" shown by the woman to demonstrate that she has been forgiven. Jesus' remarks make clear that He knows who the woman is. Simon had doubted that Jesus was a prophet because he believed He had not discerned this about the woman (7:39). The reference to her many sins shows that Jesus knows all along who the woman is. Simon should by now recognize that a prophet is present.

At first sight, the verse would seem to suggest that the woman's love for Jesus is the basis of her forgiveness. This is not the case. The wording of Jesus' parable strongly implies the woman's demonstration of love is an expression of being forgiven: The one who is forgiven much loves much. Love is the consequence of forgiveness. It is important to note that there is no simple calculus of forgiveness and gratitude in the ministry of Jesus. The passage does not tell us how the woman comes to the state of forgiveness, which is the basis of manifestation of her acts of love toward Jesus. Gratitude definitely follows the acceptance of God's undeserved mercy and forgiveness. To the Pharisee, this woman is still a sinner. Jesus does not in any way deny that her sins are "many," but that she is no longer under the burden of them. As the next verse shows, she is now forgiven. This is the message of salvation in a nutshell.

48 And he said unto her, Thy sins are forgiven.

These words to the woman are among the most precious words Jesus spoke to her or to the many who are redeemed: "Thy sins are forgiven."

Sources:

Bock, Darrell L. *Luke: 1:1–9:50*, vol. 1, Baker Exegetical Commentary on the New Testament. Grand Rapids, MI: Baker Academic, 1994.

Bovon, Francois and Helmut Koester, *Luke 1: A Commentary on the Gospel of Luke 1:1–9:50*, Hermeneia—a Critical and Historical Commentary on the Bible. Minneapolis, MN: Fortress Press, 2002.

Carroll, John T. *Luke: A Commentary.* New Testament Library. Louisville, KY: Wesminster John Knox Press, 2012.

John A. Martin, "Luke," in *The Bible Knowledge Commentary: An Exposition of the Scriptures*, eds. J. F. Walvoord and R. B. Zuck, vol. 2. Wheaton, IL: Victor Books, 1985.

Johnson, Luke Timothy *The Gospel of Luke.* Sacra Pagina vol. 3. Collegeville, MN: The Liturgical Press, 1991.

Keener, Craig S. *The IVP Bible Background Commentary: New Testament.* Downers Grove, IL: InterVarsity Press, 1993.

Lenski, R. C. H. *The Interpretation of St. Luke's Gospel.* Minneapolis, MN: Augsburg Publishing House, 1961.

Morris, Leon. *Luke: An Introduction and Commentary*, vol. 3, Tyndale New Testament Commentaries. Downers Grove, IL: InterVarsity Press, 1988.

Noland, John. *Luke 1:1–9:20*, vol. 35A, Word Biblical Commentary. Dallas, TX: Word, Incorporated, 2002.

Stein, Robert H. *Luke*, vol. 24, The New American Commentary. Nashville, TN: Broadman & Holman Publishers, 1992.

Say It Correctly

Alabaster. **AL**-uh-**BAS**-ter.
Pharisee. **FEHR**-ih-see.

Daily Bible Readings

MONDAY
God's Salvation for All People
(Isaiah 52:7–10)

TUESDAY
Your Sins Are Forgiven
(Luke 5:20–26)

WEDNESDAY
Salvation Requires Enduring Witness
(Mark 13:9–13)

THURSDAY
All Who Call Will Be Saved
(Romans 10:5–13)

FRIDAY
Treat Each Other Like Jesus Does
(John 13:12–20)

SATURDAY
Leaders Reject God's Messenger
(Luke 7:24–30)

SUNDAY
Her Many Sins Have Been Forgiven
(Luke 7:37–48)

Notes

_____

_____

_____

_____

Teaching Tips

Words You Should Know

A. Perfection (v. 9) *katartisis* (Gk.)—A state of being mended or restored so as to be fully functional

B. Farewell (v. 11) *chairete* (Gk.)—A parting salutation literally meaning "Rejoice"

Teacher Preparation

Unifying Principle—Look in the Mirror. People often set goals to achieve personal growth. What can we do to gauge our personal development? Following previous difficulties, Paul now forcibly reminds the Corinthians to examine themselves in comparison to God's standards for faithful living.

A. Read the Bible Background and Devotional Reading.

B. Pray for your students and lesson clarity.

C. Read the lesson Scripture in multiple translations.

D. Examine areas you need to strengthen as a teacher and in your relationship with Christ.

O—Open the Lesson

A. Begin the class with prayer.

B. Have the students read the Aim for Change and the In Focus story.

C. Ask students how events like those in the story weigh on their hearts and how they can view these events from a faith perspective.

P—Present the Scriptures

A. Read the Focal Verses.

B. Have the class share what Scriptures stand out for them and why, with particular emphasis on today's context.

C. Discuss the Background and The People, Places, and Times sections.

E—Explore the Meaning

A. Use In Depth or More Light on the Text to facilitate a deeper discussion of the lesson text.

B. Pose the questions in Search the Scriptures and Discuss the Meaning.

C. Discuss the Liberating Lesson and Application for Activation sections.

N—Next Steps for Application

A. Summarize the value of self-examination as a believer.

B. End class with a commitment to pray for commitment and guidance as believers in Christ.

Worship Guide

For the Superintendent or Teacher
Theme: Self-Examination
Song: "You Opened Up My Eyes"
Devotional Reading: James 1:12–18

Self-Examination

Bible Background • 2 CORINTHIANS 13:1–11
Printed Text • 2 CORINTHIANS 13:1–11 | Devotional Reading • JAMES 1:12–18

—— Aim for Change ——

By the end of the lesson, we will: IDENTIFY the standards of faithful living in Christ that guided Paul's life, SENSE the growth in faithful living by testing our lives in Christ, and EMBRACE faithful living as the basis for communal life in Christ.

—— In Focus ——

"Ethan is wrong! He knows better," Mathew thought as he sat across the dinner table from his brother, "I must tell what happened."

Ethan had been warned several times about going into the candy store with the Smith boys. They did things contrary to the way Ethan and Mathew were being taught. They were always talking back to adults, getting into fights, and stealing. Ethan knew better.

Ethan and Mathew loved going to church. They especially liked going to church with their grandparents and hearing Pastor Gray preach. The boys got baptized at the same time. They even chose the same favorite Bible verse, "If we confess our sins, He is faithful and just to forgive us our sins, and to cleanse us from all unrighteousness" (1 John 1:9).

Now Ethan was stealing and being disrespectful to Mr. King, the candy store owner. Mathew knew what Ethan was doing was wrong. He even told Ethan he was going to get in trouble because he knew better. Granddad would always say, "Boys, if you want to know if you are doing right, God is your plumb line. We examine ourselves by God's Word."

As Mathew pondered how to bring up what happened, Granddad said, "Ethan, I saw you today at the candy store. What were you doing over there?" Mathew was so relieved! Granddad had seen what happened, too.

When our sin has been called out, do we acknowledge and confess our sins? Or do we deny them? Do we examine ourselves against God's Word?

—— Keep in Mind ——

"Examine yourselves, whether ye be in the faith; prove your own selves. Know ye not your own selves, how that Jesus Christ is in you, except ye be reprobates?" (2 Corinthians 13:5, KJV)

"Examine yourselves to see if your faith is genuine. Test yourselves. Surely you know that Jesus Christ is among you; if not, you have failed the test of genuine faith" (2 Corinthians 13:5, NLT).

Focal Verses

KJV **2 Corinthians 13:1** This is the third time I am coming to you. In the mouth of two or three witnesses shall every word be established.

2 I told you before, and foretell you, as if I were present, the second time; and being absent now I write to them which heretofore have sinned, and to all other, that, if I come again, I will not spare:

3 Since ye seek a proof of Christ speaking in me, which to you-ward is not weak, but is mighty in you.

4 For though he was crucified through weakness, yet he liveth by the power of God. For we also are weak in him, but we shall live with him by the power of God toward you.

5 Examine yourselves, whether ye be in the faith; prove your own selves. Know ye not your own selves, how that Jesus Christ is in you, except ye be reprobates?

6 But I trust that ye shall know that we are not reprobates.

7 Now I pray to God that ye do no evil; not that we should appear approved, but that ye should do that which is honest, though we be as reprobates.

8 For we can do nothing against the truth, but for the truth.

9 For we are glad, when we are weak, and ye are strong: and this also we wish, even your perfection.

10 Therefore I write these things being absent, lest being present I should use sharpness, according to the power which the Lord hath given me to edification, and not to destruction.

11 Finally, brethren, farewell. Be perfect, be of good comfort, be of one mind, live in peace; and the God of love and peace shall be with you.

NLT **2 Corinthians 13:1** This is the third time I am coming to visit you (and as the Scriptures say, "The facts of every case must be established by the testimony of two or three witnesses").

2 I have already warned those who had been sinning when I was there on my second visit. Now I again warn them and all others, just as I did before, that next time I will not spare them.

3 I will give you all the proof you want that Christ speaks through me. Christ is not weak when he deals with you; he is powerful among you.

4 Although he was crucified in weakness, he now lives by the power of God. We, too, are weak, just as Christ was, but when we deal with you we will be alive with him and will have God's power.

5 Examine yourselves to see if your faith is genuine. Test yourselves. Surely you know that Jesus Christ is among you; if not, you have failed the test of genuine faith.

6 As you test yourselves, I hope you will recognize that we have not failed the test of apostolic authority.

7 We pray to God that you will not do what is wrong by refusing our correction. I hope we won't need to demonstrate our authority when we arrive. Do the right thing before we come—even if that makes it look like we have failed to demonstrate our authority.

8 For we cannot oppose the truth, but must always stand for the truth.

9 We are glad to seem weak if it helps show that you are actually strong. We pray that you will become mature.

10 I am writing this to you before I come, hoping that I won't need to deal severely with you when I do come. For I want to use the authority the Lord has given me to strengthen you, not to tear you down.

11 Dear brothers and sisters, I close my letter with these last words: Be joyful. Grow to maturity. Encourage each other. Live in harmony and peace. Then the God of love and peace will be with you.

The People, Places, and Times

Paul. Even before his conversion, Paul was instrumental in causing the church to spread from its Jerusalem roots. Paul's participation in the death of Stephen the deacon and frenzied persecution of believers after the Resurrection caused them to flee Jerusalem and take the Gospel to other parts of world. After his conversion (Acts 9:1–19), Paul embarked on three missionary journeys spreading the Gospel throughout the Roman Empire. Paul personally established numerous churches, and he also wrote at least thirteen epistles in the New Testament. The conversion of a notorious church hater such as Paul proves that even the worst of sinners can be changed, empowered, and used by God.

Corinth. A key city in ancient Greece until it was destroyed by the Romans in 146 BC. Julius Caesar rebuilt it as a Roman colony in 46 BC, and it grew and prospered. In Paul's day, Corinth was thriving because of its two seaports (to the west and the east) and had become a commercial center. The cosmopolitan center thrived on commercial entertainment and corruption. Pleasure seekers came there to spend money on immoral practices. A very active cult of Aphrodite there employed temple prostitutes. Corinth became so notorious for its evils that the term *korinthiazomai* (Gk. "to Corinth") became a synonym for debauchery and prostitution.

Background

In 2 Corinthians Paul is again writing the church because of immoral practices. Additionally, there have been attempts to besmirch Paul's reputation. Paul argues that his trials prove God's power in him rather than proving God's displeasure with him. Paul makes his argument in this letter in order to help the Corinthians so that when he comes to visit them, he will not have to be harsh.

Paul often mentions how God's power is seen in the weakness of the Cross. The Corinthian Christians were very much like the pagan culture that surrounded them.

Indisputably, Paul had Christ in him. The Corinthians must decide if Christ is in them. If they conclude Christ is in them, then they cannot deny Christ is in Paul, their spiritual father. In this letter Paul speaks of his authority for building them up (2 Corinthians 10:8) and encourages them live in the power of God.

At-A-Glance

1. The Minister's Warning
(2 Corinthians 13:1–6)
2. The Minister's Prayer (vv. 7–10)
3. The Minister's Challenge (v. 11)

In Depth

1. The Minister's Warning (2 Corinthians 13:1–6)

Paul was preparing to visit Corinth for a third time. He remembered how humbling his experience was on his second visit to Corinth. It was humbling for two reasons. One was the offense against him, and the second was that he found many people in the church living contrary to God's will. Paul was repeating his warning to them about the consequences of their sin. He assured them that if they had not changed their ways, they would have many regrets. They were asking for more than they were expecting when they asked for proof of Paul's authority. Paul recognizes that in his weakness God's power is seen. He knows how powerful the God he serves is.

Christ's experience on the Cross demonstrated humiliation and physical weakness. Paul identifies with the weakness of Christ as shown on the Cross; therefore, he also knows the power of God is with him and will sustain him as he confronts the problems plaguing the Corinthians' church. Paul wants them to understand they are not just dealing with or confronting him, but God.

Paul encourages them to be sure of their faith. If they examine themselves and find that they are not pleased with the results, they must change. The Corinthians must be accountable to God for themselves.

What methods do you use to examine yourself in the faith? How do you go about an examination of your faith?

2. The Minister's Prayer (vv. 7–10)

Paul prays for their success in the faith. If the Corinthians refuse the correction, it is to their own peril. Paul is concerned with the urgency of this need. They cannot live in sin, overlook error, and expect God to be pleased. Paul lets them know that he has the authority to give this instruction and correction. Paul makes it clear that the truth will prevail. He declares that he will not oppose the truth. Instead, he must always stand for the truth. Paul is willing to deny himself on their behalf. If Paul's weakness will help them be strong, then Paul is satisfied. His only prayer is for the full restoration of the Corinthians to fellowship and holiness.

Paul explains that he is writing to them harshly and straightforwardly because when he comes to them in person, he wants the discipline part to be out of the way. Perhaps the church at Corinth expects Paul to make some strong showing of his apostolic power. Paul does not want to have to make such a show of force. He is not trying to tear them down; rather, his intent is to build them up with the authority and power God has granted him.

What errors or sins do you see the church overlooking today? How do you speak against it?

3. The Minister's Challenge (v. 11)

Paul closes his letter with a benediction that encourages the Corinthians to aim for completeness in Christ. His benediction has four statements of encouragement. First, he tells them to be joyful. While his manner and tone may seem harsh, he wants them to rejoice in the Lord because there is hope through the Holy Spirit for them to be restored. Second, he tells them to grow to maturity. The purpose of his letter and the teaching he has provided was aimed at growing them in full maturity in Christ so that they can be strong in faith and steadfast in their love for one another. The Corinthians have faced a trying time. There have been dissensions and arguments, accusations and disputes; but now Paul says to lay aside discord and focus on encouraging one another. This is a reference to strengthening one another in the faith so the church can be stronger. Finally, he tells them to live in harmony and peace. This can only be done if their sin and disdain have been replaced by joy, maturity, and encouragement. Then, Paul says, they will be at peace with the God who loves them.

How do you remind yourself of the joyful hope Christians have in Christ?

Search the Scriptures

1. What does Paul mean when he says "if I come again, I will not spare" (v. 2) and "lest being present I should use sharpness" (v. 10)?

2. The Corinthians were told to examine and test themselves. How should they do this (v. 5)?

Discuss the Meaning

1. Paul's letter shows his love, compassion, and understanding. When we need to give correction to our brothers and sisters in the faith, how can we exhibit those same characteristics?

2. How can we be constructive and not destructive when giving reproof and correction to the people of God?

Liberating Lesson

No one likes to be corrected, young or old, female or male. However, there is a time for everything, including correction and reproof (cf. Ecclesiastes 3:3). Without discipline, we are often at odds with others and not able to please God. Often the negativity we see in our communities—the fights, murders, and crimes—are the result of undisciplined living. There is a time when we all need discipline. When discipline is handled with love, we find the dangers brought by undisciplined actions can be avoided. Paul's benediction provides the basis for liberating correction that can result in positive family and community relationships. Our discipline must be concerned with maintaining the joy of our relationships, the maturity needed to be members of the community, the encouragement that we can and must give to one another, and the harmony and peace we seek to achieve. If this is the basis of our conversation, correction, and discipline, the God of love and peace will surely bless us to live abundantly and in unity.

Application for Activation

The standard for faithful living is found in the Word of God. While we might be tempted to compare ourselves with others and to judge our actions according to whether we are better than or even not as bad as someone else, we must always look to the Bible (and to those who exhibit a wise example) to determine if our actions, thoughts, and relationships are pleasing to God. When we make comparisons between us and them, we become judgmental and often overlook our own shortcomings. As Christians, we should be more eager to examine ourselves than to judge others. We ought to measure ourselves by the standards set in Scripture. This week, examine yourself honestly to see where you may need to change or to embrace a more God-like stance. You will find when you follow God's plan that you have the power to live peaceably with people and with God.

Follow the Spirit

What God wants me to do:

_____

_____

_____

_____

Remember Your Thoughts

Special insights I have learned:

_____

_____

_____

_____

More Light on the Text

2 Corinthians 13:1–11

1 This is the third time I am coming to you. In the mouth of two or three witnesses shall every word be established. 2 I told you before, and foretell you, as if I were present, the second time; and being absent now I write to them which heretofore have sinned, and to all other, that, if I come again, I will not spare:

Having visited the Corinthians twice, Paul is coming for the third time. Paul is their pastor, and his pastoral work requires teaching and visitations. The situation in Corinth has persisted.

113

There are those who have fallen from the faith and are living in ways that are sinful and detrimental to the church. Furthermore, their actions cause dissension and deny the Cross. This has caused Paul, as their spiritual father, to chasten them as the situation demands. Paul will address the issue of sin and false doctrine according to God's law as sanctioned in Christ. His visit will be the final one, but he wants to put an end to the issues they face before he arrives. The particular actions Paul is concerned about are sexual immorality, sectarianism that is causing division, and false doctrine that is trying to keep believers in legalistic bondage rather than freedom in Christ Jesus. He addressed all of these before in 1 Corinthians and presumably during his other visits. He explains that either they will heed his correction in his letter or, when he arrives, he will not spare his words or his actions.

3 Since ye seek a proof of Christ speaking in me, which to you-ward is not weak, but is mighty in you.

There were those who sought proof of Paul's apostleship. Paul (2 Corinthians 1:1) by the will of God. Paul writes his letter to address this and other issues. Paul reminds the Corinthians that he is an apostle, sent by Christ and by God's grace. Paul had endured abuse for the sake of Christ. But when the genuineness of his apostleship is called into question, Paul draws a line. He explains that there is no weakness in Christ but mighty power that seeks to correct them. For in challenging Paul, they are challenging the Lord Himself who commissioned him. They have seen the impact of the Holy Spirit at work among them and the fruit in their lives that was planted through Paul's preaching. In reality, they have their proof already. Moreover, Christ was at work powerfully among them in Paul's absence, so they should know better than to continue to ignore or indulge sinful behavior.

4 For though he was crucified through weakness, yet he liveth by the power of God. For we also are weak in him, but we shall live with him by the power of God toward you.

The Corinthians are grappling with the paradox of Christ's power being shown through His weakness. Christ's power has transformed the Corinthians' lives, but Christ was crucified in weakness. Christ is the Prince of life (Acts 3:15), yet He died on the Cross in total humiliation (Philippians 2:8). Yet the Cross, which was a supreme spectacle of weakness and human degradation, is the source of power unto salvation for believers. The instrument of weakness became the instrument of power (2 Corinthians 4:8–12; 6:4–10; 11:23ff; 12:5–10). Christ Himself endured the sufferings of our weakness so that the believer who is united with Christ in His death will also participate in His glorious resurrection (Romans 6:3; Philippians 3:10). Christ, who died as though weak, was raised to the majestic glory as King of kings and Lord of lords. Therefore, Paul can live to say that he is Christ's apostle even in his weakness.

5 Examine yourselves, whether ye be in the faith; prove your own selves. Know ye not your own selves, how that Jesus Christ is in you, except ye be reprobates?

Now that they can prove that God is working in Paul through Christ, it is time for the Corinthians to prove to Paul whether Christ is in them. They should turn their attention to themselves. They must confirm to themselves that they have faith in Christ. Each Christian has to do his or her own self-examination. The Corinthians must be restored (v. 9) to their former faith. They must be built up if they have lost their foundation. Through Paul's ministry, they came to faith. Now they must prove their faith to Paul. If they know that Christ dwells in them, then they should also know that Paul is Christ's apostle. This could be done either through voluntary confession by individual members or though the disciplining of individual members of the church. They have to scrutinize themselves instead of scrutinizing Paul. Upon self-examination, the Corinthians will discern whether they have faith or not. So Paul hopes that they will start walking in the way of Christ.

6 But I trust that ye shall know that we are not reprobates. 7 Now I pray to God that ye do no evil; not that we should appear approved, but that ye should do that which is honest, though we be as reprobates.

Paul assures the Corinthians that after they have examined themselves and if they have found themselves to be truly in the faith, then they will surely see that Paul and his fellow missionaries are also in the faith ("not reprobates"). Paul prays that their examination of themselves and of Paul will not be tainted by sin. He is not so much concerned that a tainted examination would find him guilty, but that such a test would mean that his spiritual children were being dishonest. Paul's focus is on the spiritual well-being of the Corinthians, even as they doubt his apostleship.

8 For we can do nothing against the truth, but for the truth. 9 For we are glad, when we are weak, and ye are strong: and this also we wish, even your perfection.

In a pastoral manner, yet partially ridiculing them, Paul desires that they be strong in faith rather than weak. But he and his fellow missionaries consider themselves weak. The irony is that the Corinthians are even weaker and need to be strong. Misconduct in the congregation must be dealt with wisely in order to avoid schism. Using Paul's example, pastors must not shrink from imposing discipline when circumstances demand it. But authority must go through the proper routes and not degenerate into authoritarianism or abuse. A pastor must conform to the teaching of Christ, who is the Head of the church. Paul, therefore, longs that there should be harmony that bears fruit among members. The noun for perfection (Gk. *katartisis*, ka-TAR-tees-eess) is used only here in the New Testament, though its verb form is used often. It does not speak of moral perfection but of being made whole. It is elsewhere translated "mend" (Mark 1:19) or "restore" (Galatians 6:1) and carries the idea of putting into a proper shape so that the perfected item can do everything it is meant to do. Therefore, when the Christians reach "perfection" as the body of Christ, its members will function efficiently.

10 Therefore I write these things being absent, lest being present I should use sharpness, according to the power which the Lord hath given me to edification, and not to destruction.

Paul is accused of being bold and terrifying when he writes but weak when he is present (2 Corinthians 10:10). So, he answers the charge by saying that he does not need to act with sharpness when he comes, for he has already exercised his authority by letter. When he comes, he will act pastorally. His sharpness is that the church may become spiritually strong (12:19). He has been given this authority by the Lord (10:8). While he was challenged by his opponents, he will act as a pastor. He will still discipline the church (12:20). However, as a pastor, he will act in gentleness rather than severity. With a rod of love and a spirit of humility, he will pastor them.

11 Finally, brethren, farewell. Be perfect, be of good comfort, be of one mind, live in peace; and the God of love and peace shall be with you.

Paul concludes his letter with affectionate words to the brethren and with exhortation. The term *chairete* (Gk. **KHAY-reh-tay**), which is often translated "farewell," can more literally be translated "rejoice." Indeed Paul wants them to rejoice in the Lord (Philippians 3:1; 4:4). Joy should be a mark of every Christian community. *Katartizesthe* (Gk. **ka-tar-TEED-zess-thay**, "be perfect") is the verb form of the noun for "perfection" used above (v. 9). If all are made whole, they will live in harmony. *Parakaleisthe* (Gk. **pa-ra-ka-LACE-thay**) means "be comforted." Paul prays that the Corinthians should embrace God's comforting (cf. 1:3). "Be of one mind" means the Christians, though they hold different opinions as individuals, should always come to agreement based on the Word of God. They should respect each other. In so doing they will be united in love so that the teaching of Christ may unify them as parts of the body of Christ to promote peace and love.

Sources:

Grogan, Geoffrey. *2 Corinthians: The Glories & Responsibilities of Christian Service.* Focus on the Bible Commentary. Tain, UK: Christian Focus Publications, 2007.

Henry, Matthew. *Matthew Henry's Commentary on the Whole Bible.* WORD*search* CROSS e-book.

Lane, Eric. *Proverbs: Everyday Wisdom for Everyone.* Focus on the Bible Commentary. Tain, UK: Christian Focus Publications, 2007.

Peterson, Eugene H., trans. *The Message: The Bible in Contemporary Language.* Colorado Springs, CO: NavPress, 2002.

The Preacher's Outline & Sermon Bible – 1 Samuel. Chattanooga, TN: Leadership Ministries Worldwide, 1996.

Richards, Lawrence O. *The Teacher's Commentary.* Wheaton, IL: Victor Books, 1987.

Severance, W. Murray. *That's Easy for You to Say: Your Quick Guide to Pronouncing Bible Names.* Nashville, TN: Broadman & Holman, 1997.

Strong, James. *Strong's Talking Greek & Hebrew Dictionary.* Austin, TX: WORD*search* Corp., 2007.

Daily Bible Readings

MONDAY
Weigh the Evidence Carefully
(Deuteronomy 19:15–20)

TUESDAY
Building Up Your Faith Community
(1 Thessalonians 5:12–22)

WEDNESDAY
Preparing for the Lord's Supper
(1 Corinthians 11:26–29)

THURSDAY
Honor Your Elders
(1 Timothy 5:17–22)

FRIDAY
Test the Spirits
(1 John 4:1–8)

SATURDAY
Give Generously to Enrich Your Life
(2 Corinthians 9:10–15)

SUNDAY
Examine Yourselves in Your Faithful Living
(2 Corinthians 13:1–11)

Notes

Teaching Tips

Words You Should Know

A. Power (v. 5) *dunamis* (Gk.)—Miraculous and mighty strength; synonymous with "might" as found in Zechariah 4:6

B. Wrath (v. 10) *orge* (Gk.)—Extreme anger, indignation, and punishment

Teacher Preparation

Unifying Principle—Let It Shine. People often look for positive examples to emulate. How can we be positive examples? The Thessalonians were praised because they were positive examples to others, exhibiting strong faith and committing loving acts even in the midst of trials and persecution.

A. Read the Bible Background and Devotional Reading.

B. Pray for your students and lesson clarity.

C. Read the lesson Scripture in multiple translations.

D. Research Scriptures about love, faith, and hope that connect to the lesson text. Write a short summary of how these verses influence your understanding of today's Scripture lesson, and be sure to share these insights with your class.

O—Open the Lesson

A. Begin the class with prayer.

B. Have the students read the Aim for Change and the In Focus story.

C. Ask students how events like those in the story weigh on their hearts and how they can view these events from a faith perspective.

P—Present the Scriptures

A. Read the Focal Verses.

B. Have the class share what Scriptures stand out for them and why, with particular emphasis on today's context.

C. Discuss the Background and The People, Places, and Times sections.

E—Explore the Meaning

A. Use In Depth or More Light on the Text to facilitate a deeper discussion of the lesson text.

B. Pose the questions in Search the Scriptures and Discuss the Meaning.

C. Discuss the Liberating Lesson and Application for Activation sections.

N—Next Steps for Application

A. Summarize the value of being positive examples of Christ in our daily lives.

B. End class with a commitment to pray for developing faithful and loving actions in Christ toward others.

Worship Guide

For the Superintendent or Teacher
Theme: Be Examples of Faith
Song: "Restore In Us, O God"
Devotional Reading: 2 Corinthians 5:1–10

Be Examples of Faith

Bible Background • 1 THESSALONIANS 1:2–10
Printed Text • 1 THESSALONIANS 1:2–10 | Devotional Reading • 2 CORINTHIANS 5:1–10

——————— Aim for Change ———————

By the end of the lesson, we will: COMPREHEND the importance of the witness of the Thessalonian Christians in spite of their trials, APPRECIATE the role of faithful imitators of Christ, and BECOME positive examples of faith and love to other believers in Christ.

——————— In Focus ———————

Mary shouted, "If one more thing happens, Lord, I don't know what I'll do!" Her daughter, Sharion rushed in the room and asked, "What's the matter, Mama?" Sharion knew her mother had been struggling to keep the faith since Sharion's dad, Jack, passed so suddenly. He was a man who truly loved the Lord. He kept Mary smiling regardless of what troubles life seemed to throw their way. He would always encourage them to keep the faith. Jack would remind them that God is able, and He would bring them out.

Jack was no longer around, and things just kept happening. He was the one to take care of all their needs. He paid the bills. He made sure things were running properly. Mary didn't have to worry about anything. She was the one to cook and clean; Jack took care of the rest.

The water tank broke, the car wouldn't start, the electric bill was exceptionally high; Mary was overwhelmed. As Mary flopped down in Jack's favorite chair, she gasped. "Everything seems to be falling apart. How can I fix it all?" she thought.

Sharion walked over to her mother and picked up Jack's Bible off the table. A piece of paper fell out, written in Jack's handwriting. It said, "No matter what happens, keep the faith. God is able." Once again, Jack had encouraged them to keep the faith.

Who has set the example in your life to be faithful to God, no matter how numerous your trials may get?

——————— Keep in Mind ———————

"So that ye were ensamples to all that believe in Macedonia and Achaia. For from you sounded out the word of the Lord not only in Macedonia and Achaia, but also in every place your faith to God-ward is spread abroad; so that we need not to speak any thing" (1 Thessalonians 1:7–8, KJV).

"As a result, you have become an example to all the believers in Greece—throughout both Macedonia and Achaia. And now the word of the Lord is ringing out from you to people everywhere, even beyond Macedonia and Achaia, for wherever we go we find people telling us about your faith in God. We don't need to tell them about it" (1 Thessalonians 1:7–8, NLT)

Focal Verses

KJV **1 Thessalonians 1:2** We give thanks to God always for you all, making mention of you in our prayers;

3 Remembering without ceasing your work of faith, and labour of love, and patience of hope in our Lord Jesus Christ, in the sight of God and our Father;

4 Knowing, brethren beloved, your election of God.

5 For our gospel came not unto you in word only, but also in power, and in the Holy Ghost, and in much assurance; as ye know what manner of men we were among you for your sake.

6 And ye became followers of us, and of the Lord, having received the word in much affliction, with joy of the Holy Ghost.

7 So that ye were ensamples to all that believe in Macedonia and Achaia.

8 For from you sounded out the word of the Lord not only in Macedonia and Achaia, but also in every place your faith to God-ward is spread abroad; so that we need not to speak any thing.

9 For they themselves shew of us what manner of entering in we had unto you, and how ye turned to God from idols to serve the living and true God;

10 And to wait for his Son from heaven, whom he raised from the dead, even Jesus, which delivered us from the wrath to come.

NLT **1 Thessalonians 1:2** We always thank God for all of you and pray for you constantly.

3 As we pray to our God and Father about you, we think of your faithful work, your loving deeds, and the enduring hope you have because of our Lord Jesus Christ.

4 We know, dear brothers and sisters, that God loves you and has chosen you to be his own people.

5 For when we brought you the Good News, it was not only with words but also with power, for the Holy Spirit gave you full assurance that what we said was true. And you know of our concern for you from the way we lived when we were with you.

6 So you received the message with joy from the Holy Spirit in spite of the severe suffering it brought you. In this way, you imitated both us and the Lord.

7 As a result, you have become an example to all the believers in Greece—throughout both Macedonia and Achaia.

8 And now the word of the Lord is ringing out from you to people everywhere, even beyond Macedonia and Achaia, for wherever we go we find people telling us about your faith in God. We don't need to tell them about it,

9 for they keep talking about the wonderful welcome you gave us and how you turned away from idols to serve the living and true God.

10 And they speak of how you are looking forward to the coming of God's Son from heaven—Jesus, whom God raised from the dead. He is the one who has rescued us from the terrors of the coming judgment.

The People, Places, and Times

Thessalonica. This is the capital and largest city of the Roman province of Macedonia, a mountainous region of Greece. As a port on the shores of what is now called the Gulf of Salonika with a population of about 200,000 people, Thessalonica was one of the wealthiest and most flourishing trade centers in the Roman Empire. The city was on a trade route, the Egnatian Way, linking it to Philippi, Apollonia, and Berea— other places where Paul, Silas, Timothy, and others traveled during their missionary journeys. Many pagan religions and cultural influences also flourished in Thessalonica. These influences challenged the faith of the young Christians there.

Thessalonian Believers. The Thessalonian church was established during Paul's second missionary journey. The new Christians in Thessalonica were struggling with their newfound faith. Persecutions against them by the established order (both political and religious) were fierce. The Thessalonian believers had many unanswered questions as they struggled to hold onto their beliefs and waited for Christ's return.

Background

In ancient letters, it was common to express thanksgiving. In Paul's letter to the Thessalonians, he desired to encourage them. He wanted to be extravagant in his praise for them, so they would understand that he was pleased with what he heard and knew about their faith. The reputation of their commitment to Christ was honorable.

Generally, to be chosen or elected by God was a position the Jewish people reserved for themselves. However, Paul was applying it to a church that had many Gentile converts. Letters that are meant to counsel or persuade, more often than not, remind the reader of what they already know. Reminding them of former counsel became an indisputable means of successfully making points clear.

Teachers encourage their students to imitate them. This was commonly noted in ancient letters. Paul recognized the Thessalonians had already begun practicing this process, which made their conversion clear to the culture around them. A large number of Christians were converted from Gentile backgrounds. This resulted in their facing greater hostility and persecution as the culture rejected them. As people traveled, they would carry news with them. The other churches probably heard of the Thessalonians through the Philippian messengers, Jewish or Gentile travelers, and from Macedonians who supported Paul.

The Old Testament often referred to "wrath" as God's judgments in history, but this term was stretched in the New Testament to God's wrath in the final days, the Day of Judgment when Christ will return.

At-A-Glance

1. An Elect People (1 Thessalonians 1:2–4)
2. An Exemplary Enthusiastic People (vv. 5–8)
3. An Expectant People (vv. 9–10)

In Depth

1. An Elect People (1 Thessalonians 1:2–4)

Paul was grateful for the Thessalonians. He and his companions thought of them often and appreciated who they were. The Thessalonians had been chosen by God. It was evident in the way they lived.

Their faith guided the way they lived and caused them to work for the kingdom by influencing others to come to Christ. They did this because of the love they had for God. It was not a burden for them to show how much they loved God by being an example of the

Gospel. They did it with joy to the Lord. The Thessalonians were able to continue their labor of love without getting discouraged. They were determined to never give up. Their persistence came from their hope in Jesus Christ's return.

In what ways are you endeavoring to put your faith to work through love, and to remain steadfast in hope?

2. An Exemplary Enthusiastic People (vv. 5–8)

Paul was joyful and grateful for the Thessalonians. They received the Gospel that came to them from Paul and companions. The Holy Spirit used the Word with great power, and the Thessalonians received the message and those that brought it.

The Thessalonians were new to the faith. Because Paul was only with them for a short time, they were in some ways "babes in Christ." Like all new Christians, they needed mature Christians as examples and leaders. The Thessalonians followed or imitated their spiritual leaders, even though this led to severe persecution.

The Thessalonians' faith encouraged other churches. Although they were new in the faith, they set a good example for others by being exemplary in the way they lived. They were not perfect, but their faith and actions were commendable. They encouraged others through their faith, love, and hope, which were evident in the way they received the Word and shared the Word. They were so known for their faith that Paul heard about it everywhere he went.

Are you an exemplary Christian, enthusiastic about witnessing?

3. An Expectant People (vv. 9–10)

The Thessalonians were patient in the hope of their Savior's return. They previously worshiped idols and had no hope. However, when they trusted God, they had a living hope. The living

God has given all His children a living hope by raising Jesus Christ, His Son, from the dead.

Waiting for the Lord is not being idle but consists of activity and endurance. As we wait, we keep busy and obey God's Word. We may be tempted to stop, but the evidence that we hope in Christ's return is our diligence to stay faithful. The Thessalonians trusted Christ and looked for His return with joyful expectancy.

How do you persevere in your trials? How do you encourage others to put their faith to work, to labor in love, and to remain steadfast in hope?

Search the Scriptures

1. What evidence does Paul give that the Thessalonians were chosen by God (vv. 4–5)?

2. What proof does Paul cite to show that the Thessalonians' witness produced a godly example (v. 8)?

Discuss the Meaning

1. Why is it important for Christians' conversation (their talk) to line up with their way of living (their walk)?

2. The Thessalonians reverenced God's Word. Despite many afflictions (suffering), they maintained the joy of the Holy Spirit (1 Thessalonians 1:6). Why is it important to share suffering and joy when witnessing?

Liberating Lesson

In the world we live in today, no one wants to hear negativity. Most of us were taught that if we don't have anything good to say, then we shouldn't say anything at all. We hear people talk about how they only want good vibes, no negativity in their environment. However, as we learn in God's Word, sometimes the things we don't hope for are present. Often these things can be called afflictions.

Paul and his companions in this text remind the church that they have endured affliction— suffering while following the way of Christ

(2 Corinthians 6:4–5, 7–10). Yet Paul declares that in Christ he is more than a conqueror of all of these things (Romans 8:37). We cannot apply only some of God's Word to our lives. We cannot select the parts we like and leave out the negativity or suffering. For it is through suffering that sin is revealed, confession is made, and strength is given as we wait on Jesus' return. Remember, even Christ Himself suffered for our sakes (Isaiah 53).

Application for Activation

Are you willing to accept that suffering is part of the Christian's way of life? Would you be willing to share your testimony? Paul was not ashamed to share his suffering or to remind the Thessalonians that they had suffered. Despite this, his message is that faith prevails even in the midst of persecution. How can we apply that truth in our daily walk? Are you willing to share your struggle to win some to Christ?

Follow the Spirit

What God wants me to do:

_____

_____

_____

_____

Remember Your Thoughts

Special insights I have learned:

_____

_____

_____

_____

More Light on the Text

1 Thessalonians 1:2–10

Bible scholars speculate that while Paul was in Athens, he sent Timothy back to Thessalonica to see how the new converts were doing. Later, while Paul was in Corinth, Timothy brought back a glowing report that they were remaining firm in the faith and were unified as a body. However, Timothy also told Paul that these converts did have questions about the Second Coming that needed to be cleared up. But before Paul addressed these questions in this letter, he greeted the Thessalonian believers with encouraging words, acknowledging Timothy's report that they were "in God the Father and in the Lord Jesus Christ" (v. 1). In essence, Paul assured them that they were indeed children of the Most High God. They belonged to Him, and they were in His family—joint heirs with Jesus. Because they had believed in the Lord Jesus Christ as their personal Savior, they were also "fixed" in Him, and nothing and no one could pluck them out. Paul ended his greeting by proclaiming God's grace and peace for their lives. "Grace" in the Greek (*charis*, **KHAR-ece**) means "goodwill, favor." "Peace" in the Greek is *eirene* (**ay-RAY-nay**) and means "quietness, rest." In other words, Paul spoke about God's grace and rest in their lives. He knew that only God could give them what they needed—a sense of belonging, favor, and rest—for the spiritual battles that they had to fight.

2 We give thanks to God always for you all, making mention of you in our prayers; 3 Remembering without ceasing your work of faith, and labour of love, and patience of hope in our Lord Jesus Christ, in the sight of God and our Father.

Paul gives further encouragement by assuring the Thessalonians that the other saints are praying for them. In other words, they are not going through their battles alone. It is important for all Christians to understand this point. When believers are dealing with trials and tribulations, their brothers and sisters in the faith need to undergird them in much prayer. Besieged believers should never be isolated and left to fight Satan all alone.

To further encourage the Thessalonians, Paul acknowledges their "work of faith, and labour of love, and patience of hope in our Lord Jesus Christ" (v. 3). In this phrase, Paul joins three virtues that he names together in other letters, too (1 Corinthians 13:13): faith, hope, and love. But in addition, Paul recognizes the hardships the Thessalonians have faced in showing each of these virtues. Faith is "work" (cf. James 2:17). Love is a "labour" (Gk. *kopos*, **KOE-poce**), a word often paired with toils and travails, and elsewhere refers to a beating. The Greek word for "patience" is *hupomone* (**hoop-om-on-AY**), which means not just a willingness to wait calmly, but the endurance to suffer while undergoing something unpleasant. In summation, Paul lifted these young Christians up by commending them on their faithful labor for the Lord, all the loving deeds that they had carried out in His name, and their endurance and consistency in both the faith and in anticipating the Lord's second coming. He reminded them that the Lord saw their efforts—all that they had done did not go unnoticed by God.

4 Knowing, brethren beloved, your election of God. 5 For our gospel came not unto you in word only, but also in power, and in the Holy Ghost, and in much assurance; as ye know what manner of men we were among you for your sake.

Paul also reminded these fellow believers about God's "election" (Gk. *ekloge*, **ek-low-GAY**) of them, which refers to God choosing them from all humanity to be His children. No one need fear when hearing this term, for all

are welcomed into God's elect if we only follow Him (1 Timothy 2:6; 2 Peter 3:9). Thus, these Thessalonians were chosen—divinely selected by God Himself, who loved them and accepted them into His family. And because they were chosen by Almighty God, the Good News did not come to them "in word only, but also in power, and in the Holy Ghost" (v. 5). The Word of God, with the forcefulness to save and keep, therefore, came to them with much power— the might and capacity to transform them from sinners to new creatures by the strength of the Holy Spirit, who dwelled within them. In truth, they heard the Word, obeyed it, and their lives were transformed by it. They were saved and given eternal life. The Holy Spirit also gave them the assurance that Paul's message— the Good News of salvation—was true. Plus, this same Holy Spirit would help them remain strong in their new faith and would also help them maintain their moral character to show unconditional love toward one another, even as they underwent persecution.

6 And ye became followers of us, and of the Lord, having received the word in much affliction, with joy of the Holy Ghost: 7 So that ye were examples to all that believe in Macedonia and Achaia. 8 For from you sounded out the word of the Lord not only in Macedonia and Achaia, but also in every place your faith to God-ward is spread abroad; so that we need not to speak any thing.

Not only had Paul and his companions been an example of holy living to the believers at Thessalonica, but after the Thessalonians followed in the faith, these new believers were able to become examples or witnesses for the faith to "all that believe in Macedonia and Achaia" (v. 7)—the names of two Roman provinces that cover most of the modern Balkan states, including modern Greece, Bulgaria, and

Macedonia. In other words, in the midst of their afflictions and suffering, they imitated Paul, his companions, and the Lord, and in doing so, they planted seeds of faith that extended beyond Greece. Paul admitted to them that wherever he went, he found people telling him about the faith of the Thessalonians. They bore fruit for God that pleased both Paul and the Lord.

9 For they themselves show of us what manner of entering in we had unto you, and how ye turned to God from idols to serve the living and true God;

Other faith communities are so impressed with the Thessalonian believers, they will tell Paul the story of the Thessalonians' conversion, despite the fact that Paul was there himself! The Thessalonian church's testimony is that they turned away from idols and turned to the one true and living God. They turned from their sin to God, and they faithfully and tenaciously served God and looked forward to His Second Coming. They believed His Word. We, too, should follow the example of Paul, his companions, and the Thessalonians. We, too, should turn away from our sins to the holy God. We should encourage each other's faith, lifting up one another's efforts on behalf of God. We should be fervent in our service to Him, winning other souls to Christ, helping make disciples, and showing them how to live for Christ. Finally, we should look forward to the Second Coming and live life as though that coming could be any day. We do not know the day or the hour, but we do know that we must be ready when He comes. This is the message the Thessalonians give through their actions.

10 And to wait for his Son from heaven, whom he raised from the dead, even Jesus, which delivered us from the wrath to come.

Paul continues to recite the basic tenets of the faith that the Thessalonians have put on the lips of everyone in Macedonia and Achaia because of their faith. Paul was sure of Christ's second coming, and he did not deviate from teaching this truth. Because the Thessalonians were being persecuted and even killed, Paul encouraged them to look forward to the deliverance that would be found in Jesus Christ, writing that believers should "wait for his [God's] Son from heaven, whom he raised from the dead." There is no other one who can deliver us from the wrath of God to come. The word "wrath" (Gk. *orge*, **OR-gay**) refers to "the act of chastising or disciplining, imposing a penalty for an offense." Make no mistake, God will punish sin. As believers, then, our hope is in the Second Coming, when He will return to reign on the new earth forever and ever with His church.

Sources:

Henry, Matthew. *Commentary on the Whole Bible.* Edited by Leslie F. Church. Grand Rapids, MI: Zondervan, 1961. 1876–1877.

Life Application Study Bible. Wheaton, IL: Tyndale, 1996.

Peterson, Eugene H., trans. *The Message: The Bible in Contemporary Language.* Colorado Springs, CO: NavPress, 2002.

Richards, Lawrence O. *The Teacher's Commentary.* Wheaton, IL: Victor Books, 1987.

Severance, W. Murray. *That's Easy for You to Say: Your Quick Guide to Pronouncing Bible Names.* Nashville, TN: Broadman & Holman, 1997.

Strong, James. *Strong's Talking Greek & Hebrew Dictionary.* Austin, TX: WORDsearch Corp., 2007.

Say It Correctly

Macedonia. **MAH**-suh-**DOE**-nee-uh.
Achaia. ah-**KIE**-uh.

125

Daily Bible Readings

MONDAY
Suffering Leads to Endurance, Character, Hope
(Romans 5:1–5)

TUESDAY
Reconciliation Through Jesus Christ
(Romans 5:6–11)

WEDNESDAY
Be Ready for Christ's Coming
(Matthew 24:36–44)

THURSDAY
Live Christ's Mind and Character Daily
(Philippians 2:5–11)

FRIDAY
Under Persecution, Proclaim Jesus the Christ
(Acts 17:1–9)

SATURDAY
Facing Temptation, Stay Loyal to Christ
(2 Thessalonians 2:1–12)

SUNDAY
Examples of Faith to All Believers
(1 Thessalonians 1:2–10)

Notes

_____

_____

_____

_____

Teaching Tips

Words You Should Know

A. Purified (v. 22) *hagnizo* (Gk.)—Made holy

B. Pure (v. 22) *katharos* (Gk.)—Cleansed

Teacher Preparation

Unifying Principle—Dare to be Different! People admire and emulate those who live in accord with what they say. How can we put our beliefs into action? First Peter teaches believers that they must live holy lives and do good, loving deeds for others, thus demonstrating that they trust in God and have been born anew.

A. Read the Bible Background and Devotional Reading.

B. Pray for your students and lesson clarity.

C. Read the lesson Scripture in multiple translations.

O—Open the Lesson

A. Begin the class with prayer.

B. As a class, make a list of benefits of holy living—both temporal and eternal—as compared to following what Peter calls "the desires that you formerly had in ignorance" (v. 14).

C. Have the students read the Aim for Change and the In Focus story.

D. Ask students how events like those in the story weigh on their hearts and how they can view these events from a faith perspective.

P—Present the Scriptures

A. Read the Focal Verses.

B. Have the class share what Scriptures stand out for them and why, with particular emphasis on today's context.

C. Discuss the Background and The People, Places, and Times sections.

E—Explore the Meaning

A. Use In Depth or More Light on the Text to facilitate a deeper discussion of the lesson text.

B. Pose the questions in Search the Scriptures and Discuss the Meaning.

C. Discuss the Liberating Lesson and Application for Activation sections.

N—Next Steps for Application

A. Summarize the value of converting our beliefs into actions.

B. End class with a commitment to pray for the will and the action to do good and live holy lives.

Worship Guide

For the Superintendent or Teacher
Theme: Live Holy Lives
Song: "Holiness is What I Long For"
Devotional Reading: 1 Peter 1:3–12

Live Holy Lives

Bible Background • GALATIANS 5:22–23; 1 PETER 1
Printed Text • 1 PETER 1:13–25 | Devotional Reading • 1 PETER 1:3–12

Aim for Change

By the end of the lesson, we will: COMPREHEND the meaning and power of holy living that Peter commends to the exiled community, AFFIRM our rebirth in Christ through obedience to God, and COMMIT to living holy lives of imitating Christ.

In Focus

Nicole pulled her car into the church parking lot where she could see small clusters of young people heading into the building. The meeting was scheduled to begin in ten minutes, but Nicole remained in the car. This was the day she would be installed as the new community activity director.

When she returned home from college, she had accepted an assignment as the ministry assistant. In this role, she worked closely with Sister Woodson. Sister Woodson secured funding from local businesses to install a computer lab in the church activity room, worked with the local college to provide tutors, coordinated the seniors' monthly outings and fun activities, and so much more.

A month had passed since Sister Woodson announced that she and her husband would be leaving, retiring in another state. Nicole was surprised the pastor asked her to take the position. The pastor had assured Nicole that she was the best candidate. He had also told her that the Trustee Board had unanimously agreed, and Sister Woodson had written a letter recommending Nicole. As she walked to the church, two girls ran up and threw their arms around her. One of them looked up, smiling, and said, "We're going to miss Sister Woodson. But we're so happy you are going to be our new director."

How can we be confident in following and serving great leadership?

Keep in Mind

"As obedient children, not fashioning yourselves according to the former lusts in your ignorance: But as he which hath called you is holy, so be ye holy in all manner of conversation" (1 Peter 1:14–15, KJV).

"So you must live as God's obedient children. Don't slip back into your old ways of living to satisfy your own desires. You didn't know any better then. But now you must be holy in everything you do, just as God who chose you is holy" (1 Peter 1:14–15, NLT).

Focal Verses

KJV **1 Peter 1:13** Wherefore gird up the loins of your mind, be sober, and hope to the end for the grace that is to be brought unto you at the revelation of Jesus Christ;

14 As obedient children, not fashioning yourselves according to the former lusts in your ignorance:

15 But as he which hath called you is holy, so be ye holy in all manner of conversation;

16 Because it is written, Be ye holy; for I am holy.

17 And if ye call on the Father, who without respect of persons judgeth according to every man's work, pass the time of your sojourning here in fear:

18 Forasmuch as ye know that ye were not redeemed with corruptible things, as silver and gold, from your vain conversation received by tradition from your fathers;

19 But with the precious blood of Christ, as of a lamb without blemish and without spot:

20 Who verily was foreordained before the foundation of the world, but was manifest in these last times for you,

21 Who by him do believe in God, that raised him up from the dead, and gave him glory; that your faith and hope might be in God.

22 Seeing ye have purified your souls in obeying the truth through the Spirit unto unfeigned love of the brethren, see that ye love one another with a pure heart fervently:

23 Being born again, not of corruptible seed, but of incorruptible, by the word of God, which liveth and abideth for ever.

NLT **1 Peter 1:13** So prepare your minds for action and exercise self-control. Put all your hope in the gracious salvation that will come to you when Jesus Christ is revealed to the world.

14 So you must live as God's obedient children. Don't slip back into your old ways of living to satisfy your own desires. You didn't know any better then.

15 But now you must be holy in everything you do, just as God who chose you is holy.

16 For the Scriptures say, "You must be holy because I am holy."

17 And remember that the heavenly Father to whom you pray has no favorites. He will judge or reward you according to what you do. So you must live in reverent fear of him during your time here as "temporary residents."

18 For you know that God paid a ransom to save you from the empty life you inherited from your ancestors. And it was not paid with mere gold or silver, which lose their value.

19 It was the precious blood of Christ, the sinless, spotless Lamb of God.

20 God chose him as your ransom long before the world began, but now in these last days he has been revealed for your sake.

21 Through Christ you have come to trust in God. And you have placed your faith and hope in God because he raised Christ from the dead and gave him great glory.

22 You were cleansed from your sins when you obeyed the truth, so now you must show sincere love to each other as brothers and sisters. Love each other deeply with all your heart.

23 For you have been born again, but not to a life that will quickly end. Your new life will last forever because it comes from the eternal, living word of God.

24 For all flesh is as grass, and all the glory of man as the flower of grass. The grass withereth, and the flower thereof falleth away:

25 But the word of the Lord endureth for ever. And this is the word which by the gospel is preached unto you.

24 As the Scriptures say, "People are like grass; their beauty is like a flower in the field. The grass withers and the flower fades.

25 But the word of the Lord remains forever." And that word is the Good News that was preached to you.

The People, Places, and Times

Holiness. For people and their possessions, holiness means separation from what is common or unclean, so that consecration to God can follow. A key part of what it means to be a follower of Yahweh is to separate oneself from outside influences that are not God. Again and again, in the Law, the Israelites are told not to be like other nations and to stand out as unique because they follow God. As God's representatives to the nations and unbelievers, His people must reflect His nature. A primary characteristic of God's nature is His holiness. Around His throne, God is praised as "holy, holy, holy."

Background

In this letter, the first of the Petrine epistles (i.e., those written by Peter), the apostle is encouraging a congregation that is in the midst of persecution. This was probably a reference to the sufferings that were common to first-century Christians, whether it was ridicule, slander, or violence. Writing from Rome, referred to as "Babylon" in the text, Peter pens this epistle to "the Dispersion" using language often associated with the Jewish Diaspora to describe the state of early Christianity, where Jewish and Gentile Christians are spread throughout the Roman Empire. In the midst of the difficulty of everyday persecution, Peter offers encouragement, affirming that Christ's church lives in the world of the already and the not yet, where the kingdom of God has broken into the world but has not been fully realized. In the light of this reality, the

believer, though suffering, also awaits the greatest of joys. Ultimately, this is an epistle of hope in "an inheritance that is incorruptible, and undefiled, and that fadeth not away" and it is that hope that sustains the Christian in the midst of any trial. That hope, however, is not static but dynamic, and Peter explains what it looks like to live a life that is infused with Christian hope (1 Peter 1:13–25).

How do you usually think of hope? If your hope in Christ is imperishable, what does this mean when you face seemingly insurmountable trials?

At-A-Glance

1. Be Ye Holy; For I Am Holy
(1 Peter 1:13-16)
2. A Great Price Was Paid For You
(vv. 17-25)

In Depth

1. Be Ye Holy; For I Am Holy
(1 Peter 1:13–16)

The "wherefore" at the beginning of verse 13 refers to the fact Peter was expounding just prior to these verses: that our God has caused us to be born again to a living, active, glorious, joyful hope. In fact, God's grace, as it has been lavished upon us, is so great that the angels are almost jealous! The greatness of God and his work, however, deserves a proper response. Those to whom God has been wondrously gracious have been given marching orders by that grace. So Peter calls us to "prepare our minds for action," focusing forward on Christ, who has redeemed us. How do we do that? By seeking to be "holy in all manner of conversation" (v. 15). Apart from the Holy Spirit, such a command is impossible. But with the understanding that this is precisely one of the reasons that Christ died and rose again, such a command to be holy becomes freeing. Before Christ's death, He assured His disciples with the promise that He would send the Holy Spirit to indwell all those who are united to Him by faith. Holiness is not an option. It is a joyous imperative.

According to Scripture, where do you find the strength to live a holy life?

2. A Great Price Was Paid for You (vv. 17–25)

Peter encourages his audience that God the Father "without respect of persons judgeth according to every man's work" (v. 17). It is important to see this as encouragement, not as a burden. If one follows a message that stipulates obedience and blessing are linked so closely that if you suffer, it is purely because of your deeds, then the concept of "works" becomes a burden. God's impartial judgment might also be seen as a burden if one views it through the lens of works of righteousness, which would encourage us to work in order to gain God's favor.

Instead, Peter reminds us that God is our Father, into whose family we have been adopted. Thus, we must live out of fear, respect, and love for our Heavenly Father who showed His love for us by redeeming us with the precious blood of Christ (v. 19). That life involves forsaking the "vain conversation received by tradition from your fathers" (v. 18) and the "former lusts in your ignorance" (v. 14) and instead clothing ourselves with the Holy Spirit. This can only be done when we recognize and affirm that we have been made believers in God through our union with Christ and that our only hope rests in Him alone. With this truth firmly set in our minds and the Spirit firmly in our hearts, we can focus on loving one another, encouraging one another, and persevering in doing so because we do so with the strength of the Good News.

How can a focus on Christ bring energy to your spiritual life?

Search the Scriptures

1. What does this text tell about how to live a holy life?

2. How do we prepare our minds for action (v. 13, NLT)?

Discuss the Meaning

1. How does keeping our identity as children of God at the forefront of our minds help us to navigate the world?

2. In what practical ways does our redemption by the blood of Jesus help us face persecution and struggle?

Liberating Lesson

The holiness of conduct is not reducible to mere one-on-one relationships. It includes those, but as technology continues to develop, our webs of influence tend to grow. As these webs of influence grow, our conception of our neighbor must grow as well. As our understanding of who our neighbor is grows, our understanding of how to love our neighbor has to change with it. Thus, holiness has to be the framework within which we consider our decisions, such as where to live, where to shop, and even how to vote. Peter encourages us not to be holy in some of our conduct but in all of our conduct. Such intense self-interrogation can only happen through the lens of the Word, consistent prayer, the leading of the Holy Spirit, and the support of the Christian community.

132

Application for Activation

This passage of Scripture presents a number of concepts we should examine in our lives as we try to always demonstrate faith and love. For example, we should consider the care of the poor, the widow, and the orphan when making life decisions. If you find yourself being frustrated in attempting to do what is right, remember that your hope is not in your results but in Christ. We might expect that at times the Christian life can be difficult, but we should also expect to be given the necessary resources to persevere.

Follow the Spirit

What God wants me to do:

_____

_____

_____

_____

Remember Your Thoughts

Special insights I have learned:

_____

_____

_____

_____

More Light on the Text

1 Peter 1:13 Wherefore gird up the loins of your mind, be sober, and hope to the end for the grace that is to be brought unto you at the revelation of Jesus Christ;

The imperatives of Scripture are always grounded in the indicatives of Scripture. It is the same way with this passage. The great blessings that God has granted the believer in salvation recorded in verses 1–12 are the grounds for Peter's exhortations in verses 13–25. It is in light of the blessings described in verses 1–12 that believers are to "gird up" the loins of their minds. It is a call to keep ourselves free from addictions, either physical or otherwise, that would keep us from being mentally vigilant. "Hope" (Gk. *elpizo*, **el-PID-zo**) is "confident expectation," a certainty that what God has promised is coming.

14 As obedient children, not fashioning yourselves according to the former lusts in your ignorance:

Peter exhorts believers to refrain from a life patterned after their former ignorance of God. There was a time when they did not know God or His will, and they did whatever they desired. This can no longer be the pattern of their lives. As obedient children, believers are to live in a way that pleases God. They are children of God. He brought them into His family, and that familial relationship calls for a new kind of life, lived apart from the evil passions of their former lifestyle.

15 But as he which hath called you is holy, so be ye holy in all manner of conversation; 16 Because it is written, Be ye holy; for I am holy.

The word "but" (Gk. *gar*, **GAR**) here indicates a strong contrast. Believers are not to live a life patterned after their former evil passions. Instead, they are to pattern their lives after the one who called them, God the Father, who is holy. Thus in every aspect of their lives (i.e., KJV: "all manner of conversation"), they are to seek to be holy as well. Believers are called to imitate God in His holiness by living lives marked by holiness in every sphere. The Apostle Peter roots this exhortation in Scripture. God, who called the people of Israel to be His own special people, gave them this charge: "You shall be holy: for I the LORD your God am holy" (Leviticus 19:2). The character of our lives is to be shaped by the character of our God. We are to be holy because He is holy. When we live as God's holy people, we are living as God always intended humans to live. We are being truly human.

17 And if ye call on the Father, who without respect of persons judgeth according to every man's work, pass the time of your sojourning here in fear.

Believers are children of God. But this familial relationship with God, while giving us a sense of belonging, should not cause us to be presumptuous. Our status as His children does not give us an excuse to live recklessly. Our God is impartial. He judges us according to our works. Just because we are His children does not mean that He will overlook our disobedience. Though believers will not miss eternity because of their sin, we must certainly expect the Lord's discipline in this life when our behavior is contrary to His will. Thus, says Peter, we should "pass the time of [our] sojourning here in fear" (Gk. *phobos*, **FO-boce**), meaning reverential awe, rather than terror. It is fear born of respect. God is the Judge of all the earth and our Father as well, and as such, should command our deepest respect.

18 Forasmuch as ye know that ye were not redeemed with corruptible things, as silver and gold, from your vain conversation received by tradition from your fathers; 19 But with the precious blood of Christ, as of a lamb without blemish and without spot.

Deep respect for God should be coupled with a deep sense of gratitude and awe at the costliness of redemption. No silver or gold redeemed us from our past life of sin. God rescued them from the sinful traditions (Gk. *patroparadotos*, **pat-rop-ar-AD-ot-os**), "beliefs, values, and behavior" inherited from their ancestors, through the precious blood of Christ. Peter strengthens his point about the value of the blood of Christ by dramatically devaluing the substance used

for currency. He reminds the Christians that they were redeemed by the blood of the Lamb. The imagery that Peter uses is from the Old Testament: God's deliverance of the people of Israel from Egypt required the sacrifice of a lamb without blemish. The people were commanded to place its blood on their doorposts in order that the death angel commanded to kill the firstborn throughout Egypt might pass over them (Exodus 12:6–11). Of course, this was a foreshadowing of the sacrifice of Christ for us, the one who gave His own blood that we might be delivered from eternal death.

20 Who verily was foreordained before the foundation of the world, but was manifest in these last times for you, 21 Who by him do believe in God, that raised him up from the dead, and gave him glory; that your faith and hope might be in God.

Christ's sacrifice—His death—was no accident. Rather, events had already transpired, and Christ was "foreordained" to be our Saviour (v. 20). God planned our redemption from the foundation of the world and carried it out in Christ. In the course of human history, Christ was revealed; He came into the world for our salvation. This was all the plan of God. Through Christ alone has every believers' faith in God been established. Through Christ, the One who redeemed them is now the object of their faith. The foundation of their trust in Him is the truth that God raised Jesus from the dead and seated Him at His right hand with all power and authority. How can they not trust Him, who redeemed them and who validated that redemption by raising Jesus from the dead and glorifying Him!

22 Seeing ye have purified your souls in obeying the truth through the Spirit unto unfeigned love of the brethren, see that ye love one another with a pure heart fervently:

The first part of this verse expresses that Peter's readers are considered sincere believers. They are a people who have been purified (Gk. *hagnizo*, **hag-NID zo**, "made holy") by obeying the truth of the Gospel and responding to it in faith. The imagery of purification is from the Old Testament's ceremonial washings, which the priests and Levites serving in the Temple were commanded to do. These washings made them ritually clean. Peter picks up the imagery here to denote the spiritual cleansing that occurred once these believers put their trust in the Gospel, the Word of Truth.

They are a people who experienced the renewal of the Gospel, a fact manifested by their sincere love for fellow believers. Now they are encouraged to deepen that love for one another. Purifying their souls has also given them "pure" (Gk. *katharos*, "cleansed") hearts, with which they ought to love each other. This is what demonstrates that the renewing power of the Gospel is at work in our lives: our continued pursuit to love one another as God in Christ has loved us.

23 Being born again, not of corruptible seed, but of incorruptible, by the word of God, which liveth and abideth for ever. 24 For all flesh is as grass, and all the glory of man as the flower of grass. The grass withereth, and the flower thereof falleth away: 25 But the word of the Lord endureth for ever. And this is the word which by the gospel is preached unto you.

This call to a sincere love for one another is grounded in the new life that God has given us through His incorruptible (Gk. *aphthartos*, **AF-thartos**, the opposite of "corruptible" vv. 18, 23) Word. The Word of God is unfailing. Indeed, God's Word cannot fail because God will not fail. He lives forever, and so His Word abides forever. In verse 24, Peter quotes the words of the prophet Isaiah (Isaiah 40:6–8), and draws the comparison between the fading glory of humankind and the Word of God. The glory of humankind is like the flower of the field. Its beauty and splendor

are temporary. It lasts for but a moment. But the Word of God endures (Gk. *menounge*, **men-OON-geh**, "remains") forever. That Word comes to us today, through the Gospel. What confidence we should draw from this: The Word of God, on which our salvation is grounded and which we have believed, endures forever!

Sources:
Davids, Peter H. *The First Epistle of Peter, The New International Commentary on the New Testament*. Grand Rapids, MI: Eerdmans, 1990. 69.
Grudem, Wayne. *The First Epistle of Peter: Tyndale's New Testament Commentaries*. Leicester, England: InterVarsity Press, 1988. 77, 87.
Zodhiates, Spiros. *Complete Word Study of the New Testament with Parallel Greek*. Iowa Falls, IA: World Bible Publishers, 1992.

Daily Bible Readings

MONDAY
God's Word Is True and Reliable
(Isaiah 40:6–9)

TUESDAY
Jesus Enables Victory over Sin
(Romans 7:14–25)

WEDNESDAY
Love One Another
(Romans 13:8–10)

THURSDAY
New Life Through the Spirit
(Romans 8:1–11)

FRIDAY
Live by the Spirit
(Galatians 5:16–26)

SATURDAY
Rejoice in God's Actions in Christ
(1 Peter 1:3–12)

SUNDAY
Call to Holy Living
(1 Peter 1:13–25)

Teaching Tips

Words You Should Know

A. Add to (v. 5) *epichorego* (Gk.)—To minister to or supply with

B. Godliness (v. 6) *eusebeia* (Gk.)—Piety

Teacher Preparation

Unifying Principle—Believing Promises. People can be harmed by corruption in the world. How can we guard against those negative influences? Second Peter stresses the importance of supporting one's faith with goodness, knowledge, self-control, endurance, godliness, mutual affection, and love.

A. Read the Bible Background and Devotional Reading.

B. Pray for your students and lesson clarity.

C. Read the lesson Scripture in multiple translations.

O—Open the Lesson

A. Begin the class with prayer.

B. As a class, consider the excuses people give for not being able to live a godly lifestyle. Contrast those excuses with verse 3 of the text. Discuss how we respond to God's call and actualize his power for godliness.

C. Have the students read the Aim for Change and the In Focus story.

D. Ask students how events like those in the story weigh on their hearts and how they can view these events from a faith perspective.

P—Present the Scriptures

A. Read the Focal Verses.

B. Have the class share what Scriptures stand out for them and why, with particular emphasis on today's context.

C. Discuss the Background and The People, Places, and Times sections.

E—Explore the Meaning

A. Use In Depth or More Light on the Text to facilitate a deeper discussion of the lesson text.

B. Pose the questions in Search the Scriptures and Discuss the Meaning.

C. Discuss the Liberating Lesson and Application for Activation sections.

N—Next Steps for Application

A. Summarize the value of the importance of guarding against negative influences.

B. End class with a commitment to pray for enhancing one's faith through love, self-control, and godliness.

Worship Guide

For the Superintendent or Teacher
Theme: Stick to Your Faith
Song: "Standing on the Promises"
Devotional Reading: Psalm 90

Stick to Your Faith

Bible Background • 2 PETER 1
Printed Text • 2 PETER 1:1–15 | Devotional Reading • PSALM 90

———————— Aim for Change ————————

By the end of the lesson, we will: DISCERN the importance of faith and the call of God to authentic life and godliness, APPRECIATE a life of faith in Christ after redemption from sinfulness, and PRACTICE the virtues of goodness, knowledge, self-control, endurance, godliness, mutual affection, and love.

———————————— In Focus ————————————

"I just don't understand you," Isaac complained to his wife. "I told you that I would take care of the utility bill later this week!"

They were arguing, something that seemed to occur more and more frequently. Audrey thought Isaac was not concerned enough about their finances. Some of the bills were behind, but he had assured her that he would make sure they got paid. Why couldn't she just leave it alone? Why couldn't he just pay them? The bills had been delinquent before, but hadn't they always paid them?

Audrey and Isaac constantly fought about their poor credit rating. Audrey felt certain Isaac blamed her for not being able to purchase a new car or house. Isaac just wanted her to stop blaming him for not figuring out their finances. Why didn't she understand that he wanted reliable transportation and a home for her and their two children just as much as she did? He just didn't have the time to sit down and make a plan. The constant reminders from a bill collector's call or another late notice letter only seemed to make things worse. If she were a better wife and he a better husband, they each thought, then, their trust level for one another would increase. Could they wait for things to get better?

In today's lesson, we will see that faith is not equivalent to blind optimism. To live godly lives, we must not succumb to laziness or our own thoughts. How do you take advantage of the godly resources available to you?

———————————— Keep in Mind ————————————

"Whereby are given unto us exceeding great and precious promises: that by these ye might be partakers of the divine nature, having escaped the corruption that is in the world through lust" (2 Peter 1:4, KJV).

"And because of his glory and excellence, he has given us great and precious promises. These are the promises that enable you to share his divine nature and escape the world's corruption caused by human desires" (2 Peter 1:4, NLT)

Focal Verses

KJV **2 Peter 1:1** Simon Peter, a servant and an apostle of Jesus Christ, to them that have obtained like precious faith with us through the righteousness of God and our Saviour Jesus Christ:

2 Grace and peace be multiplied unto you through the knowledge of God, and of Jesus our Lord,

3 According as his divine power hath given unto us all things that pertain unto life and godliness, through the knowledge of him that hath called us to glory and virtue:

4 Whereby are given unto us exceeding great and precious promises: that by these ye might be partakers of the divine nature, having escaped the corruption that is in the world through lust.

5 And beside this, giving all diligence, add to your faith virtue; and to virtue knowledge;

6 And to knowledge temperance; and to temperance patience; and to patience godliness;

7 And to godliness brotherly kindness; and to brotherly kindness charity.

8 For if these things be in you, and abound, they make you that ye shall neither be barren nor unfruitful in the knowledge of our Lord Jesus Christ.

9 But he that lacketh these things is blind, and cannot see afar off, and hath forgotten that he was purged from his old sins.

10 Wherefore the rather, brethren, give diligence to make your calling and election sure: for if ye do these things, ye shall never fall:

11 For so an entrance shall be ministered unto you abundantly into the everlasting kingdom of our Lord and Saviour Jesus Christ.

NLT **2 Peter 1:1** This letter is from Simon Peter, a slave and apostle of Jesus Christ. I am writing to you who share the same precious faith we have. This faith was given to you because of the justice and fairness of Jesus Christ, our God and Savior.

2 May God give you more and more grace and peace as you grow in your knowledge of God and Jesus our Lord.

3 By his divine power, God has given us everything we need for living a godly life. We have received all of this by coming to know him, the one who called us to himself by means of his marvelous glory and excellence.

4 And because of his glory and excellence, he has given us great and precious promises. These are the promises that enable you to share his divine nature and escape the world's corruption caused by human desires.

5 In view of all this, make every effort to respond to God's promises. Supplement your faith with a generous provision of moral excellence, and moral excellence with knowledge,

6 and knowledge with self-control, and self-control with patient endurance, and patient endurance with godliness,

7 and godliness with brotherly affection, and brotherly affection with love for everyone.

8 The more you grow like this, the more productive and useful you will be in your knowledge of our Lord Jesus Christ.

9 But those who fail to develop in this way are shortsighted or blind, forgetting that they have been cleansed from their old sins.

10 So, dear brothers and sisters, work hard to prove that you really are among those God has called and chosen. Do these things, and you will never fall away.

11 Then God will give you a grand entrance into the eternal Kingdom of our Lord and Savior Jesus Christ.

12 Wherefore I will not be negligent to put you always in remembrance of these things, though ye know them, and be established in the present truth.

13 Yea, I think it meet, as long as I am in this tabernacle, to stir you up by putting you in remembrance;

14 Knowing that shortly I must put off this my tabernacle, even as our Lord Jesus Christ hath shewed me.

15 Moreover I will endeavour that ye may be able after my decease to have these things always in remembrance.

12 Therefore, I will always remind you about these things—even though you already know them and are standing firm in the truth you have been taught.

13 And it is only right that I should keep on reminding you as long as I live.

14 For our Lord Jesus Christ has shown me that I must soon leave this earthly life,

15 so I will work hard to make sure you always remember these things after I am gone.

The People, Places, and Times

Simon Peter. He was also known as Cephas, which is transliterated from the Aramaic word *kepha* and means "rock." Peter was the Galilean fisherman who, along with his brother Andrew, was chosen to be one of Jesus' twelve disciples. Peter's given name was Simon, and his father's name was Jonah (Matthew 16:17; John 1:42). Peter is often described as the bold disciple who became one of Jesus' three closest associates, along with James and John. They accompanied Jesus during His most significant events—raising Jairus's daughter (Mark 5:35–42), praying in Gethsemane (Matthew 26:36–46), and becoming radiant in glory in the Transfiguration (17:1–5). Peter answered Jesus' question, "Whom say ye that I am?" (16:15) with "Thou art the Christ, the Son of the living God." Jesus called him "blessed" and said, "Thou art Peter, and upon this rock I will build my church" (16:18). Peter had times of weakness. He told the Lord that he would never forsake Him, but when Jesus was inside being interrogated by Caiaphas and other religious leaders, Peter denied Him three times in the high priest's courtyard. Yet the disciple who denied Him became one of the strongest key leaders in the early church.

Blindness. God placed a curse on anyone who misdirected a blind person (Deuteronomy 27:18). Jesus explained that a part of His ministry entailed restoring sight to the blind (Luke 4:18), and He healed many blind people (John 9:1–41; Mark 8:22–25; Matthew 20:30–34). Blind eyes being opened is also used throughout Scripture as a metaphor for spiritual insight or visions that people could only have received from God (Numbers 22:31; 2 Kings 6:17; Luke 24:31). Spiritual blindness is worse than physical blindness because it always comes with deception and guile, specifically for the one who is blind. Jesus taught this principle to the Pharisees when He healed a blind man in the temple and used the event to castigate the "blind" Pharisees, who were more concerned with religious traditions than the power of God (see John 9:1–41).

Background

The epistle traditionally named 2 Peter is a text whose purpose is primarily to refute false teachers. In order to refute falsehood, however, one must robustly affirm the truth, which Peter is careful to do. This letter also has one of the most direct affirmations of the deity of Christ, where the author refers to "the righteousness of God and our Savior Jesus Christ" (1:1). This core Christian belief colors the rest of the book, reminding us that the truth of the Gospel is a truth of divine weight and worth. It also reminds us that the One who called us, the One who works in us, and the One who died for us is divine.

How does Scripture help us respond to false teaching about Christ's work?

At-A-Glance

1. Partakers of the Divine Nature
(2 Peter 1:1–4)
2. Is Anything To Be Added To Faith?
(vv. 5–11)
3. Remember! (vv. 12–15)

In Depth

1. Partakers of the Divine Nature
(2 Peter 1:1–4)

Here is perhaps the most profound picture of redemption found in the Scriptures. After the introductory two verses, the author turns the eyes and ears of the believer to the power of God, which is the source of all gifts, power, and promises. But verse 4 introduces an idea that has been controversial and variably understood. The goal of salvation, according to the author, is that we might be "partakers of the divine nature." We must not understand this to mean that we literally become the Creator of the universe. There is a distinction between the Creator and the creature. The reality that

Peter highlights is that the relationship to which God has called us brings us closer to Him than anything we could ever imagine. Faith in Christ unites us to God in ways that we can only fathom, and it is in awe of that reality that we live out the imperatives of the Christian life, not to earn God's favor, but as a result of our basking in His grace.

In what ways does God tell us to be like Him? In what ways are we not like Him?

2. Is Anything to Be Added to Faith?
(vv. 5–11)

Next, Peter lists the virtues needed for an ever-improving Christian life, starting with faith. Peter is not saying that faith is unnecessary. Instead, he explains what is necessary for us to sufficiently live out the Christian life. True, vibrant faith is at the core of and accompanied by virtue, knowledge, self-control, steadfastness, godliness, brotherly affection, and love. The believer must cultivate these gifts and pursue their continued development (v. 8). The qualities described are not static; rather, they must be practiced. Those who do practice these (and practice them so that their skill improves) will never fall from grace. Those who do not are not in danger of losing their salvation (which is impossible), but they are called blind, acting as though they have forgotten they are now clean from sin.

What keeps us from being diligent about these qualities? Which of these is the hardest for you?

3. Remember! (vv. 12–15)

Some complain about the repetitiveness of hearing the Good News over and over again, but Peter will have none of that complaint. As he says, he must always remind us of these things, even if we know them and are established in them (v. 12). The reminder stirs us to love and action, and it keeps it ever at the forefront of our minds. The goodness of Christ and the glory to which he has called us are far too precious to be forgotten.

What is your biggest distraction from the glory of God and the glory of the future inheritance that He has promised you upon Christ's return?

Search the Scriptures

1. How could we misinterpret 2 Peter 1:4? What are the hazards of claiming to be too much like God?

2. In the rest of the Scripture, how does God exhibit the qualities added to faith (virtue, knowledge, etc.)?

3. What are the "great and precious promises" granted to us by the knowledge of God (v. 4)?

Discuss the Meaning

1. How does the list of attributes in verses 5–7 compare with the fruit of the Spirit (Galatians 5:22–23)?

2. How ought we respond to corruption in the world?

Liberating Lesson

The word "escaped" in 2 Peter 1:4 may appear to suggest that the relationship between us and corruption is one of fear, such that we should flee from the world because it is corrupted. This, however, would be out of step with the rest of the Scriptures. Instead we are to interact with the world around us, having been freed by Christ from its corruption. This allows us to bring the Gospel into whatever spheres the Lord has placed us, whether work, school, or our local community. Having been freed by Christ, we can interact with the world with our guard up against sinful desire. No sphere is off limits to the body of Christ, and as His hands and feet, we must be willing to shine the light of truth into the darkness. By diligently doing so, we come to a deeper experience of God's grace and His mercy.

Application for Activation

Peter's advice is helpful to every Christian. It reminds us to make sure we are regularly meeting with other believers so that we can remind one another of the qualities that are developed by adherence to the Gospel. We must examine our responses to the world around us to be sure we are exhibiting self-control, virtue, and godliness. It is also important to remember that from time to time, we may find someone that we think is difficult to love. In those times we must remember the love that Christ has shown to us so that we can love those people as well.

Follow the Spirit

What God wants me to do:

_____

_____

_____

_____

Remember Your Thoughts

Special insights I have learned:

_____

_____

More Light on the Text

2 Peter 1:1–15

1 Simon Peter, a servant and an apostle of Jesus Christ, to them that have obtained like precious faith with us through the righteousness of God and our Saviour Jesus Christ: 2 Grace and peace be multiplied unto you through the knowledge of God, and of Jesus our Lord, 3 According as his divine power hath given unto us all things that pertain unto

life and godliness, through the knowledge of him that hath called us to glory and virtue:

Peter wastes no time in his epistle and jumps deep into theology. When we are born into the family of God by faith in Christ, we are born complete. God gives us "all things" we will ever need for "life and godliness" (v. 3). Nothing has to be added or taken away. Just as a baby has a definite genetic structure that determines how he or she will grow, so the believer is structured to experience glory and virtue. The divine power of God that is prepared to give us all things is the Holy Spirit, the same power that raised Jesus from the grave (Romans 8:11; 1 Peter 3:18). God has already freely "given unto us all things." We do not obtain these things on our own; by having faith in God, we will receive all the things He has for us. We must acknowledge that He is the one who has called us to "grace and peace" and "glory and virtue." Before we acknowledged or knew God, He knew us and imparted grace unto us, along with plenty of mercy. The Greek word here for "knowledge" is *epignosis* (**eh-pee-guh-NO-sis**), which implies "recognition." Because we recognize Him as God, He is eager to provide for us.

4 Whereby are given unto us exceeding great and precious promises: that by these ye might be partakers of the divine nature, having escaped the corruption that is in the world through lust.

Our Father has made great promises that lead us to a great life. Because He is a great God, He can and will keep them all. The Word of God is full of many promises for a range of situations. There are promises for eternal life, forgiveness, healing, joy, peace, and prosperity. God's greatest promise, however, was the gift of His Son, Jesus Christ. God has given us His Word, which enables us to develop new life and godliness. The Word—Jesus—in turn promised God would give the Holy Spirit to us (John 14:26).

The purpose of God's promises is to enable us to become "partakers of his divine nature." God is at work in us to transform us so we can truly live like those who bear the divine image. This promise of Scripture is one of the many "already/not yet" aspects of Christ's salvation. We are already partakers of the divine nature, as Christ's righteousness already covers our sin. We have already escaped the corruption of the world's lust, as we are no longer slaves to sin. However, we have not yet partaken in the consummation of God's glorious nature when we will enjoy full fellowship with God. We have also not yet fully escaped the world's corruption, as we still live on the earth.

We should not pine away for the "not yet" aspects of our salvation, though. One day we will be like the Lord Jesus Christ (Romans 8:29; 1 John 3:2). We shall share that glory when Jesus Christ returns and takes His people to heaven. However, we have been saved so that we might "shew forth the praises [virtues]" of God (1 Peter 2:9). We cannot wait until we get to heaven to become like Jesus Christ! In our character and conduct, we should begin to reveal His beauty and grace today.

5 And beside this, giving all diligence, add to your faith virtue; and to virtue knowledge; 6 And to knowledge temperance; and to temperance patience; and to patience godliness; 7 And to godliness brotherly kindness; and to brotherly kindness charity.

Because we are now partakers of God's divine character, we must mature spiritually. To do this, we must add (Gk. *epichorego*, **ep-ee-khor-AYG-roo**) to our faith, that is, minister to it and supply our faith with what it needs. Those needs are the virtuous qualities that Peter then lists, which grow out of our vital relationship with Jesus Christ. Peter lists seven qualities of a faithful life: virtue, knowledge, temperance (i.e., self-control), patience, godliness, brotherly kindness, and charity (i.e., divine love). The form of this list and many of the items on it would be familiar to secular philosophers of the time. This kind of list, called a *gradatio*, emphasizes the process of building one thing on top of another, rising to the climax of the final step. Terms like virtue (Gk. *arete*, **ar-uh-TAY**, moral excellence) and godliness (Gk. *eusebeia*, **ew-SAY-bay-uh**, piety) were already familiar to people trying to live good lives in Peter's day. But Peter takes these ideals and couches them in a Christian understanding. Our basis for virtue or moral excellence is not our own goodness, but our faith; we show our godliness not to an entire pantheon, but to the One True God. While other philosophers might argue over which virtue is the most important, Peter is clear here: The greatest of these is "charity" (Gk. *agape*, **ah-GAH-pay**), divine love (cf. Colossians 3:14). In a similar *gradatio*, Paul builds from trials to hope, with hope again being based on the love God shows us and gives us to show others (Romans 5:3–5).

It is impossible for human nature to manufacture these seven qualities of Christian character; the Spirit of God must produce them. Because we have a divine nature, we can grow spiritually and develop these qualities. God wants us to be "conformed to the image of his Son" (Romans 8:29).

8 For if these things be in you, and abound, they make you that ye shall neither be barren nor unfruitful in the knowledge of our Lord Jesus Christ.

The results of adding up the seven qualities mentioned earlier are that they strengthen, encourage, and improve our lives and the lives of those around us. Where these qualities are present, there will be an abundance of good works (2 Corinthians 9:8), that is, we will bring forth fruit. To "neither be barren nor unfruitful" means that we do not just sit around, idle. If these qualities are to exist within us, we must learn to cultivate them so that they produce fruitful results in our lives. There is much work to do in God's kingdom (Luke 10:2). The more we become like Jesus Christ, the more the Holy Spirit can use us in witness and service. As Christians, we are commanded to exhort, edify, and comfort one another, continuously building each other up in God's holy faith (1 Thessalonians 5:11; Hebrews 3:13).

9 But he that lacketh these things is blind, and cannot see afar off, and hath forgotten that he was purged from his old sins.

The phrase "cannot see afar off" denotes that a person is nearsighted and can only see those things that are close to them. Spiritually, believers who are nearsighted can only see things they can touch. They have no vision for the future, can only see today, and are without hope for tomorrow.

In addition, often we forget that Jesus died to cleanse us of our sins. Through the blood of Jesus Christ, we have been purged and forgiven. If we forget this, though, we will not see the ever-increasing qualities that Peter has listed. When we forget what God has done for us, when our viewpoint lacks expansive knowledge of Jesus Christ, we will not be excited to witness to others about Him. Peter determines to keep reminding believers of their freedom from sin, over and over, even when it seems like they understand, until he dies (vv. 12–15).

10 Wherefore the rather, brethren, give diligence to make your calling and election sure: for if ye do these things, ye shall never fall:

Peter admonishes us to be diligent, to exert ourselves. While it is true that God must work in us before we can do His will (Philippians 2:12–23), it is also true that we must be willing to work for God, and we must cooperate with Him. Instead of following those who are spiritually blind and suffering from forgetfulness, with diligence we are to take our invitation from God and accept the benefits of salvation. Living diligently deepens our awareness of the divine power within us (v. 3), which gives us all things needed for life (v. 5–7) and makes our "calling and election sure" (v. 10). If we as believers can apply the Word of God and live according to the will of God, then we will not fail in Christian living. God's grace has enabled us to keep the faith of our election steadfast in Christ. We must walk in righteousness and in good works. Doing so will keep us from falling into sin. Because we are growing, we can look forward to an abundant life here and entrance into heaven.

11 For so an entrance shall be ministered unto you abundantly into the everlasting kingdom of our Lord and Saviour Jesus Christ.

When we live as God wants us to, He promises us an abundant life and entrance into His kingdom. We will have riches of knowledge and holiness beyond our thoughts. Peter draws a parity here between our actions and God's. The same Greek word (*epichoregeo*) translated "add to" in verse 5 is translated "be ministered unto" here. Entrance into the kingdom is a gift from God through Christ Jesus, but it corresponds with diligence. As we add virtues to our faith, God adds the blessings of the inheritance to our salvation.

12 Wherefore I will not be negligent to put you always in remembrance of these things, though ye know them, and be established in the present truth.

Pastors, ministers, and teachers alike are to teach God's precepts with the goal of making their students "established," that is, able to stand on their own feet. Here Peter was saying that it was his responsibility to always remind the people of God's goodness toward them. He realized that although they knew the precepts of God, people's tendency to forget may cause them to take things for granted (cf. v. 9). By reminding them of God's divine grace, mercy, and goodness, Peter was reminding them to never forget the basis for their faith. The Christian who consistently reads the Bible and knows what he or she believes and why—that Christian will rarely be seduced by false teachers and their false doctrines. As we become established in the truth, we will not be shaken or moved by the problems we encounter in this world. We can stand on the truth—the Word of God!

13 Yea, I think it meet, as long as I am in this tabernacle, to stir you up by putting you in remembrance; 14 Knowing that shortly I must put off this my tabernacle, even as our Lord Jesus Christ hath shewed me. 15 Moreover I will endeavour that ye may be able after my decease to have these things always in remembrance.

Peter realizes that his death is at hand. Christ has revealed to Peter the kind of death he will face (see John 21:18–19). In the time he has left, Peter realizes he must stimulate the knowledge of the people of God. Three times in this passage, he asks them to always remember the things he taught them (2 Peter 1:12–13, 15). Peter indeed left behind something that would never die—the written Word of God. The epistles of 1 and 2 Peter have been ministering to the saints for centuries. People die, but the Word of God lives on!

Sources:
Witherington, Ben. *New Testament Rhetoric: An Introductory Guide to the Art of Persuasion in and of the New Testament.* Eugene, Oregon: Cascade Books, 2009. 230.
Zodhiates, Spiros. *Complete Word Study of the New Testament with Parallel Greek Dictionary.* Iowa Falls, IA: World Bible Publishers, 1992.

Daily Bible Readings

MONDAY
The Spirit and the Bride Say Come
(Revelation 22:14–17)

TUESDAY
Our Dwelling Place
(Psalm 90)

WEDNESDAY
One Day Like One Thousand Years
(2 Peter 3:8-10)

THURSDAY
The Coming Day of the Lord
(2 Peter 3:11–15, 17–18)

FRIDAY
This Is My Son; Listen to Him!
(Luke 9:28–36)

SATURDAY
Solid Reasons for Hope
(2 Peter 1:16–21)

SUNDAY
Always Keep the Faith
(2 Peter 1:1–15)

Notes

_____

_____

_____

_____

Honoring God

This quarter explores ways of honoring God through worship. The Old Testament sessions recall how David and Solomon honored God by establishing the center of worship in Jerusalem and building the Temple. The New Testament sessions focus on Jesus' teachings about right attitudes that honor God through worship.

UNIT 1 • David Honors God

The first three lessons are from 1 Chronicles and tell about David bringing the Ark to Jerusalem, leading the people in offering a psalm of thanksgiving, and planning to build a house for God. Lesson 4, the Christmas lesson, considers Mary's visit to Elizabeth as found in Luke. Lesson 5 returns to 1 Chronicles and David's prayer of gratitude for God's promise of a dynasty.

Lesson 1: December 1, 2019
David Worships God in Jerusalem
1 Chronicles 15:1–3, 14–16, 25–29

People are joyful and excited when they move into a new building. What is the appropriate way to celebrate? David commanded the priests to invite all the musicians and all the people to join in shouting, singing, and dancing as they rejoiced in what God had done for them.

Lesson 2: December 8, 2019
A Heart Filled with Gratitude
1 Chronicles 16:8–12, 28–36

People easily get discouraged when looking at turbulent conditions in the world. How can we find the courage to face these problems? David's

people sang a psalm of thanksgiving and a psalm of worship to God for all the great things God had done for them and for the greatness of God's being.

Lesson 3: December 15, 2019
Building God's House
1 Chronicles 17:1, 3–4, 11–14, 21:18, 21–27

People are not always able to accomplish what they desire to do for others. Is it possible to see a positive result even when our desires are not accomplished? Although God did not agree for David to build a temple, God promised that David's son would.

Lesson 4: December 22, 2019
The Lord is With You
Luke 1:39–56

People often wonder if they truly deserve the praise that others give them. How can we be gracious about the honors we receive? When Elisabeth called her blessed, Mary humbly praised God, confessing that all that had happened to her was in fulfillment of God's great plan of redemption.

Lesson 5: December 29, 2019
David's Prayer
1 Chronicles 17:16–27

When a person receives a great promise, he or she may feel honored. How does one respond when one has been so honored? When God promised to make him the head of a great dynasty, King David prayed a prayer of gratitude, praise, and petition.

UNIT 2 • Dedicating the Temple of God

These four lessons explore Solomon's dedication of the Temple in 1 Kings. Solomon honors God by providing a place for the Ark, offering blessings to God for fulfilling the promise to David, by praying that God would hear prayers offered in the Temple, by calling the people to keep God's commandments, and by offering sacrifices to God.

Lesson 6: January 5, 2020
A Place for the Ark
1 Kings 8:1–13

People have dedication ceremonies or grand openings for many different things. How are these ceremonies or grand openings celebrated? When King Solomon called an assembly to celebrate the dedication of the Temple, the glory of the Lord filled the house of God.

Lesson 7: January 12, 2020
Solomon's Speech
1 Kings 8:14–21

Many people make promises they are unable to fulfill because of unforeseen circumstances. How should people respond when they do succeed in fulfilling their promise? Solomon thanked God for fulfilling the promise made to his father, King David, when God enabled Solomon to build the Temple in which the Ark could be placed.

Lesson 8: January 19, 2020
Solomon's Dedication Prayer
1 Kings 8:22–30, 52–53

People begin new undertakings with anticipation of a better future. How can we mark such important times? Solomon presided at the dedication of the Temple by calling upon God to receive Israel's worship and to continue to be their God.

Lesson 9: January 26, 2020
Solomon's Blessing
1 Kings 8:54–61

People often mark the start of new ventures with special ceremonies or observances because they have high hopes for success. How can we know that what we propose to do will succeed? After dedicating the Temple, Solomon prayed for God's continued faithfulness toward Israel while calling on his people to renew their commitment to God.

UNIT 3 • Jesus Teaches about True Worship

This unit has four lessons that explore what Jesus says about honoring God through one's spiritual practices. Matthew points to right attitudes in obeying God only and in honoring God in almsgiving and in prayer. The prayer of Jesus provides a comprehensive life approach to honoring God. Luke teaches about perseverance in prayer as a way to honor God.

Lesson 10: February 2, 2020
Single-minded Obedience
Matthew 4:1–11

People are tempted in many ways to turn aside from what they know is right. How can we resist such temptations? Jesus resisted the devil's temptations by quoting the Scriptures, thus demonstrating His single-minded obedience to God.

Lesson 11: February 9, 2020
Piety That Honors God
Matthew 6:1–8

Eager to be well thought of, people are pulled in a multitude of contradictory directions. How can we be true to the highest principles that we have been taught? In Matthew 5, Jesus taught the disciples the Beatitudes, and in Matthew 6, He warned them against practicing their piety in order to be praised by others.

Lesson 12: February 16, 2020
The Prayer of Jesus
Matthew 6:9–15

We are often discouraged in the face of negative circumstances over which we seem to have no control. How can we experience the positive transformations we long for? Jesus taught the disciples to pray for God's kingdom to be manifested in their lives and in all creation.

Lesson 13: February 23, 2020
Perseverance in Prayer
Luke 11:5–13

It is hard to press on with a task or routine when doing so doesn't seem to produce any positive changes. How can we persevere in the absence of tangible progress? Jesus taught the disciples to continue to ask, seek, and knock, confident that God would graciously provide, and Daniel's preservation in the lions' den provides an example of God's loving protection in response to constancy in prayer.

God's Covenant: A Word That Cannot Come Back Void

by Louis H. Wilson, PhD

Promises, promises, promises. We live in a day when it seems a person's word reflects more of what is expedient than one's character, when circumstances, rather than commitments, define relationships. But according to Scripture, it is not to be this way. From God's point of view, we are members of a covenantal community, unconditionally ratified by God, a community bound to God and His people.

Many passages in Scripture provide us with a foundation for understanding what it means to have covenant relationships with God and others.

To understand the essence of what a covenant is, we begin by citing the first two contexts of the word "covenant." In Genesis 6:18 (KJV), God tells Noah, "With thee will I establish my covenant; and thou shalt come into the ark, thou, and thy sons, and thy wife, and thy sons' wives with thee." God affirms the covenant in 8:20–22 and 9:8–11. After the Flood, God tells Noah that never again will He destroy the world and all living creatures with a flood.

Our call to a covenant relationship with God is also a call to a covenant relationship with His family. God's covenant words must be confirmed by deeds. When we say yes to Jesus, we are making a promise to God and His people that we will do our best to be a positive influence on the body.

Christians are not to live in a world of double-talk and hidden agendas. Christ calls us to keep it simple: "Let your communication be, Yea, yea; Nay, nay" (Matthew 5:37, KJV). Say it and mean it. If you promise to do something, do it!

This leads to something else that influences how we live out covenants with each other—the unconditional aspect of godly covenants. God does His part by bringing us into a relationship with Himself; our part is to believe in what God is doing.

God makes direct promises to Abraham in Genesis 12; 15; and 17. In chapter 12, Abraham leaves Haran, following God day by day. In chapter 15, God clarifies the covenant by providing more details, promising to give Abraham a son through whom the nations will be blessed. Nine times in chapter 17, God says to Abraham, "This is my covenant." This covenant is about God. It is for Him and by Him, and it is by His power that covenant promises are fulfilled. Once again, Abraham responds in faith, doing as God asks by making an open confession—the rite of circumcision. He believes in all that God has said and acts on it.

Do we ask for commitments too quickly? From the time of Abraham's calling to God's request that he demonstrate complete surrender of all that was his was 15 years (12:4; 17:1). With purposeful persistence, God led Abraham to discover Him on a deeper level before taking him to another level of commitment. Covenantal relationships of substance do not happen overnight.

In the same way, when we promise fellow believers to walk, pray, and be used of God to see them through, are we really willing to covenant with them until God works it out? (Abraham made a few mistakes along with way.) Are we there for others unconditionally? Ready to stand with them when they embarrass themselves and those around them (12:10–20; 20)? We must also be willing to speak life, to share what God has said, and then, having done all, to stand (see Ephesians 6:13).

Louis H. Wilson, PhD, holds a doctorate in leadership and organizational development from the University of Phoenix and has been involved in church leadership and development for the past 25 years.

Have You Heard God's Call?

by Evangeline Carey

How we honor God involves our response to who God is to us in our lives individually and in the community. How do you honor or worship God? The following is an excerpt from an article "Have You Heard God's Call?" from Evangeline Carey, which includes the Lord establishing the community of believers and how we are to respond as a community in our honoring the Lord. The areas addressed include being open to God as a vessel, being faithful, rejoicing in the Lord, witnessing, and living in obedience. Christianity is more than studying God's Word; our actions speak to others what we believe and who we believe in—God!

As the thread of God's redemptive plan continues to weave through the Old Testament and crosses over into the New Testament, we find that God is still building His kingdom, which will reign forever. Long ago, God called Abraham to leave the comfort zone of his familiar surroundings and go to a land unknown to him but very well known to an all-knowing God (Genesis 12:1–4). This land was Canaan—today's Israel. Abraham obeyed, and it was counted unto him as righteousness (Genesis 15:6). God delivered on His promise to make Abraham "a great nation." After the timeline moves through forty-two generations, God continued to carry out His plan to bring the Messiah into the world through the lineage of this great nation (Matthew 1:17).

In the Old Testament, God's chosen people—the twelve tribes of Israel—looked forward to the Messiah's coming. Now in the four Gospels found in the New Testament, the Messiah has come. His name is Jesus—"Immanuel, which means God is with us" (Matthew 1:23, NLT). He has come to save His people from their sin.

As told again and again in the history books of the Old Testament, the twelve tribes of Israel went through cycles of covenant disobedience, suffering the consequences of God's punishment or wrath, repenting, and finally being restored by a loving God. In fact, to reestablish their personal, intimate relationship with Him, God used some of their enemies to capture and enslave them. Then, they repented and called out to God for deliverance. Subsequently, God raised up judges to deliver them. As long as the judges ruled over them, they tended to obey their God. However, when the judges died, the cycle began again: "And the children of Israel again did evil in the sight of the LORD" (Judges 4:1, KJV).

The Gospel of Luke tells how God prepared the way for the Messiah to come, establishing a new covenant, and how God would put His law "in their inward parts, and write it in their hearts" (Jeremiah 31:33, KJV). Luke tells his story of the virgin birth and announces that the Savior has come (Luke 2:1–7).

A Call to Be a Vessel

God is calling the Christian community to be united as one in Christ and become a vessel—an instrument—that He can use. He wants us to show the world that He really is the one and only true God and that He loves us unconditionally. He calls the Christian community to minister to the lost (those who do not know Him as Lord and Savior) and to the hurting and dying. He uses our minds, hands, and feet to do His work in His way to carry out His will. God uses people who are willing to walk in obedience and let Him carry out His kingdom-building initiative through them.

A Call to Be Faithful

Next, we see how Zacharias and Elisabeth served as biblical examples of how to be faithful and trust a God who never lies and is Himself faithful to His own Word (Luke 1:5–25). Even though Elisabeth was barren and post-menopausal, she still gave birth to a son, John the Baptist, the forerunner of Jesus Christ. Again, God showed that He is the Sovereign God and has control even over the reproductive cycles of humanity—He can open and close wombs. John the Baptist paved the way for the Messiah, Jesus Christ, to come and save His people from their sin.

A Call to Proclaim His Word

God also calls believers to proclaim, or tell, His Good News of salvation to lost people. He mandates us to carry out the Great Commission, commanding us to "go and make disciples of all the nations, baptizing them in the name of the Father and the Son and the Holy Spirit. Teach these new disciples to obey all the commands I have given you" (Matthew 28:19–20, NLT). Therefore, at Christmas and beyond, He expects His church to worship Him in Spirit and in truth and to lift up Jesus so He can draw the spiritually lost to Himself (John 12:32). Clearly, the church's agenda is not about conferences, seminars, or programs that lift people up. The Christian community has the answers that so many going down the fast lanes of destruction are looking for. We have Jesus Christ as Head of our lives and the love of God operating in us. Consequently, we should reach out to others

who need to know God and are still searching. God will give us His power to do what He is calling us to do.

A Call to Rejoice

Luke tells us that God is calling whoever will believe to rejoice in Him both in good and bad times (2:1–14). Through Luke's account of Jesus' birth, God shows us that He is also concerned for the poor and the oppressed, as seen in the announcement of Jesus' birth first to lowly shepherds in the fields (vv. 8–20). We can rejoice because, regardless of our station in life, we can ask God to save us from our sin and to help us mentally, physically, and spiritually—and to do His will.

A Call to Be Witnesses

As Jesus walked among men for more than thirty years, we find that God spelled out His commands for the Christian community. Luke clarified that God calls the community of faith, the church, to live out the purpose for which she was created. The church was created to show a lost and dying world what it means to live in an intimate, personal relationship with a Holy God. God calls the Christian community, not just at Christmas but beyond, to step up to the plate and be the church—the bride of Christ. He is looking for a holy people (those set apart from evil) to be holy because He is holy (Leviticus 19:2).

A Call to Obedience

As we study the life of Christ in Luke's Gospel, we must be aware that Jesus Christ was obedient to the Father—He did His Father's will. Indeed, Jesus is our example. He went about His Father's business of teaching the Word (2:41–52). He loved even His enemies unconditionally, and He commanded us to do so as well (6:27–36). Throughout the Gospels, we learn that Jesus labored in making disciples. He summoned all believers to do the same because "the harvest is great, but the workers are few" (10:2, NLT). If we are going to be in God's will, we must follow His directives. We must obey the One who is building His kingdom and who will decide who will spend eternity with Him in heaven or with Satan in hell.

Have you heard God's call? It is a call to salvation and to be a doer of His Word. It is a call to be faithful to Him and to our ministries—to be a vessel He can use in His kingdom-building initiative. Finally, it is a call to rejoice in Him and to obey His Word.

Evangeline Carey, former staff writer for UMI and a Sunday School teacher for many years.

Sources:
Life Application Study Bible, NLT. Wheaton, Ill.: Tyndale House Publishers, Inc., 1996.

Intergenerational Christian Education Opportunities

by Cheryl Price, PhD

The quarter invites us to discover the Advent Season together. Advent is a time in the Christian faith when we enjoy the anticipation of celebrating the birth of Christ at Christmas and Jesus' second coming when He returns. Forgiveness and hope are celebrated themes during this season.

Many Christian churches and other faith traditions celebrate with festive lights, meals, fun treats, as well as buying toys for children, giving to those in need, planning family events, and advocating for justice around the world. The narrative of Jesus' birth is told, displayed, sung, painted, and expressed in many forms during the season of Advent.

How can various Christian faith traditions celebrate the anticipated birth of Christ and the love of Christ throughout the year? Planning intergenerational activities provides an opportunity for many people to explore and share the faith among one another and with others who do not know Jesus.

Christmas Program—Planning the traditional Christmas program or something different? Involve various age groups and skill sets to work together in creating costumes, programs, ordering and maintaining the supplies, design sets, and writing the Christmas play/program. The committee does not have to be large unless you have a major production that requires many people. Begin each meeting with prayer by asking different people to pray. Maybe some prayers can be printed out in case someone is nervous about praying aloud. Or, have people take turns reading or playing an audio of the Scripture passages leading up to the birth of Christ.

Worship Service Participants—Allow two or three different generations to read, media, mime, step dance, sing, sign, or play a musical instrument during the worship services for children, "regular" service, and/or youth church. This allows the congregants and the participants to see how the generations can work together.

Create Fun Activities—Plan fun activities once a quarter where adults, teens, and children can work together. Storytelling, cooking, indoor/outdoor gardening, floral arrangements, creating videos of the history of a selected genre of music and dance (with live performances) are only a few examples of intergenerational activities.

Sharing the Love of Christ—Plan and implement outreach events outside of the church and in the church. For example, start collecting stuffed animals or coats in July for children at Christmas or persons who live in shelters. Provide an opportunity to create college-student care boxes. Give some to the college students or vocational/technical students who attend school in the city or nearby town where they live.

Intergenerational activities have healthy benefits that will nurture and develop everyone who participates. Additionally, intergenerational activities provide opportunities for young people to learn through seniors to support one another inside and outside of the church. Each can listen and respect each other in more loving ways.

The church can invite the community or another church to participate in these intergenerational events. Intergenerational activities open up doors for educational ministries to prepare the present and next generations to live and learn together in immeasurable ways.

Cheryl Price, PhD, is Vice President of Content at UMI. She has co-authored and edited many books.

BENJAMIN E. MAYS

(1895–1984)

Preacher, Educator, and Leader

Before 500,000 people could march on Washington, DC, before 30,000 people could march from Selma, before SNCC could sit in, before Stokely Carmichael could talk about "Black Power," before Martin Luther King Jr. could dream—certain Black men had to be bold enough, wise enough, and selfless enough to assume the awesome responsibility of preparing the ground for a harvest they might never see.

Of the handful of men called to this delicate and dangerous task, none tilled more ground than preacher Benjamin Elijah Mays,—a prophet who served as "schoolmaster" of the Civil Rights Movement during a ministry that spanned some sixty years. During this period, Mays helped lay the foundation for the new world of Black and White Americans.

Master of a variety of roles—teacher, preacher, scholar, author, newspaper columnist, activist—Mays was enormously effective in the formative years of the Black Revolution in structures of power, such as serving in many executive roles and committees. In these roles, he had a direct and pervasive influence on Black institutions, White institutions, and the Freedom Movement.

Born on August 1, 1895, Dr. Mays was a native of Epworth, South Carolina, and grew up as the last of seven children of ex-slaves and semi-literate farmers. Stunned by the assertion that Blacks were intellectually inferior to Whites, he was determined to destroy this myth. After a year at Virginia Union University, he was able to enter Bates College in Maine, where he graduated in 1920. In 1925, he entered the University of Chicago where he earned a master's degree, and later, a PhD. In 1934, Dr. Mays joined Howard University as dean of its school of religion, and in 1940, he was named the president of Morehouse College. During his presidency, the college came to be dubbed the "Black Oxford of the South," spawning a disproportionate share of Black doctors, lawyers, PhDs, college presidents, teachers, and activists.

Two years after his retirement, at the age of sixty-seven, he became the first Black president of the Atlanta Board of Education, and at the age of eighty-three, he was elected to his third term.

Sources:

Adams, Russell L. Benjamin E. Mays: 1895–1984, Preacher, Educator, Leader." *Great Negroes Past and Present*. Chicago: Afro-American Publishing Co., 1984.

Bennett Jr., Lerone. "Benjamin E. Mays: The Last of the Great Schoolmasters." *Ebony*, October 1994.

Teaching Tips

Words You Should Know

A. Sanctify (v. 14) *qadash* (Heb.)—To make oneself ceremonially clean for service to God, especially through ritual washing

B. Ephod (v. 27) *'ephod* (Heb.)—A priest's outer robe

Teacher Preparation

Unifying Principle—Celebrate! People are joyful and excited when they move into a new building. What is the appropriate way to celebrate? David commanded the priests to invite all the musicians and all the people to join in shouting, singing, and dancing as they rejoiced in what God had done for them.

A. Read the Bible Background and Devotional Reading.

B. Pray for your students and lesson clarity.

C. Read the lesson Scripture in multiple translations.

O—Open the Lesson

A. Begin the class with prayer.

B. As a class, recall worship experiences that evoked diverse emotional responses among worshipers. What happened that led to those varying responses?

C. Have the students read the Aim for Change and the In Focus story.

D. Ask students how events like those in the story weigh on their hearts and how they can view these events from a faith perspective.

P—Present the Scriptures

A. Read the Focal Verses and discuss the Background and The People, Places, and Times sections.

B. Have the class share what Scriptures stand out for them and why, with particular emphasis on today's context.

E—Explore the Meaning

A. Use In Depth or More Light on the Text to facilitate a deeper discussion of the lesson text.

B. Pose the questions in Search the Scriptures and Discuss the Meaning.

C. Discuss the Liberating Lesson and Application for Activation sections.

N—Next Steps for Application

A. Summarize the value of both order and spontaneity in worship.

B. End class with a commitment to pray for special times to celebrate the presence of God with other people of faith in different ways.

Worship Guide

For the Superintendent or Teacher
Theme: David Worships God in Jerusalem
Song: "Dance Like David Danced"
Devotional Reading:
1 Chronicles 16:7–13, 28–33

David Worships God in Jerusalem

Bible Background • 1 CHRONICLES 15 | Printed Text • 1 CHRONICLES 15:1–3, 14–16, 25–29
Devotional Reading • 1 CHRONICLES 16:7–13, 28–33

Aim for Change

By the end of the lesson we will EXAMINE the ceremony surrounding the Ark being brought to Jerusalem, APPRECIATE the diversity of responses that flow from authentic worship, and EMBRACE physical expressions as important aspects of worship.

In Focus

Allison and Mario Bishop have been for married 40 years. Three months before their anniversary they made dinner reservations at their favorite restaurant.

Their four children planned a surprise anniversary celebration. They rented a ballroom, hired a caterer, and picked out flowers and decorations, all to make the celebration special. On the day of the celebration, it was Gary's responsibility to get his parents to the site of the celebration. So he called the place his parents made reservations in advance and told them why he needed to cancel the RSVP.

"Hello. My name is Mario Bishop. My wife and I have reservations for a dinner party of 23." The manager pretended to check his list and not find their names.

"This is ridiculous! We have a large group coming here for our anniversary dinner. What should we tell them? Sorry, go home?" Mrs. Bishop was very upset. But Gary stepped in and suggested a place a mile away that had good food. Gary's wife, Gwen, told them she would call everyone about the change.

When they all arrived, Mr. and Mrs. Bishop were genuinely surprised by all the people who came to celebrate their anniversary with them. When Mr. Bishop heard the jazz ensemble playing his favorite songs, he began to laugh. Then he grabbed his wife and went onto the dance floor. Everyone enjoyed celebrating with the Bishops.

Why is it important to celebrate special occasions?

Keep in Mind

"Thus all Israel brought up the ark of the covenant of the LORD with shouting, and with sound of the cornet, and with trumpets, and with cymbals, making a noise with psalteries and harps" (1 Chronicles 15:28, KJV).

"So all Israel brought up the Ark of the LORD's Covenant with shouts of joy, the blowing of rams' horns and trumpets, the crashing of cymbals, and loud playing on harps and lyres" (1 Chronicles 15:28, NLT).

Focal Verses

KJV **1 Chronicles 15:1** And David made him houses in the city of David, and prepared a place for the ark of God, and pitched for it a tent.

2 Then David said, None ought to carry the ark of God but the Levites: for them hath the LORD chosen to carry the ark of God, and to minister unto him for ever.

3 And David gathered all Israel together to Jerusalem, to bring up the ark of the LORD unto his place, which he had prepared for it.

14 So the priests and the Levites sanctified themselves to bring up the ark of the LORD God of Israel.

15 And the children of the Levites bare the ark of God upon their shoulders with the staves thereon, as Moses commanded according to the word of the LORD.

16 And David spake to the chief of the Levites to appoint their brethren to be the singers with instruments of musick, psalteries and harps and cymbals, sounding, by lifting up the voice with joy.

25 So David, and the elders of Israel, and the captains over thousands, went to bring up the ark of the covenant of the LORD out of the house of Obededom with joy.

26 And it came to pass, when God helped the Levites that bare the ark of the covenant of the LORD, that they offered seven bullocks and seven rams.

27 And David was clothed with a robe of fine linen, and all the Levites that bare the ark, and the singers, and Chenaniah the master of the song with the singers: David also had upon him an ephod of linen.

28 Thus all Israel brought up the ark of the covenant of the LORD with shouting, and with sound of the cornet, and with trumpets, and with cymbals, making a noise with psalteries and harps.

NLT **1 Chronicles 15:1** David now built several buildings for himself in the City of David. He also prepared a place for the Ark of God and set up a special tent for it.

2 Then he commanded, "No one except the Levites may carry the Ark of God. The LORD has chosen them to carry the Ark of the LORD and to serve him forever."

3 Then David summoned all Israel to Jerusalem to bring the Ark of the LORD to the place he had prepared for it.

14 So the priests and the Levites purified themselves in order to bring the Ark of the LORD, the God of Israel, to Jerusalem.

15 Then the Levites carried the Ark of God on their shoulders with its carrying poles, just as the LORD had instructed Moses.

16 David also ordered the Levite leaders to appoint a choir of Levites who were singers and musicians to sing joyful songs to the accompaniment of harps, lyres, and cymbals.

25 Then David and the elders of Israel and the generals of the army went to the house of Obed-edom to bring the Ark of the LORD's Covenant up to Jerusalem with a great celebration.

26 And because God was clearly helping the Levites as they carried the Ark of the LORD's Covenant, they sacrificed seven bulls and seven rams.

27 David was dressed in a robe of fine linen, as were all the Levites who carried the Ark, and also the singers, and Kenaniah the choir leader. David was also wearing a priestly garment.

28 So all Israel brought up the Ark of the LORD's Covenant with shouts of joy, the blowing of rams' horns and trumpets, the crashing of cymbals, and loud playing on harps and lyres.

29 And it came to pass, as the ark of the covenant of the LORD came to the city of David, that Michal, the daughter of Saul looking out at a window saw king David dancing and playing: and she despised him in her heart.

29 But as the Ark of the LORD's Covenant entered the City of David, Michal, the daughter of Saul, looked down from her window. When she saw King David skipping about and laughing with joy, she was filled with contempt for him.

The People, Places, and Times

The Ark of the Covenant. God instructed the Children of Israel to build a Tabernacle and several pieces of furniture for it after their exodus from captivity in Egypt (Exodus 25:10–22). One piece of furniture, the Ark, measured two and a half cubits in length, and a cubit and a half in both width and height. A cubit is an ancient unit and is the measurement from the elbow to fingertip, about 18 inches. David built several buildings for himself in the City of David. He also prepared a place for the Ark of God and set up a special tent for it.

This acacia wood box was then covered in gold and carried by two staves also made of gold-covered acacia wood. Mounted on the Ark was the mercy seat, a slightly raised platform, surrounded by two cherubim made of gold, one mounted at each side of the seat. The Ark of the Covenant resided within the Holy of Holies, the innermost room of the Tabernacle. Access was only permitted to one person, a high priest, once per year, on the Day of Atonement. The high priest would enter the Holy of Holies with the blood of a goat, on behalf of the people of Israel's and his own sins. The goat's blood was sprinkled onto the mercy seat to make atonement for the sins of the people of Israel.

Background

Originally one book, Chronicles recounts the genealogy and history of Israel. It includes the spiritual heritage that shows God's hand in the life of His people from Adam through David's generation (1 Chronicles 1–9). The author is unknown; however, it is traditionally ascribed to Ezra. In the Jewish Bible, Chronicles appears at the very end, right after Ezra and Nehemiah, giving an indication that Chronicles is very different from the book of Kings, which recounts many of the same historical events. It is believed that the book was written in the fifth or fourth century BC, perhaps between 400 and 350 BC. The author devotes a large section of 1 Chronicles to the story of David's life, which took place much earlier around 1000 BC. There is little mention of David's sins. Instead, the focus is on his achievements. He loved God and accomplished much.

Why is our spiritual heritage important to our future? What are the details of your spiritual heritage, and how will you pass them on?

At-A-Glance

1. A Place for the Ark (1 Chronicles 15:1–3)
2. Transporting the Ark (vv. 14–16)
3. Praising God for the Ark's Return (vv. 25–29)

In Depth

1. A Place for the Ark (1 Chronicles 15:1–3)

David became a great warrior whose power and fame increased because of his deep faith in God. He was appointed King of Israel by God. He trusted God and recaptured Jerusalem through the help of his strong military. Jerusalem became the capital city where David built his home and other structures including a tent to house the Ark of the Covenant.

This passage indicates David's desire to move the Ark of the Covenant to Jerusalem. The Ark is the most sacred object of the Hebrew faith. It is a large box overlaid with gold that contains the two tablets of the Ten Commandments (Exodus 25:10–22). Originally it held Aaron's rod and a pot of manna from the wilderness experience. Following a battle with the Philistines, the Ark was captured and eventually ended up in Kiriath-jearim at the home of Abinadab (1 Chronicles 13:6–7) where it remained, neglected for many years.

God wants to spiritually reunite His people, so the Ark is central in reinstating the worship of God. David's initial attempt to move the ark failed because David did not follow God's directions for moving it (1 Chronicles 13:9–14). As a result, one of the men was killed when he touched the Ark. The Ark was then left at the home of Obed-edom. In despair, David learned from the experience and was determined that his second attempt to move the Ark to the tent he pitched for a sanctuary was going to be done according to the will and instructions of God in the Law. On the second try, David only permits the Levites to carry the Ark of God, which were God's directions in the Torah (15:1–3; Deuteronomy 10:8).

Why is it important to follow God's directions in carrying out our plans? What consequences might we suffer from by ignoring God's instructions?

2. Transporting the Ark (vv. 14–16)

The priests and Levites sanctify themselves in preparation to move the Ark of God. This requires physical washing and spiritual preparation. The Ark of God is considered holy, so they have to purify themselves first. Once they are prepared, they carry the Ark by placing the long poles or staves through the rings of the ark and putting them on their shoulders as the law requires (1 Chronicles 15:15).

David is a musician and recognizes the value of music to the worship experience. David commands selected Levites to sing and play a variety of instruments (v. 16). This is a time of worship and celebration for the Israelites. The instruments include psalteries and harps. While these are ancient instruments, scholars put forth ideas of what they were and how they were played. The "harp" is believed to have been a stringed instrument that may have been a bass lyre or a lute. The "psaltery" was likely a string instrument as well and was played by plucking the strings. The cymbals may have been used to announce the worship procession.

How do you prepare to worship God? How is the worship of God expressed in your church?

3. Praising God for the Ark's Return (vv. 25–29)

In response to God's deliverance of the Ark, part of the ceremony includes the sacrifice of seven bullocks and seven rams in atonement for the sins of neglecting the proper worship of God. David and the entire troop of Levites wear linen garments. As the leadership of the procession and as king, David also wears an ephod or overlaying garment.

When the Ark is brought from the home of Obed-edom, David includes all the people of Israel in the worship experience. They are rejoicing because of God's faithfulness in restoring the people to their home and allowing the Ark to return to the nation for worship. God keeps His promise. As a result, the nation can once again start worshiping God with the Ark of God in the tabernacle in Jerusalem. The people shout praises to God, along with the loud playing of instruments (1 Chronicles 15:28).

But everyone does not join in the celebration. Saul's daughter is in her house looking out the window watching King David as he dances and leaps for joy while praising God. She feels that his actions were not befitting a king (1 Chronicles 15:29). Nevertheless, this celebration is momentous and marks a turning point in the history of Israel as their worship of God indicates their unity as a nation and their remembrance of all God has done throughout their history.

How does music influence our worship experience?

Search the Scriptures

1. Who was chosen by God to carry the Ark of God (1 Chronicles 15:2)?

2. What did the priests and Levites have to do in preparation before bringing the Ark of God into Jerusalem (v. 14)?

3. What instruments did the Israelites use in praising God (v. 28)?

Discuss the Meaning

1. Why was it important to bring the Ark to Jerusalem?

2. How does this passage proclaim the importance of leading the worship of God with reverence and joy?

3. What does this passage say about the relationship of obedience to worship?

Liberating Lesson

King David returned the Ark of God to Jerusalem. He followed the laws of God concerning the movement of the Ark by using only the Levites to transport it as prescribed in the Law. David made the celebration of the Ark's return an event to be shared with all the people of Israel. Music was a central part of the celebration and worship experience. Even now, music is a special ministry in the church. However, it is important to maintain a focus on worship and to avoid allowing music or other elements of worship services to become about the satisfaction of our "taste" in music. On the other hand, we can also evaluate the place of quiet meditation and prayer in our worship times. How can we maintain the sacredness of worship while allowing our God-given creativity and joy to be focused on worshiping God? Do you believe there is a role for quiet reflection as part of personal or congregational worship? Why or why not?

Application for Activation

This text is about the joy of celebrating God's deliverance and restoration. This week, reflect on how God has delivered you and restored joy and hope to your life after a period of pain, despair, or some other "dry place" in your spiritual life. What acts of worship can you engage in that show your gratitude for His grace?

Follow the Spirit

What God wants me to do:

_____

_____

_____

_____

Remember Your Thoughts

Special insights I have learned:

_____

_____

_____

_____

More Light on the Text

1 Chronicles 15:1–3, 14–16, 25–29

In order to understand the significance of the Ark, it is important to examine its placement, construction, contents, and purpose. The Ark, which was supposed to be placed permanently in the inner sanctuary of the Tabernacle, did not have an attached lid. Instead, the mercy seat that had cherubs at each end became the lid for the Ark. The Ark itself was made of wood and was covered inside and out by gold. The mercy seat, however, was composed of a solid sheet of pure gold beaten or pounded into shape. The Ark and mercy seat were symbols that God's mercy was the vehicle with which the priest was able to come before God on behalf of the people. During the time that Israel was in the wilderness, Moses was instructed to place three items inside the finished Ark: Aaron's rod, a container of the manna that the Children of Israel had been fed in the wilderness, and the stone tablets inscribed with the terms of the covenant. We call these the Ten Commandments. These three items served as symbols of God's selection, provision, and relationship with His chosen people (see Exodus 16:32–34, Numbers 17:10–11, Deuteronomy 10:2–5).

1 And David made him houses in the city of David, and prepared a place for the ark of God, and pitched for it a tent. 2 Then David said, None ought to carry the ark of God but the Levites: for them hath the LORD chosen to carry the ark of God, and to minister unto him for ever. 3 And David gathered all Israel together to Jerusalem, to bring up the ark of the LORD unto his place, which he had prepared for it.

David has built houses in Jerusalem for himself and his family. He also prepared a place for the Ark in Jerusalem. David knows that the role of the Levites and priests is to lead people in the sacrifices and worship of God; therefore, David assigns the Levites the task of moving the Ark in accordance with the Law. He also gives them additional responsibility for the ministry of music. David's preparation for returning the Ark includes involving all of the people of Israel in corporate worship. This is a momentous occasion. It symbolizes the restoration of worship to the nation and victory over Israel's enemies. God prospered the Levite, Obed-edom, when the Ark resided with him (2 Samuel 6:11). David is certain that God will prosper the nation when this symbol of communion with God is restored to national prominence. Furthermore, God is not just the God of the leaders. He is the God of the nation. All of the people are to participate and to witness what is done on that day. Through this procession, celebration, and worship, David establishes his kingdom as being loyal only to Jehovah, the self-existent God, who chose Abraham and his descendants and later took the Children of Israel out of bondage and through the wilderness. The return of the Ark will be celebrated and the beauty of the procession will be discussed throughout Israel's generations.

14 So the priests and the Levites sanctified themselves to bring up the ark of the LORD God of Israel. 15 And the children of the Levites bare the ark of God upon their shoulders with the staves thereon, as Moses commanded according to the word of the LORD. 16 And David spake to the chief of the Levites to appoint their brethren to be the singers with instruments of musick, psalteries and harps and cymbals, sounding, by lifting up the voice with joy.

Before the Ark could be moved, the priests and Levites sanctify themselves. In the Hebrew, the term "sanctify" (*qadash*, **kah-DAHSH**) refers to a process of becoming ceremonially clean by washing oneself in preparation for service to the Lord (Exodus 29:1–37). Strict adherence to the ritual of washing and sacrifice is necessary in order to avoid the penalty of death when approaching the Ark and the Tabernacle. In transporting the Ark, David makes sure the instructions given to Moses are followed.

The priests are the descendants of Aaron, the brother of Moses. God chose Aaron to be the first priest. As was God's plan, David makes sure that the priests have the responsibility of conducting worship through the offering of sacrifices. The law clearly specifies which animals are to be used for sacrifice and the manner in which sacrifice is to be carried out. The priest is just one line of the tribe of Levi, but all Levites help in worship. The Levites, one of the twelve tribes of Israel, are the descendants of Levi, the third son of Jacob and Leah. They are set apart by God to minister Him on behalf of the people. In the wilderness, the Levites had the responsibility for moving the Ark of the Covenant along with all of the furnishings of the Tabernacle.

It is also critical that the Ark is carried in a specific manner. David saw firsthand what transgression of God's instructions meant (2 Samuel 6). In this second attempt, David follows the Law completely. Only the Levites are to take responsibility for the Ark (1 Chronicles 15:2). The Levites follow God's instructions explicitly. According to the law, the Ark is to be carried. It is to be laid upon the shoulders of the Levites as symbols of their carrying the worship of the Lord before the people. It is to be held only by its staves, which, like the Ark, are made of acacia wood overlaid with gold. The staves are placed through rings of pure gold, which are affixed to each corner of the Ark. Through its materials and construction, the Ark represents the protection and covering of God over His chosen people. The rings represent God's direction.

David's ability as a musician is well known, and he believes that the return of the Ark must be accompanied by praise. The worship of God is accompanied by music and singing—a joyful noise. The instruments of David's time are described in these verses. The "psaltery" (Heb. *nebel*, **NEH-bell**) was similar in shape to a lyre and was probably played like its modern sister, the guitar. The "harp" (Heb. *kinnor*, **kee-NOHR**) was named because of its "twanging" sound. The cymbals (Heb. *metseleth*, **mets-AY-leth**) were probably double cymbals and gave a high pitch as they would today. This music is accompanied by the voices of Levite singers. This entire musical praise is described as a "sounding" and uses the Hebrew term *shama'* (**shah-MAH**), which means "to listen attentively." At this resounding music and song, the nation is to pay strict attention and to rejoice because of the return of God's presence.

25 So David, and the elders of Israel, and the captains over thousands, went to bring up the ark of the covenant of the LORD out of the house of Obededom with joy. 26 And it came to pass, when God helped the Levites that bare the ark of the covenant of the LORD, that they offered seven bullocks and seven rams. 27 And David was clothed with a robe of fine linen, and all the Levites that bare the ark, and the singers, and Chenaniah the master of the song with the singers: David also had upon him an ephod of linen. 28 Thus all Israel brought up the ark of the covenant of the LORD with shouting, and with sound of the cornet, and with trumpets, and with cymbals, making a noise with psalteries and harps. 29 And it came to pass, as the ark of the covenant of the LORD came to the city of David, that Michal, the daughter of Saul looking out at a window saw king David dancing and playing: and she despised him in her heart.

David leads the return of the Ark with a joyous and orderly procession, which includes Israel's older leaders and captains. The Israelites offer sacrifices to express their gratitude to God and to ask His blessing upon their nation as the Ark is returned to prominence in the worship of the people. This voluntary gesture is made in accordance with the law for the sins of the people (Leviticus 1:1–7). A sacrifice of seven animals of each type is made. In Scripture, the number seven refers to completeness and corresponds to the number of days in creation. The sacrifice, therefore, symbolizes the complete atonement of the people as they seek the complete forgiveness and presence of God in their nation and national affairs.

The leaders follow strict guidelines even regarding attire. David, as well as the Levites, wear fine linen, and he also wears an *ephod* (Heb. '*ephod*, **ay-FOHD**), a priest's outer robe. David is not attempting to step into the place of the priest. Rather, his attire represents him as the leader and as a worshiper who has donned the finest vestments in this celebration of restoration.

Verse 28 of this text summarizes the mood of the celebration and symbolizes the restored relationship between God and the nation of Israel. The "shouting" (Heb. *teruah*, **ter-oo-AH**) can also refer to a battle cry. This is a historic moment in the nation's history. All surrounding nations will know by the sound that God has given victory to Israel. Here, additional instruments are mentioned. The "cornet" (Heb. *shophar*, **shoh-FAR**) is a ram's horn, which was blown in battle, to sound the alarm as a warning and to call the people to solemn assemblies. The "trumpet" (Heb. *chatsotserah*, **khaw-tsoh-tser-AH**) added to the sound of the cymbals, the harps, and the voices to signify that God returned to Israel and that the symbol of His presence would reside with His people. The procession of the Ark into the city of Jerusalem takes three days. David knows that he is declaring the restored prominence of worship.

His installation of the Ark, using worship with singers, musicians, and apparently dancers, is not just a spectacle. David is ushering in God's presence and ushering in a new direction for the nation. The Bible clearly tells us that the violence and bloodshed of David's reign did not stop with the entrance of the Ark, but David's action in restoring the priority of worship over violence also created a mindset among the people.

In the return of the Ark the great Jehovah, who chose Abraham and promised him a great nation, is being honored. In this procession, the nation is remembering that Jehovah delivered their fathers from Pharaoh's hand and brought them across the Red Sea. Through the restoration of worship, the nation is declaring before their enemies that the one true God who brought their forefathers out of the wilderness and across the Jordan indeed delivered the Promised Land into their hands. David is shown to be a great king who is dependent upon the Lord and in whom the Lord is pleased. The Ark of the Covenant is brought into the city, and David himself rejoices by dancing and playing.

David is an expressive participant in the worship to God and celebration in thanks to God's presence among His people. David does not let his position as king of Israel keep him from praising God with all that he has. He is subject to God who is worthy of praise just as all the other Israelites are, and he recognizes and honors God as a result. However, his wife Michal who is Saul's daughter is offended and embarrassed that David does not maintain his status and decorum as a king (2 Samuel 6:15–23). She is angered by his expressive praise and feels it more important to maintain his status above the common people in worship. Yet David is the man after God's own heart and refuses to let human praise be more important to him than praising God (2 Samuel 6).

As we reflect on today's lesson, we must remember that whether we are worshiping

God in the church building or in our home, we should respond to God with expressions of praise and gratitude for who He is in our lives, for His power in the universe, and for what He has done for us. In Jesus Christ, God has fulfilled the promise of the Ark of the Covenant. God has made His abode with humanity and brought to earth the divinity that enables us to offer true worship and praise.

Say It Correctly

Ephod. **EE**-fud.
Kiriath-jearim. **KEER**-ee-ath jeh-ar-**EEM**.

Daily Bible Readings

MONDAY
Duties of the Levitical Priesthood
(Deuteronomy 18:1–5)

TUESDAY
David Delivers Ark to Obed-edom
(1 Chronicles 13:5–8, 13–14)

WEDNESDAY
Leader to Bring Ark to Jerusalem
(1 Chronicles 15:4–13)

THURSDAY
Ark Placed in Tent in Jerusalem
(1 Chronicles 16:1–6)

FRIDAY
Regular Worship Services Resumed
(1 Chronicles 16:37–43)

SATURDAY
Engaging in Spiritual Worship
(Romans 12:1–8)

SUNDAY
Rejoice in God's Faithfulness
(1 Chronicles 15:1–3, 14–16, 25–29)

Notes

Teaching Tips

Words You Should Know

A. Sing (v. 9) *shiyr* (Heb.)—To sing, especially a religious song

B. Sing (v. 9) *zamar* (Heb.)—To sing, especially while accompanied by a stringed instrument

Teacher Preparation

Unifying Principle—Keep Your Promises. People easily get discouraged when looking at turbulent conditions in the world. How can we find the courage to face these problems? David's people sang a psalm of thanksgiving and a psalm of worship to God for all the great things God had done for them and for the greatness of God's being.

A. Read the Bible Background and Devotional Reading.

B. Pray for your students and lesson clarity.

C. Read the lesson Scripture in multiple translations.

O—Open the Lesson

A. Begin the class with prayer.

B. Invite the class to write a prayer of thanksgiving. Use David's song in 1 Chronicles 16:8–36 as a model to have students write a personal prayer of thanksgiving to God for His acts of faithfulness and deliverance.

C. Have the students read the Aim for Change and the In Focus story.

D. Ask students how events like those in the story weigh on their hearts and how they can view these events from a faith perspective.

P—Present the Scriptures

A. Read the Focal Verses and discuss the Background and The People, Places, and Times sections.

B. Have the class share what Scriptures stand out for them and why, with particular emphasis on today's context.

E—Explore the Meaning

A. Use In Depth or More Light on the Text to facilitate a deeper discussion of the lesson text.

B. Pose the questions in Search the Scriptures and Discuss the Meaning.

C. Discuss the Liberating Lesson and Application for Activation sections.

N—Next Steps for Application

A. Summarize the value of expressions of thankfulness as part of worship.

B. End class with a commitment to pray for showing gratitude to others.

Worship Guide

For the Superintendent or Teacher
Theme: A Heart Filled with Gratitude
Song: "In the Lord I'll Be Ever Thankful"
Devotional Reading: Deuteronomy 26:1–11

A Heart Filled with Gratitude

**Bible Background • 1 CHRONICLES 16:7–36 | Printed Text • 1 CHRONICLES 16:8–12, 28-36
Devotional Reading • DEUTERONOMY 26:1–11**

Aim for Change

By the end of the lesson we will: ANALYZE the psalm David sung when he brought the Ark to Jerusalem, REJOICE in the wonderful things God has done on behalf of His people, and EXPRESS thanks for God's greatness and provision.

In Focus

A few weeks ago, the family heirloom, an old wooden clock, arrived at Jessica's house. She was excited to see the clock that her great-grandma Brown had been praying about for years. The clock belonged to her great-great-grandmother's grandfather. Grandma Brown had told stories to each new generation about the significance of the clock and the fun times family members had regarding the heirloom.

The wood that framed the clock was from a family tree that had been planted on the land they owned in North Carolina. Later, the land would be seized and stolen from the family. The family heirloom was passed down to each generation as a reminder of their past and an inspiration for their future.

Through the years, various family members kept the clock in their homes. Unfortunately, a fire in Jessica's uncle and aunt's home damaged the clock. Although the clock was rescued and repaired, no one knew where it was until now. Jessica's cousin, Jasmine, contacted family members to say that the clock was in their great-uncle Jerald's attic. He had forgotten about the clock until he went to the attic to look for a model train his grandchildren wanted to see. Everyone praised God for the clock's return.

How does your family praise and thank God? Why do you praise and thank God?

Keep in Mind

"Give thanks unto the LORD, call upon his name, make known his deeds among the people" (1 Chronicles 16:8, KJV).

"Give thanks to the LORD and proclaim his greatness. Let the whole world know what he has done" (1 Chronicles 16:8, NLT).

Focal Verses

KJV **1 Chronicles 16:8** Give thanks unto the LORD, call upon his name, make known his deeds among the people.

9 Sing unto him, sing psalms unto him, talk ye of all his wondrous works.

10 Glory ye in his holy name: let the heart of them rejoice that seek the LORD.

11 Seek the LORD and his strength, seek his face continually.

12 Remember his marvellous works that he hath done, his wonders, and the judgments of his mouth;

28 Give unto the LORD, ye kindreds of the people, give unto the LORD glory and strength.

29 Give unto the LORD the glory due unto his name: bring an offering, and come before him: worship the LORD in the beauty of holiness.

30 Fear before him, all the earth: the world also shall be stable, that it be not moved.

31 Let the heavens be glad, and let the earth rejoice: and let men say among the nations, The LORD reigneth.

32 Let the sea roar, and the fulness thereof: let the fields rejoice, and all that is therein.

33 Then shall the trees of the wood sing out at the presence of the LORD, because he cometh to judge the earth.

34 O give thanks unto the LORD; for he is good; for his mercy endureth for ever.

35 And say ye, Save us, O God of our salvation, and gather us together, and deliver us from the heathen, that we may give thanks to thy holy name, and glory in thy praise.

36 Blessed be the LORD God of Israel for ever and ever. And all the people said, Amen, and praised the LORD.

NLT **1 Chronicles 16:8** Give thanks to the LORD and proclaim his greatness. Let the whole world know what he has done.

9 Sing to him; yes, sing his praises. Tell everyone about his wonderful deeds.

10 Exult in his holy name; rejoice, you who worship the LORD.

11 Search for the LORD and for his strength; continually seek him.

12 Remember the wonders he has performed, his miracles, and the rulings he has given,

28 O nations of the world, recognize the LORD, recognize that the LORD is glorious and strong.

29 Give to the LORD the glory he deserves! Bring your offering and come into his presence. Worship the LORD in all his holy splendor.

30 Let all the earth tremble before him. The world stands firm and cannot be shaken.

31 Let the heavens be glad, and the earth rejoice! Tell all the nations, "The LORD reigns!"

32 Let the sea and everything in it shout his praise! Let the fields and their crops burst out with joy!

33 Let the trees of the forest sing for joy before the LORD, for he is coming to judge the earth.

34 Give thanks to the LORD, for he is good! His faithful love endures forever.

35 Cry out, "Save us, O God of our salvation! Gather and rescue us from among the nations, so we can thank your holy name and rejoice and praise you."

36 Praise the LORD, the God of Israel, who lives from everlasting to everlasting! And all the people shouted "Amen!" and praised the LORD.

The People, Places, and Times

Psalm. Any sort of ancient religious song can be considered a "psalm," whether it offers a cry for help, a shout of thanks, or simply adoration. The words of many Jewish religious songs have been preserved in the Scriptures. The book of Psalms is a well-known source for these songs, but some of the psalms are also repeated in other parts of the Scriptures. In today's lesson, we have a psalm that parallels several psalms found in the book of Psalms.

David. As king of Israel, David was responsible for unifying the nation, building Jerusalem as its capital, and bringing the Ark of the Covenant to a proper place of worship. King David composed many songs, some of which are recorded in the Scripture.

Background

Readers should be aware of two backgrounds when interacting with this text. First there is the background of David's story, and second, there is the background of the writing of Chronicles. David ruled in Israel around 1000 BC. The date of Chronicles' writing is between 400 and 350 BC. There is no specific scriptural reference to the author, but according to Jewish tradition, the writer of Chronicles was Ezra.

The original audience of Chronicles was the Jewish people who returned from the exile. The book was written to provide perspective and historical continuity as they returned to Israel from Babylonia. They had to rebuild the Temple, restore worship, including the Levitical sacrificial system, and rebuild the cities. Many negative events of David's reign are left out of Chronicles. This was not because the author wanted to erase those events from history books; rather, the book of Chronicles focuses on relaying the key elements of Jewishness that were considered foundational in rebuilding the nation.

Chronicles' post-exilic audience saw newfound meaning in David's previous establishment of a center for national worship. Generations ago, when David brought the Ark into Jerusalem, he sent the message that every Israelite should worship Yahweh, and Yahweh alone. He also sent the message that Jerusalem would be the center of this worship, the one special place on earth where God chose to dwell, as represented by the Ark. David called the Israelites to joyously remember all God had done to bring them to this point.

At-A-Glance

1. A Call to Thanksgiving
(1 Chronicles 16:8–12)
2. Nature called to Praise God (vv. 28–33)
3. Petition for Israel's Deliverance
(vv. 34–36)

In Depth

1. A Call to Thanksgiving (1 Chronicles 16:8–12)

This first part of this psalm of thanksgiving (vv. 8–22) parallels Psalm 105:1–15. David invites all those who accompanied him to Jerusalem for the installation of the Ark to give thanks unto the Lord (v. 8) for all His wondrous works (v. 9), His holy name (v. 10), and for the judgments of His mouth (v. 12). These verses demonstrate what should comprise a song of worship to God: adoration not just for what God has done, but also for who He is.

In writing Chronicles, Ezra recounts this psalm to encourage the Jews to engage Yahweh in worshipful praise. The Jews who just returned from exile are to thank God for keeping His everlasting covenant with their forefathers, fulfilling His promise of settlement into the land of promise (Psalm 105:8–11), and bringing them back to the land of promise after years in exile.

There is also a place for shouting aloud to God in praise. The call requested here is not that of lament or deliverance but of a loud shout to God in praise. In recounting this time that David leads the Israelites to praise God for establishing them in Jerusalem, Ezra hopes to lead the Jews to praise God for bringing them back from exile.

Verse 8 says, "Make known his deeds among the people." These words challenge the Israelites to share what the Lord has done for them among the people of other faiths, tribes, languages, and countries. The Israelites of David's time had many groups living close by in Canaan to show God's deeds to the Philistines, Moabites, Amorites, and so forth. The Israelites of Ezra's time had broadened their worlds through the exile and would think to spread the news of God's deeds to Egypt, Mesopotamia, and Greece. Verse 9 commands the listeners to sing. David assigns the Levites the duty of singing praise to God, but today we are all called to sing unto the Lord as an expression of our gratitude to him.

The reference to God's "strength" (v. 11) likely refers to the Ark of the Covenant, which they are moving. The Ark is seen as a symbol of the strength of God. Ezra, therefore, encourages his audience to continuous dependence on the Lord, both in good times and bad. Verse 12 declares that Israel should "Remember his marvelous works." This is a reference to the Exodus from Egypt (Psalm 105:5, 26–27). The phrase "judgments of his mouth" (v. 12) refers to God's verdict against those who offend Him.

What did the Israelites thank God for? Is your thanksgiving to God different?

2. Nature Called to Praise God (vv. 28–33)

We also read 1 Chronicles 16:24–33 in Psalm 96:3–13. The first invitation to thanksgiving is specifically to the Israelites, while the second call is general. In these verses families of nations and all nature are invited to praise God. The audience is called to bring various gifts to the Lord, like glory, strength, and offerings.

Nature is also invited to praise God. Both the tumultuous sea and orderly fields shout their praises to Yahweh. These verses call us to consider the injustices humans inflict on God's creation via polluting the sea or chopping down forests. When we abuse the natural habitat and animals around us, we deprive God of the worship His creation brings Him. Taking care of natural resources is another way to show our gratitude to God.

How should your praise of God include enabling nature to show His glory?

3. Petition for Israel's Deliverance (vv. 34–36)

These last three verses parallel Psalm 106:1, 47, and 48. It is a transition from praise to petition. These verses depict what comprises a proper attitude for the worshiper: gratitude for what God has done, followed with a humble prayer for God's constant help and deliverance.

The prayer for God to "gather" (v. 35) them and hold the people together reflects the fears of a people surrounded by enemies. While the Israelites of David's time felt pressure from the surrounding nations of Philistines and Moabites, the Israelites of Ezra's time were probably thinking of the threat of the Egyptians and Persians. The Israelites finally learn their lesson and cry out for deliverance from the Lord, not from their leaders or prophets. Verse 36 encourages the people to say Amen. It was a common practice and the usual way to respond in the public worship to the priests' and Levites' prayer (Deuteronomy 27:15–26; Nehemiah 8:6). "All the people" here refers to those who accompanied David to Jerusalem in bringing the Ark.

What do you do in your time of crisis? Whom do you call, and how can they help you?

Search the Scriptures

1. What blessings should the nation thank God for in these verses (1 Chronicles 16:8–12)?

2. How was Israel to tell other people of God's greatness (v. 28)?

3. What elements in nature praise God (vv. 30–33)? How?

Discuss the Meaning

1. Discuss the injunction to give thanks to the Lord. What effect did this have on the attitudes of the returnees? How does it impact us?

2. What do you think the statements about nature and the earth meant to the Hebrew people?

Liberating Lesson

We are in a society where people want things done in a jiffy, and this attitude has penetrated into our worship service. People rush in and out of God's presence without spending time to appreciate Him for specific things He has done for them. Some who wish to thank Him are often at a loss on what to thank Him for. David and the chronicler offer us specific things to thank the Lord for: all His wondrous works, His holy name, and the judgments of His mouth. We can thank Him for the daily victories He gives us, the gift of eternal life, and the gift of His Word that teaches, rebukes, and corrects us, as well as the Holy Spirit who reminds us of all things and convicts us. We are called to be grateful for all these things. Often pains and challenges of life blind us from observing these immeasurable blessings.

Expression of our gratitude to God should be seen in our relationship with nature. It is our responsibility to care for the natural resources around us in order to enhance their worship of God. When we pollute and waste the environment by chopping trees and pouring waste into the sea, it destroys them, thereby depriving God the praise they bring Him.

Application for Activation

Having seen the various ways the Israelites were encouraged to praise God, we are also called to express our gratitude to God. First, remember God's miracles in your life and write them in a journal or notebook as a record of His grace. Then tell three people, especially those of other faiths and unbelievers, about God's blessings. Second, as you consider the practical steps you could take to preserve nature around you, spend about 30 minutes each day tending to God's creation. Third, turn your eyes from hope in people and instead cry unto the Lord concerning situations you are going through. Take time to petition the Lord for those issues that are on your heart and for His grace upon others, making sure that you praise Him in anticipation of His answers.

Follow the Spirit

What God wants me to do:

_____

_____

_____

_____

Remember Your Thoughts

Special insights I have learned:

_____

_____

_____

_____

More Light on the Text
1 Chronicles 16:8–12, 28–36

In Exodus 25, God commanded Moses to build a Tabernacle and the Ark of Covenant that would to represent the center of worship for the people and be a symbol of Yahweh's presence among His people. When the Lord was to meet with the people, He was to appear above the Ark between the two cherubim placed on the cover of the Ark (Exodus 25:22). In the times of Eli, the priest, the Philistines captured the Ark during the war (1 Samuel 4). This brought the wrath of the Lord heavily upon the Philistines, and after seven months, they were compelled to send the Ark back to Israel. It was deposited at Kiriath-Jearim in the house of Abinadab.

During the reign of King Saul, the Ark was neglected. However, when David became king, he sought means to bring the Ark to Jerusalem. After a first attempt that failed for lack of preparation, which resulted in a death of Uzza (2 Samuel 6:4–11). David in a second attempt, with all the care required, brought the Ark to Jerusalem to be the center of worship life in Israel. The psalm in 1 Chronicles 16:8–36 is sung at the occasion of the coming of the Ark to Jerusalem. The placement of the Ark in Jerusalem is the manifestation of God's presence in the center of the people's lives and the transformation of their entire pattern of worship.

8 Give thanks unto the LORD, call upon his name, make known his deeds among the people.

Three actions are outlined in this verse: to express gratitude to the Lord, to call upon His name, and to proclaim His deeds among people. The Hebrew term *yadah* (**yaw-DAW**) translates as "give thanks," to profess or celebrate, with the idea of extending one's hands. It is a sign of gratitude. Gratitude should be expressed to someone for what the person has done. However, when directed to God, our gratitude is to celebrate who He is. His character implies His actions. He fulfills His promises because He is faithful. The Ark is a symbol of His faithful presence in the midst of His people.

To "call upon [God's] name" is an invitation to pray to God with dependency, confidence, and praise. The Hebrew word *qara'* (**kaw-RAW**), translated "call," means "to cry out" or "shout aloud." In other psalms, too, the Lord urges His people to call on His name in the days of their trouble, and He would deliver them (Psalm 50:15, 91:15). The Ark serves as a place for the gathering of the nation to worship the Lord and to pray to Him in any circumstance they might experience. When Solomon dedicates the Temple where the Ark will be laid, he will ask God to answer His people or even the nations when they come to the Temple (1 Kings 8:31–52). The word "name" translates the Hebrew word *shem* (**SHAME**) and connotes the personality revealed by someone's character and actions. The Lord's name reveals His character (self-existing) and is evident in His choosing of His people and making them His own. His name, symbolizing who God is, deserves praise.

Verse 8 encourages the Israelites to proclaim the deeds of the Lord among the people, which could include Gentile nations. His deeds (Heb. *'alilah*, **ah-lee-LAW**) certainly comprise what God has done for His people starting with the covenant with Abraham and continuing until Israel inherited the land. These deeds are embedded in their history. They should proclaim the wonderful works of the Lord to other nations.

9 Sing unto him, sing psalms unto him, talk ye of all his wondrous works.

The Hebrew language has two synonymous verbs for to sing: *shir* (**SHEER**) and *zamar* (**zaw-MAR**). *Shir* usually denotes a religious praise as rendered in a historical hymn. *Zamar* is used for singing and for accompanying oneself on a stringed musical instrument as part worship.

Singing is an important part of celebrating the Lord. Music has been part of public worship throughout the history of Israel. After the Egyptians were drowned in the Red Sea after their pursuit of the Israelites, Moses and the whole people sang to the Lord to proclaim His mighty deeds (Exodus 15). Hannah (1 Samuel 2) and Mary (Luke 1:46–55) magnified the Lord with praises to share of His wondrous work in giving them children. The importance of songs in the proclamations of God's word and works are tremendous. God, the supreme King, deserves beautiful songs and poetic skills to stress His might and greatness.

10 Glory ye in his holy name: let the heart of them rejoice that seek the LORD. 11 Seek the LORD and his strength, seek his face continually.

Glory (Heb. *halal*, **haw-LOL**) here has the sense of bragging about something and is used here to indicate not just pride but happiness as well. As the prophet would tell Israel, pridefully boasting is foolish, unless done to brag about what an awesome God they serve (Jeremiah 9:24). God is worthy to be praised for what He has already done, but this phrase could also be a direction for a worship service. Praise is to be offered with an attitude of delight and joy, perhaps with music, singing, and dancing.

These verses contain three references of seeking God. However, the three occurrences are expressed by two Hebrew words: *baqash* (**baw-KASH**, vv. 10, 11) and *darash* (**daw-RASH**, v. 11). Hebrew poetry, like this psalm, often relies on repetition of a concept to reinforce its point. The emphasis is not on the words' slightly different nuances but on how the words are synonyms. Both words refer to seeking someone out to ask (or demand) something of them. We ought to "continually" seek out God's judgment and strength rather than

rely on our own, as His is infinitely better. The result of seeking the Lord is joy and deliverance from all our fears (Psalm 34:4). The implication of seeking the Lord in this instance requires going to the place where the Ark is placed, as "his strength" is a reference to the Ark itself.

12 Remember his marvellous works that he hath done, his wonders, and the judgments of his mouth;

To remember something is to keep it fresh in your mind. Remembrance is often paired with action in the Bible. Because they remember God's works, they will worship Him. The subject of this remembrance is to be God's marvelous works, specifically His wonders and His judgments. The wonders of the Lord are probably a reference to the wonders God performed from the days of Egypt to the possession of the Promised Land. The word for judgments (Heb. *mishpat*, **meesh-POT**) may be a reference to the condemnation of Israel's enemies.

28 Give unto the LORD, ye kindreds of the people, give unto the LORD glory and strength.

After calling "the people" (v. 8), the song now calls the "kindreds of people" to honor God and glorify Him. Both of these refer to all people everywhere, the nation of Israel and other nations. The Hebrew word for people is plural in both cases, better translated as "peoples," that is, several different people groups. Here, David is more specific about inviting everyone, calling on each "kindred" (Heb. *mishpach*, **meesh-PACH**, tribe or clan) of each people group to glorify God. The other nations have to glorify God because, as verse 14 states, His rulings are over the whole earth while the gods of other nations are only idols who do not perform anything worthy of praise (v. 26). Obviously, no one can truly give the Lord anything, since everything is already His. When worshiping, however, it is common to talk about "giving" the Lord blessing and honor. Elsewhere, this word is translated "ascribe," showing the song means to acknowledge that God already possesses all the glory and strength.

29 Give unto the LORD the glory due unto his name: bring an offering, and come before him: worship the LORD in the beauty of holiness.

The people of Israel are encouraged not to appear before the Lord empty-handed (cf. Exodus 23:15). They are to bring an offering into His presence. This verse is echoed in Psalm 96:8. There the writer records the phrase "come before him" as "come into his courts." This change is understandable given the circumstances of the psalm. The Temple with its courts was not yet built during David's time, but by the time the song was recorded in the book of Psalms, it could be more specific about where a worshiper could encounter the presence of God. The presence of the Ark represents the presence of the Lord Himself.

30 Fear before him, all the earth: the world also shall be stable, that it be not moved. 31 Let the heavens be glad, and let the earth rejoice: and let men say among the nations, The LORD reigneth.

The word "fear" (Heb. *chul*, **khool**) in the Old Testament often describes respect, reverence, and awe when God is the object of that fear. "All the earth" refers to the inhabitants of the earth, but it is followed by "the world" (Heb. *tebel*, **tay-BALE**), which refers to the physical globe. The call is to both the people and the world itself. God is the sustainer of the universe. All the laws of physics by which there is balance in the entire cosmos have been set by Him. Humanity only discovered these laws. While the stability of the world (the physical globe) is firmly established by God and will "be not moved," the stability of the world

(all people) depends solely on the reverence humankind has for God. The various troubles the world goes through are the result of human refusal to acknowledge God as the author of life and the universe and to follow His precepts.

The praise started with telling Israel to reach the nations, and now the whole universe is required to express joy and gladness because the Lord is King. God is not only the King over Israel; He is the King over every nation of the earth. He reigns over the universe.

32 Let the sea roar, and the fulness thereof: let the fields rejoice, and all that is therein. 33 Then shall the trees of the wood sing out at the presence of the LORD, because he cometh to judge the earth.

The elements of the universe and nature are personified and urged to sing to the Lord who is the supreme Judge. Chaotic elements like the sea and the trees of the forest are called to praise God alongside the domesticated, orderly fields. This should give us hope and assurance in the midst of confusion, chaos, iniquity, and inequality. The One we serve rules the affairs of this world with justice, and eventually, His reign will prevail. Sin in the world may darken our horizons and paint a gloomy picture of the future world. But we must prayerfully and patiently await the restoration of the universe (cf. Romans 8:19–23) when the King will subdue all His adversaries and reign forever and ever.

34 O give thanks unto the LORD; for he is good; for his mercy endureth forever.

This verse is a common refrain in the Psalms (Psalm 106:1, 107:1, 118:1, 136:1). The Hebrew word translated "mercy" (KJV), and "faithful love" (NLT) here and steadfast love elsewhere is *chesed* (**KHEH-sed**). The word expresses an idea of love, devotion, and faithfulness to a promise or covenant. When the word is used to describe God, it highlights God's faithfulness to His covenant with His people.

35 And say ye, Save us, O God of our salvation, and gather us together, and deliver us from the heathen, that we may give thanks to thy holy name, and glory in thy praise. 36 Blessed be the LORD God of Israel for ever and ever. And all the people said, Amen, and praised the LORD.

Verse 35 is a prayer for salvation and deliverance. Calling the Lord "God of our salvation" establishes the prayer on the basis of God's past actions. The prayer will be answered in two steps: first, gathering together, and then, deliverance. David prays for the nation to be gathered together and delivered from the threat of Canaanite nations like the Philistines. When Ezra reminds the people of the hymn, it gains even greater significance as a prayer to gather the people back from exile to far off countries. We often find throughout Scripture and our present lives that God will answer prayer and then answer it again in an even greater way years later.

The psalm promises that after God has gathered and delivered His people, they will thank and praise Him. While we can offer God our thanks and praise anywhere at any time, we are better able to devote our whole bodies, minds, and hearts to worship when we are able to do it corporately in a designated place of worship.

The psalm is concluded with a blessing to Yahweh, the God of Israel, who forever deserves to be praised. The people responded "Amen" (Heb. *'amen*, **ah-MANE**), which means "let it be so" or "truly," and they praised the Lord.

Sources:

Bennett, W. H. 1947. "Books of the Chronicles," *The Jewish Encyclopedia* New York and London: Funk and Agnalls Company.

Bratcher, R. G., & Reyburn, W. D. (1991). *A Translator's Handbook on the Book of Psalms.* New York, NY: United Bible Societies.

Coggins, R. J., ed. 1976. *The First and Second Books of the Chronicles: Commentary. The Cambridge Bible Commentary on the New English Bible.* Cambridge, England: Cambridge University Press.

Earle, Ralph, and W. T. Purkiser, eds. 1964. *Beacon Bible Commentary.* Kansas City, MO: Beacon Hill Press.

Harris, L. R., Archer, Jr., G. L., & Waltke, B. K. (1980). *Theological Wordbook of the Old Testament.* Chicago, IL: Moody Bible Institute.

Keil, Carl F. "Introduction." *Commentary on the Old Testament.* Grand Rapids, MI: Wm. B. Eerdmans Publishing Company.

Klein, Ralph W., and Thomas Kruger. 2006. *1 Chronicles: A Commentary. Hermeneia—a Critical and Historical Commentary on the Bible.* Minneapolis, MN: Fortress Press.

Selman, M. J. (1994). *Tyndale Old Testament Commentaries: 1 Chronicles, An Introduction & Commentary.* D. J. Wiseman, Ed. Downers Grove, IL: InterVarsity Press.

Tuell, Steven S. 2001. *First and Second Chronicles.* Interpretation, a Bible Commentary Louisville, KY: John Knox Press.

VanGemeren, W. A. (1997). *New International Dictionary of Old Testament Theology and Exegesis (Vol. I).* Grand Rapids, MI: Zondervan.

Williamson, H. G. (1982). *The New Century Bible Commentary: 1 & 2 Chronicles.* R. E. Clements, Ed. Grand Rapids, MI: Wm. B. Eerdmans.

Say It Correctly

Kiriath-Jearim. **KEE**-ree-ath **JEH**-ah-reem.
Abinadab. ah-**BEN**-an-**DAB**.

Daily Bible Readings

MONDAY
All Nations Invited to Worship God
(Isaiah 45:20–25)

TUESDAY
Response to God's Generosity
(Deuteronomy 26:1–11)

WEDNESDAY
God's Saving Deeds
(Psalm 105:1–15)

THURSDAY
God's Gracious Compassion
(Psalm 106:40–48)

FRIDAY
God's Forever Covenant
(1 Chronicles 16:14–18)

SATURDAY
God's Forever Steadfast Love
(1 Chronicles 16:28–36)

SUNDAY
God's Wondrous Deeds for all People
(1 Chronicles 16:8–13, 28–36)

Notes

_____

_____

_____

_____

Teaching Tips

Words You Should Know

A. Servant (v. 4) *'ebed* (Heb.)—Slave, a devoted follower

B. Forever (v. 12) *'olam* (Heb.)—Without end; an indefinite, long period

Teacher Preparation

Unifying Principle—Negotiating Obedience. People are not always able to accomplish what they desire to do for others. Is it possible to see a positive result even when our desires are not accomplished? Although God did not agree for David to build a temple, God promised that his son would.

A. Read the Bible Background and Devotional Reading.

B. Pray for your students and lesson clarity.

C. Read the lesson Scripture in multiple translations.

O—Open the Lesson

A. Begin the class with prayer.

B. As a class, offer personal examples of times when participants made plans that were thwarted or postponed and how they discerned God providing different and better plans.

C. Have the students read the Aim for Change and the In Focus story.

D. Ask students how events like those in the story weigh on their hearts and how they can view these events from a faith perspective.

P—Present the Scriptures

A. Read the Focal Verses and discuss the Background and The People, Places, and Times sections.

B. Have the class share what Scriptures stand out for them and why, with particular emphasis on today's context.

E—Explore the Meaning

A. Use In Depth or More Light on the Text to facilitate a deeper discussion of the lesson text.

B. Pose the questions in Search the Scriptures and Discuss the Meaning.

C. Discuss the Liberating Lesson and Application for Activation sections.

N—Next Steps for Application

A. Summarize the value of demonstrating our gratitude to God by dedicating ourselves, our gifts, and special places of worship to God.

B. End class with a commitment to pray for God's wisdom and guidance as they make plans for their futures.

Worship Guide

For the Superintendent or Teacher
Theme: Building God's House
Song: "Behind the Veil" by Juanita Bynum
Devotional Reading: Psalm 138

Building God's House

Bible Background • 1 CHRONICLES 17:1–15; 21:18–30 | Printed Text • 1 CHRONICLES 17:1, 3–4, 11–14; 21:18, 21–27 | Devotional Reading • PSALM 138

Aim for Change

By the end of the lesson, we will: CONTRAST the "house" David wanted to build for God with the "house" that God promised to David, REFLECT on how God's plans for us are greater and more satisfying than our plans for ourselves, and SEEK God's wisdom in planning for the future.

In Focus

A major nonprofit corporation wanted to give back to the community and make a real difference for the city. For the first four months, things went very well, but at midyear, the project was losing ground. The project supervisor, Margaret, was pushing people to work harder, and while she wanted to be the first team to make the goal, her approach wasn't working. New ideas were definitely needed.

Within three months, the management moved Margaret, and a new manager, Barbara, came on board. Barbara's style was just different enough that team members felt more included in the vision. Team meetings took on new life as people began to see this as an achievable goal for the team and not just the leader.

After reaching new goals and receiving recognition from the national office, the vice president of the division hosted a luncheon to recognize each team member. The vice president said, "When Margaret felt that she had taken it as far as she could, she asked that we consider Barbara, and we did. It takes a true leader to accept when it is time to pass the work to the person who can take it to the next level. Margaret laid a good foundation, and because of that, Barbara and the team were able to succeed."

When in your life has God said for you "to pass the torch" for the greater glory of God's mission?

Keep in Mind

"And it shall come to pass, when thy days be expired that thou must go to be with thy fathers, that I will raise up thy seed after thee, which shall be of thy sons; and I will establish his kingdom. He shall build me an house, and I will stablish his throne for ever" (1 Chronicles 17:11–12, KJV).

"For when you die and join your ancestors, I will raise up one of your descendants, one of your sons, and I will make his kingdom strong. He is the one who will build a house—a temple—for me. And I will secure his throne forever" (1 Chronicles 17:11–12, NLT).

Focal Verses

KJV 1 Chronicles 17:1 Now it came to pass, as David sat in his house, that David said to Nathan the prophet, Lo, I dwell in an house of cedars, but the ark of the covenant of the LORD remaineth under curtains.

3 And it came to pass the same night, that the word of God came to Nathan, saying,

4 Go and tell David my servant, Thus saith the LORD, Thou shalt not build me an house to dwell in:

11 And it shall come to pass, when thy days be expired that thou must go to be with thy fathers, that I will raise up thy seed after thee, which shall be of thy sons; and I will establish his kingdom.

12 He shall build me an house, and I will stablish his throne for ever.

13 I will be his father, and he shall be my son: and I will not take my mercy away from him, as I took it from him that was before thee:

14 But I will settle him in mine house and in my kingdom for ever: and his throne shall be established for evermore.

21:18 Then the angel of the LORD commanded Gad to say to David, that David should go up, and set up an altar unto the LORD in the threshingfloor of Ornan the Jebusite.

21 And as David came to Ornan, Ornan looked and saw David, and went out of the threshingfloor, and bowed himself to David with his face to the ground.

22 Then David said to Ornan, Grant me the place of this threshingfloor, that I may build an altar therein unto the LORD: thou shalt grant it me for the full price: that the plague may be stayed from the people.

23 And Ornan said unto David, Take it to thee, and let my lord the king do that which is good in his eyes: lo, I give thee the oxen also for burnt offerings, and the threshing instruments for wood, and the wheat for the meat offering; I give it all.

NLT 1 Chronicles 17:1 When David was settled in his palace, he summoned Nathan the prophet. "Look," David said, "I am living in a beautiful cedar palace, but the Ark of the LORD's Covenant is out there under a tent!"

3 But that same night God said to Nathan,

4 "Go and tell my servant David, 'This is what the LORD has declared: You are not the one to build a house for me to live in.

11 For when you die and join your ancestors, I will raise up one of your descendants, one of your sons, and I will make his kingdom strong.

12 He is the one who will build a house—a temple—for me. And I will secure his throne forever.

13 I will be his father, and he will be my son. I will never take my favor from him as I took it from the one who ruled before you.

14 I will confirm him as king over my house and my kingdom for all time, and his throne will be secure forever.'"

21:18 Then the angel of the LORD told Gad to instruct David to go up and build an altar to the LORD on the threshing floor of Araunah the Jebusite.

21 When Araunah saw David approaching, he left his threshing floor and bowed before David with his face to the ground.

22 David said to Araunah, "Let me buy this threshing floor from you at its full price. Then I will build an altar to the Lord there, so that he will stop the plague."

23 "Take it, my lord the king, and use it as you wish," Araunah said to David. "I will give the oxen for the burnt offerings, and the threshing boards for wood to build a fire on the altar, and the wheat for the grain offering. I will give it all to you."

24 But King David replied to Araunah, "No, I insist on buying it for the full price. I will not

24 And king David said to Ornan, Nay; but I will verily buy it for the full price: for I will not take that which is thine for the LORD, nor offer burnt offerings without cost.

25 So David gave to Ornan for the place six hundred shekels of gold by weight.

26 And David built there an altar unto the LORD, and offered burnt offerings and peace offerings, and called upon the LORD; and he answered him from heaven by fire upon the altar of burnt offering.

27 And the LORD commanded the angel; and he put up his sword again into the sheath thereof.

take what is yours and give it to the LORD. I will not present burnt offerings that have cost me nothing!"

25 So David gave Araunah 600 pieces of gold in payment for the threshing floor.

26 David built an altar there to the LORD and sacrificed burnt offerings and peace offerings. And when David prayed, the LORD answered him by sending fire from heaven to burn up the offering on the altar.

27 Then the LORD spoke to the angel, who put the sword back into its sheath.

The People, Places, and Times

Nathan. A prophet in the royal court of David and for some of Solomon's reign, Nathan was a personal adviser to David and spoke for God. His name means "gift." Nathan was not afraid to speak the truth. He was divinely appointed to keep David accountable. Throughout David's life, Nathan was able to help David see his own sins.

Threshing floor. A smooth, hard plot of land used to beat grain in order to separate the wheat from the chaff.

Background

For much of Israel's history, it was nomadic. Established as a nation enslaved within a nation, the Lord delivered them, only for them to end up wandering in the wilderness for forty years as a result of disobedience and lack of faith. Israel then spent centuries engaged in cycles of idolatry, enslavement, repentance, and deliverance. These deeds are recorded in the book of Judges and began before Saul was chosen to be the first king. Saul is known for having led the nation through battles with its neighboring enemies, and David spent the beginning of his own reign battling many

surrounding enemies. Now, after years of wandering and fighting, 2 Samuel 7 indicates that God gave them rest in their own land. With his mind rested and able to dream about the future, David made a plan to build a grand temple for God.

After a time of relative peace, however, 2 Samuel 24:1 indicates that Israel angered the Lord, who then "incites" David to take a census. The parallel account in 1 Chronicles 21:1 states that Satan rose up against Israel. While this may seem contradictory, we know that God does not lead us to sin. He does, however, on occasion allow Satan to have access to tempt people (cf. Job 1).

David's sin was not in taking the census but the pride behind his decision. God built the nation of Israel, defeated their enemies, and established David's kingship, and in arrogance, David wanted an account of the kingdom "he" built. Despite warnings from Joab, captain of Israel's army, that a census would bring the Lord's judgment, David proceeded. Nine months and twenty days later, the census was completed, and David regretted his decision. God, in His displeasure, sent the prophet Gad to give David three options to choose as a discipline: three years of famine, three months of enemies' attacks, or three days of a plague. David chose the plague. God sent the prophet Gad again with further instructions of how to end the plague: consecrate the spot that would eventually be built up into the Temple.

At-A-Glance

1. David's Intentions (1 Chronicles 17:1, 3–4)
2. God's Promises (vv. 11–14)
3. David's Sacrifice
(1 Chronicles 21:18, 21–27)

In Depth

1. David's Intentions (1 Chronicles 17:1, 3–4)

With Israel finally at peace, David is securely established as her king. David built houses for himself. He dedicated himself to freeing the people of God from their enemies and to leading them back to worship Yahweh, the one true God. The Ark of Covenant, the sign of God's presence, which was neglected during Saul's reign, is now in Jerusalem but only in a tent (1 Chronicles 15:1).

As he surveys his home, he is convicted that he should not reside in a more permanent and stately home than the Lord's Ark of the Covenant. So, with the prophet Nathan's blessing, David purposes in his heart to build a more suitable home for the Ark. However, David's intentions were premature. God comes to Nathan that night, sending him back to David to remind him that He did not ask for a "house of cedar," and in fact, God has been the one doing the building. God turned a shepherd into a king with a great name and lasting legacy, and He turned a people into a nation, loved and protected by the one true God.

Recall a time when you changed course based upon the wise, godly counsel of another, and it proved to be an unexpected blessing?

2. God's Promises (vv. 11–14)

Throughout the Old Testament we see the significance placed in birthrights and lineage. People are identified by the households, tribes, and clans of their fathers or grandfathers. Legacy matters. God promises that long after David is gone, his name and legacy will live on. God also speaks of a coming son who will not only build a temple for the Lord, but will become king with his throne established by the Lord forever. God promises that their relationship will be one of steadfast love—and God will never withdraw from him as he did when Saul disobeyed. While this promise has its initial fulfillment in David's son, Solomon, it also points toward a greater King to come from the line of David—Jesus.

What is God prompting you to leave behind as a godly legacy?

3. David's Sacrifice (1 Chronicles 21:18, 21–27)

Following David's sin in taking a census, God punishes him by sending a plague that kills 70,000 men of Israel before God stops the angel by Ornan (NLT: Araunah) the Jebusite's threshing floor (vv. 14–15). David sees the angel with his sword stretched out over Jerusalem and repents. His repentance leads him to sacrifice. Both Ornan (who also saw the angel, v. 20) and David recognize God's mercy. David seeks to build an altar for burnt offerings and peace offerings, symbolizing his and Israel's complete surrender to God, and desire to reconcile in order to repair the breach caused by their sin. In gratitude, Ornan offers all that was required for the sacrifice—the land, oxen, grain, and wood. David, however, recognizing that his disobedience led to these consequences, determines that a true sacrifice would require his investment. God's answer is fire from heaven, indicating that God is pleased.

How seriously do you take repentance? Is there currently something for which you need to repent? Do so.

Search the Scriptures

1. Who does God say will build His house? (17:12)

2. What promise did God make for David's offspring? (17:13–14)

3. What requirement did David make of Ornan? Why? (21:22)

Discuss the Meaning

1. How does this passage speak to the significance of lineage in ancient Israel? How does that apply today?

2. What does this passage reveal about God's character and His promises?

3. What do you believe the threshing floor symbolizes? (21:22)

Liberating Lesson

In today's society, people seem to struggle accepting responsibility for their actions. We are naturally self-preservers, seeking to shift blame. As a result, society as a whole suffers. David took individual responsibility for his role in the destruction of the plague. His example of repentance, investment, and action is one for us all. Significant and overwhelming problems exist in our neighborhoods, communities, and families. But David shows us that one person taking responsibility and obediently following the Lord can have a life-altering impact on the masses.

Application for Activation

Although we are Christians, we can have a tendency to take God's grace and mercy for granted. Because of Christ's sacrifice, repentance can seem too easy and get pushed aside. However, verbally and decisively "turning away" from our sin has the same effect as we see here—it pleases God, repairs a breach in our relationship, serving as an act of worship.

Consider any breaches that exist in your relationships. Are there people you need to forgive? Pray that God will give you strength to do so. Are there ways that you have sinned against others that have impacted them—in minor or major ways? Accept responsibility for your actions. Seek forgiveness and see what actions can be taken to restore the relationship.

Follow the Spirit

What God wants me to do:

_____

_____

_____

_____

Remember Your Thoughts

Special insights I have learned:

_____

_____

_____

_____

More Light on the Text

1 Chronicles 17:1, 3–4, 11–14; 21:18, 21–27

David devoted his monarchy to the restoration of public worship. He instituted liturgical worship and praise with the introduction of the musicianship of the Levites. The entrance of the Ark into the national capital of Jerusalem moved the people into a realm of prominence among the other nations in ways that Israel never before experienced. All of this was centered on their worship and praise of Jehovah, the one true God. Our text today moves beyond David's restoration of worship as a national practice and introduces the idea that David had come to a point in his life where he felt uncomfortable living in secure surroundings that were, in his opinion, grander than where the Ark was kept.

17:1 Now it came to pass, as David sat in his house, that David said to Nathan the prophet, Lo, I dwell in an house of cedars, but the ark of the covenant of the LORD remaineth under curtains.

3 And it came to pass the same night, that the word of God came to Nathan, saying, 4 Go and tell David my servant, Thus saith the LORD, Thou shalt not build me an house to dwell in:

David's home may have been built with timber from a species of cedar, *Cedrus libani,* an evergreen that grows to a huge size and is known for its durability. Cedar wood will be used in Solomon's palace as well and in the Temple. The use of cedar in the building became synonymous with affluence (Song of Solomon 8:9, Jeremiah 22:14). David's statement to Nathan implies that the idea of the Lord's dwelling being insufficient has either been bothering him or is a revelation that now takes hold and causes him concern. David has done for the Lord what he thinks is good. In fact, the return of the Ark and the new priority of worship were very good. Now, however, less concerned with external enemies, David realizes that he can do better and wants to fully honor the dwelling place of the Ark of the Covenant.

Part of David's concern is probably that the entire Tabernacle and its furnishings are not in Jerusalem. The Levites continue to worship God in Jerusalem before the Ark, but the priests are also presenting the offerings and sacrifices of the people before the brazen altar in Gibeon (see 1 Chronicles 16: 37–43). Theologians and biblical scholars alike are at a loss regarding why David did not return the Tabernacle and all of its furnishings to Jerusalem at the same time he returned the Ark. Perhaps the focus is on restoring the prominence of the Ark by showing those who took it that the nation is now unified under God. Whatever the reason, only the Ark itself resides in Jerusalem, and now David expresses his concern for unified worship in a more appropriate place.

Nathan is David's chief advisor, and on this occasion, David shares his innermost thoughts with Nathan regarding the place of the Ark. Nathan is a prophet about whom little is known except for his role as advisor to David and later to Solomon and his mother, Bathsheba. Nathan is not afraid to speak the truth to David and always spoke to the king with sound counsel based on his own faithfulness to God (2 Samuel 12:1–14). Prior to this lesson text, Nathan sought God before giving David advice, and David obviously respected Nathan as a confidant and friend. Nathan's original response is to tell David to move forward with his plans (v. 2).

Apparently, to both Nathan and David it seems that David's heart is in the right place. But when the Lord visits Nathan that night, the prophet is told to go back to David and tell him not to build the house because God is not in the plan. This does not imply that God is not with David; God refers to David as his "servant" (Heb. '*ebed,* **EH-bed**). But God does make clear that He does not want David to establish a permanent dwelling place for the Ark and the furnishings of the Tabernacle.

11 And it shall come to pass, when thy days be expired that thou must go to be with thy fathers, that I will raise up thy seed after thee,

which shall be of thy sons; and I will establish his kingdom. **12 He shall build me an house, and I will stablish his throne for ever. 13 I will be his father, and he shall be my son: and I will not take my mercy away from him, as I took it from him that was before thee: 14 But I will settle him in mine house and in my kingdom for ever: and his throne shall be established for evermore.**

David's son, Solomon, will build a house for the Ark and the throne of Solomon will be established "forever" (Heb. *'olam*, **oh-LAHM**). This Hebrew phrase means without ending and for an indefinite period. Although David is denied the privilege of building a house for the Ark, God let him know that the Ark will continue to be a focal point of worship for the Israelites. Solomon will be the one to build the house for the Ark. God promises that unlike Saul, from whom God took the kingdom, Solomon will always have God's mercy. These are powerful words that Nathan delivers to David.

In addition, these verses indicate that ultimately, through David's lineage, Christ will come, who will rule forever. As Christians, it should bring us great joy to know that we can and do live in covenant with God. Moreover, we can find great comfort in knowing that God delivers on His promises—nothing can occur that will void God's Word.

21:18 Then the angel of the LORD commanded Gad to say to David, that David should go up, and set up an altar unto the LORD the threshingfloor of Ornan the Jebusite.

21 And as David came to Ornan, Ornan looked and saw David, and went out of the threshingfloor, and bowed himself to David with his face to the ground.

David sins against the Lord by taking a census when he should not have, even when

his general Joab warns him not to do it (1 Chronicles 21:1–6). As a result of the prophet Gad, a seer, tells David the Lord will give him an option of punishment. David prays for God's mercy, and God's judgment is limited to a three-day plague (21:7–15). The angel of the Lord is on its way to destroy Jerusalem because of David's disobedience, but David intercedes for his city, taking responsibility for his action and pleading for God's mercy on Jerusalem (21:16–17). The angel responds, speaking to Gad the seer, that David is to build an altar to the Lord in the threshing floor owned by Ornan. Ornan, whose name is also spelled Araunah (NLT), is a Jebusite. He sees the angel and hides, bowed to the ground (21:19–20).

There is an interesting parallel here in that David bows himself to the angel and Ornan bows himself to both the angel and to David. The man reverences the anointed ones of God, both angelic and earthly. He is terrified that the angel of the Lord came to destroy him. He responds to the situation with humility, waiting for instruction for how he should respond to God's messenger and the king. Ornan is also of note because he is a Jebusite. He is a foreigner, not an Israelite or even a follower of God (cf. 2 Samuel 24:23). Jerusalem had been a Jebusite city before David conquered it, which makes it surprising that a Jebusite still lives here instead of being cleansed from the land (as God commanded with all Canaanites). Nevertheless, God chooses a foreigner's threshing floor as the place for His altar.

22 Then David said to Ornan, Grant me the place of this threshingfloor, that I may build an altar therein unto the LORD: thou shalt grant it me for the full price: that the plague may be stayed from the people. 23 And Ornan said unto David, Take it to thee, and let my lord the king do that which is good in his eyes: lo, I give thee the oxen

189

also for burnt offerings, and the threshing instruments for wood, and the wheat for the meat offering; I give it all. 24 And king David said to Ornan, Nay; but I will verily buy it for the full price: for I will not take that which is thine for the LORD, nor offer burnt offerings without cost. 25 So David gave to Ornan for the place six hundred shekels of gold by weight.

David can take the field from Ornan by force or try to exercise his power and authority as king to receive it for free. Ornan certainly wants the plague to stop and is willing to give up what he has to protect himself and his family. This man certainly recognizes that his own life and the lives of others are more important than property. He goes a step further by offering everything that he has to provide for his family to the Lord. Ornan recognizes the power and severity of God and the king and willingly submits all he has to their service. But David acts in honesty and responsibility, placing the blame for the Lord's judgment back on himself. He will not let an innocent man pay the cost for his sin.

This is definitely a lesson for believers in positions of authority. When we are leaders—whether in our homes, organizations, congregations, or communities—we must take responsibility for our wrong actions and face the consequences rather than making those we lead pay for our poor decisions. David is also using the opportunity to buy the land at full price. He is willing to pay the full amount for what he needed from Ornan because of the use of the land for the Lord was worth it.

David's words in verse 24 are piercing for us as believers. He will not try to give a sacrifice to God that did not cost him anything. Indeed if he takes the offerings from Ornan for nothing, they will not be sacrifices for

David at all. According to some scholars, the amount of gold David paid was worth around two hundred thousand dollars. God is worthy of the offerings that cost us something; that reminds us that the things we offer are far less important than the God we offer things to. It is God who gives us the ability to offer in the first place. David shows a truly repentant heart by showing God is worthy of his costly sacrifice.

26 And David built there an altar unto the LORD, and offered burnt offerings and peace offerings, and called upon the LORD; and he answered him from heaven by fire upon the altar of burnt offering. 27 And the LORD commanded the angel; and he put up his sword again into the sheath thereof.

David is faithful by obeying the Lord's instructions. He builds an altar at Ornan's field and sacrifices offerings to God there. David prays, and the Lord answers by fire, which foreshadows the way God will respond to Solomon's offering at the dedication of the Temple near this very spot (2 Chronicles 7:1). The Lord is pleased with David's offering and shows mercy by having the angel stop the plague and the potential destruction of Jerusalem.

Sources:

Global Study Bible, English Standard Version. Wheaton, IL: Crossway Publishers, 2012. 572–576.

Keener, Craig S., *The IVP Bible Background Commentary: Old Testament.* Downers Grove, IL: Intervarsity Press, 1993. 332–333, 353–354.

Radmacher, Earl D., ed. *Nelson Study Bible, New King James Version.* Nashville, TN: Thomas Nelson Publishers, 1997. 690–696.

Ryrie, Charles C. *Ryrie Study Bible, New International Version.* Chicago, IL: Moody Press. 1986. 560–564.

Unger, Merrill F. *The New Unger's Bible Dictionary.* Chicago, IL: Moody Press, 1988. 692–693.

Walvoord, John F., and Roy B. Zuck, eds. *The Bible Knowledge Commentary: Old Testament.* Wheaton, IL: Victor Books, SP Publications, Inc., 1983. 607, 610–611.

Zondervan Study Bible, New International Version. Grand Rapids, MI: Zondervan Publishers, 2002. 606–610.

Say It Correctly

Araunah. uh-**RAW**-nuh.
Ornan. or-**NON**.

Daily Bible Readings

MONDAY
David Cannot Build the Temple
(1 Chronicles 22:6–13)

TUESDAY
Solomon to Build the Temple
(1 Chronicles 28:2–10)

WEDNESDAY
Ornan's Land Is Site of Temple
(1 Chronicles 21:28–22:1)

THURSDAY
God Needs No House
(2 Samuel 7:1–11)

FRIDAY
God's Makes a House for David
(1 Chronicles 17:7–10)

SATURDAY
The Lord Regards the Lowly
(Psalm 138)

SUNDAY
Two Houses Firmly Settled
(1 Chronicles 17:1, 3–4, 11–14; 21:18, 21–27)

Notes

_____

_____

_____

_____

Teaching Tips

Words You Should Know

A. Magnify (v. 46) *megaluno* (Gk.)—To enlarge, to ascribe greatness to someone

B. Handmaiden (v. 48) *doule* (Gk.)—Female servant or slave

Teacher Preparation

Unifying Principle—Graciously Accepting Praise. People often wonder if they truly deserve the praise that others give them. How can we be gracious about the honors we receive? When Elisabeth called her blessed, Mary humbly praised God, confessing that all that had happened to her was in fulfillment of God's great plan of redemption.

A. Read the Bible Background and Devotional Reading.

B. Pray for your students and lesson clarity.

C. Read the lesson Scripture in multiple translations.

O—Open the Lesson

A. Begin the class with prayer.

B. Recite what God has done for you and your family. Name God's promises. What promises do you rely on? What promises have you seen God fulfill?

C. Have the students read the Aim for Change and the In Focus story.

D. Ask students how events like those in the story weigh on their hearts and how they can view these events from a faith perspective.

P—Present the Scriptures

A. Read the Focal Verses and discuss the Background and The People, Places, and Times sections.

B. Have the class share what Scriptures stand out for them and why, with particular emphasis on today's context.

E—Explore the Meaning

A. Use In Depth or More Light on the Text to facilitate a deeper discussion of the lesson text.

B. Pose the questions in Search the Scriptures and Discuss the Meaning.

C. Discuss the Liberating Lesson and Application for Activation sections.

N—Next Steps for Application

A. Summarize the value of God's indwelling presence in their lives through the presence and power of the Holy Spirit.

B. End class with a commitment to pray for the roles we play in furthering God's kingdom.

Worship Guide

For the Superintendent or Teacher
Theme: The Lord Is with You
Song: "Mary's Song of Praise: The Magnificat"
Devotional Reading: 1 Samuel 2:1–10

The Lord Is with You

Bible Background • LUKE 1:39–56
Printed Text • LUKE 1:39–56 | Devotional Reading • 1 SAMUEL 2:1–10

Aim for Change

By the end of the lesson, we will: SURVEY the themes present in Mary's song of praise, VALUE Mary's place in the unfolding story of God's saving work, and COMMIT to our own roles in furthering God's kingdom.

In Focus

Tyrone was an account executive for one of the biggest accounting firms in the country. He praised God for his great success and his climb up the corporate ladder. What separated him from other account executives was his integrity. His reputation added value to his company. Now the company wished to use Tyrone's name to cheat their vendors out of excess revenues. They offered Tyrone a substantial salary increase, more perks, and a spot in the Who's Who in the business sector.

He wrestled with the decision. Refusing to go along with the company's plan would likely damage his career and cost him financially. As a young newlywed with a child on the way, what should he do? Could Tyrone stay committed to his Christian convictions with his social status and such great material rewards at stake?

After fasting and praying with his wife for three days, Tyrone gave his company a response. Although he was committed to excelling in his career and providing for his family, he understood that devotion to God came first. Therefore, he respectfully declined their offer. Instead, he presented an alternative plan to the senior partners, one designed to increase the company's revenue. The proposal was adopted and eventually successfully implemented.

How are your values shaped? Compare your prayer life at home and at church.

Keep in Mind

"And Mary said, My soul doth magnify the Lord, And my spirit hath rejoiced in God my Saviour" (Luke 1:46-47, KJV).

"Mary responded, 'Oh, how my soul praises the Lord. How my spirit rejoices in God my Savior!'" (Luke 1:46–47, NLT).

Focal Verses

KJV Luke 1:39 And Mary arose in those days, and went into the hill country with haste, into a city of Juda;

40 And entered into the house of Zacharias, and saluted Elisabeth.

41 And it came to pass, that, when Elisabeth heard the salutation of Mary, the babe leaped in her womb; and Elisabeth was filled with the Holy Ghost:

42 And she spake out with a loud voice, and said, Blessed art thou among women, and blessed is the fruit of thy womb.

43 And whence is this to me, that the mother of my Lord should come to me?

44 For, lo, as soon as the voice of thy salutation sounded in mine ears, the babe leaped in my womb for joy.

45 And blessed is she that believed: for there shall be a performance of those things which were told her from the Lord.

46 And Mary said, My soul doth magnify the Lord,

47 And my spirit hath rejoiced in God my Saviour.

48 For he hath regarded the low estate of his handmaiden: for, behold, from henceforth all generations shall call me blessed.

49 For he that is mighty hath done to me great things; and holy is his name.

50 And his mercy is on them that fear him from generation to generation.

51 He hath shewed strength with his arm; he hath scattered the proud in the imagination of their hearts.

52 He hath put down the mighty from their seats, and exalted them of low degree.

53 He hath filled the hungry with good things; and the rich he hath sent empty away.

54 He hath helped his servant Israel, in remembrance of his mercy;

55 As he spake to our fathers, to Abraham, and to his seed for ever.

NLT Luke 1:39 A few days later Mary hurried to the hill country of Judea, to the town

40 where Zechariah lived. She entered the house and greeted Elizabeth.

41 At the sound of Mary's greeting, Elizabeth's child leaped within her, and Elizabeth was filled with the Holy Spirit.

42 Elizabeth gave a glad cry and exclaimed to Mary, "God has blessed you above all women, and your child is blessed.

43 Why am I so honored, that the mother of my Lord should visit me?

44 When I heard your greeting, the baby in my womb jumped for joy.

45 You are blessed because you believed that the Lord would do what he said."

46 Mary responded, "Oh, how my soul praises the Lord.

47 How my spirit rejoices in God my Savior!

48 For he took notice of his lowly servant girl, and from now on all generations will call me blessed.

49 For the Mighty One is holy, and he has done great things for me.

50 He shows mercy from generation to generation to all who fear him.

51 His mighty arm has done tremendous things! He has scattered the proud and haughty ones.

52 He has brought down princes from their thrones and exalted the humble.

53 He has filled the hungry with good things and sent the rich away with empty hands.

54 He has helped his servant Israel and remembered to be merciful.

55 For he made this promise to our ancestors, to Abraham and his children forever."

56 And Mary abode with her about three months, and returned to her own house.

56 Mary stayed with Elizabeth about three months and then went back to her own home.

The People, Places, and Times

Mary. After marrying Joseph, Mary bore several children: James, Joseph, Judas (Jude), Simon, and some daughters. She gave birth to Jesus in Bethlehem while she and Joseph were engaged, but not yet married.

Elisabeth. The meaning of Elisabeth's name is "Oath of God." Her kinship ties included being the wife of the priest Zacharias, the cousin of Mary, and the mother of John the Baptist. Before the birth of Jesus, Mary spent months with Elisabeth.

Judea. Bound by the Jordan River and the Dead Sea on the east across to the Mediterranean Sea on the west, Judea was first used as a name for a Persian province (Ezra 5:8). It later became a Roman province (Matthew 2:1). North of the province were the other Roman provinces of Galilee and Phoenicia.

Background

Two women, Mary and Elisabeth, whose lives probably seemed very different were joined together in the most spectacular event known to humanity. Both women miraculously conceived. Elisabeth was well past the normal childbearing years. Her relative, Mary, was propelled into motherhood sooner than she anticipated and in a manner she could not have imagined. Both Mary and Elisabeth were joyous over the events taking place in their lives. Both were pleased that God somehow saw fit to use them as part of His divine plan. Motherhood did not fit conveniently into the lifestyle of either woman at the time each conceived. Nevertheless, each woman yielded herself to the will of God. After the angel Gabriel left Mary, she paid a visit to Elisabeth, who was in the final months of pregnancy. Luke tells their story of honoring Mary's baby, Jesus, before His birth because He would become the Savior of the world.

At-A-Glance

1. Elisabeth Honors God
(Luke 1:39-45)
2. Mary Honors God Personally (vv. 46–49)
3. Mary Honors God for Her Community
(vv. 50–56)

In Depth

1. Elisabeth Honors God (Luke 1:39-45)

Mary's visit to Elisabeth brings together the two events that are first mentioned in Luke's account. The visit gives readers more insight into the relationship between the two women's sons. At the sound of Mary's voice, the baby inside Elisabeth's womb leaps, and Elisabeth is filled with the Holy Spirit. The phrase "filled with the Holy Spirit" lets us know that Elisabeth is prophesying in the power of the Holy Spirit as she declares Mary's baby to be her Lord. She gives honor to Jesus before He is even born.

The attention then shifts to Mary, who will give birth to the world's Savior. Once again it affirms that Mary is blessed among women. Elisabeth, John the Baptist's mother, proclaims her unworthiness to be honored by a visit from the mother of the Savior. By leaping in his mother's womb, John the Baptist, the forerunner of Christ, gives testimony to the coming Messiah even before he is born. The angel Gabriel already said that John would be filled with the Holy Spirit even before birth (v. 15). God owes Elisabeth nothing, yet through His grace, He gives her so much. Elisabeth calls Mary blessed and praises her for her obedience. She gives honor to God for allowing her to take part in His glorious plan.

Why is it important to celebrate those who are honored by God?

2. Mary Honors God Personally (vv. 46–49)

Mary's song is called "The Magnificat" (vv. 46–55) and it is about how blessed she is. From a worldly perspective, this might not seem like a blessing. She is poor and a woman, two things that may have made her contemporaries think of her as inferior. Mary comes from Nazareth, a town that is poorly thought of in the area. Most importantly, she is pregnant while she is engaged to a respectable man who is not the father of her child. Where are the blessings in such a situation? Because Mary understands, she gives honor to God her Savior. Then, thinking about the news from the angel Gabriel, Mary praises God for choosing her for this blessing, in spite of her humble status. She realizes that her status is not a disadvantage in the sight of the Lord.

How can we focus on God's blessing despite the circumstances around us?

3. Mary Honors God for Her Community (vv. 50–56)

Mary trusts the Lord to show mercy to His people because she knows that the Scripture details how God blessed His people in the past. This hope is based on the knowledge of how God worked before. God kept His promise to give Israel the Messiah and as a result is keeping the covenant to restore justice, blessing, and His presence among His people. Based upon how He blessed His people, Mary knows that He will continue to do so in the future. As we look closely at the things that Mary sings about concerning how God acts, we see that when Jesus comes to the earth, He brings about a moral revolution regarding pride. Pride (v. 51)

has no place in the Christian life because our standard is Jesus Christ. When we see ourselves compared to Him, we realize how far we are from how God desires us to be. Then, we see a social revolution (v. 52). Jesus brings an end to the labels and titles that people think elevate them. In the sight of our Lord, the lowest person is just as important as the person with money and power. Jesus also brings an economic revolution, seen when the first Christians come together and share their wealth, the rich with the poor, such that everyone has what they needed (Acts 2:44-45). We live in a very materialistic and greedy society, but God is merciful and remembers His promises (vv. 54–55). Mary's song reminds us that, because of Jesus, Christians should have a different set of values than those of the world.

How does Mary's song encourage us to honor God and help our community?

Search the Scriptures

1. What specific blessings does Mary thank God for (Luke 1:46–49)?

2. What sort of people does God bless (vv. 50–53)?

3. What attributes of God does Mary recite (vv. 50–55)?

Discuss The Meaning

1. How can we honor God and bless others during the Christmas season instead of focusing on ourselves?

2. How have you seen God at work in your family to fulfill His promises and advance His will?

Liberating Lesson

Mary's Magnificat declares that the birth of Jesus Christ dethrones the powerful, humbles the proud, and brings provision to the poor. The hungry are fed while the wealthy are left empty at the coming of Jesus. Often we do not

197

talk about this great reversal that Jesus brings when we think about Christmas. We can easily get caught up in the commercialization and secularization of Jesus' birth that permeates our culture. Children think of Santa Claus, presents, and vacations. Adults think of shopping, big meals, and decorations. We may think about special worship services where we sing Christmas carols about a baby. But when was the last time we talked about Christmas as the coming of God's justice to the earth? Today's lesson reminds us that Jesus was not born to bring presents and holiday cheer. He came to bring justice, righteousness, and the reign of God to the earth. Those who are great must humble themselves before Jesus; those who are least find their hope of provision and exaltation in Him. We are called to share God's peace and goodwill during the holiday season, but we are also called to share His truth and justice for the oppressed.

How will you honor God's call to justice and care for the poor this Christmas?

Application for Activation

When we study God's Word, we are reminded of His promises. Our faith is shown in the way we obey God. Let's take a closer look at how we express honor for God in our actions. It can often be easier to honor God with special worship services, repeating Christian sayings, or being kind to those who are kind to us. But Mary and Elisabeth surrender and obey God when He places them in unexpected positions. They proclaim God's faithfulness and devote themselves to nurturing their children who are called by God to unexpected lives. What has God called you to do to honor Him that may take you out of your comfort zone or differ from the expectations of others or yourself? Will you serve someone less fortunate? Care for a child in your extended family? Speak about the cause of the poor? Give a gift to someone who isn't expecting one from you? Mary's obedience amid her unexpected situation gives honor to God! In the upcoming week, follow Mary's lead and honor God in the way you obey Him despite your circumstances.

Follow the Spirit

What God wants me to do:

_____

_____

_____

_____

Remember Your Thoughts

Special insights I have learned:

_____

_____

_____

_____

More Light on the Text

Luke 1:39–56

39 And Mary arose in those days, and went into the hill country with haste, into a city of Judah;

Mary loses no time in paying a visit to her relative, Elisabeth. She reacted when she learns from the angel that God also blessed Elisabeth (Luke 1:36). Mary is an ordinary girl of flesh and blood who has been chosen for a gigantic and unique task. Her visit to Elisabeth is to someone who has also been miraculously blessed. She is able to find encouragement and understanding. In Elisabeth's sixth month (v. 36), the angel Gabriel spoke to Mary. Her visit with Elisabeth lasts for approximately three months, just before the birth of John (vv. 56–57). Therefore, Mary must have left her home to go to visit Elisabeth almost immediately after the angel's visit. This immediacy is reflected in the wording that "Mary arose …and went … with haste." The expression "the hill country … into a city of Judah" does not locate the home of Elisabeth with any precision, but it shows that she is living in a rural area. Like many priestly families, Zacharias and Elizabeth live outside Jerusalem.

40 And entered into the house of Zacharias, and saluted Elisabeth. 41 And it came to pass, that, when Elisabeth heard the salutation of Mary, the babe leaped in her womb; and Elisabeth was filled with the Holy Ghost:

When Mary arrives at Elisabeth's home, not only does she find that Elisabeth is miraculously pregnant as the angel said but that Elisabeth knows, by the inspiration of the Holy Spirit, that Mary is going to be the mother of the Messiah (vv. 41–44). The moment that Mary greets Elisabeth, the baby leaps (Gk. *skirtao*, **skeer-TAH-oh,** to jump for joy) in his mother's womb. It is a natural phenomenon for an unborn child to make frequent movements, but John's movement this time is extraordinary. Elisabeth is filled with the Holy Spirit and interprets the movement of her baby as an expression of joy.

42 And she spake out with a loud voice, and said, Blessed art thou among women, and blessed is the fruit of thy womb.

The Greek word translated "spake out" (*anaphoneo*, **ah-na-fo-NEH-oh**) means "to raise the voice" or "to call out." Elisabeth raises her voice with a great cry of excitement. She greets Mary as blessed among women and names the same blessing for Mary's child.

"Blessed" here in Greek is *eulogeo* (**yew-low-GEH-oh**), which means to bless or speak well of. "Fruit of thy womb" refers to the baby inside Mary but also indicates the full humanity of Jesus. We confess that Jesus is fully divine and fully human, and this text reminds us that Christ truly comes into the world in a way that completely identifies with us.

43 And whence is this to me, that the mother of my Lord should come to me?

The use of the title "my Lord" suggests that Elisabeth recognizes, through the Holy Spirit, that Mary's child will be the Messiah (see 2:25–30; Psalm 110:1). She acknowledges that a much greater honor has been granted to Mary than to her. In humility of heart, she expresses her amazement and her privilege at being visited by the mother of her Lord. Elisabeth accepts, in grateful worship, God's gift to her. When she reconnects with Mary, to whom a greater gift has been given, she does not become jealous. She humbles herself and gives honor to Mary as the vessel God chooses and honors Jesus, recognizing that He is the long-awaited Messiah and Lord. Elisabeth's humility is also instructive. Her humble attitude opens the gates to true joy.

44 For, lo, as soon as the voice of thy salutation sounded in mine ears, the babe leaped in my womb for joy.

The Greek word *idou* (**ee-DOO,** "lo") often announces an unexpected and extraordinary event. Elisabeth explains to Mary that at her greeting, her own baby exulted for joy in her womb. The exultation of her baby is the sign from the Holy Spirit that enables her to recognize Mary for who she is.

45 And blessed is she that believed: for there shall be a performance of those things which were told her from the Lord.

Elisabeth further blesses (Gk. *makarios*, **mah-KAR-ee-oce**, "blessed," "happy") Mary. She tells Mary that the Lord blesses her faith. The Greek word for the word "for" is *hoti* (**HOE-tee**) and can be understood in two ways. Mary is either blessed because through her faith she believes God's promises will come true, or simply blessed because God's promises will come true. First, *hoti* can mean "that" as an object of "believed." In that case, it is to be translated as "Blessed is she that believed that there shall be a performance of those things which were told her from the Lord." This makes the statement an indication of Mary's faith. Second, *hoti* can be rendered as "because." In that case, it is to be translated as "Blessed is she that believed because there shall be a performance of those things which were told her from the Lord." Thus, the statement is an explanation of the happiness of Mary. Elisabeth affirms that the fulfillment will certainly happen. Mary believes and goes on believing the message from the Lord. She bores the immense honor and the immeasurable burden without losing faith. She remains humble and committed to the Lord. True faith gives happiness, and there is no true happiness without faith.

46 And Mary said, My soul doth magnify the Lord, 47 And my spirit hath rejoiced in God my Saviour. 48 For he hath regarded the low estate of his handmaiden: for, behold, from henceforth all generations shall call me blessed.

Mary's song is commonly referred to as "The Magnificat." It has several striking features. First, it is filled with Old Testament concepts and phrases, plus it seems to have been modeled on Hannah's prayer (1 Samuel 2:1–10). Second, the song reveals Mary's deep piety and knowledge of the Old Testament; a familiarity with the Scriptures is not unusual for that time. Third, in its essence, the song reveals a God who vindicates the downtrodden and ministers to the hungry (cf. 1 Samuel 2:5),

makes the poor sit with the nobles (v. 8), judges those who arrogantly oppose God (vv. 3, 7, 10; cf. Luke 1:51, 53), and topples the nobles from their places of power (Luke 1:52).

Mary's song can be divided into four parts. Verses 46–48 praise God for what He has done for Mary, a theme that continues into the first part of the next section. Verses 49–50 mention God's power, holiness, and mercy. Verses 51–53 show God's sovereign action in reversing certain social conditions. Finally, verses 54–56 recall God's mercy to Israel.

Mary responds to Elisabeth's Spirit-inspired utterances in a song. The word "magnify" (Gk. *megaluno*, **meh-gah-LOO-no**) literally means "to enlarge." Here it ascribes greatness to God. To magnify means to make something appear larger than what it already is in order to have a better and proper perception of it. Yet God cannot appear larger because He is already bigger than we can ever imagine. We often have a picture of God that is too small and contrived, so we need to magnify Him so we can have a bigger and better picture of Him. The song is an expression of praise for what God has done for Mary. It opens with the declaration of her intention to magnify God in song (v. 46), which parallels the affirmation that she finds joy in God who, enabling her in a miraculous way to become pregnant with the child of messianic hopes, now intervenes as Savior (v. 47). This happy state exists because God regards the afflicted state of His servant (v. 48). It is not that it indicates Mary has some personal and individual affliction; her affliction is simply that of God's people awaiting His saving intervention on their behalf. The Messiah has long been a symbol of liberation, freedom, and salvation to the Israelites (Isaiah 9:6). Israel believed that the coming of the Savior meant God was saving them from oppression.

This Savior bestows grace on Mary, and she responds with humility. She restates that she is only a "handmaiden" (Gk. *doule*, **DOO-lay**) of the Lord, as she said to the angel (v. 38). Mary is one of the lowest and most powerless people in that world, yet God uses her to bring salvation to all. Mary realizes that the grace God gives her is more than she deserves, and so she praises the Lord with a humble heart. Mary proclaims God and His glorious mercy to humanity. She proclaims the salvation of God, that comes through the promised Messiah, her Savior. The greatness of the work of God is that it is a universal blessing to all; Jesus comes so all people will be blessed. God blesses all because He is mighty and holy. He does a mighty work in the life of Mary that affects all people everywhere for all time. The King has come and will bring salvation.

49 For he that is mighty hath done to me great things; and holy is his name. 50 And his mercy is on them that fear him from generation to generation.

Mary proclaims God's power. She is in awe of "he that is mighty," the One whose great power has touched her life. The Greek word translated "great things" (*megaleios*, **meh-gah-LAY-oce**) recalls "magnify" (v. 46) as both share a root word meaning great or large. Mary proclaims God's holiness because God is to be set apart from all others. His very nature, His very being, is different. In this context, God's holy (Gk. *hagios*, **HA-gee-oce**) name has overtones of power and may be defined as His transcendent mightiness. Verse 50 is strongly reminiscent of Psalm 103:17, as Mary proclaims God's mercy. This act of God's mercy is for "generation upon generation", that is forever. God's mercy is His active faithfulness to His covenant with Israel, or more specifically, with those who follow Him. God has done mighty works through history for His followers and continues to do so even now.

51 He hath shewed strength with his arm; he hath scattered the proud in the imagination of their hearts. 52 He hath put down the mighty from their seats, and exalted them of low degree. 53 He hath filled the hungry with good things; and the rich he hath sent empty away.

Mary proceeds from adoration to celebration. She speaks about the future and proclaims what the Messiah's coming will accomplish. She prophetically speaks merging past and future, as though the child yet to be born has already lived and done His mighty work in the world. She recognizes the strength of God's "arm" which, in old days, wrought such mighty things for Israel. Mary shows that God will reverse the order of things on earth. In times past and now more fully with the coming of the Messiah, the Lord will scatter the proud "in the imagination of their hearts." The Greek word *dianoia* (**dee-ah-NOY-ah**), translated "imagination," ordinarily refers to the "mind" as a distinct aspect of self, apart from the "heart" (Gk. *kardia*, **kar-DEE-ah**). Here, however, the heart and mind work together to puff up the proud. The Lord will dethrone the mighty and exalt the humble. The mighty are those who sit in positions of power, authority, and influence over others. Those who are rich only in the things of this world will be stripped of all their earthly goods and sent away empty. And those who have nothing of this world but who put their trust in God will receive all the good things that God will provide.

54 He hath helped his servant Israel, in remembrance of his mercy; 55 As he spake to our fathers, to Abraham, and to his seed for ever. 56 And Mary abode with her about three months, and returned to her own house.

Mary recognizes that the salvation her Son will bring is rooted in God's covenant with Abraham. Mary recalls what God has done both for the nation and its patriarchs. She mentions two specific times God provided for His people. First, God remembered His mercy, which Israel desperately needed. In Mary's day, God's people were oppressed by the Romans. They were desperate in their need and search for deliverance, so desperate that many were turning to false messiahs to escape their predicament. Some were even finding their security in the Roman state and in humanistic answers instead of God. It was at such a time Mary proclaims the Lord remembered His mercy. Second, and more importantly, God remembered His promise of the Messiah made to Israel. The promise has now been fulfilled. God sent the Messiah, the Savior of the world.

Sources:

Cox, Steven L. "Angel." *Holman Illustrated Bible Dictionary*. Nashville, TN: Holman Reference, 2003. 66–67.

Hughes, R. Kent. *Luke (Volume One): That You May Know the Truth. Preaching the Word*. Wheaton, IL: Crossway, 1998.

Keener, Craig S. *The IVP Bible Background Commentary: New Testament*. Downers Grove, IL: IVP Academic, 1994.

Unger, Merrill F., R. K. Harrison, Howard Vos, and Cyril Barber. *The New Unger's Bible Dictionary*. Chicago, IL: Moody Publishers, 1988.

Say It Correctly

Magnificat. mag-**NIH**-fih-**COT**.

Daily Bible Readings

MONDAY
John the Baptist Born to Elizabeth
(Luke 1:57-66)

TUESDAY
Zechariah Blesses God for John's Ministry
(Luke 1:67-79)

WEDNESDAY
Young Woman's Pregnancy Is Sign of Immanuel
(Isaiah 7:10-17)

THURSDAY
Virgin Conception Announced to Mary
(Luke 1:26-33)

FRIDAY
Mary Accepts Miracle of Pregnancy
(Luke 1:34-38)

SATURDAY
Joseph Obediently Honors Mary's Role
(Matthew 1:18-25)

SUNDAY
Blessed Mothers of the Faithful
(Luke 1:39-56)

Notes

Teaching Tips

Words You Should Know

A. House (v. 16) *bayit* (Heb.)— Household, lineage

B. Servant (v. 17) *'ebed* (Heb.)—Slave, bondservant, subject (of a king), or worshiper

Teacher Preparation

Unifying Principle—A Greater Plan. When a person receives a great promise, he or she may feel honored. How does one respond when one has been so honored? When God promised to make him the head of a great dynasty, King David prayed a prayer of gratitude, praise, and petition.

A. Read the Bible Background and Devotional Readings.

B. Pray for your students and lesson clarity.

C. Read the lesson Scripture in multiple translations.

O—Open the Lesson

A. Begin the class with prayer.

B. Have students discuss their responses to "What does David's prayer teach each of us about God?"

C. Have the students read the Aim for Change and the In Focus story.

D. Ask students how events like those in the story weigh on their hearts and how they can view these events from a faith perspective.

P—Present the Scriptures

A. Read the Focal Verses and discuss the Background and The People, Places, and Times sections.

B. Have the class share what Scriptures stand out for them and why, with particular emphasis on today's context.

E—Explore the Meaning

A. Use In Depth or More Light on the Text to facilitate a deeper discussion of the lesson text.

B. Pose the questions in Search the Scriptures and Discuss the Meaning.

C. Discuss the Liberating Lesson and Application for Activation sections.

N—Next Steps for Application

A. Summarize the value of praying and being thankful to the Lord.

B. End class with a commitment to pray for listening and being obedient to God.

Worship Guide

For the Superintendent or Teacher
Theme: David's Prayer
Song: "Holy, Holy, Holy! Lord, God Almighty!"
Devotional Reading: Psalm 89:19–37

David's Prayer

Bible Background • 1 CHRONICLES 17:16–27
Printed Text • 1 CHRONICLES 17:16–27 | Devotional Reading • PSALM 89:19–37

Aim for Change

By the end of the lesson, we will: RECOGNIZE the significance of David's prayer in its historical context, ASPIRE to become faithful in the way David expresses in his prayer, and EMBRACE David's prayer as a model for our own prayers of gratitude and praise.

In Focus

Michelle worked for 40 years at the telephone company. She started working there as a high school graduate and faithfully stayed with the company. She notified her boss in October that she would be retiring at the end of November.

The week before her retirement, Michelle was in her office and had tears in her eyes thinking about how grateful she was to be employed for so long. She heard a knock on her door. Mr. Butler, a co-worker stopped by.

"Hey, the boss called for a staff meeting this afternoon," said Mr. Butler.

"Oh no! I thought I could escape before Mr. Hensley called for another staff meeting."

"OK. I will see you at 3:00 p.m." Mr. Butler left her office.

After her lunch, Michelle went to the meeting. As she opened the door everyone in the room shouted, "Congratulations, Michelle!" Michelle stood at the door in shock.

Mr. Hensley said, "Michelle, we wanted to thank you for all you have contributed to the company. I want you to come take the seat at the head of the table. On behalf of the company, I would like to present you with two tickets for a fourteen-day vacation to anywhere in the world! I hope you enjoy your retirement."

"I do not feel like I deserve all of this, but thank you," Michelle said.

How does it feel when you receive unexpected blessings?

Keep in Mind

"O LORD, there is none like thee, neither is there any God beside thee, according to all that we have heard with our ears" (1 Chronicles 17:20, KJV).

"O LORD, there is no one like you. We have never even heard of another God like you!"
(1 Chronicles 17:20, NLT).

Focal Verses

KJV **1 Chronicles 17:16** And David the king came and sat before the LORD, and said, Who am I, O LORD God, and what is mine house, that thou hast brought me hitherto?

17 And yet this was a small thing in thine eyes, O God; for thou hast also spoken of thy servant's house for a great while to come, and hast regarded me according to the estate of a man of high degree, O LORD God.

18 What can David speak more to thee for the honour of thy servant? for thou knowest thy servant.

19 O LORD, for thy servant's sake, and according to thine own heart, hast thou done all this greatness, in making known all these great things.

20 O LORD, there is none like thee, neither is there any God beside thee, according to all that we have heard with our ears.

21 And what one nation in the earth is like thy people Israel, whom God went to redeem to be his own people, to make thee a name of greatness and terribleness, by driving out nations from before thy people whom thou hast redeemed out of Egypt?

22 For thy people Israel didst thou make thine own people for ever; and thou, LORD, becamest their God.

23 Therefore now, LORD, let the thing that thou hast spoken concerning thy servant and concerning his house be established for ever, and do as thou hast said.

24 Let it even be established, that thy name may be magnified for ever, saying, The LORD of hosts is the God of Israel, even a God to Israel: and let the house of David thy servant be established before thee.

25 For thou, O my God, hast told thy servant that thou wilt build him an house: therefore thy servant hath found in his heart to pray before thee.

NLT **1 Chronicles 17:16** Then King David went in and sat before the LORD and prayed, "Who am I, O LORD God, and what is my family, that you have brought me this far?

17 And now, O God, in addition to everything else, you speak of giving your servant a lasting dynasty! You speak as though I were someone very great, O LORD God!

18 "What more can I say to you about the way you have honored me? You know what your servant is really like.

19 For the sake of your servant, O LORD, and according to your will, you have done all these great things and have made them known.

20 "O LORD, there is no one like you. We have never even heard of another God like you!

21 What other nation on earth is like your people Israel? What other nation, O God, have you redeemed from slavery to be your own people? You made a great name for yourself when you redeemed your people from Egypt. You performed awesome miracles and drove out the nations that stood in their way.

22 You chose Israel to be your very own people forever, and you, O LORD, became their God.

23 "And now, O LORD, I am your servant; do as you have promised concerning me and my family. May it be a promise that will last forever.

24 And may your name be established and honored forever so that everyone will say, 'The LORD of Heaven's Armies, the God of Israel, is Israel's God!' And may the house of your servant David continue before you forever.

25 "O my God, I have been bold enough to pray to you because you have revealed to your servant that you will build a house for him—a dynasty of kings!

26 And now, LORD, thou art God, and hast promised this goodness unto thy servant:

27 Now therefore let it please thee to bless the house of thy servant, that it may be before thee for ever: for thou blessest, O LORD, and it shall be blessed for ever.

26 For you are God, O LORD. And you have promised these good things to your servant.

27 And now, it has pleased you to bless the house of your servant, so that it will continue forever before you. For when you grant a blessing, O LORD, it is an eternal blessing!"

The People, Places, and Times

Redemption. The main idea of redemption is that of buying back someone from bondage, or ransoming or avenging them. God is the Redeemer of Israel (Isaiah 43:1, 14), purchasing them from their literal slavery in Egypt and their metaphorical slavery to sin. Redemption of the firstborn (Exodus 13:2, Numbers 18:15–16) was a ceremony performed to redeem the child back to his or her parents from God through sacrificial offerings and to recognize God as the owner and giver of life. Christ is the Redeemer of the Church (Galatians 3:13), redeeming us from the law. God paid an inestimable price to redeem us and restore us to a full relationship with him (cf. 1 Corinthians 6:20). Instead of silver or gold, we were redeemed with the precious blood of God's only Son. The mission of God's Son was to "redeem" or to emancipate from slavery to the law those who were heirs to the promise, in order that they might receive the inheritance, namely "the adoption of sons."

Background

King David oversaw the move of the Ark of the Covenant to Jerusalem (1 Chronicles 15–16). He obeyed the law and only permitted the Levites to carry the Ark to its new location. King David incorporated praise and worship as part of the celebration. The musicians sang; played instruments such as harps, lyres, and cymbals; and gave shouts of praise as they celebrated the occasion. It was a joyful event!

David soon realized as he sat in his beautiful house made of cedar that the Ark of the Covenant was inside a tent (1 Chronicles 17:1–15). When David talked with the prophet Nathan, Nathan gave his personal opinion that David should do as he desired because God was with him. However, later Nathan had to retract his opinion after God spoke to him (cf. 2 Samuel 7:1–17). David's son, Solomon would be the one who built the Temple (1 Chronicles 17:11, 22:6–10). God also promised "I will establish his throne forever" (17:12). This is fulfilled in Solomon and his heirs, which includes Jesus Christ (Luke 1:31–33). God was going to establish a dynasty through King David's family. Nathan shared this promise with David. This is known as the Davidic Covenant. The following section is David's prayer to God which in its totality is similar to 2 Samuel 7:18–29.

How does it feel when God gives you different directions than you originally expected?

At-A-Glance

1. Thanksgiving for God's Promise
(1 Chronicles 17:16–22)
2. Request for Confirmation of the Promise
(vv. 23–27)

In Depth

**1. Thanksgiving for God's Promise
(1 Chronicles 17:16–22)**

David loved God, and God loved David. When he received the promise of God from the prophet Nathan, he responded by going into the presence of God through prayer. David was a man who diligently prayed and sought God. But it is clear David was surprised by God's promise. He opened his prayer with a question and then comments about his unworthiness to receive such blessings from God. David calls himself "servant" ten times, which gives him the designation of someone of low status, showing he is humble before God (vv. 16–18). David did not feel like an important person, but God viewed him differently.

David did not have adequate words to express his gratitude to God. But he praised God, understanding that He had promised him something unearned and undeserved (vv. 19–20). It was all God's work. This is the same God who by His mighty power redeemed Israel from slavery in Egypt. And the other nations witnessed His power when He defeated them to make way for His chosen nation, the Israelites (vv. 21–22). David was grateful for God's blessings throughout the generations.

Why is it important to remain humble and grateful when God blesses us?

2. Request for Confirmation of the Promise (vv. 23–27)

David asks God to keep His promise concerning his house. David is hopeful but desires more assurance. In keeping His promise, God's name will be honored and praised for eternity (v. 24). When someone keeps their word, it gives them a good reputation. God's fulfillment of His promise would continue to do just that.

The closing words of David's prayer speak to who God is and once again requests, if it is God's pleasure, for God to keep His promise (vv. 26–27). Throughout the Bible, we can identify many of God's people who doubted and asked for confirmation of God's promises. We too may sometimes need help believing God's

Word when it seems so unimaginable and grand. Doubts are normal, but God's plans are trustworthy.

When we have doubts, what can we rely on to restore our faith?

Search The Scriptures

1. What was King David's posture when he prayed to God (1 Chronicles 17:16)?

2. What did God do for the people of Israel in the past (vv. 21–22)?

3. How would God's reputation be affected by keeping His promise to David (v. 24)?

Discuss The Meaning

1. Why did David use the term "servant" so often in his prayer?

2. What parts of the prayer reveal David's confidence in God's promise? How?

3. Based on Psalm 89:19–37, what further information can we learn about the Davidic Covenant?

Liberating Lesson

King David's intention to build a house for the Ark of the Covenant was admirable. He did not desire to live in a beautiful house while the Ark was in a tent. But God had other plans. Sometimes we have to change our plans because God desires to go in a different direction. It is better to yield and accept His will rather than follow our own ideas. King David felt humbled by the blessing, praised God, and accepted His decision. When we have to give up our plans to follow God, God wants us to trust Him. Based on God's faithfulness to us in the past, we can be guaranteed He will keep His promises now and in the future.

Application for Activation

Think about an occasion when God bestowed on you an undeserved blessing. Discuss how you felt. Did you share your testimony about

God's blessing with others? Write a prayer of thanksgiving and praise using King David's prayer as a model.

Follow the Spirit
What God wants me to do:

_____

_____

_____

_____

Remember Your Thoughts
Special insights I have learned:

_____

_____

_____

_____

More Light on the Text
1 Chronicles 17:16–27

David, the sweet psalmist of Israel prayed to the Lord in a manner similar to his songs and psalms (e.g., 1 Chronicles 16:7–36). David's prayer has three movements: (1) submission to God's will (17:16–19), (2) confession about God's person (17:20–22), and (3) petition for God's fulfillment of His promise (17:23–27). David's prayer is in response to God's declaration that David could not build a "house" (temple) for God, but that God would build a "house" (dynasty) for David. Although previously content to inquire of the Lord through Nathan the prophet (17:1–2), David is so moved by God's promise to build a "house" for him that he does not respond to

God through the prophet. Instead, he responds directly to God.

16 And David the king came and sat before the LORD, and said, Who am I, O LORD God, and what is mine house, that thou hast brought me hitherto? 17 And yet this was a small thing in thine eyes, O God; for thou hast also spoken of thy servant's house for a great while to come, and hast regarded me according to the estate of a man of high degree, O LORD God. 18 What can David speak more to thee for the honour of thy servant? for thou knowest thy servant. 19 O LORD, for thy servant's sake, and according to thine own heart, hast thou done all this greatness, in making known all these great things.

These introductory words are significant as they indicate David's position and his posture. This is but the second time that the chronicler mentions David's position as king, saying, the king "sat before the Lord." David is acutely aware that he is in the presence of the true King of Israel, the One who not only rules his life, but also the lives of his people Israel.

Since standing or lying prostrate were the more customary positions for prayer, some have questioned whether sitting was an appropriate posture for David to assume. There are a couple of ways to understand this posture, though. First, David might have sat down as one might collapse into a chair at hearing some astounding news. He was blown away at God's great news and could not support himself on his own feet anymore. Otherwise, David also might have taken a kneeling position, sitting down on His feet. This posture is easily recognized today as a worshipful one and was then as well. David provides a great example to us of the posture that we should assume when we pray. It should be the spiritual posture of seeking God's will and then submitting to it even when it may not be in alignment with our desire.

209

In the ancient world, a king could render no greater service than to build a house for his god as an act of homage to the deity responsible for establishing him on the throne. Therefore, it was natural for David to seek to honor his God in like manner and build a house for Him. Additionally, David was ashamed that the true King of Israel was confined to a tent-sanctuary (17:1), while he lived in a magnificent house of cedars (17:1). During Israel's grand celebration while bringing the Ark to Jerusalem, David danced before the Lord in praise (15:29). After the formal installation of the Ark of the Covenant, all the people went to their homes, and David returned to his home (16:43). David told the prophet, Nathan, that he wanted to build a permanent house for the Ark (17:1). It can probably be assumed that the return of the Ark and the celebration of praise played a role in David's desire to build a permanent sanctuary for the Lord. The covenant that God made with the house of David (17:3–15) is heightened in light of Israel's covenant renewal with God once the Ark, representing God's covenant and presence with His people, was now formally installed in Jerusalem.

The movement of the Ark to Jerusalem leads thematically to the establishment of God's covenant with David. Although David's desire was to honor God with a permanent temple, he was not permitted to build a house for God (17:4). On the other hand, it was God's expressed desire to honor his servant by building a house for David. "House" is the Hebrew *bayit* (**BAH-yeeth**) and is a key term, occurring fourteen times in 1 Chronicles 17. David's "house" would be a royal house, a dynasty that would originate with David but would never end. His kingdom and throne were to be understood as permanent (17:14). However, the Davidic Covenant gave the promise of kings from David's lineage. This was also a fulfillment of a provision in the Abrahamic Covenant that "kings will come out

of thee" (Genesis 17:6). Both covenants find their ultimate fulfillment in the person of Jesus Christ, Son of David and Son of Abraham the friend of God, the One who will reign and rule forever.

It is important to note that the Ark of the Covenant represented the presence of God as well as the corresponding blessings that flowed to God's people. For example, when the Ark was in the home of Obed-edom, God blessed his household (1 Chronicles 13:14). After installing the Ark in Jerusalem, "David returned to bless his house" (1 Chronicles 16:43), and now it is God who will bless the "house" or family of David (17:27). Similarly, when the presence of God abides fully and freely in our homes and hearts (2 Timothy 2:21–22), when we honor God with clean hands and pure hearts (Psalm 24:4–5), when we prepare our bodies as a fit dwelling place to "house" the Holy Spirit (1 Corinthians 6:19–20), then we are in a position to receive unexpected, unsolicited blessings from the Lord.

This first movement in David's three-fold prayer highlights his submission to God's will. David is undoubtedly disappointed by the divine "no" that he received to his request to build a house for his God. God simply stated that He does not require a temple to be built for Him (17:5–6). After all, even the heavens cannot contain Him (1 Kings 8:27). Consequently, David's prayer does not have the usual features of exuberant thanksgiving (cf. 1 Chronicles 16:8–9). Nevertheless, there is excitement as David is awed and humbled by God's divine, unsolicited promise to build David's house. So he begins his prayer by asking three rhetorical questions that reflect his humility and awe at God's promise: (1) "Who am I," (2) "What is mine house," and (3) "What can I speak more to thee for the honor of thy servant?" David is in awe, recognizing that he has done nothing to merit the honor God bestowed on him.

Although he is king, he is genuinely surprised that God is treating him like someone great. In fact, David expressed his humility by calling himself God's servant four times in this section (vv. 16–19), and six times in the last section (vv. 23–27).

The Hebrew word for servant is *'ebed* (**EH-ved**) and can refer to a slave, a bondservant, a subject of a king, or a worshiper. In speaking to Nathan, God referred to David as his servant twice (17:4, 7), and David willingly affirmed his role as a servant for he was indeed a loyal subject of the true King and a true worshiper of God. This is the example we too must follow. Like King David, King Jesus willingly took on the role of servant and humbled himself by being obedient to God's will to die on a cruel cross (Philippians 2:7–8, Mark 10:45). Therefore, all who want to be great in God's kingdom must become the servant of all (Mark 10:43–44). It is an imperative, not an option. After all, the highest commendation anyone can receive from God is, "Well done good and faithful servant" (Matthew 25:21, 23). One of the requirements of a faithful servant is submission to the Master's will, especially when, like David, God says "no" to our request and provides little explanation. Even if we are disappointed, our response must be, "Father knows best," realizing that our loving God always acts with our best interest at heart.

20 O LORD, there is none like thee, neither is there any god beside thee, according to all that we have heard with our ears. 21 And what one nation in the earth is like thy people Israel, whom God went to redeem to be his own people, to make thee a name of greatness and terribleness, by driving out nations from before thy people whom thou hast redeemed out of Egypt? 22 For thy people Israel didst thou make thine own people for ever; and thou, LORD, becamest their God.

In this second movement of David's prayer, there is a distinct shift. If it were a song, this is the point where the song begins to build and gets louder. Here David moves from talking about himself and looking inward, to talking about God and looking upward. David's twofold confession is focused and intense. First, he unequivocally declares that there is no one like the Lord (17:20). He lifts up and exalts the God of Israel as the only true God, emphatically stating that there is not even a mention of anyone that can compare to Him. The second part of his declaration increases in intensity as he asserts that there is no other nation like Israel whom God specifically chose as a people for Himself (17:21–22). He did it by delivering them from the horrors of Egyptian bondage, and by faithfully bringing them through the wilderness into the Promised Land. There He fought for them, conquering nations that were stronger than Israel, keeping His covenant promise to Abraham, and giving them the land of Canaan as their possession. This selection of people for Himself was not temporary. God made Israel his very own forever, just as the selection of David's house was forever.

God's desire to have a people for Himself is a key part of redemptive history. When God entered into a covenant with Abraham, He promised that Abraham's descendants would be His people and He would be their God (Genesis 17:7–8). When God came to Israel in Egypt, He promised that "I will take you to me for a people, and I will be to you a God" (Exodus 6:7). God instructed Israel to set up the tabernacle in the wilderness for this grand purpose, "that I may dwell among them" (Exodus 25:8). When the Tabernacle was completed, God's glory descended (Exodus 40:34–35), and therein His sanctuary, He would dwell among His people and be their God (Exodus 29:45). And when Solomon completed the Temple, this same

Shekinah glory "filled the house of the Lord" (1 Kings 8:11).

It is this intense desire of God, this promise, that is at the heart of the New Covenant that was declared through Jeremiah the prophet, "[I] will be their God, and they shall be my people" (Jeremiah 31:33). This was fulfilled in the Messiah who came as Immanuel, "God with us," dwelling among His people. Before ascending to heaven Jesus promised to send the Holy Spirit to be with us always (Matthew 28:20). The Apostle Paul reminds us that this promise is fulfilled in us today because we are the "temple of the living God." This is the grace God has granted to us, to have His perpetual presence with us always. In return, our reasonable service is to honor God's presence by maintaining our temples as a fit dwelling place through worship in Spirit and truth, profuse praise, and a willing sacrifice that is acceptable to Him. Ultimately, this promise will be fully accomplished when the New Jerusalem descends from heaven with this grand announcement, "Behold, the tabernacle of God is with men, and he will dwell with them, and they shall be his people, and God himself shall be with them, and be their God" (Revelation 21:3).

23 Therefore now, LORD, let the thing that thou hast spoken concerning thy servant and concerning his house be established for ever, and do as thou hast said. 24 Let it even be established, that thy name may be magnified for ever, saying, The LORD of hosts is the God of Israel, even a God to Israel: and let the house of David thy servant be established before thee. 25 For thou, O my God, hast told thy servant that thou wilt build him an house: therefore thy servant hath found in his heart to pray before thee. 26 And now, LORD, thou art God, and hast promised this goodness unto thy servant: 27 Now therefore let it please thee to bless the house of thy servant that it may be before thee for ever: for thou blessest, O LORD, and it shall be blessed for ever.

This is the third and final movement in David's prayer. It begins softly with his submission to God before building in intensity in his confession about God and then reaching a crescendo in his petition to God. This section has two parts: (1) the petition itself (17:23–24), and (2) the acknowledgment of divine blessing (17:25–27). Verse 23 begins with the words, "Therefore now, LORD," indicating the climatic conclusion that leads to the outcome David desires. Verse 23 also contains the single imperative in the prayer: do as thou hast said. After expressing what was in his heart in the first two movements, David now petitions the Lord to do as He promised, which is to establish David's dynasty forever so that everyone will acknowledge that the Lord of Hosts is the God of Israel. The name of God will be honored and established forever just as David's dynasty is forever.

The crescendo in this prayer centers on the name of the Lord. In essence, David raises his voice and cries out, "thy name may be magnified for ever." To magnify is the Hebrew word *gadal* (**gaw-DOLL**) that means to become great or important, to praise and promote, to make powerful by doing great things. Therefore David invokes the supreme name for God ten times throughout his prayer. Then he magnifies His name by giving Him praise (17:20), and by promoting the great deeds He accomplished in delivering Israel from bondage, defeating her enemies, bringing her into the land of Promise, and establishing Israel as His people (17:21–22). The name David magnifies is the Hebrew name *Yahweh* (**YAH-way**).

The name Yahweh speaks of God's eternal self-existence. Additionally, the name is related to God's relationship with His people as the covenant-keeping God (Deuteronomy 7:9). Therefore, it is significant that this is the name David chose to use throughout his prayer. It signifies his absolute trust in the Lord, and His ability to do the great things for David that He said He would do. Because the Lord is undeniably trustworthy, David acknowledges that the future blessing that He has promised is certain to be fulfilled. Therefore, with a strong sense of confidence in God, David magnifies the Lord by closing his prayer with this noteworthy proclamation, "bless the house of thy servant that it may be before thee for ever: for thou blessest, O LORD, and it shall be blessed for ever."

Jesus Christ is indeed the same yesterday, today and forever (Hebrews 13:8). He hears and answers the prayers of the righteous by doing great things that ultimately bring glory to His name (1 John 5:14). Therefore, when you cry out in prayer to the covenant-keeping God, praying according to His will and in the name of Jesus, you too can rest assured that you will receive that which you have requested of the LORD (John 15:16).

Sources:
Allen, Leslie C. *The Communicator's Commentary Series, Old Testament, Volume 10: 1, 2 Chronicles.* Waco, TX: Word Books, 1987.
Arnold, Bill T. *The NIV Application Commentary: 1 and 2 Samuel.* Grand Rapids, MI: Zondervan, 2003.
Douglas, J. D., ed. *New Bible Dictionary (Second Edition).* Downers Grove, IL: Intervarsity Press. 1982. 187–188.
Hicks, John Mark. *The College Press NIV Commentary: 1 & 2 Chronicles.* Joplin, MO: College Press Publishing Company, 2001.
Hill, Andrew E. *The NIV Application Commentary: 1 and 2 Chronicles.* Grand Rapids, MI: Zondervan, 2003.
Jonker, Louis C. *1 & 2 Chronicles.* Grand Rapids, MI: Baker Books, 2003.
Life Application Study Bible, New Revised Standard Version. Wheaton, IL: Tyndale House Publishers, Inc., 1989. 669–670.
The NIV Study Bible (Tenth Anniversary Edition). Grand Rapids, MI: Zondervan Publishing House 1995. 601–602.
Unger, Merrill F. *The New Unger's Bible Handbook.* Chicago, IL: Moody Press. 1984. 110-112.
Unger, Merrill F. *Unger's Bible Dictionary.* Chicago, IL: Moody Press. 1985. 196–197, 243–248.
Walvoord, J. F., & Zuck, R. B. *The Bible Knowledge Commentary: Old Testament.* Wheaton, IL: Victor Books, 1985.

Say It Correctly

Yahweh. **YAH**-way.
Shekinah. sheh-**KIE**-nah.

Daily Bible Readings

MONDAY
God's Forever Covenant with David
(Psalm 89:19–37)

TUESDAY
The Lord Will Build David's House
(2 Samuel 7:11–17)

WEDNESDAY
No God Like Our God
(2 Samuel 7:18–22)

THURSDAY
No People Like Our People
(2 Samuel 7:23–29)

FRIDAY
David Selects Materials for Temple
(1 Chronicles 22:2–5)

SATURDAY
David Orients Builders about Temple Construction
(1 Chronicles 22:14–19)

SUNDAY
David's Prayer of Praise and Thanksgiving
(1 Chronicles 17:16–27)

Teaching Tips

Words You Should Know

A. Heads (v. 1) *ro'sh* (Heb.)—Mature, older men who oversaw one of the twelve tribes

B. Oracle (v. 8) *debir* (Heb.)—The Holy of Holies

Teacher Preparation

Unifying Principle—A Long-Anticipated Celebration. People have dedication ceremonies or grand openings for many different things. How are these ceremonies or grand openings celebrated? When King Solomon called an assembly to celebrate the dedication of the Temple, the glory of the Lord filled the house of God.

A. Read the Bible Background and Devotional Readings.

B. Pray for your students and lesson clarity.

C. Read the lesson Scripture in multiple translations.

O—Open the Lesson

A. Begin the class with prayer.

B. Debate the need to have a permanent location to worship God.

C. Have the students read the Aim for Change and the In Focus story.

D. Ask students how events like those in the story weigh on their hearts and how they can view these events from a faith perspective.

P—Present the Scriptures

A. Read the Focal Verses and discuss the Background and The People, Places, and Times sections.

B. Have the class share what Scriptures stand out for them and why, with particular emphasis on today's context.

E—Explore the Meaning

A. Use In Depth or More Light on the Text to facilitate a deeper discussion of the lesson text.

B. Pose the questions in Search the Scriptures and Discuss the Meaning.

C. Discuss the Liberating Lesson and Application for Activation sections.

N—Next Steps for Application

A. Summarize the value of God's promises that are worthy of prayer and praise.

B. End class with a commitment to pray for togetherness in celebrating God's presence.

Worship Guide

For the Superintendent or Teacher
Theme: A Place for the Ark
Song: "How Firm a Foundation"
Devotional Reading: Deuteronomy 31:7–13

A Place for the Ark

Bible Background • 1 KINGS 8:1-13, 2 CHRONICLES 5:1–14
Printed Text • 1 KINGS 8:1–13 | Devotional Reading • DEUTERONOMY 31:7–13

Aim for Change

By the end of the lesson, we will: CONSIDER the significance of Solomon's Temple dedication, CONTEMPLATE how the people of Jerusalem felt as the glory of God filled the Temple, and CELEBRATE God's presence among those who gather in the name of the Lord today.

In Focus

Marcus had prayed and prayed for this day to come. He grew up in a really rough neighborhood, and his family struggled. Some days he didn't know if he would live. He enjoyed the time he spent at church because he always felt safe there. Going off campus or just hanging out could be scary because he never knew what might happen. But today, Marcus stood proudly as his name was called and he walked across the stage to receive his college degree.

Marcus's parents had died two years apart before he finished junior high school. His Aunt Sheila and Uncle Michael raised him along with their three children. Marcus was grateful for his aunt and uncle's love and for his fun-loving cousins. They had been quite the crew when all four of them were in youth group at once for a couple of years. He couldn't believe how blessed he was. Before the graduation ceremony started, he cried as he wished his parents could have been there to see it. He was also grieved to not be joined by some friends who had not made it past their seventeenth birthdays because of drugs and gangs. Today was his day to show others the mighty work God had done through him.

When you reflect on the amazing things God does in your life? How do you say thanks to God for your many blessings?

Keep in Mind

"I have surely built thee an house to dwell in, a settled place for thee to abide in for ever" (1 Kings 8:13, KJV).

"Now I have built a glorious Temple for you, a place where you can live forever!"
(1 Kings 8:13, NLT).

Focal Verses

KJV **1 Kings 8:1** Then Solomon assembled the elders of Israel, and all the heads of the tribes, the chief of the fathers of the children of Israel, unto king Solomon in Jerusalem, that they might bring up the ark of the covenant of the LORD out of the city of David, which is Zion.

2 And all the men of Israel assembled themselves unto king Solomon at the feast in the month Ethanim, which is the seventh month.

3 And all the elders of Israel came, and the priests took up the ark.

4 And they brought up the ark of the LORD, and the tabernacle of the congregation, and all the holy vessels that were in the tabernacle, even those did the priests and the Levites bring up.

5 And king Solomon, and all the congregation of Israel, that were assembled unto him, were with him before the ark, sacrificing sheep and oxen, that could not be told nor numbered for multitude.

6 And the priests brought in the ark of the covenant of the LORD unto his place, into the oracle of the house, to the most holy place, even under the wings of the cherubims.

7 For the cherubims spread forth their two wings over the place of the ark, and the cherubims covered the ark and the staves thereof above.

8 And they drew out the staves, that the ends of the staves were seen out in the holy place before the oracle, and they were not seen without: and there they are unto this day.

9 There was nothing in the ark save the two tables of stone, which Moses put there at Horeb, when the LORD made a covenant with the children of Israel, when they came out of the land of Egypt.

10 And it came to pass, when the priests were come out of the holy place, that the cloud filled the house of the LORD,

NLT **1 Kings 8:1** Solomon then summoned to Jerusalem the elders of Israel and all the heads of the tribes—the leaders of the ancestral families of the Israelites. They were to bring the Ark of the LORD's Covenant to the Temple from its location in the City of David, also known as Zion.

2 So all the men of Israel assembled before King Solomon at the annual Festival of Shelters, which is held in early autumn in the month of Ethanim.

3 When all the elders of Israel arrived, the priests picked up the Ark.

4 The priests and Levites brought up the Ark of the LORD along with the special tent and all the sacred items that had been in it.

5 There, before the Ark, King Solomon and the entire community of Israel sacrificed so many sheep, goats, and cattle that no one could keep count!

6 Then the priests carried the Ark of the LORD's Covenant into the inner sanctuary of the Temple—the Most Holy Place—and placed it beneath the wings of the cherubim.

7 The cherubim spread their wings over the Ark, forming a canopy over the Ark and its carrying poles.

8 These poles were so long that their ends could be seen from the Holy Place, which is in front of the Most Holy Place, but not from the outside. They are still there to this day.

9 Nothing was in the Ark except the two stone tablets that Moses had placed in it at Mount Sinai, where the LORD made a covenant with the people of Israel when they left the land of Egypt.

10 When the priests came out of the Holy Place, a thick cloud filled the Temple of the LORD.

11 So that the priests could not stand to minister because of the cloud: for the glory of the LORD had filled the house of the LORD.

12 Then spake Solomon, The LORD said that he would dwell in the thick darkness.

13 I have surely built thee an house to dwell in, a settled place for thee to abide in for ever.

11 The priests could not continue their service because of the cloud, for the glorious presence of the Lord filled the Temple of the LORD.

12 Then Solomon prayed, "O LORD, you have said that you would live in a thick cloud of darkness.

13 Now I have built a glorious Temple for you, a place where you can live forever!"

The People, Places, and Times

King Solomon's Temple. The blueprints for this magnificent structure are described in great detail in 1 Kings 5–6. Solomon strengthened his diplomatic ties with King Hiram of Tyre to use their lumber, labor, and craftsmen to complete the construction project. All the best materials of stone, precious gems, gold, and fine woods of cedar and olive were used to construct the Temple. The project took seven years total. While the blessing of a good king respecting and instituting the worship of the true God cannot be overstated, the knowledge that Solomon completed this great work must also be held with the knowledge that he used many slaves and foreigners to build it. Just as much literary attention is devoted to the building of the Temple as is given to the building of Solomon's palace, which took thirteen years and used all the same precious building materials. This Temple stood from around 970 BC until the Babylonians destroyed Jerusalem in 587 BC.

Background

During his reign, King David declared that he wanted to build a house for the Lord. However, the Lord told David through the prophet Nathan that his son would build a house instead of him (2 Samuel 7:13). After Solomon became king, he proposed that he would build a house for the Lord. Solomon's building projects were extensive. Some scholars suggest that building the Temple lasted seven years. Solomon contracted with King Hiram to provide and cut the wood for the Temple because no one was skilled like the Sidonians, and Solomon wanted the best for the Temple. Solomon created a labor force of 180,000 men and 3,300 supervisors to work on all of the different aspects of the Temple project (1 Kings 5:5–18).

The Temple was huge. It was about 90 feet long, 30 feet wide, and 45 feet high. The grandeur of the Temple furnishings matched its size. This was particularly true for the inner sanctuary, the Most Holy Place. Not only were the floors and walls overlaid with gold like the rest of the Temple, but he also overlaid the altar and the cherubim in the Most Holy Place with gold (1 Kings 6:20–28).

God told David that his son would build a Temple. The word of the Lord came to Solomon emphasizing that God will fulfill the promise to dwell with the Children of Israel if he will be obedient (1 Kings 6: 11–13).

Why was obedience to God so important to the Temple project?

At-A-Glance

1. King Solomon Gathers the People (1 Kings 8:1–3, 5)
2. The Priests Bring the Ark to the Inner Sanctuary (vv. 4, 6–9)
3. God's Glory Fills the Temple (vv. 10–13)

In Depth

1. King Solomon Gathers the People (1 Kings 8:1–3, 5)

This text marks the beginning of the dedication of the Temple as a sacred place of worship for the Lord. At the time of the dedication, there were many Israelites in Jerusalem because they had come for their national festival. King Solomon called upon all of the elders and leaders of the Israelites to come as the priests carried the Ark (v. 3). The leaders and the people joined Solomon in worshiping the Lord outside of the Temple. The sacrifices they made could not be numbered. We might imagine that the area was full like the National Mall during the Presidential Inauguration. Yet the symbolism of this event was even greater than our political celebrations. The celebration of Solomon and the nation was not about establishing a man as a national leader; it was about establishing a throne for the God of Israel on earth.

How do you think the Israelites felt about finally dedicating the Temple?

2. The Priests Bring the Ark to the Inner Sanctuary (vv. 4, 6–9)

The construction of the Temple had been complete for nearly a year, but the project was not finished. The Ark of the Covenant was still in a tent sanctuary where King David placed it. Transporting the Ark from the City of David to the new Temple in Jerusalem was the focal point of this dedication. Every group of people including the elders and all of the leaders present had a role during the ceremony. The priests carried the Ark, and King Solomon and the people worshiped God before the Ark with many sacrifices as the Ark was placed in the Most Holy Place. The Ark made the Temple the center of their religious life. This ark contained the tablets that represent the covenant that God made with the Israelites when God delivered them out of bondage in Egypt.

What is the center of your religious life? What role does the church have in your walk with God?

3. God's Glory Fills the Temple (vv. 10–13)

The moment of truth finally arrived. Would the Lord choose to dwell in the Temple? Although Solomon spent a lot of resources building the Temple, hired the best people to work on the project, and sacrificed many animals for the dedication, none of that meant anything unless the Lord approved. As soon as the priests walked out of the holy place, God's glory filled the entire temple. God's glory came in the form of a cloud just as it did when God led the Children of Israel through the wilderness during the exodus and when God met them at Mt. Sinai before giving the Ten Commandments. God's glory was so thick that the priests could no longer minister inside the Temple. Solomon then told the gathered people that "The Lord has said that he would dwell in thick darkness." Solomon believed the thick cloud of darkness to be a sign of God fulfilling His promise to be with the Children of Israel. And now the Lord was present. Solomon's project to build a house for the Lord was complete. God was with His people in His house.

Solomon's final phrase sums up what this text means to the Children of Israel: "I have built you an exalted house, a place for you to dwell in forever." The Children of Israel endured many times of instability: wandering in the wilderness, warring with other tribes to acquire the Promised Land, changing leadership during the time of the judges, warring during the times of Saul and David. Here at the Temple, they had finally arrived as a people. They had peace, their land, and a strong king. They only needed their God to dwell among them. With this dedication, God finally had a permanent residence amongst them.

How has God shown up in your life to confirm that He was moving on your behalf?

Search the Scriptures

1. What items are mentioned that were brought to the Temple? (1 Kings 8:4–5)

2. What was in the Ark and what was its significance? (v. 9)

3. Name in order the events that showed God's approval of the Temple. (vv. 10–12)

Discuss the Meaning

1. Whenever the Temple is mentioned in this text, it is called "a house" (vv. 6, 11, 13). Solomon proclaims that he has built the Lord an exalted house. Why is it significant that the children of Israel understand the Temple to be "the house of the Lord" and not just a place to meet the Lord?

2. There were multiple items that the priest and Levites brought up from the City of David in addition to the Ark of the Covenant, yet the Ark is the only item placed in the Most Holy Place. Why is the Ark so significant?

Liberating Lesson

This text demonstrates a beautiful story of Israel's true victory, restoration, and completeness. God is on their side. After everything they have experienced—all of the past sufferings and transgressions—God continues to choose them. Any community of people who have been neglected, abandoned, and exploited by the larger society needs to know that God is on their side, individually and collectively. Knowing God has chosen us and will remain with us as He did from slavery to freedom provides a message of hope, triumph, and truth that the people of the African Diaspora can embrace.

As believers, how can we be more intentional about sharing our testimonies of God's redemption with the larger community?

Application for Activation

Sometimes when we suffer, it is easy to forget the redemption we experience through Jesus Christ and the hope we have on earth. Our collective worship in church allows us to remember God's redemption and the hope we have in Him.

- During the next church celebration, designate a place where members can write about and then display their testimonies regarding critical times when God confirmed His love to members of the congregation.

- Create a display with drawings from the church youth depicting what their dreams are. Pray to God to help those children realize their dreams and to create a community where their dreams can thrive.

Follow the Spirit

What God wants me to do:

_____

_____

_____

_____

Remember Your Thoughts

Special insights I have learned:

_____

_____

_____

_____

More Light on the Text

1 Kings 8:1–13

1 Kings 8 records the high point of the reign of Solomon over Israel and his most noteworthy accomplishment as king. Having brought into the house of the Lord all the vessels and furnishings that David had set apart for this exact purpose, Solomon prepared to bring up the Ark into the Temple as well. This celebration included innumerable sacrifices by the elders, tribal heads, family leaders, and all the men of Israel Solomon had assembled in Jerusalem. Once the Ark was set in place, Solomon delivered a series of public prayers and blessings that recounted the past, the plans of David, as well as the future role of the Temple as a place toward which the people could pray.

1 Then Solomon assembled the elders of Israel, and all the heads of the tribes, the chief of the fathers of the children of Israel, unto king Solomon in Jerusalem, that they might bring up the ark of the covenant of the LORD out of the city of David, which is Zion.

The Ark had previously been housed in Zion, the City of David. As a first step in bringing the Ark to Jerusalem, Solomon assembled every segment of Israelite leadership—the "elders," the "heads," and the "chiefs"—to participate in bringing the Ark to its new resting place in the Temple. The word "elder" (Heb. *zaqen*, **zaw-KANE**) reflects an ancient tribal league. The elders were older, respected leaders who advised the king on various national matters. The "heads" of the tribes were also mature, older men who oversaw one of the twelve tribes; and the "chiefs" of the fathers were leaders who administered the clans and villages within the tribes. The engagement of the entire community was important because the transfer of the Ark from the city of David to Solomon's Temple in Jerusalem was a change of the national religious center. The entire nation was on hand to recognize and enact this transfer.

2 And all the men of Israel assembled themselves unto king Solomon at the feast in the month Ethanim, which is the seventh month.

All the common men joined the procession indicating that Solomon had broad-based involvement in moving the heart of Israel's national worship to the new site. This important event took place during the celebration of the Feast of Booths in the month of Ethanim, the seventh month in the Hebrew calendar. It was a feast that commemorated the end of the wilderness wanderings and the fact that God had brought His people home into Canaan and given them rest (Deuteronomy 12:8–11). During this feast, Moses renewed the covenant with the second generation of freed Israelites. He also commanded that Israel read the Law every seven years during this observance (Deuteronomy 31:9–13). Solomon's choice of the Feast of Booths for the dedication was strategic in that it was a traditional time of gathering the nation for a time of religious renewal.

3 And all the elders of Israel came, and the priests took up the ark. 4 And they brought up the ark of the LORD, and the tabernacle of the congregation, and all the holy vessels that were in the tabernacle, even those did the priests and the Levites bring up.

The priests, who brought the Ark according to the Law, were followed by the elders who carried the tabernacle and all the holy vessels to Jerusalem. These items were carefully wrapped by the priests before the Levites carried them (Numbers 4:4–12). These vessels included the table for the shewbread, the altar of incense, the lampstand, and all the items needed to display and use them properly. The Levites were prohibited from directly touching the sacred items on pain of death. It is important to note that unlike David's decision to transport the Ark on a cart made for such occasions—something that resulted in a disaster (2 Samuel 6:3, 6–7)—the priests carried the Ark from the city to the Temple precinct on poles, reminiscent of the way the priests first carried it across Jordan as Israel entered the land (Joshua 3–4). An important lesson to learn here is that God's work must be done in God's way.

5 And king Solomon, and all the congregation of Israel, that were assembled unto him, were with him before the ark, sacrificing sheep and oxen, that could not be told nor numbered for multitude.

During this occasion, King Solomon and the summoned congregation sacrificed before the Ark in the courtyard outside of the Temple. The joyous occasion of transporting the Ark was commemorated with sacrifices to provide both honor to God and a feast for his people. At the ceremony dedicating the Temple later that day, Solomon and the priests slaughtered about 144,000 sheep and oxen (1 Kings 8:63). It is unclear if the animals being sacrificed here as the Ark is moving are part of that estimated total or not. The point is to emphasize the extravagance of the event.

6 And the priests brought in the ark of the covenant of the LORD unto his place, into the oracle of the house, to the most holy place, even under the wings of the cherubims. 7 For the cherubims spread forth their two wings over the place of the ark, and the cherubims covered the ark and the staves thereof above. 8 And they drew out the staves, that the ends of the staves were seen out in the holy place before the oracle, and they were not seen without: and there they are unto this day.

The Ark was eventually installed in the inner sanctuary, "into the oracle of the house." "Oracle" here is *debir* (Heb. **duh-BEER**), which is related to the Hebrew for word or speech. This is why

it is translated "oracle"; in context, however, it clearly simply refers to the room of the Holy of Holies. While the Ark itself had cherubim on each side of the mercy seat that acted as its lid, the "cherubims" mentioned here are the statues which Solomon had constructed within the Holy of Holies (1 Kings 6:23). These cherubim were half the size of the room (1 Kings 6:20), so it is easy to imagine their wings spreading over the place where the Ark stood. The description here also includes the staves that were placed through the rings and used to carry the Ark.

The priests partially drew out the staves through the rings so that someone standing inside the Holy Place directly in front of the doors to the holiest place could see the poles. They could not be seen from the outer courtyards, however. The poles were a reminder of what was inside the Temple. They were not removed completely because that was expressly forbidden (Exodus 25:15; Numbers 4:6).

9 There was nothing in the ark save the two tables of stone, which Moses put there at Horeb, when the LORD made a covenant with the children of Israel, when they came out of the land of Egypt.

At an earlier point in Israel's history, there were three items in the Ark. They were the golden pot that had the manna (Exodus 16:33), Aaron's rod that budded (Numbers 17:6–11), and the tablets of the covenant (Exodus 25:16). This is confirmed by Hebrews 9:4, which says that the Ark "had the golden censer, and the ark of the covenant overlaid round about with gold, wherein was the golden pot that had manna, Aaron's rod that budded, and the tables of the covenant." It is not clear what happened to the golden pot of manna and Aaron's rod, but they were not in the Ark when Solomon set it in the Most Holy Place. Scholars have suggested that although they were not actually inside the Ark of the testimony, they formed part of the witness during the days of Moses. These items also reminded Israel of their rebellious spirit and lack of trust in God while simultaneously testifying of God's provision, deliverance, and selection of the nation. However, the importance of the Ark did not lie in what it contained but in the fact that it signified the presence of God or, more precisely, the presence of God's glory with his people. Hence its loss to the Philistines in the time of Samuel was lamented with the words, "The glory has departed from Israel" (1 Samuel 4:21–22), and the psalmist records the same event by saying that God "delivered ... his glory to the hand of the foe" (Psalm 78:61).

10 And it came to pass, when the priests were come out of the holy place, that the cloud filled the house of the LORD, 11 So that the priests could not stand to minister because of the cloud: for the glory of the LORD had filled the house of the LORD.

Once the Ark is placed, the Lord makes His presence known with the cloud of His glory, which fills the Temple so that the priests go out because they could not perform their service. The cloud, the symbol of the divine glory and presence, appears to have filled not only the holy of holies but the whole temple, court and all. All the people experienced it. The connection between the Ark and the presence of God's glory is evident in these verses.

12 Then spake Solomon, The LORD said that he would dwell in the thick darkness. 13 I have surely built thee an house to dwell in, a settled place for thee to abide in for ever.

When the thick darkness took abode in the magnificent Temple, Solomon recognized the glory cloud for what it was. The thick and dark cloud of glory made Solomon recall that the Lord said He would dwell in a dark cloud (cf. Exodus 19:7–9). This cloud of glory being too much even for God's ministers also happened

before when the Tabernacle was completed (Exodus 40:34–35). Because of this, Solomon knew that God had honored the place with His presence and taken it for His habitation. He saw in it God's approval and His promised presence. Solomon's response to this gracious manifestation is to proclaim that he has built a house for the Lord so that he might sit enthroned in regal splendor as befits his majesty.

There is also a parallel to the presence of the Lord coming that is important to Christians today. It occurs in Acts 2:1–4 when God marks the inception of the church, as the Holy Spirit makes His presence known through the sound of a mighty rushing wind and by filling the people with the Holy Spirit.

Sources:

Bimson, John J. "1 and 2 Kings." *New Bible Commentary: 21st Century Edition*. D. A. Carson, et al., eds. 4th ed. Downers Grove, IL: InterVarsity Press, 1994.

House, Paul R. "1, 2 Kings." Vol. 8. *The New American Commentary*. Nashville, TN: Broadman & Holman Publishers, 1995.

Patterson Richard D. and Hermann J. Austel. "1, 2 Kings." in *The Expositor's Bible Commentary: 1 Samuel–2 Kings* (Revised Edition). Tremper Longman III and David E. Garland, eds. Vol. 3. Grand Rapids, MI: Zondervan, 2009.

Poole, Matthew. *Annotations upon the Holy Bible, vol. 1*. New York: Robert Carter and Brothers, 1853.

Rosscup, James E. *An Exposition on Prayer in the Bible: Igniting the Fuel to Flame Our Communication with God*. Bellingham, WA: Lexham Press, 2008.

Van Groningen, Gerard. "1–2 Kings." *Evangelical Commentary on the Bible*. Vol. 3. Baker Reference Library. Grand Rapids, MI: Baker Book House, 1995.

Winslow, Karen Strand. *1 & 2 Kings: A Commentary in the Wesleyan Tradition*. Alex Varughese and Roger Hahn, eds. New Beacon Bible Commentary. Kansas City, MO: Beacon Hill Press, 2017.

Say It Correctly

Cherubim. **CHAIR**-oo-bim.
Ethanim. ay-thaw-**NEEM**.

Daily Bible Readings

MONDAY
Heavenly Vision of the Ark
(Revelation 11:15–19)

TUESDAY
An Orderly Worship Service
(1 Corinthians 14:26–33)

WEDNESDAY
The Law Is Read at Booths Festival
(Deuteronomy 31:9–13)

THURSDAY
Ark Brought to the Temple
(2 Chronicles 5:2–7)

FRIDAY
Priests Praise God with Music
(2 Chronicles 5:11–14)

SATURDAY
All Temple Furnishings Completed
(2 Chronicles 4:19–5:1)

SUNDAY
Preparing to Dedicate the Temple
(1 Kings 8:1-13)

Notes

_____

_____

_____

_____

Teaching Tips

Words You Should Know

A. Performed (v. 20) *qum* (Heb.)—To stand, arise, rise up, establish

B. Word (v. 20) *dabar* (Heb.)—Speech, saying, utterance; matter, thing

Teacher Preparation

Unifying Principle—I Promise! Many people make promises they are unable to fulfill because of unforeseen circumstances. How should people respond when they do succeed in fulfilling their promise? Solomon thanked God for fulfilling the promise made to his father, King David, when God enabled Solomon to build the Temple in which the Ark could be placed.

A. Read the Bible Background and Devotional Readings.

B. Pray for your students and lesson clarity.

C. Read the lesson Scripture in multiple translations.

O—Open the Lesson

A. Begin the class with prayer.

B. Discuss how church leaders establish the necessity of congregants to pray and praise God.

C. Have the students read the Aim for Change and the In Focus story.

D. Ask students how events like those in the story weigh on their hearts and how they can view these events from a faith perspective.

P—Present the Scriptures

A. Read the Focal Verses and discuss the Background and The People, Places, and Times sections.

B. Have the class share what Scriptures stand out for them and why, with particular emphasis on today's context.

E—Explore the Meaning

A. Use In Depth or More Light on the Text to facilitate a deeper discussion of the lesson text and discuss the Liberating Lesson and Application for Activation sections.

B. Pose the questions in Search the Scriptures and Discuss the Meaning.

N—Next Steps for Application

A. Summarize the value of trust that God is faithful.

B. End class with a commitment to pray for being a faithful witness to God's faithfulness.

Worship Guide

For the Superintendent or Teacher
Theme: Solomon's Speech
Song: "Count Your Blessings"
Devotional Reading: Proverbs 3:1–10

Solomon's Speech

Bible Background • 1 KINGS 8:14–21; 2 CHRONICLES 6
Printed Text • 1 KINGS 8:14–21 | Devotional Reading • PSALM 132:1–5, 11–18

Aim for Change

By the end of the lesson, we will: EXAMINE how Solomon's building of the Temple fulfills a promise God made to Solomon's father, David; APPRECIATE that God keeps promises, even if the fulfillment takes many years; and REJOICE wholeheartedly when God's promises come to pass.

In Focus

Another empty promise! The store owner, Mr. Young, had promised to give the traditional Christmas bonuses, but then he told the employees that his family-owned store was losing money. Everyone believed him and worked extra hours to keep the store afloat. The yearly end-of-the-season sale was great.

When the store managers Joyce and Ian stepped forward and asked all the employees to gather around. As Ian began to speak, the joyous occasion became somber. He was trying to explain why there would be no bonuses. Joyce stepped forward and tried to further explain what was happening.

Then, someone shouted, "Mr. Young promised us a bonus. Where are our bonuses? We sacrificed and made him, his family, and the company money." Mr. Young appeared and asked the upset employees to quiet down. It took a few moments, but they stopped shouting. Eventually, Mr. Young spoke. He and the accountant went back over the numbers. Although the bonus would not be as large as he had planned, each employee would receive a bonus and a $100 gift card from the community grocery store. Mr. Young did indeed keep his promise.

What is your response when you are unable to keep a promise or when someone breaks a promise to you? How much do you trust or doubt God's promises?

Keep in Mind

"And he said, Blessed be the LORD God of Israel, which spake with his mouth unto David my father, and hath with his hand fulfilled it, saying" (1 Kings 8:15, KJV).

"Praise the LORD, the God of Israel, who has kept the promise he made to my father, David. For he told my father" (1 Kings 8:15, NLT).

Focal Verses

KJV **1 Kings 8:14** And the king turned his face about, and blessed all the congregation of Israel: (and all the congregation of Israel stood;)

15 And he said, Blessed be the LORD God of Israel, which spake with his mouth unto David my father, and hath with his hand fulfilled it, saying,

16 Since the day that I brought forth my people Israel out of Egypt, I chose no city out of all the tribes of Israel to build an house, that my name might be therein; but I chose David to be over my people Israel.

17 And it was in the heart of David my father to build an house for the name of the LORD God of Israel.

18 And the LORD said unto David my father, Whereas it was in thine heart to build an house unto my name, thou didst well that it was in thine heart.

19 Nevertheless thou shalt not build the house; but thy son that shall come forth out of thy loins, he shall build the house unto my name.

20 And the LORD hath performed his word that he spake, and I am risen up in the room of David my father, and sit on the throne of Israel, as the LORD promised, and have built an house for the name of the LORD God of Israel.

21 And I have set there a place for the ark, wherein is the covenant of the LORD, which he made with our fathers, when he brought them out of the land of Egypt.

NLT **1 Kings 8: 14** Then the king turned around to the entire community of Israel standing before him and gave this blessing:

15 "Praise the LORD, the God of Israel, who has kept the promise he made to my father, David. For he told my father,

16 'From the day I brought my people Israel out of Egypt, I have never chosen a city among any of the tribes of Israel as the place where a Temple should be built to honor my name. But I have chosen David to be king over my people Israel.'"

17 Then Solomon said, "My father, David, wanted to build this Temple to honor the name of the LORD, the God of Israel.

18 But the LORD told him, 'You wanted to build the Temple to honor my name. Your intention is good,

19 but you are not the one to do it. One of your own sons will build the Temple to honor me.'

20 "And now the LORD has fulfilled the promise he made, for I have become king in my father's place, and now I sit on the throne of Israel, just as the LORD promised. I have built this Temple to honor the name of the LORD, the God of Israel.

21 And I have prepared a place there for the Ark, which contains the covenant that the LORD made with our ancestors when he brought them out of Egypt."

The People, Places, and Times

The Name of the Lord. In the ancient Near East, when an emissary came "in the name of" their king, they had all the power the king commanded. They were also to be treated with all the respect and dignity the king himself would enjoy. This is because the "name" of a person represented all their power and reputation. We speak even today of someone trying to preserve their "good name." The name of the Lord, therefore, refers to all of God's power and greatness. To glorify His name is to add to His reputation. As God is worthy of all honor and glory, He is rightfully offended when people do not respect His name, either in their words or actions. To keep from using the name of the Lord "in vain"—that is, lightly—one must not only refrain from throwing around His personal, covenantal name (Yahweh) without due respect, but one must also refrain from sullying His reputation through unrighteous action.

Background

The scene for our Scripture text is just one in a string of many events that display Solomon's wisdom and thoughtfulness as he began his reign as King of the Israelites. After forty years of leadership as the king of Israel, Solomon's father David dies at seventy years of age (1 Kings 2). However, before he dies, David instructs Solomon about maintaining obedience to God and making diplomatic decisions while dealing with surrounding nations. Solomon takes his father's words to heart and is credited with having complete control of his kingdom—eliminating potential threats while making peace treaties with potential allies. Solomon is approached by God in a dream and given permission to "ask what I shall give thee," to which Solomon famously asks God for the wisdom to lead His people with a discerning heart (1 Kings 3:5, 9). This request pleases God so much that God grants Solomon the wisdom he requested and the riches, long life, and wealth that he did not ask for. Through this exchange, Solomon confirms he can be trusted and is given the wisdom, resources, and clearance to begin the building of the Temple.

To be sure, the building of the temple proves to be a massive undertaking, fueled by the labor of thirty thousand Israelites (1 Kings 5:13), "threescore and ten thousand [seventy thousand] that bare burdens, and fourscore thousand [eighty thousand] hewers

in the mountains ... three thousand and three hundred [thirty-three hundred], which ruled over the people that wrought in the work" (from 5:15–16) and seven years to complete the work (1 Kings 6:38). After beginning construction on his own palace and completing and furnishing the temple, Solomon "brought in the things his father David had dedicated." He summoned all of the leadership in Israel to bring the Ark of the Lord's Covenant to the Lord's temple in Jerusalem. All of Israel came to see the Ark brought into the Temple, and when the priests withdrew from the Holy Place, the glory of the Lord filled the Temple in a dark cloud of smoke. This was a sign to Solomon that God would dwell in the Temple for generations (1 Kings 8:10–13).

At-A-Glance

1. A Prelude of Praise (1 Kings 8:14–16)
2. A Proper Perspective of the Past (vv. 17–19)
3. A Promise-Keeping God (vv. 20–21)

In Depth

1. A Prelude of Praise (1 Kings 8:14–16)

The cloud of smoke is confirmation to Solomon that he is still in step with God and God's plan for the Temple and God's people. This project was literally two generations in the making! Here he was looking at what was only a dream for his father David who wanted to build a permanent dwelling place for the God of his ancestors. This was not a shabby house but a house of worship beautifully adorned with silver and gold. Solomon was the man leading the charge—successfully managing the Temple into existence after seven long years. The completion of the Temple and the confirmation of God's presence through the cloud could

229

have led Solomon to begin the festivities with a sense of great pride. Instead, Solomon uses this moment to provide great praise.

Solomon's posture at this moment of the completion of the Temple is instructive for us. As we achieve major milestones in our lives, careers, or ministries, we too can be tempted to become prideful. We can look at the finished product of our efforts and become intoxicated by memories of our own efforts, ideas, and ingenuity. To be sure, taking pride in our work is not sinful, but becoming blind to God's role in our successes and opportunities is. Solomon recognizes that to have the opportunity to see through to the end of the project his father envisioned is a gift, an opportunity fulfilled through his leadership by the grace of God. For Solomon, the appropriate response is not to pat himself on the back or to praise his own efforts but to praise "LORD God of Israel, which spake with his mouth unto David my father" (1 Kings 8:15).

How do you resist the temptation to take credit for an accomplishment for which God should have been praised?

2. A Proper Perspective of the Past (vv. 17–19)

Maybe one of the most impressive things about Solomon's blessing and address to the people at the completion of the Temple is his ability to see the current moment in light of history. Solomon is aware enough to understand that the work of completing the Temple is the continuation and completion of a promise that God made to his father. While Solomon is the king who is allowed to complete this important work, this accomplishment could not be divorced from the promises of the past and from the history God had with his father David. Solomon remembers and repeats the desires of his own father and the conversations God had with David around the completion of

the Temple (vv. 17–19). This portion of the text is instructive in at least two ways. Solomon is able to see the work he does in completing the Temple as a continuation of what God already began in the past. The work of the Temple does not begin with him. Moreover, the text also implies that a proper perspective of the past is shaped through intergenerational conversation. The reader can assume that Solomon knows the intimate details of David's conversations with God about the Temple because David made a point to share this history with his son, and his son remembered it. We, too, would do well to see the milestones we achieve in our own lives as the continuation of God's ongoing work through our personal, family, and human history.

In what ways can you see God's work in your life as a continuation of the dreams and goals of your ancestors and family?

3. A Promise-Keeping God (vv. 20–21)

Solomon concludes the initial address to the people of Israel by affirming that God is a promise keeper! Solomon says, "the LORD has fulfilled the promise he made" (1 Kings 8:20). He recounts the two promises that God made to David that were now manifested for all to see. God promised that Solomon would succeed his father David and that Solomon would build the Temple for the name of the Lord. Solomon pauses to remind the people that what God said is what they now see (vv. 20–21). Solomon's wisdom is on display as he intentionally positions the Ark of the Covenant, the sign of God's presence that would always dwell at the center of the promised Temple. It is a reminder that the proper response to a promise-keeping God is to always make room and preparations to ensure that God is properly honored and at the center of what we do.

What considerations have you made to ensure that God remains in a central position in your life following the realization of a fulfilled promise God made you?

Search the Scriptures

1. According to verse 15, how did God speak, and how did He fulfill His promise?

2. Why did God commend David? (vv. 17–18)

3. What promises does Solomon say God fulfilled? (v. 20)

Discuss the Meaning

1. One of the themes throughout this text is Solomon's honor and reverence for his father David. Why do you think Solomon honors his father's memory and mission with such high regard?

2. What promises have you seen God keep in your own life? Are there any places you can look in your community or nation where God has kept a promise to a group of people at one time?

3. What role do our church buildings or worship centers have in sharing the goodness of God and testimony of God's faithfulness within our communities?

Liberating Lesson

Following the election of President Barack Obama in 2008, many media outlets and political pundits pushed the idea that America had finally become a "post-racial" society where the race of a human being bore no weight on the heights one could achieve or the way one was treated in this country. It did not take long for many to realize that society was not nearly as post-racial as some had hoped, but seeing a man of color in the White House was a symbol of *some* progress being made by people of color in the political arena and beyond. Solomon's story in 1 Kings 8 reminds us that we cannot take full credit for the advances and milestones we experience. Our personal and cultural victories must never be seen as

events disconnected from our history but as the continuation of the progressive work of a promise-keeping and praiseworthy God.

Application for Activation

Make a list of some of your proudest moments and greatest achievements. For each moment and achievement listed, identify the people who contributed most to the completion of the work, inspired you, or provided a "blueprint" to achieve the task. Spend some time writing thank-you notes or emails to three to five of those people and express to them how their work, dreams, and inspiration were continued and completed in your own work and accomplishments.

Follow the Spirit

What God wants me to do:

_____

_____

_____

Remember Your Thoughts

Special insights I have learned:

_____

_____

_____

More Light on the Text

1 Kings 8:14–21

With the Ark safely in place, Solomon now turns his face toward the assembly of Israel to bless them. One must notice the portrait of Solomon turning to the people, then to God, and back to the people. This illustrates the position of Solomon as the king and the responsibilities that are to attend his position. The king is to be the vice-regent of God with great responsibility and privilege of mediating between God and the people and between the people and God alongside the priests.

All the groups and individuals described in 1 Kings 8:1–5 are addressed in Solomon's blessing. They hear the king give God credit for this significant day. His blessing is a reminder of three significant concepts. First, the basis of the Lord's covenant with David is the earlier deliverance of Israel from Egypt. That concrete historical evidence of God's commitment to saving the chosen people paved the way for future saving events. Included in these subsequent saving acts is God's eternal covenant with David.

14 And the king turned his face about, and blessed all the congregation of Israel: (and all the congregation of Israel stood;) 15 And he said, Blessed be the LORD God of Israel, which spake with his mouth unto David my father, and hath with his hand fulfilled it, saying, 16 Since the day that I brought forth my people Israel out of Egypt, I chose no city out of all the tribes of Israel to build an house, that my name might be therein; but I chose David to be over my people Israel.

The king turned his face to the standing congregation from the Temple where he was observing the thick and extraordinary darkness. Solomon had been speaking to God. He now turns to the people and blesses them. The blessing takes the form of praise to God for fulfilling his promise to David (v. 15; cf. 2 Samuel 7), not only for providing him with a son to continue the dynasty but also in providing a permanent resting place for the Ark, the symbol of God's presence. The expressions "with his own hand" and "with his own mouth" refer to the sovereign power of God

in fulfilling His promises. Since the Davidic covenant implied benefit to Israel through God-appointed leadership and ultimately the coming Messiah, God has clearly begun the fulfillment of the covenant. Israel can expect to receive the bounty of God's blessings if the people walk in His ways.

What started as a blessing on the congregation standing before Solomon suddenly shifts to a prayer of praise to God. God's fidelity to David is the underpinning of Solomon's subsequent prayer that God would faithfully respond to prayers in or toward this Temple. Solomon's prayer also shows the importance of praise. Praises ought to form part of our prayers as we learn to thank God for his past mercies and goodness toward us. Solomon is fully aware of what the Lord has promised and done. The Lord brought Israel from Egypt, and the Lord chose David to rule. David desired to build a Temple, but the Lord indicated that David's son was to build the house for the Lord's name. All this had taken place, and every promise made had been kept. The blessings for Israel that were initially given in the exodus are now fully realized with the Lord's permanent residence in the Temple. The Lord keeps His covenant; the presence of the Ark of the Covenant in the Temple gives full assurance of this.

Furthermore, Solomon reflects on the delay between Israel's entry into Canaan and the building of the Temple. After all, as verse 16 states, the Lord did not choose a city for a temple for His name, but rather He chose a king, David. God chose David and recognized David's desire to build a temple for His name but gave that task to David's son. This emphasis on God's choice of David, not a city, must be remembered together with Deuteronomy's repeated phrase regarding Israel's future place of sacrifice. No city is named in these passages, but they assert firmly that God would choose a place. The logic of Solomon's claim that God had instead chosen a king proceeds like this: the chosen king, David, chose to build a temple; the Lord delayed this procedure to the time of David's son. This son, Solomon, chose the place: Jerusalem, on a hill outside of the city of David.

17 And it was in the heart of David my father to build an house for the name of the LORD God of Israel. 18 And the LORD said unto David my father, Whereas it was in thine heart to build an house unto my name, thou didst well that it was in thine heart. 19 Nevertheless thou shalt not build the house; but thy son that shall come forth out of thy loins, he shall build the house unto my name.

The plan to build a house for God's name was not originally conceived of by Solomon but by David, his father. David had purposed to build a house for the Lord but God prevented him from doing so because of the many wars and the shedding of blood in the wars (2 Samuel 7:13; 1 Kings 5:3–5). Here, Solomon reviews that episode: David's heart had been warm with a passion to build a temple (1 Kings 8:17) and that God had responded to David by commending the motivation. Solomon's attribution of the plan to David is contrary to human nature that seeks glory for itself. Although it may seem insignificant, we must learn to give credit to whom it is due and recognize people for what we may consider intangible contributions to our success in life.

It is important to note that the house is for the name of the Lord God of Israel (vv. 16, 17, 18, 20). The recurring phrase "a house for God's name" echoes God's words to David through Nathan (2 Samuel 7:13). David wanted to build a house for the Ark of God (2 Samuel 7:2). God said in response (v. 5): "Shalt thou build me an house for me to dwell in?" He states that David's son would build a house for his name (v. 13). In sum, the Lord interprets shelter for the Ark as a house for Himself and later declares this will

be for His name (2 Samuel 7). Solomon says the same thing throughout this passage. The Temple of Solomon, according to this chapter, was a house for the Ark, for the Lord, and for the Lord's name.

We must understand what God's name is, He is. In other words, God's name denotes the Lord Himself. Moreover, the idea of the Temple as a "house for the name" of the Lord can be understood by comparison with the phrase, "city of David." Zion was called "city of David" (1 Kings 8:1) not simply because David lived there but because his conquest of the city made it his possession. In the same manner, the Temple in Jerusalem is known by God's name, not because it contains Him (since He cannot be contained) but He dwells there spiritually and it is His possession.

What is the motivation behind what we do? What are our intentions? These questions come to fore as we look at God's response to David's desire to build a house for God's name. There are two important lessons. First God knows our intentions. He saw into David's heart and knew David's reasons for wanting to build a house. It was not to magnify himself but to be a place for the name of the Lord. Second, sincere good intentions can be graciously approved and accepted by God, though we may be prevented from executing our plans for them at a specific time. God may have other plans. God accepted David's good will, yet would not permit him to do the good work, reserving the honor of it for his son (v. 19): "He shall build the house unto my name." What Solomon did was not for his own glory, but the work itself was according to his father's design and his doing it was according to God's designation.

20 And the LORD hath performed his word that he spake, and I am risen up in the room of David my father, and sit on the throne of Israel, as the LORD promised, and have built

an house for the name of the LORD God of Israel. 21 And I have set there a place for the ark, wherein is the covenant of the LORD, which he made with our fathers, when he brought them out of the land of Egypt.

The blessing begins and ends with the statement that God brought his people Israel out of Egypt (vv. 16, 21). This suggests that the fulfillment of God's promise to David through Solomon is not an end in itself. It serves the larger purpose of providing a permanent resting place for the Ark. Moses' prophetic words as he rejoiced with the Israelites when they walked through the Red Sea are now fulfilled: "Thou shalt bring them in, and plant them in the mountain of thine inheritance, in the place, O LORD, which thou hast made for thee to dwell in, in the Sanctuary, O LORD, which thy hands have established" (Exodus 15:17).

Solomon uses a repeated wordplay to emphasize the Lord's actions in making him king of Israel. The words translated "hath performed" and "am risen up" are from the same Hebrew verb *qum* (**KOOM**), but used differently. The root meaning of the verb is "to stand," but when first used in verse 20, the grammatical nuance is "to cause to stand." Solomon acknowledges that because God caused His promise to stand, he now can stand in the place of David. He also repeatedly uses the word *dabar* (**daw-BAR**), which as a noun means "word" and as a verb means "to speak." Solomon uses this root three times in verse 20: "And the LORD hath performed his word (*dabar*) that he spake (*dabar*), ..., as the LORD promised (*dabar*)." This repetition emphasizes the power and surety of God's Word. We must always listen when God speaks, and we can always count on God to keep His promises.

Solomon portrays himself as the heir and fulfillment of the Davidic promises and as the link of the Exodus traditions—represented by the Ark and the tent of meeting—and the

Temple in Jerusalem. Two things had been fulfilled, and they must be understood together. First, a son of David had indeed ascended to the throne of Israel, as promised. Second, this son built the Temple for the name of Israel's God as a fulfillment of God's promises to the man, Solomon, whom God chose to rule Israel (2 Samuel 7:13). Thus, Solomon's speech effectively ties the Ark produced by the freed slaves of the Exodus period to the Temple he built in Jerusalem. This had the effect of emphasizing the unity of the tribes and the traditions of all Israel. In the same manner as Solomon, we must recognize that whatever good we do, or whatever we accomplish in life, we must look upon as the fulfillment of God's promise to us, an act of His faithfulness, rather than the performance of our promises to Him or the result of our works of obedience or faithfulness.

Furthermore, the purpose of this Temple had been fulfilled. It provided a place for the Ark, which held the tablets of the covenant God made with Israel in the wilderness. The Ark is not a throne for God or a localization of His presence. The Almighty God cannot be domesticated, limited to, or contained in a space. But the God of the universe chose to be in a relationship with this Temple, this place, and this people.

Sources:

Bimson, John J. "1 and 2 Kings." *New Bible Commentary: 21st Century Edition.* D. A. Carson et al., eds. 4th ed. Downers Grove, IL: InterVarsity Press, 1994

House, Paul R. *1, 2 Kings.* Vol. 8. The New American Commentary. Nashville, TN: Broadman & Holman Publishers, 1995.

Patterson, Richard D. and Hermann J. Austel. "1, 2 Kings." *The Expositor's Bible Commentary: 1 Samuel–2 Kings (Revised Edition).* Tremper Longman III and David E. Garland, eds. Vol. 3. Grand Rapids, MI: Zondervan, 2009.

Poole, Matthew. *Annotations Upon the Holy Bible.* Vol. 1. New York: Robert Carter and Brothers, 1853.

Rosscup, James E. *An Exposition on Prayer in the Bible: Igniting the Fuel to Flame Our Communication with God.* Bellingham, WA: Lexham Press, 2008.

Van Groningen, Gerard. "1-2 Kings." *Evangelical Commentary on the Bible.* Vol. 3. Baker Reference Library. Grand Rapids, MI: Baker Book House, 1995.

Winslow, Karen Strand. *1 & 2 Kings: A Commentary in the Wesleyan Tradition.* Alex Varughese and Roger Hahn, ed. New Beacon Bible Commentary. Kansas City, MO: Beacon Hill Press, 2017.

Say It Correctly

Davidic. dah-**VID**-ik.

Daily Bible Readings

MONDAY
A House of Prayer
(2 Chronicles 6:12–21)

TUESDAY
Forgive and Restore Broken Relationships
(2 Chronicles 6:22–25)

WEDNESDAY
Send the Rain
(2 Chronicles 6:26–31)

THURSDAY
Welcome the Stranger
(2 Chronicles 6:32–33)

FRIDAY
Forgive and Restore the Captive
(2 Chronicles 6:34–39)

SATURDAY
Plea for God's Steadfast Love
(2 Chronicles 6:40–42)

SUNDAY
Solomon Reviews Temple Developments
(1 Kings 8:14–21)

Notes

Teaching Tips

January 19
Bible Study Guide 8

Words You Should Know

A. Prayer (v. 28) *tefillah* (Heb.)—Intercession

B. Supplication (v. 28) *tekhinnah* (Heb.)—Plea or entreaty

Teacher Preparation

Unifying Principle—A Bright Future. People begin new undertakings with anticipation of a better future. How can we mark such important times? Solomon presided at the dedication of the Temple by calling upon God to receive Israel's worship and to continue to be their God.

A. Read the Bible Background and Devotional Readings.

B. Pray for your students and lesson clarity.

C. Read the lesson Scripture in multiple translations.

O—Open the Lesson

A. Begin the class with prayer.

B. As a class, list characteristics of a worshipful lifestyle believers could adopt in response to God's goodness.

C. Have the students read the Aim for Change and the In Focus story.

D. Ask students how events like those in the story weigh on their hearts and how they can view these events from a faith perspective.

P—Present the Scriptures

A. Read the Focal Verses and discuss the Background and The People, Places, and Times sections.

B. Have the class share what Scriptures stand out for them and why, with particular emphasis on today's context.

E—Explore the Meaning

A. Use In Depth or More Light on the Text to facilitate a deeper discussion of the lesson text.

B. Pose the questions in Search the Scriptures and Discuss the Meaning.

C. Discuss the Liberating Lesson and Application for Activation sections.

N—Next Steps for Application

A. Summarize the value of having a building in which to worship God.

B. End class with a commitment to pray, trusting that God will hear and answer their prayers.

Worship Guide

For the Superintendent or Teacher
Theme: Solomon's Dedication Prayer
Song: "Let Us Break Bread Together"
Devotional Reading: 1 Timothy 2:1–6

Solomon's Dedication Prayer

Bible Background • 1 KINGS 8:22–53; 2 CHRONICLES 6:12–42
Printed Text • 1 KINGS 8:22–30, 52–53 | Devotional Reading • 1 TIMOTHY 2:1–6

Aim for Change

By the end of the lesson, we will: ANALYZE the importance of a national temple for Israel, EXPRESS gratitude for God's faithfulness in covenant relationships, and EMBRACE a worshipful lifestyle in light of God's continuing goodness.

In Focus

Claudine and her husband, Gus, moved to Miami, Florida, after they both retired from the Ohio State Police Department. The winter season in Ohio was harsh. They desired to live in a warmer climate. They liked the weather and the people they met. But there was one aspect of living in Miami they disliked. They could not find a church similar to home.

One day Brian, their next-door neighbor, invited Gus and Claudine to join him and his wife at church on Sunday. Gus hesitated in responding because Brian attended a nondenominational church. Gus had to convince his wife to go with him. "It will not hurt to just go this one time. I know they are of a different race and worship experience. Maybe it will be a good experience." Claudine reluctantly went.

They attended the 8:00 a.m. worship service with Brian and his wife. When they entered the sanctuary, the praise and worship team was leading the congregation in songs. There were multigenerational families of different nationalities in attendance. After a few minutes, Claudine whispered to Gus, "I feel God's presence in this place." The pastor's sermon inspired them to make a commitment to return for another visit.

Why is it important in the midst of life transitions to be in a covenant relationship with God and others?

Keep in Mind

"And hearken thou to the supplication of thy servant, and of thy people, Israel, when they shall pray toward this place, and hear thou in heaven thy dwelling place; and when thou hearest, forgive" (1 Kings 8:30, KJV).

"May you hear the humble and earnest requests from me and your people Israel when we pray toward this place. Yes, hear us from heaven where you live, and when you hear, forgive" (1 Kings 8:30, NLT).

Focal Verses

KJV **1 Kings 8:22** And Solomon stood before the altar of the LORD in the presence of all the congregation of Israel, and spread forth his hands toward heaven:

23 And he said, LORD God of Israel, there is no God like thee, in heaven above, or on earth beneath, who keepest covenant and mercy with thy servants that walk before thee with all their heart:

24 Who hast kept with thy servant David my father that thou promisedst him: thou spakest also with thy mouth, and hast fulfilled it with thine hand, as it is this day.

25 Therefore now, LORD God of Israel, keep with thy servant David my father that thou promisedst him, saying, There shall not fail thee a man in my sight to sit on the throne of Israel; so that thy children take heed to their way, that they walk before me as thou hast walked before me.

26 And now, O God of Israel, let thy word, I pray thee, be verified, which thou spakest unto thy servant David my father.

27 But will God indeed dwell on the earth? behold, the heaven and heaven of heavens cannot contain thee; how much less this house that I have builded?

28 Yet have thou respect unto the prayer of thy servant, and to his supplication, O LORD my God, to hearken unto the cry and to the prayer, which thy servant prayeth before thee to day:

29 That thine eyes may be open toward this house night and day, even toward the place of which thou hast said, My name shall be there: that thou mayest hearken unto the prayer which thy servant shall make toward this place.

30 And hearken thou to the supplication of thy servant, and of thy people Israel, when they shall pray toward this place: and hear thou in heaven

NLT **1 Kings 8:22** Then Solomon stood before the altar of the LORD in front of the entire community of Israel. He lifted his hands toward heaven,

23 and he prayed, "O LORD, God of Israel, there is no God like you in all of heaven above or on the earth below. You keep your covenant and show unfailing love to all who walk before you in wholehearted devotion.

24 You have kept your promise to your servant David, my father. You made that promise with your own mouth, and with your own hands you have fulfilled it today.

25 And now, O LORD, God of Israel, carry out the additional promise you made to your servant David, my father. For you said to him, 'If your descendants guard their behavior and faithfully follow me as you have done, one of them will always sit on the throne of Israel.'

26 Now, O God of Israel, fulfill this promise to your servant David, my father.

27 But will God really live on earth? Why, even the highest heavens cannot contain you. How much less this Temple I have built!

28 Nevertheless, listen to my prayer and my plea, O LORD my God. Hear the cry and the prayer that your servant is making to you today.

29 May you watch over this Temple night and day, this place where you have said, 'My name will be there.' May you always hear the prayers I make toward this place.

30 May you hear the humble and earnest requests from me and your people Israel when we pray toward this place. Yes, hear us from heaven where you live, and when you hear, forgive.

52 May your eyes be open to my requests and to the requests of your people Israel. May

239

thy dwelling place: and when thou hearest, forgive.

52 That thine eyes may be open unto the supplication of thy servant, and unto the supplication of thy people Israel, to hearken unto them in all that they call for unto thee.

53 For thou didst separate them from among all the people of the earth, to be thine inheritance, as thou spakest by the hand of Moses thy servant, when thou broughtest our fathers out of Egypt, O LORD God.

you hear and answer them whenever they cry out to you.

53 For when you brought our ancestors out of Egypt, O Sovereign LORD, you told your servant Moses that you had set Israel apart from all the nations of the earth to be your own special possession."

The People, Places, and Times

The Temple Altar. The altar built in Solomon's Temple was made of cedar and gold. It stood directly in front of the Temple gates, between the gates and the inner sanctuary. Priests needed to use a ramp to reach the top of the altar, as it was about 15 feet high. There was space on the altar to burn several offerings at once, since it was about 900 square feet (2 Chronicles 4:2). Even when no one was giving an offering to God, a fire always burned on the altar as a reminder of God's constant presence with His people. Jewish tradition says that Solomon's altar was built on the exact spot where God took the dust from the ground to make Adam. With the old covenant's emphasis on sacrifice, the altar served as the center of godly worship until the Temple was destroyed.

Background

King David was very old and living out his last days as ruler of Israel when he was faced with a crisis (1 Kings 1). His son, Adonijah, crowned himself the next king outside of Jerusalem. This was not God's plan. Once King David was informed of Adonijah's self-appointment as the next king, he had to take corrective action.

As King David instructed him, the priest Zadok anointed Solomon with sacred oil in the city of Gihon and declared him the next king.

Adonijah's plans were thwarted, and he was granted a reprieve.

Before he died, King David's last instructions to his son Solomon were for him to be strong, courageous, and totally obedient to God in all aspects of life (1 Kings 2). It was the only way to be a successful ruler. Solomon also had to deal with any opposition to his reign as king from Adonijah and others before his kingdom was firmly established.

God spoke to King Solomon in a dream and told him to ask for anything he wanted (1 Kings 3:5ff.). King Solomon asked for wisdom to lead the people, so it was granted by God. He was the wisest man to have ever lived. He wrote Ecclesiastes, Song of Solomon, many of the Proverbs, and some of the Psalms.

King Solomon set his mind to build the Temple (1 Kings 5). His father David was forbidden by God to do so. But God promised David his son who sat on the throne would be the one who built the Temple. King Solomon gathered the materials, some from across the world, and had the Temple built (1 Kings 6–7). He brought in all the vessels His father David had dedicated and stored them in the Temple.

Why is it important to obey the commands of God to ensure a better future?

At-A-Glance

1. Pray and Give Thanks (1 Kings 8:22–26)
2. Pray and Believe (vv. 27–30, 52–53)

In Depth

1. Pray and Give Thanks (1 Kings 8:22–26)

King Solomon waited until the end of the harvest seasons, during the Festival of Booths, to dedicate the Temple (8:1). Before the dedication of the Temple, the Ark of the Covenant was transferred from the Tabernacle (tent) to the Temple. The Temple represented a permanent place for the people to worship God. King Solomon offered three prayers during the dedication ceremony: the first in verses 14–21; second in verses 22–53; and the third in verses 54–61. The first prayer concentrates on God's promise to Solomon's father, David, to always have an heir from his family sitting on the throne throughout eternity (2 Samuel 7:5–16). The second prayer is the fundamental core of the dedication ceremony.

King Solomon showed reverence to God. He entered into the inner sanctuary and knelt in front of the altar with hands stretched toward heaven as he prayed (v. 22). King Solomon expressed gratitude to God for being faithful to the covenant made with his father (2 Samuel 7:13). God is faithful even when we may not be. And as time passed, the people of Israel were not always faithful in keeping God's commands. But in spite of their (our) sinful ways, God would always have a successor to sit on the throne of Israel, which King Solomon petitioned God to fulfill (v. 25–26). God's promise (1 Kings 2:4) was fulfilled through the birth of the Messiah who was a part of the Davidic line.

Why is expressing gratitude to God important?

2. Pray and Believe (vv. 27–30, 52–53)

God's presence was manifested in the Temple through the visibility of a cloud. King Solomon acknowledged in his prayer that in spite of the beautiful Temple he had built for God, not even heaven was vast enough to contain His presence (v. 27). God is omnipresent, so He cannot be confined to one specific location. No one can rightfully say God is only present at their place of worship. Our God can be wherever and with whomever He desires. Today God does not need a temple as a visible symbol of His invisible presence. God lives in our hearts.

King Solomon asked God to hear his prayers and pleas to be forgiven, as well as those of the people of Israel (v. 30). This included when they were in the Temple and in other locations. It is traditional for the Israelites to pray facing the Temple in Jerusalem if they are not actually able to pray in the Temple. As Christians, we can pray and seek forgiveness no matter our physical position. God only requires we have a humble, repentant heart. He hears us and will respond.

King Solomon closed the prayer by reminding God about the covenant made at Mount Sinai with Moses and the Israelites after the exodus from Egypt (vv. 52–53; Exodus 19:5–7). The Mosaic covenant set the commands the Israelites had to obey as God's chosen people. Since they were still God's chosen people, King Solomon petitioned God to remember and respond to His people's prayers.

Why is prayer vital in our relationship with God?

Search the Scriptures

1. What posture did King Solomon take at the altar before he prayed (8:22)?

2. What promise did God make to David (8:25)?

3. When and whom did God speak to concerning the Israelites being His inheritance (chosen people) (8:53)?

Discuss the Meaning

1. King Solomon understood the importance of building a place where people could worship God. What benefits would the Israelites gain from having a new national temple? What benefits do we enjoy in coming together in a specific place for worship?

2. The dedication of the Temple was an exciting and inspirational event in the Israelites' lives. What role does prayer take in our worship of God? How would the Temple dedication influence their future?

Liberating Lesson

It is a blessing to have a space dedicated to worshiping God. The space may or may not be in a church building. Sometimes believers gather in hospital rooms, prisons, parks, open fields, or under trees for worship. This does not mean God's presence is not with them. We have to be careful not to box God in and think God is only present in our faith community. God is omnipotent and omnipresent. God is always present with His people. He lives in our hearts.

God has been faithful toward us. Even when we have not done what is right, God still blesses us. All that God requires is that we pray and repent of our sins. God can and will restore us just like He repeatedly did for the Israelites. It is not too late to make things right between you and God. Today is the day. He loves us. Take a moment and think about all the ways God has blessed you. Why not give thanks and worship God? God is worthy.

Application for Activation

Since God is present at all times, we can call on God in prayer and know God hears us. Our circumstances may seem dismal, but God knows about it. The world seems to be more and more hateful and divisive. Instances of hate crimes are present via various mediums. What can we do? "Pray without ceasing" (1 Thessalonians 5:17). God hears us and will provide guidance in what steps to take. Moreover, we have to take advantage of every opportunity to worship God. When we develop an attitude of praise and thanksgiving for all God has done and has yet to do, it will change our lives and those around us as well. This will help future generations know about God's faithfulness to His promises.

Follow the Spirit

What God wants me to do:

_____

_____

_____

_____

Remember Your Thoughts

Special insights I have learned:

_____

_____

_____

_____

More Light on the Text

1 Kings 8:22–30, 52–53

We read in 2 Samuel 7 that David had proposed to build a house for the Lord, a place of worship where the Ark of the Covenant of God would rest. Instead of David, the Lord promised him that his offspring and the heir to his throne would be the one to build the Lord's temple (2 Samuel 7:12–14). Solomon inherits his father David's throne; he becomes the king and assumes the task of building the Temple for the Lord (1 King 2). The Temple is completed with specified details and furnishings according to the Lord's promise to his father David (1 Kings 6–7). The people assemble in Jerusalem to dedicate the Temple. The Ark of God's covenant is brought from Zion, David's city, and placed in its place in the Temple (1 Kings 8:1–13). Solomon addresses the people explaining God's fulfilling His promise to his father David (vv. 14–21). He then addresses the Lord in prayer on behalf of his people (vv. 22–53).

22 And Solomon stood before the altar of the LORD in the presence of all the congregation of Israel, and spread forth his hands toward heaven:

After assembling the people in the Temple courts, Solomon stands before the altar of the Lord. In other words, Solomon stands in front of the altar of the Lord, rather than inside the Temple building reserved only for the priestly and Levitical order in worship. It appears that Solomon positioned himself between the altar and the congregation, facing the people.

The verb "stood" describes Solomon's posture during the prayer. It is customary for the Jews to stand or kneel with hands raised in prayer, petition, and praise to the Lord (Exodus 9:29, Isaiah 1:15). This posture in prayer was also practiced by New Testament Christians and is still practiced by contemporary Christians. The posture implies looking up toward heaven to God in faith and total surrender and expectancy as they wait for the answer. The Chronicler's account of this event says that Solomon knelt on the special platform near the altar as he offered this prayer, lifting his hands to heaven (2 Chronicles 6:13). The lifting or raising up

of one's hand also represents total surrender, helplessness, and dependency to a superior or higher authority—in this case to God.

23 And he said, LORD God of Israel, there is no God like thee, in heaven above, or on earth beneath, who keepest covenant and mercy with thy servants that walk before thee with all their heart: 24 Who hast kept with thy servant David my father that thou promisedst him: thou spakest also with thy mouth, and hast fulfilled it with thine hand, as it is this day.

Lifting up his hands to heaven, King Solomon begins his prayer of dedication with worship and thanksgiving to the covenant-keeping God for His faithfulness in keeping His promises. Using the personal name "LORD" *Yehovah* (**yeh-ho-VAW**), Solomon describes Him as the supreme "God" *'elohiym* (**eh-low-HEEM**) of Israel. The Bible places Israel as God's chosen people (Exodus 19:5-6; Deuteronomy 9:26, 29; 14:2). Peter equates all believers also as God's unique and chosen people (1 Peter 2:9). Solomon's phrasing of "God of Israel" can be read as acknowledging that God has chosen Israel and also as promising that Israel has chosen God. King Solomon then expresses the uniqueness of Yahweh: "There is no God like Thee in heaven above, or on earth beneath" (cf. Exodus 15:11). The uniqueness of this God is that He keeps "covenant" (Heb. *berith*, **beh-REETH**) and "mercy" (Heb. *khesed*, **KHE-sed**) with those who walk before Him with all their heart. A covenant is a solemn agreement between two parties, often a king and his subjects, defining the rights and responsibilities of each party in the relationship. God's relationship with His people has been defined by covenant since Noah, through Abraham, and to Moses. God's mercy has always been one of His defining characteristics, one of the first times He is named is when He reveals Himself to Moses (Exodus 34:6).

Solomon then refers to God's promise made to his father, David, that one of his sons would be heir to the throne and the builder of the Temple (2 Samuel 7:12–15). By fulfilling the blessing promised to His people through Solomon, the Lord has proved Himself to be the faithful God in heaven above and the earth beneath. Israel could not deny God's faithfulness in keeping His promises and covenant.

25 Therefore now, LORD God of Israel, keep with thy servant David my father that thou promisedst him, saying, There shall not fail thee a man in my sight to sit on the throne of Israel; so that thy children take heed to their way, that they walk before me as thou hast walked before me. 26 And now, O God of Israel, let thy word, I pray thee, be verified, which thou spakest unto thy servant David my father.

Solomon prays to God to fulfill His promise to David—the perpetuity of a Davidic dynasty. Based on God's past faithfulness, Solomon asks for the ultimate fulfillment of this promise to keep someone on the throne of Israel as long as they walk righteously before God. He then concludes invoking God's personal relationship with His people with the phrase "O God of Israel." This promise is conditional, which God reiterated to Solomon (1 Kings 6:12–13). God will allow disobedience for a time, waiting for us to repent or not wanting to appear too harsh to pagan nations. Ultimately, though, God's blessings are only for those who faithfully follow His ways. So long as the Israelites obeyed, God would keep a continuous line of kings on David's throne. The ultimate realization of this promise is in Christ Jesus (Luke 1:26–33, 67–75; Acts 2:29–30; Romans 1:3).

27 But will God indeed dwell on the earth? behold, the heaven and heaven of heavens cannot contain thee; how much less this house that I have builded? 28 Yet have thou respect unto the prayer of thy servant, and to his supplication, O LORD my God, to hearken unto the cry and to the prayer, which thy servant prayeth before thee today:

Solomon is overwhelmed by the greatness of God in contrast to the insignificance of the work he had done in building the Temple. He realizes with the improbability of such a mighty God dwelling on earth, how much less would He be in the Temple made by man's hand. He rhetorically questions, "But will God indeed dwell on the earth?" and supplies the answer by an affirmation of the truth. Since not even "the highest heaven" is big enough to accommodate Him, there is no way "this house that I have built" could do so. Solomon had expressed the same truth to King Hiram of Tyre before he began to build (2 Chronicles 2:6). The Lord affirmed this truth through the Prophet Isaiah, "The heaven is my throne, and the earth is my footstool: where is the house that ye build unto me?" (from Isaiah 66:1). Stephen referred to these words from Solomon and Isaiah in his defense before the Jewish council (Acts 7:47–50). Preaching to the Athenian Gentiles on Mars Hill, Paul emphasized the same truth about God whom they unknowingly worshiped (Acts 17:22–25). It is amazing that, though heaven cannot contain God, He is willing to live in the hearts of those who love Him. He cannot be restricted, He is omnipresent, and His presence can be felt everywhere His name is called. How comforting to know the God of the universe takes up residence in His people. This is amazing grace!

Such knowledge leads King Solomon to solicit God's attention to prayer and supplication, which he makes to Him. Here Solomon uses two complementary nouns for "prayer" *tefillah* (teh-feel-LAW) meaning "intercession," and "supplication" and *techinnah* (teh-kheen-NAW) meaning "plea or entreaty." Here prayer or intercession speaks of a petition on behalf of somebody or something. In this case, Solomon is interceding on behalf of his people Israel. Supplication speaks of an appeal or plea made to somebody in authority, one who has the power to grant the request. With the use of these two words, Solomon emphasizes the urgency of his plea on behalf of his subjects and the need for God to "hearken" (Heb. *shama'*, shaw-MAW, listen closely or pay attention) to his cry and to the prayer, which he presently brings before Him. Solomon then proceeds to lay his petitions and requests to God on behalf of his people (vv. 29–53).

29 That thine eyes may be open toward this house night and day, even toward the place of which thou hast said, My name shall be there: that thou mayest hearken unto the prayer which thy servant shall make toward this place. 30 And hearken thou to the supplication of thy servant, and of thy people Israel, when they shall pray toward this place: and hear thou in heaven thy dwelling place: and when thou hearest, forgive.

Solomon continues his prayer by asking the Lord to keep His watchful eyes over the Temple "night and day"—to hear the prayer of His people. The phrase "night and day" speaks of the constancy and consistency of God's attention toward the Temple. That is to say, God will make the Temple His residence because He will manifest His gracious presence there. Not only does Solomon ask for God's watchful eyes over the Temple, he solicits, figuratively speaking, that God's ears be open to the prayers of the people and to answer them when they prayed toward the Temple.

A good relationship must be in place before one can ask for a favor from another. So it is

with God. Sin hurts the relationship between God and His people (Isaiah 59:1–2). Solomon is aware of the impact of sin and the terms of God's covenant relationship with His people Israel (Deuteronomy 28–29). He also knows the calamities the Lord promised to send as a discipline if Israel disobeyed His law. Therefore Solomon asks the Lord to forgive the sins of his people when they pray in or toward the Temple. Solomon is equally aware of the Lord's grace of forgiveness and restoration if God's people would repent and turn to the Lord (Deuteronomy 30). The clause, "when they shall pray toward this place" indicates that when an Israelite is unable to pray in the Temple, he or she is to direct his or her prayers toward the Temple where the Lord had pledged to be present among His people. It was customary for Jews, wherever they might be, to pray facing toward Jerusalem or the Temple. Daniel prayed for his people looking toward Jerusalem (Daniel 6:10); Jonah looked toward the Temple and prayed, and God forgave him (Jonah 2:4). Although God dwells in heaven, He says "My house shall be called a house of prayer for all nations" (Isaiah 56:7, Mark 11:17).

52 That thine eyes may be open unto the supplication of thy servant, and unto the supplication of thy people Israel, to hearken unto them in all that they call for unto thee. 53 For thou didst separate them from among all the people of the earth, to be thine inheritance, as thou spakest by the hand of Moses thy servant, when thou broughtest our fathers out of Egypt, O LORD God.

In verses 31–51 King Solomon presents seven specific requests, which cover different calamities that would befall the people as a result of disobedience and sin. These calamities are listed in Deuteronomy as curses on Israel for breaking the covenant (Deuteronomy 28:22, 25, 38, 42, 59; 31:17, 29; 32:24). In verses 52 and

53, Solomon concludes his petitions by calling on God to hear His people whenever they cry out in prayer. To wrap up the section, Solomon ends the same way he started his petition. He again asks the Lord to keep His eyes open to both his and his people's prayers and to hearken to their requests. Solomon then appeals to God's covenant relationship toward His people Israel. The word "separate" comes from the Hebrew verb *badal* (**baw-DOLL**), meaning to "sever, distinguish or select." Solomon seems to remind the Lord that among all the nations of the world, He singled Israel out to be God's own inheritance. This is a promise God made with Moses at Mount Sinai when He brought them out of Egypt. It is generally referred to as the Mosaic or Sinaitic covenant (Exodus 19:5).

In this whole prayer (1 Kings 8:23–53) Solomon called on God, who had been faithful to His promises in the past, to continue to be faithful and to show mercy to His people in the future. The outcome of a genuine confession and forsaking of sin is God responding to His people's prayers. It is comforting to know that our God is not restricted to a place, in a man-made cathedral or temple, but He is everywhere His name is worshiped and magnified. Jesus says, "For where two or three are gathered together in my name, I am in the midst of them" (Matthew 18:20). More importantly, He dwells in the hearts of those who worship Him in spirit and in truth (John 4:23–24).

Sources:

Interlinear Transliterated Bible. Biblesoft, Inc., 2006.

Life Application Study Bible, New Revised Standard Version. Wheaton, IL: Tyndale House Publishers, Inc., 1989. 550–555.

New Exhaustive Strong's Numbers and Concordance with Expanded Greek-Hebrew Dictionary. Biblesoft, Inc., 2006

The NIV Study Bible (Tenth Anniversary Edition). Grand Rapids, MI: Zondervan Publishing House 1995. 459–464, 480–484.

"The Temple Institute: Articles: The Altar." *The Temple Institute.* https://www.templeinstitute.org/altar.htm (accessed January 15, 2019).

Unger, Merril F. *Unger's Bible Dictionary.* Chicago, IL: Moody Press. 1985. 632–633, 1035–1037.

Zondervan NIV Study Bible. Grand Rapids, MI: Zondervan, 2008.

Daily Bible Readings

MONDAY
Pray for all Secular Leaders
(1 Timothy 2:1–6)

TUESDAY
Forgiveness of Sin Against Another
(1 Kings 8:31–32, 41–44)

WEDNESDAY
Forgive Each Other Generously
(Colossians 3:8–13)

THURSDAY
Encourage Each Other in Facing Difficulties
(1 Corinthians 15:1–11)

FRIDAY
A House of Prayer for All Peoples
(Isaiah 56:3–8)

SATURDAY
Captives Receive God's Gifts
(Ephesians 4:1–8, 11–16)

SUNDAY
God's Promises Are Kept
(1 Kings 8:22–30, 52–53)

Say It Correctly

Sinaitic. sie-nee-**IH**-tick.

Teaching Tips

Words You Should Know

A. Rest (v. 56) *menuach* (Heb.)—To repose or relax peacefully; consolation, peace and quietness

B. Perfect (v. 61) *shalem* (Heb.)—Complete, whole

Teacher Preparation

Unifying Principle—Commitment to Success. People often mark the start of new ventures with special ceremonies or observances because they have high hopes for success. How can we know that what we propose to do will succeed? After dedicating the Temple, Solomon prayed for God's continued faithfulness toward Israel while calling on his people to renew their commitment to God.

A. Read the Bible Background and Devotional Readings.

B. Pray for your students and lesson clarity.

C. Read the lesson Scripture in multiple translations.

O—Open the Lesson

A. Begin the class with prayer.

B. Ask participants to discuss their experiences of God's faithfulness and how these experiences motivated their commitment to God.

C. Have the students read the Aim for Change and the In Focus story.

D. Ask students how events like those in the story weigh on their hearts and how they can view these events from a faith perspective.

P—Present the Scriptures

A. Read the Focal Verses.

B. Have the class share what Scriptures stand out for them and why, with particular emphasis on today's context.

C. Discuss the Background and The People, Places, and Times sections.

E—Explore the Meaning

A. Use In Depth or More Light on the Text to facilitate a deeper discussion of the lesson text.

B. Pose the questions in Search the Scriptures and Discuss the Meaning.

C. Discuss the Liberating Lesson and Application for Activation sections.

N—Next Steps for Application

A. Summarize the value of prayer.

B. End class with a commitment to pray for obedience to God's commands.

Worship Guide

For the Superintendent or Teacher
Theme: Solomon's Blessings
Song: "Come Let Us Worship and Bow Down"
Devotional Reading: Psalm 136:1–16, 23–25

247

Solomon's Blessing

Bible Background • 1 KINGS 8:54–66
Printed Text • 1 KINGS 8:54–61 | Devotional Reading • PSALM 136:1–16, 23–25

———————— Aim for Change ————————

By the end of the lesson, we will: EXAMINE Solomon's prayer of dedication, AFFIRM God's continued faithfulness to His people, and COMMIT ourselves to obeying God's commands.

———————— In Focus ————————

Charlotte had dreamed of opening a flower shop. She and husband Gerald had saved and invested their money quite well. After praying and seeking God, Gerald and Charlotte found a space not too far from where they lived. Next, they scheduled the grand opening two months later.

Gerald walked around admiring the flowers. "This flower shop is going to do great. I am amazed at the variety of flowers you have."

"Thanks. But we have to have customers to buy flowers. I invited everyone at church and put an ad in the local paper. I also put flyers in our neighbors' mailboxes at the community center. I pray we have a good turnout for our grand opening tomorrow."

The next day Charlotte and Gerald arrived early to attend to every detail. Charlotte was in the back of the store preparing more flowers to sell. Gerald went to the back of the store and said, "I think you need to come up front for a moment."

Charlotte could not believe her eyes as the tears welled up. There were over a hundred people lined up outside waiting for the opening of the store. Gerald said, "Let's just go ahead and open the doors for these people. They want flowers." Charlotte nodded. Their grand opening was a success, and the flower shop continued to do great business.

Why is it important to seek God's direction before implementing a plan?

———————— Keep in Mind ————————

"The LORD our God be with us, as he was with our fathers: let him not leave us nor forsake us: That he may incline our hearts unto him, to walk in all his ways, and to keep his commandments, and his statutes, and his judgments, which he commanded our fathers" (1 Kings 8:57–58, KJV).

"May the LORD our God be with us as he was with our ancestors; may he never leave us or abandon us. May he give us the desire to do his will in everything and to obey all the commands, decrees, and regulations that he gave our ancestors" (1 Kings 8:57–58, NLT).

Focal Verses

KJV 1 Kings 8:54 And it was so, that when Solomon had made an end of praying all this prayer and supplication unto the LORD, he arose from before the altar of the LORD, from kneeling on his knees with his hands spread up to heaven.

55 And he stood, and blessed all the congregation of Israel with a loud voice, saying,

56 Blessed be the LORD, that hath given rest unto his people Israel, according to all that he promised: there hath not failed one word of all his good promise, which he promised by the hand of Moses his servant.

57 The LORD our God be with us, as he was with our fathers: let him not leave us, nor forsake us:

58 That he may incline our hearts unto him, to walk in all his ways, and to keep his commandments, and his statutes, and his judgments, which he commanded our fathers.

59 And let these my words, wherewith I have made supplication before the LORD, be nigh unto the LORD our God day and night, that he maintain the cause of his servant, and the cause of his people Israel at all times, as the matter shall require:

60 That all the people of the earth may know that the LORD is God, and that there is none else.

61 Let your heart therefore be perfect with the LORD our God, to walk in his statutes, and to keep his commandments, as at this day.

NLT 1 Kings 8:54 When Solomon finished making these prayers and petitions to the LORD, he stood up in front of the altar of the LORD, where he had been kneeling with his hands raised toward heaven.

55 He stood and in a loud voice blessed the entire congregation of Israel:

56 "Praise the LORD who has given rest to his people Israel, just as he promised. Not one word has failed of all the wonderful promises he gave through his servant Moses.

57 May the LORD our God be with us as he was with our ancestors; may he never leave us or abandon us.

58 May he give us the desire to do his will in everything and to obey all the commands, decrees, and regulations that he gave our ancestors.

59 And may these words that I have prayed in the presence of the LORD be before him constantly, day and night, so that the LORD our God may give justice to me and to his people Israel, according to each day's needs.

60 Then people all over the earth will know that the LORD alone is God and there is no other.

61 And may you be completely faithful to the LORD our God. May you always obey his decrees and commands, just as you are doing today."

The People, Places, and Times

Solomon. David's second son by Bathsheba was special to the Lord from the very beginning of his life, as the prophet Nathan told David to call the boy Jedidiah, "beloved to God" (2 Samuel 12:25). Several of David's other sons attempted to take the throne after their father, but Bathsheba knew God had chosen her son to take the kingship. She reminded David of this, and David used his kingly power to ensure Solomon would rule after him. At the beginning of his reign, God offered to grant Solomon any wish, and when Solomon humbly asked for wisdom, God granted him wisdom and all the wealth and power he could have asked for, too. Solomon undertook the massive building project of the Temple that his father David had prepared for him to do. Solomon also built a grand palace for himself. Solomon affirmed the worship of the Lord God throughout Israel, and the nation prospered. However, Solomon also took wives from all the surrounding nations as a way to establish good relations between the peoples. These wives brought their gods with them and led Solomon and the nation into idolatry. Solomon's successor, Rehoboam, was not a wise ruler, and the nation split into two kingdoms soon after Solomon's reign ended.

Background

King Solomon was the successor to the throne after his father David died. He was known as the wisest man to have lived in his time. God granted him the privilege of building the Temple. He was able to use the finest building materials to erect the Temple and make its appearance splendid. It would be a permanent place of worship for the Israelites and contain the Ark of the Covenant.

As recorded in 1 Kings 8, King Solomon offered three prayers during the dedication ceremony: the first in verses 14–21; second in verses 22–53; and the third in verses 54–61. The first prayer in verses 14 through 21 concentrated on God's promise to Solomon's father, David, to always have an heir from his family sitting on the throne throughout eternity (2 Samuel 7:5–16).

The second prayer in verses 22 through 53 concentrates on the expression of gratitude to God for His faithfulness to His promises and a plea to believe God hears our prayers. King Solomon reminded the people that God's presence is not confined to a building. God is everywhere. Therefore, the message was that when they found themselves far away from the Temple in Jerusalem, if they would physically turn toward the Temple and pray, God would hear and respond. Today, Christians only need to call on the name of Jesus in prayer wherever they find themselves. Our location and physical posture are not important. It is the spiritual condition of our hearts that matters.

What role does prayer have in our success as we engage in new endeavors?

At-A-Glance

1. Renewed Commitment (1 Kings 8:54–58)
2. Requesting God's Help (vv. 59–61)

In Depth

1. Renewed Commitment (1 Kings 8:54–58)

The third prayer King Solomon offered during the dedication of the Temple is in verses 54–61. After the conclusion of the second prayer in verses 22 through 53, he stands up and faces the people. He has humbled himself in the sacred space that will be used to worship and honor God. He understands the historical and spiritual importance of the dedication of the Temple for the Israelites at that moment and in the future. Now he has to address the people of Israel who have assembled for the historic occasion (vv. 54–55).

The priests were the ones who blessed the people (Numbers 6:23–27). However, Solomon's "blessing" here is actually a prayer of blessing and praise to God. King Solomon praises God for rest from Israel's enemies and His faithfulness (v. 56). His father, David, was a great warrior who defeated many of the nations who were enemies of Israel (2 Samuel 7; 1 Kings 5:3–4). These nations had not been eradicated when Israel took possession of the Promised Land in Canaan (Judges 1). The nation is now at rest from the threat of attacks because David defeated these enemies. However, this made David a warrior who had shed blood, which disqualified him from building the Temple. God was gracious and promised David that his son would be the one to do it.

Solomon and his generation of Israelites need God's presence just as much as their ancestors did (v. 57). God promised to "not fail thee, nor forsake thee" (Deuteronomy 31:6). But King Solomon knew there was a commitment needed on their part to "incline our hearts to him" to keep the covenant. The Israelites, like us, had a tendency to stray away from God. If we love God, we should obey His laws and commands, not our own desires. We have to yield our hearts, minds, and souls totally to Him.

How does God's presence make a difference in our lives?

2. Requesting God's Help (vv. 59–61)

King Solomon was appointed by God to serve. However, he recognized his and the people's necessity of requesting God's help meeting daily needs (v. 59). We, too, have to seek God to provide our daily needs so we will not yield to the temptations of the world. God will provide for His people. We can depend on Him.

As the people obeyed God and daily needs were provided, King Solomon hoped that God's glory would be known in the world (vv. 60–61). People are always watching those who call themselves Christians. They want to see if we are living the life we confess to believe in. What will people conclude by watching you? The world needs God to be a light in your life so they can know He is real.

How does God provide help in meeting our daily needs?

Search the Scriptures

1. Why did King Solomon say, "blessed be the LORD" (1 Kings 8:56)?

2. How could the Israelites "incline our hearts" toward God (v. 58)?

3. How can the world know "the LORD is God" (vv. 59–60)?

Discuss the Meaning

1. For a long period of time, the Israelites did not have a permanent place to worship God. How do you think the building and dedication of the Temple influenced them to recommit their lives to God?

2. We need God's presence in our lives. How can we draw closer to God and discern His will?

Liberating Lesson

When we endeavor to develop a church project or ministry, it must begin and end with prayer. Prayer is necessary to discern the will of God. Every good idea is not God's plan. Sometimes, when we do not have success with our church projects or ministry ideas, perhaps it is because the flesh is trying to get the glory and not God. We can become competitive in the church and want to outdo other churches that have flourishing ministries.

King Solomon prayed that God's presence would be with him and the nation of Israel. He recalled God's faithfulness to their ancestors and desire for God's presence to continue to be with them. When we have God's presence and know we are following His commands, our church projects will succeed. But do not get caught up in the number of people reached. Maybe the purpose of the project or ministry is to reach one specific person or a small select group. For example, you may pool your resources over five years to help one inmate be exonerated and released from prison. It is a success since it fulfills God's divine plan.

Application for Activation

We may find achieving our goals does not bring the result that we imagined. God desires for us to submit to His will by obeying His laws and commands. Once we align our lives with God, He can direct us according to His divine plan. It becomes easier to know what to do because the Holy Spirit helps us understand the needs of others. In today's world, there are people who need help enrolling in health plans, obtaining housing, finding a job, someone to listen to them, court advocates, mental health counseling, treatment for addictions, food for their families, warm coats, and so on. Even if we help one person, that is success. Why? You changed their life with one act of kindness and love. This enables others to see God in you. Then, God gets the glory, which is the ultimate goal.

Follow the Spirit

What God wants me to do:

_____

_____

_____

_____

Remember Your Thoughts

Special insights I have learned:

_____

_____

_____

_____

More Light on the Text

1 Kings 8:54–61

The construction of the Temple of the Lord has been completed; the whole congregation of Israel has gathered at the Temple courts for its dedication. The Ark of the Covenant, which was brought from Zion, the city of David, is now positioned in its place in the Temple (vv. 1–13). King Solomon stands in front of the altar and addresses the people. He recites the promises God made to David: that his heir would be the one to build the Temple in His name, and that God would faithfully fulfill His Word. Solomon has ascended the throne of his father David and has completed the Temple (vv. 14–21). He then devotes much time to addressing God, interceding on behalf of his people in prayer. He asks God to forgive his people when they sinned, to have mercy on them when they repent, and deliver them from calamities pronounced upon them as consequences of their sin (vv. 22–51). Then Solomon turns his attention to blessing the people and praising the Lord for His faithfulness (vv. 54–61).

54 And it was so, that when Solomon had made an end of praying all this prayer and supplication unto the LORD, he arose from before the altar of the LORD, from kneeling on his knees with his hands spread up to heaven.

Verse 54 serves as a transition from the previous thought to the next part of the narrative. The verse starts with the phrase, "And it was so," which translates to the Hebrew word *hayah* (**HAW-yaw**). It is often rendered "it came to pass, it happened," or "it follows that." It connects the preceding thought to the subsequent; it also introduces the next part of a story.

After Solomon has concluded his "prayer and supplication" to the Lord, he gets up "from kneeling on his knees with his hands spread up to heaven." The words for prayer,—*tephillah* (**teh-feel-LAW**), which means "intercession" and "supplication," and *techinnah* (**teh-kheen-NAW**), which means "entreaty or plea,"—are used synonymously here (see last week's study under v. 27). The use of the two words shows the intensity and gravity of Solomon's prayer "unto the LORD." Here "the LORD" is the Hebrew word, *Yahweh* (**YAH-way**), which means "the Self-Existent or Eternal"; it is also rendered *Jehovah* (**yeh-ho-VAW**), "the existing One." Yahweh is the Jewish proper name of the one true God. The name is considered sacred to the Jews, and in reverence, it is never pronounced.

After the somewhat extended prayer, Solomon stands from his kneeling position with his hands stretched toward heaven. At the beginning of the prayer, "kneeling" is omitted. Rather, it reads, "Solomon stood before the altar of the LORD in the presence of all the congregation of Israel, and spread forth his hands toward heaven" (v. 22). However, the same account in 2 Chronicles reads, "he stood, and kneeled down upon his knees before all the congregation of Israel, and spread forth his hands toward heaven" (2 Chronicles 6:13–14). It means that Solomon stands on the platform and, facing the audience, he addresses them (vv. 14–21). After speaking to the people, Solomon kneels facing the altar and with outstretched hands toward heaven, he prays to Yahweh.

This is the first time kneeling in prayer is mentioned in the Bible. Kneeling is a common posture for prayer and worship in the Bible (Ezra 9:5, Daniel 6:10, Luke 22:41, Ephesians 3:14). Socially, kneeling down before a superior is a show of humility, respect, and worship. This practice is common in some African traditions where respect is extremely important; one kneels down or prostrates when one meets or sees an elder, king, or traditional ruler to greet him. Solomon and other biblical figures seem to be conscious of this. So he humbly and in reverence kneels before the sovereign, promise-keeping God and prays.

After praying, Solomon rises from his kneeling position "with his hands spread up to heaven." At the beginning of this prayer, we read that he "spread out his hands toward heaven" (v. 22, cf. 2 Chronicles 6:13). It implies that

Solomon had his hands stretched out toward heaven throughout the prayer—he never let them down. One raises one's hands before an officer of the law when under arrest as a show of surrender and vulnerability—under the mercy of a superior, especially God. Lifting hands is also a common posture for worship in both the Old and New Testaments. It is also a common mode of worship among Christians in many contemporary churches.

55 And he stood, and blessed all the congregation of Israel with a loud voice, saying, 56 Blessed be the LORD, that hath given rest unto his people Israel, according to all that he promised: there hath not failed one word of all his good promise, which he promised by the hand of Moses his servant.

Solomon has been kneeling in prayer on the platform near the altar, with his hands lifted toward God. He now stands to give his people a blessing. The word "blessed" is used twice here, once for the people and the other for God (vv. 55–56). It is the Hebrew *barak* (**baw-RAK**). The same word, used with slightly different meanings. The first blessing to the congregation of Israel means that he pronounced a blessing or benediction on the people—normally a priestly duty (Numbers 6:22–27). However, in a ceremonial occasion such as this, the king could give the blessing as David did after the Ark was brought to Jerusalem (2 Samuel 6:17–18). The use of *barak* in verse 56 seems to focus on God but is also directed toward the people.

The phrase "Blessed be the LORD" is an act of adoration and worship; it can also be rendered "praise be to God." It is an outburst of praise aimed at expressing the faithfulness of God for all He has done for them and for giving His people rest as He promised. Solomon emphasizes this truth with the clause, "there hath not failed one word of all his good promise." The word "rest" comes from *menuchah* (**men-oo-KHAW**),

254

which means "to repose or relax peacefully, consolation, peace, and quietness."

As Solomon reviews the history of the Jewish nation, his conclusion is that the promises of God have never failed, not even once. He promised Moses that He would give the nation rest (Exodus 33:14, Deuteronomy 25:19). He empowered Joshua to defeat the nations in Canaan and claim the land for Israel's inheritance. He also promised Moses that when they had entered into the promised rest, God would give them a sanctuary where they could offer their sacrifices and worship God (Deuteronomy 12:1–14). Now that sanctuary has been provided. And after the conquest of Canaan under Joshua, the Lord gave Israel a period of rest from their enemies (Joshua 11:23, 21:44–45, 22:4).

Solomon knows the history of Joshua, and he says, "There hath not failed one word of all his good promise, which he promised by the hand of Moses his servant." This is a quotation he gleans directly from Joshua's farewell speech to the leaders where Joshua emphasized the same truth of God's faithfulness (Joshua 21:45; 23:14–15). Although rest from their wilderness wandering was granted to the people under Joshua, there still remained land left to possess (Joshua 13:1; Judges 1). It was only after David's conquests that complete and lasting rest was granted to Israel (2 Samuel 7:1; 1 Kings 5:4). That promise is now totally fulfilled without missing an iota and was now being celebrated at the dedication ceremony.

57 The LORD our God be with us, as he was with our fathers: let him not leave us, nor forsake us: 58 That he may incline our hearts unto him, to walk in all his ways, and to keep his commandments, and his statutes, and his judgments, which he commanded our fathers.

In addition to the previous blessing, Solomon highlights God's faithfulness in keeping one important promise God gave to his ancestors and often repeated throughout their history: the promise that the Lord would never leave His people or forsake them. The Lord made this promise to Abraham (Genesis 17:19, 21); He promised to be with Isaac (Genesis 26:3, 24) and with Jacob (Genesis 28:15; 31:3; 46:1–4). The promise was renewed with Moses (Exodus 3:12; 33:14); Moses repeated it to Joshua (Deuteronomy 31:7–8).

The Lord Himself also reassured Joshua of the promise (Joshua 1:5, 9; 3:7) and fulfilled it (Joshua 6:27). Gideon received the promise (Judges 6:15–16), and the prophet Samuel repeated it to the nation (1 Samuel 12:22). Solomon obtained the same promise from David when he chose him to build the Temple.

Solomon now calls on God to help him and his people to have hearts inclined to the Lord and to be willing to walk in His ways and eager to obey His commandments. Solomon asks God for divine work of grace within his people to enable them to be faithful to their own part of the covenant (Deuteronomy 30:6; Psalm 51:10–12). Without God, we can do nothing. Our faith is a gift; even our desire to obey is the work of grace (Ephesians 2:8–9).

59 And let these my words, wherewith I have made supplication before the LORD, be nigh unto the LORD our God day and night, that he maintain the cause of his servant, and the cause of his people Israel at all times, as the matter shall require: 60 That all the people of the earth may know that the LORD is God, and that there is none else.

To conclude his prayer, Solomon appeals to the Lord to remember all the prayer and supplication he brought before Him on behalf of himself and of his people. He further asks the Lord to keep watch over all the requests and to meet his and the needs of his people accordingly. It is gratifying to know that no sincere prayer offered to the Lord is ever forgotten; He hears and remembers our prayers and answers them in His time and in His own way (see Revelation 5:8 and 8:3). The purpose of the people's faithful obedience and the Lord's faithfulness to answer their prayers is that all the nations of the world will also come to "know that the Lord is God, and that there is no other god besides the Lord." Their obedience coupled with answers to their prayer will encourage other nations to trust the Lord God of Israel. How encouraging to know that the prayer of one man could touch and influence a whole world!

61 Let your heart therefore be perfect with the LORD our God, to walk in his statutes, and to keep his commandments, as at this day.

Solomon ends the prayer part of the dedication ceremony by calling on the people to maintain a good relationship with the Lord as they have that day. He asks three things from them. First, "Let your heart be perfect with the Lord our God." The word "perfect" comes from the Hebrew *shalem* (**shaw-LEM**), which means complete, whole. That is, they should have undivided obedience to the Lord—they should yield totally, and wholly devote themselves to God and not to other gods (1 Kings 9:6). Unfortunately, Solomon later failed in this area (1 Kings 11:4). Second, they should walk in His statutes; and third, they should keep His commandments. In this nontechnical context, there is no meaningful distinction between statutes and commandments. Keeping them is how Israel will keep their hearts perfect before God. Solomon ends by encouraging the people that they are to keep God's commandments "as at

this day." He assures them they are currently doing everything correctly in their worship of the Lord. All they have to do now is keep it up.

Sources:
Biblesoft's New Exhaustive Strong's Numbers and Concordance with Expanded Greek-Hebrew Dictionary. Biblesoft, Inc., 2006.
Dake, Finis Jennings. *Dake's Annotated Reference Bible.* 1963.
Douglas, J. D., ed. *New Bible Dictionary (Second Edition).* Downers Grove, IL: Intervarsity Press. 1982. 1127–1131.
Interlinear Transliterated Bible. Biblesoft, Inc., 2006.
Life Application Study Bible NIV. Carol Stream, IL; Tyndale House Publishers, Inc.
Life Application Study Bible, New Revised Standard Version. Wheaton, IL: Tyndale House Publishers, Inc., 1989. 550–555.
The NIV Study Bible (Tenth Anniversary Edition). Grand Rapids, MI: Zondervan Publishing House, 1995. 459–464, 480–484.
Unger, Merril F. *Unger's Bible Dictionary.* Chicago, IL: Moody Press. 1985. 632–633, 1035–1037.
Zondervan NIV Study Bible. Grand Rapids, MI; Zondervan, 2008.

Daily Bible Readings

MONDAY
Hezekiah Restores the Temple
(2 Chronicles 29:3–11)

TUESDAY
Solomon Seeks Wisdom to Govern
(1 Kings 3:5–14)

WEDNESDAY
Solomon's Success Based on His Obedience
(1 Kings 9:1–9)

THURSDAY
Solomon and God's Glory Compared
(Matthew 6:25–30)

FRIDAY
Temple Completed and Dedicated
(2 Chronicles 7:1–6)

SATURDAY
Festivities Ended; People Return Home
(2 Chronicles 7:8–11)

SUNDAY
Solomon Blesses the People; Urges Faithfulness
(1 Kings 8:54–61)

Teaching Tips

Words You Should Know

A. Tempted (v. 1) *peirazo* (Gk.)—To test or entice to sin

B. Ministered (v. 11) *diakonein* (Gk.)—To serve

Teacher Preparation

Unifying Principle—Passing the Tests. People are tempted in many ways to turn aside from what they know is right. How can we resist such temptations? Jesus resisted the devil's temptations by quoting the Scriptures, thus demonstrating His single-minded obedience to God.

A. Read the Bible Background and Devotional Reading.

B. Pray for your students and lesson clarity.

C. Read the lesson Scripture in multiple translations.

O—Open the Lesson

A. Begin the class with prayer.

B. As a class, explore the individual and systemic nature of power—good and bad; how power is used and misused. Identify ways the church is tempted to achieve control and dominion, historically and today.

C. Have the students read the Aim for Change and the In Focus story.

D. Ask students how events like those in the story weigh on their hearts and how they can view these events from a faith perspective.

P—Present the Scriptures

A. Read the Focal Verses.

B. Have the class share what Scriptures stand out for them and why, with particular emphasis on today's context.

C. Discuss the Background and The People, Places, and Times sections.

E—Explore the Meaning

A. Use In Depth or More Light on the Text to facilitate a deeper discussion of the lesson text.

B. Pose the questions in Search the Scriptures and Discuss the Meaning.

C. Discuss the Liberating Lesson and Application for Activation sections.

N—Next Steps for Application

A. Summarize the value of staying focused only on God's Word.

B. End class with a commitment to pray for true worship and obedience to God.

Worship Guide

For the Superintendent or Teacher
Theme: Single-Minded Obedience
Song: "Jesus, Tempted in the Desert"
Devotional Reading: Psalm 91

Single-Minded Obedience

Bible Background • MATTHEW 4:1–11
Printed Text • MATTHEW 4:1–11 | Devotional Reading • PSALM 91

Aim for Change

By the end the lesson, we will: EXPLORE the story of Jesus' temptation in the wilderness, ASPIRE to obey God as Jesus demonstrated, and DEVELOP spiritual habits that can strengthen them in times of temptation.

In Focus

As Valerie boarded the train, she felt optimistic about the next phase in her life. She had always loved living in the big city, and after college, she couldn't wait to return to the same neighborhood where she was born and raised. Her life's passion was helping troubled teens in her community turn their lives around, and six years ago, God blessed her with the opportunity to work in full-time ministry with them.

Valerie thought she was set for life. But then the ministry lost its building and most of its funding, and it had to let go most of its employees, including Valerie. Just when she thought things couldn't get any worse, her health began to fail. The mounting hospital bills plunged her into so much debt she could no longer pay her mortgage. She lost her home. So now, Valerie was on a train headed to her uncle's place in a small town.

"How could you be so happy about losing everything and having to leave here?" her friend asked the day before.

"I ain't gonna lie. I had to remember all the rough spots God got me through. I believe He will get me through this one."

Valerie knew that her only hope was in God. Just as He had taken care of her before, He would again. How has God taken care of you in a time of crisis?

Keep in Mind

"Then saith Jesus unto him, Get thee hence, Satan: for it is written, Thou shalt worship the Lord thy God, and him only shalt thou serve" (Matthew 4:10, KJV).

"'Get out of here, Satan,' Jesus told him. 'For the Scriptures say, 'You must worship the LORD your God and serve only him'" (Matthew 4:10, NLT).

Focal Verses

KJV **Matthew 4:1** Then was Jesus led up of the Spirit into the wilderness to be tempted of the devil.

2 And when he had fasted forty days and forty nights, he was afterward an hungred.

3 And when the tempter came to him, he said, If thou be the Son of God, command that these stones be made bread.

4 But he answered and said, It is written, Man shall not live by bread alone, but by every word that proceedeth out of the mouth of God.

5 Then the devil taketh him up into the holy city, and setteth him on a pinnacle of the temple,

6 And saith unto him, If thou be the Son of God, cast thyself down: for it is written, He shall give his angels charge concerning thee: and in their hands they shall bear thee up, lest at any time thou dash thy foot against a stone.

7 Jesus said unto him, It is written again, Thou shalt not tempt the Lord thy God.

8 Again, the devil taketh him up into an exceeding high mountain, and sheweth him all the kingdoms of the world, and the glory of them;

9 And saith unto him, All these things will I give thee, if thou wilt fall down and worship me.

10 Then saith Jesus unto him, Get thee hence, Satan: for it is written, Thou shalt worship the Lord thy God, and him only shalt thou serve.

11 Then the devil leaveth him, and, behold, angels came and ministered unto him.

NLT **Matthew 4:1** Then Jesus was led by the Spirit into the wilderness to be tempted there by the devil.

2 For forty days and forty nights he fasted and became very hungry.

3 During that time the devil came and said to him, "If you are the Son of God, tell these stones to become loaves of bread."

4 But Jesus told him, "No! The Scriptures say, 'People do not live by bread alone, but by every word that comes from the mouth of God.'"

5 Then the devil took him to the holy city, Jerusalem, to the highest point of the Temple,

6 and said, "If you are the Son of God, jump off! For the Scriptures say, 'He will order his angels to protect you. And they will hold you up with their hands so you won't even hurt your foot on a stone.'"

7 Jesus responded, "The Scriptures also say, 'You must not test the LORD your God.'"

8 Next the devil took him to the peak of a very high mountain and showed him all the kingdoms of the world and their glory.

9 "I will give it all to you," he said, "if you will kneel down and worship me."

10 "Get out of here, Satan," Jesus told him. "For the Scriptures say, 'You must worship the LORD your God and serve only him.'"

11 Then the devil went away, and angels came and took care of Jesus.

The People, Places, and Times

Satan. In Hebrew, the name means "adversary" or "accuser." God's people's understanding of evil developed over the course of time, but by Jesus' day, the Jewish understanding of Satan was an embodied force of evil, a fallen angel who had rebelled against God before Creation. He is the chief of the demons and is called many names and titles: the devil, Beelzebub, the prince of the power of the air. He is very mighty and tries to tempt or harm God's children, but in the end, he will be captured and defeated by God and his angelic hosts.

Background

The Gospel of Matthew makes numerous references to Old Testament Scriptures that foretell the coming of the Messiah. The Jews were anticipating the arrival of the Messiah in the midst of Roman occupation. Matthew writes to provide evidence to Jews that Jesus of Nazareth is the Son of God, the Messiah. In Matthew 3, John the Baptist, as the forerunner for Christ, called for the Children of Israel to repent. In doing that, he fulfilled Isaiah's prophecy (Isaiah 40:3). Jesus makes His public appearance and asks John to baptize Him in the Jordan River. John does, and at that moment the Holy Spirit descends in the form of a dove to bear witness to this truth and God makes an audible public statement identifying Jesus as His beloved Son. (Matthew 3:13–17).

What Scriptural evidence can you cite to prove that Jesus Christ is the Son of God?

At-A-Glance

1. Passing the Flesh Test (Matthew 4:1–4)
2. Passing the Power Test (vv. 5–7)
3. Passing the Pride Test (vv. 8–11)

In Depth

1. Passing the Flesh Test (Matthew 4:1–4)

Shortly following God's pronouncement of Jesus as His beloved Son in whom He is well pleased (Matthew 3:17), Jesus is led by the Holy Spirit to the wilderness where He fasts for forty days. The Scriptures do not give details on why Jesus was led to the wilderness, but wilderness throughout the Old Testament is indicative of a place of solitude, consecration, and revelation. After fasting and no doubt praying during the forty days of solitude, Jesus is met by the devil (the Tempter) who brings Jesus His first test. Satan hearkens back to the visible blessing of God during Jesus' baptism. The Tempter says that if Jesus is who God says He is (the Son of God), then Jesus should prove it by using His power to provide food for Himself. Jesus stands firm in His identity,

trusting God for His provision and not seeking to satisfy His hunger. Jesus does not depart from the commandment of God; He treasures the words of God more than His necessary food. Therefore, Jesus replied to Satan's suggestion by quoting Deuteronomy 8:3. He selects this passage because God used the wilderness to test and prove the Children of Israel and to humble them (Deuteronomy 8:2) so that they would know that they were to remain completely dependent on Him. Jesus cites this verse to make a statement to the devil that although He is the Son of God and came from God, He remains completely yielded to His Father. Jesus' answer reminds us that food is not what really sustains life. The Word of God is.

What can we learn from Jesus about remaining resolute in our dependence on God's provision?

2. Passing the Power Test (Matthew 4:5–7)

The devil is not done with his discourse and sought yet another opportunity to question Jesus' identity and move Jesus from His faithfulness to God. The devil leads Jesus to the height of the Temple in the holy city of Jerusalem. He then asks Jesus to prove who He is by a display of power—throwing Himself off the building. The devil even cites Psalm 91:11–12 in his attempt to back up his challenge. He wants Jesus to frivolously use His divine power, but Jesus does not take the bait. Instead, Jesus responds by referencing Deuteronomy 6:16 where the Lord God commands Israel not to put Him to useless, vain tests to prove His care for them. Rather than flaunting His power by calling on angels to rescue Him to prove a point to the devil, Jesus relies again on the knowledge of who He is. He remains faithful to His Father.

Why is it important for God's people to be secure in their identity in Christ?

3. Passing the Pride Test (Matthew 4:8–11)

In what will be his last attempt for this encounter with Jesus, the devil leads Jesus to the top of a mountain and suggests that if Jesus bows down and worships him, he will give Him the world and all its glory. This is the devil's most audacious offer. He attempts to give Jesus what already belongs to Him (Daniel 7:13–14, Matthew 28:18). At this point, Jesus has had enough of Satan and tells him to get behind Him, be gone, get out! Jesus then quotes Scripture to let the devil know that as the Son of God He will worship God alone and remains subject to His Father (Exodus 34:14). After this last attempt, the devil leaves, and Jesus is refreshed, replenished, and served by the angels. When believers withstand tests, it is imperative to get rest in the presence of God to be restored and renewed.

How can we use Jesus' example to withstand the devil's schemes?

Search the Scriptures

1. Jesus met every temptation from the devil by remaining true to His purpose. What Scriptures did He use in His responses? (Matthew 4:4, 7, 10)

2. What Scripture did the devil misuse in his attempt to persuade Jesus? (Matthew 4:6, Psalm 91:11–12)

Discuss the Meaning

1. What can we learn from Jesus about how to meet everyday challenges to our character and identity?

2. How can we ensure that we remain focused on God's eternal purpose for our lives and not get caught up in selfish pursuits?

3. What did Jesus do in the wilderness that enabled Him to withstand temptation?

Liberating Lesson

In today's context, Christians are met with many opportunities to compromise their standards in order to achieve some goal. However, our belief system must remain rooted and grounded in what the Scriptures teach for right living and moral and ethical behavior in spite of cultural shifts. As God's standard bearers, like Jesus, we must also remain humble and let our light shine so that the world will see how we live as a testimony to the power of the God we serve and turn to Him. We must stand up for what is right at every level, no matter who agrees or disagrees. We must hold every system accountable to God's standards for making decisions for the common good.

Application for Activation

Hebrews 4:14 says that Jesus is our High Priest, He is able to sympathize with struggles of our human condition because He was tempted as we were but did not sin. Jesus was able to withstand. How did Jesus do it? He knew His identity, stuck to His purpose, and remained submitted to the will of the Father. Examine your life for areas in need of strengthening to withstand in these times knowing that you have an Advocate in Jesus who lives to make intercession for you.

Follow the Spirit

What God wants me to do:

_____

_____

_____

_____

Remember Your Thoughts

Special insights I have learned:

_____

_____

_____

_____

More Light on the Text
Matthew 4:1–11

Jesus' dialogue with John the Baptist (Matthew 3) and with the devil (Matthew 4:1–11) provides a foundation for His ministry throughout the remainder of the Gospel. Interpreters have understood the temptations outlined here in a variety of ways. Some scholars place emphasis on Jesus being tempted in a fully human manner with the temptations that typically befall the Christian. In that light, Matthew 4:1–6 attempts to show how Jesus withstood the human temptations of gluttony, glory, and greed as an example to His followers. A variant of this interpretation is psychological. Consequently, the temptation of Jesus shows how faithful persons can overcome the temptations of materialism, self-centered actions, and power over the world. Other scholars argue that Jesus' temptations are the distinctive temptations of the Savior, who is preparing to undertake His necessary role in salvation history. In this case, a particular focus is placed on His obedience throughout the ordeal. Those scholars see this as the decisive struggle between Jesus and Satan. These struggles represent the three basic dimensions of messiahship: 1. the prophetic (the Word of God); 2. priestly (the Temple); and 3. royal (the kingdoms of the world). A third group of scholars identifies an apologetic (a way to defend the Gospel) role for the temptation story. In this view, the account challenges false understandings of the Messiah in the Jewish world at the time. It is also possible that the temptation story serves to address an internal church dispute regarding Jesus. In some cases, this reflects the insistence by early Christians that Jesus was the Messiah, despite the fact that He did not fit the prescribed categories—most notably that the Messiah would not be killed. None of these, however, appears capable of explaining fully what unfolds here.

1 Then was Jesus led up of the Spirit into the wilderness to be tempted of the devil.

The role of the Spirit in leading Jesus to the wilderness should be taken as a model for the whole ministry of Jesus to come. Mountainous wilderness can be found immediately outside the Jordan valley. The word "wilderness" (Gk. *eremon*, **EY-ray-mon**) looks back to Matthew 3:1 and 3 as well as forward to other elements that form a typology based on the Old Testament testing of Israel in the wilderness. The agency of the devil in this verse is important to understanding what it means for Jesus to be tempted. Judaism in Jesus' day struggled with the idea of the source of sin, wondering if God sent temptation or simply allowed it. Even though Jesus is being led by the Spirit, the temptation comes from the devil. James is clear in his teaching that God does not tempt people (James 1:13–14). However, the sense that God was involved was never lost in Jewish thought. This can be seen in this verse through the action of the Spirit in leading Jesus into the wilderness.

Because of the role of the Spirit and the role of the devil, the message appears to be that Satan tempts and, thereby, God tests (see also Job 1–2). Consequently, the actions of the devil aside, the same word "tempted" (Gk. *peirazo*, **pay-RAD-zo**) that is used to refer to God's testing of Israel in the wilderness is echoed here (Exodus 16:4, 20:20). The actions of the devil are not the central focus of this story. The focus is rather on the temptations themselves and the nature of their rebuff. Later in this Gospel, the devil will be identified as the one who sows the weeds (Matthew 13:39) and the one for whom the eternal fire has been prepared (Matthew 25:41). He is called "the tempter"(Matthew 4:3) and "Satan" (Matthew 4:10) when he is sent away by Jesus. This will be echoed later, when Peter is identified with Satan (Matthew 16:23). His role as prince of the demons comes up when he is called "Beelzebub" (Matthew 12:27).

2 And when he had fasted forty days and forty nights, he was afterward an hungred.

Matthew identifies Jesus' failure to eat with the religious practice of fasting (cf. Luke 4:2). The Bible offers no particular theory of fasting, but it takes place in a variety of contexts. It is fundamentally a practice of mourning, generally with repentance.

In Israel, it was a practice of ritualized mourning in the face of disaster (see Isaiah 58:3–6; Jeremiah 14:12; Joel 1:14). Fasting is also associated with seeking God's guidance, petitioning for God's assistance in a matter of immediate concern, and with an intense focus on God. Because of its public character, fasting is discussed critically in Matthew 6:16–18. The most likely reason for Jesus' fasting is consecrating Himself as He enters His earthly ministry. Thus, fasting brings the issues facing Jesus into sharp focus. The resulting hunger has a clear parallel in the testing of Israel in the wilderness (Deuteronomy 8:2–3), while "forty days and forty nights" echoes the forty years the Israelites spent in the wilderness. Such an association with the time of Moses makes it clear that Jesus' fasting is extraordinary.

3 And when the tempter came to him, he said, If thou be the Son of God, command that these stones be made bread.

Having been presented in Matthew 4:1, the devil is now introduced into the story as "the tempter." Jesus' hunger becomes the occasion for the first temptation. The devil's use of "if" is not an expression of doubt on his part, nor is it an attempt to suggest that Jesus should doubt. Rather, it is on the basis of Jesus' status as the Son of God that He is being encouraged to act. Jesus knows that He is the Son of God and thus has a special status. The devil, then, suggests that this status is something to be exploited— that Jesus should use His opportunities as the Son of God to see to his own needs (i.e.,

satisfying His hunger). We can imagine that the stones involved are of the size and general shape that loaves of bread would have been. The bread would satisfy Jesus' hunger and allow the devil to declare a victory over God.

4 But he answered and said, It is written, Man shall not live by bread alone, but by every word that proceedeth out of the mouth of God.

Jesus responds to the devil with words from Deuteronomy 8:3, which take us once again to the wilderness testing of Israel. When the Israelites were hungry in the wilderness and longed for the bread of Egypt (Exodus 16:3), God provided "manna" to nourish them (Deuteronomy 8:3). Specifically, Deuteronomy 8:2–5 was concerned with the way God led the people of Israel during the forty years in the wilderness by testing to see whether they would keep His commandments, in order to train them like children. This passage makes it clear that our attention should not be focused on bread or any desire for fulfilling our natural needs or yearnings, especially if that means moving our attention from God's promises and truths in order to seek satisfaction for ourselves. We are to seek God's kingdom above all else (Matthew 6:33).

Thus, the desire for bread does not influence Jesus to erroneously use His power and authority. Satan implies that turning stones into bread in the midst of hunger would be a sign of Jesus' privileged position as the Son of God, but Jesus' answer operates in more general terms and focuses the issue on how followers should live before God. While Jesus is unique as the Son of God, the nature of the temptation to rely on ourselves instead of God is no different from what faces all human beings. Here the noun *rhema* (**RAY-mah**) is used in a narrow fashion as "word," but elsewhere in Matthew it is sometimes used in the general sense of "thing" or "matter." Given this narrow usage, what is likely meant here is that listening to God is life-sustaining.

5 Then the devil taketh him up into the holy city, and setteth him on a pinnacle of the temple,

The wilderness location is abandoned in the second and third temptations, although this story still echoes the wilderness experience of Israel. The devil "taketh" Jesus here, as he will do again for the third temptation (Matthew 4:8). The word involved, *parelaben* (Gk. **pah-RAY-lah-ben**), was also used for Joseph's taking Jesus (and his mother) to Egypt, as well as for the return journey (2:14, 21). It is likely that Matthew takes up the word here to establish a contrast between Joseph and the devil: Joseph acts to protect the child Jesus, while the devil seeks to entice the adult Jesus to His doom. The status of Jerusalem is highlighted in the use of "the holy city" to describe it. The Temple location within the city takes this even further since it is the official dwelling place of the presence of God, pointing to the reality of God's help (cf. 1 Kings 8:22–53). It is not entirely clear what is meant by the translation "pinnacle" (Gk. *pterugion*, **puh-teh-ROO-gee-on**, literally "wing"), since the Temple is not described as having tall spires. Its role here, though, is just to provide a high-enough point from which Jesus can be encouraged to jump.

6 And saith unto him, If thou be the Son of God, cast thyself down: for it is written, He shall give his angels charge concerning thee: and in their hands they shall bear thee up, lest at any time thou dash thy foot against a stone.

The first temptation rested on the immediacy of Jesus' hunger. This second temptation operates in a larger framework. The devil points to the promise in Psalm 91:11–12 of protection for the godly. However, Jesus is being asked to create the situation of need first. Jesus is called upon to force the hand of divine protection by provoking a life-threatening situation. Jesus is to demand that God, on the basis of His status

as the Son of God, rescue Him from a threat upon His life. According to the devil's theory, Jesus can test God by throwing Himself off the pinnacle since His life will be preserved through angelic help. But this test hearkens forward to another significant scene where Jesus will refuse to obey the scribes who taunt Him as the Son of God, tell him to come down from the Cross and save Himself (Matthew 27:40). Thus, what is happening here in the second temptation points forward to the obedience of the Son of God not only throughout His life and ministry on earth but especially during His Passion, the suffering He experienced before dying on the Cross.

7 Jesus said unto him, It is written again, Thou shalt not tempt the Lord thy God.

Jesus resists Satan's twisted logic. In response, He quotes Deuteronomy 6:16, where Israel is challenged to do better than they had at Massah. There they had confronted Moses about the preservation of their lives (Exodus 17:3; cf. 17:7). But it is not the people's place to dictate to God how God is to express His covenant commitment to them. Doubt, demand, and dissatisfaction appear to be the core components of the wilderness test of God (Exodus 17:2, 7; Numbers 14:22; Deuteronomy 6:16). In those verses we understand that instead of grumbling, the Israelites were admonished to accept God's pledge that He will do well by the people. Again, despite the particularity of the temptation in the specific case of Jesus, its fundamental form is not different from any temptation that faces other human beings.

8 Again, the devil taketh him up into an exceeding high mountain, and sheweth him all the kingdoms of the world, and the glory of them; 9 And saith unto him, All these things will I give thee, if thou wilt fall down and worship me.

The word "again" now introduces the third time that the devil takes Jesus to a new place. The devil promises to give Jesus not just the holy land, but "all the kingdoms of the world." Satan phrases this so that it appears that the devil has ownership of all that can be seen from the mountain and all the kingdoms of the world. In other words, it is the devil's gift so that the promise to give it comes from the devil, not God. The mountain location clearly underscores the importance of the event, as it does when mountains appear elsewhere in the Gospel. There is a steady rise in altitude, from the wilderness to the Temple pinnacle to a mountaintop, a climactic start to the third temptation. The two previous temptations were perversions of Jesus' calling as the Son of God. In this final temptation, the stakes are much higher. If He complies, Jesus would be abandoning His calling as the Son of God and transferring His allegiance to the devil. (Notice that the "if thou be the Son of God" drops out.) If Jesus were to take as His goal the possession of "all the kingdoms of the world, and the glory of them," then He would pursue this by following the ways of the world, desiring glory for Himself in this world, and becoming indebted to Satan. Indeed, this final temptation brings into the open what is to be understood as the goal of the prior two trials.

Jesus views the devil's offer in the light of the warning that He will later give others: "For what is a man profited, if he shall gain the whole world, and lose his own soul?" (Matthew 16:26) But "the whole world" is not an offer to other human beings as it is to Jesus here. In fact, the scale of the offer only highlights the unique status of Jesus as the Son of God. The glory of all the kingdoms of the world, as offered to Jesus, is to be contrasted with the heavenly glory of God's kingdom (see Matthew 16:27). After His ministry, death, and resurrection, God gives Jesus the positive counterpart to the Satanic counterfeit offered here in Matthew 4:8–9. The devil erroneously believes he has given Jesus a choice between following the devil's imagined authority and committing to the true authority of God as given to His only begotten son.

10 Then saith Jesus unto him, Get thee hence, Satan: for it is written, Thou shalt worship the Lord thy God, and him only shalt thou serve.

In this last account of Jesus' response—its climax—the devil is now called "Satan," the Greek form for the Hebrew word for "adversary." In line with the sense of climax for this third temptation, we find Jesus' decisive repudiation: "Get thee hence, Satan." Jesus follows His rebuff of Satan with another quotation from Deuteronomy 6:13. We should note that Jesus' response focuses on what is to be the proper demeanor before God, and once more He alludes to Israel in the wilderness setting. Even if giving Jesus all the kingdoms of the earth and their glory was within Satan's power, Jesus knows the ends would not have justified the means had He worshiped Satan to gain the world. No prize is worth breaking faith so severely with God who alone is worthy of worship.

11 Then the devil leaveth him, and, behold, angels came and ministered unto him.

Jesus has withstood every attempt of the devil to deflect Him from His calling as the Son of God. He has stood the test, and the devil has been rebuffed. Satan can do nothing other than withdraw. It is the nature of temptation to press at certain times. Jesus here faced, in a fundamental way, issues designed to tempt Him to take a life path different from that set for Him by His Father. Having withstood the temptations, angels come to Jesus' aid. The word "ministered" (Gk. *diakonein*, **dee-ah-KO-nayn**) can mean "serve" in a broad sense, but in the context of this passage, the imagery of being served at a table makes a reference to providing food. Jesus, who refused to turn stones into bread, receives food from heaven. The message is, God is no one's debtor.

Sources:

Aland, Kurt, ed. *Synopsis of the Four Gospels (10th edition)*. Stuttgart, Germany: German Bible Society, 1993.

Blount, Brian K. et al., eds. *True to Our Native Land: An African American New Testament Commentary*. Minneapolis, MN: Fortress Press, 2007.

Nolland, John. *The Gospel of Matthew (NIGTC)*. Grand Rapids, MI: Eerdmans, 2005.

Say It Correctly

Beelzebub. bee-**EL**-zeh-bub.
Massah. mass-**SAH**.

Daily Bible Readings

MONDAY
Don't Test the Lord
(Deuteronomy 6:16–25)

TUESDAY
Angels Guard Tempted Believers
(Psalm 91)

WEDNESDAY
Do Not Forget the Lord
(Deuteronomy 8:11–20)

THURSDAY
Jesus' Priestly Ministry
(Hebrews 4:14–5:10)

FRIDAY
Jesus, God's Beloved Son
(Matthew 3:13–17)

SATURDAY
The Kingdom of Heaven Is Here
(Matthew 4:12–17)

SUNDAY
Jesus Rejects Satan's Temptations
(Matthew 4:1–11)

Notes

Teaching Tips

Words You Should Know

A. Secret (v. 4) *kruptos* (Gk.)—Hidden, inner, private

B. Closet (v. 6) *tameion* (Gk.)—An inner storage room in a house

Teacher Preparation

Unifying Principle—The Pitfalls of Showing Off. Eager to be well thought of, people are pulled in a multitude of contradictory directions. How can we be true to the highest principles that we have been taught? In Matthew 5, Jesus taught the disciples the Beatitudes, and in Matthew 6, he warned them against practicing their piety in order to be praised by others.

A. Read the Bible Background and Devotional Reading.

B. Pray for your students and lesson clarity.

C. Read the lesson Scripture in multiple translations.

O—Open the Lesson

A. Begin the class with prayer.

B. Discuss ways to practice simplicity and humility in daily life.

C. Have the students read the Aim for Change and the In Focus story.

D. Ask students how events like those in the story weigh on their hearts and how they can view these events from a faith perspective.

P—Present the Scriptures

A. Read the Focal Verses.

B. Have the class share what Scriptures stand out for them and why, with particular emphasis on today's context.

C. Discuss the Background and The People, Places, and Times sections.

E—Explore the Meaning

A. Use In Depth or More Light on the Text to facilitate a deeper discussion of the lesson text.

B. Pose the questions in Search the Scriptures and Discuss the Meaning.

C. Discuss the Liberating Lesson and Application for Activation sections.

N—Next Steps for Application

A. Summarize the value of praying with humility.

B. End class with a commitment to prayer with pure motivations.

Worship Guide

For the Superintendent or Teacher
Theme: Piety That Honors God
Song: "Make Me a Channel of Your Peace"
Devotional Reading: Luke 11:1–13

Piety That Honors God

Bible Background • ECCLESIASTES 5:1-6; MATTHEW 6:1–8
Printed Text • MATTHEW 6:1–8 | Devotional Reading • LUKE 11:1–13

Aim for Change

By the end of this lesson, we will: UNDERSTAND Jesus' teachings about not practicing one's piety in order to be noticed by others, REPENT of making a show of religiosity in order to receive praise from others, and PRACTICE simplicity and humility in our devotional lives.

In Focus

Georgia and James sat at their desks with hands folded, heads bowed, and eyes closed. It was the lunch hour, and they had decided to forgo lunch and pray. Georgia and James needed to hear from God. After ten years of employment at the university, they were both wondering if they would be laid off.

Georgia had transferred into the position only seven months earlier when her former job had been phased out. Up until now, her work record had been impeccable. Now her new supervisor was telling her that her work was unsatisfactory. James had worked in his department for seven years.

"Dear Lord," Georgia prayed. "Please give us the strength to endure whatever comes our way and help us have the right attitude, especially toward my supervisor. I trust in you and not the situation. Show us what to do, Lord, as we prepare for our immediate and distant future." After work, James and Georgia decided to call a couple of their good friends and invite them over for dinner on Friday evening. This would be a good time to discuss what their future may hold with close and trusted friends. On Monday, they would know for sure what would happen.

Where did you turn in times of trouble? Is God your first choice for help and are you willing to trust God's Word?

Keep in Mind

"Take heed that ye do not your alms before men, to be seen of them: otherwise ye have no reward of your Father which is in heaven" (Matthew 6:1, KJV).

"Watch out! Don't do your good deeds publicly, to be admired by others, for you will lose the reward from your Father in heaven" (Matthew 6:1, NLT).

Focal Verses

KJV **Matthew 6:1** Take heed that ye do not your alms before men, to be seen of them: otherwise ye have no reward of your Father which is in heaven.

2 Therefore when thou doest thine alms, do not sound a trumpet before thee, as the hypocrites do in the synagogues and in the streets, that they may have glory of men. Verily I say unto you, They have their reward.

3 But when thou doest alms, let not thy left hand know what thy right hand doeth:

4 That thine alms may be in secret: and thy Father which seeth in secret himself shall reward thee openly.

5 And when thou prayest, thou shalt not be as the hypocrites are: for they love to pray standing in the synagogues and in the corners of the streets, that they may be seen of men. Verily I say unto you, They have their reward.

6 But thou, when thou prayest, enter into thy closet, and when thou hast shut thy door, pray to thy Father which is in secret; and thy Father which seeth in secret shall reward thee openly.

7 But when ye pray, use not vain repetitions, as the heathen do: for they think that they shall be heard for their much speaking.

8 Be not ye therefore like unto them: for your Father knoweth what things ye have need of, before ye ask him.

NLT **Matthew 6:1** "Watch out! Don't do your good deeds publicly, to be admired by others, for you will lose the reward from your Father in heaven.

2 When you give to someone in need, don't do as the hypocrites do—blowing trumpets in the synagogues and streets to call attention to their acts of charity! I tell you the truth, they have received all the reward they will ever get.

3 But when you give to someone in need, don't let your left hand know what your right hand is doing.

4 Give your gifts in private, and your Father, who sees everything, will reward you.

5 When you pray, don't be like the hypocrites who love to pray publicly on street corners and in the synagogues where everyone can see them. I tell you the truth, that is all the reward they will ever get.

6 But when you pray, go away by yourself, shut the door behind you, and pray to your Father in private. Then your Father, who sees everything, will reward you.

7 When you pray, don't babble on and on as the Gentiles do. They think their prayers are answered merely by repeating their words again and again.

8 Don't be like them, for your Father knows exactly what you need even before you ask him!"

The People, Places, and Times

Prayer. Any kind of communication from the heart of man to the ear of God can be called prayer. Throughout the Scriptures, we find God answering the prayers of those people who need Him. Abel's blood cried out, and God heard and avenged him (Genesis 4:10–12). The Hebrews, while in Egypt, cried out because of their hard taskmasters, and God sent Moses to deliver them (Exodus 3:1–4:17). David prayed for forgiveness and restoration after being caught in sin, and God heard his prayer (Psalm 51). Elisha prayed for his servant's eyes to be opened to see the army of the Lord, and God made it so (2 Kings 6:17). The disciples asked Jesus to teach them to pray after they had watched Him (Luke 11:2–4). Peter prayed, and Tabitha woke up from the dead (Acts 9:40–41). Both faith (Mark 11:24) and forgiveness (Mark 11:25) are needed in order for prayers to be answered.

Background

The Gospel according to Matthew emphasizes the authoritative teaching ministry of Jesus Christ and records five sermons. These are found in chapters 5–7; 10; 13; 18–20; and 24–25. There are more sermons recorded in Matthew than any of the other Gospels. Throughout his Gospel, Matthew uses terminology and references that would be well-known to Jews because he is writing to prove to them that Jesus is their Messiah, and the promised King.

The first sermon is frequently referred to as the Sermon on the Mount (Matthew 5–7). The multitudes followed Jesus "from Galilee, Decapolis, Jerusalem, Judea and beyond the Jordan" (Matthew 4:25). They were witnesses as Jesus healed the sick, the paralyzed, the demon-possessed, and the diseased. After they gathered, Jesus began to teach His disciples in the presence of the multitudes. Teaching regarding a new view of life was necessary because these followers, mostly Jewish, would have been largely familiar with and influenced by the Pharisees, who were well-learned, religious experts, but legalistic and hypocritical, far from the heart of God.

How can Jesus' example of meeting the needs of the people before He instructs them on the way to live affect the way the church serves unbelievers?

At-A-Glance

1. Giving in Secret (Matthew 6:1–4)
2. Praying in Secret (vv. 5–8)

In Depth

1. Giving in Secret (Matthew 6:1–4)

Jesus addresses three acts of righteousness often touted by Pharisees to prove their piety, or devotion to God: giving, praying, and fasting. This lesson, however, focuses on two of those areas: giving and prayer.

Jesus warns His disciples not to follow the example of those who give so that they can be seen and praised by people (vv. 1–2). Their actions do not show authentic worship of God. The word "alms" refers to what is given by someone for the benefit of a person in need. When He uses the word "when" instead of "if," Jesus is making it clear that everyone is expected to give alms; however, the manner and attitude of the good deed counts. Jesus uses entertaining exaggeration throughout this sermon (e.g., Matthew 7:3–5). Here, obviously, no one was going to the synagogue blowing a horn to announce their arrival at the offering box. Sounding a trumpet is a figure of speech that makes its point by exaggerating the fanfare these hypocrites' desire by looking for praise. Jesus cautions that improper motives carry their own reward because the actions are acknowledged only by others, thus forfeiting any reward from God.

Christ then provides instruction regarding how God expects good deeds to be done (vv. 3–4). "Let not thy left hand know what thy right hand doeth" doesn't seem to make literal sense. Jesus is using a figure of speech that explains a concept that should be taken to heart. We might rephrase this to say, "When your right hand does a good deed, don't lift your left hand to pat yourself on the back!" When good deeds are done secretly and without fanfare for "thy Father which seeth in secret," that will openly let others know that you are devoted to Him.

The Greek word we use for "hypocrite" can mean a play actor or pretender. How does this information affect your understanding of the word hypocrite as Jesus uses it?

2. Praying in Secret (Matthew 6:5–8)

Again, Christ warns His followers to not be like the pharisaical play-actors who pretend to have a relationship with God by showcasing their prayers in public. We cannot take this to mean that Jesus was condemning public prayer. After all, when He teaches His disciples later in this same sermon (Matthew 6:9–13), He is not only modeling a prayer but praying one! Jesus' concern is the internal motivation for praying in public. One should not pray in public to be heard and praised by others. Jesus gives the example of hypocrites who enjoy making a show of praying by "standing in the synagogues and in the corners of the streets" to be seen by others. He again reminds them how doing so cheats them of a greater reward.

Jesus teaches them the proper attitude for prayer (v. 6). He contrasts the "corners of the street" with going "into thy closet," and praying privately. A "closet" refers to an inner chamber used for storage (usually of food). Jesus wanted His listeners to understand the secret, private, and personal nature their communication with God should have.

Jesus warns his audience about praying like the pagans (v. 7). Greek prayers would mindlessly repeat as many of the names and titles of their gods as possible, endlessly listing favors and sacrifices performed. These prayers were like business contracts. Their hope was to inform, to gain the gods' or goddesses' attention in order to earn a response. Christ reminds them that God is different. He is not a business partner. He is their God and Father. The all-knowing, ever-present Lord does not need to be informed or reminded of their past actions. He already knows their future.

Why do you believe prayer is still important, when "your Father knows what you need before you ask Him"?

Search the Scriptures

1. What contrasts about attitudes and actions are made in these verses?

2. What does Jesus say the Father will do as a result of the proper attitude in giving and in praying?

3. What words are repeated in Matthew 6:1–8?

Discuss the Meaning

1. What does Jesus' teaching in these verses tell us about His views on prayer and giving?

2. We offer public prayers in churches and gatherings all the time. How can public prayer maintain the proper attitude that Jesus describes? What examples can you offer when public prayer did not demonstrate the proper attitude?

3. Consider how modern churches collect offerings. How can we avoid giving with the wrong attitude? What would be modern examples of an improper attitude in giving?

Liberating Lesson

The Pharisees were men who knew the law of Moses and studied the prophets, but somehow, they still missed the Messiah and failed to apply His teachings. This is a potential danger in today's churches, too. We can become so focused on maintaining our individual comforts and images that we neglect following Christ's commands to simply love God and love others.

Social media feeds into this temptation. It provides us with ample opportunities to give the illusion of righteousness by posting photos of good deeds as "examples" to others, announcing quiet times and lessons learned from them. If we are not careful, what begins as a great intention can easily slip into an improper motivation. When this happens, that disenfranchised community, that foreign village, that worthy cause, that life-changing revelation becomes a tool to gain attention, likes, or followers. And sadly, that becomes its own sham of a reward.

Application for Activation

This lesson suggests three things you can do this week to evaluate and demonstrate the attitude Jesus describes.

1. Pay attention to those around you who may be in need. It could be a co-worker who needs assistance, your child who needs you at an inconvenient time, someone at church who needs support, or a homeless person on the street who needs a meal. Meet the need. Then, tell no one. If you are not thanked, choose to be at peace, knowing that your Father in heaven rewards.

2. Be intentional about prayer this week. Set aside time with your Father, not just because you have a need, but to continue to develop an intimate relationship with the One who loves and knows you.

3. If you are on social media, pay attention to the things you choose to post this week. Evaluate your motivation for posts, photos, responses, or shares.

Follow the Spirit

What God wants me to do:

_____

_____

_____

_____

Remember Your Thoughts

Special insights I have learned:

_____

_____

_____

_____

More Light on the Text
Matthew 6:1–8

In this part of the Sermon on the Mount, Jesus talks about two important aspects of the holy life: almsgiving and prayer. The overall theme is that these activities of righteousness should be done with the right motivation.

1 Take heed that ye do not your alms before men, to be seen of them: otherwise ye have no reward of your Father which is in heaven.

Verse 1 starts with a warning to take heed. Jesus wants His audience to take special care to understand the teaching He is about to give. He begins with the issue of alms. These are the gifts one brings to share with those in need. Jesus tells His listeners not to bring alms to seek the attention of others. If one seeks attention from others, then the reward of others is all they will receive. There will be no reward from God. If one's actions are for the benefit and admiration of others, then they accomplish nothing. Jesus is directly contrasting His teaching with the actions of the Pharisees his hearers would have seen often publicly. The Pharisees were regarded as very pious for their devotion to the Law of God, but Jesus is teaching that following their actions to be seen rather than giving of out of humble obedience to the Law of God is unrighteous.

2 Therefore when thou doest thine alms, do not sound a trumpet before thee, as the hypocrites do in the synagogues and in the streets, that they may have glory of men. Verily I say unto you, They have their reward. 3 But when thou doest alms, let not thy left hand know what thy right hand doeth: 4 That thine alms may be in secret: and thy Father which seeth in secret himself shall reward thee openly.

Those who do such outlandish giving (v. 1) are called hypocrites. They look pious and righteous, but they are seeking to glorify themselves and not God. Jesus tells us that to give with an expectation of being noticed and rewarded by people is to give with the wrong attitude. Today we call this "blowing our own horn," and Jesus uses a similar phrase here, "sound a trumpet" (Gk. *salpizo*, **sall-PEED-zo**). We might do this by naming the amounts and frequency of our donations. Some people might expect to be rewarded and acknowledged by those in authority or by having their names placed on a pew or an offering plate. Such vanity in giving will be the extent of the reward.

Jesus expected that everyone would give alms. He makes this clear by saying "when" you give alms. Yet He goes on to say, "Let not your left hand know what thy right hand doeth." This figure of speech cannot be explained literally. The right hand generally refers to a good deed or a proper position while the left hand implies a negative action or a bad position. Jesus uses this same concept in Matthew 25:33 when speaking of judgment where the sheep are on His right hand, but the goats are on the left. By using this idiom, Jesus tells His listeners that if they wish to please God, they must avoid letting their ego and pride exaggerate what they have done. We must do our giving in secret, even from ourselves to some extent. There is a human tendency to brag, to tell ourselves what we can expect from God in response to our generosity. We should not feel a sense of self-importance and pride in doing something that we are supposed to do in humility and reverence for God. We are simply to do what God commands.

Jesus emphasizes the importance of our actions being done in "secret" (Gk. *kruptos*, **KROOP-toce**). This word is often used in negative contexts but can also simply refer to inner, private matters as it does here. When we give in secret, we give because it is the right thing to do, not because we will get something out of it. Still, this verse does assure us that if we give without seeking attention, God will see and reward us openly.

5 And when thou prayest, thou shalt not be as the hypocrites are: for they love to pray standing in the synagogues and in the corners of the streets, that they may be seen of men. Verily I say unto you, They have their reward. 6 But thou, when thou prayest, enter into thy closet, and when thou hast shut thy door, pray to thy Father which is in secret; and thy Father which seeth in secret shall reward thee openly.

Jesus applies this same "secrecy" principle to prayer. Jesus declares that praying to impress others makes people into hypocrites. He describes the hypocrites as those who find conspicuous places to stand and pray in the synagogue and even on the street corners. Their objective is to have everyone see them and admire their devotion and dedication. Instead, we should go into a secret closet (Gk. *tameion*, **tah-MAY-on**). This does not refer to a modern closet used to hang clothes or coats but to an inner room in a house, often used for storage. Even though no one else may know what we are doing, God will see, know, and reward us. This is not to say we should avoid praying in public, but we should not pray to show the public how pious and spiritual we are. Even in public, our motivation should be to glorify and seek God and God alone.

7 But when ye pray, use not vain repetitions, as the heathen do: for they think that they shall be heard for their much speaking. 8 Be not ye therefore like unto them: for your Father knoweth what things ye have need of, before ye ask him.

Jesus continues His instructions about prayer (v. 7). Not only are we to avoid praying in order to be seen by others, but we are to avoid the practice that was common to the Gentiles of using lots of words to try to impress or manipulate God.

The Gentiles had so many gods and so many names for them that they would try to list them all to make sure they included the right one. Also, they would try to flatter the gods in order to convince them to answer the prayer. Their prayers would often include mantra-like repetition, thinking that if they said the right words the right number of times, their god would have to respond. Jesus said specifically not to be like them. He assures us that God, our Father, the omniscient One, knows already what we need even before we ask. And God cannot be manipulated. God stands ready to answer our prayers and bless us because of the love He has for us.

Sources:

Global Study Bible, English Standard Version. Wheaton, IL: Crossway Publishers, 2012. 1329.

Keener, Craig S. *The IVP Bible Background Commentary: New Testament.* Downers Grove, IL: InterVarsity Press, 1993. 61–62.

Radmacher, Earl D., ed. *Nelson Study Bible, New King James Version.* Nashville, TN: Thomas Nelson Publishers, 1997. 1573–1574,1585.

Ryrie, Charles C. *Ryrie Study Bible, New International Version.* Chicago, IL: Moody Press. 1986. 1323.

Unger, Merrill F. *The New Unger's Bible Dictionary.* Chicago, IL: Moody Press, 1988. 997-998,1141–1143.

Walvoord, John F., and Roy B. Zuck, eds. *The Bible Knowledge Commentary: New Testament.* Wheaton, IL: Victor Books, SP Publications, Inc., 1983. 13–16, 32.

Zondervan Study Bible, New International Version. Grand Rapids, MI: Zondervan Publishers, 2002. 1463, 1477–78.

Say It Correctly

Decapolis. de-**KA**-poe-liss.

Daily Bible Readings

MONDAY
Listen and Act with Integrity
(Ecclesiastes 5:1–6)

TUESDAY
Work and Play Are God's Gifts
(Ecclesiastes 5:18–20)

WEDNESDAY
Express Your Faith through Actions
(Isaiah 1:11–17)

THURSDAY
A Doxology of Praise to God
(1 Chronicles 29:10–13)

FRIDAY
Forgive from the Heart
(Matthew 18:21–35)

SATURDAY
God's Will and Our Needs
(Matthew 6:16–21)

SUNDAY
Piety That Honors God
(Matthew 6:1–8)

Notes

Teaching Tips

Words You Should Know

A. Daily (v. 11) *epiousious* (Gk.)—That which is needed for tomorrow

B. Debts (v. 12) *opheilema* (Gk.)—That which is incurred after failure to pay what is due

Teacher Preparation

Unifying Principle—Ask for What Really Matters. We are often discouraged in the face of negative circumstances over which we seem to have no control. How can we experience the positive transformations we long for? Jesus taught the disciples to pray for God's kingdom to be manifested in their lives and in all creation.

A. Read the Bible Background and Devotional Reading.

B. Pray for your students and lesson clarity.

C. Read the lesson Scripture in multiple translations.

O—Open the Lesson

A. Begin the class with prayer.

B. As a class, write a contemporary version of the Lord's Prayer to express its deeper transformational meaning.

C. Have the students read the Aim for Change and the In Focus story.

D. Ask students how events like those in the story weigh on their hearts and how they can view these events from a faith perspective.

P—Present the Scriptures

A. Read the Focal Verses.

B. Have the class share what Scriptures stand out for them and why, with particular emphasis on today's context.

C. Discuss the Background and The People, Places, and Times sections.

E—Explore the Meaning

A. Use In Depth or More Light on the Text to facilitate a deeper discussion of the lesson text.

B. Pose the questions in Search the Scriptures and Discuss the Meaning.

C. Discuss the Liberating Lesson and Application for Activation sections.

N—Next Steps for Application

A. Summarize the value of praying like Jesus.

B. End class with a commitment to pray with pure motivations for ourselves and one another.

Worship Guide

For the Superintendent or Teacher
Theme: The Prayer of Jesus
Song: "The Lord's Prayer"
Devotional Reading: Psalm 40:1–10, 16–17

The Prayer of Jesus

Bible Background • MATTHEW 6:9–15
Printed Text • MATTHEW 6:9–15 | Devotional Reading • PSALM 40:1–10, 16–17

Aim for Change

By the end of the lesson, we will: IDENTIFY the place of the Lord's Prayer in the life of the church, LONG for the kingdom of God described in the Lord's Prayer to be manifested in our lives, and PRAY the Lord's Prayer with deeper appreciation for its meaning.

In Focus

Virginia knelt beside her bed and bowed her head. She knew that only God could loosen the grip that fear had on her. After nine years of remission from cancer, she had begun to feel similar symptoms as before. Virginia thought cancer may have returned.

She had made an appointment, and the doctor had run tests. Virginia had sat patiently for several blood tests and even an MRI. When the doctor called back, Virginia hoped she would get some answers, but the doctor decided they needed to run additional tests. At the same time, at work she was being considered for a promotion. Virginia wanted the promotion and already had ideas of how she could renovate the department. However, if the cancer returned, she would not have enough strength to supervise several people and do her work.

"Our Father, who art in heaven," Virginia prayed. "Thy kingdom come, Thy will be done in earth, as it is in heaven. Give us this day our daily bread. And forgive our debts, as we forgive our debtors. And lead us not into temptation, but deliver us from evil: For thine is the kingdom, and the power, and the glory, for ever. Amen."

Have you ever had something happen to you that was not in your control? Where did you turn? Today we want to examine God's teachings on prayer.

Keep in Mind

"Thy kingdom come, Thy will be done in earth, as it is in heaven" (Matthew 6:10, KJV).

"May your Kingdom come soon. May your will be done on earth, as it is in heaven" (Matthew 6:10, NLT).

Focal Verses

KJV **Matthew 6:9** After this manner therefore pray ye: Our Father which art in heaven, Hallowed be thy name.

10 Thy kingdom come, Thy will be done in earth, as it is in heaven.

11 Give us this day our daily bread.

12 And forgive us our debts, as we forgive our debtors.

13 And lead us not into temptation, but deliver us from evil: For thine is the kingdom, and the power, and the glory, for ever. Amen.

14 For if ye forgive men their trespasses, your heavenly Father will also forgive you:

15 But if ye forgive not men their trespasses, neither will your Father forgive your trespasses.

NLT **Matthew 6:9** Pray like this: Our Father in heaven, may your name be kept holy.

10 May your Kingdom come soon. May your will be done on earth, as it is in heaven.

11 Give us today the food we need,

12 and forgive us our sins, as we have forgiven those who sin against us.

13 And don't let us yield to temptation, but rescue us from the evil one.

14 "If you forgive those who sin against you, your heavenly Father will forgive you.

15 But if you refuse to forgive others, your Father will not forgive your sins."

The People, Places, and Times

The Lord's Prayer. Jesus taught His disciples how to pray by giving them a model, which is recorded both in Matthew 6:9–13 and Luke 11:1–4. Matthew places his telling of the prayer as part of the Sermon on the Mount near the beginning of Jesus' ministry. Luke, however, recounts the model prayer later, after His ministry has taken a turn out of Galilee and toward Jerusalem where Jesus would be killed. No doubt the subject of prayer is important enough that Jesus could have repeated Himself to forgetful disciples. The only other significant variation between the Gospel writers' records of the prayer is whether we should ask for forgiveness of "debts" (Matthew) or of "sins" (Luke). This is an interesting insight into the Jewish mind at the time. Debt is considered the same as sin, or just as bad as sin. Even today, we often speak of Jesus' sacrifice to forgive our sin as "paying the debt" for us.

Background

Jesus taught that the true righteousness of the kingdom must be applied in the everyday activities of life. He cautioned against practicing piety to impress other people. Almsgiving was designed to be a display of mercy, but the Pharisees had distorted it to demonstrate their devotion to religious duties in almsgiving and prayer. Giving without fanfare and quietly praying will receive its rewards.

Just as the Pharisees made a public display in giving, so they did in praying. They prayed in public places to be seen and heard by men. Jesus says they got their reward in the applause of the people. Instead of condemning prayer in general, though, the Lord purified the practice by directing us into a private place to be alone and pray to our Father. Jesus went on to give us an example of how to pray with certain guidelines.

At-A-Glance

1. Our Prayer (Matthew 6:9–13)
2. Our Forgiveness (vv. 14–15)

In Depth

1. Our Prayer (Matthew 6:9–13)

Jesus gave His followers a model prayer known as the Lord's Prayer. We should use this prayer as a pattern, as Jesus said to pray "after this manner." The purpose of prayer is to glorify God, and these are the guidelines for prayer: 1. it should involve worship, reverence, and exaltation of our Father; 2. it should concern itself with the work God is engaged in, namely, the establishment of God's kingdom and His will be done on earth; 3. it should be concerned with daily needs; 4. it should contain confession and seek forgiveness; and finally, 5. it should seek protection and deliverance from the evil one.

Notice this model prayer begins with the phrase "Our Father." We put God's concerns first; then we can bring in our own needs. This is the God-appointed way of having our needs met because prayer also prepares us for God's answer.

How do you pray most often? Is your prayer structured like the Lord's Prayer, another prayer, or not structured at all?

2. Our Forgiveness (vv. 14–15)

Forgiveness puts you in the right relationship with your brothers and sisters and with God. This enables you to pray effectively; therefore, forgiveness is an important part of prayer. We must pray with a forgiving spirit toward others. Christians must be prepared and willing to forgive the offenses of others. As Christ just taught earlier in this same sermon: "Blessed are the merciful, for they shall obtain mercy" (Matthew 5:7). If you do not forgive offenders, God will not forgive you.

We all need forgiveness. To be forgiven is to be released from all guilt and condemnation. Forgiving means we should not be bitter or hostile, seek revenge, or hold hard feelings against another person. We should not rejoice when others fall on hard times.

How do we reconcile Jesus' message that God's willingness to forgive is limited to our own willingness to forgive, with the message that Jesus offers forgiveness of sin free to all?

Search the Scriptures

1. How is forgiveness connected to prayer (v. 14)?

2. What does verse 13 mean in light of Matthew 4:1–11 (Lesson 10)? What does verse 11 mean in light of Matthew 6:2–4 (Lesson 11)?

Discuss the Meaning

1. What is prayer?

2. Why must we pray that God "lead us not into temptation" when we know that God does not tempt anyone (James 1:13)?

3. What elements of prayer are modeled in the Lord's Prayer? Are our prayers ineffective if we do not use these exact words or follow this exact outline?

Liberating Lesson

Many of us are tempted to spiritualize the meaning of "give us today our daily bread" as seeking a daily spiritual insight to feed our souls. However, this is not what Jesus was talking about. The majority of people in Jesus' day (and even until the 18th century) were food insecure, meaning they didn't know how (or even if) they would get their next meal. While this is not a worry for middle- and upper-class America, there are many around the world and even in the wealthiest cities who are food insecure today. These people understand the necessity of praying to God to give them just the barest minimum of food for just that day. Those of us who have never had to worry about how to afford groceries must remember that this is only by the grace of God, our only Provider. If we are so blessed as to be sure of having food in our pantries today and tomorrow, we can thank God for removing a terrible weight of worry from our shoulders.

Application for Activation

Prayer is needed today more than ever. This week, set aside a specific time each day for prayer. Jesus and the psalmist prayed in the morning, but anytime is good to talk to God (Mark 1:35, Psalm 63:1). Ask the Father to bring to your mind those people who have hurt you or persecuted you. Then ask Him to help you to forgive those people. If you can contact any of them, do so, and resolve whatever differences you may have. Remember, prayer changes things.

Follow the Spirit

What God wants me to do:

_____

_____

_____

_____

Remember Your Thoughts

Special insights I have learned:

_____

_____

_____

_____

More Light on the Text

Matthew 6:9–15

In verses 9 through 14, Jesus tells the disciples how they should pray in a model prayer that we commonly call the Lord's Prayer. While it is an excellent prayer, used publicly for various reasons, it was not given just for us to memorize and recite. It was not intended to replace the corporate prayer in the synagogue, but to give His disciples (and us) a model for their own private prayer time. Entire books have been written analyzing this prayer. It is rich in meaning and subject to various interpretations. Although it is short, it is a powerful model for the way that we should pray in our own prayer closets. This prayer format begins with words of worship, expresses a desire for God's will to be done, thanks, God for supplying one's physical needs, and asks forgiveness for sins and the help to stand against temptation.

9 After this manner therefore pray ye: Our Father which art in heaven, Hallowed be thy name.

Jesus starts by affirming that God is the Father, the one in the heavens. This was typical of many formal Jewish prayers. We know that Jesus referred to God as "Abba" (**AH-bah**), which is an affectionate, familiar term, similar to our current use of the term "dad." It shows the kind of relationship He had with God, the Father. We should seek to have that same kind of closeness and intimacy in our relationship with God. But in this prayer, God is addressed as "Father," not as "Dad." The Greek for "Father" is pater (**PAH-tare**). This is His title. He is the parent. We are reminded that our Father is the God of heaven. He is absolute holiness. He is *our* Father, the Father of all who have received Jesus Christ.

Fatherhood is a very sensitive and delicate issue in African American communities and for others who have experienced absent or negative relationships with their fathers. Whether we blame personal irresponsibility, the lingering effects of slavery, the current evils of racism, or other forms of oppression, we can identify forces that contribute to the negative feelings associated with the term father. Some modern theologians question whether we really should address God as Father since the term father can evoke powerfully negative feelings related to the absence of fathers or negative relationships with fathers who are present in the home. But this is the wrong strategy to adopt because God has revealed Himself as Father. To those who have not experienced the love and security of a father in the home, we look at Psalm 68:5 to replace that bad image and give assurance of our God who is a father to the fatherless. We cannot take away the fact that Jesus addressed God as Father. God has repeatedly revealed Himself to be our holy and loving Father. This image of the father-child relationship can guide us as we work to repair damaged hearts and heal those who have been wounded in relationships.

After this opening address, the Lord's Prayer contains seven petitions. There are three "Thou" or "Thy" God petitions—things we are praying God will do for His glory. There are four "we" petitions—things we want God to do for His children. The first "Thy" petition, "Hallowed be thy name" (Matthew 6:9), would more accurately be stated, "Let Thy name be hallowed." This means that God's name should be sanctified, revered, and considered holy. For Jewish people, the name of God was considered so holy, it could not be spoken or even written in its entirety. The name of God was treated with reverence because it was considered synonymous with God. For us, the prayer is a request that in all the earth the name of God would speak of God's holiness and kingdom. This is both a personal request and a communal, missionary request.

10 Thy kingdom come. Thy will be done in earth, as it is in heaven.

In one respect, "thy kingdom come" refers to the end times, when there will be the fulfillment of all prophecies and expectations. At that time, God's kingdom will prevail, and God will rule and reign on earth as He does in heaven. This is what we look forward to as Christians and

what we seek to make a reality in our daily lives while we wait for the kingdom to come in totality. Jesus is asking us to live in ways that demonstrate our faith that the kingdom will, indeed, come. Not only are we to pray that the fullness of God's kingdom will be evident on earth, but we are to live in ways that reveal God is the King of our lives even now.

The prayer continues with the desire for the coming of the kingdom—that is, God's ultimate will for the earth and humanity. As we pray these words, we have to consider what we are doing day to day to witness to God's kingdom on earth. What do we see on earth that is not like God's will and not like the kingdom of heaven? Jesus prays that the earth will mirror heaven according to God's will. Jesus manifests that reality in His earthly ministry. In heaven, there is no sickness, so He heals the sick. In heaven, there is no demonic oppression, so He casts out demons. In the kingdom, there is no hunger, so He feeds the hungry. In heaven there is no bondage, so He frees the captives. The Kingdom of God is of peace, righteousness, and justice. Jesus lives that kingdom and calls us to pray and live out the same. It is also a prayer for God's will to be done in our individual lives and our communities. We can ask this prayer in complete confidence because we know that God loves us and would not do anything in our lives that would ultimately be bad for us. While something we desire may look good to us today, God knows whether it will truly be good in our future. Likewise, we may go through situations that are uncomfortable or difficult, but it is God's will to work it out for our good (Romans 8:28). We can pray this in confidence because God has all wisdom and our faith is in Him.

11 Give us this day our daily bread.

At this point, the "we" petitions begin, as we request things from God. Some scholars have debated whether this means literal bread in terms of our daily physical needs, or whether "daily bread" should be taken in the spiritual sense, or even in the understanding of what will be consumed at the heavenly banquet. The Greek word for "daily" is *epiousios* (**ep-ee-OO-see-oce**), and since this prayer is its only occurrence in Scripture, it is difficult to translate. Most likely it refers to that which is needed just for tomorrow. Each day, we are to ask God for just enough to get by through the next day. This simple request is not about money. We are not asking God to set up a large bank account for us. We are simply asking Him to give us what we need for today and the most immediate future. Whether we have need of food, shelter, clothing, hope, healing, or grace, we are to pray as trusting children, asking our Father for what is needful for today. This is a prayer that may have called to mind the story of God providing manna in the wilderness to Israel for Jesus' hearers. That was an instance in which God literally provided bread for God's people each day and only enough for that day. It is God's sovereign will and Jesus' prayer that people receive enough daily food to eat. That makes it our prayer and call as Jesus' body in the earth.

Many of us pass over this verse quickly because we have never known days without enough to eat, but people in many parts of the world are hungry—some do not live very far from us. They have learned what it means to truly have to trust God to provide for their basic needs. When we pray this prayer, we should remember those who are hungry.

12 And forgive us our debts, as we forgive our debtors.

The object of our prayer for forgiveness is the most widely varied word in this passage. Some translations use the word "debts" (KJV); others seek to harmonize with Luke's record and use "sins" (NLT). When the early Bible translator John Wycliffe translated the passage, he pulled the word "trespasses" from a few verses down (Matthew 6:14). This version was used in the *Book of Common Prayer* and therefore entered the liturgy of many church traditions. The best understanding of this word is perhaps a combination of all three. The Greek word for "debts" is *opheilema* (**oh-FAY-lay-mah**), which literally means failure to pay what is due. Common people in Judea in Jesus' day struggled with having enough money with the threat of debtors prison looming. The situation is not unlike the plight of many today. In a spiritual context, though, all of us have failed to live up to our duties to both God and humankind. The word also has the sense of a moral failure or a fault. Sin is a universal disease in all of us. This verse literally means that we are asking God to forgive us in the same proportion in which we forgive others. That is pretty scary. This means that if we say, "I will never forgive so-and-so for what he has done" or "I will never forget what you did to me," we are actually asking God not to forgive us! Human forgiveness and God's forgiveness are all wrapped up together.

As we have experienced the initial forgiveness of God at the Cross, we have been made capable of forgiving others. Let's remember how much God has forgiven us and have that same attitude toward others.

13 And lead us not into temptation, but deliver us from evil: For thine is the kingdom, and the power, and the glory, for ever. Amen.

This is a difficult passage to understand because it implies God actively "leads" us into temptation. The expression is intended as a petition for God's help when we face the inevitable temptations and trials that come in this life. The epistle of James cautions us never to say that God is tempting us (James 1:13–14). Other translations of this verse give a more helpful interpretation of what Jesus is praying such as "don't let us yield to temptation". This interpretation helps to point out that the desire is to have God keep us faithful when we are tempted to become unfaithful by the lusts of the world, the difficulties of life, or the ways of the ungodly. Another possible example of this is when Jesus tells Peter that he will deny Him because the enemy desires to sift him as wheat (tempt him to unfaithfulness), but Jesus has already prayed for him that his faith will not fail him and that he will be kept in that trial.

The Lord's Prayer continues with a request to be delivered from evil (Matthew 6:13). The more accurate translation of the Greek word *poneros* (**poe-nay-ROCE**) is used here as "evil one." When times of testing come, as they will, then we pray to be delivered from the evil one—Satan. These two petitions—to resist temptation and to be rescued from evil—go together. Some people feel Christians should not undergo trials and temptations. But Jesus said we would have tribulation in the world (John 16:33). We should be of good cheer in the midst of them, however, because we know that He has overcome the world. So when we are tempted, when we suffer, when we are tossed and driven by the storms of life, we pray for the strength to bear it, to come through it, and to be liberated from the evil one.

14 For if ye forgive men their trespasses, your heavenly Father will also forgive you: 15 But if ye forgive not men their trespasses, neither will your Father forgive your trespasses.

Finally, Jesus goes back to the subject of forgiveness, mentioned in the prayer. These verses are not part of the Lord's Prayer but are included to emphasize the importance of forgiveness and the fact that forgiveness must go two ways in the life of the Christian. As seen in Jesus' parable of the Unforgiving Servant, our Master will show us just as much mercy as we show those subordinate to us (Matthew 18:21–35). We forgive in part because we realize we too have been forgiven much. We also forgive because we recognize the image of God in our neighbor. Whether or not they ask for forgiveness, whether or not they even think they need forgiveness, we are to forgive because they are God's child as much as we are.

We sing and pray the Lord's Prayer so often that it can become rote and lose its meaning for us. But when we look at it with fresh eyes, the prayer can come alive again and give us, as Jesus intended, clear instructions on how to pray effectively. How serious are we in wanting God's kingdom to come and His will to be done? Do we live as kingdom people, aware of who and whose we are? How easy or difficult is it for us to forgive others when they do something wrong to us? How satisfied are we with having just our daily needs met, as opposed to all our wants and desires? And, in the course of going about our daily lives, how much awareness do we show— in our thoughts, actions, and treatment of others—of the truth of Matthew 6:14–15? These are all questions that arise when we take time to really reflect and meditate on the Lord's Prayer.

Sources:
Barclay, William. *The Gospel of Matthew, Vol. 1* (Chapters 1 to 10). Rev. ed. Philadelphia, PA: The Westminster Press, 1975. 219–24.
Greek and Hebrew Lexicons. Eliyah.com. http://www.eliyah.com/lexicon.html/greek/kjv (accessed June 1, 2010).

Daily Bible Readings

MONDAY
God's Name Is "Our Father"
(Isaiah 63:15–16; 64:8–9)

TUESDAY
The Adopted Children of God
(Romans 8:12–17)

WEDNESDAY
Enticed by Temptation
(James 1:12–15)

THURSDAY
Forgive the Sins of Fellow Believers
(Luke 17:1–4)

FRIDAY
Forgive the Offender
(2 Corinthians 2:5–11)

SATURDAY
Forgive Like God in Christ Forgives
(Ephesians 4:25–5:2)

SUNDAY
Praying and Living the Lord's Prayer
(Matthew 6:9–15)

Notes

Teaching Tips

Words You Should Know

A. Friend (v. 5) *philos* (Gk.)—A loved one, a dear and friendly person, associate, or neighbor

B. Ask (v. 9) *aiteo* (Gk.)—To request in a way that suggests the petitioner is lower in position than the one to whom the petition is made

Teacher Preparation

Unifying Principle—Making the Request. It is hard to press on with a task or routine when doing so doesn't seem to produce any positive changes. How can we persevere in the absence of tangible progress? Jesus taught the disciples to continue to ask, seek, and knock, confident that God would graciously provide.

A. Read the Bible Background and Devotional Reading.

B. Pray for your students and lesson clarity.

C. Read the lesson Scripture in multiple translations.

O—Open the Lesson

A. Begin the class with prayer.

B. Have the class discuss: "In what ways do people seek, ask, and knock? What response do they hope to receive?"

C. Have the students read the Aim for Change and the In Focus story.

D. Ask students how events like those in the story weigh on their hearts and how they can view these events from a faith perspective.

P—Present the Scriptures

A. Read the Focal Verses.

B. Have the class share what Scriptures stand out for them and why, with particular emphasis on today's context.

C. Discuss the Background and The People, Places, and Times sections.

E—Explore the Meaning

A. Use In Depth or More Light on the Text to facilitate a deeper discussion of the lesson text.

B. Pose the questions in Search the Scriptures and Discuss the Meaning.

C. Discuss the Liberating Lesson and Application for Activation sections.

N—Next Steps for Application

A. Summarize the value of the power of perseverance in prayer.

B. End class with a commitment to pray for practicing true worship.

Worship Guide

For the Superintendent or Teacher
Theme: Perseverance in Prayer
Song: "Lord, Teach Us How to Pray Right"
Devotional Reading: Psalm 13

Perseverance in Prayer

Bible Background • LUKE 11:1-13
Printed Text • LUKE 11:5-13 | Devotional Reading • PSALM 13

—————————— Aim for Change ——————————

By the end of the lesson, we will: DISCOVER the meaning of Jesus' exhortation to ask, seek, and knock; DESIRE God to give the Holy Spirit the greatest possible gift; and DEDICATE ourselves to praying daily as a vital aspect of our lives.

———————————— In Focus ————————————

Kenny could not understand why, after five years on the job, he had not been promoted. He showed up on time, he did his job properly, and he was always upbeat and positive; he had even trained some of the people who moved up the ladder ahead of him. What was the problem? Troubled by this situation, he began to share his frustrations with a friend one evening while attending mid-week Bible study.

"I don't get it, man. What am I doing wrong? I like my job. I like the company, but they just won't give me a break. I apply for new and better positions, but I can't seem to move up. I'm qualified; I've got the skills; I just don't get it," Kenny told his friend Brad.

"Um," replied Brad. "How's your prayer life?"

"You know what? Initially, I prayed for God to lead me to the right employer and He did, but after I got the job, I stopped praying about it."

"Well, I think it's time you started praying about it. There are three of us who get together every morning at 6:30 on a conference call for prayer. Join us."

"That's a good idea. I think I will join all of you brothers. Let me get your number."

In today's text, Jesus teaches that persistent prayer helps through life's many twists and turns. He taught we have a loving Heavenly Father to whom we can persistently bring our needs in prayer. How often do you actually bring your needs to Him?

—————————— Keep in Mind ——————————

"And I say unto you, Ask, and it shall be given you; seek, and ye shall find; knock, and it shall be opened unto you" (Luke 11:9, KJV).

"And so I tell you, keep on asking, and you will receive what you ask for. Keep on seeking, and you will find. Keep on knocking, and the door will be opened to you" (Luke 11:9, NLT).

Focal Verses

KJV **Luke 11:5** And he said unto them, Which of you shall have a friend, and shall go unto him at midnight, and say unto him, Friend, lend me three loaves;

6 For a friend of mine in his journey is come to me, and I have nothing to set before him?

7 And he from within shall answer and say, Trouble me not: the door is now shut, and my children are with me in bed; I cannot rise and give thee.

8 I say unto you, Though he will not rise and give him, because he is his friend, yet because of his importunity he will rise and give him as many as he needeth.

9 And I say unto you, Ask, and it shall be given you; seek, and ye shall find; knock, and it shall be opened unto you.

10 For every one that asketh receiveth; and he that seeketh findeth; and to him that knocketh it shall be opened.

11 If a son shall ask bread of any of you that is a father, will he give him a stone? or if he ask a fish, will he for a fish give him a serpent?

12 Or if he shall ask an egg, will he offer him a scorpion?

13 If ye then, being evil, know how to give good gifts unto your children: how much more shall your heavenly Father give the Holy Spirit to them that ask him?

NLT **Luke 11:5** Then, teaching them more about prayer, he used this story: "Suppose you went to a friend's house at midnight, wanting to borrow three loaves of bread. You say to him,

6 'A friend of mine has just arrived for a visit, and I have nothing for him to eat.'

7 And suppose he calls out from his bedroom, 'Don't bother me. The door is locked for the night, and my family and I are all in bed. I can't help you.'

8 But I tell you this—though he won't do it for friendship's sake, if you keep knocking long enough, he will get up and give you whatever you need because of your shameless persistence.

9 And so I tell you, keep on asking, and you will receive what you ask for. Keep on seeking, and you will find. Keep on knocking, and the door will be opened to you.

10 For everyone who asks, receives. Everyone who seeks, finds. And to everyone who knocks, the door will be opened.

11 You fathers—if your children ask for a fish, do you give them a snake instead?

12 Or if they ask for an egg, do you give them a scorpion? Of course not!

13 So if you sinful people know how to give good gifts to your children, how much more will your heavenly Father give the Holy Spirit to those who ask him."

The People, Places, and Times

Hospitality. The virtue of hospitality was mandatory in ancient Jewish and Mediterranean cultures. It is commanded and commended throughout the Bible. Moses spoke about it in Exodus 22:21 and Deuteronomy 14:28–29. Abraham was hospitable to three strangers and discovered that he had entertained the Lord and two angels (Genesis 18, Hebrews 13:2). When we share with others, we share with Christ (Matthew 25:35, 43). Jesus enjoyed hospitality when He was on earth and so did the apostles (see Acts 18;17; Philippians 2:2). Christ shows us the epitome of hospitality by receiving us into His kingdom and preparing a place for us (John 14:2-3). A believer's hospitality to others is a reflection of God's hospitality to us (Luke 14:16 ff.).

Background

The Scriptures reveal how important prayer was to Jesus' earthly existence. Time alone with His Father reflected His pre-incarnate existence, and Jesus' prayer showed His total dependence on His Father (John 5:19, 30). The outcome of His prayer life was marked with unexplainable wisdom and power (Luke 4:18, Acts 10:38). Jesus' disciples asked that He teach them to pray as John the Baptist taught his disciples. (Luke 11:1–4; cf. Matthew 6:9–15). What we know as the "Lord's Prayer" serves as a model for approaching God in prayer as Father who is holy. In every prayer recorded in the Gospels, Jesus addressed God as Father, which was groundbreaking. Jesus shared a new norm in approaching God as Father and through prayer made the relationship and conversation personal. Jesus made access to the Father attainable by changing the perspective on what it means to pray without lofty, pious words (Matthew 6:5-7). He also radically changed who was able to approach God by inviting everyone who believes in Him to call God Father (Matthew 23:9).

How do you view God, and how does it affect how you approach God in prayer?

At-A-Glance

1. The Picture of Perseverance (Luke 11:5–8)
2. The Results of Perseverance (vv. 9–10)
3. The Response to Perseverance (vv. 11–13)

In Depth

1. The Picture of Perseverance (Luke 11:5–8)

Jesus uses an illustration to underscore His point in teaching on God as Father. He shares with His audience an example that places them in the scenario. Jesus asks His listeners to suppose that a friend comes by at an inconvenient hour to ask a favor. At the heart of this is the issue of hospitality. In Jewish culture, hospitality was an important custom because it speaks of the love modeled by God toward Israel and is replicated by all members of the community.

Jesus' parable presents quite a problem for the listeners. A friend who has a visitor of his own is unprepared to show hospitality and so requests help for his situation. However, when he knocks on his neighbor's door, the person approached does not open the door. Instead, he sends his friend away, saying that he and his family have retired to bed. What Jesus makes apparent is that the untimely visitor kept knocking on the door to receive a response. It is also important to note that the man was not asking for himself. He was asking in order to help someone else. Jesus ends the parable with the words, "I say to you" meaning that Jesus is about to tell the point of the parable. Despite the friendship of the two men, the door was answered—not out of an obligation as a friend—but because of the person's persistence, his relentless pursuit of a resolution to his situation. His perseverance led to his receiving what he asked for.

How are we persistent in prayer on behalf of others?

2. The Results of Perseverance (vv. 9–10)

Jesus then clarifies the focal point of His teaching. He instructs His audience to keep pursuing God by asking, seeking and knocking. To ask is more than just politely making a request. Jesus is telling us to earnestly beg the Lord for what we need. Second, we are to seek God. This implies looking with the expectation of finding a solution to our situation. Finally, we are to knock. Knocking cannot be done from across the street or in the next suburb! Knocking requires that you go directly to the person's door. Our knocking then means stepping into the presence of the Lord so that our request can be made known. Notice that as we ask, seek, and knock, we are getting closer in a relationship with the person we are asking to help. So it is with God.

Jesus always placed emphasis on going after God and pursuing fellowship with Him. Everything needed in life is found in Him (Matthew 6:33). The outcome of such a prayer life is to live in the will of the Father who always gives us what is best for us because that accomplishes His purpose in us. As a result of an ongoing pursuit of God through prayer, believers have what they need (Psalm 37:3–5, Matthew 6:6, 25–26).

Does asking, seeking, and knocking give us a blank check to ask God for whatever we want? Does it obligate God to give it to us?

3. The Response to Perseverance (vv. 11–13)

Jesus shared another relatable illustration with His disciples to show the goodness of God and His response to the one who pursues Him. In short, Jesus said that if human fathers provide for their children and take the time to listen, then believers should expect that their heavenly Father will do the same. God's response to our pursuit of Him in prayer is that He will give us His Holy Spirit who is our unlimited power supply. The Holy Spirit is not given to us for selfish pursuit or gain, but to keep us connected to the Father and to trust His purpose. Every good and perfect gift comes from the Father for it is the Father's good pleasure to give and be gracious to us (Psalm 84:11, Luke 12:32, James 1:17).

Why should we approach God as a trustworthy Father?

Search the Scriptures

1. Describe the two illustrations Jesus used to display how to approach God and how He responds to prayer? (Luke 11:5–8, 11–12)

2. What will God give to us freely if we ask in prayer? (Luke 11:13)

3. What three approaches to asking does Jesus give us?

Discuss the Meaning

1. Why does Jesus end this discourse on being persistent in prayer (ask, seek, knock) with God's good gift of the Holy Spirit?

2. Why is it important to keep the focus of our pursuit of God?

3. Is it ever appropriate to ask God to meet our wants and desires, or are we only to ask about our physical needs?

Liberating Lesson

We are able to pursue God in prayer and trust Him for what we need, but when we ask, seek, and knock, it should not be for selfish gain. The body of Christ is set apart to be salt and light in the earth. When we ask, seek, and knock in our pursuit of God, we can expect that God will answer prayer. But we should also be mindful of how what we ask, seek, and knock for can bless others.

The church should bear witness of the Father's willingness to hear and answer prayer and serve as a testimony to lead others to Christ. We should ask, seek, and knock for God to use us in the earth to bring His will on earth as it is in heaven. When the church is in lockstep with God, His power is the key to bringing forth justice for the poor and oppressed (Psalm 10:17–18, Isaiah 1:17) because pure religion cares for the world (James 1:27).

Application for Activation

James teaches that we do not have because we do not ask, and when we do ask, we do not receive because we ask amiss due to our worldly passions (James 4:2–3). As believers, we need to purify our hearts to ensure that our pursuit of God is with the right motives. We must seek His kingdom and His righteousness. We must place our trust in God's character and His love for us, knowing that everything we need is in Him. Therefore, we can come boldly to the throne of grace and be persistent in prayer. We are able to come to God as Father as instructed by Jesus and believe that He can reward those who diligently seek Him (Hebrews 11:6).

Follow the Spirit

What God wants me to do:

_____

_____

_____

_____

Remember Your Thoughts

Special insights I have learned:

_____

_____

_____

_____

More Light on the Text

Luke 11:5–13

In today's text, Jesus has just finished teaching His disciples how to pray. He taught them a model prayer, which we refer to today as the Lord's Prayer.

5 And he said unto them, which of you shall have a friend, and shall go unto him at midnight, and say unto him, Friend, lend me three loaves; 6 For a friend of mine in his journey is come to me, and I have nothing to set before him?

Needs give rise to prayers, which are usually in the form of supplications or requests. This lesson begins with a parable in which Jesus portrays a situation where a need arises, and a neighbor has to ask a friend for help. *Philos* (**FEE-los**) is the Greek word translated "friend." It denotes a "loved one, a dear and friendly person, associate, or neighbor." The person to whom supplication is made is usually seen as a supplier of the need. Even though God is the ultimate supplier of all needs, there are times when we need help from a friend or a neighbor. While our need may be urgent, we must realize that sometimes a need arises when the circumstances are not favorable. The person may lack the resources to help. At other times, the need may arise at the wrong time of the day or out of season so that the friend cannot help, no matter how pressing it is.

In Jesus' parable, the neighbor went to call upon his friend at midnight to make a supplication. He beseeches his friend to lend him three loaves of bread. The man seeking to borrow three loaves has a sense of obligation because he realizes that he is expected to provide refreshments for the person who has come to visit him. All of this occurs at midnight. In a parable, the darkness of midnight implies a calamity, sorrow, or unfavorable situation. Jesus' listeners understood, like us, that when you go to someone for help "at midnight," the welcome may not be good, leaving us with a pressing need in the midst of an awkward and trying state of affairs.

For believers, such an end-of-the-rope situation is likely to inspire us to pray. We should be motivated to pray with a sense of need and a sense of obligation. When we are motivated by need, we are usually asking for ourselves, but when we are driven by obligation then we feel a sense of duty to pray for or make intercession for others. In his letter to the Ephesians, the apostle Paul urges us to be alert and always praying, interceding for all the saints (6:18). This means "standing in the gap" for another person whose need you see as urgent.

7 And he from within shall answer and say, Trouble me not: the door is now shut, and my children are with me in bed; I cannot rise and give thee.

The refusal to open the door created an impediment to the friend's chances of having his needs met. The man felt troubled by his friend's request. This gives us the idea that the supplicant's request was a disturbance to his friend—so much so that the friend may become weary of being bothered. Without opening the door and giving any hope of access, the man answer's his friend with four statements. First, he states that his friend is troubling him. The word translated "trouble" is *kopos* (**KOH-poce**), which means "weariness, laborious toil." This gives us the idea that the supplicant's request was a disturbance to his friend and will make the friend weary himself or give him such laborious toil in the process of opening the door and going to give the supplicant what he requests. The friend seems to say, "Don't bother me because I will not go through the trouble of opening the door to get what you need." Second, the door is shut. The implication is that it is well past the time of shutting the door. It simply too late. Third, the man says that his children are in bed with him, meaning that the entire household is being upset by his friend's persistence. Finally, he says, for these reasons it is impossible for him to get out of his bed to answer the friend's request. We are all familiar with times when we can't seem to get our prayer needs met; despite praying, it seems answers are not forthcoming.

8 I say unto you, Though he will not rise and give him, because he is his friend, yet because of his importunity he will rise and give him as many as he needeth.

In this parable, the man was unwilling to give his friend what he requested. When we look to people for help, we will find that some are unwilling to extend themselves for another person's request, regardless of the reason or need. Some people are stingy and cruel. Others lack the resources or are reluctant to share. Despite his familiarity with his friend, the homeowner will not go through the trouble to help. The Greek word for "importunity" is *anaideia* (**ah-NIE-day-ah**). The use of this term means that the friend is shamelessly persistent in seeking help from his neighbor. He is not shy about asking his friend for help. When one's need is pressing, he or she will go beyond the bounds of modesty, casting away dignity and any pretense of decorum in order to get the needed response.

Another interpretation of the word *anaideia* focuses on the giver. The request is honored simply because the reputation of the giver is at stake. Jesus uses this parable to emphasize the need for earnestness and perseverance in prayer to God. From this vantage point, the focus is on God's nature as a generous giver who responds to all manner of requests, even those that arise under less than ideal circumstances. In these verses, Jesus strongly encourages us to bring all of our requests to God, particularly those that are most urgent. Even if we have a need at midnight, Jesus enjoins us to seek God with persistence and determination, believing fully that God will and can answer our prayer.

9 And I say unto you, Ask, and it shall be given you; seek, and ye shall find; knock, and it shall be opened unto you. 10 For every one that asketh receiveth; and he that seeketh

findeth; and to him that knocketh it shall be opened.

Here we are made to know three forms of outward actions in the process of requesting: asking, seeking, and knocking. In this passage, Jesus' encouragement for us to do these three things elevates them to the status of command backed by divine authority. Hebrews 11:1 says, "Faith is the substance of things hoped for, the evidence of things not seen." Jesus provides these three commands as a way for us to gain the substance of our faith by making requests of God. Asking, seeking, and knocking are different forms of petition. Here the Greek word *aiteo* (**eye-TEH-oh**) is translated as ask. Its use suggests that the petitioner is lower in position than the one to whom the petition is made. The Greek word translated "seek" is *zeteo* (**dzay-TEH-oh**). *Zeteo* signifies a seeking that is aggressive and therefore the seeker strives, endeavors, and desires that which is sought. Its use suggests that seeking is not a passive inquiry. *Krouo* (**KROO-oh**) is the Greek word translated "knock." When we knock at another's door, we are close to their place of abode. When we think of this term in regard to petitioning God, we are knocking on the door of heaven.

The coveted privileges of receiving, finding, and experiencing an open door is for everyone, without discrimination. Though Jesus was speaking to His disciples, His statement seems to apply to a general audience—believers and nonbelievers—because of its axiomatic nature. In practice, followers of Christ are instructed to make petitions in the name of Jesus. We must have a fundamental belief in Jesus (John 14:12–14), the reality of abiding in Him and His words abiding in us (John 15:7). The fact that He chose us and ordained us so that we should bear fruit (John 15:16) gives us authentic grounds to petition God in the name of Jesus. God is the ultimate source of our needs.

Jeremiah 17:7 says, "Blessed is the man that trusteth in the LORD, and whose hope the LORD is." A consistent attitude of petitioning God in times of need is sure to breed trust and reliance on Him. As we go through the challenges of life, we can always petition our Heavenly Father, being fully assured that we will receive what we need. The three terms—ask, seek and knock—are each followed by a resultant action. If we bring our needs before the Lord in prayer, then Jesus gives us the assurance that if we ask, we will receive; if we seek, we will find; and if we knock, the door will be opened.

11 If a son shall ask bread of any of you that is a father, will he give him a stone? Or if he ask a fish, will he for a fish give him a serpent? 12 Or if he shall ask an egg, will he offer him a scorpion?

Jesus uses a comparison here to point out God's generosity and His desire to respond to our petitions. Understanding this example hinges on the significance of the items identified here. Jesus' parable is about a son and his father, but it applies to any parent and their child. There is an expectation here of a nurturing father and a proper parental relationship, just as a loving and caring father is willing and expected to please his son and to give him what is right and good. Given the expected relationship between parent and child, Jesus provides a common example to prove his point regarding God's generosity and love.

Jesus poses three questions. He asks what father would give his son a stone in place of bread. The child's request for bread is based on an innate desire to live. Bread is used figuratively of food in general. But bread also provides the sustenance of life, spirit, and eternal life because Jesus is the Bread of Life. It is abnormal for a parent to offer a stone instead of the requested cake of bread. Stones were used as a means of punishing offenders. Those who committed certain evils were stoned to death. Any parent who would do such a thing as substituting a stone for bread is cruel and wicked. Another request a child might make is for some fish. In biblical times fish constituted one of the staple foods, and the fish trade was highly developed as indicated by the fact that some of the apostles of Christ were fishermen. To offer a serpent in place of a fish would be indicative of giving the son something that would definitely bring pain instead of sustenance. It is not clear that the snake is poisonous, but its intent to harm and hurt the child is clear. To give a child a scorpion in place of an egg is another way of providing that which brings harm instead of life. But the scorpion goes further; it is known to bring sudden death.

13 If ye then, being evil, know how to give good gifts unto your children: how much more shall your heavenly Father give the Holy Spirit to them that ask him?

Man is evil from birth (Psalm 51:5), and as such he is prone to evil. *Poneros* (**poe-nay-ROCE**) is the Greek word translated "evil." It can mean "wicked, bad, vicious" and is used to describe the moral or ethical condition of people. Jesus addresses His disciples in a way that lets them know that they are inherently evil as a result of the Fall yet they still have the capacity to give good gifts to their children. This is indicative of their fatherly love, their willingness to do good to their children, and the fact that they feel the imperative to perform their fatherly responsibilities. Jesus then compares their character of evil, which produces the good that cares for their child, with the essential character of goodness, love, generosity, and kindness with which our Heavenly Father abounds. Based on God's intrinsic nature, and the fact that He is our Father, He will give us what is good for us.

In concluding His explanation, Jesus encourages His followers to come to God with their requests and with the expectation that God will provide for them because God desires to give good things to His children. Spiritual development is essential for every child of God, and the Holy Spirit is the agent of that development. In every believer, development should begin with an aspiration to grow. It is this aspiration that leads us to petition God. Spiritual development is characterized by an increase in the sanctifying influence of the Holy Spirit. Believers must desire to grow and to exhibit the fruit of the Spirit. Our spiritual development is seen when we yield to the leading of the Holy Spirit, desire and receive the gifts of the Spirit, and consistently receive the revelation of truth as guided by the Spirit. As children of God, we must grow in the knowledge of Christ as well as in wisdom and understanding. These are laudable areas upon which we should petition God to help us as we grow in our trust of Him. He will grant our requests.

Sources:

Cabal, Ted et. al., *The Apologetics Study Bible*. Nashville, TN: Holman Bible Publishers, 2007. 1507, 1536–1537.

Van der Mass, Ed M. *Halley's Bible Handbook: Deluxe Edition (25th Edition)*. Grand Rapids, MI: Zondervan, 2007. 604.

Daily Bible Readings

MONDAY
Daniel Prays Despite Legal Prohibition
(Daniel 6:6–13)

TUESDAY
God Forms the Holy Nation
(Ezekiel 36:22–28)

WEDNESDAY
Jesus Prays for Future Believers
(John 17:20–26)

THURSDAY
The Holy Spirit Empowers Believers
(Acts 1:6–11)

FRIDAY
Justice for Those Who Pray Fervently
(Luke 18:1–8)

SATURDAY
Ask, and It Is Yours!
(Matthew 7:7–11)

SUNDAY
Ask, Seek, and Knock!
(Luke 11:5–13)

Notes

_____

_____

_____

_____

Justice

The study this quarter focuses on justice as presented in Scriptures from the prophets and in the reading for Easter Sunday, which is taken from First Corinthians. The prophets communicated God's will to the people. They called for repentance and justice.

UNIT 1 • God Requires Justice

This is a five-lesson study from four of the minor prophets. The prophets issue God's call for justice in the conduct of human affairs. Amos, Habakkuk, Micah, and Malachi convey that the laws of God require justice for the poor and the oppressed. The last two lessons from Micah and Malachi are a study of the responsibilities of leaders for practicing justice.

Lesson 1: March 1, 2020
Called to Accountability
Amos 5:18–24

Often, people ignore or disregard the plight of the disenfranchised. How will the cause of these disadvantaged be addressed? The prophet Amos affirms that the justice and righteousness of God always champion the poor and oppressed.

Lesson 2: March 8, 2020
A Prayer for Justice
Habakkuk 1:1–4, 12–14

People wonder about the seeming prevalence of injustice. How will justice and fairness be established for all? Habakkuk appeals to God to end wickedness and injustice.

Lesson 3: March 15, 2020
Consequences for Injustice
Habakkuk 2:6–14

People seem not to suffer for their unjust actions. When will acts of the unjust be punished? The psalmist affirms that God will reward the just, and Habakkuk declares that the unjust will be punished for wickedness.

Lesson 4: March 22, 2019
Corrupt Leaders
Micah 3:1–3, 9–12, 6:6–8

Leaders often struggle with expectations of being examples of justice. How can leaders become models of justice worthy of emulation? Micah confronts the leaders of Israel for their failure to pursue justice and suggests that doing justice should be the basis of their lives.

Lesson 5: March 29, 2020
Leading Justly
Malachi 2:1–9, 3:5–6

Just leaders act honorably toward constituents. How do just leaders act toward others? Malachi admonishes the priests to turn from their wickedness, revere God, and reap a rich harvest for promoting godly justice.

UNIT 2 • God Promises a Just Kingdom

The lessons for Palm Sunday and Easter examine the promised Messiah as the defender of justice. In Lesson 8, Esther's triumph is reviewed as demonstrating the prevailing of God's justice. For children, the unit concludes with the narrative from Solomon as an example of God's justice while adults study the Lord's proclamation of the redeemed nation where justice and righteousness are restored.

Lesson 6: April 5, 2020 (Palm Sunday)
God's Just Servant
Isaiah 42:1–9

People seek a champion of justice. Who can and will defend and uphold the cause of justice? In Matthew 21, Jesus upholds God's justice in the Temple, fulfilling Isaiah 42's vision of the Messiah.

Lesson 7: April 12, 2020 (Easter)
Resurrection Hope
1 Corinthians 15:1–8, 12–14, 20–23, 42–45

People struggle with the probability and possibility of life after death. How can resurrection from death provide life that is different from what is experienced before death? In 1 Corinthians and Mark, only life through the resurrection of Christ engenders hope for authentic justice.

Lesson 8: April 19, 2020
Injustice Will Be Punished
Esther 7:1–10

Ignoble people often seem to attain great power and wealth. What evidence is there that people will receive the recompense their evil deeds deserve? The story of Esther's triumph over Haman provides assurance that evil does not prevail.

Lesson 9: April 26, 2020
The Lord Loves Justice
Isaiah 61:8–11, 62:2–4

When people feel helpless and angry, they seek help from others. What hope is there that the conditions of the powerless will be addressed? Solomon's wise decision confirms that God loves justice, and Isaiah affirms that the righteous will be vindicated.

UNIT 3 • Called to God's Work of Justice

This unit has five lessons that explore ways that people are called to participate in God's work of justice. Zephaniah presents both a judgment against the wickedness and injustice of Jerusalem and a vision of restoration. Zechariah calls for a return to God's ways of justice. In Jeremiah, God's rigorous standards for justice are defined and God's people are given a choice either to repent injustices by executing justice or to face destruction. Hosea uses early history to call the people to love and justice.

Lesson 10: May 3, 2020
A Vision of Restoration
Zephaniah 3:14–20

Oppression of the poor and powerless seems pervasive in our world. Is there any hope for reversal of this condition? The prophet Zephaniah proclaims the day of restoration when God's people shall be returned to righteousness, justice, and peace.

Lesson 11: May 10, 2020
Peace and Justice Reign
Zechariah 8:1–8, 11–17

Sometimes people respond to evil conditions in the world with a sense of hopelessness, regret, and doom. Where can they find motivation for continuing? The prophet Zechariah delivers God's promise of a new world of peace and prosperity for God's people.

Lesson 12: May 17, 2020
Practice Justice
Jeremiah 21:8–14

Evil is pervasive throughout human society. Can people continue to do evil without consequence? Jeremiah tells us that God is a God of justice and will recompense evil.

Lesson 13: May 24, 2020
Repent of Injustice
Jeremiah 22:1–10

Society often ignores and even condones the oppression of the vulnerable. Will righteousness be rewarded, and will evil face retribution? Through the prophet Jeremiah, God exhorts the people either to repent of injustice and deliver those who are oppressed or to face destruction.

Lesson 14: May 31, 2020
Return to Love and Justice
Hosea 11:1–2, 7–10, 12:1–2, 6–14

People often equate prosperity with righteousness. Is prosperity the standard by which people and society should be judged? Hosea reminds us that love and justice are God's standards.

A First Century Text for a Twenty-first Century Church

by Marvin A. McMickle, PhD

In Galatians 3:26–28 the Apostle Paul addresses what were the three major social divisions within all of the cultures of the Mediterranean in the 1st century AD. Those divisions were gender (male and female), class (slave and free), and ethnicity (Jew and Gentile). These three divisions were especially true for Israel and for all the towns and regions of the Mediterranean region where Paul conducted his three missionary journeys. In all those contexts there was a clear, almost impenetrable divide between Jews and Gentiles, men and women, and slaves and free folk.

There was a prayer in the Jewish prayer book called the Siddur that was invoked every morning by every Jewish male that said, "I thank You, O God, that you did not make me a Gentile, a slave, or a woman." In uttering those words, those men were self-identifying as a person who occupied a preferred social status within their society. That position of privilege was even reinforced by both law and custom. In terms of influence, economic opportunities, the chance to exercise leadership in the community, the right to own property, and the right to speak and participate in synagogue services, the advantage clearly belonged to men in general and to Jewish men in particular. Given this reality, gender, class, and ethnicity were

matters of paramount importance. Male identity mattered in every aspect of daily life.

What is startling about this passage in Galatians is that Paul directly attacks the premise that neither gender, ethnicity, nor social status should matter at all when it comes to membership in the Christian community. Paul's triumphant declaration resounds to this day:

For ye are all the children of God by faith in Christ Jesus. For as many of you as have been baptized into Christ have put on Christ. There is neither Jew nor Greek, there is neither bond nor free, there is neither male nor female: for ye are all one in Christ Jesus (Galatians 3:26-28).

Paul's proclamation about a community unrestricted by gender, class, or ethnicity was not just an assault on the sensibilities of Jewish males in the first century AD. This notion was equally disturbing to the Roman Empire where the vast majority of inhabitants in that far-flung realm of influence were either slaves or other free people who did not enjoy Roman citizenship. To suggest that there was no difference between slaves and free people or both of those groups and a full-fledged Roman citizen was a politically destabilizing notion that Rome went to great lengths to resist and suppress.

It must be remembered that one of the things that Paul used to his great advantage was the fact that he was a Roman citizen who had to be treated with all the preferential status that came with that designation. This was on display when the magistrates in Philippi realized that Paul and Silas had been beaten by their jailers without a trial, which was a violation of Roman law (Acts 16:37–39). It was on display again when Paul avoids being flogged by Roman soldiers when they discover that he is a Roman citizen (Acts 22:25–29). In both instances, the attitude and behavior of the magistrate in Philippi and the centurion in Jerusalem changed dramatically when they discovered that Paul was a Roman citizen.

Paul fit into all three categories of preferential status as a male, a Jew, and a free person—with the added bonus of enjoying Roman citizenship. All of this must be kept in mind when Paul says that none of that mattered once he came to Christ where "all are one." He goes even further in this direction of abandoning his own privileged position when he says:

> But what things were gain to me, those I counted loss for Christ. Yea doubtless, and I count all things but loss for the excellency of the knowledge of Christ Jesus my Lord: for whom I have suffered the loss of all things, and do count them but dung, that I may win Christ, And be found in him, not having mine own righteousness, which is of the law, but that which is through the faith of Christ, the righteousness which is of God by faith. (Philippians 3:7–9)

What makes these three social divisions so startling is that they continue to be a reality in so many places within the twenty-first century society, including within the very church that Paul was so instrumental in helping establish. There are cultures in the twenty-first century world where the rights of women are severely restricted. That is not just true in nations like Saudi Arabia and other extremely conservative Muslim nations where women cannot drive cars, own property, pursue higher education, or participate in the political process. It is true in the United States where the quality of life is abysmal for Native Americans living on reservations and migrant workers who move from crop to crop throughout this country. Women still earn seventy-five cents for every dollar earned by a man.

In recent days, two Muslim girls were verbally assaulted on a commuter train in Portland, Oregon. When three men came to their defense they were stabbed by a man who told those girls to "get out of my country." With more than 80% of our nation's wealth is controlled by 10% of America's families, poverty and the wage gap only grow. It has been reported that it would take the average worker at a McDonald's restaurant one million hours to earn what that company's CEO takes home in one year. The rise of human trafficking, both for purposes of sexual and labor exploitation, means that human slavery is alive and well in the United States and around the world.

While these things may be true in the secular order, Paul says that none of these things should be true in the church. Here again this powerful word of liberation, equality, and justice: "There is neither Jew nor Greek, there is neither bond nor free, there is neither male nor female: for ye are all one in Christ Jesus" (Galatians 3:28). Whatever social and cultural biases and bigotries we may have held prior to coming to Christ should be the first things we abandon once we are in Christ. It is not just individual sin that is forgiven when we become followers of Christ, but we are also forgiven of how we look at and interact with other people, especially people who are different from us in terms of gender, class, or religious affiliation. That is what is meant by the hymn that says, "What a wonderful change in my life has been wrought since Jesus came into my heart."

The question is, does the twenty-first century church reflect the values of this first century text? While much progress has been made in society as a whole, there are some areas where the church is lagging far behind. The Southern Baptist Theological Seminary acknowledged only in 2018 that many of its founders and early funders were involved in the slave trade that was built on the assumption of class and color distinctions. There are many congregations, indeed entire denominations, where women cannot be ordained to the ministry, cannot speak from a pulpit, or cannot even hold lay leadership positions. What is particularly galling about this is that this is true even in African American churches that have spent the last 200 years battling against racism, but seem content with sexism. It is as if they only want two-thirds of what is promised in Galatians 3:28. They would fight with all they have against issues of racism and class division. They would work for the alleviation of poverty and oppression. But when it comes to women in ministry they seem entrenched in their opposition. Such churches and church leaders would do well to read *An End to This Strife* by Demetrius Williams.

Think about four New Testament texts, each of which challenges us to think differently about racism, sexism, and class divisions. Think about the slave named Onesimus found in Philemon for whose freedom Paul makes a compelling appeal when he tells Philemon to treat Onesimus as a brother beloved and to receive him as he would have welcomed Paul himself (Philemon 17). Think about the Roman centurion named Cornelius, a representative of the oppressive Roman regime and a member of the Gentile elite. Yet he was converted and later baptized by the Apostle Peter (Acts 10:34–48). Think about Phoebe, a female member of the church in Cenchreae whom Paul refers to as "a deacon," who likely was charged with delivering Paul's letter to the Romans (Romans 16:1). Think about Simeon the Niger and Lucius of Cyrene, two men described by their dark-skinned appearance or country of origin as of obvious North African background, who were among those who laid hands on Paul and Barnabas and commissioned them for their first missionary journey (Acts 13: 1–3). Each of these four texts points to what can and should happen when the church embraces the idea that in Christ there is neither male nor female, slave nor free, Jew nor Gentile, for all is one in Christ Jesus.

There is a well-known hymn sung to a melody popularized by the African American singer and composer Harry T. Burleigh that points to the promise of Galatians 3:28:

> In Christ, there is no east nor west,
> In Him no south or north;
> But one great fellowship of love,
> Throughout the whole wide earth.

May this become true in our churches and in our own lives today.

Marvin A. McMickle, PhD, is the President of Colgate Rochester Crozer Divinity School. There he is also the director of the Doctor of Ministry Program and Professor of African American Religious Studies. He has authored seventeen books.

Sources:
Griffen, Wendell. "White Baptists and racial reconciliation: There's a difference between lament and repentance." *Baptist News Global.* https://baptistnews.com/article/white-baptists-and-racial-reconciliation-theres-a-difference-between-lament-and-repentance/#.XD9wac9TmV5 (published January 3, 2019).
Mirsky, Yehudah. Three Blessings. *Jewish Ideas Daily.* http://www.jewishideasdaily.com/848/features/three-blessings/(published March 23, 2011).
Rolf, David. *The Fight for $15: The Right Wage for a Working American.* New York: The New Press, 2016.
Williams, Demetrius. *An End to This Strife: The Politics of Gender in African American Churches.* Minneapolis, MN: Fortress Press, 2004.

Christian Education in Action

Walking in the Light We Share through Forgiveness

by Rukeia Draw-Hood, PhD

As God's Word tells us, God so loved the world that He sent His only begotten Son as a sacrifice to amend for our sins so that forgiveness could be offered and reconciliation achieved. As the story continues, those who accept this reality are to extend this forgiveness and love to one another and be reconciled (Matthew 6:14; Mark 11:25; Ephesians 4:32; Colossians 3:13). So why is it that the world recognizes believers more by their hypocrisy than by their love for one another?

Alexander Pope is famous for saying, "To err is human; to forgive, divine." Journalist Elizabeth Large reports that it is human nature to respond to an offense with anger, grudges, or vengeance. In spite of religious instruction, many believers respond with all three. Lots of Christians have lives controlled by anger and bitterness. Many are touchy and easily provoked. Others don't know how to let go of grudges. Like the second-grader who is full of rage and yells at his teacher, like the abused woman who has rehearsed the acts of molestation and retaliation in her mind a million times over the past twenty years, like the streetwise young man who refuses to let go of payback for the business venture gone sour with his childhood friend, how is it that many of God's children never adequately learned how to cope with the disappointments and injuries experienced at the hands of others?

The church should dedicate more resources to facilitating forgiveness. It starts with the theologians, the great minds, whose task it is to challenge the church to reflect on issues of great importance. There are many systematic theology textbooks, and although they are supposed to cover all the major authoritative teachings of the church, they rarely, if ever, address the topic of love and forgiveness. This trend continues among distinguished Black theologians (with the exception of J. Deotis Roberts and Dwight Hopkins). In contemporary Black theology, freedom and justice overshadow forgiveness and reconciliation. There is, however, ample preaching on forgiveness in local churches. In spite of this, many believers have not moved beyond knowing about forgiveness and believing in its goodness. Christian education in the local church has not typically given congregants the educational experiences they need to practice forgiveness in their daily lives.

Forgiveness helps Christians fulfill God's commandment to love one another (Matthew 22:39; John 13:34; 1 John 3:23). To love another brother or sister in Christ is to walk in the light they share (1 John 2:10). Love is the bond that holds Christian communities together, and forgiveness is an expression of that love. Mother Theresa said, "If we really want to love we must learn how to forgive." This agrees with Paul's writing that love keeps no record of wrongs (1 Corinthian 13:5). Healthy loving relationships are impossible without forgiveness because, as Peter Ustinov says, "Love is an act of endless forgiveness." Jesus tries to communicate this to Peter when He encourages him to forgive one person a lavish number of times (Matthew 18:22).

Forgiveness is a moral response to injustice. It's a choice to lay down the right to pay an offender back, absorbing the evil and suffering the pain of an injury instead. Based on the merciful character of God and the forgiveness He has already extended to the believer for far greater offenses, such a choice is informed by a conviction that unwillingness to forgive another Christian is hypocritical (Luke 6:36; Ephesians 4:32). The International Forgiveness Institute says forgiveness also reaches out to the offender in moral love by seeking the rehabilitation and betterment of the injurer.

An unforgiving believer walks in darkness because every part of his or her being is negatively affected—mind, body, and spirit. An unforgiving person drinks poison and expects someone else to die from it. The point is that harboring hostility can be deadly for individuals and those who come too close to them!

Recent studies have found that people who hold grudges have diminished health compared to those in the general population. They have more visits to the doctor, more stress-related disorders (anxiety, restlessness, sadness, and depression), lower immune system functioning, and higher rates of cardiovascular disease (high blood pressure, heart disease, and abnormal heart rate).

Jesus warns that God is like the lender who forgave an enormous debt (Matthew 18:35) because He expects a believer's character and treatment of others to reflect His own character and treatment toward the believer. Forgiven people forgive others, and there are consequences when they don't.

Believers are an integral part of a loving community, linked by the Spirit of God. Everyone will inevitably, if not regularly, be offended in this imperfect community. Love can only prosper where there is forgiveness. You can begin to walk in the light of love and facilitate forgiveness in your life or congregation in a myriad of ways: consider keeping gratitude journals, providing training in communication skills and conflict resolution, participating in role plays and simulations, completing the weekly REMEMBER YOUR THOUGHTS, MAKE IT HAPPEN, and FOLLOW THE SPIRIT sections in this book, seeing a professional (minister, therapist, social worker, life coach) who can accompany you through the process, researching a forgiveness curriculum for congregational use, hiring a consultant to design an intervention, or formulating a congregational theology of forgiveness through honest dialogue and Bible study. Whatever method you use, please address reconciliation, repentance, process, and abuse cycles.

Practicing forgiveness allows believers to be healthy and whole, thereby contributing to the stability, unity, and maturity of the entire Christian community. Remember unforgiveness has serious consequences. Begin using what resources you have to let go of grudges or help others do so today!

Rukeia Draw-Hood, PhD, received an MA in Christian education from Oral Roberts University and a PhD in educational studies from Trinity International University. She is an active member of the The Church Without Walls in Houston, Texas.

Sources:

James, Larry. *How to Really Love the One You're With.* http:// www.celebratelove.com (accessed July 7, 2005).

Large, Elizabeth. "Forgiveness is hot: Researchers cite health, personal benefits." Reprint. *Baltimore Sun.* January 12, 2005. http:// www.azcentral.com/health/wellness/articles/0112forgiveness12.html (accessed July 5, 2005).

Rhodes-Wickett, Sharon. "Judge Not--Forgive A Lot" [sermon online]. Westwood United Methodist Church. September 15, 2002. http://www.westwoodumc.org/sermons/2002sermons/s091502.htm (July 5, 2005).

Xenos Christian Fellowship. "Christian Community: Part #6 Forgive One Another." http://www.xenos.org/ct_outln/forgive1another.htm (July 6, 2005).

Teaching the Adult Learner

by A. Okechukwu Ogbonnaya, PhD

Because adults come to any learning situation with life experiences that have been fundamental in the formation of their identities, teaching adults is much more complex than teaching children. Christian education for adults is the process whereby, through the Scriptures, the power of the Holy Spirit's light shines upon the experiences of the adult. The purpose of Christian education is to transform the whole life of the adult Christian learner into conformity with the image of God as revealed in Christ.

To accomplish their transformation, adult Christian students need to receive tools and skills with which they can act out their Christian vocations in their everyday lives. Therefore, simply providing ready-made responses will be insufficient. The process of educating Christian adults must engage them at a level where the learning becomes theirs, not merely "what the Sunday School teacher said." The goal of educating Christian adults is to provide a process in which their faith becomes real and experiential.

Therefore, the adult educator must ask, "What does it mean to treat the learner as an adult?" A corollary question is, "What results can be expected from adult learning processes?" Further questions include: "Are the students growing in their understanding of their Christian vocation? Are they conforming their everyday walk more and more to their understanding of the life of Christ? Is the education process helping to actualize the spiritual freedom promised in the Scripture?"

In order to develop the possibility of achieving these goals, adult Christian educators are called to several practices. First, you should **model maturity** within your classroom, promoting the spirit of Christ by treating your students as adults. There is no substitute for the respect and dignity you offer adult learners. Second, **model love** and **respect** within the classroom. Both educators and students need love and respect in teaching and learning. Third, **model enthusiasm** for what you teach. If you do not seems interested in what you are teaching, your students will not be interested either and chances are it will not be effective. Fourth, **model freedom** and **grace**. Adult learners need the sense that they have contributed to the process of their own learning. While time may constrain class participation and sharing, you as the educator are still responsible for creating a comfortable learning context. The worst enemy of effective learning is fear of being dismissed or even ridiculed for saying the "wrong thing."

Given the dynamic and experiential nature of adult learning, one effective way to educate is to ask for the students' experiences as they relate to the lesson. In this way, you will discover some of the class members' needs and are better able to minister to them effectively.

There is a false notion in teaching circles that adults enjoy listening to lectures. While lecturing may be appropriate sometimes, it is not usually the most effective way to educate adult learners. Like children, adults appreciate variety in their learning environments. In response to this, you should develop a repertoire of a variety of methods for interacting with your class. No one method is sufficient for all times and circumstances. Only those that enhance a greater understanding of freedom in Christ will lead your students to discover deeper truths from the Word of God and orient them toward Christian action.

Jesus Himself taught by using parables, proverbs, riddles, silence and direct action, particularly as it related to the miraculous. Sometimes He exhorted; at other times He was confrontational. However, His methods always related to the context and the people with whom He was communicating.

Dr. A. Okechukwu Ogbonnaya is a former VP of Editorial at UMI, a noted pastor, and speaker.

NATHANIEL R. JONES

1926–

Civil Rights Lawyer and Judge

Just a few blocks from the Smoky Hollow community in Youngstown, Ohio, where Nathaniel R. Jones grew up, stands the Nathaniel R. Jones Federal Building and U.S. Courthouse. This was certainly not something that Jones had dreamed of.

He was a good student and caught the eye of African American newspaper publisher, Maynard Dickerson, while he was still in high school. Jones was soon writing a sports column for the *Buckeye Review*. When Jones finished high school, he was enlisted into the US Army Air Corps and served in Dayton, Ohio.

After his army experience, he returned home and attended Youngstown State University, followed by Youngstown State University Law School. He worked for four years as a private practice lawyer and then, in 1961, was appointed executive director of the Fair Employment Practices Commission, where he could work on a federal level assuring that African Americans had equal opportunities in employment. After this, he served on the Kerner Commission, which investigated the causes of the race riots that began with the assassination of Dr. Martin Luther King Jr. in 1968.

Then Roy Wilkins, the Executive Director of the NAACP, asked him to lead their law team. In Jones' acceptance speech, he said, "We still live in the basement of the great society." As general counsel for the NAACP, he worked for integration of northern schools, affirmative action, and equality in the US armed services.

In 1979, President Jimmy Carter nominated Jones as judge of the US Court of Appeals, and he served in this position for twenty-three years. He retired in 2002, and he continues to work as a lawyer in private practice. He has a wife and four children.

Sources:
The History Makers. https://www.thehistorymakers.org/biography/
honorable-nathiel-r-jones (accessed March 28, 2019).

Teaching Tips

Words You Should Know

A. Burnt Offerings (v. 22) *'olah* (Heb.)—A sacrifice that consumed the whole animal with fire.

B. Judgment (v. 24) *mishpat* (Heb.)—Proper treatment of all people; a judge's final verdict; right action according to the Law.

Teacher Preparation

Unifying Principle—Seeking Justice. Often, people ignore or disregard the plight of the marginalized. How will the cause of these disadvantaged be addressed? The prophet Amos affirms that the justice and righteousness of God always champion the poor and oppressed.

A. Read the Bible Background and Devotional Reading.

B. Pray for your students and lesson clarity.

C. Read the lesson Scripture in multiple translations.

O—Open the Lesson

A. Begin the class with prayer.

B. Divide the classroom board into two columns: "Reasons the Day of the Lord excites me" and "Reasons the Day of the Lord frightens me." Brainstorm ideas for both columns.

C. Have the students read the Aim for Change and the In Focus story.

D. Ask students how events like those in the story weigh on their hearts and how they can view these events from a faith perspective.

P—Present the Scriptures

A. Read the Focal Verses and discuss the Background and The People, Places, and Times sections.

B. Have the class share what Scriptures stand out for them and why, with particular emphasis on today's context.

E—Explore the Meaning

A. Use In Depth or More Light on the Text to facilitate a deeper discussion of the lesson text.

B. Pose the questions in Search the Scriptures and Discuss the Meaning.

C. Discuss the Liberating Lesson and Application for Activation sections.

N—Next Steps for Application

A. Summarize the value of supporting the cause of the poor and oppressed.

B. End class with a commitment to pray for justice for the disenfranchised.

Worship Guide

For the Superintendent or Teacher
Theme: Called to Accountability
Song: "Let Justice Flow Like Streams"
Devotional Reading: Psalm 97

Called to Accountability

Bible Background • AMOS 5
Printed Text • AMOS 5:18-24| Devotional Reading • PSALM 97

──────────── **Aim for Change** ────────────

By the end of the lesson, we will: COMPREHEND advocating for all oppressed as a commitment to divine justice and righteousness, DESIRE fairness for the disadvantaged, and CHOOSE to become activists supporting the cause of the poor and oppressed.

──────────── **In Focus** ────────────

Shanice and Tamara had been friends since college. After graduation, the two decided to share an apartment. Shanice wanted to live in the renovated townhomes where many people who lived in the former housing project were forced out.

After touring the homes with the realtor, Tamara began talking to a man who was standing around outside. Shanice thought he was a bum. Tamara shook her head. "His name is Albert. He used to live here before they renovated this building. He told me that several former residents of this building are now either homeless or living in a shelter."

"Why is that my concern?" asked Shanice.

Tamara knew that Shanice was materialistic. She prayed that her friend would learn to lead a more selfless life. Concerned, Tamara asked, "Do you think that my conversation with Albert was just a coincidence? You've given your life to God, right?" asked Tamara.

"Yes. I go to church and I give my tithes. That should be enough," retorted Shanice.

"Well, it's not. When we see something that is unfair, God wants us to take action. After you give your life to God, He expects your life to reflect Jesus Christ. It's not about you, Shanice; it's about God and living for Him."

When have you responded to a situation like Tamara and Shanice? Discuss ways you keep yourself from choosing to be unethical.

──────────── **Keep in Mind** ────────────

"But let judgment run down as waters, and righteousness as a mighty stream" (Amos 5:24, KJV).

"Instead, I want to see a mighty flood of justice, an endless river of righteous living" (Amos 5:24, NLT).

Focal Verses

KJV **Amos 5:18** Woe unto you that desire the day of the LORD! to what end is it for you? the day of the LORD is darkness, and not light.

19 As if a man did flee from a lion, and a bear met him; or went into the house, and leaned his hand on the wall, and a serpent bit him.

20 Shall not the day of the LORD be darkness, and not light? even very dark, and no brightness in it?

21 I hate, I despise your feast days, and I will not smell in your solemn assemblies.

22 Though ye offer me burnt offerings and your meat offerings, I will not accept them: neither will I regard the peace offerings of your fat beasts.

23 Take thou away from me the noise of thy songs; for I will not hear the melody of thy viols.

24 But let judgment run down as waters, and righteousness as a mighty stream.

NLT **Amos 5:18** What sorrow awaits you who say, "If only the day of the LORD were here!" You have no idea what you are wishing for. That day will bring darkness, not light.

19 In that day you will be like a man who runs from a lion—only to meet a bear. Escaping from the bear, he leans his hand against a wall in his house—and he's bitten by a snake.

20 Yes, the day of the LORD will be dark and hopeless, without a ray of joy or hope.

21 "I hate all your show and pretense—the hypocrisy of your religious festivals and solemn assemblies.

22 I will not accept your burnt offerings and grain offerings. I won't even notice all your choice peace offerings.

23 Away with your noisy hymns of praise! I will not listen to the music of your harps.

24 Instead, I want to see a mighty flood of justice, an endless river of righteous living."

The People, Places, and Times

Feast Days. There were three major feast days in the nation of Israel: the Feast of Unleavened Bread (Passover), the Feast of Harvest (Pentecost), and the Feast of Ingathering (Tabernacles or Booths). These were pilgrimage festivals that required participation from the entire Israelite community. All work was to cease, and travelers made their way from all over Israel to celebrate these festivals in Jerusalem.

Background

Amos was a shepherd and keeper of sycamore fig trees. From Tekoa, a town ten miles south of Jerusalem, in the hill country of Judah. Although a resident of the Southern Kingdom, God called him to be a prophet to warn the Northern Kingdom of coming judgment (Amos

7:14–15). Amos prophesied during the reigns of Jeroboam II, the king of Israel, in the north (792–753 B.C.), and Uzziah, king of Judah, in the south (792 – 740 B.C.).

His prophecies would come at a time when both kingdoms were experiencing stability, expansion, political influence, and material prosperity. They attributed all of these to favor and blessings from God. However, they were grossly mistaken. In actuality, their prosperity was rooted in evil, the result of the exploitation of the poor—both through systems of law and of money. Israel's first king, also named Jeroboam, was responsible for the division of the kingdoms. He established Bethel as a center of worship, encouraging the Israelites to worship in Bethel instead of Jerusalem. Over the years, while morality and true commitment to God declined, religious activities—such as festivals and sacrifices—flourished, causing Israel to erroneously believe that they were immune to God's wrath.

This was the climate in which Amos would preach. For several months, he delivered a message of judgment to Israel, warning her leaders that failure to repent of the injustices they committed against the poor and vulnerable would lead to Israel's destruction. Amos began his message with a series of oracles pronouncing judgment against Israel's pagan neighbors—Damascus, Gaza, Tyre, Edom, Ammon, and Moab (1:1–2:3). Then, the remainder of the message was dedicated to condemning Judah and Israel.

Do you find any similarities between this description of Israel and the current state of our country? Describe them.

At-A-Glance

1. False Hope (Amos 5:18–20)
2. False Sacrifices (vv. 21–24)

In Depth

1. False Hope (Amos 5:18–20)

One can imagine the sense of satisfaction and pride God's chosen people would have to hear the initial proclamations against the sins of the other nations. This would have supported the popular belief that in the "day of the Lord," God would exact vengeance on Israel's enemies and restore her to a time of greatness. However, Amos reveals that Israel is also worthy of condemnation, even more so because of their habitual sins, frequently violating their covenant relationship with God.

"Woe" was a funeral cry, the wailing in grief over the dead. When referring to the living, it serves as a prediction of death. Here, the "woe" is for those eagerly awaiting the day of the Lord, expecting light and abundant life, who will instead be met with darkness and death.

Amos illustrates the futility of such hope using images of a lion, bear, and poisonous snake to describe the terror one will experience when, after escaping one danger, finding himself face to face with an equally terrifying one. Then, upon finally believing that rest and relief are available in their own home, meeting even more danger. There will be no safe haven when judgment comes.

Why is it important to be critical of ourselves instead of believing we are above criticism?

2. False Sacrifices (vv. 21-24)

"I hate … I despise … I will not smell … I will not accept … nor regard … I will not hear." In three short verses, God vehemently rejects multiple aspects of Israel's hypocritical religious rituals. Although their outward practices imitate a commitment to the Lord, their hearts are far from him. He begins with his displeasure with their feasts. Moses gave instructions for three feasts that the Israelites were to celebrate annually—the Passover with the Festival of Unleavened Bread, honoring God for His protection, and the Festival of Harvest and Festival of Shelters, honoring His provision (Deuteronomy 16). God's disdain for their celebrations of these stems from the reality that in daily activities they make a mockery of them.

Amos then addresses the assemblies, offerings, and sacrifices. The Israelites offer sacrifices that are required by law. They are supposed to be a representation of lives totally surrendered to God—acknowledging and repenting of sin, reconciling to Him, and seeking His pleasure. However, these offerings are refused because they are not authentic—Israel is blatantly disobedient and their "worship" is self-seeking. Even their music, previously prescribed and valued by God as worship, is disregarded as useless noise.

Instead of these insincere ritualistic performances, God calls for repentant hearts committed to doing what is morally right, just, and fair. However, justice and righteousness are not to be an occasional action, but exacted continuously and abundantly, as with rolling water and an ever-flowing stream.

In what ways do believers sometimes get caught up on rituals and neglect the command to love our neighbors?

Search the Scriptures

1. What made the Israelites' sacrifices unacceptable (Amos 5:22)?

2. What standard is set regarding what God requires when it comes to worshiping Him (v. 24)?

3. How are the Israelites to worship God if not with offerings and music (v. 24)?

Discuss the Meaning

1. When we read Amos, it is tempting to focus on the cultural aspects of ancient Israel and ignore the prophecy's relevance to today. If Amos were to address today's church, what would his message of warning to the church be? Complete this statement, "Woe to you who..."

2. God indicates that justice and righteousness are to be integral parts of the life of His people. What can today's followers of Christ do to help justice and righteousness flow?

Liberating Lesson

In recent years, debates have arisen about the Gospel's place in addressing justice issues—particularly issues of ethnicity and race, and the injustices often experienced by those in minority cultures in America. The Bible is clear:

God's judgment of Israel came because their mistreatment, exploitation, and neglect of the poor and vulnerable did not show their worship of God, but instead their love of power, comfort, money, and idols. Anyone can succumb to the temptation to elevate the pursuit of money and comfort above loving God and loving others. It is our duty as Christians to stand up for the oppressed.

Application for Activation

Compare the amount of money, energy, and time you spend on entertainment, pleasure, and leisure to the money, energy, and time you reserve for ministry and serving others. What does this say about where your true affections reside? A path to contentment is to practice gratitude. Spend time this week thanking and worshiping God for what He has provided for you. Ask God to open your eyes to ways you can use your time, talents, money, and other resources to serve others. Make a list of how you will follow God's leading.

Follow the Spirit

What God wants me to do:

_____

_____

_____

_____

Remember Your Thoughts

Special insights I have learned:

_____

_____

_____

_____

More Light on the Text

Amos 5:18–24

18 Woe unto you that desire the day of the LORD! to what end is it for you? the day of the LORD is darkness, and not light. 19 As if a man did flee from a lion, and a bear met him; or went into the house, and leaned his hand on the wall, and a serpent bit him. 20 Shall not the day of the LORD be darkness, and not light? even very dark, and no brightness in it?

"The day of the LORD" is a term that refers to the Lord appearing and judging the nations and punishing wickedness (Isaiah 13:6; Joel 2:1). Amos implies that some Israelites longed for this Day of Judgment. The Israelites are expected to be on the side of safety during the Day of the Lord. They are God's covenant people, and Amos' hearers are anticipating the Lord punishing their enemies for how they treated Israel. Yet, these same people are involved in oppressing the poor. Amos announces that God comes to punish unrighteousness and injustice, and Israel and Judah will be included in the judgment rather than exempt. Amos directly speaks judgment against the high priest Amaziah in the temple at Bethel and, by implication, King Jeroboam II of Israel for their false worship (Amos 7:10-17).

God does not tolerate us saying we love God while not showing love to our neighbors. Amos calls out the Israelites for their sin. It is sinful and hypocritical to expect God to execute justice on our behalf while condoning our unjust acts. God included many systems in the Mosaic Law to help free those in bondage and debt and to defend the accused. But these laws are being neglected while meaningless rituals and sacrifices are being made.

The images of running from a lion only to meet a bear or running into a house only to be bitten by a serpent describe the Day of the Lord as a time where they will not be able to escape God's judgment. The Asian lion (now extinct), the Syrian bear, and the snake are the major animal predators of the region. Serpent (Heb. *nakhash*, naw-KHASH) refers specifically to a poisonous snake. As one cannot escape darkness at night, Israel will not escape God's deadly judgment on the Day of the Lord.

21 I hate, I despise your feast days, and I will not smell in your solemn assemblies. 22 Though ye offer me burnt offerings and your meat offerings, I will not accept them: neither will I regard the peace offerings of your fat beasts.

God's heart is not moved by outwardly impressive religious acts of goodwill that are selfishly done. The phrase "your feast days" (Heb. *khag,* **KHAG**) refers to the three main festivals that God established in Israel: Passover, Pentecost, and the Feast of Tabernacles (Exodus 23:14–19; Deuteronomy 16:16–17). Israel is abusing all of these festivals at this time. The Israelites' hypocritical celebration of God's protection at Passover, His Law at Pentecost, and His provision at the Feast of Tabernacles is meaningless while they also pray to other gods (Amos 5:5). God says He despises (Heb. *ma'as,* **maw-AHS**) their false feasts and celebrations. This term can also mean reject and is often used in the context of breaking covenant. God rejects what Israel has done during these feasts, which is a form of religious practice but lacks the power of true worship. The implication is that God establishes events, activities, and rituals, but His people pervert, abuse, and misuse them to achieve their own selfish ends.

The Lord says He will not smell the smoke of the animal sacrifices made during Israel's assemblies. The scent imagery used here is common throughout the Bible. As the fragrant smoke from the offerings goes up, the smell is thought to rise to God in heaven. Amos is possibly referring to the solemn assembly on the seventh day of Feast of Unleavened Bread and the eighth day of the Feast of Tabernacles (Leviticus 23:8, 36). But none of the offerings prescribed in the law will please God. The Lord will not accept their burnt offerings (Heb. *'olah,* **oh-LAH**) in which the whole animal is consumed with fire. This is a symbol of the total commitment of the worshiper's life to God. He will not accept their meat or grain (Heb. *minkhah,* **meen-KHAH**) offerings that are supposedly intended as gifts to the Lord. Lastly, He will not accept their peace offerings (Heb. *shelem,* **SHEH-lehm**), as these gifts are to be a sign of reconciliation or friendship, but this is not the state of their relationship with God. All of the worship rituals here are supposed to be symbols of the people's real-life walk with the Lord, and offering them without true worship behind them is hypocritical.

23 Take thou away from me the noise of thy songs; for I will not hear the melody of thy viols.

Celebrations and rejoicing in God's presence play an important part in Israel's temple worship, which God established. The Israelites use many kinds of musical instruments to praise God for His goodness and faithfulness (2 Chronicles 7; Psalm 149). In this instance, the Lord actually calls their songs noise. "Viols" in this case refers to lyre-shaped stringed instruments that are used to play music during worship. Instead of rendering the joyful noise of Psalm 100:1, the confusion and insincerity of their false actions creates a noise that the Lord does not want to hear. The Lord is not interested in music and singing that does not match the truth of a worshipful lifestyle. He is not pleased with the songs of celebration at Temple given while the Israelites continue to treat the people around them, especially the poor, unjustly.

24 But let judgment run down as waters, and righteousness as a mighty stream.

In this verse, often quoted by Martin Luther King Jr. during the Civil Rights Movement, God illustrates the nature of judgment (justice) and righteousness by using the phrases "run down as waters" and "as a mighty stream," which speak of the ongoing and unobstructed movement of an ever-flowing body of water. The word for stream, *nakhal* (Heb. **NAH-khall**), is the word for the desert wadi. These small narrow valleys lay dry and barren for much of the year until a torrent of rain flooded them and made them into flowing streams. The Lord already laid out the stipulations of justice in His covenant, and He is waiting for His people to fill the dry and barren land with justice and righteousness as the rain fills up a desert wadi.

Note that Amos does not call the Israelites to simply "love your neighbor like rolling waters" but to practice justice. God wants His people to care not just for those in their same socioeconomic spheres, but for the lesser ones too. The Israelites' righteousness is supposed to attract the Gentiles to God. Today, we must attract non-Christians not by our worship services alone but by showing that Christians uphold justice and righteousness in the world.

The word judgment here refers to the proper treatment of all people. The Hebrew word *mishpat* (**meesh-POT**) can refer both to the judge's final verdict (judgment, KJV), and to that which is right according to the law (justice, NLT). When verdicts flow down like waters, the accused are tried quickly without lingering for years in jail pretrial. When that which is right runs down like waters, there is no stopping the forces of good from cleansing and nourishing the world. Elsewhere in the Bible, the words judgment and righteousness are also used together to describe God's presence: "righteousness and judgment are the habitation of his throne" (Psalm 97:2). We do not invite God's presence with our empty worship and sacrifices. We invite His presence with our attention to justice and righteousness that flows down from His very throne into our lives, neighborhoods, and the world. The core problem in the book of Amos is that the people in power are outwardly keeping the covenant of God in worship practices but are perverting justice and oppressing the poor and vulnerable (Amos 5:5–15).

Sources:

Alexander, David, and Pat Alexander. *Zondervan Handbook to the Bible*. Grand Rapids, MI: Zondervan, 1999. 490.

Burge, Gary M., and Andrew E. Hill, eds. *Baker Illustrated Bible Commentary*. Grand Rapids, MI: Baker Books, 2012. 834–835, 837–838.

Kaiser, Walter C., and Duane Garrett, eds. "Prophets in the Bible and Pagan Nations." *Archaeological Study Bible*. Grand Rapids, MI: Zondervan, 2005.

Keck, Leander, ed. *The Twelve Prophets*. The New Interpreter's Bible. Vol. 7. Nashville, TN: Abingdon Press, 1996. 384–397.

Phillips, Timothy, and Dennis Okholm, eds. *Christian Apologetics in the Postmodern World*. Westmont, IL: InterVarsity Press, 1995.

Stuart, Douglas. *Word Biblical Commentary: Hosea–Jonah*. Nashville, TN: Thomas Nelson, 1987. 340–356.

Walton, John H., Victor H. Matthews, and Mark W. Chavalas. *The IVP Bible Background Commentary: Old Testament*. Downers Grove, IL: InterVarsity Press, 2000. 769–771.

Say It Correctly

Tekoa. teh-**KOH**-uh.
Uzziah. oo-**ZEYE**-uh.
Amaziah. **AH**-muh-**ZEYE**-uh.
Jeroboam. **JARE**-uh-**BOE**-um.

Daily Bible Readings

MONDAY
The Coming Day of the Lord
(Zephaniah 1:14–18)

TUESDAY
Judgment Coming to the Nation
(Amos 5:1–3, 16–17)

WEDNESDAY
Seek the Lord, Establish Justice
(Amos 5:4–5, 14–15)

THURSDAY
Injustice Leads to Ruin
(Amos 5:6–7, 10–13)

FRIDAY
Lord of Creation and Judgment
(Genesis 1:4–9; Amos 5:8–9)

SATURDAY
God Loves All Peoples
(Hosea 2:14–23)

SUNDAY
Justice for the Poor and Distressed
(Amos 5:18–24)

Notes

_____

_____

_____

_____

Teaching Tips

Words You Should Know

A. Burden *massa'* (Heb.)—A load, or that which is lifted up and carried.

B. Spoiling *shod* (Heb.)—Destruction and oppression of the weak; the wealth that one might obtain through destruction or oppression.

Teacher Preparation

Unifying Principle—Ending Injustice. People wonder about the seeming prevalence of injustice. How will justice and fairness be established for all? Habakkuk appeals to God to end wickedness and injustice.

A. Read the Bible Background and Devotional Reading.

B. Pray for your students and lesson clarity.

C. Read the lesson Scripture in multiple translations.

O—Open the Lesson

A. Begin the class with prayer.

B. As a class, brainstorm a list of circumstances to which one may respond with the words, "It's not fair!" Then help the class categorize them as either a true injustice or justice that the person did not like.

C. Have the students read the Aim for Change and the In Focus story.

D. Ask students how events like those in the story weigh on their hearts and how they can view these events from a faith perspective.

P—Present the Scriptures

A. Read the Focal Verses and discuss the Background and The People, Places, and Times sections.

B. Have the class share what Scriptures stand out for them and why, with particular emphasis on today's context.

E—Explore the Meaning

A. Use In Depth or More Light on the Text to facilitate a deeper discussion of the lesson text.

B. Pose the questions in Search the Scriptures and Discuss the Meaning.

C. Discuss the Liberating Lesson and Application for Activation sections.

N—Next Steps for Application

A. Summarize the value of celebrating God as the source and model of justice.

B. End class with a commitment to pray for God to end wickedness and injustice—even when unjust leaders triumph.

Worship Guide

For the Superintendent or Teacher
Theme: A Prayer for Justice
Song: "God Will Take Care of You"
Devotional Reading: Psalm 73:1–3, 21–28

A Prayer for Justice

Bible Background • HABAKKUK 1
Printed Text • HABAKKUK 1:1-4, 12-14 | Devotional Reading • PSALM 73:1–3, 21–28

Aim for Change

By the end of the lesson, we will: EXPLAIN the justice of God in contrast to human injustice, ASPIRE to the establishment of justice and fairness for all, and CELEBRATE God as the source and model of justice.

In Focus

Michael could hear the clock ticking on the wall. He waited in silence for the phone to ring. His foot kept tapping, he knew it was his nerves. When he stopped tapping his foot, he began to tap the pen on the table. *Why haven't they called already?* He thought to himself.

For Michael, waiting any longer was too long. He just had an interview after months of getting no response from any of the companies he applied to. The bills were piling up, and he began to wake up at night wondering how he was going to care for his wife and kids. He wondered if God even cared about his family. There was nothing left for Michael to do. He felt like he could not go on any longer without an answer from God. Michael thought for a moment about their situation. He knew that God was in control of it all. He also knew that God deserved to be praised before he even got a job. So Michael sang softly at first, "Trust and obey for there's no other way..." He felt his spirit raising with the song of praise and started shouting "Hallelujah!" and "Thank You, Jesus" as an act of faith in God's care. While he was shouting and praising God, the phone rang.

Sometimes things look impossible or as if they will not work out. Trusting God is often difficult for people to do. What do you do to praise God for what He has done, is doing, and will do?

Keep in Mind

"Thou art of purer eyes than to behold evil, and canst not look on iniquity: wherefore lookest thou upon them that deal treacherously, and holdest thy tongue when the wicked devoureth the man that is more righteous than he?" (Habakkuk 1:13, KJV).

"But you are pure and cannot stand the sight of evil. Will you wink at their treachery? Should you be silent while the wicked swallow up people more righteous than they?" (Habakkuk 1:13, NLT).

Focal Verses

KJV **Habakkuk 1:1** The burden which Habakkuk the prophet did see.

2 O LORD, how long shall I cry, and thou wilt not hear! even cry out unto thee of violence, and thou wilt not save!

3 Why dost thou shew me iniquity, and cause me to behold grievance? for spoiling and violence are before me: and there are that raise up strife and contention.

4 Therefore the law is slacked, and judgment doth never go forth: for the wicked doth compass about the righteous; therefore wrong judgment proceedeth.

12 Art thou not from everlasting, O LORD my God, mine Holy One? we shall not die. O LORD, thou hast ordained them for judgment; and, O mighty God, thou hast established them for correction.

13 Thou art of purer eyes than to behold evil, and canst not look on iniquity: wherefore lookest thou upon them that deal treacherously, and holdest thy tongue when the wicked devoureth the man that is more righteous than he?

14 And makest men as the fishes of the sea, as the creeping things, that have no ruler over them?

NLT **Habakkuk 1:1** This is the message that the prophet Habakkuk received in a vision.

2 How long, O LORD, must I call for help? But you do not listen! "Violence is everywhere!" I cry, but you do not come to save.

3 Must I forever see these evil deeds? Why must I watch all this misery? Wherever I look, I see destruction and violence. I am surrounded by people who love to argue and fight.

4 The law has become paralyzed, and there is no justice in the courts. The wicked far outnumber the righteous, so that justice has become perverted.

12 O LORD my God, my Holy One, you who are eternal—surely you do not plan to wipe us out? O LORD, our Rock, you have sent these Babylonians to correct us, to punish us for our many sins.

13 But you are pure and cannot stand the sight of evil. Will you wink at their treachery? Should you be silent while the wicked swallow up people more righteous than they?

14 Are we only fish to be caught and killed? Are we only sea creatures that have no leader?

The People, Places, and Times

Habakkuk. Information about Habakkuk is very limited. There are two references to him in the Bible that bears his name. He was a prophet of God who probably lived during some portion of the reigns of Josiah, Jehoiakim, and other kings that followed. This dating is derived from a reference in Habakkuk 1:6 to the impending arrival of the Chaldeans in 605 B.C. It is possible that Habakkuk witnessed the decline and fall of the Assyrian Empire and knew about the fall of the Assyrian capital of Nineveh in 612 BC. The sinful conditions in Judah he wrote about were also consistent with this time in history, which would make him a contemporary of the prophets Jeremiah, Zephaniah, and Nahum. Habakkuk was commissioned to announce the Lord's intention to punish Judah by the coming deportation into Babylon. The central theme of the book of Habakkuk is faith in the midst of problems and is beautifully expressed in 2:4, which says, "The just shall live by his faith." The name Habakkuk may mean "one who embraces," a fitting name for a man who struggled through the conflicts of life while continuing to "embrace" God.

Background

The powerful country of Babylonia exercised total control over large portions of the Middle East, including Israel. In 722 BC Assyria was responsible for the breakup of Israel's Northern Kingdom. They invaded the land and carried many of its inhabitants into captivity. While Judah, the Southern Kingdom, was not attacked, it still lived in the shadow of the Assyrian Empire and was careful not to do anything that would invite its wrath.

In 612 BC, however, the Babylonians destroyed Nineveh, the Assyrian capital, which changed the balance of power in the ancient Near East. The era of Assyrian control came to an end while the Babylonians began to emerge as the world power. The Babylonians' conquering armies moved westward from Nineveh, eventually reaching Carchemish, along the Euphrates River at the modern Turkey/Syrian border. There they decisively defeated the Egyptians in 605 BC.

During this transition in world politics, King Jehoiakim was on the throne of Judah. He was a worldly man and an oppressive ruler who, among his many faults, rejected the message of Jeremiah (see Jeremiah 22:13–17). Jehoiakim's reign was characterized by religious idolatry. He was the son of Josiah, a good king and one who had turned the people back to God away from idolatry. This made the situation especially tragic. Under Jehoiakim's rule, the people of Judah were in a downward spiral moving further and further away from God and the truth. Habakkuk, a prophet of God, concluded that divine intervention was necessary if the people were to be saved from destruction. When the intervention did not happen, Habakkuk questioned God's failure to act.

At-A-Glance

1. Habakkuk's First Question (Habakkuk 1:1–4)
2. Habakkuk's Second Question (vv. 12–14)

In Depth

1. Habakkuk's First Question (Habakkuk 1:1–4)

When Habakkuk looks around his country, he sees a few encouraging situations. Everywhere he turns in Judah, he sees violence and bloodshed. The wicked always seems to have the upper hand over the righteous. The legal system is corrupt. Jehoiakim, Judah's king, is an unspiritual man, more concerned with the trappings of power than in providing leadership for God's people. The prophet Jeremiah has the occasion to denounce Jehoiakim's leadership (see Jeremiah 22:13–19). By comparison, Jehoiakim's father, Josiah, had been a good king who had initiated many religious reforms that encouraged the Jews to live up to their covenant promises. Unfortunately, Jehoiakim does not follow in his father's moral footsteps.

It is in this context of social chaos that Habakkuk exclaims, "O Lord, how long shall I cry, and thou will not hear!" (v. 1) Habakkuk expects God to intervene directly in this crisis, to judge and punish the wrongdoers and save the righteous. His prayer of complaint has been voiced not once, but many times. Habakkuk is distressed because it seemed as though God is "asleep at the wheel." Sin and injustice seem to increase the more the prophet cries (v. 2). God allows Habakkuk to see violence, iniquity, plundering, strife, contention, and a crooked, worthless government that is powerless to stop such rebellion in the land. The wicked are so entrenched in their wickedness that they make fun of those who are perplexed about the problem. To Habakkuk, it seems as though no one cares about God's standard of righteousness, including God Himself!

How do you respond when you see or hear about injustice?

2. Habakkuk's Second Question (vv. 12–14)

The Lord responds to Habakkuk's first question in verses 5–11 as to what He would do about all of the violence and wickedness in the land. He would not continue to have mercy on the injustice in Judah. God has heard Habakkuk and the cries of the righteous; He would punish the injustice. God would use the Babylonians, who already have a reputation for their ruthless destruction and conquest, to conquer and punish Judah for their sin.

Habakkuk responds with this second question: if God is going to use Babylon to punish Judah, will He punish them for their wickedness as well? How can God use wicked people to punish His own people's unrighteousness? Judah is bad but not as bad as Babylon. God should spare some of the Judeans in order for the covenant to be renewed, Habakkuk argues. Furthermore, Habakkuk is concerned the Babylonians will think it is their own strength that has allowed them to conquer Judah rather than the power of God that has allowed it. Habakkuk is upset with the state of His own people and the injustice in the land, but he is offended that the most unjust people he could think of would be used to punish the injustice.

This is Habakkuk's attempt to circle back on his own first complaint. He wants God to intervene and give justice, but does not like God's plan to use people who are ignorant of God to do it. Habakkuk is caught in a comparison between what he sees as the little sins of Judah and the big sins of Babylon. Clearly, God's sense of justice is different from Habakkuk's. In fact, God is simply keeping His word in the Law to punish Israel by raising up enemies to defeat them so they will repent (Leviticus 26:14–17, 33, 40–41). God will judge any injustice, and God can use whom He chooses to correct it. God has already said that Babylon is guilty as well, and God will handle the injustice of Babylon as well.

How is God's justice sometimes different than our sense of justice?

Search the Scriptures

1. Identify the specific injustices and evil that distressed Habakkuk (Habakkuk 1:2–4).

2. Why was Habakkuk troubled by God's lack of intervention in the life of Judah?

Discuss the Meaning

1. What are some of the conditions in our society that you wish God would intervene and change? Is there anything you can do now to help make changes?

2. How should we respond when an injustice is punished in a way that we didn't expect? Are all injustices equal?

Liberating Lesson

The dismal picture that Habakkuk paints of his society sounds all too familiar to us today. Many believers are deeply troubled by what they see in the world, their country, and in their own neighborhoods. Murders and violence are headline news in most major cities. Truth sometimes seems in short supply, and lies and half-truths are accepted as truth. We now have alternative facts and fake news as everyday vocabulary. There are people being silenced and killed in their countries for speaking out. There is corruption making the rich super-rich while in the same nation the poor starve. Believing that God is on the side of justice and righteousness, many Christians wonder, as did Habakkuk, why doesn't God do something about the situation right now? Habakkuk was a prophet of God, and yet he questioned God. God is not afraid of our questions. We can always ask God for His response in prayer. When God answers Habakkuk, God's plan is different from what Habakkuk expected. But God will restore justice and allow Habakkuk to participate in sharing His plan and helping it come to pass. God likewise is inviting us to intercede in prayer and advocacy about injustice in our communities and our world. Our responsibility is to listen and respond to God's direction to play our part in seeking justice for all.

Application for Activation

Take the opportunity this week to learn about injustice in your community or the world. Research the issue using the Internet, local library, or other resources including those who might be most impacted near you. Then cry out! Gather together with others or a prayer partner to pray about the issue. Share some of the information you learned on social media or in your congregation to bring attention to the issue. Donate your time or money to a charity that seeks to right the injustice. Most of all, trust that God hears your cries and will answer them in His timing.

Follow the Spirit

What God wants me to do:

_____

_____

_____

_____

Remember Your Thoughts

Special insights I have learned:

_____

_____

_____

_____

More Light on the Text
Habakkuk 1:1–4, 12–14

Habakkuk's name means "embracer or wrestler," which might give us some insight into the character of this man of God. Habakkuk willingly embraces the burden he is given and then relentlessly wrestles with God in prayer for Him to act in accordance with His covenant promise and judge the sin of His people (Deuteronomy 28:15; Leviticus 26:15–21). How needful we are today for more modern-day Habakkuks. One does not need to be a prophet to wrestle in prayer with God for our nation and our leaders who have strayed from acting according to godly principles (Micah 6:8), and instead are doing what seems "right in their own eyes" (Judges 21:25).

Habakkuk's prophecy is articulated as a prayer for justice, a dialogue between Habakkuk and Yahweh, because of God's people's gross sin. The prophet's prayer in Habakkuk 1 is a petition that is stated in the form of two sets of questions in his plea for justice. In his first set of questions (1:2–4), Habakkuk asks the Lord why He continues to tolerate sin among the people of Judah. Yahweh's first response, that He is raising up the wicked Babylonians to punish Judah, does not satisfy the prophet (1:5–11). Therefore, Habakkuk asks a second set of questions where he rephrases, intensifies, and expands his original question (1:12–17). God gives His detailed response in Habakkuk

2 that justice delayed is not justice denied, that God is sovereign and is working His purposes according to His wisdom. Habakkuk then concludes his short book with a prayer of praise for justice that is imminent, though it may not yet be evident (3:1–19). Interestingly, this poetic prayer of praise is actually sung by Habakkuk himself (v. 1). Although little is known historically about this prophet, the fact that he sings his poetic prayer indicates that he may have also been an official temple musician (1 Chronicles 25:1). Additionally, at the end of the song, Habakkuk gives instructions to the choir director that the prayer should be accompanied by string instruments (3:19).

1 The burden that Habakkuk the prophet did see.

This little known minor prophet characterizes his entire prophecy as a "burden" (Heb. *massa',* **mas-SAW**), which means a load, or that which is lifted up and carried. Habakkuk wants the reader to know that he is carrying a load that is personally and emotionally heavy. He is totally involved. He is not above God's people, but an integral part of the people. That is why the sinful condition of the nation is so disturbing to Habakkuk, prompting him to wonder why God seems unconcerned. In fact, Habakkuk is in a position very similar to Jeremiah, who also prophesied during that same time to the same Israelites that stubbornly refused to repent. Jeremiah got so discouraged, he tried to quit, but simply could not do it (Jeremiah 20:9). Like Habakkuk, Jeremiah had to carry his burden and obey the call of God for his life, even though the rebellious nation did not respond to his message. When we choose to follow Christ, we too have a burden, a cross that we must carry in order to do God's will (Matthew 16:24). Although the "cross" may be different for each person, everyone must be willing to carry it. Salvation is free, but there is a cost to following Christ.

This prophecy, this burden, is something the prophet "did see," indicating that God gave him this prophecy through a vision. God often uses this method of revelation for His prophets such as Amos (1:1), Isaiah (1:1), and Obadiah (1:1). Not surprisingly, one term used for prophet is *chozeh* (Heb. **kho-ZEH**), or seer.

2 O LORD, how long shall I cry, and thou wilt not hear! even cry out unto thee of violence, and thou wilt not save! 3 Why dost thou shew me iniquity, and cause me to behold grievance? for spoiling and violence are before me: and there are that raise up strife and contention.

Habakkuk's first set of questions come in rapid succession like waves crashing on the seashore during a violent storm. He prays with an intensity combined with a deep sense of frustration. This is not the first or second time Habakkuk had prayed to the Lord about this burden he is carrying, but he feels that his incessant cries to God seem to fall on deaf ears. He received no response. To understand the reason for his urgent plea, some historical context is imperative. Habakkuk's desperate prayer comes at a time when hope for justice and righteousness in Judah has been raised and dashed again and again. Josiah, a godly king, had returned the nation to righteous living after the rediscovery of the Book of the Law in 622 BC (2 Kings 22–23). Unfortunately, Josiah was killed in battle in 609 BC, and kingship went to his corrupt son, Jehoiakim who ruled from 609–598 BC (2 Kings 23:35–37). Habakkuk's prophetic prayer comes during Jehoiakim's ruthless reign, characterized by greed, dishonesty, the murder of the innocent, and oppression of the poor (Jeremiah 22:13–19).

The violence and corruption rampant under Jehoiakim's rule is the main historical context for Habakkuk's complaint. The prophet's cry against violence is a legal plea for God to act.

325

After all, God's covenant promise to hear the cry of his people means that He would also act in accordance with His Word (Exodus 2:23–25, 22:23). If the people obey His Law, the Mosaic Covenant, they would be abundantly blessed (Deuteronomy 28:1–14). Conversely, if they turn away from His Law, they would be cursed (Deuteronomy 28:15–68). Indeed, the purpose of the curses is not simply for punishment, but also to get them to repent so that a gracious God could restore them (Leviticus 26:14–44). The same is true for us today. Under the new covenant, there is a blessing for obeying God's Word, and believers are disciplined when they disobey (Hebrews 12:5–11). Discipline is for the exact same reason as the curses—to encourage repentance for the purpose of restoration.

Habakkuk further complains that by not acting, God is forcing him to "behold" (nabat, naw-BAT), that is "to stand by and watch" such atrocities (1:3, 13). Habakkuk cannot do anything about evil but always has it in front of him. There is nowhere he can look and not see it. Habakkuk knows if he can see all this iniquity, surely God can too, and it must grieve God to see it (cf. v. 13).

Habakkuk's prayer continues as he enumerates the six obvious problems in Judah that are being tolerated and not addressed by God (1:3). These problems are addressed as matched pairs that are flip sides of the same coin. They are: (1) iniquity and grievance, (2) spoiling and violence, and (3) strife and contention. The first couplet is iniquity and grievance. In Hebrew, iniquity is the word 'aven (aw-VEN) meaning wickedness like idolatry, and the grievance is the word 'amal (aw-MAUL), which is wrongful suffering, toil, or trouble. In pairing these together in his cry for justice, Habakkuk emphasizes that the wickedness of the perpetrator causes the wrongful suffering of the victim. Spoiling and violence are paired next. Spoiling is the word shod (SHODE) and refers to destruction and

oppression of the weak or the wealth that can be obtained through those. Such destruction leads to violence (khamas, khaw-MOSS), which wreaks havoc on the community and infrastructure as well as relationships. The third pair of problems mentioned are strife (rib, REEB) and contention (madon, maw-DON). "Strife" is a legal term, and contention is often paired with it (Proverbs 15:18; Jeremiah 15:10), indicative of the numerous lawsuits and legal quarrels in Judah's courts as a result of the violence and destruction.

We have all been in a situation like Habakkuk, praying about a situation and getting no answer, as if the prayers hit the ceiling and bounced back to earth. Jesus tells us the appropriate response during such times: "Men ought always to pray, and not to faint" (Luke 18:1). That's what Habakkuk does. He is constant in prayer like the persistent widow with the unjust judge (Luke 18:1–7). The widow got an answer, Habakkuk eventually got an answer, and you too will get an answer if you do not faint (Galatians 6:9).

4 Therefore the law is slacked, and judgment doth never go forth: for the wicked doth compass about the righteous; therefore wrong judgment proceedeth.

The word judgment is the key to Habakkuk's complaint. Mentioned twice in verse 4, it is the Hebrew word mishpat (meesh-POT), literally justice. Justice speaks of the verdict, favorable or unfavorable, that is pronounced judicially, and includes the crime committed and the associated penalty that is required so that the society can function properly. In other words, justice brings about the order ordained by God for His covenant people (Isaiah 42:1–4, Jeremiah 5:1–9). However, society is out of order. The six problems (v. 3) have so negatively impacted the society that there is no justice: (1) the law is so slack that justice never prevails, and (2) the wicked hem in the righteous so that justice is perverted.

The law is slacked (Heb. *pug*, **POOG**), or lies still so that the courts no longer work, and laws are not enforced. Consequently, wrongdoers go unpunished and are never corrected. If that were not bad enough, the wicked hem in those who are trying to do right so that they are totally frustrated. Those with the responsibility to uphold the law accept bribes and rule in favor of wrongdoers, thereby perverting justice. The result is chaos, a society full of crime, violence, corruption, legal trials that are a farce, and the defeat of the righteous.

No one pays attention to priestly or prophetic instruction. In fact, it was so bad that the very priests ignored the Law (Jeremiah 2:8), and false prophets preached their own opinions or soothing words that the people wanted to hear (Jeremiah 23:16–20). During the reign of Jehoiakim, Judah abandoned the righteous order intended by God for their society, in spite of the fact that only twelve years prior they had renewed their covenant with the Lord and undergone sweeping religious reform in the time of King Josiah.

Given all of this, Habakkuk could not understand why Yahweh tolerated such wickedness. Yes, the society was out of order, but the reason there was no justice was that God did not dispense divine justice (*mishpat*) on a rebellious people. However, it is important to remember that God has promised to judge sin, and He will. It is not a question of whether He will judge, but when. So the prophet's question about how long will God wait before He judges His people is appropriate. Therefore, we too can take heart knowing that God sees the injustices that occur in our nation today. We can pray with confidence for God to intervene, knowing that He will do so in due season.

12 Art thou not from everlasting, O LORD my God, mine Holy One? we shall not die. O LORD, thou hast ordained them for judgment; **and, O mighty God, thou hast established them for correction. 13 Thou art of purer eyes than to behold evil, and canst not look on iniquity: wherefore lookest thou upon them that deal treacherously, and holdest thy tongue when the wicked devoureth the man that is more righteous than he?**

God reassures His prophet that He has the situation well in hand and is going to handle it in a way Habakkuk would not believe (1:5). His plan is to raise up the cruel Chaldeans (Babylonians) and make them a world power that will conquer many lands, including Judah and Jerusalem (1:6–7). On one hand, Habakkuk accepts and repeats, in his own words, what has been stipulated: God has chosen Babylonia to be their judgment (1:12). Habakkuk recognizes the sovereignty of God by addressing Him as "O LORD" and "O mighty God" in the same sentence. He acknowledges that God has ordained the Babylonians to punish Judah and dispense justice (*mishpat*) sometime in the future.

This plan, however, still leaves a big question in Habakkuk's mind. How does God's plan square with God's character? How can the everlasting, holy God continue to "behold," to stand back and watch evil with His pure eyes? How can God continue to tolerate evil, not only by Judah but also by the Babylonians, who are even more wicked than the Israelites (1:13). To allow the Babylonians to invade Judah and take the Israelites as captives to Babylon is more than the prophet could comprehend.

However, Habakkuk should not have been confused because God's plan of action is not at all mysterious or even new. As a matter of fact, it is already spelled out in the Law, in the Mosaic Covenant that God used as the means of governing His people Israel. If they did not listen to and obey God's commandments, He would punish them, especially by allowing their enemies to conquer them. God told Israel

327

He would "scatter you among the heathen" (Leviticus 26:33). What is happening is exactly what God said would happen.

God uses whomever He chooses as His instrument of justice. In this case, God told Israel that defeat by their enemies would be one of the curses for disobedience and lawlessness. So why is Habakkuk surprised? Perhaps in his overwhelming distress, Habakkuk is not concentrating on God's Word, and what God had already said about the situation he is praying about.

This is a lesson for us as well. God will always act in concert with His written Word. Therefore, when we pray about a matter, we can have confidence, for "if we ask anything according to His will He hears us" (1 John 5:14). His will is clearly expressed in His Word. In fact, the only reason Habakkuk could say, "We shall not die" (1:12) is because of God's covenant promise: "when they be in the land of their enemies, I will not cast them away, neither will I abhor them, to destroy them utterly, and to break my covenant with them" (Leviticus 26:44). His Word is His covenant, His unfailing promise to us. Therefore, it is critical to know God's Word, and then to pray in accordance with that Word.

14 And makest men as the fishes of the sea, as the creeping things, that have no ruler over them?

In the next few verses, Habakkuk uses a fishing metaphor to explain his questions and objections more fully (1:14–17). The Israelites are like the fish in the sea, and the Babylonians are the fishermen. Habakkuk offers several objections about their hideous activities: (1) the wicked fishermen catch the more righteous in their nets, (2) strings them up on their hooks, (3) rejoices and celebrates over their success, (4) sacrifices to their false gods while living in luxury, enjoying the choicest food. It seems as if the wicked Gentiles are flourishing, and God is tolerating it. However, again and again in Scripture, God assures His people that evildoers will be punished (Psalms 37:1–2). The success of wicked people is only temporary. As we observe and pray for our society and our nation today in light of all the evil in it (mass murders, racism, voter suppression, etc.), we do well to remember these words of admonition and take hope in the God who will ultimately judge all evildoers. He uses Babylon to judge Judah, and then He uses the Medio-Persians to judge Babylon. Truth and justice will ultimately prevail.

Sources:

Achtemeier, Elizabeth. *Interpretation: A Bible Commentary for Teaching and Preaching.* Atlanta, GA: John Knox Press, 1986.

Bruckner, James. *The NIV Application Commentary: Habakkuk.* Grand Rapids, MI: Zondervan, 2004.

Old-Time Gospel Hour. Liberty Bible Commentary, Old Testament, Volume 1. Nashville, TN: Thomas Nelson, Inc., Publishers, 1982.

Walvoord, J.F., & Zuck, R.B. *The Bible Knowledge Commentary: Old Testament.* Wheaton, IL: Victor Books, 1985.

Winward, Stephen. *A Guide to the Prophets.* Atlanta, GA: John Knox Press, 1969. 412-436.

Say It Correctly

Habakkuk. **HAB**-uh-kuhk.
Chaldean. kal-**DEE**-uhn.
Jehoiakim. juh-**HOY**-ah-kim.
Jehoiachin. Juh-**HOY**-ah-khin.

Daily Bible Readings

MONDAY
Job's Cry for Justice Frustrated
(Job 19:1–7)

TUESDAY
The Rock's Work Is Justice
(Deuteronomy 32:1–4)

WEDNESDAY
God's People Ravaged for Sin
(Jeremiah 5:14–19)

THURSDAY
Chaldeans to Ravage the Nations
(Habakkuk 1:5–11)

FRIDAY
The Destructive Character of the Enemy
(Habakkuk 1:15–17)

SATURDAY
Assyrians Punished for Arrogance
(Isaiah 10:12–14)

SUNDAY
Why, Lord, Does Injustice Prevail?
(Habakkuk 1:1–4, 12–14)

Notes

_____

_____

_____

_____

Teaching Tips

Words You Should Know

A. Taunting (v. 6) *melitsah* (Heb.)—A mocking poem or satirical song

B. Vex (v. 7) *zua'* (Heb.)—To make tremble and shake

Teacher Preparation

Unifying Principle—Lost and Found. People seem not to suffer for their unjust actions. When will acts of the unjust be punished? The psalmist affirms that God will reward the just, and Habakkuk declares that the unjust will be punished for wickedness.

A. Read the Bible Background and Devotional Reading.

B. Pray for your students and lesson clarity.

C. Read the lesson Scripture in multiple translations.

O—Open the Lesson

A. Begin the class with prayer.

B. Discuss modern examples of oppression and people who waited for God's judgment (e.g. Martin Luther King, Jr.).

C. Have the students read the Aim for Change and the In Focus story.

D. Ask students how events like those in the story weigh on their hearts and how they can view these events from a faith perspective.

P—Present the Scriptures

A. Read the Focal Verses and discuss the Background and The People, Places, and Times sections.

B. Have the class share what Scriptures stand out for them and why, with particular emphasis on today's context.

E—Explore the Meaning

A. Use In Depth or More Light on the Text to facilitate a deeper discussion of the lesson text.

B. Pose the questions in Search the Scriptures and Discuss the Meaning.

C. Discuss the Liberating Lesson and Application for Activation sections.

N—Next Steps for Application

A. Summarize the value of following God's commandment to act with justice.

B. End class with a commitment to pray for clarity on where to serve the cause of justice locally.

Worship Guide

For the Superintendent or Teacher
Theme: Consequences for Injustice
Song: "The Vision"
Devotional Reading: Psalm 130

Consequences for Injustice

Bible Background • HABAKKUK 2
Printed Text • HABAKKUK 2:6–14 | Devotional Reading • PSALM 130

———— Aim for Change ————

By the end of the lesson, we will: RECOGNIZE why injustice will be punished, APPRECIATE the fairness of divine punishment of injustice, and DECIDE to follow God's commandment to act with justice.

———— In Focus ————

Terri struggled to keep her car on the road as she sped home from the office. After 13 years with the school district, the administrators had decided to eliminate her position. As Terri drove, she thought about the hundreds of overtime hours she had freely given.

Worst of all was that two of the special education people, Lauren and Crystal, were remaining after Terri had covered for both of them countless times. Yet the district cut her job. Since her husband's death, Terri was the sole supporter of their three kids.

She related the whole story to her friend Karla over coffee. Karla listened patiently through the long, angry rant. "What do you think of that?" Terri finally asked.

"Terri," Karla softly began. "Do you think God doesn't know all of this already? Do you think He's not watching you?" Karla held Terri's hand. "Be patient. He will protect you, and He will bring justice to them. Just watch!"

Just as Terri's severance pay was going to end, she was hired by a Christian charity at a higher salary than her last job. The next month, Terri turned on her computer to check the news,and the first headline said that her former district supervisor and several staff were under investigation for fiscal mismanagement. Terri shook her head and said, "Won't He do it?"

Why do you think God delays justice? Where have you seen delayed justice in your life?

———— Keep in Mind ————

"Woe to him that buildeth a town with blood, and stablisheth a city by iniquity!"
(Habakkuk 2:12, KJV).

"What sorrow awaits you who build cities with money gained through murder and corruption!" (Habakkuk 2:12, NLT).

Focal Verses

KJV Habakkuk 2:6 Shall not all these take up a parable against him, and a taunting proverb against him, and say, Woe to him that increaseth that which is not his! how long? and to him that ladeth himself with thick clay!

7 Shall they not rise up suddenly that shall bite thee, and awake that shall vex thee, and thou shalt be for booties unto them?

8 Because thou hast spoiled many nations, all the remnant of the people shall spoil thee; because of men's blood, and for the violence of the land, of the city, and of all that dwell therein.

9 Woe to him that coveteth an evil covetousness to his house, that he may set his nest on high, that he may be delivered from the power of evil!

10 Thou hast consulted shame to thy house by cutting off many people, and hast sinned against thy soul.

11 For the stone shall cry out of the wall, and the beam out of the timber shall answer it.

12 Woe to him that buildeth a town with blood, and stablisheth a city by iniquity!

13 Behold, is it not of the LORD of hosts that the people shall labour in the very fire, and the people shall weary themselves for very vanity?

14 For the earth shall be filled with the knowledge of the glory of the LORD, as the waters cover the sea.

NLT Habakkuk 2:6 "But soon their captives will taunt them. They will mock them, saying, 'What sorrow awaits you thieves! Now you will get what you deserve! You've become rich by extortion, but how much longer can this go on?'

7 Suddenly, your debtors will take action. They will turn on you and take all you have, while you stand trembling and helpless.

8 Because you have plundered many nations, now all the survivors will plunder you. You committed murder throughout the countryside and filled the towns with violence.

9 What sorrow awaits you who build big houses with money gained dishonestly! You believe your wealth will buy security, putting your family's nest beyond the reach of danger.

10 But by the murders you committed, you have shamed your name and forfeited your lives.

11 The very stones in the walls cry out against you, and the beams in the ceilings echo the complaint.

12 What sorrow awaits you who build cities with money gained through murder and corruption!

13 Has not the LORD of Heaven's Armies promised that the wealth of nations will turn to ashes? They work so hard, but all in vain!

14 For as the waters fill the sea, the earth will be filled with an awareness of the glory of the LORD."

The People, Places, and Times

The Babylonians. The battle of Carchemish in 605 BC (Jeremiah 46:2) was an important one because the king of Babylon defeated the Egyptians and added Syria-Palestine to the Babylonian Empire, including Judah. For several years, King Jehoiakim was loyal to his new Babylonian masters. But after three years he rebelled against Nebuchadnezzar. Later the Babylonian army invaded Jerusalem.

During the siege, Jehoiakim died or was possibly killed in action. Jehoiakim's son, Jehoiachin, took the throne after his father's death but surrendered the city after a reign of three months. He and his staff were taken to Babylon as captives along with ten thousand

333

others (2 Kings 24:14). This was the beginning of the Babylonian captivity.

Background

In the age of goal setting seminars and vision boards, Christians and non-Christians alike have likely heard some paraphrase of Habakkuk 2:2: "Write the vision, make it plain upon tables, that he may run that readeth it." While many reference this Scripture as part of conversations around the importance of writing down one's goals and dreams, in context, these words serve as a much more pointed rebuttal to the prophet Habakkuk's charges toward God on behalf of the people. The book of Habakkuk reads as both a prophecy and a heated conversation between God and the prophet. Habakkuk begins the conversation with a complaint against God. For the prophet, God seemingly cannot or will not hear His people's cries for help and refuses to save them from the violence, wrongdoing, and injustice in their land (Habakkuk 1:2–11). God answers Habakkuk's complaint by promising to do something unthinkable—raising up the ruthless and lawless Babylonians to execute God's judgment (Habakkuk 1:6). In response, the prophet first affirms the holiness and wisdom of God but questions why God continues to tolerate the wickedness and injustice that the people of God faced in Jerusalem. The prophet questions the silence of God while the righteous seem to be "swallowed up" and compares God's people to a sea of fish being hooked, tangled, and caught with ease by their foes, whom he compares to fishermen who worship their nets and hooks (Habakkuk 1:13–16). At the end of this second complaint, Habakkuk steps back and declares that he will wait to hear what answer God desires him to give to the believers (Habakkuk 2:1). It is out of this context that God responds with "write the vision, make it plain" as a way of instructing Habakkuk to ensure that everyone is able to hear the response from the Lord—a piece of which we examine in our text for this lesson.

At-A-Glance

1. The Power of The People (Habakkuk 2:6)
2. Destroyed by Their Own Devices (vv. 6–11)
3. God Will Get the Glory (vv. 12–14)

In Depth

1. The Power of The People (Habakkuk 2:6)

In response to Habakkuk's second complaint of questioning God's silence in the face of violence and injustice and what felt like an unwillingness of God to intervene on behalf of His people, God describes the enemy as puffed up, not upright in his desires, betrayed by wine, arrogant, restless, and greedy (Habakkuk 2:4–5) and chronicles how the enemy has prioritized taking captive the peoples of all nations. However, God then provides Habakkuk with a unique prophecy, declaring that at some point, those same people whom the enemy captured will overcome the enemy, taunting him and speaking unavoidable truths of the enemy's demise (v. 6). This small portion of the text is packed with some big implications, namely that the beginning of the work of restoration is when God's oppressed people tap into their own power to use their voices to speak to and against the injustices that they have witnessed. As in the day of Habakkuk, today God's people have the power and obligation to speak to people, policies, and systems that are unjust and oppressive. This power is given to us like a spark plug for the change that God will bring about in His perfect time.

What injustices and oppression have you seen or experienced that God may be calling you to speak against?

2. Destroyed by Their Own Devices (vv. 6–11)

Next, God reveals at least three warnings or "woe" statements that the people would speak

334

against the enemy. What is interesting about these statements is that, in each scenario, the enemy is destroyed utilizing the same methods that they used against God's people. God reveals that those who gain their wealth by stealing and exhorting God's people would come to ruin at the hands of their creditors (vv. 6–7). God declares that those who plunder many nations would eventually be plundered by the nations that remain (v. 8). Finally, God says that those who try to escape ruin by ruining others would be ruined during the end (vv. 9–10). These three woe statements illustrate the great irony of injustice—eventually, the very devices one uses to destroy others will be the devices of one's own demise. This lesson foreshadows the lesson Jesus seeks to teach Peter: "All they that take the sword shall perish with the sword" (from Matthew 26:52).

Can you recall a time when the methods someone used to destroy others were eventually used to destroy them?

3. God Will Get the Glory (vv. 12–14)

The final statement of the text contains the good news! In the final "woe" statement of our text, God speaks directly to the violence and injustice that Habakkuk gave his initial complaint about. God declares that these efforts are ultimately futile as the Lord Almighty predetermines that the final glory would not be given to the work of the oppressors but that "the earth shall be filled with the knowledge of the glory of the LORD" (Habakkuk 2:14). This text serves as a reminder to Habakkuk and to the reader today that injustice, violence, and oppression cannot win. In the end, God will get the glory!

Can you name some instances where justice was delayed but ultimately was achieved on a local, national, or global level?

Search the Scriptures

1. Paraphrase God's "woe" statements (Habakkuk 2:6, 9, 11). Where else in the Bible do we find "woe" statements and who is being warned?

2. Why is Israel being set upon by its enemies (v. 8)?

3. What promise does God mention in verse 13?

Discuss the Meaning

1. Why is it important to maintain hope that God will punish injustice as believers in Jesus Christ?

2. What does it look like to act justly and pursue godly justice in our private and public lives?

3. What hope does God provide in the midst of our despair regarding our need for justice?

Liberating Lesson

The theme of injustice has been a mainstay of American public discourse over the last decade—particularly as it relates to the violence experienced within black and brown communities. The murder of Trayvon Martin at the hands of an acquitted vigilante and the countless cases of unarmed black women and men killed at the hands of law enforcement with painfully few convictions have caused citizens and clergy to sing Habakkuk's song. *How long will this continue to go on? How long will we cry violence and God does not intervene? How long will God allow injustice to persist?* The lesson of the text is that God is not asleep and God will ultimately get the glory—but God's people must use their power to speak against the systems of oppression and injustice to spark the desired change.

Application for Activation

Justice work is not a cultural phenomenon but a biblical requirement. Micah reminds the believer that the Lord requires us "to do justly, and to love mercy, and to walk humbly" with God (Micah 6:8). As a group, create a list of potential justice issues that exist within the area where your congregation is situated. Expand the list by discussing major justice issues in your city and state. Now discuss justice issues that interest the group on a national level. From your list, select one local, state, and national issue and discuss practical ways that the congregation can be proactive in "lending a voice" and resources to these causes.

Follow the Spirit

What God wants me to do:

_____

_____

_____

_____

Remember Your Thoughts

Special insights I have learned:

_____

_____

_____

_____

More Light on the Text
Habakkuk 2:6–14

Habakkuk was a pre-exilic prophet (i.e., he lived prior to the Babylonian captivity), writing the book that bears his name before the Babylonian captivity in the seventh century BC. Every prophet of God communicates God's word to his own generation and beyond. Habakkuk is assigned to prophesy concerning the kingdom of Judah. Chapter 1 begins with Habakkuk's ongoing cry to God, who has not yet answered him. Habakkuk wants to know how long God would continue to allow the righteous to suffer and the ungodly to prosper. The moral and spiritual condition of Judah is getting worse and worse (2 Kings 21–22), and Habakkuk could not understand why God is allowing this to continue. It is extremely hard for Habakkuk to continue to look on sin, and he wants to know how a holy God could tolerate it. God answers Habakkuk by telling him that He is going to do a work that Habakkuk would not believe. He is going to raise up that bitter, terrible, and dreadful nation of the Chaldeans (Babylonians) to punish His people. Habakkuk has such a good relationship with God that he could ask God about anything that was troubling him. So Habakkuk asks God another question: Why would God use a wicked nation to punish Judah? After all, even the worst things that Judah had done were not as bad as the deeds of the wicked Chaldeans. Habakkuk has learned patience from his previous experience. This time, he would wait and watch expectantly for God's answer. The Lord answers him in a vision.

6 Shall not all these take up a parable against him, and a taunting proverb against him, and say, Woe to him that increaseth that which is not his! how long? and to him that ladeth himself with thick clay!

The Hebrew word translated "parable" is *mashal* (**maw-SHAWL**), referring to an aphorism or proverb. The downfall of this wicked people will be told as a cautionary tale to all. The Hebrew word translated "taunting" is *melitsah* (**meh-lee-TSAW**) and refers to a mocking poem or a satirical song. One usually hears taunting songs or mocking from the wicked about the righteous, as when Job was mocked by his enemies, who made up a song to tease him about his afflictions (Job 30:9). But when the righteous finally see God punish the unrighteous, they will boldly mock the wicked with their taunting songs. In the text that follows, God uses this sarcastic song or poem that the captives will sing to explain how He will punish the wicked Chaldeans. The song has several woes and addresses the Chaldeans as individuals. The first woe is directed at those who increase their wealth with things that do not belong to them. "Thick clay" here could be read two ways. It could be a euphemism for gold or silver, which come out of the ground like clay, and are just as worthless as clay when one gives proper weight to the truly important things of life. Otherwise, it is a mistranslation of the text that Jewish scholars have long since clarified. Instead of being translated as "clay," it should be translated as "pledge," referring to a piece of property a lender might take as collateral. Either way, this first woe is to those who gain by theft and cruel lending practices.

7 Shall they not rise up suddenly that shall bite thee, and awake that shall vex thee, and thou shalt be for booties unto them? 8 Because thou hast spoiled many nations, all the remnant of the people shall spoil thee; because of men's blood, and for the violence of the land, of the city, and of all that dwell therein.

"Booties" refers to the spoils of war. When a city was captured, everything belonging to the people of that city became the property of the conquerors. How the spoil was to be divided among the Israelites was called the "law of booty." The distribution of spoils became a joyous occasion (Isaiah 9:3). Now the tables are turned; instead of the righteous becoming spoil for the wicked, the wicked would become spoil for the righteous. The righteous would suddenly despoil the wicked, as if awakening them out of deep sleep, to "vex" (Heb. *zua'*, **ZOO-ah**) them, or make them tremble and shake. The "remnant" (Heb. *yether*, **YEH-ther**)—those who are left in the land—will despoil the wicked; the very people most harmed by the Chaldeans will be the ones to regain the possessions that

were originally theirs. What the Chaldeans have done to others will be done to them. All of this is punishment for the human blood that was shed and the violence inflicted on Judah.

9 Woe to him that coveteth an evil covetousness to his house, that he may set his nest on high, that he may be delivered from the power of evil! 10 Thou hast consulted shame to thy house by cutting off many people, and hast sinned against thy soul. 11 For the stone shall cry out of the wall, and the beam out of the timber shall answer it.

Verse 9 contains the second woe of the taunting song. This woe refers to the household of "him that coveteth [Heb. *batsa'*, **baw-TSAH**] evil covetousness [Heb. *betsa'*, **BEH-tsah**]." Both Hebrew words are from the same root and include the idea of violently cutting away to take the coveted thing. Everything the object of this taunt gains is illegally obtained through unnecessary violence, just so that he could build a high place in order to be delivered from those who would harm him. Evil people know what evil people do and how they think, so they must constantly protect themselves from other evil people and from those whom they have victimized. The evildoer has "consulted" (Heb. *ya'ats*, **yaw-OTS**) shame to come to his own house. He sits down, considers, and consults with himself and still thinks it is wise to treat people with violence and sin. The materials of the house itself speak in a call-and-response chorus, with the stone walls starting and the wooden beams answering, testifying to the evil that has been done. The familiar saying "If only these walls could talk" certainly applies here.

12 Woe to him that buildeth a town with blood, and stablisheth a city by iniquity!

Here we have the third woe of the taunting song. The Hebrew word translated "stablisheth" is *kun* (**KOON**), which means to fix or establish.

Verse 8 spoke of violence and the shedding of innocent blood to support the individual evildoer's theft or usury. Here, blood and iniquity build up and establish entire towns. The city of the oppressors has been built with human blood; it has been prepared with iniquity or injustice. These three woes increase in scope, from the individual to the city. We tend to think on an individual level, hoping our sin only affects the victim or maybe our household, but in truth, our entire community is affected.

13 Behold, is it not of the LORD of hosts that the people shall labor in the very fire and the people shall weary themselves for very vanity?

By referring to God as the "LORD of hosts," Habakkuk answers the war imagery of spoils (vv. 7–8). The Babylonians had been taking spoils from Israel, but now the Lord of hosts is fighting for Israel. He fights their battles (Exodus 15:3) and controls their military operations. The taunting song turns into the question, "Is it not of the LORD of hosts …," that is, "Is it not [a promise from] the LORD of hosts …." God's decision is to destroy Babylon so that the people who labored and wearied themselves building it will have done so in vain. Babylonia is the land of the Chaldeans, and this verse is describing how the LORD will destroy them with fire (cf. Jeremiah 51:58). Any attempt to stop the destruction will be in vain. The Chaldeans wear themselves out for nothing.

14 For the earth shall be filled with the knowledge of the glory of the LORD, as the waters cover the sea.

Verse 14 is a promise from God that one day there will be as much knowledge of God around the world as there is water in the sea. Isaiah uses a nearly identical phrase to describe a time of complete peace and harmony among nature, animals, and people (11:9). At that time, the Messiah will rule the earth justly (v. 10) and will call all His people from all over the earth (v. 11). God knew that it would be many decades before His promises would be fulfilled in the Jews' return from Babylonian exile (even long before the Messiah would come, and longer still before the Messiah comes to rule the earth). This was why God comforts Habakkuk before He gives him the vision, telling him that the vision is for an appointed time and that he should wait for it because it would surely happen (2:3). Even though things look as though they are not going to change, God tells Habakkuk to keep waiting because he would see the fulfillment of God's promise in the end. Meanwhile, God encourages him with the knowledge that "the just shall live by his faith" (v. 4), a refrain the people of God remember throughout the Bible (Romans 1:17; Galatians 3:11; Hebrews 10:38).

Say It Correctly

Chaldeans. kal-**DEE**-ans.
Pre-exilic. **PREE**-ex-**ILL**-ic

Daily Bible Readings

MONDAY
Wait for Divine Intervention
(Psalm 130)

TUESDAY
Pay Attention to the Sentinel
(Ezekiel 33:1–9)

WEDNESDAY
The Risk of Ignoring the Needy
(Matthew 25:41–46)

THURSDAY
The Righteous Live by Faith
(Habakkuk 2:1–5)

FRIDAY
Violence Leads to Destruction
(Habakkuk 2:15–17)

SATURDAY
Compare an Idol with the Lord
(Habakkuk 2:18–20)

SUNDAY
You Reap What You Sow
(Habakkuk 2:6–14)

Notes

_____

_____

_____

_____

Teaching Tips

Words You Should Know

A. Abhor (v. 3:9) *ta'av* (Heb.)—To loathe, detest, or make abominable

B. Justly (v. 6:8) *mishpat* (Heb.)—Justice, judgment, that which is right and has been laid down as proper practice in a lawful society

Teacher Preparation

Unifying Principle—Doing Justice. Leaders often struggle with expectations of being examples of justice. How can leaders become models of justice worthy of emulation? Micah confronts the leaders of Israel for their failure to pursue justice and suggests that doing justice should be the basis of their lives.

A. Read the Bible Background and Devotional Reading.

B. Pray for your students and lesson clarity.

C. Read the lesson Scripture in multiple translations.

O—Open the Lesson

A. Begin the class with prayer.

B. As a class, brainstorm a list of leaders whose lives demonstrate what God requires of leaders.

C. Have the students read the Aim for Change and the In Focus story.

D. Ask students how events like those in the story weigh on their hearts and how they can view these events from a faith perspective.

P—Present the Scriptures

A. Read the Focal Verses and discuss the Background and The People, Places, and Times sections.

B. Have the class share what Scriptures stand out for them and why, with particular emphasis on today's context.

E—Explore the Meaning

A. Use In Depth or More Light on the Text to facilitate a deeper discussion of the lesson text.

B. Pose the questions in Search the Scriptures and Discuss the Meaning.

C. Discuss the Liberating Lesson and Application for Activation sections.

N—Next Steps for Application

A. Summarize the value of expecting leaders to be models of justice.

B. End class with a commitment to pray for justice, kindness, and humility to be cardinal human virtues.

Worship Guide

For the Superintendent or Teacher
Theme: Corrupt Leaders
Song: "Seek Justice, Love Mercy"
Devotional Reading: Zechariah 7:8–10;
Deuteronomy 24:17–22

Corrupt Leaders

Bible Background • MICAH 3-6 | Printed Text • MICAH 3:1-3, 9-12; 6:6-8
Devotional Reading • ZECHARIAH 7:8–10; DEUTERONOMY 24:17–22

Aim for Change

By the end of the lesson, we will: UNDERSTAND God's requirements for people and leaders; VALUE justice, kindness, and humility as key human virtues; and DECIDE to be just, kind, and humble people and leaders.

In Focus

On Monday morning, the headlines in many newspapers and reports on TV stated that an alderman in a major urban city was being indicted for taking bribes and kickbacks from companies and individuals who were seeking to do business with the city. All this came on the back of reports that priests across the country were being brought up on charges for sexually molesting minors for more than forty years.

Pastor Clarence addressed many of these issues with his congregation, but now he was preparing to speak at the semi-annual meeting of denominational leaders. He reminded them that leaders are expected to have compassion and respect for the people in their care. However, time and time again, greed and corruption have caused many to fall into a cesspool of crime and broken vows.

"Today, I want to remind you that God is not pleased when leaders refuse to lead by His standards and stand on His Word. Examine your own heart and actions to see if your motives in serving God and others are pleasing to Him. God does not want empty sacrifices but pure hearts that love Him and appreciate what He did on Calvary."

In what ways are people capable of giving "empty sacrifices" to the Lord? How does this impact or reflect on their relationship with God?

Keep in Mind

"He hath shewed thee, O man, what is good; and what doth the LORD require of thee, but to do justly, and to love mercy, and to walk humbly with thy God?" (Micah 6:8, KJV).

"No, O people, the LORD has told you what is good, and this is what he requires of you: to do what is right, to love mercy, and to walk humbly with your God" (Micah 6:8, NLT).

Focal Verses

KJV **Micah 3:1** And I said, Hear, I pray you, O heads of Jacob, and ye princes of the house of Israel; Is it not for you to know judgment?

2 Who hate the good, and love the evil; who pluck off their skin from off them, and their flesh from off their bones;

3 Who also eat the flesh of my people, and flay their skin from off them; and they break their bones, and chop them in pieces, as for the pot, and as flesh within the caldron.

9 Hear this, I pray you, ye heads of the house of Jacob, and princes of the house of Israel, that abhor judgment, and pervert all equity.

10 They build up Zion with blood, and Jerusalem with iniquity.

11 The heads thereof judge for reward, and the priests thereof teach for hire, and the prophets thereof divine for money: yet will they lean upon the LORD, and say, Is not the LORD among us? none evil can come upon us.

12 Therefore shall Zion for your sake be plowed as a field, and Jerusalem shall become heaps, and the mountain of the house as the high places of the forest.

6:6 Wherewith shall I come before the LORD, and bow myself before the high God? shall I come before him with burnt offerings, with calves of a year old?

7 Will the LORD be pleased with thousands of rams, or with ten thousands of rivers of oil? shall I give my firstborn for my transgression, the fruit of my body for the sin of my soul?

8 He hath shewed thee, O man, what is good; and what doth the LORD require of thee, but to do justly, and to love mercy, and to walk humbly with thy God?

NLT **Micah 3:1** I said, "Listen, you leaders of Israel! You are supposed to know right from wrong,

2 but you are the very ones who hate good and love evil. You skin my people alive and tear the flesh from their bones.

3 Yes, you eat my people's flesh, strip off their skin, and break their bones. You chop them up like meat for the cooking pot.

9 Listen to me, you leaders of Israel! You hate justice and twist all that is right.

10 You are building Jerusalem on a foundation of murder and corruption.

11 You rulers make decisions based on bribes; you priests teach God's laws only for a price; you prophets won't prophesy unless you are paid. Yet all of you claim to depend on the LORD. "No harm can come to us," you say, "for the LORD is here among us."

12 Because of you, Mount Zion will be plowed like an open field; Jerusalem will be reduced to ruins! A thicket will grow on the heights where the Temple now stands.

6:6 What can we bring to the LORD? Should we bring him burnt offerings? Should we bow before God Most High with offerings of yearling calves?

7 Should we offer him thousands of rams and ten thousand rivers of olive oil? Should we sacrifice our firstborn children to pay for our sins?

8 No, O people, the LORD has told you what is good, and this is what he requires of you: to do what is right, to love mercy, and to walk humbly with your God.

The People, Places, and Times

False Prophets. While there were many true prophets in Israel, there were also false prophets. These false prophets often offered messages of hope and peace. These messages comforted the people without pointing out their sin or challenging them to repent from their evil ways. The false prophets became rich from the fees they charged for their services. These prophets chose to seek after money rather than speak God's truth to the people. They prophesied according to how much money their words might bring them. Often they would use pagan methods of divination or fortune-telling, which were strictly forbidden in the Law of the Old Testament (Deuteronomy 18:9–14). The Lord told Israel to evaluate false prophets to see if the message they had spoken came to pass (vv. 21–22) and if they enticed the people to worship idols (v. 20).

What false prophets attempt to mislead the church today? How might profits corrupt a true prophet into a false one?

Background

Micah's prophecy began with a general announcement to Samaria and Jerusalem that God had a case to present against the nations of Israel and Judah. He then laid out the first of two series of judgments against the divided nation by describing the sins that they had committed against God as well as their fellow citizens. The Neo-Assyrian Empire was the dominant and real threat to Jerusalem during Micah's time. One of the many ways Jerusalem prepared for conflict was to strengthen the economy so they would have the necessary resources to fight off both foreign and domestic threats. But as today's text suggests, the ways they pursued economic stability were immoral and did not align with the precepts of the Lord. Their stimulus plan was based on greed, exploitation, and senseless taxes, and as a result, moral corruption slowly

crept in. The rulers and leaders convinced themselves that their methods of governing were necessary because of the impending dangers; thus, treachery soon became merely business as usual. The culture of corruption and abuse spread, and soon landowners began taking advantage of farmers. The poor were subjugated, and they had no social or economic power. Individually and collectively, the nation claimed to depend on God, whom they knew and believed to be the ultimate lover of justice; however, the leaders were cynical and perverted righteousness.

What should we do as Christians when we see corruption in our political or religious leaders?

At-A-Glance

1. Leader's Evil Desires (Micah 3:1–3)
2. Leaders' Corruption (vv. 9–12)
3. God's Call (6:6–8)

In Depth

1. Leaders' Evil Desires (Micah 3:1–3)

The leaders of Israel—including government leaders, priests, prophets, business leaders, and more—had turned their hearts from God's will. They had been given God's covenantal law and were supposed to be examples of righteous behavior for all those around them. Yet they had perverted what was right and used their position to take advantage of those they were supposed to lead. Israel's leaders had neglected their duties and led the people astray. Rather than protecting and instructing their citizens, they exploited and misled them. Micah uses the image of cannibalism to describe how the leaders fed off those they were called to protect. Jerusalem's leaders are being accused of increasing their power by using violence and oppression.

2. Leaders' Corruption (vv. 9–12)

Amid all of this, Micah stands up for justice by the power of the Spirit of the Lord. The prophet accuses leaders of not just disobedience but of hating justice and perverting the very meaning of righteousness. Micah says the leaders are attempting to build up the city but at the expense of the poor. The false prophets are not the only corrupt citizens in Samaria and Jerusalem; leaders in almost every area of their society have gone astray. As a nation and individually for many leaders, the focus quickly became prosperity by any means necessary. Despite the fact that the nation had adopted a culture of cheating, lying, stealing, and marginalizing the poor, they profess that their "growth and success" is due to their dependence on and protection by God. Micah ends by telling people that the city they are working so hard to build will ultimately be destroyed.

3. God's Call (6:6–8)

What can Israel do to correct its broken relationship with God? Their immediate response would be to offer the traditional burnt offerings as sacrifices to God. The prophet points out that no matter how much they give, God won't be pleased. Even the offer of human sacrifice, which was customary of pagan sacrifice but prohibited by the covenant law (Leviticus 18:21; 20:2–5) is suggested to show how ridiculous and insulting their erroneous attempts were. Micah's prophecy, in keeping with other Israelite prophecies, clearly indicates that the inward condition of one's heart and the importance of acting justly towards neighbors are of more concern to God than outward religiosity. God doesn't require outrageous sacrifice; He has already said what He requires. As communicated earlier in Micah's prophecy,

God requires that His people would once again be a just society that loves mercy. He desires protection for the oppressed and poor. He desires that His people act mercifully toward one another. God requires that they (and we) continue to walk in covenant fellowship with Him.

Search the Scriptures

1. Based on Micah's prophecy, what was the primary source of motivation during this period in Jerusalem (3:11)?

2. What outward religious activities did Israel think would please God (vv. 6–7)?

3. What sacrifices does God require (6:8)?

Discuss the Meaning

1. What makes a leader corrupt? Be sure to consider thoughts, words, and actions.

2. Micah's message to the people indicated that God is more concerned with the inward state of one's heart than outward shows of piety. What causes us to try to look outwardly spiritual while secretly knowing that we're out of step with God's will?

Liberating Lesson

We live in a polarized society today where injustice abounds. Children are separated from their families. People go without food and shelter. People are persecuted for their beliefs and behaviors. God's faithful people know, however, that God will restore true justice to the land. They realize that no matter what others do, they must continue in their faith with just actions, love, and humility. We may or may not be able to effect change at a societal level, but we are always required to make sure our own personal actions are in step with God's law.

Application for Activation

Discuss modern leaders and whether they are models of justice and humility. List and discuss God's requirements for people and leaders. Have participants write a litany of commitment to become just, kind, and humble people and leaders. If you can share this litany in a worship service, be sure to include acts of appreciation for leaders in the congregation whose lives demonstrate what God requires.

Follow the Spirit

What God wants me to do:

_____

_____

_____

_____

Remember Your Thoughts

Special insights I have learned:

_____

_____

_____

More Light on the Text

Micah 3:1–3, 9–12; 6:6–8

The prophet Micah, a contemporary of Isaiah, speaks to the Southern Kingdom of Judah. At this time, the Northern Kingdom of Israel has been under threat of destruction and will eventually fall into the hands of the Assyrians in 722 BC. Micah's warning to Judah is that the same could happen to them if they continue in their evil ways.

3:1 And I said, Hear, I pray you, O heads of Jacob, and ye princes of the house of Israel; **Is it not for you to know judgment? 2 Who hate the good, and love the evil; who pluck off their skin from off them, and their flesh from off their bones; 3 Who also eat the flesh of my people, and flay their skin from off them; and they break their bones, and chop them in pieces, as for the pot, and as flesh within the caldron.**

The book of Micah is a prophetic judgment against the royal family and other leaders in Judah during the reigns of kings Jotham, Ahaz, and Hezekiah as well as those who support them. Micah is accusing these leaders of treating the people badly, as though they are meat. The leaders of both nations are taking from the poor and oppressed in order to make themselves wealthy in a kingdom of utter corruption. They are so corrupt that those who try to do good are despised while those who do evil are celebrated. The prophet intentionally exaggerates the violence of the times in the same way that someone who feels used or taken advantage of might say someone "took the shirt off my back" (vv. 2–3). In this case, the corrupt leaders are accused of being even worse, taking the flesh off people's bones and using them as stew meat to feed themselves. Greed rules the day in a way that values profits over human lives.

9 Hear this, I pray you, ye heads of the house of Jacob, and princes of the house of Israel, that abhor judgment, and pervert all equity.

Micah particularly addresses the political and religious groups of Judah. He calls out the heads and princes responsible for establishing the religious and political moral standards for the people. The Lord, through Micah, accuses them of hating or abhorring what is just. The word "abhor," (Heb. *ta'av*, **tah-AHV**, to loathe, detest, or make abominable) is a strong indication of how far those who rule over the Israelites have fallen from God. They are not instructing people with fairness but seeking their own gain and pursuing personal agendas. Not only do these rulers and chiefs abhor justice, but they also pervert "equity" (Heb. *yashar,* **yah-SHAR**, that which is straight, right, or just). This word also denotes fairness and being honest and aboveboard. Those who rule over Judah do not practice such honesty.

10 They build up Zion with blood, and Jerusalem with iniquity.

The prophet continues to personalize the accusation against Judah. In the name of religion and sacrifice to God, the people have erected buildings using perverse and deceitful means. Instead of using tithes and offerings to establish places of worship, the religious leaders have taken from the poor and, in some instances, killed to expand Jerusalem. Archaeology testifies to the building activities underway in Jerusalem during Micah's prophecy to build themselves up against the coming Assyrian invasion. Such capital activities are performed at the expense of the oppressed and less fortunate. Jeremiah makes reference to similar activities, mentioning those who build their homes by unrighteousness (22:13). The prophet Habakkuk also records official building with bloodshed (2:12). The name "Zion" refers to the hill between the Kidron and Tyropoeon valleys that David captured from the Jebusites (2 Samuel 5:7). The city of Jerusalem by Micah's time also includes a second hill, Moriah, between the Tyropoeon and Hinnum valleys. After the building of the temple to the north of the hill of Zion, it became the center of the Lord's activity, since the Temple was where Yahweh dwelt. The term "Zion" may refer specifically to the Temple vicinity or Jerusalem in general. Thus, Micah's reference to the people building Zion up with blood shows how this holy habitation has been defamed and desecrated.

11 The heads thereof judge for reward, and the priests thereof teach for hire, and the prophets thereof divine for money: yet will they lean upon the LORD, and say, Is not the LORD among us? none evil can come upon us.

Micah again compels Judah to reexamine its political and social ethics. The rulers who govern civic and state affairs are corrupt. The priests who dictate religious standards practice evil. The prophets who speak the Word of the Lord only do it for money. Micah contends that Judah's leadership has turned away from the Lord. Those in power only want to be compensated by their subjects for what God has gifted and instructed them to do. Rulers give judgment for a bribe, priests teach for a price, and prophets give oracles for money. Micah stresses the greed and insatiable materialism pervading Judah. These leaders, however, believe that what they do is good and pleasing in the eyes of the Lord. They are convinced that since Zion is the dwelling place of God and that since the Hebrews are God's chosen people, all is well, and their transgressions can be overlooked.

Speaking rhetorically, Micah states that those in authority do not lean on the Lord. The word "lean" (Heb. *sha'an,* **shah-AWN**), means to lie, rely on, or rest on, often with reference to God (2 Chronicles 14:11). Isaiah uses another verb for leaning in, stating how Judah must depend on God (48:2). Such leaning implies a need to find favor and obtain support. Judah wishes to engage in wrongdoing while claiming to depend on the Lord for safety. The leaders, despite their unscrupulous conduct, believe that God will protect them because of His faithfulness and promises. The people do not see the error of their ways. They are so obstinate and spiritually blind that they are convinced that because the Lord dwells in Zion, no harm can come to them, even when they sin against God. These leaders mistake leniency for indulgence. God is patiently waiting for and encouraging them through His prophets to return to keeping the Law. In the meantime, He is being lenient, holding off the proper punishment for their crimes. The Israelites interpret this holding off of punishment, however, as a mitigation of punishment. They think they have escaped the consequences of their actions.

12 Therefore shall Zion for your sake be plowed as a field, and Jerusalem shall become heaps, and the mountain of the house as the high places in the forest.

Because Judah has become prideful and sinful, the Lord, through Micah, predicts its ensuing destruction. The crassness of the leaders will result in the leveling of Jerusalem and its Temple. Micah made a similar pronouncement earlier stating that Samaria would be a heap and a place for planting vineyards, that is, an unused, open land (1:6). This prophecy is remembered a century later when the people of Israel observe its fulfillment (Jeremiah 26:18–19). Both prophets foretell the captivity of Judah by the Babylonians and the exile afterward. Judah, during Micah's time, is already a vassal state of the Assyrians; further enslavement is the next step. Again, the prophet specifically names Zion and Jerusalem, the center of Israelite worship, as places to be destroyed. Micah personalizes the message and the plans of God to show Judah's leaders their ill behavior. No place is beyond God's wrath when evil has been committed. The Israelites perhaps had hoped that God's desire to preserve the honor of His own name would outweigh His desire to let Israel feel the consequences of their actions. Various times before, righteous Israelites had pleaded with God to spare punishment so that other nations would not think that God was not powerful enough to protect His people (Exodus 32:9–14). God's people now use this mercy as an excuse to continue in unrighteous action.

6:6 Wherewith shall I come before the LORD, and bow myself before the high God? shall I come before him with burnt offerings, with calves of a year old? 7 Will the LORD be pleased with thousands of rams, or with ten thousands of rivers of oil? shall I give my firstborn for my transgression, the fruit of my body for the sin of my soul? 8 He hath shewed thee, O man, what is good; and what doth the LORD require of thee, but to do justly, and to love mercy, and to walk humbly with thy God?

Micah 6:1–8 is written like a court trial between God and Israel. In the rhetorical trial, first God takes the side of the defendant. God asks them what He has done that would cause the people of Israel to turn their backs on him? What did God do that would make them pursue wickedness instead of righteousness? He invites Israel to bring witnesses to testify against Him, whether from nature or their history together. God uses the opportunity to point out His history of doing great works in His covenant with Israel, from creation through the Exodus and beyond. God had blessed and protected them. God was not guilty.

Then Micah's prophecy switches sides. If God is not guilty, then Israel must pay restitution to God. They must give God what He is owed for their injustice against Him. They are the ones who failed in keeping the covenant, not God. Verse 6 continues the metaphor of sentencing in this court trial. What do the Israelites owe God for what they have done? Does God want offerings of calves or rams? An exaggerated number is given to show not only how deep the debt is to God for sin, but also how much they could try to pay to please God. The exaggerated amount to be given continues with rivers of olive oil or even their children to atone for their sins.

We know as believers that nothing we could give God could atone for our sin—the debt is too great. Israel is in a position to lose the case and be unable to pay damages for violating the covenant. Then God tells them what He wants (v. 8). He wants them to do justly, be merciful, and walk in humility with Him. The Hebrew word translated "justly" here is *mishpat* (**meesh-POT**), which is also translated justice, judgment, and law. It refers to that which is right and has been laid down as proper practice in a lawful society. God's first answer to how they should pay restitution is to look at what He has already told them. Just do the Law that He has already revealed to them. It is not a great mystery or too hard (cf. Deuteronomy 30:11–14). Secondly, they are to love "mercy" (Heb. *khesed*, **KHE-sed**), which is also translated loving-kindness and goodness. In many ways, it is the Hebrew equivalent of *agape* (Gk. **ah-GAH-pay**), which is unconditional, divine love (1 Corinthians 13). Lastly, they are to walk (Heb. *halak*, **ha-LOCK**, here: to live one's life) humbly (Heb. *tsana*, **tsaw-NAH**). In an honor-shame society as the ancient Mediterranean, where social regard was based on where you fit in a rigid hierarchy, humility could very easily be misunderstood as shame. Voluntarily and overtly living your life to show you were subservient to another was unheard of in neighboring nations. But this is just how God expects the Israelites to behave. However, in God's great mercy, when we are humble and do not think of ourselves as higher than we are, He humbles Himself too, to walk "with" us.

God requires obedience in our relationship with Him. Obedience to God is better than sacrifices (1 Samuel 15:22). God wants His people to pursue justice, care for the poor, and be merciful—meaning nonjudgmental and patient with others, the same way He is patient with us. God wants us to recognize we are all sinful and make mistakes. He also wants us to receive His grace in humility. We do not deserve God's grace. The debt of our sin is too great to repay God. So God gives this "second chance" to Israel to obey Him and keep His covenant. The covenant calls for justice, mercy, and humility. It is summed up as love God and our neighbors as ourselves. We must obey as living sacrifices because we cannot atone with material sacrifices.

This same sentiment is prophesied again in Jeremiah 7:21–23 which happens one hundred years later. God is giving Judah an opportunity to repent and be faithful here in Micah during the reign of King Hezekiah after the Northern Kingdom of Israel had fallen. They repent for a time but then are unfaithful again and eventually face God's judgment when the Southern Kingdom of Judah is destroyed by Babylon during Jeremiah's lifetime. Israel still is not able to be righteous after this chance God gives them to get it right. Like all of us, they sin again by not living justly, being merciful, and walking with God in humility. They do not keep God's covenant, and their sin debt is still hanging over their heads. It is because of that debt of sin and the need for righteousness to please God that we need salvation through Jesus Christ. Jesus comes as the one who perfectly keeps the law of justice, mercy, and humility. Jesus then gives His life and releases us from our debt of sin. He bears witness of how to live justly for God and then empowers us to do the same.

Sources:
Achtemeier, Paul J., ed. *The HarperCollins Bible Dictionary*. New York: HarperCollins Publishing, 1996. 680, 888.
Smith, Ralph L. *Micah–Malachi. Word Biblical Commentary*. Waco, TX: World Books Publishers, 1984. 32–34.
Waltke, Bruce K. *A Commentary on Micah*. Grand Rapids, MI: Eerdmans 2007. 181–183.

Say It Correctly

Jebusite. **JEB**-you-site
Tyropoeon. **TIE**-row-**PEE**-on.
Hinnum. **HIN**-num

Daily Bible Readings

MONDAY
The Lord Acts Justly
(Psalm 146)

TUESDAY
The Results of Social Injustice
(Isaiah 5:18–24)

WEDNESDAY
Justice Actions by the Expected Messiah
(Isaiah 11:1–5)

THURSDAY
Prophets Fail on Their Watch
(Micah 3:5–8)

FRIDAY
Remember God's Righteous Actions
(Micah 6:1–5)

SATURDAY
Cheating and Violence Will Be Punished
(Micah 6:9–16)

SUNDAY
God Requires Justice for All
(Micah 3:1–3, 9–12; 6:6–8)

Notes

_____

_____

_____

_____

Teaching Tips

Words You Should Know

A. Corrupt (3:2) *ga'ar* (Heb.)—To rebuke or reprove

B. Seed (3:2) *zera'* (Heb.)—Seed for growing a crop; often used metaphorically for sperm and therefore descendants

Teacher Preparation

Unifying Principle—Justice for All. Just leaders act honorably toward constituents. How do just leaders act toward others? Malachi admonishes the priests to turn from their wickedness, revere God, and reap a rich harvest for promoting godly justice.

A. Read the Bible Background and Devotional Readings.

B. Pray for your students and lesson clarity.

C. Read the lesson Scripture in multiple translations.

O—Open the Lesson

A. Begin the class with prayer.

B. Ask the class: "Give an example of how modern leaders act toward constituents and others. Are they honorable and just?"

C. Have the students read the Aim for Change and the In Focus story.

D. Ask students how events like those in the story weigh on their hearts and how they can view these events from a faith perspective.

P—Present the Scriptures

A. Read the Focal Verses.

B. Have the class share what Scriptures stand out for them and why, with particular emphasis on today's context.

C. Discuss the Background and The People, Places, and Times sections.

E—Explore the Meaning

A. Use In Depth or More Light on the Text to facilitate a deeper discussion of the lesson text.

B. Pose the questions in Search the Scriptures and Discuss the Meaning.

C. Discuss the Liberating Lesson and Application for Activation sections.

N—Next Steps for Application

A. Summarize the value of covenanted reverence of God for leadership.

B. End class with a commitment to pray for opportunities to set a godly example that will not cause others to stumble.

Worship Guide

For the Superintendent or Teacher
Theme: Leading Justly
Song: "Make Me a Blessing"
Devotional Reading: Psalm 50:1–15

Leading Justly

Bible Background • MALACHI 2–3
Printed Text • MALACHI 2:1–9; 3:5–6 | Devotional Reading • PSALM 50:1–15

——— Aim for Change ———

By the end of the lesson, we will: DETERMINE the significance of justice for spiritual leadership, AFFIRM the value of covenanted reverence of God for leadership, and PRACTICE just spiritual leadership.

——— In Focus ———

It was the last Sunday Pastor Long would address his congregation. Sitting behind his desk, he reflected on the first time he addressed his congregation. Pastor Long remembered how humble he felt that the congregation had chosen him as their leader after a two-year search.

That was forty years ago. Pastor Long remembered he prayed that his new church would be a community of faith that would live just lives and pray. He prayed that God would keep him safe from temptation and scandal. He prayed for honest elders and deacons to help him lead the congregation. He prayed he would learn the personal stories of his congregants so he would feel the heartbeat of the congregation. He prayed the members of the congregation would show compassion toward one another and strengthen and challenge each other. He prayed for a community of faith that would bear each others' burdens and help the oppressed, the fatherless, and the poor. Finally, he prayed that his leadership would bring others to Christ.

On this last Sunday, Pastor Long walked out in front of the congregation feeling confident that God had answered all his prayers—God had done all he asked.

How does God bless honest leaders in His church? What is His reaction to dishonest leaders?

——— Keep in Mind ———

"If ye will not hear, and if ye will not lay it to heart, to give glory unto my name, saith the LORD of hosts, I will even send a curse upon you, and I will curse your blessings: yea, I have cursed them already, because ye do not lay it to heart" (Malachi 2:2, KJV).

"'Listen to me and make up your minds to honor my name,' says the LORD of Heaven's Armies, 'or I will bring a terrible curse against you. I will curse even the blessings you receive. Indeed, I have already cursed them, because you have not taken my warning to heart'" (Malachi 2:2, NLT).

Focal Verses

KJV **Malachi 2:1** And now, O ye priests, this commandment is for you.

2 If ye will not hear, and if ye will not lay it to heart, to give glory unto my name, saith the LORD of hosts, I will even send a curse upon you, and I will curse your blessings: yea, I have cursed them already, because ye do not lay it to heart.

3 Behold, I will corrupt your seed, and spread dung upon your faces, even the dung of your solemn feasts; and one shall take you away with it.

4 And ye shall know that I have sent this commandment unto you, that my covenant might be with Levi, saith the LORD of hosts.

5 My covenant was with him of life and peace; and I gave them to him for the fear wherewith he feared me, and was afraid before my name.

6 The law of truth was in his mouth, and iniquity was not found in his lips: he walked with me in peace and equity, and did turn many away from iniquity.

7 For the priest's lips should keep knowledge, and they should seek the law at his mouth: for he is the messenger of the LORD of hosts.

8 But ye are departed out of the way; ye have caused many to stumble at the law; ye have corrupted the covenant of Levi, saith the Lord of hosts.

9 Therefore have I also made you contemptible and base before all the people, according as ye have not kept my ways, but have been partial in the law.

3:5 And I will come near to you to judgment; and I will be a swift witness against the sorcerers, and against the adulterers, and against false swearers, and against those that oppress the hireling in his wages, the widow, and the fatherless, and that turn aside the

NLT **Malachi 2:1** "Listen, you priests—this command is for you!

2 Listen to me and make up your minds to honor my name," says the LORD of Heaven's Armies, "or I will bring a terrible curse against you. I will curse even the blessings you receive. Indeed, I have already cursed them, because you have not taken my warning to heart.

3 I will punish your descendants and splatter your faces with the manure from your festival sacrifices, and I will throw you on the manure pile.

4 Then at last you will know it was I who sent you this warning so that my covenant with the Levites can continue," says the LORD of Heaven's Armies.

5 "The purpose of my covenant with the Levites was to bring life and peace, and that is what I gave them. This required reverence from them, and they greatly revered me and stood in awe of my name.

6 They passed on to the people the truth of the instructions they received from me. They did not lie or cheat; they walked with me, living good and righteous lives, and they turned many from lives of sin.

7 "The words of a priest's lips should preserve knowledge of God, and people should go to him for instruction, for the priest is the messenger of the LORD of Heaven's Armies.

8 But you priests have left God's paths. Your instructions have caused many to stumble into sin. You have corrupted the covenant I made with the Levites," says the Lord of Heaven's Armies.

9 "So I have made you despised and humiliated in the eyes of all the people. For you have not obeyed me but have shown favoritism in the way you carry out my instructions."

3:5 "At that time I will put you on trial. I am eager to witness against all sorcerers and stranger from his right, and fear not me, saith the LORD of hosts.

6 For I am the LORD, I change not; therefore ye sons of Jacob are not consumed.

adulterers and liars. I will speak against those who cheat employees of their wages, who oppress widows and orphans, or who deprive the foreigners living among you of justice, for these people do not fear me," says the LORD of Heaven's Armies.

6 "I am the LORD, and I do not change. That is why you descendants of Jacob are not already destroyed."

The People, Places, and Times

Malachi. The book of Malachi is the last of the Minor Prophets and the last prophetic voice to God's people before John the Baptist. The book is believed to have been written between 450–430 BC, a century after Cyrus, the king of Persia, issued a decree allowing the Jews to return to Judah after their Babylonian exile. The Temple had been rebuilt in 515 BC, and houses were reconstructed; however, their spiritual lives remained in ruins. It is debated as to whether Malachi, which means, "My messenger," is the name of an actual person or simply a title attributed to a prophet tasked with relaying God's message to His sinful people. The issues that Malachi addresses are similar to those found in Ezra and Nehemiah, which means he either preached during their time or in the generation following them.

Background

One hundred years after their return, the Jews had expectations of how life should be for God's chosen people. They had rebuilt the Temple and reinstated Temple worship as instructed by Haggai and Zechariah years prior. And yet, they were still in economic turmoil, suffered from poor crops, and were a far cry from the major independent nation that they once were. There was little evidence of the blessings promised to Abraham and Moses. This suffering, though brought about

from their forefathers' repeated disobedience, caused them to question God's love. As a result of their disappointment and disillusionment, their hearts were indifferent or hardened toward God. The priests and the people violated many requirements of the Mosaic Law—haphazardly making sacrifices, tithes and offerings, marrying pagans, divorcing freely, and living morally bankrupt lives in general.

Why do you believe people ask "Does God really love me?" in the face of trials? What can this indicate about a person's view of God?

At-A-Glance

1. God's Warning to the Priests
(Malachi 2:1–4)
2. Priestly Examples (vv. 5–7)
3. The Priests' Sins (Malachi 2:8–9, 3:5–6)

In Depth

1. God's Warning to the Priests (Malachi 2:1–4)

First, the Lord lays out His case against the priests (Malachi 1:6–11). There were specific requirements for offerings and sacrifices according to Mosaic Law. The priests, in their indifference to the Lord, failed to comply, complaining that His requirements were "too hard." They allowed offerings that were not true sacrifices—from stolen animals to animals that were unfit for any other use, presenting "gifts" to God that would not even be appropriate for an earthly leader. These priests defiled the Temple and dishonored the Lord. Not only were they offensive, but also they failed to acknowledge their offensiveness, feigning ignorance and seeking to justify their actions.

In response, God commanded that they choose to honor Him. He warned them that failure to do so would lead to curses. These curses would be so effective that even those things that were expected to be blessings would be cursed, like the required provisions to the Levites from other Jews. However, this destruction would not stop with them; it would extend to their descendants. Ironically, the cause of their current suffering stemmed from the disobedience of their forefathers, and they were on the path of continuing the cycle.

The graphic picture the Lord provides is that of smearing feces on their faces. Not only would they be made unclean and unfit for service, they would be discarded and exposed. This would happen so that the priestly Levitical line could be purified and restored, and His covenant with them could continue.

Why do some people believe it is "too hard" to follow God and His ways?

2. Priestly Examples (vv. 5–7)

Following the incident of the Golden Calf (Exodus 32), the Levites came forward when Moses asked for those who were for the Lord. The Levites then obeyed Moses' command to kill those who had rebelled. God instructed Moses to set these descendants of Levi apart for His service. Those who rebelled against the covenant with God died amidst the turmoil of sin and rebellion. The Levites, however, were obedient and faithful to the covenant. It is in this context that the Lord reminds these disobedient priests that the covenant He made with Levi was one of life and peace.

The prophet delineates the characteristics of those who are examples of positive and godly leadership. Truth, peace, and equity are benchmarks for the lifestyle that does not accept inequity. Faithful leaders seek God for the truth as His messengers. The Levites revered and honored the Lord, speaking truth, living righteously, and obeying the Lord. The Levitical priests of old did as they were ordained: they instructed the people and preserved the knowledge of God. While prophets were typically called messengers of God, here Malachi uses it for those priests.

How can considering the examples of the past help us to live more faithfully in the present?

3. The Priests' Sins (Malachi 2:8–9, 3:5–6)

In contrast to how the former Levites lived, these priests were not committed to the truth. Not only did they allow Israel to fall away from the Lord, but they caused them to sin with false teaching. They showed favoritism in serving, cheating, and oppressing the vulnerable, involving themselves in all types of ungodliness. The all-knowing, ever-present, self-existent God would be His own witness against them and the judge. There would be no escape. And because of the public nature of their sins and positions, the judgment would be for all to see.

How can we resist temptation to abuse positions of authority, and how can we help those who are taken advantage of by those in power?

Search the Scriptures

1. What did God say about the blessings of those who are disobedient (Malachi 2:2)?

2. How did God characterize Levi (v. 6)?

3. What wicked groups are described in Malachi 3:5?

Discuss the Meaning

In the Bible we see the detrimental effects of leaders who strayed away from the Lord. Throughout 1 and 2 Kings, Israel and Judah's kings are characterized by whether they followed in their forefathers' footsteps in obedience or disobedience. Here we see that even after exile, Israel still struggles to be who God called them to be. We see who they are, but what do we learn about God's character in these examples?

Liberating Lesson

"We do not sin in isolation." This statement is applicable to everyone, but it is particularly impactful for those who are leaders. History has shown that one leader with a bent toward injustice, evil, and selfish ambition can have a devastating effect on the masses. Consider Andrew Jackson's Indian Removal Act, which set the stage for the Trail of Tears. However, history has also shown that one leader, such as Alexander Crummell, who served as a missionary in Liberia for twenty years and planted the first independent black Episcopal church in Washington DC, can spiritually impact generations to come. God told the priests to "make up your minds to honor my name." We get to choose what type of impact we will have. It all begins with a sincere commitment to follow and obey the Lord.

Application for Activation

Reflect on a few leaders in your life, past and present. How have their actions impacted your life—positively and negatively? Identify what you learned about being a godly (or ungodly) leader from them.

Then evaluate your relationship with the Lord and influence over others—at home, work, church, and so on. How would God describe your current relationship with Him and others? More like the zealous Levitical priests of old, or like the resentful priests in Malachi?

Follow the Spirit

What God wants me to do:

_____

_____

_____

_____

Remember Your Thoughts

Special insights I have learned:

_____

_____

_____

_____

More Light on the Text
Malachi 2:1–9; 3:5–6

Malachi used a rhetorical, interactive style of writing designed to have a persuasive effect on his rebellious audience. Each of his six messages begin with a serious charge against these post-exile Jews who had returned to Judah after their seventy-year captivity in Babylon. True to his call as God's messenger, Malachi presented six charges against the post-exilic community. However, they challenged each of his commands with a sarcastic rebuttal question: (1) charged to respond to God's love, they rebut, "How has He loved us?" (1:2–5); (2) charged to honor God as He deserves, they rebut, "How have we ever shown Him contempt?" (1:6–2:9); (3) charged to be faithful to God, they rebut, "Why doesn't God accept our worship?" (2:10–16); (4) charged that they have wearied the Lord, they rebut, "How have we wearied the Lord?" (2:17–3:6); (5) charged with robbing God, they rebut,

"How have we ever robbed You?" (3:7–12); and (6) charged with saying terrible things about God, they rebut, "What have we said against God?" (3:13–4:3). In their rebuttal, they try to claim that the charges are false, but Malachi proves in his persuasive messages that the charges are indeed true. The expected response is confession and repentance because there is hope in the God who keeps His covenant even when His people do not.

In spite of God's willingness to forgive, these Israelites were indifferent and resentful, but why? Although they had returned to their native land (538 BC), they were still under the political domination of the Persians. These former captives reconstructed the Temple (515 BC), but lacking the type of resources Solomon had, this Temple was but a mere shadow of Solomon's exquisite Temple. Life was difficult. Harvests were poor and subject to locust damage (3:11). In short, they felt that God did not deliver on the covenant blessings that He had promised them, and their behavior exhibited several indications of hidden resentment, specifically stagnant worship, lack of praise, blemished offerings, defensive responses to correction, and disparaging remarks about God.

1 And now, O ye priests, this commandment is for you. 2 If ye will not hear, and if ye will not lay it to heart, to give glory unto my name, saith the LORD of hosts, I will even send a curse upon you, and I will curse your blessings: yea, I have cursed them already, because ye do not lay it to heart.

Here, Malachi's focus is on the priests. The priests are from the tribe of Levi, the third son of Jacob. However, only the descendants of Levi's great-grandson Aaron, the first high priest, can legitimately serve as priests and offer sacrifices on the altar on behalf of the people. As intermediaries, the priests represented the people before a holy God through sacrifice and

instructed the people in the Word and the will of God. In so doing, they played a crucial role in the spiritual life of the nation. But now, instead of instructing the people, the priests were the ones receiving instruction, a command from the Lord through the Lord's messenger, Malachi. This rebuke was necessary because the priests, who knew better, were accepting blind, crippled, and diseased animals from the people and offering them as sacrifices (1:7–10). This was in direct defiance of the regulations in the book of Leviticus, which served as a handbook for the priests for offering sacrifices. The regulations specifically stated, "Whosoever offereth a sacrifice unto the LORD, it shall be perfect to be accepted; there shall be no blemish therein … Ye shall not offer unto the LORD that which is bruised, or crushed, or broken, or cut" (Leviticus 22:21, 24).

God was so displeased with their conduct that He gave the priests a severe warning. If they refused to listen and make the appropriate changes, God would curse them. Curses, which are hardships and difficulties, were nothing new to Israel. In fact, curses for disobedience to God's Law were embedded in the Mosaic Covenant. The covenant of Law was the means by which God governed His people Israel. Blessings were the incentive to obey (Deuteronomy 28:1–14), while curses were the deterrent to disobedience (vv. 16–68). The priests were not exempt from the Law, and God was warning them that their violation of their sacred duty to lead the people in proper worship would result in curses. In fact, even the very blessings they received would be cursed. Indeed, because of their hearts' condition, the curse was already in effect. The curse was so complete, even the priestly blessings they pronounced on the people would be cursed (Numbers 6:22–27).

3 Behold, I will corrupt your seed, and spread dung upon your faces, even the dung

of your solemn feasts; and one shall take you away with it. 4 And ye shall know that I have sent this commandment unto you, that my covenant might be with Levi, saith the Lord of hosts.

Because the priests dishonored God, God would in turn dishonor the priests as well as their descendants. He had already announced that the priests would be cursed for their refusal to honor Him with proper sacrifices (2:2), but that was only part of the consequences for their sinful behavior. God now focuses their attention on the additional dramatic action He would take against them with the phrase "behold [me]" (Heb. *henni*, **heh-NIE**). In other words, look and take notice of what I will do. Not only will the current priests be punished for their misdeeds, but their seed (Heb. *zera'*, **ZEH-rah**), their descendants, would suffer an even sterner punishment. To corrupt (Heb. *ga'ar*, **gaw-AR**) is to rebuke or reprove. The manner in which this will occur is by spreading "dung upon your faces." Dung, or the excrement from the sacrificial animals, was normally burned outside the camp along with other unused parts of the sacrifice (Leviticus 4:11). In other words, this was a symbolic and graphic way for God to announce that He would make the priests unclean, therefore unable to serve, and remove them from the priesthood just as the dung was removed and burned. The stated penalty for the priests was severe for the purpose of getting them to repent so that God could restore them. Once restored, they could honor God once again by leading the people in true worship with acceptable sacrifices. These severe words of warning were unmistakably from God.

It is important to note that even in the midst of judgment, a gracious, loving God was still reaching out to His rebellious priests, letting them know that the ultimate purpose of His judgment was redemption and restoration, not just punishment. He wanted to purify the priesthood so that His covenant with Levi could continue. It is the same with us today. As a royal priesthood we are charged with the responsibility to proclaim the praises of God (1 Peter 2:9) to those who are still trapped in a dark world of sin. We are charged with offering our bodies as a living sacrifice to Him (Romans 12:2). That is simply our reasonable service, nothing extra, nothing extraordinary. And yet, we often fail to fulfill this solemn duty. So we too are admonished to repent, to remember that God has honored us by making our bodies His holy temple, so that we are to glorify God by giving Him our complete selves—body, soul, mind, and strength—as a worthy sacrifice.

5 My covenant was with him of life and peace; and I gave them to him for the fear wherewith he feared me, and was afraid before my name. 6 The law of truth was in his mouth, and iniquity was not found in his lips: he walked with me in peace and equity, and did turn many away from iniquity. 7 For the priest's lips should keep knowledge, and they should seek the law at his mouth: for he is the messenger of the Lord of hosts.

This covenant was made after Israel was freed from bondage in Egypt and camped at the foot of Mt. Sinai. After spending forty days and nights on the mountain receiving the Law of God for the people, Moses returned to find that they had committed idolatry by worshiping the golden calf that Aaron, his brother and high priest, had made (Exodus 32). Moses was so angry he broke the tablets of stone with the Ten Commandments and gave the command for those on the Lord's side to remove themselves as a sign of their fidelity to the Lord. The Levites obeyed. As a result, God set them apart as the priestly tribe with these words: "Today you have ordained yourselves for the service of the LORD, for you obeyed him even though it meant killing your own sons and brothers" (from Exodus 32:29, NLT). Thus God joined Himself to Levi through the covenant He made with him declaring that "no Israelites except priests or Levites may approach the Tabernacle. If they come too near, they will be judged guilty and will die" (Numbers 18:22).

The covenant with Levi was for life and peace. It brought spiritual life because the priests offered the blood of the animal sacrifices to God for the sin of the people. As a result of receiving forgiveness of sin, it brought peace with God, which resulted in the peace of God.

As God's representatives, the priests were the messengers of the Lord, tasked with the responsibility "to teach your regulations to Jacob; to give your instructions to Israel" (Deuteronomy 33:10). When the lips of the priests teach the truth of God with integrity, then the people will come and seek out the priests to hear the Word. Pastors and teachers are similarly tasked with that solemn responsibility today. They must teach and preach God's Word, not opinion or tradition, but rightly divide the Word of truth and then be an example before the people. When teachers and preachers live out the truth, it increases the possibility that the people will follow their example.

8 But ye are departed out of the way; ye have caused many to stumble at the law; ye have corrupted the covenant of Levi, saith the LORD of hosts. 9 Therefore have I also made you contemptible and base before all the people, according as ye have not kept my ways, but have been partial in the law.

The priests were mandated to teach the Law to the people of Israel (Deuteronomy 33:10). As teachers, each priest was to be God's messenger. However, since they were not giving true instruction, they were rebuked by the prophet. The priests' teaching caused many to stumble because they themselves had departed from the way. Telling the people that defiled and diseased

animals were acceptable for sacrifice violated the covenant God made with the Levites and the warning they were given to be held responsible for any covenant breaking. Because of their offenses, the priests were despised and humiliated before all the people. They suffered public disgrace because they disobeyed and despised the honor they had been given. Only the priests, the descendants of Aaron, could approach the awesome presence of God to offer sacrifices on behalf of the people. Instead of gratitude for that honor, they demeaned it by offering defiled sacrifices.

3:5 And I will come near to you to judgment; and I will be a swift witness against the sorcerers, and against the adulterers, and against false swearers, and against those that oppress the hireling in his wages, the widow, and the fatherless, and that turn aside the stranger from his right, and fear not me, saith the LORD of hosts. 6 For I am the LORD, I change not; therefore ye sons of Jacob are not consumed.

Israel's judgment would not be limited to the Levites but would include the whole nation. Usually when God says He will "come near," it is for blessing (Genesis 18:1–14; Exodus 33:12–23; 1 Kings 3:3–9). But in this instance, God comes near to His people for judgment. Judgment is the word *mishpat* (Heb. **meesh-POT**), which also means justice. Justice speaks of the act of deciding a case and then issuing a verdict with the associated penalty that is required in order to restore order (Isaiah 42:1–4). Notice the unusual nature of this particular court case brought against the people (3:5). God is not only the judge, He is also the witness against the people and the prosecutor who brought the charges. His verdict is that every aspect of the society is guilty: (1) the family is afflicted with adulterers, (2) the workplace is infected with employers who cheat employees of their wages, (3) the community leaders oppress the widows and orphans and mistreat strangers (immigrants), (4) the courts are corrupted with perjurers ("false swearers," KJV), and (5) sorcerers in the society practice evil with the aid of evil spirits. The overarching charge is that all of these transgressions occur because the people do not fear the Lord. But will this judgment bring about the end of Israel? Will the people be consumed by the refiner's fire (3:2)? No! The descendants of Jacob will not be destroyed because of God's covenant promise to the nation of Israel. God's Word, like Himself, is immutable, and that is the basis for Israel's hope (Deuteronomy 4:31, Ezekiel 36:22–32). We too have the same basis for hope whenever we mess up and go astray. Our Covenant-Keeping God is true to His Word and will forgive and cleanse us if we but confess (1 John 1:9).

Sources:
Hanson, P. *The Harper Collins Bible Commentary.* New York: Harper Collins, 2000.
Hindson, E. *Liberty Bible Commentary.* Nashville, TN: Thomas Nelson Inc, 1982.
Walvoord, J.F., and Zuck, R.B. *The Bible Knowledge Commentary: Old Testament.* Wheaton, IL: Victor Books. 1985.

Say It Correctly

Malachi. **MAL**-uh-kay.
Haggai. **HAH**-guy.

Daily Bible Readings

MONDAY
Offer Sacrifice of Thanksgiving to God
(Psalm 50:1–15)

TUESDAY
Bring Acceptable Offerings to the Lord
(Leviticus 22:17–25)

WEDNESDAY
God's Name Is Great among Nations
(Malachi 1:11–14)

THURSDAY
Be Faithful to One Another
(Malachi 2:10–16)

FRIDAY
Messenger of Judgment Coming
(Malachi 2:17–3:4)

SATURDAY
God's Blessings and Delights Await
(Malachi 3:7–12)

SUNDAY
Leading in Troubled Times
(Malachi 2:1–9; 3:5–6)

Notes

_____

_____

_____

_____

Teaching Tips

April 5
Bible Study Guide 6

Words You Should Know

A. Uphold (v. 1) *tamak* (Heb.)—To sustain or support.

B. Righteousness (v. 6) *tsedeq* (Heb.)—Right, just, normal, standard, justice, equity.

Teacher Preparation

Unifying Principle—Seeking a Champion of Justice. People seek a champion of justice. Who can and will defend and uphold the cause of justice? In Matthew 21, Jesus upholds God's justice in the Temple, fulfilling Isaiah 42's vision of the Messiah.

A. Read the Bible Background and Devotional Readings.

B. Pray for your students and lesson clarity.

C. Read the lesson Scripture in multiple translations.

O—Open the Lesson

A. Begin the class with prayer.

B. As a class, list and discuss ways in which God may be seen as either just or unjust in certain circumstances facing individuals and groups in society.

C. Have the students read the Aim for Change and the In Focus story.

D. Ask students how events like those in the story weigh on their hearts and how they can view these events from a faith perspective.

P—Present the Scriptures

A. Read the Focal Verses.

B. Have the class share what Scriptures stand out for them and why, with particular emphasis on today's context.

C. Discuss the Background and The People, Places, and Times sections.

E—Explore the Meaning

A. Use In Depth or More Light on the Text to facilitate a deeper discussion of the lesson text.

B. Pose the questions in Search the Scriptures and Discuss the Meaning.

C. Discuss the Liberating Lesson and Application for Activation sections.

N—Next Steps for Application

A. Summarize the value of loving and revering Jesus as the Messiah who teaches us to desire justice.

B. End class with a commitment to pray for the courage and strength to live just lives as required by the Gospel.

Worship Guide

For the Superintendent or Teacher
Theme: God's Just Servant
Song: "In the Name of the Lord"
Devotional Reading: Psalm 98

God's Just Servant

Bible Background • ISAIAH 42
Printed Text • ISAIAH 42:1–9 | Devotional Reading • PSALM 98

Aim for Change

By the end of the lesson, we will: EXPLORE the concept of Messiah, SENSE the wonder of Jesus' role as servant to the nations, and IMITATE Jesus as a servant of God who executes justice.

In Focus

David Boyd worked for five years as a mail sorter for Harts Distribution Service, a private postal company. David was a hard worker and really enjoyed his job. When a senior management position opened in the mail department. David applied for the job and interviewed well.

"David, I don't know how to say this, but … you didn't get the job." David was stunned. He asked Mr. Carter who received the promotion. "Mrs. Betty Howser," said Mr. Carter. David couldn't understand. Betty had only been with the company six months. Everyone enjoyed working with David. He was a man of integrity. Betty was just the opposite. She was lazy, did just enough work to get by, and was usually late for work.

Several months later, Mr. Carter approached David as he was having lunch. "May I sit down with you?" asked Mr. Carter. As the two men ate, Mr. Carter told David that Betty's promotion was political. "She has contacts in high places with the company." In fact, Mr. Carter threatened to report her to the board of directors. Four weeks later, David was promoted to senior management. Mr. Carter's tenacious attitude and his willingness to fight for justice on behalf of David paid off in a positive way.

This week, our Bible Study Guide focuses on the Servant who provides justice for all people. What has been your reaction to injustice and other negative forces in your life?

Keep in Mind

"Behold my servant, whom I uphold; mine elect, in whom my soul delighteth; I have put my spirit upon him: he shall bring forth judgment to the Gentiles" (Isaiah 42:1, KJV).

"Look at my servant, whom I strengthen. He is my chosen one, who pleases me. I have put my Spirit upon him. He will bring justice to the nations (Isaiah 42:1, NLT).

Focal Verses

KJV **Isaiah 42:1** Behold my servant, whom I uphold; mine elect, in whom my soul delighteth; I have put my spirit upon him: he shall bring forth judgment to the Gentiles.

2 He shall not cry, nor lift up, nor cause his voice to be heard in the street.

3 A bruised reed shall he not break, and the smoking flax shall he not quench: he shall bring forth judgment unto truth.

4 He shall not fail nor be discouraged, till he have set judgment in the earth: and the isles shall wait for his law.

5 Thus saith God the LORD, he that created the heavens, and stretched them out; he that spread forth the earth, and that which cometh out of it; he that giveth breath unto the people upon it, and spirit to them that walk therein:

6 I the LORD have called thee in righteousness, and will hold thine hand, and will keep thee, and give thee for a covenant of the people, for a light of the Gentiles;

7 To open the blind eyes, to bring out the prisoners from the prison, and them that sit in darkness out of the prison house.

8 I am the LORD: that is my name: and my glory will I not give to another, neither my praise to graven images.

9 Behold, the former things are come to pass, and new things do I declare: before they spring forth I tell you of them.

NLT **Isaiah 42:1** "Look at my servant, whom I strengthen. He is my chosen one, who pleases me. I have put my Spirit upon him. He will bring justice to the nations.

2 He will not shout or raise his voice in public.

3 He will not crush the weakest reed or put out a flickering candle. He will bring justice to all who have been wronged.

4 He will not falter or lose heart until justice prevails throughout the earth. Even distant lands beyond the sea will wait for his instruction."

5 God, the LORD, created the heavens and stretched them out. He created the earth and everything in it. He gives breath to everyone, life to everyone who walks the earth. And it is he who says,

6 "I, the LORD, have called you to demonstrate my righteousness. I will take you by the hand and guard you, and I will give you to my people, Israel, as a symbol of my covenant with them. And you will be a light to guide the nations.

7 You will open the eyes of the blind. You will free the captives from prison, releasing those who sit in dark dungeons.

8 I am the LORD; that is my name! I will not give my glory to anyone else, nor share my praise with carved idols.

9 Everything I prophesied has come true, and now I will prophesy again. I will tell you the future before it happens."

The People, Places, and Times

Isaiah. Bearing the name "Yahweh is salvation," Isaiah was one of the greatest prophets of his time. He had a vision of God and was called by God to do God's work bringing His nation to repentance in order to save it from a whirlpool of destruction. Isaiah came to the people with messages of judgment tempered with hope. He ministered for sixty years or more and prophesied during the reign of five kings of Judah: Uzziah, Jotham, Ahaz, Hezekiah, and Manasseh. He pleaded with the people to turn from their wicked ways back to a loving God who would forgive and restore them. Isaiah saw the deliverance of Jerusalem from her enemies, the Assyrians.

Through his prayers and by the intervention of God, Jerusalem was spared from Assyrian destruction. Many of the promises God gave through Isaiah have been fulfilled in Jesus Christ.

Background

Isaiah 41 opens with the nations being challenged by God, who reminds them of His greatness, power, wisdom, and foreknowledge (Isaiah 41:1). More than 150 years before Cyrus was born, the Lord revealed to Isaiah that He was going to raise him up to be used by God to conquer the nations and protect Israel (vv. 2–6). Cyrus was king of Persia from 559–530 BC (see Isaiah 44:28; 45:1). God used him to free Israel from captivity under Babylonian rule during the time of Nebuchadnezzar. Though the king was not a righteous man, Cyrus was God's instrument to fulfill His divine purpose and to be a blessing to His chosen people. God had made a promise to Israel that He would use them as His channel of redemption. Therefore, they were encouraged not to be fearful in the midst of their captivity. In fact, the written revelation of God by which salvation would be offered to all the earth would come through Israel (Isaiah 41:8). Because God loved His people, they had no reason to doubt Him since He promised to be with them and impart His grace in their lives. God assured Israel that they would be kept in times of crisis and that their enemies would eventually be destroyed. In other words, God would sustain His people and be their Advocate. As Isaiah concludes chapter 41, he affirms that the Messiah would bring good tidings to the people (v. 27). Though Cyrus would allow the people to return to the Promised Land, it is only Jesus Christ who can provide God's people with the safety, protection, and justice they desperately need.

At-A-Glance

1. A Judge to the Nations (Isaiah 42:1–4)
2. A Light for the Nations (vv. 5–7)
3. A Hope for the Nations (vv. 8–9)

In Depth

1. A Judge to the Nations (Isaiah 42:1–4)

Just like Isaiah 49:1–9; 50:4–11; and 52:13—53:12, Isaiah 42 is a clear reference to the "Servant Songs." These passages of Scripture identify the Servant whom God has chosen to be His instrument of righteousness for His people. Though many Jewish scholars traditionally identify the "Servant" as the nation of Israel, as Christians we see in the Suffering Servant a prophecy of Jesus Christ, the Messiah, who is the true Israel, faithfully fulfilling all the Law that God gave Israel to make it holy. Writing on behalf of God, Isaiah declared that God would send His Servant whom He would uphold. Isaiah identifies God's Servant as "elect, referring to the Chosen One who was appointed by God for a specific task and purpose. Thus the Servant is the One in whom the Father "delighteth" (v. 1). The prophet declares that the Servant will neither "cry nor lift up, nor cause his voice to be heard in the street"; that is, He will not have to cry out to be heard and obeyed. The Servant would be meek and humble, not breaking a bruised reed or putting out smoking flax. The Servant would completely embody gentleness and yet righteous judgment. Isaiah reminds us that the Messiah will neither fail in His ministry, nor will He get discouraged because there is work yet to be done. God's righteous judgment has not fully been implemented in the earth. Until the Second Coming, the kingdom of God is ever expanding as God's people are in the world ministering to others and bringing them into a right relationship with the Father.

2. A Light for the Nations (vv. 5–7)

Isaiah writes that this is God, the One who made the heavens and earth and all aspects of creation. Isaiah takes his declaration from Genesis 1, where Scripture affirms that God not only put His seal of approval upon all creation, but also His spirit into human beings so that they might be in the image and likeness of God (cf. Genesis 1:27; 2:1–4). This is the God who has raised up His Servant in righteousness. The word "righteousness" encompasses integrity, moral honesty, purity, and having a right heart before God. The Messiah was given the assignment to come to His creation to speak righteousness into the lives of people. God would "hold his hand and keep him" (v. 6). Thus, the Messiah was the fulfillment of God's "covenant" for the Jews and the "light" for the Gentiles who trust in Him. The word "covenant" has to do with a treaty or an alliance of friendship that is accompanied by signs and solemn oaths and is sealed by a relationship between two parties. Despite their rebellion, God is Israel's friend. He loves His people and has sent His Servant to bring them back to Him. At the same time, God loves the Gentiles, those who are not Jacob's descendants. Jesus Christ is the fulfillment of these prophecies for Christians. Jesus Christ came so that He might destroy the work of the enemy (1 John 3:8) and bring light to the Gentiles (Acts 26:23). He has come to bring illumination and revelation to those who will receive Him.

3. A Hope for the Nations (vv. 8–9)

Isaiah gives the nations a glimpse of the Servant's identity: "I am the Lord" (v. 8). God will not give this "name" or His glory to any other, because none is worthy but Him. When Jesus claims himself to be the fulfillment of the prophecies (Luke 4:16–21) and the early New Testament writers use this language when describing Jesus (Mark 1:11), it is clear confirmation that Jesus Christ is the promised Messiah and Lord. Philippians says that one day every knee shall bow and every tongue will confess that Jesus Christ is Lord (Philippians 2:10–11). The word "glory" indicates the majesty and splendor of Almighty God. He alone is worthy to be praised.

One interpretation of verse 9 is that everything we see will come to an end. Those institutions and systems that have created such havoc and confusion in our lives will be gone. Paul says that the things we see are only temporary. What we cannot see are the eternal and "weighty" things of God's infinite glory (2 Corinthians 4:17–18). The "new things" are what Jesus Christ has declared unto His people. One day we shall see new heavens and a new earth where Jesus, God's Servant, shall be known as Lord of all (Revelation 21:1–2). We can trust God's word to us about the future where God reigns physically as He reigns in our hearts today. He was faithful to His word in the past to deliver Israel, we see Him delivering us today from sin and its effects, and we can trust His word that His kingdom come and His will be done in our future. Justice and righteous judgment shall be for every person, and we will experience God's peace and love because He has promised to make all things new.

Search the Scriptures

1. What is the Servant's primary responsibility? (Isaiah 42:1)

2. How did Isaiah describe God? (v. 5)

Discuss the Meaning

1. Is it possible for Jesus' ministry to be fulfilled before He returns to the earth for His people? Why or why not?

2. If God is just, why is there so much injustice in our nation and communities? Discuss.

Lesson in Our Society

The good news of Jesus Christ is liberating for all aspects of life. This is the news that our neighborhoods and country need. The division, anger, and incivility we see in our streets and on the news are so prevalent that they seem to be the way we expect and accept the world to behave. While some might think that younger generations or people from particular socioeconomic groups accept today's violence as the norm, that is not true. God's truth has a place in every generation. When your words and deeds share the truth of Jesus the Servant who brings the Good News to all cultures and communities, you can see how that message can make the difference we all need.

Make It Happen

Think about the new heavens and earth that God has promised us. Spend time rejoicing in the fact that one day injustice and oppressive systems will be gone and that God's righteous judgment will be the standard for all. Read the Daily Bible Readings for added encouragement. Then, be prepared to share the lesson with at least one person this week.

Follow the Spirit

What God wants me to do:

_____

_____

_____

_____

Remember Your Thoughts

Special insights I have learned:

_____

_____

_____

_____

More Light on the Text
Isaiah 42:1–9

The concluding verses of chapter 41 speak of the futility of idols and their messengers, whose works amount to nothing. There, especially in verse 27, God says that He is the One to declare the good news to Zion and Jerusalem regarding the bearer of the good news, not the idols. This good news bearer is now introduced to us in chapter 42.

1 Behold my servant, whom I uphold; mine elect, in whom my soul delighteth; I have put my spirit upon him: he shall bring forth judgment to the Gentiles.

Isaiah begins this section of prophecy with "Behold," which calls attention to a great message about to unfold. The word "behold" can also be rendered as "here is," in which case the opening phrase would read, "Here is my servant." The speaker introduces His Servant to His audience, which includes the nation of Israel and all who hear the message. They are to turn their attention away from the idols and their messenger and turn instead to the Servant who brings the good news of salvation to His people. The Hebrew word for "servant" (Heb. *ebed*, **EH-bed**) means "one who works" (in any sense), and by implication "one who serves." There are different suggestions about whom "servant" refers to, but the most logical and reasonable answer (generally accepted by the majority of scholars) is that it refers to the awaited Messiah. This Servant is unique and differs from an ordinary servant as humans understand it. His uniqueness is demonstrated in the series of qualifying or identifying attributes and the special relationship He has with the Lord God—He belongs to God.

The first of these designations, "whom I uphold" (Heb. *tamak*, **taw-MAK**) here means "to sustain" or "to support." But God "upholds" His Servant and causes Him to be sustained. The idea is that God will sustain and support Him throughout His ministry. The second designation, which is also one of honor, is that He is God's "elect" or "Chosen One." Translated from the Hebrew word *bakhir* (**baw-KHEER**), this designation carries the idea of being chosen with ultimate and eternal significance. Christ had been chosen before time—in eternity—for the special task of redemption. The word "elect" is used to express the subject's exclusive relationship to God. The Chosen One is also the One in whom God delights. The phrase "my soul delighteth" speaks of being "deeply pleased" or "passionately delighted with." This delight involves the whole being; it is not a one-time event as the verb might suggest; rather, God continues to have pleasure in His Servant. Speaking of Christ on two occasions in the New Testament, the Lord says, "This is my beloved Son, in whom I am well pleased" (Matthew 3:17; 17:5).

The Servant, the speaker says, has been endued with God's Spirit. The phrase "my spirit" definitely refers to the Holy Spirit, who equips and works through people to accomplish their given tasks. The Lord Himself testifies of being filled with the power of the Holy Spirit for His work of deliverance, healing, and preaching the good news (Isaiah 11:1–2; 61:1–2). This prophecy is fulfilled in the New Testament during the Baptism of Jesus (Matthew 3:16–17; Luke 3:16; John 3:34; cf. Acts 10:38). John the Baptist testified concerning Christ: "I saw the Spirit descending from heaven like a dove, and it abode upon him" (John 1:32). Here the Lord says, "I have put My Spirit upon Him." The tense here signifies a completed action, which shows that even before it is manifested—indeed, even before the prophecy is revealed to the prophet—the Lord had already equipped the Servant for His task with the infilling of the Holy Spirit. This also points to the eternal pre-existence of Christ, meaning Christ always existed even before He became incarnate. Here we get a glimpse of the concept of the Trinity.

The Servant is equipped from eternity for a specifically assigned mission—to "bring judgment to the Gentiles." The word translated as "judgment" is the Hebrew noun *mishpat* (**meesh-POT**), which also can mean justice, ordinance, or verdict. The verb "to bring forth" comes from the Hebrew word *yatsaʻ* (**yot-SAW**), which has a variety of meanings, including "to cause to go" or "to come out," "to lead out," and so on. The idea is more than that of announcing or proclaiming judgment, but of establishing justice or the law among the Gentiles, that is, foreign or heathen nations (non-Jewish people). The Jews referred to all non-Jews as Gentiles because they were aliens from the worship, rites, and privileges of Israel. The word "Gentiles" was used contemptuously by the Jews. Up until the time of this prophecy, only Israel possessed the type of "law" or "ordinance" spoken of here (Deuteronomy 4:5–8; Psalm 147:19–20). Although other nations had their own laws and decrees (Deuteronomy 4:7–8), theirs was not the true law and justice because it was founded on the worship of false gods and idols. True justice has its foundation in the knowledge of the true God. From verse 4, we assume that "judgment" or "justice" is synonymous with "law." Therefore, the Servant's mission is to establish the divine ordinance among the Gentiles, an idea that is repeated in verse 4 and is similar to the meaning of Isaiah

2:2–4 and 51:4–5. From these passages, we learn that the Servant is not an ordinary person, prophet, or teacher of the law who announces God's ordinance or judgment to the people, but the Lawgiver Himself. Hence, He taught with authority (cf. Matthew 7:29).

2 He shall not cry, nor lift up, nor cause his voice to be heard in the street. 3 A bruised reed shall he not break, and the smoking flax shall he not quench: he shall bring forth judgment unto truth.

Next, Isaiah's prophecy identifies the manner in which the Servant will fulfill His mission: He will do it unassumingly, or unpretentiously (vv. 2–3). This fact is presented here (v. 2) with three negative verbs: He shall "not cry," He shall "not lift up," and He shall "not cause His voice to be heard in the street." All this describes the quiet manner in which the Servant will carry out His task. These phrases are synonymous. The Servant's demeanor will differ from that of an ordinary person such as the merchant who goes out advertising his wares with a loud voice on the street. As a teacher, He will speak with quietness and calmness. As a prophet, He will not proclaim His message with a loud voice or with sensationalism; neither will He present His message argumentatively (i.e., he will not "strive," Matthew 12:19), nor will He push His teaching "down the throat" of the people. He does not need to, because the Holy Spirit is the One who will convince them. This prophecy is fulfilled in Matthew 12:17–21 consequent to Jesus' charge to His disciples "that they should not make him known" (v. 16).

His modesty and the quiet manner in which He carries out His mission are also reflected in His attitude toward and treatment of the weak. This is graphically expressed in the imagery of the "reed" and the "smoking flax" or "lamp wick" (v. 3).

A "bruised" (Heb. *ratsats*, **raw-TSATS**) reed is cracked in many places or has breaks. God says to His servant that he should not "break" (Heb. *shabar*, **shaw-BAR**) this reed; that is, he should not burst it or break it down or break it off (or into pieces) any further. In keeping with the botanical theme, God says that the "smoking flax," which is feeble or obscure, is not to be "quenched" by His Servant. The "reed" (Heb. *qaneh*, **kaw-NEH**) is a gigantic hollow-stemmed grass that grew along riverbanks and in moist areas of Egypt and Palestine. The word is used to refer to the marsh plants of the Bible. They form a large order of plants, such as flax, flags, bulrush, cane, and papyrus. The reeds were used as various objects, including walking sticks, fishing poles, musical instruments, and pens. People also used them for weaving baskets, mats, and other domestic objects. The "bruised reed" is a picture of the reed at a tender age, bruised or bent due to strong wind (cf. Matthew 12:20). The "smoking flax" refers to a lamp wick that is burning with a feeble flame because the oil has burned out. The flame can be blown out easily. Both the flickering, weak light and the bruised reed are symbols of frailty and weakness. The Servant will neither quench the flickering, weak light nor break the already bruised reed, which is another way of saying that He will sustain and uphold the weak (cf. 50:4). His activities will be marked with gentleness, compassion, and mercy (Matthew 11:28). This passage is applied to Jesus' healing ministry (Matthew 12:13, 20).

The last clause, "he shall bring forth judgment," echoes verse 1. The phrase "unto truth" simply shows the manner in which He will establish judgment—in faithfulness or in a dutiful and effectual manner.

4 He shall not fail nor be discouraged, till he have set judgment in the earth: and the isles shall wait for his law.

The first part of this verse is a play on words using the Hebrew metaphors from the previous verse: He will not "fail" (Heb. *kahah*, **kaw-HAW**) also meaning "to grow dim," recalling the dim, failing smoking flax from the previous verse. Nor will He "be discouraged" (Heb. *ratsats*, **rat-SOTS**), also meaning "to be crushed, or bruised," recalling the bruised reed from the previous verse. Affirming the Servant will not fail or be discouraged implies that the ministry of the Servant will not be easy; He will encounter difficulties and resistance. This is expressively prophesied of Him that He was "wounded" and "bruised" (Isaiah 49:50, 53) However, He will never grow weary or faint, nor will He be discouraged, but He will continue conscientiously until He accomplishes His task—until He establishes mishpat in the earth.

The setting of "judgment" is His act of salvation, and it is not restricted to the Jewish people only but is universal and includes both Jews and Gentiles (v. 1). The last part of this verse says that "the isles will wait for His law." "The isles" (Heb. *'i*, **EE**) brings to mind far-off places and emphasizes how far God's law will spread. The "law" (Heb. *torah*, **TOW-rah**) is synonymous with justice or judgment. Torah generally refers to teaching, precepts, and statutes, especially the Decalogue or the Pentateuch. Note the possessive pronoun "His" used here, which implies that it is not merely a reference to the Law of Moses but also to the divine precepts and instructions for living that the Servant of the Lord as the Lawgiver (v. 1) will bring to the people of the earth. Therefore, all humankind will eagerly wait for His law until He comes to take over the kingdoms of this world (Zechariah 14; Acts 15:13–18; Revelation 11:15).

5 Thus saith God the Lord, he that created the heavens, and stretched them out; he that spread forth the earth, and that which cometh out of it; he that giveth breath unto the people upon it, and spirit to them that walk therein:

Verse 5 is transitional in nature. The prophet again introduces the one who sends His Servant and with the introduction directs our attention to God, who is about to speak directly to the Servant to confirm His calling. The prophet appeals to the person of God as the Creator and Sustainer of all things. He is the one who created and stretched out the heavens, who spread forth the earth and everything in it. Since God is the Creator of everything, He has power and authority over everything. The One speaking is the one that gives "breath" (Heb. *neshamah*, **nesh-aw-MAW**) and "spirit" (Heb. *ruach*, **ROO-akh**) to all people on earth. These synonyms indicate that God breathed life into all of His creation. These qualifications authenticate the authority of the Servant of the Lord, who is to come to establish the law of God for all nations of the world. The Servant who comes in the name and power of the Creator has the authority of the Creator too.

6 I the Lord have called thee in righteousness, and will hold thine hand, and will keep thee, and give thee for a covenant of the people, for a light of the Gentiles;

Now the Lord identifies Himself as the Speaker, confirming His call to the Servant. The first word in this verse is the singular personal pronoun "I"; it is actually rare to find a pronoun standing alone as the subject of a Hebrew sentence. It is used here for emphasis to establish the authority of the calling and to assure the Servant of the identity of the One who is behind the calling. He is the Lord, the covenant-keeping God of Israel, the One who is faithful to keep His promises and never fails. With such a God behind Him, the Servant cannot "fail" or "be discouraged" (v. 4) even in the face of obstacles or resistance.

371

The call is made "in righteousness." This mission will have its foundation in God's righteousness. The word "righteousness" (Heb. *tsedeq*, **TSEH-dek**), which, among other things, means what is right, just, normal, or standard. It can also be translated as "justice" or "equity." Righteousness is one of the attributes of God, and in Him is absolute justice. Therefore, in this attribute has the Servant been called, and in it will He accomplish the mandate of His calling. This will manifest itself in the salvation of those who yield to Him and punishment for those who reject Him. Jeremiah prophesied concerning Him, "Behold, the days come, saith the LORD, that I will raise unto David a righteous Branch, and a King shall reign and prosper, and shall execute judgment and justice in the earth. ... and this is his name whereby he shall be called, THE LORD OUR RIGHTEOUSNESS" (Jeremiah 23:5–6; 33:16).

Not only has God called Him in righteousness, but He will also hold the Servant's hand and keep Him. The phrase "will hold thine hand" is similar in meaning to "whom I uphold" (v. 1), which means that the Lord will sustain; it again calls attention to the fact that the task of the Servant is not going to be an easy one. Hence, the Lord reaffirms His commitment with the phrase "and will keep thee." God will more than hold His Servant's hand; He will not let go of it. This signifies that the Lord will guide and protect the Messiah as a man guides and protects his child when he holds him by the hand.

The clause "and give thee for a covenant of the people" states the purpose of the Servant's mission. Pay special attention to the preposition "of," which indicates that it is a covenant belonging to the people. This reference to the "people" is not restricted to Jews alone but extends to all people, even to the Gentiles, as stated in the phrase which follows: "for a light of the Gentiles." The Messiah is identified as "covenant" and "light," in which case it is through Him that salvation will be mediated to the earth to both Jews and Gentiles. Being a "covenant" and a "light" implies more than being the source through which salvation comes to the people. The Servant is the embodiment of the covenant and light, the origin and dispenser of the covenant and the radiance of light Himself. John identified Christ as the Light that is coming into the world (John 1:7–8).

7 To open the blind eyes, to bring out the prisoners from the prison, and them that sit in darkness out of the prison house.

This verse begins with the imperative "to open" (Heb. *paqakh*, **paw-KAKH**). The purpose of the Servant's mission, which is idiomatically expressed in the previous verse, is now made more explicit, although in different figurative terms. "To open the eyes of the blind" does not only mean healing of those who are physically blind (although Jesus did that during His ministry) but also refers to those blinded because of sin—those who reject the love relationship the Lord has offered to them. All sinners are blind because of sin. This includes both Jews and Gentiles. Therefore, the task of the Messiah, called the Light, is to open their eyes and deliver them from the darkness of sin. The same idea applies to the next two phrases. God literally sets captives free (Matthew 27:26; Acts 16:40). In addition to this, though, those without the knowledge of God are in bondage to sin and darkness, and they need to be liberated. They cannot liberate themselves; therefore, they need a Deliverer—not as a warrior, but as One who comes as God's righteousness to impart God's love and righteousness to them.

8 I am the Lord: that is my name: and my glory will I not give to another, neither my praise to graven images.

Again, the Lord identifies Himself as Yahweh, the covenant-keeping God of Israel, the eternal and self-existing God. The phrase "I am the Lord" does not merely identify who He is; it reassures the Servant of the power and authority behind that name and emphasizes His faithfulness. It is the same name used when He revealed Himself to Moses in Exodus 3 (cf. Exodus 6:3), a name that reflects His nature: the unchanging and sovereign God who forever stands by His word. The phrase "that is my name" adds further emphasis to the assurance He has given to the Servant.

This assurance of God's faithfulness in keeping His promises is further stated in the last two phrases of this verse, which are synonymous: "my glory will I not give to another, neither my praise to graven images." This is to say that "what I promise, I will perform." He will not let the Servant down. What an assurance! Letting Him down or failing Him is tantamount to letting Satan take the essence of His being or His "glory" and letting the praise that belongs to God be taken by idols ("images"). Worship and praise belong only to God and therefore must not be given to any creature—neither human beings nor man-made graven images nor Satan, the enemy of all righteousness. The following statements (v. 9) further strengthen the certainty that all that the Lord has promised will definitely be fulfilled.

9 Behold, the former things are come to pass, and new things do I declare: before they spring forth I tell you of them.

The speaker of this utterance, whether God through the prophet or the prophet himself, is difficult to identify. Nonetheless, the speaker talks about the former things that have been fulfilled, which indicates that the new things or the present predictions he is making will also surely come to pass. "The former things" most likely refers to the entire past history of Israel, particularly the redemption of Israel through the exodus from Egypt, which is referred to in the next chapter (43:12–19).

Here the prophet, inspired by the Holy Spirit, recalls the faithfulness of God in keeping His word and promises in the past, reassures the people of the certain fulfillment of the present prediction, and reminds them that God is to be fully trusted. The certainty and assurance of these prophecies are further strengthened with the following phrase: "before they spring forth I tell you of them." These new predictions and promises will "spring forth" (i.e., will be fulfilled) like a seed in the ground. At first unseen, they will eventually germinate, and Israel will remember them and honor the Lord. Confident in the faithfulness of the Lord to keep His promises even before they "spring forth," Isaiah calls on the people, both Jews, and Gentiles and all who would hear this prophecy—indeed the whole earth—to start celebrating by singing "a new song to the Lord" (vv. 10–12).

Sources:
Life Application Study Bible, New Living Translation. Wheaton, IL: Tyndale House Publishers, Inc., 1996. 1055–1056.

Say It Correctly

Decalogue. **DEH**-kah-log.
Penteteuch. **PEN**-teh-took
Uzziah. you-**ZIE**-uh.
Jotham. **JAH**-thum.

Daily Bible Readings

MONDAY
Faith Heroes Acted Justly
(Hebrews 11:29–35)

TUESDAY
Your King Comes Humbly
(Matthew 21:1–11)

WEDNESDAY
House of Prayer for All Nations
(Mark 11:15–19)

THURSDAY
Neglect Justice at Your Peril
(Luke 11:42–44)

FRIDAY
Jesus, God's Servant Messiah
(Matthew 12:15–21)

SATURDAY
God Will Not Forsake the People
(Isaiah 42:10–17)

SUNDAY
God's Servant to Establish Justice Everywhere
(Isaiah 42:1–9)

Notes

Teaching Tips

Words You Should Know

A. Born out of due time (v. 8) *ektroma* (Gk.)—Abnormally born through miscarriage or stillbirth

B. Preaching (v. 12) *kerusso* (Gk.)—To proclaim or herald, as one would herald the coming of a king

Teacher Preparation

Unifying Principle—Hope for a Better Life. People struggle with the probability and possibility of life after death. How can resurrection from death provide life that is different from what is experienced before death? In 1 Corinthians, only life through the resurrection of Christ engenders hope for authentic justice.

A. Read the Bible Background and Devotional Readings.

B. Pray for your students and lesson clarity.

C. Read the lesson Scripture in multiple translations.

O—Open the Lesson

A. Begin the class with prayer.

B. As a class, roleplay the scene of Mary Magdalene, Mary the mother of James, and Salome coming to the tomb early and encountering the young man, and what follows from there (Mark 16:1–8). Discuss how the story of the Resurrection relates to Paul's teaching about the Resurrection in 1 Corinthians 15.

C. Have the students read the Aim for Change and the In Focus story.

D. Ask students how events like those in the story weigh on their hearts and how they can view these events from a faith perspective.

P—Present the Scriptures

A. Read the Focal Verses.

B. Have the class share what Scriptures stand out for them and why, with particular emphasis on today's context.

C. Discuss the Background and The People, Places, and Times sections.

E—Explore the Meaning

A. Use In Depth or More Light on the Text to facilitate a deeper discussion of the lesson text.

B. Pose the questions in Search the Scriptures and Discuss the Meaning.

C. Discuss the Liberating Lesson and Application for Activation sections.

N—Next Steps for Application

A. Summarize the value of hope the Resurrection brings.

B. End class with a commitment to pray for resurrection renewal and restoration in the present life, looking forward to spiritual life in Christ.

Worship Guide

For the Superintendent or Teacher
Theme: Resurrection Hope
Song: "Risen" by Israel Houghton
Devotional Reading: Isaiah 53:4–12

Resurrection Hope

Bible Background • MARK 16; 1 CORINTHIANS 15 | Printed Text • 1 CORINTHIANS 15:1–8, 12–14, 20–23, 42–45 | Devotional Reading • ISAIAH 53:4–12

Aim for Change

By the end of the lesson, we will: CONTRAST the first Adam and the last, ANTICIPATE a new resurrected life different from the present one, and EMBRACE the call to proclaim the death and resurrection of Jesus Christ despite ridicule or resistance.

In Focus

Anthony stood and looked at the cell he had called home for the last 10 years. He was just a twenty-two-year-old kid when he came into this place, scared and angry. To make matters worse, he was innocent! His court-appointed lawyer had convinced him that it was better to plea bargain and serve some time than to risk a full sentence from a jury trial.

As he walked through the long corridors saying his goodbyes, Anthony tried to focus on the good in his unjust incarceration. He realized that prison had slowed him down, maybe even saved his life. Even though he didn't do the crime he was accused of, Anthony's lifestyle back then was leading him to certain destruction.

Anthony thought about the college degree he earned while in prison. His parents had begged him to go after high school, but, no, he was too cool for college back then.

The most important benefit from prison, Anthony knew for sure, was his salvation. He accepted Jesus Christ as his Lord and Savior nearly five years ago. It was difficult for Anthony to be bitter about his experience. God had yielded many positive things from something negative.

In our study we will observe how God turned Jesus' negative experience of death into the positive experience of the resurrection. What "resurrections" has God performed in your life?

Keep in Mind

"If in this life only we have hope in Christ, we are of all men most miserable. But now is Christ risen from the dead, and become the firstfruits of them that slept" (1 Corinthians 15:19–20, KJV).

376

"And if our hope in Christ is only for this life, we are more to be pitied than anyone in the world. But in fact, Christ has been raised from the dead. He is the first of a great harvest of all who have died" (1 Corinthians 15:19–20, NLT).

Focal Verses

KJV **1 Corinthians 15:1** Moreover, brethren, I declare unto you the gospel which I preached unto you, which also ye have received, and wherein ye stand;

2 By which also ye are saved, if ye keep in memory what I preached unto you, unless ye have believed in vain.

3 For I delivered unto you first of all that which I also received, how that Christ died for our sins according to the scriptures;

4 And that he was buried, and that he rose again the third day according to the scriptures:

5 And that he was seen of Cephas, then of the twelve:

6 After that, he was seen of above five hundred brethren at once; of whom the greater part remain unto this present, but some are fallen asleep.

7 After that, he was seen of James; then of all the apostles.

8 And last of all he was seen of me also, as of one born out of due time.

12 Now if Christ be preached that he rose from the dead, how say some among you that there is no resurrection of the dead?

13 But if there be no resurrection of the dead, then is Christ not risen:

14 And if Christ be not risen, then is our preaching vain, and your faith is also vain.

20 But now is Christ risen from the dead, and become the firstfruits of them that slept.

21 For since by man came death, by man came also the resurrection of the dead.

22 For as in Adam all die, even so in Christ shall all be made alive.

23 But every man in his own order: Christ the firstfruits; afterward they that are Christ's at his coming.

NLT **1 Corinthians 15:1** Let me now remind you, dear brothers and sisters, of the Good News I preached to you before. You welcomed it then, and you still stand firm in it.

2 It is this Good News that saves you if you continue to believe the message I told you—unless, of course, you believed something that was never true in the first place.

3 I passed on to you what was most important and what had also been passed on to me. Christ died for our sins, just as the Scriptures said.

4 He was buried, and he was raised from the dead on the third day, just as the Scriptures said.

5 He was seen by Peter and then by the Twelve.

6 After that, he was seen by more than 500 of his followers at one time, most of whom are still alive, though some have died.

7 Then he was seen by James and later by all the apostles.

8 Last of all, as though I had been born at the wrong time, I also saw him.

12 But tell me this—since we preach that Christ rose from the dead, why are some of you saying there will be no resurrection of the dead?

13 For if there is no resurrection of the dead, then Christ has not been raised either.

14 And if Christ has not been raised, then all our preaching is useless, and your faith is useless.

20 But in fact, Christ has been raised from the dead. He is the first of a great harvest of all who have died.

21 So you see, just as death came into the world through a man, now the resurrection from the dead has begun through another man.

22 Just as everyone dies because we all belong to Adam, everyone who belongs to Christ will be given new life.

23 But there is an order to this resurrection: Christ was raised as the first of the harvest; then all who belong to Christ will be raised when he comes back.

42 So also is the resurrection of the dead. It is sown in corruption; it is raised in incorruption:

43 It is sown in dishonour; it is raised in glory: it is sown in weakness; it is raised in power:

44 It is sown a natural body; it is raised a spiritual body. There is a natural body, and there is a spiritual body.

45 And so it is written, The first man Adam was made a living soul; the last Adam was made a quickening spirit.

42 It is the same way with the resurrection of the dead. Our earthly bodies are planted in the ground when we die, but they will be raised to live forever.

43 Our bodies are buried in brokenness, but they will be raised in glory. They are buried in weakness, but they will be raised in strength.

44 They are buried as natural human bodies, but they will be raised as spiritual bodies. For just as there are natural bodies, there are also spiritual bodies.

45 The Scriptures tell us, "The first man, Adam, became a living person." But the last Adam—that is, Christ—is a life-giving Spirit.

The People, Places, and Times

Gospel. The Gospel is literally "good news." The equivalent Greek word, *euangelion* (ew-an-**GHEL**-ee-on), was used in relation to the announcement that Augustus Caesar was proclaimed ruler over the Roman Empire and would bring peace and joy. The biblical writers used this word to announce God's grace and the coming of His kingdom in the life, death, and resurrection of Christ. This is the substance of the message the apostles preached. In the Gospel's bare essentials, it is the telling of Jesus' life, death, and resurrection and how we can be forgiven and welcomed into God's kingdom.

How do you usually share the Gospel?

Background

Throughout 1 Corinthians, Paul dealt with issue after issue. He addressed the divisions in the church (1:10–4:21), sexual immorality including incest (5:1–13) and fornication (6:12–20), marriage and divorce (7:1–40), idolatry (8:1–11:1), and different aspects of public worship (11:2—13:13). In 1 Corinthians 14, Paul addressed the spiritual gifts of speaking in tongues and prophecy. The apostle instructed the Corinthians to pursue love and the gift of prophecy because it builds up the whole church. Paul wrote that proper worship will result in even unbelievers admitting, "God is truly here among you" (from 1 Corinthians 14:25, NLT). The chapter ends with Paul describing the proper order of worship. With all of these other issues dealt with, Paul finally launched into explaining the significance of Christ's resurrection.

At-A-Glance

1. Resurrection Clarified
(1 Corinthians 15:1–4)
2. Resurrection Witnessed (vv. 5–8)
3. Resurrection Guaranteed (vv. 12–14, 20–23)
4. Resurrection Promises (vv. 42–45)

In Depth

1. Resurrection Clarified (1 Corinthians 15:1–4)

There were some in the Corinthian church who did not believe in the resurrection of the dead. Paul reminds them that he had already preached the Good News to them and they had, or so it seemed, fully accepted it. Before explaining the foundation of the Gospel message, Paul asserts that the message he had given them and he had received himself was valid. He then explains the foundation of the Christian faith: (1) Christ died for our sins. If this had not occurred, eternal damnation would await us all, but God presented Jesus as the sacrifice for sin (Romans 3:23). (2) Christ was buried. To ensure Jesus was dead, a rock was sealed across the tomb and guards placed outside (Matthew 27:62–66). (3) Christ rose on the third day. Death needed to be conquered so that salvation could be secured (2 Timothy 1:10). Paul notes that the Scriptures support what he says, and though Paul does not indicate specific verses, his references could include Psalm 69:9, Isaiah 53:4–12, Hosea 6:2–3, Jonah 1:17, and others.

How do you interact with people who profess to be Christians, but do not hold strictly to core doctrines?

2. Resurrection Witnessed (vv. 5–8)

Paul refers even more validity to the Resurrection by listing the witnesses. Peter and the Twelve saw the resurrected Jesus (John 20:19–29). They had been chosen to be witnesses (Acts 10:40–43). More than five hundred of His followers saw Jesus, including Jesus' half-brother James and other apostles (v. 6; Luke 24:33, 36–53). Perhaps a criterion for being an apostle, from Paul's perspective, was that one had to have been divinely chosen to see the resurrected Christ. They were sent out to preach the Gospel because they could personally testify to its truth. Paul was the last witness. Although he had not lived and journeyed with Jesus, he too had been chosen when Jesus appeared to him on the road to Damascus (Acts 9). The phrase "born out of due time" refers to a miscarried or stillborn

baby. In essence, Paul was someone who was spiritually dead and therefore unfit to be an apostle because he had persecuted believers. However, God, in His grace, still chose Paul to be a witness. Paul mentions this in response to those in Corinth who were questioning his authority (1 Corinthians 9). Whether the other apostles or Paul preached the Gospel, it was the same message that the Corinthians had already believed.

3. Resurrection Guaranteed (vv. 12–14, 20–23)

Paul refutes the people's belief that there is no resurrection of the dead. Paul's line of reasoning, in essence, concludes that if there is no resurrection, Christ did not rise and their faith would be useless. They would all still be in their sin, condemned forever. However, Paul reassures his audience that Jesus had indeed risen from the dead. He continues to explain the benefit of this fact. Jesus did not conquer death only for Himself. He is the first of all who have died. His resurrection ensures that all who believe in Him shall have eternal life. To illustrate this truth, Paul compares Jesus to Adam. Just as Adam brought death for all, Jesus has brought eternal life for those who believe in Him. This was Christ's purpose all along; the Father sent Him so "that whosoever believeth in him should not perish, but have everlasting life" (from John 3:16). Jesus Christ was resurrected first so that all who belong to Him might be resurrected as well.

Many see Christ as being foreshadowed as far back as Adam's Fall (Genesis 3:17). What does this reveal about God?

4. Resurrection Promises (vv. 15:42–45)

Bible scholars disagree on the exact nature of the Corinthian church's doubts concerning the resurrection. Some argue that some Corinthians held that there was no such thing as

Resurrection. Others think that the Corinthians held that Jesus Himself was not resurrected. Still others believe that the Corinthians were at odds about the status of the believers who had already died and the ability of these believers to be raised from the dead at the return of Christ.

Paul is emphasizing that the Resurrection is not simply a tenet but the cornerstone of Christian faith. If, he reasons, Christ died for their sins but He was not resurrected, then they have not been justified, and Jesus' death was in vain. The heart of Paul's argument is that although human lives are subject to death and the body will disintegrate, decay, and decompose—that is not the end of the story. They are also subject to the will of God, who through His Son, Jesus Christ, will bring forth resurrection of the dead.

Therefore, after death, there is continuity rather than a conclusion. Next, Paul launches into the "mystery" of death that he obviously believes plagues these believers. Because of the sin of the first man, Adam, the "natural" bodies of all humankind are subject to death. However, praise be to God, because of the redemptive act of the "last Adam," Jesus Christ, believers now possess "spiritual" bodies. Paul asserts that these bodies are "incorruptible"; they are no longer subject to the laws of nature and the penalty of sin (i.e., death). If believers were only subject to the inheritance of Adam, it would be fitting that we return to dust since it is through Adam's sin that mankind dies. However, through faith, believers are joined to Jesus Christ. The bodies of the believers, through their faith in Him, now bear "the image of the heavenly." (1 Corinthians 15:49) It is these glorified "heavenly bodies" that are subject to be resurrected. Part of this glorious inheritance in Christ is the resurrection!

How does Christ's bodily resurrection give us hope in this life and the next?

Search the Scriptures

1. What is the Gospel message (1 Corinthians 15:3–4)?

2. How do Jesus and Adam differ (vv. 21–22)?

Discuss the Meaning

Many engage in frivolous activities attempting to understand who they are. As believers, the Resurrection has already determined our identity. How has the resurrection of Christ impacted your life? How can you begin to value your identity in Christ?

Liberating Lesson

Jesus was executed when found guilty of false charges during a trial that failed to follow due process. Resurrection on Easter morning, however, is God's first fulfillment of true justice for all. Even if we fail in a fight against a system stacked against us, we know that God has the final word. Until that final word, we know we have the Resurrection power of Christ on our side. If He can conquer such an enemy as death, what can He not do? Meditate on ways the Resurrection motivates us to work for justice with hope.

Application for Activation

We love to celebrate life-changing events with others. We book banquet halls a year in advance and hire the best caterers so people can spend a few hours with us on our special day. The greatest event to ever happen to us is the Resurrection, and we should find ways to share it. Pray about at least three people with whom you can share the Good News and create a special occasion for the sharing. For example, meet for breakfast, schedule time at the gym, or invite them to a church function.

Follow the Spirit

What God wants me to do:

_____

_____

_____

_____

Remember Your Thoughts

Special insights I have learned:

_____

_____

_____

_____

More Light on the Text

1 Corinthians 15:1–8, 12–14, 20–23, 42–45

1 Moreover, brethren, I declare unto you the gospel which I preached unto you, which also ye have received, and wherein ye stand; 2 By which also ye are saved, if ye keep in memory what I preached unto you, unless you have believed in vain.

The opening of this chapter introduces Paul's concerns and lays the foundation for the argument he develops in the verses that follow. Some in the Corinthian church exalted the spiritual in a way that devalued the physical. Consequently, this path led to the denial of bodily resurrection. Paul begins with what they have in common. Paul uses the *euaggelion* (Gk. **ew-an-GHEL-ee-on**), which means good news message or Gospel, to describe what he preached and they, in turn, received as a means for salvation. They owe their existence as a community of faith to the Gospel he brought them. He warns if they cannot

hold on to the same Gospel that saved them, their faith is in jeopardy of being ineffective and producing no fruit.

3 For I delivered unto you first of all that which I also received, how that Christ died for our sins according to the scriptures; 4 And that he was buried, and that he rose again the third day according to the scriptures: 5 And that he was seen of Cephas, then of the twelve.

Paul presents the basics of the Gospel by highlighting three points of emphasis: Jesus died, was buried, and rose again on the third day, all in accordance with the Scriptures. This essence of the Gospel was passed down to Paul. It is generally accepted that these verses reflect an early creed, which would have developed out of some ecumenical gathering of churches rather than simply Paul himself. Being of primary importance, the creed was, in turn, passed along by Paul to the church in Corinth. Although Paul covers a wide range of subjects in his letters, not everything he discusses is central to the Gospel. Nor does every instruction carry equal weight. In this passage, Paul highlights the elements of the Gospel message that are critical to the church and its health and vitality. The death, burial, and resurrection of Jesus are presented as an objective reality. There is a grave, and there were witnesses. It is not merely a spiritual phenomenon.

In addition to misconceptions about the Resurrection, it is likely that the church in Corinth had some misgivings about Paul's authority. Paul therefore grounds his argument not in himself but in tradition, Scripture, and apostolic authority. First, he appeals to tradition by referencing an early church creed. Then, he asserts that these things have happened according to Scripture. Last, he states that Cephas, or Peter, and the Twelve can attest to the validity of his claims. The twelve apostles had an especially close relationship with Jesus and a special role in the founding of the church.

6 After that, he was seen of above five hundred brethren at once; of whom the greater part remain unto this present, but some are fallen asleep. 7 After that, he was seen of James; then of all the apostles. 8 And last of all he was seen of me also, as of one born out of due time.

Paul continues to build the credibility of his position by adding an additional source of authority—eyewitness testimony of believers, apostles, and him. Paul affirms that Jesus was seen by a number of people in a variety of settings after his resurrection, more than five hundred believers, according to Paul. Many of the witnesses were still alive at the time of the writing, and their accounts could be verified firsthand, although some had already "fallen asleep," a common euphemism at the time for death. Next, Paul says that the resurrected Jesus was seen by James, Jesus' half brother. He was also a major leader in the Jerusalem church. This would have given Paul even more credibility, as James had major influence with the church at large due to his natural relation to Jesus. Paul also speaks of the resurrected Jesus being seen by the apostles. This is obviously not the Twelve because they were just mentioned in verse 5. Paul must have been referring to others outside of the Twelve who had been commissioned to represent Christ, perhaps those Jesus had sent out earlier in His ministry (Luke 10:1–20). Paul establishes a connection between the apostolic tradition and himself, even though there is no evidence he was regarded as one of the Twelve. He is likely referring to his encounter with the risen Lord on the road to Damascus (Acts 9). Paul uses the Greek word *ektroma* (**ECK-troh-ma**), which is often translated abnormally born, to describe his apostolic calling. The Twelve had years of mentoring and

close relationship with Jesus during His time on earth. Paul, however, did not become an apostle this way. He may have been expressing feelings of being born out of season since his apostolic calling was out of the ordinary.

12 Now if Christ be preached that he rose from the dead, how say some among you that there is no resurrection of the dead? 13 But if there be no resurrection of the dead, then is Christ not risen: 14 And if Christ be not risen, then is our preaching vain, and your faith is also vain.

Here Paul makes a bold statement to the Corinthians about the resurrection that is demonstrated again and again in the New Testament. The resurrection of Jesus Christ is at the core of the Gospel of Jesus Christ. Paul and the apostles are persecuted for preaching the resurrection (Acts 4:1–23, 17:18–32, 23:6–10). The Greek word for preaching is *kerusso* (**kay-ROOS-so**) and means to proclaim or herald, as one would herald the coming of a king. Proclaiming the presence of King Jesus is directly connected to announcing His resurrection from the dead. Paul argues that it is essential that Jesus Christ rose from the dead for our faith in Him to be valid.

Paul addresses the fact that there was a division among Jews about whether or not there is a resurrection from the dead. The Pharisees believed that there was a resurrection from the dead, but the Sadducees (which were another major faction of Jewish leaders) did not believe in a resurrection. Paul is asserting that the resurrection for all people will happen because the resurrection of Christ happened; the debate should be ended for everyone who believes in Jesus Christ. Paul takes it a step further: if Christ's resurrection is not preached, then our faith in Him is in vain (v. 14). This should serve as a fundamental doctrine for all Christians, Paul proclaims. Jesus Christ was resurrected from the dead, and because He was, we can place our faith in Him. Without the resurrection, there is no hope for our resurrection, and Jesus could be treated as just another prophet at best or a heretic at worst. But because Jesus was resurrected, we have a hope of life after death and our preaching has power.

20 But now is Christ risen from the dead, and become the firstfruits of them that slept. 21 For since by man came death, by man came also the resurrection of the dead. 22 For as in Adam all die, even so in Christ shall all be made alive.

Paul emphasizes the benefits of the resurrection for believers. Christ's resurrection made the resurrection of the dead necessary and inevitable. God raised Christ from the dead based on His own authority and sovereignty. Resurrection is required for the final victory over death so God can be "all in all" (v. 28). Paul uses the Greek word *aparche* (**ah-par-KHAY**), meaning a sacrifice of the harvest's "firstfruits" to sanctify the whole harvest, to describe the work of Christ. He is the first fruit of a larger harvest (2 Thessalonians 2:13; 1 Corinthians 16:15). This agricultural metaphor has eschatological significance. Christ's resurrection is not bound to one annual harvest, but it foreshadows the resurrection of all believers for eternity. For this to happen, Christ had to be human because death is a part of humanity, not divinity.

God's command, which resulted in the introduction of sin and its natural result, death, into the world. This was the beginning of all the death and dying that followed. Since it was through a human being that death came into the world, likewise the resurrection of the dead had to come through a human being.

New life and resurrection for believers are inevitable because we share in the new nature of the Resurrected Christ through the grace of God.

23 But every man in his own order: Christ the firstfruits; afterward they that are Christ's at his coming.

There is an order to this plan, which Paul now begins to explain. First, Christ the first fruits (the redeemer) must be resurrected; then when He arrives those who belong to Christ (the redeemed) shall be resurrected. The word order also carries the meaning of military ranking, like the ordering of troops for battle. The word "coming" (Gk. *parousia*, **pah-roo-SEE-ah**) was a term used to indicate the arrival, presence, or coming of someone, especially someone like an emperor. It is used especially in Christian writing to indicate the appearance of God. Christ will become the King who sits at the right hand of God. His troops will be readied for battle against His foes. This imagery of the royal coronation is found in Psalm 110:1 and quoted from that Psalm in Acts 2:34–35.

42 So also is the resurrection of the dead. It is sown in corruption; it is raised in incorruption.

The thrust of this section is to answer the question raised earlier in verse 35 with respect to how the dead are to be raised. Using various examples from agriculture, the animal world, and the heavenly bodies, Paul explains one central point: the resurrection body is going to be different from the present body in four significant respects. First, the present body is sown (an agricultural metaphor for death/interment) as perishable, but it will be raised imperishable. Contrary to Greek thought that regards all bodies as subject to decay, Paul says while the present body is subject to decay, the resurrection body is not going to be subject to decay though it is a body all the same.

43 It is sown in dishonour; it is raised in glory: it is sown in weakness; it is raised in power:

Since the present body is subject to decay, it follows naturally that it would be treated with dishonor. There is nothing honorable in the whole process of the body decaying. It is partly to reduce the dishonor that death brings to the present body that it is buried or cremated. But even this is a form of dishonor as it is actually getting rid of the body. In the Old Testament, the corpse is regarded as something capable of defiling (Numbers 19:11). That is how we treat anything that is decaying, and the same is no less true of our present body in spite of the colossal amount we spend on cosmetics. At resurrection, the saints will assume a glorious body that is no longer subject to the dishonor of the present body because the resurrection body will not be capable of decay. All the dishonor that attends this present body will not affect the resurrection body because death will have no power over it. Instead, the resurrection body is going to be an honorable body. In this state, it is going to be comparable to the glorified body of Christ after He was raised from the dead (Ephesians 3:21). The resurrection is a divine act. As such it is characterized by the glory typical of such divine acts as Christ's resurrection (Romans 6:4).

The present body is subject to weaknesses of various kinds, such as fatigue, hunger, disease, pain, and death. In its present state this body is limited by time and space. It is not a body designed to endure for eternity or to transcend material barriers. The reality of our present body's weakness confronts us daily in our experience of pain, suffering, and death. This physical weakness will be a thing of the past as far as the resurrection body is concerned. When God raises the saints at the resurrection of the dead, He is going to bless them with a powerful body that is no longer subject to physical weaknesses and limitations. The resurrection body will not know weariness, hunger, disease, or death.

44 It is sown a natural body; it is raised a spiritual body. There is a natural body, and there is a spiritual body.

The word translated as "natural" is *psuchikos* (Gk. **psoo-khee-KOCE**). Depending on the context, it describes the immaterial, natural, or physical part of humanity. Here it contrasts with that which is spiritual and seems to refer to the quality of the material body, which is taken from the physical world. The resurrection body is "spiritual" (Gk. *pneumatikos*, **puh-new-mah-tee-KOCE**) and refers to that quality of the resurrection body, which is able to exist in the heavenly realm. There is a realm for physical (natural) existence, and there is another for spiritual existence. Each realm has a distinct body fashioned for it.

45 And so it is written, The first man Adam was made a living soul; the last Adam was made a quickening spirit.

Here Paul quotes Genesis 2:7 to support his argument concerning the physical and spiritual distinctions between the present body and the resurrection body. The first Adam became a living soul and thereby represents the source of this present body that is subject to all kinds of suffering and pain. God created Adam's body directly, while the rest of humanity inherited the same kind of body through its descent from Adam. Adam represents the natural body from the previous verse, as he comes a living "soul" (Gk. *psuche*, **psoo-KHAY**). Jesus, on the other hand, is identified as the last Adam, who was made a life-giving "spirit" (Gk. *pneuma*, **puh-NEW-ma**). Jesus is not just a living Spirit but a life-imparting Spirit. The word translated "quickening" is *zoopoieo* (Gk. **dzoo-poy-EH-oh**), which literally means "to make living." In contrast to the first Adam, Jesus is the life-giving source of the spiritual body in which saints are raised at the resurrection. So, just as the two sources are different, so also are the qualities of both bodies different.

385

Sources:

Barnes, Albert. 1 Corinthians. *Barnes' Notes on the New Testament*. Grand Rapids, MI: Kregel Publications, 1980. 314.

Fee, Gordon D. The First Epistle to the Corinthians. *New International Commentary on the New Testament*. Grand Rapids, MI: Eerdmans, 1987.

Furnish, Paul Victor. "First Letter of Paul to the Corinthians: Introduction and 1 Corinthians 15:1–11; 20–22 notes." *The Harper Collins Study Bible*. NRSV. San Francisco, CA: Harper Collins Publishers, 2006. 1932–34, 1952–53.

Keener, Craig S. *The IVP Bible Background Commentary: New Testament*. Downers Grove, IL: InterVarsity Press, 1993. 647–50, 670–71.

Horsley, Richard A. 1 Corinthians. *Abingdon New Testament Commentaries*. Nashville, TN: Abingdon Press, 1998.

Lane, William L. Hebrews 9–13. *Word Biblical Commentary*, Vol. 47B. Dallas, TX: Word Inc., 1991.

Life Application Study Bible. King James Version. Wheaton, IL: Tyndale House Publishers, Inc., 1997. 2154–55, 2170–72.

Morris, Leon. 1 Corinthians. *Tyndale New Testament Commentaries*. Leicester, England: InterVarsity Press, 1995. 221.

Radmacher, Earl D., ed. *Nelson's New Illustrated Bible Commentary: Spreading the Light of God's Word into Your Life*. Nashville, TN: Thomas Nelson Publishers, 1999. 1648–53.

Soards, Marion L. "Back to the Basics: 1 Corinthians 15:1–11." *Understanding the Bible Commentary Series*. Grand Rapids, MI: Baker Books. 2011.

Unger, Merrill F. *The New Unger's Bible Dictionary*. R.K. Harrison, ed. Chicago, IL: Moody Press, 1988. 255–56, 968–69.

Vincent, Marvin. *Vincent's Word Studies in the New Testament*. Peabody, MA: Hendrickson Publishers, Inc., 1985. 284.

Daily Bible Readings

MONDAY
Women Find Jesus' Tomb Empty
(Mark 16:1–8)

TUESDAY
Saul Meets Jesus on Damascus Road
(Acts 9:1–9)

WEDNESDAY
Free Gift of Grace and Hope
(Romans 5:12–17)

THURSDAY
The Dead in Christ Will Rise
(1 Thessalonians 4:13–18)

FRIDAY
All Things under God's Control
(1 Corinthians 15:24–28)

SATURDAY
Victory through Our Lord Jesus Christ
(1 Corinthians 15:50–58)

SUNDAY
All Are Made Alive in Christ
(1 Corinthians 15:1–8, 12–14, 20–23, 42–45)

Say It Correctly

Eschatological. es-ka-toe-**LAH**-gih-kal.

Notes

_____

_____

_____

_____

Teaching Tips

Words You Should Know

A. Afraid (v. 6) *ba'at* (Heb.)—To be terrified, overwhelmed, troubled

B. Gallows (v. 10) *'ets* (Heb.)—Tree, branch, spike

Teacher Preparation

Unifying Principle—Justice Prevails. Ignoble people often seem to attain great power and wealth. What evidence is there that people will receive the recompense their evil deeds deserve? The story of Esther's triumph over Haman provides assurance that evil does not prevail.

A. Read the Bible Background and Devotional Readings.

B. Pray for your students and lesson clarity.

C. Read the lesson Scripture in multiple translations.

O—Open the Lesson

A. Begin the class with prayer.

B. Ask the class: "The name of God never appears in the entire book of Esther, yet we see God at work throughout it. How do we see God at work in our own lives, even when He does not draw attention to Himself?"

C. Have the students read the Aim for Change and the In Focus story.

D. Ask students how events like those in the story weigh on their hearts and how they can view these events from a faith perspective.

P—Present the Scriptures

A. Read the Focal Verses.

B. Have the class share what Scriptures stand out for them and why, with particular emphasis on today's context.

C. Discuss the Background and The People, Places, and Times sections.

E—Explore the Meaning

A. Use In Depth or More Light on the Text to facilitate a deeper discussion of the lesson text.

B. Pose the questions in Search the Scriptures and Discuss the Meaning.

C. Discuss the Liberating Lesson and Application for Activation sections.

N—Next Steps for Application

A. Summarize the value of courage and faith in encountering those with power over us.

B. End class with a commitment to pray for knowledge of how and when to use our positions for justice.

Worship Guide

For the Superintendent or Teacher
Theme: Injustice will be Punished
Song: "Born for This (ESTHER)" by Mandisa
Devotional Reading: Luke 19:11–26

Injustice Will Be Punished

Bible Background • ESTHER 3; 5; 7
Printed Text • ESTHER 7:1–10 | Devotional Reading • LUKE 19:11–26

———————————— **Aim for Change** ————————————

By the end of the lesson, we will: EXPLICATE the story of Esther as a triumph of justice, SENSE that treachery and wickedness will not win, and CHOOSE to act justly in every situation with the assurance that good triumphs over evil.

———————————— **In Focus** ————————————

In church, James and Mariah were leading the adult class discussion on why fighting injustice takes a willingness to take a stand even when you are afraid. After this discussion, Mariah spoke about God's love for justice. Then, she reviewed Esther's heroic deeds and James shared how Esther was a reluctant hero but eventually changed her mind to stand up for her people. He added how Mordecai's instruction to his cousin-daughter, Esther, and his determination for justice provided the catalyst to help save the Jewish people. They reminded the class that Mordecai and Esther literally changed the course of history.

Then, they asked the class to identify historical figures that represented risk takers and freedom fighters. Class members named persons like Fannie Lou Hamer, Mary McLeod Bethune, and Fredrick Douglass. Next, they asked the class to reflect on the sentence on the board, "When you look over your life, how many instances can you recall that you stood up for justice, especially when it was in a very stressful situation?" The class gave different responses about marches they had organized or participated in."

After this discussion, James and Mariah asked the class to find three Scriptures during the week which encourage them to stand up for justice.

How do you stand up for God's justice? Identify when you did not stand up for justice.

———————————— **Keep in Mind** ————————————

"So they hanged Haman on the gallows that he had prepared for Mordecai. Then was the king's wrath pacified" (Esther 7:10, KJV).

"So they impaled Haman on the pole he had set up for Mordecai, and the king's anger subsided" (Esther 7:10, NLT).

Focal Verses

KJV **Esther 7:1** So the king and Haman came to banquet with Esther the queen.

2 And the king said again unto Esther on the second day at the banquet of wine, What is thy petition, queen Esther? and it shall be granted thee: and what is thy request? and it shall be performed, even to the half of the kingdom.

3 Then Esther the queen answered and said, If I have found favour in thy sight, O king, and if it please the king, let my life be given me at my petition, and my people at my request:

4 For we are sold, I and my people, to be destroyed, to be slain, and to perish. But if we had been sold for bondmen and bondwomen, I had held my tongue, although the enemy could not countervail the king's damage.

5 Then the king Ahasuerus answered and said unto Esther the queen, Who is he, and where is he, that durst presume in his heart to do so?

6 And Esther said, The adversary and enemy is this wicked Haman. Then Haman was afraid before the king and the queen.

7 And the king arising from the banquet of wine in his wrath went into the palace garden: and Haman stood up to make request for his life to Esther the queen; for he saw that there was evil determined against him by the king.

8 Then the king returned out of the palace garden into the place of the banquet of wine; and Haman was fallen upon the bed whereon Esther was. Then said the king, Will he force the queen also before me in the house? As the word went out of king's mouth, they covered Haman's face.

9 And Harbonah, one of the chamberlains, said before the king, Behold also, the gallows fifty cubits high, which Haman had made for Mordecai, who spoken good for the king, standeth in the house of Haman. Then the king said, Hang him thereon.

NLT **Esther 7:1** So the king and Haman went to Queen Esther's banquet.

2 On this second occasion, while they were drinking wine, the king again said to Esther, "Tell me what you want, Queen Esther. What is your request? I will give it to you, even if it is half the kingdom!"

3 Queen Esther replied, "If I have found favor with the king, and if it pleases the king to grant my request, I ask that my life and the lives of my people will be spared.

4 For my people and I have been sold to those who would kill, slaughter, and annihilate us. If we had merely been sold as slaves, I could remain quiet, for that would be too trivial a matter to warrant disturbing the king."

5 "Who would do such a thing?" King Xerxes demanded. "Who would be so presumptuous as to touch you?"

6 Esther replied, "This wicked Haman is our adversary and our enemy." Haman grew pale with fright before the king and queen.

7 Then the king jumped to his feet in a rage and went out into the palace garden. Haman, however, stayed behind to plead for his life with Queen Esther, for he knew that the king intended to kill him.

8 In despair he fell on the couch where Queen Esther was reclining, just as the king was returning from the palace garden. The king exclaimed, "Will he even assault the queen right here in the palace, before my very eyes?" And as soon as the king spoke, his attendants covered Haman's face, signaling his doom.

9 Then Harbona, one of the king's eunuchs, said, "Haman has set up a sharpened pole that stands seventy-five feet tall in his own courtyard. He intended to use it to impale Mordecai, the man who saved the king from assassination." "Then impale Haman on it!" the king ordered.

10 So they hanged Haman on the gallows that he had prepared for Mordecai. Then was the king's wrath pacified.

10 So they impaled Haman on the pole he had set up for Mordecai, and the king's anger subsided.

The People, Places, and Times

The Book of Esther. In the Jewish community, the Book of Esther is read every year during the festival of Purim, which commemorates this story. Internally, the Book of Esther does not mention God's name in any of its ten chapters. God is not seen or heard to offer direct guidance to anyone. When Esther calls for a period of fasting, no direct reference to prayer is made (Esther 4:15ff). Even though it was canonized with the rest of Scripture during the middle of the first millennium AD, the first Christian commentary on the book of Esther did not appear until the ninth century. Consequently, some in the Christian community have critically questioned the book of Esther's use for revealing the nature of God. These concerns, however, have not dampened the book's capacity to encourage Christian believers to defend what is morally right.

Background

Here in this passage, we find Esther making her plea and request to King Xerxes, also called Ahasuerus. The story of Esther began in 483 BC, which was 103 years after Nebuchadnezzar took the Jewish people into captivity. Mordecai's family went into exile from Jerusalem because of Nebuchadnezzar. Even after King Cyrus allowed them to return, many Jews stayed and lived in Persia because they experienced great freedom. Xerxes was the fifth king of Persia (the kingdom that overthrew and ruled much the same territory as Babylonia) and during that time was considered a dominant force to be reckoned with both in wealth and influence. At the beginning of Esther's story, Vashti was Xerxes' queen, and because of her perceived disobedience to the king, she was banished. Xerxes sought to look for a new queen who was both young and a virgin. Esther's family had chosen to stay in Persia and as such, Esther was considered for queen and ultimately given the title because of her beauty and charm. As the queen, Esther kept her background as a Jew a secret. She was given very few rights as a queen, and because of the behavior of Vashti in particular, there was a weariness to relinquish any rights to her. However, she would ultimately be the one to save Mordecai from death because he refused to bow down or kneel to Haman, the highest official in the king's court. Haman's ancestors, the Amalekites, were a long-time ancient enemy of the Jews, and they were warned to "blot out the name of Amalek from under heaven" (Deuteronomy 25:19; cf. Exodus 17:14; 1 Samuel 15:3). Although Jews did show honor and reverence to government officials, Mordecai could not extend that same honor to Haman. As a result, Haman plotted to kill Mordecai and all the Jews, which is why Esther found herself pleading with King Xerxes to reverse the decree to kill all the Jews.

How might Esther have felt bearing the weight of saving the lives of herself, family, and people?

At-A-Glance

1. Esther's Petition (Esther 7:1–6)
2. Haman's Demise (vv. 7–10)

In Depth

1. Esther's Petition (Esther 7:1–6)

Esther hosted two banquets and invited the King to bring Haman to each, Esther 7 records the events of the second banquet and Esther's hopes of pleading with the king to save the lives of her people and Mordecai. But it was not an easy task. Esther understood that she had minimal rights as a queen. The text does not mention the name of God; however, it assumes that in her fasting it was God who had covered her as she prepared herself to ask the king her request. Esther was going up against not only the power of the king's decree but also Haman, the most powerful noble in the land. Haman had a direct hatred against the Jews. Unfortunately, when he entered the banquet of the queen, he was unaware of her identity as a Jewish woman. The king had already proclaimed that he was both willing to hear and approve her requests, which is evidence that God had honored the prayers and fasting to provide her with favor from the king even before she made her requests known. The king boldly states, "What is your petition? It will be given to you." Esther requests that the King save her people from annihilation and makes the case that if her people were sold into slavery that she would have kept quiet. She emphasizes this is not because the Jewish people have offended the government but because the hatred and prejudice of one man is the potential cause of their destruction.

What strategy did Esther formulate in her approach to the king, and how was that important in her achieving her outcome to save her people?

2. Haman's Demise (vv. 7–10)

Once the king realizes what Haman had done, he becomes outraged. The king in his anger walks to the garden to cool off and comes to the realization that Haman fooled him. Haman is afraid as what was at one point a banquet of joy quickly turned into terror as he realized that he was in the line of judgment. Haman, a once proud noble, finds himself at the foot of the woman he wished to destroy; the roles were now reversed. God's rule declares that those who choose to persecute God's chosen ones will ultimately become beholden to them. As Haman pleads for his life, the king enters, more enraged, and the King's servants quickly covered Haman's face. It was practice to cover the face of the one who was condemned to death because the Persian kings refused to look at them. The king then orders that the pole Haman had built to be the demise of Mordecai should become the measure by which his own life is taken. Haman's prejudice and hatred are what led to his destruction. Mordecai is now given the position of honor, and Haman the execution.

Search the Scriptures

1. What is Esther's answer when the king tells her to make her request (Esther 7:3)?

2. How does Esther describe the plot against Mordecai and the Jews (v. 4)

3. Where does the idea of the method of Haman's death come from? Why is it important?

Discuss the Meaning

1. Why was it essential for Esther to prepare the king's heart through fasting for her petition?

2. Does it seem just that Haman was put to death with the same pole that he had initially designed to kill Mordecai on? Why or why not?

3. Have you ever found yourself in Esther's position, having to speak for the dignity of a person or group of people that you witnessed being wrongfully persecuted by those in authority?

Liberating Lesson

In our world today many people find themselves persecuted, marginalized, and oppressed because of their race, immigration status, and position in society. We are desperately in need of individuals who will stand up to modern-day Hamans who wish to destroy the well-being of others. If we look closely at our elected officials, we note that those who come from marginalized communities have had to fight to get a seat at the table. When they finally get to the table, they feel a responsibility to speak and advocate on behalf of their respective communities. Unfortunately, there are systems and individuals that wish to tarnish our democratic process by doing everything in their power to stop change from coming to fruition. Nevertheless, the efforts, spirit, heart, and conviction of those who seek liberation and hope are able to call attention to the social ills in this country. It is our job as a community to continue uplifting voices who speak out against unjust practices, to keep them in our prayers, and when called upon, to also use our privilege and voice to uplift the silenced voices in our world.

Application for Activation

As you find yourself witnessing the continued marginalization of individuals in this country, seek out and support organizations using their platform to elevate and alleviate the plight of the marginalized. Secondly, continue praying for and voting for elected officials who will attempt not to harm and oppress the least of these but will establish and fight for policies that will make their lives better. Lastly, through prayer and fasting, bring all your cares and worries regarding how people are treated to God and trust that God will bring forth justice and righteousness.

Follow the Spirit

What God wants me to do:

_____

_____

_____

_____

Remember Your Thoughts

Special insights I have learned:

_____

_____

_____

_____

More Light on the Text
Esther 7:1–10

1 So the king and Haman came to banquet with Esther the queen. 2 And the king said again unto Esther on the second day at the banquet of wine, What is thy petition, queen Esther? and it shall be granted thee: and what is thy request? and it shall be performed, even to the half of the kingdom.

The narrative of Queen Esther has been building up to this point. Esther is very beautiful and was chosen by the king from a number of candidates to be the queen of Persia. Haman, one of the king's officials, was an Agagite, a tribe that had warred with Israel from the days of Joshua (Exodus 17, 1 Samuel 15, 1 Samuel 30). It was on the basis of this generational hatred that Mordecai, Esther's uncle, refused to bow before Haman. In retaliation, Haman decided to punish all Jews. To this end, he tricked the king into signing a decree to search for and kill the entire population of Jews in the empire. Mordecai informed Esther of Haman's plot and encouraged her to use her position to help the Jews who were scattered throughout the Persian Empire. Esther gains the attention of the king and invites him and Haman to a banquet where she makes her request. In the revelry of the second banquet, the king asks Esther to make her request known and obligates himself to fulfill her desire.

3 Then Esther the queen answered and said, If I have found favour in thy sight, O king, and if it please the king, let my life be given me at my petition, and my people at my request: 4 For we are sold, I and my people, to be destroyed, to be slain, and to perish. But if we had been sold for bondmen and bondwomen, I had held my tongue, although the enemy could not countervail the king's damage.

Queen Esther is very clever. The king loves her, is very proud of her, and is taken with her beauty. She wisely sets up the situation to liberate her people by seizing the opportunity to ask the king to spare her life and the lives of her Jewish people. She informs him that she herself and the Jewish people have been sold out to be killed. She follows up that by saying that if they had simply been sold as slaves, it would not even be worth mentioning to someone as important as the king. She says the "enemy" (Heb. *tsar*, **TSAR**, trouble, distress) would not have been severe enough to damage the king's time and energy. "Enemy" here probably refers to the situation rather than Haman himself. Esther's wording simultaneously flatters the king and expresses the direness of her situation. She appeals to his ego, his relationship with her, and his sense of reason all at the same time.

5 Then the king Ahasuerus answered and said unto Esther the queen, Who is he, and where is he, that durst presume in his heart to do so? 6 And Esther said, The adversary and enemy is this wicked Haman. Then Haman was afraid before the king and the queen.

King Xerxes (Ahasuerus, KJV), the king of Persia, is deeply troubled at this news. How dare someone try to kill his beautiful queen? How dare someone decide who should die in his kingdom without him knowing? He wants to know who had the boldness to do such a thing. Esther does not hesitate to tell the king the truth. It was Haman who had been plotting to destroy the Jews in Persia, and she calls out his wickedness and injustice plainly. Haman cannot help but be afraid (Heb. *ba'at*, **bah-AT**). This is not the usual word for being afraid but is mostly reserved for poetic expressions. The heightened diction shows the extent of Haman's fear. He had just been bragging to his friends and family about being invited to this exclusive banquet, and now the banquet has turned into a trap. He has been exposed for trying to wield the power of life and death, a power reserved only for the king in his kingdom. He has been called out for his injustice to his face, in front of the one person in the kingdom that could do something to punish him.

7 And the king arising from the banquet of wine in his wrath went into the palace garden: and Haman stood up to make request for his life to Esther the queen; for he saw that there was evil determined against him by the king. 8 Then the king returned out of the palace garden into the place of the banquet of wine; and Haman was fallen upon the bed whereon Esther was. Then said the king, Will he force the queen also before me in the house? As the word went out of king's mouth, they covered Haman's face.

The king was furious. He walked out of the party and went into the garden, presumably to calm himself down. While he was outside, Haman got up and went to plead for his life from Queen Esther as she reclined on her "bed" (Heb. *mittah*, **meet-TAH**). The word sometimes refers to a bed for sleeping, but here refers to a dining couch (cf. Ezekiel 23:41). He had put himself in this situation with his own wickedness toward Esther; now Esther was the only one who could save him. The king was clearly angry and willing to kill him for his arrogance and injustice. He was placed at the mercy of the woman he had made his enemy. But when the king came back in from trying to cool his head before he made a rash decision, his anger was reignited. Again the comedic irony comes to play as the king misinterprets the situation. He saw Haman falling on the couch where Queen Esther was eating and believed he was trying to sexually assault her. In reality, he was pleading for his own life; he had gone from aggressor to beggar in reality and was being mistaken as going from subservient to subversive. As soon as the king finishes speaking, Haman's face is covered by the palace guards to take him, prisoner.

9 And Harbonah, one of the chamberlains, said before the king, Behold also, the gallows fifty cubits high, which Haman had made for Mordecai, who spoken good for the king, standeth in the house of Haman. Then the king said, Hang him thereon. 10 So they hanged Haman on the gallows that he had prepared for Mordecai. Then was the king's wrath pacified.

Here is the ultimate irony. Haman had already built the dreaded device to kill and display Mordecai and ends up being killed on it himself. Although the KJV translates "gallows," the more likely translation is NLT's "sharpened pole." The Hebrew here (*'ets*, **ETS**) literally means tree, and so only implies that

the structure is made of wood. The king's command to kill Haman is to "hang" (Heb. *talah*, **tah-LAH**) him on the instrument. To the modern Western mind, an execution by "hanging" on a "tree" would clearly speak of being hanged by a noose on a gallows. However, this sort of execution was rare in Persia at the time. Also, this same wording is used for the baker whose dream Joseph interprets in jail, who was beheaded before being "hanged" on a "tree" (Genesis 40:19), making the use of a noose impossible. Impaling one's enemies as execution or displaying their bodies after death was more common at that time and therefore the more likely translation.

Haman had been plotting genocide against the Jews as an incredible act of evil and injustice because of Mordecai's refusal to bow before him. He wanted to make an example of Mordecai, not only to have him killed but to let the whole kingdom know he was killed. Now that Haman's evil plot was exposed, the very pole he was going to use to impale Mordecai would be used to impale him. Justice was fully exacted in kind for the injustice that Haman intended upon the innocent man and his people. This reminds us that those who prepare traps for others may fall in themselves (Psalm 5:9–10).

Say It Correctly

Xerxes. **ZURK**-sees.
Ahasuerus. uh-**HAZ**-er-us.
Harbonah. har-**BONE**-ah.

Daily Bible Readings

MONDAY
Mordecai Refuses to Bow to Haman
(Esther 3:1–6)

TUESDAY
Haman Sets Decree to Destroy the Jews
(Esther 3:7–11)

WEDNESDAY
Haman Builds Gallows to Hang Mordecai
(Esther 5:9–14)

THURSDAY
Decree against Jews Struck Down
(Esther 8:3–8, 16–17)

FRIDAY
Festival of Purim Established
(Esther 9:18–23, 29–32)

SATURDAY
Mordecai Advances Welfare of the Jews
(Esther 10:1–3)

SUNDAY
Esther's Plea and Haman's Punishment
(Esther 7:1–10)

Notes

Teaching Tips

Words You Should Know

A. Robbery (61:8) *gazel* (Heb.)—Plunder, that which is taken away by violence

B. Diadem (62:3) *tsanif* (Heb.)—A type of turban worn by kings, often adorned with jewels

Teacher Preparation

Unifying Principle—What Goes Around Comes Around. When people feel helpless and angry, they seek help from others. What hope is there that the conditions of the powerless will be addressed? Isaiah affirms that the righteous will be vindicated.

A. Read the Bible Background and Devotional Reading.

B. Pray for your students and lesson clarity.

C. Read the lesson Scripture in multiple translations.

O—Open the Lesson

A. Begin the class with prayer.

B. Ask the class: "Are there any ways a person might be unintentionally involved in acts of injustice? Reflect on your own lives. Are you perpetuating injustice in any way?"

C. Have the students read the Aim for Change and the In Focus story.

D. Ask students how events like those in the story weigh on their hearts and how they can view these events from a faith perspective.

P—Present the Scriptures

A. Read the Focal Verses.

B. Have the class share what Scriptures stand out for them and why, with particular emphasis on today's context.

C. Discuss the Background and The People, Places, and Times sections.

E—Explore the Meaning

A. Use In Depth or More Light on the Text to facilitate a deeper discussion of the lesson text.

B. Pose the questions in Search the Scriptures and Discuss the Meaning.

C. Discuss the Liberating Lesson and Application for Activation sections.

N—Next Steps for Application

A. Summarize the value of God's salvation and restoration.

B. End class with a commitment to pray for help from God when we are victims of injustice.

Worship Guide

For the Superintendent or Teacher
Theme: The Lord Loves Justice
Song: "Beauty for Ashes"
Devotional Reading: Isaiah 42:1-9

The Lord Loves Justice

Bible Background • ISAIAH 61:8—62:12
Printed Text • ISAIAH 61:8–11; 62:2–4 | Devotional Reading • ISAIAH 42:1–9

Aim for Change

By the end of the lesson, we will: EXPLAIN the hope of vindication for the righteous and faithful, DESIRE salvation and restoration for God's people, and COMMIT to making just decisions in everyday life.

In Focus

It was the thirty-fifth high school reunion for West Side High School's class of 1967. Everyone was excited and ready to have a good time. Jacqui and Darrell were the organizers.

As everyone gathered to make a toast to their present and future, Darrell asked if they could have a moment of silence and remember the two brothers, Reginald and Stephen Phillips. Everyone remembered how kind they were back in their high school days. After graduation, the brothers established themselves as outstanding men in the community, in their families, and in the teen club they started. As they were walking down the street just a few months ago, a car rode past them, and shots were fired. Later, it was revealed the brothers were not even the intended targets.

After a moment of silence, Jacqui and Darrell decided to make their announcements. They shared with everyone that a memorial plaque honoring Stephen and Reginald would be placed in the hallway near the principal's office and a program to combat bullying and promote economic development for the high school and the community would start in the fall, and everyone was invited to participate.

In today's lesson, we learn about God's promise to honor His people, even after hardship. How have you seen God bestow honor on His children in this world?

Keep in Mind

"For I the LORD love judgment, I hate robbery for burnt offering; and I will direct their work in truth, and I will make an everlasting covenant with them" (Isaiah 61:8, KJV).

"For I, the LORD, love justice. I hate robbery and wrongdoing. I will faithfully reward my people for their suffering and make an everlasting covenant with them" (Isaiah 61:8, NLT).

Focal Verses

KJV Isaiah 61:8 For I the LORD love judgment, I hate robbery for burnt offering; and I will direct their work in truth, and I will make an everlasting covenant with them.

9 And their seed shall be known among the Gentiles, and their offspring among the people: all that see them shall acknowledge them, that they are the seed which the LORD hath blessed.

10 I will greatly rejoice in the LORD, my soul shall be joyful in my God; for he hath clothed me with the garments of salvation, he hath covered me with the robe of righteousness, as a bridegroom decketh himself with ornaments, and as a bride adorneth herself with her jewels.

11 For as the earth bringeth forth her bud, and as the garden causeth the things that are sown in it to spring forth; so the LORD God will cause righteousness and praise to spring forth before all the nations.

62:2 And the Gentiles shall see thy righteousness, and all kings thy glory: and thou shalt be called by a new name, which the mouth of the LORD shall name.

3 Thou shalt also be a crown of glory in the hand of the LORD, and a royal diadem in the hand of thy God.

4 Thou shalt no more be termed Forsaken; neither shall thy land any more be termed Desolate: but thou shalt be called Hephzibah, and thy land Beulah: for the LORD delighteth in thee, and thy land shall be married.

NLT Isaiah 61:8 "For I, the LORD, love justice. I hate robbery and wrongdoing. I will faithfully reward my people for their suffering and make an everlasting covenant with them.

9 Their descendants will be recognized and honored among the nations. Everyone will realize that they are a people the LORD has blessed."

10 I am overwhelmed with joy in the LORD my God! For he has dressed me with the clothing of salvation and draped me in a robe of righteousness. I am like a bridegroom dressed for his wedding or a bride with her jewels.

11 The Sovereign LORD will show his justice to the nations of the world. Everyone will praise him! His righteousness will be like a garden in early spring, with plants springing up everywhere.

62:2 The nations will see your righteousness. World leaders will be blinded by your glory. And you will be given a new name by the LORD's own mouth.

3 The LORD will hold you in his hand for all to see— a splendid crown in the hand of God.

4 Never again will you be called "The Forsaken City" or "The Desolate Land." Your new name will be "The City of God's Delight" and "The Bride of God," for the LORD delights in you and will claim you as his bride.

The People, Places, and Times

Names. In Bible times, names held meaning for their bearers. They often reflected a parent's hope for their child's life or the parent's concerns at their child's birth. Rachel knew she would die in childbirth and wanted to name her son Ben-oni, "son of my sorrow." Jacob, however, saw hope in his favorite wife's son and named him Benjamin, "son of my right hand" (Genesis 35:18). Sometimes names are foretold for children whom God has already chosen to do His work (Matthew 1:21; Luke 1:13). Renaming, especially when the new name is from God, expresses a kind of rebirth into a new person. Abram, "great father," became Abraham, "father of many nations" (Genesis 17:5). Jacob, "supplanter," became Israel, "wrestles with

God" (Genesis 32:26–29). Jesus changed Simon, "he has heard," to Peter, "rock," to reflect his character and his place in the church (Matthew 16:18). Saul, "asked for" in Hebrew, began to go by Paul, "small," the most similar sounding Latin name, to reflect his calling as an apostle to the Gentiles (Acts 13:9).

Background

The prophet Isaiah articulates a message about justice from an unlikely place—in the midst of Babylonian captivity. In that place, God has seemingly forsaken the people of Israel and has used a more corrupt nation to punish God's own people for their corruption. This timeless spirit and commitment to calling out injustice becomes immortalized in the words of Isaiah 61:1–4, the very words that Luke records Jesus using as the text for his initial sermon in Luke 4. This illustrates that God's love affair with justice transcends time, space, and communities. Even people who find themselves in diaspora can comfort themselves in knowing that God is still in love with justice and that God is committed to righting the wrongs that have been inflicted upon them.

How can we think about God's commitment to justice in diaspora in line with our own history?

At-A-Glance

1. Divine Adoration for Justice
(Isaiah 61:8–9)
2. Divine Attire of Justice (vv. 10–11)
3. Divine Attraction to Justice (62:1–4)

In Depth

1. Divine Adoration for Justice (Isaiah 61:8–9)

Our text follows the form of much Hebrew poetry where the lines of couplets communicate similar ideas but with different nuances. In verse 8, the Lord declares that He loves justice. Then for further clarification, the next line puts forward the Lord's declaration of His hatred for robbery and wrongdoing. In both lines, the subject is the same—the Lord. The verbs are antonyms, and thus the predicates are polar opposites. If justice is on one side, then robbery and wrongdoing are on the complete another side. The two are incompatible. They warrant opposing responses from the Lord. However, the focus of verses 8 and 9 are not on the Lord's hatred; rather, they center on the Lord's love for those who have been mistreated and suffer injustice. These verses are for those on the margins of empire (in this case the Babylonian Empire) and for those who feel that God has forgotten them because it seems like evil has won the day. To those people, the Lord writes a love letter to justice about them and shares how He will settle the accounts, because His covenant is everlasting, and His blessings can relocate them from a place of shame to a place of prominence.

What would God's love letter about justice say to our society today?

2. Divine Attire of Justice (vv. 10–11)

Verse 10 marks a change in speaker. It moves from the Lord's speech to the Lord's servant, Israel, speaking about a celebration. This is not an ordinary occasion. It is at the level of wedding ceremony significance. Therefore, similar to how the bride and bridegroom put on their best outfits, this celebration and rejoicing demand a wardrobe change. This type of formal attire is what the Lord provides for God's people Israel through a robe of justice. The Lord also provides garments of salvation. It is important to remember that salvation in the Hebrew Bible has a wide meaning that includes "to rescue." This shade of meaning is helpful in this passage, because it depicts how the Lord is going to take God's people who have been treated as insignificant and stripped of their dignity and envelop them in garments of rescue. Their very clothes will make them witnesses to all other people that the Lord sides with the vulnerable and exploited.

We should be keen to observe the oppression and nakedness that the Lord has had to clothe in our communities. In considering African Americans, who have been historically dispossessed in the U.S., how significant is it for us to recognize that God has provided a possession of justice as clothes?

3. Divine Attraction to Justice (62:1–4)

These verses depict how the Lord is drawn to his people in spite of their oppressed status and in spite of how the forces in power have rendered them as forsaken. The prophet's zeal will not allow him to remain silent, and he is certain that the Lord will liberate in such a dynamic way that every group of people in the world will be dazzled by the Lord's commitment to justice. Israel will arise as crown jewels. Such a significant transformation is marked by a name change. Israel will no longer be called Forsaken or Desolate. Instead the Lord will give the nation names that only the Lord can give. They may not look like a name in English but they are one word in Hebrew. One of the names is "My Delight Is in Her." This is a powerful message for those who can only see destruction around them and for those who struggle to see pleasantness in themselves or in their tragic situations. The Lord wants those folks to know that they are not forgotten and that His delight is in them.

For people who have been systematically reminded that their lives don't matter, how significant is a message that declares that they are not forsaken and that God delights in them?

Search the Scriptures

1. How is the Lord's love for justice discussed? What is it opposed to? What type of commitment does it entail? Who sees this love?

2. For those who are in situations that seem impossible and face obstacles that appear insurmountable, what are the reasons to rejoice in the Lord? What is the role of the future tense in verses 10–11?

3. What does Isaiah 62:1–4 teach us about the power of naming? Whom should we allow to name us? What types of names should we accept?

Discuss the Meaning

The Lord has a special affinity for justice, and God pays special attention to those who are on the underside of oppressive forces. The Lord is committed to rescuing God's people, not primarily because they are chosen, but because the Lord takes up for those who are robbed and mistreated. The Lord is a fan of the underdog, and those connected to the Lord cannot remain silent when they see others victimized. Not only should the Lord's eyes see the vulnerable, so should those of us who profess to have a relationship with the Lord. If we truly love the Lord, then we should love what the Lord loves, and the Lord loves justice. Whose side do we need to take today to be on the same side as the Lord?

Liberating Lesson

Many leading Black studies thinkers discuss the forced transportation of African bodies around the globe as diaspora. This term originally applied to the people of Judah in passages like our focus text. Now it has been appropriated to think about the experience of Africans around the world that correlates to the experiences of the people of Judah. Bodies were forcibly moved by imperial powers. Those powers attempted to destroy the culture of the people whom they stole.

The stolen people had to create a new identity in spaces where people actively despised them. God reaffirms His unending love for those who were forced into slavery. God reminds them that their name is not what their oppressors call them. Their land is not barren like the oppressors call it. Their culture is not savage like the oppressors label it. Rather, they are the beloved, and they are the ones in whom God takes delight. To God, the wretched of the earth, the dispossessed, and people who are black are beautiful. In the sight of the Lord, Black lives matter. Their name is "Delightful."

Application for Activation

Often it is easy to become cynical when we look at the affairs of the world. As African Americans, it is difficult to observe the progress that we have made without becoming discouraged by looking at how far we have to go. However, we are not called to solve all of the problems that face our community and our world. We are called to fall in love with justice like God has. By falling in love with justice, we are to keep one eye on the big picture while focusing our other eye on ways that we can remind individuals and communities that they are not forsaken by God. We may not be able to change all of the educational inequality, but we can mentor one student who feels forgotten. We may not be able to undo mass incarceration, but we can vote and rally around people who prioritize prison divestment and critical rethinking of incarceration. We may not be able to transform corrupt capitalism, but we can be fair to those whom we employ and be generous to servers. We may not be able to transform the perception of African Americans in the United States, but we can prevent ourselves from internalizing toxic images. Even though living in the diaspora can make us feel naked, God clothes His people with luxurious garments of justice and salvation.

Follow the Spirit

What God wants me to do:

_____

_____

_____

_____

Remember Your Thoughts

Special insights I have learned:

_____

_____

_____

_____

More Light on the Text
Isaiah 61:8–11; 62:2–4

Isaiah 59 portrays the deplorable and gloomy condition of the nation of Israel as a result of their sin and rejection of the Lord their God. The chapter paints a picture of total collapse in their relationship with God. Their sin, the prophet laments, has separated them from the Lord, and consequently, the Lord has turned His back on them (vv. 1–2). They are left in utter darkness, figuratively speaking, without hope of deliverance from their enemies. The enemies are being used by God as instruments for discipline; they had no mercy on them; they denied them justice (vv. 9–15). In the midst of this gloomy situation, there comes a ray of hope to Zion; she is promised justice, deliverance, and a Redeemer. The chapter concludes with a climax: "And the Redeemer shall come to Zion, and unto them that turn from transgression in Jacob, saith the LORD" (Isaiah 59:20).

The next three chapters of Isaiah (60–62) follow up the announcement and give an optimistic detailed description of the coming Redeemer and His work for God's people. They record promises of great things that will come to Zion and the joy that will follow when the promises are fulfilled. In these chapters are a number of themes, such as righteousness, salvation, joy, and justice. In chapter 60, the Redeemer will be the Light that will lighten and draw all nations; Zion would be the object of the nations' blessings and service, no longer in servitude of the nation. Chapter 61 begins with the description of the Messiah and His mission of the good news of salvation to God's people. We learn that the Messiah, endowed with the "Spirit of the Lord GOD" will bring physical, emotional, and spiritual healing, deliverance, and comfort to God's people (vv. 1–3); this was fulfilled by Jesus Christ, the Messiah (Luke 4:18–21). Verses 4–7 speak about the change that will come to Zion—Jerusalem will be rebuilt, the nations will serve them, and their former glory will be restored.

8 For I the LORD love judgment, I hate robbery for burnt offering; and I will direct their work in truth, and I will make an everlasting covenant with them.

In the following verses, the Lord gives the reason for changing their situation. The statement, "For I the Lord love judgment, I hate robbery for burnt offering" describes God's character, who He is. He is a fair and just God. The Hebrew word translated "judgment" is *mishpat* (**meesh-POT**); it is also rendered as "justice." Often justice is used synonymously with "righteousness" (Heb. *tsedaqah*, **tseh-daw-KAW**), and the words are often used in parallel structure (Isaiah 1:21, 27). So God is both just and righteous in judgment. A number of suggestions have been made for the interpretation of the phrase "robbery for burnt

offering." It appears that the phrase refers to the improper manner in which such offerings were made: people stole an animal and then used that dishonest gain as an offering to God. It refers to Israel's past sin and hypocritical sacrifice that resulted in their long captivity.

However, in context, this doesn't seem to be the case. The idea here is that God hates "robbery and wrongdoing" (NLT). The word here "robbery" is the Hebrew *gazel* (**gaw-ZALE**), which also refers to plunder or things taken away by violence. This is in particular reference to what the Babylonians did to Judah and the surrounding nations. Robbery through plunder is paired with the Hebrew word *'olah* (**oh-LAW**), which is very often translated "burnt offering," from the root *'alah* meaning "to lift up." However, the word *'olah* can also come from the root word *'owal*, in which case it means "evil deeds, immorality, wickedness." Therefore, the sentence "For I the LORD love judgment, I hate robbery for burnt offering" can be rendered better as "For I the Lord love justice, I hate plunder and evil." Rather than to blame Israel for hypocritical sacrifices, God says this to aver the injustice against the Babylonians.

Furthermore, the Lord promises, "I will make an everlasting covenant with them." The word "covenant" comes from the Hebrew *berit* (**beh-REET**), with the idea of making a pledge between two or more peoples, such as between nations. In certain cultures, a treaty was consummated by killing an animal or by making a small cut on the finger of each of the parties and leaking one another's blood. Hence the Hebrew phrase can literally be translated as "cutting a covenant." A covenant is simply a legally binding agreement or contract between two parties; it typically includes certain expectations from all parties concerned and the benefits to be enjoyed by each party. In the divine covenant, God always takes the initiative for the benefit of His people.

When God promises to make an "everlasting covenant" here, He is indeed renewing an already existing covenant relationship with His people. This "everlasting covenant" is also described in Jeremiah 31:31–37; it includes the blessings of the New Covenant that Jesus Christ instituted by His death (Matthew 26:28; Hebrews 10:1–18).

9 And their seed shall be known among the Gentiles, and their offspring among the people: all that see them shall acknowledge them, that they are the seed which the LORD hath blessed.

All these blessings are for posterity. As a result of these blessings and because of the eternal nature of their covenant with the Lord, Israel's descendants will be noted by all nations. The idea here is that Israel will be a distinct nation among the nations. The sentence structure here is parallelism in which the first sentence is deliberately repeated for emphasis. The word "seed" is synonymous with "offspring," and "Gentiles" and "the people" are synonymous. Other nations will notice the uniqueness of Israel's descendants and will recognize Israel as the ones the Lord has blessed. They will see God's blessing radiating around them. This divine promise to be a blessing among other nations has been part of God's covenant with His chosen ones going all the way back to Abraham (Genesis 12:1–3). This promise is not limited to Israel's natural descendants, but to all spiritual children of Abraham—all believers in Christ—the Church.

10 I will greatly rejoice in the LORD, my soul shall be joyful in my God; for he hath clothed me with the garments of salvation, he hath covered me with the robe of righteousness, as a bridegroom decketh himself with ornaments, and as a bride adorneth herself with her jewels.

The Lord has been the one speaking (vv. 8–9), but now the voice changes to the first person speaking of the Lord in the third person. There is no consensus on who the speaker is here. Is it the voice of the Messiah who was the speaker in verses 1–7, or Isaiah rejoicing on behalf of the people whom God has blessed? Some suggest that it was the voice of Zion—the people of God—those whom the Lord will bless. We assume, though not with certainty, that Isaiah is speaking for Israel or Zion, God's people. He rejoices in their relationship with Yahweh who will prove faithful and generous in His dealings with His people. The clause "I will greatly rejoice in the Lord ..." is similar to the joy expressed in Mary's song (Luke 1:46–47), joy at the recognition of redemption coming soon.

This redemption is expressed metaphorically as ceremonial attires and ornaments. Salvation (Heb. *yesha‘*, **yeh-SHA**) is referred to as the inner dress or garment, while righteousness (*tsedaqah*) represents the outer coat. While modern thought might disassociate a person's dress or outer appearance from who they are inside, in Isaiah's time the clothes really did make the man. One's outer appearance was thought to reflect one's inner being. Therefore to be clothed in salvation and righteousness was to absorb those qualities into your core self. This dressing is more of a ceremonial outfit than protective—such as a wedding ceremony. We have here a picture of a wedding party, dressed in beautiful wedding garments and decorated with costly jewels. The Bible uses the bride/bridegroom imagery again to express God's (or Christ) relationship with the Church (Ephesians 5:25–27, Revelation 21:2, 9).

11 For as the earth bringeth forth her bud, and as the garden causeth the things that are sown in it to spring forth; so the Lord GOD will cause righteousness and praise to spring forth before all the nations.

405

Using joyous botanical and horticultural imagery, the prophet describes how righteousness and praises will suddenly emerge. Just as new leaves and flowers add new colors to the tree, and seeds emerge from the ground in springtime, so will righteousness and praise shoot up everywhere. God controls the springtime growth, and so He can control righteousness and praise as well. Notice the pairing now is righteousness (*tsedaqah*) and praise (Heb. *tehillah*, **teh-heel-LAH**). When God sows His goodness in us, we can respond in one of two ways: by reflecting His righteousness in ourselves or by offering up our praise directly to God. As with all that has been going on with Israel in this prophecy, this budding is "before all the nations." That means righteousness will be a common thing in all the earth—not only Zion will benefit from this.

62:2 And the Gentiles shall see thy righteousness, and all kings thy glory: and thou shalt be called by a new name, which the mouth of the LORD shall name. 3 Thou shalt also be a crown of glory in the hand of the LORD, and a royal diadem in the hand of thy God. 4 Thou shalt no more be termed Forsaken; neither shall thy land any more be termed Desolate: but thou shalt be called Hephzibah, and thy land Beulah: for the LORD delighteth in thee, and thy land shall be married.

Chapter 62 opens with the assurance of God's determination to fulfill His promise to Zion. He reassures Jerusalem that He would never relent until the promise of righteousness shines brightly (62:1). It should be noted that Zion and Jerusalem are used synonymously—Jerusalem was built on Mount Zion. Both are often used interchangeably to refer to Israel or Judah—God's people. Because the righteousness and salvation will shine so brightly, it will be seen by the Gentiles and their kings—they will

behold Zion's glory. This is akin to His earlier pronouncement in the previous chapter (61:9) where "all that see them shall acknowledge them, that they are the seed which the LORD hath blessed." Righteousness will be so outstanding that all the Gentile nations will see and experience the glory of God radiating through Israel.

Zion will become the regalia of God. "Crown" is the Hebrew *'atarah* (**ah-taw-RAW**), a specially decorated headpiece for royalty, and "diadem," *tsanif* (**TSAW-neef**) is like a type of turban worn by kings—often adorned with jewels. Both words are synonymous. This is poetic parallelism in which the second sentence emphasizes the first. The imagery sets up Israel as God's crowning glory. They are the sign to all who see them that God is mighty, glorious, and authoritative. Oddly, though Israel is called a crown or diadem, they are still held "in the hand" of the Lord. This shows that even as the nation is made righteous, they are still protected in God's hand. They are also not elevated above God but subject to Him.

At one time, during their exile and as a consequence of sin, Israel felt forsaken and thought their land was rendered desolate. Because of the severity of their suffering, they assumed the names "Forsaken" (49:14); God called her forsaken (60:15); howbeit it was for a short term. Now the Lord had completely altered the situation for them, as their new names show.

Israel will acquire "a new name." Names are very important in Bible times—they often reflect a person's fundamental character, and renaming expresses a significant change of character or calling. Hence Abram became Abraham because he would be "father of many nations" (Genesis 17:5); Jacob was given Israel (which means wrestled with God) after wrestling with the angel (Genesis 32:26—29). Jesus changed Simon to Peter (Rock) to reflect his character (Matthew 16:18), and Saul became Paul (Greek equivalent to the Hebrew Saul) to reflect his calling as an apostle to the Gentiles (Acts 13:9). Israel's new names are "Hephzibah" and "Beulah," which mean "delight" and "husband or marry" respectively. The notion of giving Zion a new name symbolizes a new and closer intimate relationship between God and His people Israel. This promise is renewed for the Church when we have been fully transformed in heaven (Revelation 2:17; 3:12).

Sources:
Barnes' Notes Electronic Database. Biblesoft, Inc., 2006.
New Exhaustive Strong's Numbers and Concordance with Expanded Greek-Hebrew Dictionary. Biblesoft, Inc., 2006.
Interlinear Transliterated Bible. Biblesoft, Inc., 2006.
Life Application Study Bible NIV. Grand Rapids, MI: Zondervan, 2011.
Zondervan NIV Study Bible. Grand Rapids, MI: Zondervan, 2008.

Say It Correctly

Hephzibah. **HEFF**-zih-buh.
Beulah. **BEE**-you-lah.

Daily Bible Readings

MONDAY
Solomon Makes a Just Decision
(1 Kings 3:16—28)

TUESDAY
Jesus Issues His Platform for Justice
(Luke 4:14—21)

WEDNESDAY
The Year of Jubilee Established
(Leviticus 25:8—17)

THURSDAY
A Light to the Nations
(Isaiah 49:1—7)

FRIDAY
A New Vision for the People
(Isaiah 61:1—7)

SATURDAY
Zion Welcomes the Redeemed Home
(Isaiah 62:5—12)

SUNDAY
The Lord Brings the People Justice
(Isaiah 61:8—11; 62:2—4)

Notes

_____

_____

_____

_____

Teaching Tips

May 3
Bible Study Guide 10

Words You Should Know

A. Sing (v. 14) *ranan* (Heb.)—To give a joyous shout

B. Mighty (v. 17) *gibbor* (Heb.)—Strong; hero, warrior

Teacher Preparation

Unifying Principle—The Return of Joy. Oppression of the poor and powerless seems pervasive in our world. Is there any hope for reversal of this condition? The prophet Zephaniah proclaims the day of restoration when God's people shall be returned to righteousness, justice, and peace.

A. Read the Bible Background and Devotional Readings.

B. Pray for your students and lesson clarity.

C. Read the lesson Scripture in multiple translations.

O—Open the Lesson

A. Begin the class with prayer.

B. Give the students time to write just a few verses of a psalm of praise to God for His workings in their past, present, and future. Let those who wish to do so share their writing.

C. Have the students read the Aim for Change and the In Focus story.

D. Ask students how events like those in the story weigh on their hearts and how they can view these events from a faith perspective.

P—Present the Scriptures

A. Read the Focal Verses.

B. Have the class share what Scriptures stand out for them and why, with particular emphasis on today's context.

C. Discuss the Background and The People, Places, and Times sections.

E—Explore the Meaning

A. Use In Depth or More Light on the Text to facilitate a deeper discussion of the lesson text.

B. Pose the questions in Search the Scriptures and Discuss the Meaning.

C. Discuss the Liberating Lesson and Application for Activation sections.

N—Next Steps for Application

A. Summarize the value of God's mighty works and salvation.

B. End class with a commitment to pray for God's intervention in restoring creation.

Worship Guide

For the Superintendent or Teacher
Theme: A Vision of Restoration
Song: "Sing Out, All God's People!"
Devotional Reading: Psalm 47

A Vision of Restoration

Bible Background • ZEPHANIAH 3
Printed Text • ZEPHANIAH 3:14–20 | Devotional Reading • PSALM 47

—————————————— **Aim for Change** ——————————————

By the end of the lesson, we will: DISCERN the need for the just restoration of God's people, PURSUE trusting God for victory, hope, and renewal, and CELEBRATE the return of joy and God's glory in salvation.

————————————————— **In Focus** —————————————————

Truly, it was a day of rejoicing! People were singing and praising God. A few years earlier, Theresa had been diagnosed with kidney disease. The only cure was a kidney transplant. The doctors were not hopeful because her blood type was rare, and she was in her early thirties. Her mother and aunt were mighty prayer warriors, and the church was supportive, but she was not sure if God was going to answer this prayer with a new kidney. Theresa's father's faith was waning, but he tried to put on a good front for her.

One day her doctor called and asked if she could come to his office within the hour. As she rushed out of the office, she called her parents and asked if they could meet at the doctor's office. They agreed and were there as Theresa walked quickly up the stairs to the doctor's office. The nurse asked them all to take a seat in the doctor's office. The doctor walked in and Theresa could see the sparkle in his eyes. She started smiling herself and jumped with joy when he said, "Theresa, we have found your kidney match."

During prayer service, Theresa shared her wonderful news, and everyone began singing and praising God.

How do you celebrate your blessings from God? Identify ways you respond to God when God blesses you the way you want or when God responds in a different way?

————————————————— **Keep in Mind** —————————————————

"Behold, at that time I will undo all that afflict thee: and I will save her that halteth, and gather her that was driven out; and I will get them praise and fame in every land where they have been put to shame" (Zephaniah 3:19, KJV).

"And I will deal severely with all who have oppressed you. I will save the weak and helpless ones; I will bring together those who were chased away. I will give glory and fame to my former exiles, wherever they have been mocked and shamed" (Zephaniah 3:19, NLT).

Focal Verses

KJV **Zephaniah 3:14** Sing, O daughter of Zion; shout, O Israel; be glad and rejoice with all the heart, O daughter of Jerusalem.

15 The LORD hath taken away thy judgments, he hath cast out thine enemy: the king of Israel, even the LORD, is in the midst of thee: thou shalt not see evil any more.

16 In that day it shall be said to Jerusalem, Fear thou not: and to Zion, Let not thine hands be slack.

17 The LORD thy God in the midst of thee is mighty; he will save, he will rejoice over thee with joy; he will rest in his love, he will joy over thee with singing.

18 I will gather them that are sorrowful for the solemn assembly, who are of thee, to whom the reproach of it was a burden.

19 Behold, at that time I will undo all that afflict thee: and I will save her that halteth, and gather her that was driven out; and I will get them praise and fame in every land where they have been put to shame.

20 At that time will I bring you again, even in the time that I gather you: for I will make you a name and a praise among all people of the earth, when I turn back your captivity before your eyes, saith the LORD.

NLT **Zephaniah 3:14** Sing, O daughter of Zion; shout aloud, O Israel! Be glad and rejoice with all your heart, O daughter of Jerusalem!

15 For the LORD will remove his hand of judgment and will disperse the armies of your enemy. And the LORD himself, the King of Israel, will live among you! At last your troubles will be over, and you will never again fear disaster.

16 On that day the announcement to Jerusalem will be, "Cheer up, Zion! Don't be afraid!

17 For the LORD your God is living among you. He is a mighty savior. He will take delight in you with gladness. With his love, he will calm all your fears. He will rejoice over you with joyful songs.

18 I will gather you who mourn for the appointed festivals; you will be disgraced no more.

19 And I will deal severely with all who have oppressed you. I will save the weak and helpless ones; I will bring together those who were chased away. I will give glory and fame to my former exiles, wherever they have been mocked and shamed.

20 On that day I will gather you together and bring you home again. I will give you a good name, a name of distinction, among all the nations of the earth, as I restore your fortunes before their very eyes. I, the LORD, have spoken!"

The People, Places, and Times

Zephaniah. The first verse of Zephaniah's book of prophecy identifies his father as a Cushite, or Ethiopian, descended from King Hezekiah. Because he mentions the presence of pagan priests, the worship of Baal, and the practice of astrology in Judah, Zephaniah's ministry probably began around the time of the religious reforms undertaken by King Josiah in 621 BC. His position among other prophets is unique in that he prophesied during a period of revival. Zephaniah's message is clear: Judah's indifference and stubborn refusal to obey God would bring His wrathful judgment. This judgment would be threefold and would involve purifying, purging, and restoration. Zephaniah was a contemporary of Jeremiah and was one of the last prophets before the captivity.

Background

In Zephaniah 1 we learn that he is a prophet during the reign of King Josiah. Josiah led a religious reform that focused on serving the Lord alone and removing all other religious relics, attire, and practices. Many scholars assume that Zephaniah prophesied before Josiah's reform and perhaps while the king was a child (cf. 2 Kings 22:1).

According to Zephaniah, the day of the Lord is coming, and it is a day of judgment. God will judge the Children of Israel for worshiping foreign gods and mixing worship of the Lord with other religious practices (Zephaniah 1:5–6). God will judge the princes, judges, priests, and prophets who lie, oppress, and eagerly increase corruption—despite all of God's warnings (3:3–7). God will judge the enemies of Israel who at one time have oppressed them. God will not spare the wicked. They will be cut off, ruined, and desolated. In the process, God will judge the whole earth. But there will be a remnant of humble people from near and far that God will bring together. This remnant shall serve the Lord and do no wrong.

It can be hard to read about God's judgment. What reactions do you have when you learn about it in Zephaniah?

At-A-Glance

1. Zion Sings a Song of Joy (Zephaniah 3:14–15)
2. God Sings a Song of Joy (vv. 16–18)
3. Full Restoration (vv. 19–20)

In Depth

1. Zion Sings a Song of Joy (Zephaniah 3:14–15)

After nearly two and a half chapters of judgment, it is only fitting that Zephaniah would pen this song of joy and invite the Children of Israel to sing and rejoice. Just five

verses prior, the prophecies of judgment turned into a message of hope. God's wrath is not the final word. God will give the people clean lips, and all of God's scattered children will worship and serve God on one accord. There will be peace, and they will have nothing to fear. This vision of unity and serenity invites the Children of Israel to praise the Lord because God acts on their behalf. God has removed any judgments against them. God has removed their enemies from oppressing them. And that same God is among them.

What song would you sing in response to how God has moved in your life?

2. God Sings a Song of Joy (vv. 16–18)

God's love restores the soul and spirit of the Children of Israel. In these verses, Zephaniah declares that there is a new day. This day is the day God will be a warrior who brings victory. This day brings God's rejoicing and renewal of God's people. Previously, the Israelites had undergone distress, anguish, and bitter cries (Zephaniah 1:14–15); now is the day of God singing. How great must this day be if it causes God to bring forth a song? He promises to lovingly gather the mournful and remove their disgrace with His love.

Close your eyes and imagine how you would feel if God started singing over you. What would cause the Lord to sing today?

3. Full Restoration (vv. 19–20)

In these final verses, we are reminded that God's restoration is complete. While the previous verses deal with the remnant's spiritual, emotional, and mental wellness, these verses address their social location. They have been oppressed, cast away, and robbed of their fortune. They did not get to experience whatever goodness came with their identity. Instead they were mocked and shamed for it. Due to their social location, they were treated as inferior.

God promises to do more than remove their oppressors. God promises to bring the remnant together, give them a good name, and restore their fortunes. In this final vision, there is no lack in the remnant. They are full relationally because God loves them. They have an identity, and they have a community of gathered people. They are full socially because those who were not able to help themselves are in God's care, and they have full access to their fortunes.

What makes our restoration complete?

Search the Scriptures

1. God promises to do a lot of things in these verses, yet the Children of Israel are only asked to do two things: sing and fear not. Why do you think that these are the actions the prophet and the Lord asked them to take?

2. How is God's forgiveness at work in this text? (v. 15)

Discuss the Meaning

In order to truly appreciate today's readings, one must read the entire book of Zephaniah. It is only then that the full weight of God's redemption and restoration is clear. Just when it looked like there was no hope for redemption, God turns it all around and establishes a new world order with God, the King of Israel, in charge. The Lord creates a kingdom where there is no suffering, no oppression, no shame, no enemies, and no disaster. Even their enemies are turned away or have clean lips (cf. 3:9), and they are forgiven people. All of their idolatry is behind them. The Children of Israel can live free from fear. Their God has given them the victory.

How do we trust God to bring victory in our lives today?

Liberating Lesson

Zephaniah paints a complex picture of restoration. Many changes are necessary in order for God's children to be fully restored to a new day. God must turn from wrath, God's people must turn toward serving God only, God's people must turn away from oppressing each other, and enemies must turn away from oppressing God's people. It seems nearly impossible to believe that all of this change can come, especially when we have suffered for so long. Yet there are two lessons from this reflection. We as God's people can make different decisions that turn us in the right direction and make us active participants in our own restoration. Furthermore, Zephaniah reminds us that we do not act alone. God turns from wrath, God changes us, and God turns away our enemies. Restoration is only possible because God is in our midst.

How can we as a church participate in our own restoration? How has God changed us?

Application for Activation

1. Replace praise and worship with a traditional testimony and song service during a regular service to focus on responding to the Lord with joy.

2. Read Martin Luther King, Jr.'s book *Strength to Love.*

3. Plan a trip to your local museum that focuses on Black history and has a debriefing session on the impact.

Follow the Spirit

What God wants me to do:

_____

_____

_____

_____

Remember Your Thoughts
Special insights I have learned:

_____

_____

_____

_____

More Light on the Text
Zephaniah 3:14–20
The book of Zephaniah begins with incredible descriptions of God's wrath, but it ends in almost indescribable joy. For those who heard the earlier words of the prophet, this final section of the book must have been nothing but mind-boggling. A bewildered remnant now realizes that God's displeasure with them is gone, and the tension between the Lord and the nations is now resolved. Here we find a message of hope and encouragement based on the knowledge that with God all things are possible and that God is the Lord in spite of human circumstances and situation. Now that the judgment has passed, the people may sing for joy at the blessings and goodness of God.

14 Sing, O daughter of Zion; shout, O Israel; be glad and rejoice with all the heart, O daughter of Jerusalem. 15 The LORD hath taken away thy judgments, he hath cast out thine enemy: the king of Israel, even the LORD, is in the midst of thee: thou shalt not see evil any more.

Zephaniah 3:14–17 functions as a prophetic response to the divine declarations in the preceding verses. The command to rejoice was used by town heralds calling the city to rejoice when messengers from the battlefield brought the good news of victory and deliverance. The term *ranan* (Heb. **raw-NAN**, "sing") represents a joyous shout. The verse contains four imperative verbs that are similar in meaning ("sing," "shout aloud," "be glad," "rejoice") and three vocatives that refer to the people of Israel in general and Jerusalem in particular ("O Daughter of Zion," "O Israel," "O Daughter of Jerusalem"). The redeemed people should be glad and rejoice with all their heart. Their praise must not be perfunctory. They have real cause to rejoice.

In verse 15, the three reasons for rejoicing are given: (1) The punishment and the enemy have been turned away. "Judgments" refers to the punishment of the Lord's sentence of condemnation against the city. These are the judgments that have fallen upon Israel through all her history. (2) The enemy is cast out. This prediction and promise are in the singular. The "enemy" is not specified but may refer to those who collaborated with the Assyrians in the past, but it is most likely refers to all Judah's enemies. However, the chief enemy of Israel was sin in conduct and sin in the heart. God's salvation from sin here is total. There is nothing now to alienate the Holy One; atonement has been achieved. (3) The Lord is king in the midst of her. He is there to protect, and therefore Israel need have no more fear. The idea of the Lord as King is common in the Old Testament. Early in Old Testament history, Israel praised the Lord, who "will reign forever and ever" (Exodus 15:18). The Lord manifested himself as "king over Jeshurun" (Deuteronomy 33:2–5). Gideon would not accept the people's desire to crown him king because "the Lord will rule over you" (Judges 8:23).

16 In that day it shall be said to Jerusalem, Fear thou not: and to Zion, Let not thine hands be slack.

What a difference the presence of God makes! It gives peace of heart. So, "in that day" refers to the day when the judgment is complete and God's blessings completely manifest. Then Zion, a synonym for Jerusalem that specifically refers to the temple mount, will have no reason to fear. The expression "do not let your hands hang slack" is unfamiliar to our culture. In Hebrew thought, the hand symbolized strength or power. Letting the hands hang slack referred to a feeling of weakness or powerlessness, a sense of discouragement. Slack hands are a symbol of despair and an indication of the loss of power (Deuteronomy 32:36), so now with Yahweh in their midst and with nothing to fear, let the fallen hands be lifted up.

17 The LORD thy God in the midst of thee is mighty; he will save, he will rejoice over thee with joy; he will rest in his love, he will joy over thee with singing.

Here is the real basis of courage and hope. The Lord is in the midst of His people. When His people slide into idolatry and sin, He withdraws Himself from them (cf. Ezekiel 11:22–24). The word translated "mighty" is *gibbor*, (Heb. **gih-BORE**), an adjective usually used as a noun, often translated "hero" or "warrior" (cf. 1:14). It is used most frequently with military activities to describe one who has already distinguished himself by performing heroic deeds. In this case, the Word speaks of God who is a warrior who brings salvation. In other contexts as well, God is called by the name "mighty God" (*'el gibbor*, **EL gib-BORE**, cf. Isaiah 9:6; 10:21). Here the Divine Warrior has declared peace. He will save. He will issue no more battle cries. He will wreak no more havoc. His people have no reason for fear except a healthy "fear of the Lord" (3:7, 15–16). He has accomplished his purpose. He has vanquished the proud. The holy, humble remnant now seeks him in righteousness.

The rest of the verse is a vivid description of God's love for his people. Here we have an expression of the deepest joy and satisfaction of God Himself in His love for His people. God is ecstatic over the return of His wandering people. He is portrayed as rejoicing over them with singing. The last three lines should be taken together with the general sense that God delights in the people whom He has redeemed.

The middle phrase has presented a particular difficulty. The phrase expresses the renewal of the relationship between God and His estranged lovers. Such a conceptualization would draw on the well-known tradition of Israel/Zion as Yahweh's bride to portray God's return to His long-forsaken bride (see Hosea 2; Jeremiah 2; Ezekiel 16). Yahweh joins the people's singing and soothes them with divine love. This amazing love of God for human beings is inexplicable. Human minds would never dream up such a God. Human actions or human character could never deserve such love. In the core of His being, God is love (1 John 4:8). Zephaniah thus sings the prelude to the kind of love Jesus reveals on the Cross, a love that "surpasses knowledge" (Ephesians 3:19). How can this not cause God's people to praise! Surely the greatest reason for them to offer praise is found here.

18 I will gather them that are sorrowful for the solemn assembly, who are of thee, to whom the reproach of it was a burden.

Only Yahweh speaks in 3:18–20. At this point, He summarizes His acts of grace by saying He will deal with Israel's oppressors and bring her scattered people home. The prophecy's plot is now also complete. Jehovah will demonstrate His love for the pious of Israel by gathering them together to Himself. But before this can be done, Judah must be scattered among the nations in judgment at hand. Through this refining experience, those would be restored who yearn for the presence of Yahweh, and to whom scattering from the presence of the Lord was considered a great reproach or disappointment. The prophet pictures a day when all of the sorrows associated with the people's sin and judgment would be removed. Their sorrow might refer to sorrow over the loss of Jerusalem as well as the feasts associated with it. Whatever grief the prophet sees among the people of God, he promises relief. The enemy's destruction will vanish. Worship opportunities will be purified and renewed. Social injustice will disappear from Israel's agenda. God's elect people will participate in joy and thanksgiving in God's appointed times of worship. People will rejoice, and God will be glorified.

19 Behold, at that time I will undo all that afflict thee: and I will save her that halteth, and gather her that was driven out; and I will get them praise and fame in every land where they have been put to shame.

God announced that He was about to do something about Jerusalem's oppressors. He would deal with those who would afflict His people: they would not escape the fire of His wrath. The use of "all" for the oppressors widens the picture and points to include everyone who had ever afflicted Zion, including Assyrians and Babylonians, as well as neighbors who took advantage of Jerusalem when the Babylonians attacked (Isaiah 60:14; Nahum 1:12). The people would no longer suffer oppression, because the Lord would gather them and bring them home (3:20). Those who "halteth" who are the lame, and those "driven out," referring to the banished or exiled, indicates the state of the people in a hapless, helpless, and homeless condition. As the Lord has made a promise to make of these a "strong nation" (Micah 4:6–7), so now He will make of them a "praise" instead of the shame they had been and that had been brought upon them. Thus, a change in status would also result in a change in reputation. Israel had been profaned by the experience of their exile. God promises this experience would never happen again. What a loving Savior God is, who turns mourning into dancing, sorrow into joy, and weeping into laughter.

20 At that time will I bring you again, even in the time that I gather you: for I will make you a name and a praise among all people of the earth, when I turn back your captivity before your eyes, saith the LORD.

With some slight change in wording, the first part of the verse closely repeats the promise made in the preceding verse. This is probably to give emphasis to God's determination to accomplish that which he has purposed. In language reminiscent of other promises of restoration from exile (Amos 9:14–15; Ezekiel 36:34–37), God promises to restore the fortunes of the people of Israel. He would again make them prosperous in the land. The restoration would occur "before your very eyes," that is, in your own day. The use of the personal pronoun "I" is striking (vv. 18–20). God takes personal responsibility for Israel's redemption and restoration. He would fulfill His promise so that all would see it. God would return the people to their land, and the people would experience praise and renown rather than shame and reproach.

The book ends where it began with a scene of the reversal of the whole world order. It began with devastating overthrow. It ended with the blessings of God's people being returned to the land. God's restoration of the nation in chapter three is as complete as His destruction of the world in chapter one. He is now a judge who pardons. The promise of Zephaniah will find its immediate fulfillment in the return from the seventy years of exile. At that time the people will be rescued and their reputation restored. In some sense, however, the fulfillment better describes the glorious promise of the Messianic age when the Lord promised through His Son to "take great delight in you … quiet you with his love, [and] … rejoice over you with singing" (Zephaniah 3:17).

Sources:

Allen, L. C. *The Books of Joel, Obadiah, Jonah, and Micah.* NICOT. Grand Rapids, MI: Eerdmans, 1976.

Baldwin, J. *Haggai, Zechariah, Malachi.* TOTC. Downers Grove, IL: InterVarsity Press, 1972.

Barker, Kenneth L. *Micah, Nahum, Habakkuk, Zephaniah.* Vol. 20, The New American Commentary. Nashville, TN: Broadman & Holman Publishers, 1999.

Keil, C. F. *The Twelve Minor Prophets: Biblical Commentary on the Old Testament.* Trans. J. Martin. Grand Rapids, MI: Eerdmans, 1954.

Ralph L. Smith. *Micah–Malachi.* Vol. 32. Word Biblical Commentary. Dallas, TX: Word, Incorporated, 1998.

Sweeney, Marvin A. *Zephaniah: A Commentary.* Editor Paul D. Hanson. Hermeneia—A Critical and Historical Commentary on the Bible. Minneapolis, MN: Fortress Press, 2003.

Say It Correctly

Jeshurun. ye-**SHOO**-run.
Zephaniah. **ZEH**-fuh-**NYE**-uh.

Daily Bible Readings

MONDAY
God Promises Restoration of Israel's Fortunes
(Deuteronomy 30:1–6)

TUESDAY
God Will Shepherd the People
(Ezekiel 34:11–16)

WEDNESDAY
God Will Strengthen the People
(Zechariah 10:6–12)

THURSDAY
Christ's Forgiveness of Israel's Sins
(Acts 5:27–32)

FRIDAY
Leaders, Priests, and Prophets Don't Listen
(Zephaniah 3:1–7)

SATURDAY
God Will Preserve a Remnant
(Zephaniah 3:8–13)

SUNDAY
Rejoice in God's Glory and Salvation
(Zephaniah 3:14–20)

Notes

_____

_____

_____

_____

Teaching Tips

Words You Should Know

A. Truth (v. 3) *'emet* (Heb.)—True doctrine, faithfulness, sureness, stability

B. Marvellous (v. 6) *pala'* (Heb.)— Remarkable, difficult, miraculous

Teacher Preparation

Unifying Principle—A New Day Is Coming! Sometimes people respond to evil conditions in the world with a sense of hopelessness, regret, and doom. Where can they find motivation for continuing? The prophet Zechariah delivers God's promise of a new world of peace and prosperity for God's people.

A. Read the Bible Background and Devotional Readings.

B. Pray for your students and lesson clarity.

C. Read the lesson Scripture in multiple translations.

O—Open the Lesson

A. Begin the class with prayer.

B. Ask learners to share occasions when they've been part of a "How many times do I have to tell you?" scenario.

C. Have the students read the Aim for Change and the In Focus story.

D. Ask students how events like those in the story weigh on their hearts and how they can view these events from a faith perspective.

P—Present the Scriptures

A. Read the Focal Verses.

B. Have the class share what Scriptures stand out for them and why, with particular emphasis on today's context.

C. Discuss the Background and The People, Places, and Times sections.

E—Explore the Meaning

A. Use In Depth or More Light on the Text to facilitate a deeper discussion of the lesson text.

B. Pose the questions in Search the Scriptures and Discuss the Meaning.

C. Discuss the Liberating Lesson and Application for Activation sections.

N—Next Steps for Application

A. Summarize the value of staying in tune with God's will by listening to what He says in His Word.

B. End class with a commitment to pray to live in a way that invites unbelievers to accept God's eternal peace and justice.

Worship Guide

For the Superintendent or Teacher
Theme: Peace and Justice Reign
Song: "We're Marching to Zion"
Devotional Reading: Zechariah 8:18–23

Peace and Justice Reign

Bible Background • ZECHARIAH 8
Printed Text • ZECHARIAH 8:1–8, 11–17 | Devotional Reading • ZECHARIAH 8:18–23

———————————— Aim for Change ————————————

By the end of the lesson, we will: COMPREHEND the impact of God's presence in a community, YEARN for God's perpetual presence and the promise of justice it brings, and PRAY for God's presence to result in a communal sense of justice, prosperity, and unity.

———————————— In Focus ————————————

Christine and Michael walked slowly through the immense destruction of their house. They were searching and hoping to find some photos of their children and Michael's wedding ring. He had just taken the ring off to work on their car when the tornado siren sounded. Michael's only thought was to run to the house to gather his children and wife. They met as he bounded up the steps of the porch. They went to the special room he had just completed for a storm like this. He never thought they would really use it or at least not this soon. After two minutes that felt like forever, the winds ceased. Michael slowly opened the door and walked cautiously up the steps. The darkness was replaced with bright sunshine. As his eyes adjusted, he had seen utter destruction. In the midst of this chaos and calamity, how would they ever find his wedding ring or the pictures?

Michael decided he and Christine should stop and pray. As they prayed, others joined them. After the prayer, they walked and found the family photo of all the children and themselves. They smiled and hugged each other. Even if they did not find the ring, the picture was a reminder of how God had shown mercy and blessed them in many ways.

What would you look for if your possessions were devastated in a powerful storm or an unbelievable situation? Do you pray and trust God right away, or do you turn to God later? What are ways God blesses people even when all hope is lost?

———————————— Keep in Mind ————————————

"So again have I thought in these days to do well unto Jerusalem and to the house of Judah: fear ye not" (Zechariah 8:15, KJV).

"But now I am determined to bless Jerusalem and the people of Judah. So don't be afraid" (Zechariah 8:15, NLT).

Focal Verses

KJV **Zechariah 8:1** Again the word of the LORD of hosts came to me, saying,

2 Thus saith the LORD of hosts; I was jealous for Zion with great jealousy, and I was jealous for her with great fury.

3 Thus saith the LORD; I am returned unto Zion, and will dwell in the midst of Jerusalem: and Jerusalem shall be called a city of truth; and the mountain of the LORD of hosts the holy mountain.

4 Thus saith the LORD of hosts; There shall yet old men and old women dwell in the streets of Jerusalem, and every man with his staff in his hand for very age.

5 And the streets of the city shall be full of boys and girls playing in the streets thereof.

6 Thus saith the LORD of hosts; If it be marvellous in the eyes of the remnant of this people in these days, should it also be marvellous in mine eyes? saith the LORD of hosts.

7 Thus saith the LORD of hosts; Behold, I will save my people from the east country, and from the west country;

8 And I will bring them, and they shall dwell in the midst of Jerusalem: and they shall be my people, and I will be their God, in truth and in righteousness.

11 But now I will not be unto the residue of this people as in the former days, saith the LORD of hosts.

12 For the seed shall be prosperous; the vine shall give her fruit, and the ground shall give her increase, and the heavens shall give their dew; and I will cause the remnant of this people to possess all these things.

13 And it shall come to pass, that as ye were a curse among the heathen, O house of Judah, and house of Israel; so will I save you, and ye shall be a blessing: fear not, but let your hands be strong.

NLT **Zechariah 8:1** Then another message came to me from the LORD of Heaven's Armies:

2 "This is what the LORD of Heaven's Armies says: My love for Mount Zion is passionate and strong; I am consumed with passion for Jerusalem!

3 And now the LORD says: I am returning to Mount Zion, and I will live in Jerusalem. Then Jerusalem will be called the Faithful City; the mountain of the LORD of Heaven's Armies will be called the Holy Mountain.

4 This is what the LORD of Heaven's Armies says: Once again old men and women will walk Jerusalem's streets with their canes and will sit together in the city squares.

5 And the streets of the city will be filled with boys and girls at play.

6 This is what the LORD of Heaven's Armies says: All this may seem impossible to you now, a small remnant of God's people. But is it impossible for me? says the LORD of Heaven's Armies.

7 This is what the LORD of Heaven's Armies says: You can be sure that I will rescue my people from the east and from the west.

8 I will bring them home again to live safely in Jerusalem. They will be my people, and I will be faithful and just toward them as their God.

11 But now I will not treat the remnant of my people as I treated them before, says the LORD of Heaven's Armies.

12 For I am planting seeds of peace and prosperity among you. The grapevines will be heavy with fruit. The earth will produce its crops, and the heavens will release the dew. Once more I will cause the remnant in Judah and Israel to inherit these blessings.

13 Among the other nations, Judah and Israel became symbols of a cursed nation. But no longer! Now I will rescue you and make you both a symbol and a source of blessing. So don't

14 For thus saith the LORD of hosts; As I thought to punish you, when your fathers provoked me to wrath, saith the LORD of hosts, and I repented not:

15 So again have I thought in these days to do well unto Jerusalem and to the house of Judah: fear ye not.

16 These are the things that ye shall do; Speak ye every man the truth to his neighbour; execute the judgment of truth and peace in your gates:

17 And let none of you imagine evil in your hearts against his neighbour; and love no false oath: for all these are things that I hate, saith the LORD.

be afraid. Be strong, and get on with rebuilding the Temple!

14 For this is what the LORD of Heaven's Armies says: I was determined to punish you when your ancestors angered me, and I did not change my mind, says the LORD of Heaven's Armies.

15 But now I am determined to bless Jerusalem and the people of Judah. So don't be afraid.

16 But this is what you must do: Tell the truth to each other. Render verdicts in your courts that are just and that lead to peace.

17 Don't scheme against each other. Stop your love of telling lies that you swear are the truth. I hate all these things, says the LORD."

The People, Places, and Times

Zechariah. One of the twelve minor prophets whose collective work concludes the Old Testament. Zechariah wanted to motivate the Jews to rebuild the Temple after their return from exile in Babylonia, but he used a different approach from that of his contemporary Haggai. Prophesying between August and December of 520 BC, Haggai promised the Jews an end to their crop failures and economic misery, giving God's message that "from this day will I bless you" (Haggai 2:19). Zechariah, prophesying from 520 BC to perhaps 480 BC, promised them a Messiah and a return to the glorious days of King David.

Background

Zechariah's prophetic ministry began in the summer of 520 BC in Jerusalem, in the years between the arrival of the first group of returning captives from Babylonia (536 BC) and the completion of the rebuilding of the temple (516 BC). Both Zechariah and Haggai prophesied about the situation in Jerusalem immediately after the Babylonian captivity. Most of the city was still desolate. There was no Temple; it had been destroyed by Nebuchadnezzar. Everything around them

was in ruins. The people found this situation too daunting; could this land ever recover? Could the Lord ever return to Zion? Could life come back to these dried bones (Ezekiel 37)? Ezra tells us that soon after the remnant Jews arrived in Jerusalem, they embarked on the work of restoring the Temple, starting with the altar (Ezra 3). Their intention was to rebuild the Temple as well, but their drive to work petered out. There were too many distractions, especially from the numerous enemies around them. Haggai, who prophesied at the same time as Zechariah, tells us of the state of the Temple at the time. The people had settled down in durable houses while the Lord's house remained in ruins (Haggai 1:3–5). Zechariah emerged to be one of the prophets speaking hope and encouragement to the people. He is generally characterized as a prophet who challenges the remnants to believe that the Lord would actually remember Zion. He was a visionary prophet who inspired the people as they sought to rebuild the Temple.

Think of a situation in your life, your neighborhood, or even in your state/the country that seems desolate. What is your innermost response to the desolation?

At-A-Glance

1. God is Jealous for Judah (Zechariah 8:1–2)
2. God will restore Judah (vv. 3-8, 11–12)
3. Judah must Return to God (vv. 13–17)

In Depth

1. God is Jealous for Judah (Zechariah 8:1–2)

Zechariah ministered among a discouraged and indifferent community of people who had returned from Babylon to a city they called home but that looked nothing like it. When the people were too discouraged to care about God's house, God still cared for them enough to send prophets to help them build the Temple (for the people's own good). The Lord is quite stern in his assertion, "I was jealous for Zion with great jealousy, and I was jealous for her with great fury." God is jealous with a true kind of jealousy and, here, we see how that jealousy shapes God's relationship with Judah. On the one hand, God wants to be the only one receiving Judah's worship. Israel was not supposed to worship any other gods because the Lord, their God, is a jealous God. When they showed interest in other gods or started to follow the gods of the Gentiles, God's wrath was unleashed upon them, and they were severely punished. These punishments often took the form of foreign invasions by other nations that God used to chastise Israel. However, here we learn that God's jealousy compels Him to return to His people and bring them hope for the future.

Do you ever feel God being jealous over other things that try to take His place in your life?

2. God will Restore Judah (vv. 3–8, 11–12)

God does not just rescue Judah from captivity both in the east and in the west. God's people will return to Jerusalem. They will rebuild the city, and God will dwell in it again. The Temple that lay in ruins at the time of the Babylonian captivity was to be rebuilt. The worship of Yahweh would take place in Jerusalem again. But with all this, the Lord would restore the people of Jerusalem. There will be peace and economic growth again in the city even though it seems desolate at the time of Zechariah. Where there is now only death and destruction, God will bring life and hope. Joy and gladness will replace the sorrow and mourning that characterized life for the captives. There will be large families again in the city, with grandparents and grandchildren seen in the streets of the city without a care for their safety. The earth will yield her increase. This is a far-fetched "dream" of a future that seems unrealistic to the hearers, yet God is asking for the people's trust.

How do you respond when God says something to you that sounds impossible?

3. Judah must Return to God (vv. 13–17)

God is eager to bless Israel as they re-establish themselves and re-devote themselves to rebuilding the Temple. He reminds Israel why they are in this state: God had to punish their ancestors for their sin, but now their punishment is complete, and He is pleased to bless His people again. However, the Israelites do have a part to play in their restoration. They must promise to obey the God who is blessing them. The Lord requires the Jews to avoid the negative policies that precipitated their fall into exile. They must reform their justice system so that the truth is told and peace is sought. Schemes and perjury have no place in a nation God is restoring to fellowship with Him.

Search the Scriptures

1. Zechariah promises the day when the Lord will dwell in Jerusalem. Who else makes such

a prophecy? What were the circumstances that caused the Lord to leave Zion?

2. What scenes of peace does Zechariah's prophecy highlight (vv. 4–5, 12)?

3. What must Israel do now that God is with them again (vv. 16–17)?

Discuss the Meaning

The Lord has previously told the Israelites that His name is Jealousy (Exodus 34:14), which He reaffirms here. Yet, in our culture today, jealousy is usually spoken of as a negative emotion that should be avoided. Is there such a thing as healthy or holy jealousy?

Liberating Lesson

The principle theme of the text is that God will return to Jerusalem to be the God of His people once again. This is unbelievably good news to the people. Thus, we are reminded that God's wrath does not endure forever. Only His loving kindness does (Psalm 136). He forgives, and if we return to the covenant that we have with Him, He rescues us from whatever or whoever is holding us captive, drawing us back to Himself. We must return to all parts of the covenant though to protect us from falling again into a place removed from God's presence. Covenant keepers do not lie. Covenant keepers practice good judgment, especially in a legal setting. Covenant keepers want good and not evil for our neighbors. What social systems that God set up in His covenant with Israel could help us today bring good judgment to our courts?

Application for Activation

God is with us, and He is in control. That is the chill-pill that we all need: to know that God is with us. We are in a covenant with the faithful God who can never break a promise. He will cause the sun to shine on us again and the dew to water our efforts. He will heal us from our sicknesses and save us from the schemes of the enemy. However, He asks us to trust Him with our very lives and obey His every word. How different would our lives be if we trusted Him in everything? Take some time, this week, to think and write about an area where you can give God more trust. Share your desire with someone close to you so they can help encourage and remind you.

Follow the Spirit

What God wants me to do:

_____

_____

_____

_____

Remember Your Thoughts

Special insights I have learned:

_____

_____

_____

_____

More Light on the Text
Zechariah 8:1–8, 11–17

Zechariah paints a picture of the radical change for the better that had begun in Jerusalem, while the nations that chastised Judah would soon be punished. He looks forward to the future in hope. Against the negative and pessimistic tone of his message in Zechariah 7, here the message is balanced with a positive and optimistic series of oracles. The rebuke of chapter 7 changes into a promise of a glorious future for Judah in chapter 8. Indeed, in chapter 7, Judah was admonished to repent and live righteously after the punishment of her time in captivity, while in chapter 8, she is to repent and live righteously because of the promise of her future restoration—a restoration that apparently has already started. In this spirit of optimism, each of the seven oracles in chapter 8 contains a few words of encouragement for the remnant—those who have returned from Babylonia. Overall, these seven oracles are thought to form a theological summary of the book; language and themes are rehearsed in this chapter in a rapid staccato style that emphasizes the centrality of Zion in God's plan, the need for ethical living, and the need to see God's hand at work in the midst of current events. Zechariah 8:1–17 promises that the Lord will return to Zion, focuses on the changes that the Lord's presence in Jerusalem will produce, and then implores the people to be faithful to God and one another in this restored city of Jerusalem.

1 Again the word of the LORD of hosts came to me, saying, 2 Thus saith the LORD of hosts; I was jealous for Zion with great jealousy, and I was jealous for her with great fury.

The situation is dire. There is no hope in the city, and there is no hope for the city. Each person takes care of their own property and has no desire or energy to pay attention to the larger community projects, the most important of which is the house of the Lord. Yet, to these people in this condition, the word of the Lord of hosts comes through Zechariah. Here and in five other oracles, the Lord is called the "LORD of hosts," Yahweh who commands angel armies. This Lord of the mighty heavenly hosts always comes through for God's people, and often, when the Lord breaks through to deliver God's people, it is through the word of the prophet. The presence of the prophets—Haggai,

Zechariah, and later, Malachi—shows that God still cared for Judah. As a matter of fact, it is this passionate caring that causes the Lord to be jealous for His people.

Here, as in Zechariah 1:14, the Lord's jealousy is declared. The dispiriting situation of Israel as a renewed political state caused the people to doubt that God would uphold His covenant with them, choosing to favor the nations instead. The Lord being a jealous God is a well-known fact among the remnant. Jehovah was always known to be a jealous God whose possessiveness and extreme intolerance to idols often expressed themselves in anger. The first of the Ten Commandments essentially states, "Thou shalt have no other gods before me ... for I the LORD thy God am a jealous God" (Exodus 20:3, 5). Later, we learn that one of the Lord's names is "Jealous" (34:14). Over and over again, we read of the Lord being a jealous God who threatens to punish Israel if provoked to anger (Deuteronomy 6:15; Joshua 24:19; Ezekiel 39:25; Nahum 1:2). The Lord's jealousy is a result of the covenant relationship that exists between God and Israel. The Lord cares so passionately for Zion that exclusive worship is expected, and when Israel went after other gods, punishment followed. Thus, in the past, God's jealousy had brought many great hardships upon Israel whenever she broke her covenant.

This time though, God's wrath is directed not to God's people but to the surrounding nations who took advantage of Judah when God punished her. This jealousy promises comfort to Jerusalem since it leads to the punishment of the nations oppressing her. Just like a jealous husband would protect his wife, God's protective love over Judah now causes God's wrath to go after the nations that oppressed her. The Lord promises to act on Zion's behalf and to protect her from the surrounding nations that threaten her welfare. This burning love results in an exclusive relationship between the Lord and Judah and would ultimately result in a glorious future.

3 Thus saith the LORD; I am returned unto Zion, and will dwell in the midst of Jerusalem: and Jerusalem shall be called a city of truth; and the mountain of the LORD of hosts the holy mountain.

Here, Zechariah recalls the theme of the Lord's return to Jerusalem as had already been prophesied (1:16; 2:10). Earlier on, Ezekiel revealed that the Lord left both the Temple and Jerusalem, allowing the city to be destroyed by Nebuchadnezzar (Ezekiel 10:18–19; 11:22–23). Now, the Lord is promising to return to Jerusalem just as Ezekiel (43:1–5) and Haggai (1:8) had said. The sin that is spoken of by the prophets, even by Zechariah himself (Zechariah 7), has been reversed. The Lord now promises not just to return to Zion, but also to dwell among God's people in Jerusalem. This promise of the Lord's return to an abandoned city offers the strongest imaginable encouragement that the Lord is still with Judah and that, because of this, her future is secure.

With the Lord living in Jerusalem, the city will be renamed the city of truth. Thus, with the change of name comes the transformation of character. Jerusalem will no longer be only the city of peace; it will also be the truthful city—or a city of faithfulness, since "truth" (Heb. *'emet*, **EH-met**) can also be translated "faithfulness." Elsewhere, the city is a prostitute (Isaiah 1:21; Hosea 1–3), but this is not the case anymore. Her reputation is restored. The mountain of the Lord will again be known as the holy mountain of the Lord in the new city characterized by faithfulness. The Lord and the people will be faithful to the covenant between them. The Lord's faithfulness would be an assurance to the people that God will execute judgment to Israel's enemies on her behalf (Psalm 146:6). It would give them confidence

in God's protection from all external threats. In return, Judah's faithfulness means that the people will be obedient to God like never before. Consequently, they should no longer fear that the Lord will abandon them.

4 Thus saith the LORD of hosts; There shall yet old men and old women dwell in the streets of Jerusalem, and every man with his staff in his hand for very age. 5 And the streets of the city shall be full of boys and girls playing in the streets thereof.

The Lord continues here to make promises to Zion. There is a shift in the promises made from the spiritual type in the preceding verses—like the faithfulness that will cover the city—to some real-life implications of the Lord's presence in the city. Life will return to an unbelievable normalcy; there will be large, growing families in the city, for blessings always mean fertility. Old men and women will sit in the streets peacefully while young boys and girls play in the same streets. There will be no need to be concerned about their health or safety. Peace will reign, and people will live to an old age once again. The mention of the extreme ends of a human lifespan suggests that the entire population will enjoy an atmosphere of renewal and blessings. When the young and the old thrive, it shows the entire population is doing well. Rather than measuring the city's health by business or commerce, its wealth will be in two often-overlooked groups: the old and the young. May we measure the significance of our cities by their effect on how the young and the old live!

6 Thus saith the LORD of hosts; If it be marvellous in the eyes of the remnant of this people in these days, should it also be marvellous in mine eyes? saith the LORD of hosts.

It seems here that Zechariah's audience found it difficult to believe the oracles given in the chapter so far. To them, it was "marvellous"

(Heb. *pala'*, **paw-LAW**), a word referring to things that are remarkable or difficult, and by extension, a miracle of God. In all fairness, the promises seem impossible. It should make sense then that the people's response to Zechariah's message is that of wonder and doubt. Could far-fetched prophecies like these actually come to pass? Everything around them says otherwise. Their circumstances are discouraging—it is almost impossible to have hope. But the Lord answers their questions before they verbalize them. Is anything too hard for the Lord? Should an action be too difficult for the Lord to accomplish merely because it exceeds human reach? Zechariah had prophesied earlier that the reestablishment of the people and the Temple in Jerusalem would happen "not by power, nor by might, but by the spirit of the Lord" (Zechariah 4:6).

God Almighty, the Lord of hosts, can do what the remnant of His people thinks is impossible. There is nothing too hard for the Lord (Genesis 18:14, Jeremiah 32:27). Doubting the Lord simply shows that these people did not know the Lord for who He truly is. Doubt often weakens our faith and causes us to look to other "false gods" for support.

7 Thus saith the LORD of hosts; Behold, I will save my people from the east country, and from the west country; 8 And I will bring them, and they shall dwell in the midst of Jerusalem: and they shall be my people, and I will be their God, in truth and in righteousness.

Again, the Lord of hosts is speaking through Zechariah, making a four-fold promise to God's people that (1) the Lord will save His people from the east and the west, (2) the Lord will bring His people back to Jerusalem where they will dwell, and that (3) the Lord will be their God and they will be the Lord's people and (4) all this will happen in truth and righteousness. Indeed,

this is more than a promise; it is a declaration, hence the word "Behold" (Heb. *hennei*, **heh-NYE**), which could also be translated "Look at me." It is likely the phrase "east and west" means the land of the sun's rising and setting—the entire known world. Thus, the promise is not just to those who remain in Babylonia; it is to all scattered sons and daughters of Abraham around the world. The Lord will deliver these people, scattered in many places around the world, and bring them back to Jerusalem.

Once back in Jerusalem, they will live in truth (*'emet*) and righteousness (Heb. *tsedeqah*, **tseh-daw-KAW**; justice, salvation, truthfulness). Both the Lord and the people will be recognized and celebrate their covenant relationship. This fulfills the Lord's promise going all the way back to Abraham, "I will be their God" (Genesis 17:8). The same promise is also found throughout the Old Testament Scriptures (Exodus 6:7; Jeremiah 24:7; Ezekiel 11:20). Once again, the Lord declares that He will be their God and they will be His people. No other statement could evoke stronger memories of the covenant than this one. In saying, "I will be their God," the people are reminded of God's faithfulness—of how God kept them through the generations. They would also be encouraged to trust God for their future. If God is with them, nothing can destroy them.

11 But now I will not deal with the remnant of this people as in the former days, says the Lord of hosts. 12 For there shall be a sowing of peace; the vine shall yield its fruit, the ground shall give its produce, and the skies shall give their dew; and I will cause the remnant of this people to possess all these things. 13 Just as you have been a cursing among the nations, O house of Judah and house of Israel, so I will save you and you shall be a blessing. Do not be afraid, but let your hands be strong.

The Lord continues to make promises to the remnants; things would change for Israel now that the Temple is being rebuilt and worship is being restored. Their fortunes are about to change because the Lord will deal differently with them from the former days. These "former days" are likely the days of the exile, which Zechariah will soon reference more clearly (v. 14).

Now that they have returned, the Lord's attitude toward Israel is changing, and with it, the Lord's actions among the people. The Lord is reversing the economic depression that has made life difficult for the remnant. Again, in this promise, the Lord moves beyond the rebuke we find in the previous chapters. The people will do their farming in peace on fertile soil and with great weather conditions. Economic growth will return and with it, prosperity and normalcy. In its scattered state, Israel was like a curse, a byword, and a laughing stock among the nations, but the Lord reversed their condition. The Lord would rescue His people and change the attitudes of the nations toward them. Instead of being a curse, both Israel and Judah (as a people reunited) would become a blessing after the Lord had delivered them. Here, Zechariah once again evokes the covenant, echoing the promises that God gave to Abraham (Genesis 12:1–3), that he would be blessed to become a blessing among the nations. Furthermore, Zechariah realizes that the fulfillment of the promises may take both time and work and, therefore, he urges his audience to let their hands be strong.

14 For thus says the LORD of hosts: Just as I purposed to bring disaster upon you, when your ancestors provoked me to wrath, and I did not relent, says the LORD of hosts, 15 so again I have purposed in these days to do good to Jerusalem and to the house of Judah; do not be afraid. 16 These are the things that ye shall do; Speak ye every man the truth to his neighbour; execute the judgment of truth and peace in your gates: 17 And let none of you imagine evil in your hearts against his neighbour; and love no false oath: for all these are things that I hate, saith the LORD.

Here, the Lord is reconfirming the desire and the purpose to bless Israel. It is a strong commitment to do them good, and the Lord cannot relent from it. Before then, when the Lord purposed to bring disaster upon the people, it surely came to pass. There was no turning back. Here, it is with the same resolution that the Lord wants to bless His people. In response, the Lord wants the people to not be afraid. In other words, the Lord calls the people to put their trust in God's faithfulness. He had made a promise, and it would be fulfilled.

Still, the Lord places some ethical requirements upon the people. The people should, as a society, be truthful and just to one another, and seek to live in peace with one another. The Lord adds that the people should not devise evil against each other, nor should they love false oath, for the Lord hates these things. Indeed, the people should hate them as well, since they were covenanted to the Lord. In so doing, there seems an expectation of health and peaceful relationships among the people. This leads to further normalcy among the remnant.

Sources:

Collins, John J. Joel, Obadiah, Haggai, Zechariah, Malachi. *The New Collegeville Bible Commentary Old Testament*. Collegeville, MN: Liturgical Press, 2013.

Klein, George L. Zechariah: An Exegetical and Theological Exposition of Holy Scripture. *The American Commentary*. Nashville, TN: B&H Publishing Group, 2008.

Nogalski, James. The Book of the Twelve: Micah—Malachi. *The Smyth & Helwys Bible Commentary*. Macon, GA: Smyth & Helwys Pub., 2011.

Smith, Ralph L. Micah-Malachi. *Word Biblical Themes*. Dallas, TX: Word Pub., 1990.

Say It Correctly

Zechariah. ze-ka-**REYE**-uh.
Nebuchadnezzar. **NEH**-buh-kad-**NEZZ**-ar.

Daily Bible Readings

MONDAY
God's Worldwide Covenant with Abraham
(Genesis 12:1–8)

TUESDAY
A New Covenant of the Heart
(Jeremiah 31:31–34)

WEDNESDAY
Divided Peoples to Become One
(Ezekiel 37:15–23)

THURSDAY
Just Living in Church and World
(Romans 12:9–21)

FRIDAY
Cultivate Peaceful and Just Relations
(1 Thessalonians 5:12–22)

SATURDAY
Joyful Feasts Draw Newcomers
(Zechariah 8:18–23)

SUNDAY
Enjoy Fruits of Peace and Justice
(Zechariah 8:1–8, 11–17)

Notes

_____

_____

_____

_____

Teaching Tips

Words You Should Know

A. Prey (v. 9) *shalal* (Heb.)—Spoils, booty, goods captured in war

B. Evil (v. 10) *ra'ah* (Heb.)—Moral evil and wickedness; misfortune, trouble, disaster

Teacher Preparation

Unifying Principle—Just Rewards. Evil is pervasive throughout human society. Can people continue to do evil without consequence? Jeremiah tells us that God is a God of justice and will recompense evil.

A. Read the Bible Background and Devotional Readings.

B. Pray for your students and lesson clarity.

C. Read the lesson Scripture in multiple translations.

O—Open the Lesson

A. Begin the class with prayer.

B. As a class, discuss evils that continue to perpetuate in the world and why some people or groups are not punished.

C. Have the students read the Aim for Change and the In Focus story.

D. Ask students how events like those in the story weigh on their hearts and how they can view these events from a faith perspective.

P—Present the Scriptures

A. Read the Focal Verses.

B. Have the class share what Scriptures stand out for them and why, with particular emphasis on today's context.

C. Discuss the Background and The People, Places, and Times sections.

E—Explore the Meaning

A. Use In Depth or More Light on the Text to facilitate a deeper discussion of the lesson text.

B. Pose the questions in Search the Scriptures and Discuss the Meaning.

C. Discuss the Liberating Lesson and Application for Activation sections.

N—Next Steps for Application

A. Summarize the lesson that God is always fair—even when situations seem difficult to understand.

B. End class with a commitment to pray for courage to take unpopular stances.

Worship Guide

For the Superintendent or Teacher
Theme: Practice Justice
Song: "I'm Gonna Live So"
Devotional Reading: Psalm 86:1–13

Practice Justice

Bible Background • JEREMIAH 21
Printed Text • JEREMIAH 21:8–14 | Devotional Reading • PSALM 86:1–13

———————————— **Aim for Change** ————————————

By the end of the lesson, we will: DISCOVER divine justice described by Jeremiah, EXPRESS gratitude that God is a God of justice, and ENDEAVOR to be just and advocate for justice.

———————————————— **In Focus** ————————————————

The judge pounded her gavel after sentencing John to five years in prison. John couldn't believe this. He had turned his life around and volunteered with the youth in the church and the community. Yet the judge said that he made the mistake of trusting someone who really meant him harm. John thought it was okay to hang with his old friends this one time. Little did he know what they were planning. Had he realized they were serious about stealing the boxes off the delivery truck, he would have stayed in the store or returned to his car. John realized God had given him a chance to walk away before things happened, but John stayed, trying to convince his friends not to steal the packages. By the time he was ready to leave, the police were already there and it was too late.

After a year and a half in prison, two of his friends put in writing that John was not a part of the plan and that they had proof. The Community Criminal Defense Fund took up John's case. After three years in prison, John was released and his record expunged. John was ready for a new beginning and new friends.

Identify a time when you decided not to listen to the Lord. What were the results? Describe a time when someone asked you for your advice. Was your advice received or was it rejected?

———————————————— **Keep in Mind** ————————————————

"O house of David, thus saith the LORD; Execute judgment in the morning, and deliver him that is spoiled out of the hand of the oppressor, lest my fury go out like fire, and burn that none can quench it, because of the evil of your doings" (Jeremiah 21:12, KJV).

"This is what the LORD says to the dynasty of David: Give justice each morning to the people you judge! Help those who have been robbed; rescue them from their oppressors Otherwise, my anger will burn like an unquenchable fire because of all your sins" (Jeremiah 21:12, NLT).

Focal Verses

KJV Jeremiah 21:8 And unto this people thou shalt say, Thus saith the LORD; Behold, I set before you the way of life, and the way of death.

9 He that abideth in this city shall die by the sword, and by the famine, and by the pestilence: but he that goeth out, and falleth to the Chaldeans that besiege you, he shall live, and his life shall be unto him for a prey.

10 For I have set my face against this city for evil, and not for good, saith the LORD: it shall be given into the hand of the king of Babylon, and he shall burn it with fire.

11 And touching the house of the king of Judah, say, Hear ye the word of the LORD;

12 O house of David, thus saith the LORD; Execute judgment in the morning, and deliver him that is spoiled out of the hand of the oppressor, lest my fury go out like fire, and burn that none can quench it, because of the evil of your doings.

13 Behold, I am against thee, O inhabitant of the valley, and rock of the plain, saith the LORD; which say, Who shall come down against us? or who shall enter into our habitations?

14 But I will punish you according to the fruit of your doings, saith the LORD: and I will kindle a fire in the forest thereof, and it shall devour all things round about it.

NLT Jeremiah 21:8 "Tell all the people, 'This is what the LORD says: Take your choice of life or death!

9 Everyone who stays in Jerusalem will die from war, famine, or disease, but those who go out and surrender to the Babylonians will live. Their reward will be life!

10 For I have decided to bring disaster and not good upon this city, says the LORD. It will be handed over to the king of Babylon, and he will reduce it to ashes.'

11 Say to the royal family of Judah, 'Listen to this message from the LORD!

12 This is what the LORD says to the dynasty of David: Give justice each morning to the people you judge! Help those who have been robbed; rescue them from their oppressors. Otherwise, my anger will burn like an unquenchable fire because of all your sins.

13 I will personally fight against the people in Jerusalem, that mighty fortress—the people who boast, "No one can touch us here. No one can break in here."

14 And I myself will punish you for your sinfulness, says the LORD. I will light a fire in your forests that will burn up everything around you.'"

The People, Places, and Times

Jerusalem During the Time of the Prophets (750–586 BC). Jerusalem was a walled city during the time of the prophets. Located between the Hinnom and Kidron Valleys, Jerusalem was surrounded by the Mount of Olives. Refugees arrived in Jerusalem about the time of the fall of the Northern Kingdom (722 BC). Settlement spread to the western hill, and a new wall was added for protection. Hezekiah carved an underground aqueduct out of solid rock to bring an ample water supply inside the city walls, enabling Jerusalem to survive the siege of Sennacherib in 701 BC.

Jeremiah. Jeremiah is one of the giants of Old Testament prophecy. The son of a priest, he was born in Anathoth, a village three miles northeast of Jerusalem. Jeremiah received his calling as a prophet in 626 BC during the thirteenth year of King Josiah's reign. The book of Jeremiah reveals a lot about the inner turmoil and conflict out of which Jeremiah delivered his prophetic burden. Jeremiah's life demonstrates the hardships that sometime accompany the task of bringing God's word to His people. Perhaps anticipating the difficulties of being a prophet, Jeremiah resisted his call to prophetic ministry, citing his youth as an obstacle (Jeremiah 1:6–9). But God's will cannot be resisted. Jeremiah followed his calling faithfully, but the road was hard. He was rejected by his people (Jeremiah 15:10). He was frustrated by their hardheartedness (Jeremiah 5:3). He was cut off from the normal joys and pleasures of life (Jeremiah 16:9). In spite of all of the difficulties that Jeremiah experienced, he found that he could not resist God's call to prophesy. He had to declare the word of the LORD as the LORD had directed him. It was a compulsion. It was a dynamic, powerful inner motivation that made him prophesy. "Then I said, I will not make mention of him, nor speak any more in his name. But his word was in mine heart as a burning fire shut up in my bones, and I was weary with forbearing, and I could not stay" (Jeremiah 20:9).

Background

Jeremiah first began to prophesy under King Josiah (639–609). Jeremiah witnessed a great spiritual revival and awakening in Jerusalem that took place when Josiah was in office. Then Josiah was killed attempting to stop an Egyptian Pharaoh from marching through Judah. For a brief period, Judah was under the control of Egypt. This event marked the beginning of a terrible time for Judah. Eventually, Nebuchadnezzar of Babylon took control of countries north of Judah, leaving them sandwiched in between these two powerful nations. At various times both threatened to wipe out God's chosen nation. God spoke through Jeremiah during these alarming, turbulent times. He attempted to persuade them to repentance and faithfulness to Yahweh and laid before them the consequences of their rebellion against Yahweh.

Unfortunately, the people chose to listen to false prophets who spoke comfort and peace

to them in the midst of their unfaithfulness. Jeremiah to them was a nuisance. They rejected the word of the Lord from the mouth of Jeremiah. It is a stern cautionary tale to people who claim to be in a relationship with the just God but prioritize oppression and self-centeredness. God does not prioritize oppressors even if they consider themselves to be His chosen people. God's chosen people are the weak and vulnerable. This could seem contradictory since the Babylonians are more corrupt people; however, the prophet frames the Babylonians' destruction of Jerusalem as a prime example of God's zero tolerance for exploitation. In the same way that Judah receives its punishment, the Babylonians' turn is coming too. Jeremiah calls us to remember that we must consistently consider whose side we are on, because God will not stand by us if we are wrong and wronging others. We should consider the following: Where are we standing against God? And how can we move to God's side before its too late?

At-A-Glance

1. The Paradox of the Malpractice of Justice (Jeremiah 21:8–10)
2. The Priority of the Practice of Justice (vv. 11–12)
3. The Price of the Malpractice of Justice (vv. 13–14)

In Depth

1. The Paradox of the Malpractice of Justice (Jeremiah 21:8–10)

Because the people of Judah had practiced evil, they were given only two bleak options: Submit to Babylonian domination or fight unsuccessfully. The prophet frames their dire condition as a result of their own lack of concern for the lowly. Neither of their options is desirable, but their lack of options is directly correlated to their not providing options to the most vulnerable. The people of Judah that would be taken away as captives would have been the elite who had benefited from exploiting others. The land that would be burned with fire would be the land that had produced an abundance, but the fruit of the land had been marked up, overpriced, and placed outside of the reach of the poor who worked the land so that the wealthy could live even more luxuriously. Although it looks like they have no options, they do. They had chosen the wrong ones, which led to their current collision with Babylonia.

It is important to consider whose oppression we benefit from. Whose exploitation, low wages, or immigration status secures us a more stable life?

2. The Priority of the Practice of Justice (vv. 11–12)

God's command is for justice to be the priority that is taken up as the first order of business. It cannot be secondary or ignored. God cares about the lived experiences of people who are trapped by hands that steal from them, devalue them, and benefit from their powerlessness. Since these are God's priorities, they should also be the priorities of God's people, especially leaders. That is why Jeremiah directs his prophecy to the house of David. The work of leaders demands a commitment to equity. Equity is not the same as equality. The passage does not only express that leaders should treat everyone the same, which is equality. It compels them to right the wrongs and do more for those who have been mistreated. That is equity. Making this type of justice a priority aligns with God's values and prevents God's wrath from breaking out on behalf of the marginalized.

How can we prioritize justice? Why is it important to distinguish between equity and equality?

3. The Price of the Malpractice of Justice (vv. 13–14)

We should never become desensitized to the harshness of the language in these verses. The prophet raises the tone and allows for the audience to hear God testifying against and declaring war on people that God no longer calls by God's name or their name. They are referred to only as "inhabitant of the valley." God declares that He will allocate their punishment by their actions. Unfortunately for them, their actions are highly flammable, and their punishment is a kindled fire. These verses highlight the significance of one's actions, especially when he or she thinks that they can get away with wrongdoing. Even if those who are weak cannot defend themselves against the strong, they have an advocate who will remember their cause and fight for them. This passage should serve as an impetus to make sure that one's actions are geared to seeking and pursuing justice, because if they are not, you may find yourself fighting against God.

What does God's anger about injustice communicate to us about how we should view oppression?

Search the Scriptures

1. What are the two options that the Lord sets before the people of Judah? What do these options indicate to us about the Lord's tolerance for evil, oppression, and marginalization? What option would you choose?

2. To whom is the word of the Lord addressed, and why is this specifically significant to the Lord's concern for practicing justice?

Discuss the Meaning

The Lord stands squarely against those who oppress. However, the Babylonians are also oppressive and employ imperial domination. What does the Lord's use of the Babylonians indicate to us about the Lord's commitment to justice? In what way is the Babylonian destruction of Judah a part of the same system of violence that the Jerusalem elite perpetuated against the poor and marginalized? How does violent imagery function to compel God's people to actively resist injustice?

Lesson in Our Society

This lesson compels us to take stock of the ways in which we have been an active or complicit participant in the oppression of others. It is important that we regularly examine how the corporate elite benefit from low wages to workers and the suppression of unions. We should not forget how global capitalism leaves many people around the world in poverty in order to provide inexpensive clothing and technology for us. We also have to be conscious of how our tax dollars go to fund a military whose destructive capacity makes Babylon's imperial force look like child's play. This should cause us to repent and resist so that we can find ourselves on God's side and not on the side of making excuses for oppression.

Make It Happen

What people's pain do you feel the most? Is it children, the elderly, the homeless, immigrants, the poor, victims of racial or gender discrimination, the falsely incarcerated, the over-policed, those affected directly by climate change? Find one way to stand on their side, which is to stand on God's side. Perhaps it can be through donating to an organization that deals with those issues. Perhaps it is volunteering. Perhaps it is to boycott a restaurant that uses discriminatory hiring practices. Perhaps it is to protest a store that uses problematic images in its marketing materials. Take an issue that is close to you and choose to stand with those people and God.

Follow the Spirit

What God wants me to do:

_____

_____

_____

_____

Remember Your Thoughts

Special insights I have learned:

_____

_____

_____

_____

More Light on the Text

Jeremiah 21:8–14

8 And unto this people thou shalt say, Thus saith the LORD; Behold, I set before you the way of life, and the way of death.

Nebuchadnezzar, the king of Babylon, has come against Jerusalem to destroy it, and King Zedekiah of Judah is hopeful that the Lord will deliver them. After all, he has saved them so many times in the past (see Jeremiah 21:2). But this time will be different. Not only will he not save them, but the Lord himself is against his own people because of their constant sin and rejection of his kingship over them. So the prophet Jeremiah first addresses Zedekiah and dashes his hopes by declaring that the Lord will ensure that Jerusalem and its people are captured by Nebuchadnezzar (see vv. 4–7).

Now, he turns to address the people of the city (v. 8). God had already been patient with His people for centuries as they worshiped other gods and disregarded His laws, and now the time for judgment has finally arrived. Yet even now, God graciously provides a way of escape. He could have simply destroyed them, which would have been entirely justified, since "the wages of sin is death" (Romans 3:23). Instead, He tells them that there still remains a "way of life." For Israel this way of life involves obedience to God's commands, loving Him, fearing Him, and serving Him. Their failure in this task causes them to now face God's judgment, yet God sets before them the way of life one more time.

9 He that abideth in this city shall die by the sword, and by the famine, and by the pestilence: but he that goeth out, and falleth to the Chaldeans that besiege you, he shall live, and his life shall be unto him for a prey.

God now describes "the way of life" and "the way of death" for the inhabitants of Jerusalem. Those who choose to remain in the city and hide behind its walls during the Babylonian siege will face death. Jeremiah often refers to sword, famine, and pestilence to summarize the various ways in which God will judge His people for their unfaithfulness to Him and the covenant. All three bring about death, but from different sources: "sword" refers to war, "famine" to the lack of food due to the lack of rain, and "pestilence" to diseases or plagues. All three are among the covenant curses that God had promised to bring upon the people in Leviticus 26 and Deuteronomy 28 if they did not remain loyal to Him.

While those who stay in the city will eventually die, those who leave the city will save their lives. The people are encouraged to "fall to the Chaldeans" ("Chaldeans" being another name for the Babylonians). Although the Hebrew word *nafal* (**naw-FALL**) often refers to "falling" in battle (in other words, "dying"), in this case, it refers to falling to the ground

before the enemy in an act of submission and surrender. They will not survive by fighting but by giving themselves up. The Hebrew word *shalal* (**shaw-LALL**), translated as "prey" by the KJV, typically refers to the spoil or captured goods won through battle. In this case, even though Jerusalem will lose the battle, those who leave the city will at least "win" their own lives. This option may not be the best-case scenario that the people may have hoped for, but it is at least better than dying.

It would not be easy to follow "the way of life" in this case. Even though the Babylonians possess a powerful and superior army, it would be natural to find security behind the walls of Jerusalem and to hope that they could hold out against the siege. Those who are more religious may trust in the invincibility of the Temple in their city and assume that remaining would surely be the path that God would bless. Surrendering to the enemy would be unpopular, treasonous, and dangerous. It would take faith to believe that their lives will be spared if they leave the city. God's ways are sometimes quite different from what we would think. God is calling the people to trust Him for a way of escape, even as He is bringing judgment.

10 For I have set my face against this city for evil, and not for good, saith the LORD: it shall be given into the hand of the king of Babylon, and he shall burn it with fire.

It is certain that Jerusalem will fall to Babylon. But this is not because Babylon is more powerful than Jerusalem, although this is true in terms of human strength. Jerusalem is certain to fall because God Himself is against the city and is directing these events for His own purposes. Nebuchadnezzar is simply God's "servant" (cf. Jeremiah 25:9; 27:6), God's instrument of judgment. Babylon does not "take" Jerusalem. Rather, Jerusalem is "given" into their hand.

Since God is good and not evil, it may be difficult to understand how he has determined to bring "evil" against Jerusalem, as we read in the KJV. The Hebrew word *ra'ah* (**ra-AH**) often refers to moral evil or wickedness, but can also refer to misfortune, trouble, or "disaster" (NLT). In this case, "disaster" serves as a better translation since God is bringing a deserved and just form of judgment against the people for their sin.

11 And touching the house of the king of Judah, say, Hear ye the word of the LORD; 12 O house of David, thus saith the LORD; Execute judgment in the morning, and deliver him that is spoiled out of the hand of the oppressor, lest my fury go out like fire, and burn that none can quench it, because of the evil of your doings.

God provides one last opportunity for the people to escape with their lives (vv. 8–10). Now, He turns back to address the Davidic kings. There is no specific king named here, but we might assume Zedekiah is in mind since he was the recipient of the prior message, but this new message is the first of a number of short messages addressed to various kings during Jeremiah's ministry that run through the next chapter. Also, in Hebrew the commands to "execute judgment" and "deliver him" are plural, so multiple kings are addressed here. In light of this, these verses appear to address the kings of Judah in general and summarize the expectations placed upon them and the consequences if they fail.

God's message for the kings begins with a command to judge with *mishpat* (Heb. **meesh-POT**), the most common word in the Old Testament for "justice." Although this justice is to be dispensed literally "in the morning," the NLT translation "each morning" better communicates the intended meaning that justice is to be a continual and top priority for

the king. The following line explains the kind of justice that God has in mind: kings ought to come to the defense of those who have been robbed by "delivering" them from those who have oppressed them. It is clear from as early as the eighth century from the prophets Hosea and Amos that the abuse of the poor at the hands of the rich was a significant problem in Israel's society. Two hundred years later, the situation remains unchanged as the wealthy and powerful continue to take advantage of the lower classes.

It is one of the primary responsibilities of the king in Israel to perform "justice and righteousness" throughout the land by maintaining God's laws and promoting the economic and social welfare of the entire population. Sadly, it becomes clear from the next two chapters of Jeremiah that the Davidic kings had failed miserably in their responsibility toward the lower class. The penalty is severe if the kings fail in their duty. They may not have thought of these matters as all that important. But turning a blind eye to the plight of the poor is such a great evil in God's eyes that He will unleash his just wrath on them, wrath so great that it is like a raging fire that cannot be put out.

13 Behold, I am against thee, O inhabitant of the valley, and rock of the plain, saith the LORD; which say, Who shall come down against us? or who shall enter into our habitations? 14 But I will punish you according to the fruit of your doings, saith the LORD: and I will kindle a fire in the forest thereof, and it shall devour all things round about it.

Here God continues to describe the judgment He will bring against the kings of Judah and on the whole city. In the previous verse God had given them a strong warning, encouraging them to change their ways to avoid judgment. Here it becomes clear that the verdict is already in:

they have failed, and God's judgment is certain. God has often intervened as the divine warrior on behalf of His people, as in the Exodus deliverance when He fought for them (Exodus 15). But this time He is against them.

God here addresses the "inhabitant of the valley" and "rock of the plain," both unusual descriptions. These are references to Jerusalem, which is surrounded on three sides by valleys and was a relatively strong, rock-like fortress. The kings are still in view here, but now the broader population of the city is addressed as well.

It appears that the people were quite confident that they were safe and secure. Nebuchadnezzar led the most powerful army in the world at that time. The small and powerless nation of Judah had little chance against them from a human point of view. Although the people are described as wicked, they were still pious and religious. Many believed that God would protect them and that He would never allow His Temple, His city, and His king to be taken (cf. Jeremiah 7:4–15). This is a kind of faith in God, but it is a faith that assumes that righteous living does not really matter.

In response to their boastful claim that no one can enter the city, God says that He will do so Himself to punish "the fruit of your doings." This could refer to many violations of God's laws, but it likely mainly refers to the one issue described at the beginning of God's message in verse 12: the failure of kings and people to deal justly with the needy in the land. As before (vv. 10–12), God's judgment will take the form of fire, a fire that will "devour" and consume everything around them. The whole city will be destroyed.

Sources:
Adeyemo, Tokunboh, gen. ed. *Africa Bible Commentary*. Grand Rapids, MI: Zondervan, 2006. 874.
Craigie, Peter C., Page H. Kelley, and Joel F. Drinkard, Jr. Jeremiah 1–25. WBC. Dallas, TX: Word, 1991. 292–94.
Wright, Christopher J. H. *The Message of Jeremiah*. Downers Grove, IL: InterVarsity, 2014. 236.

Say It Correctly

Chaldeans. kal-**DEE**-uhns.
Hinnom. **HIH**-nom.
Kidron. **KID**-ron.
Anathoth. **AH**-nath-oth.

Daily Bible Readings

MONDAY
Seeking Divine Help in Troubled Times
(Psalm 86:1–13)

TUESDAY
Land Now Belongs to Babylon
(Jeremiah 27:1–11)

WEDNESDAY
Choose to Love and Obey the Lord
(Deuteronomy 30:15–20)

THURSDAY
Surrender and the People Will Live
(Jeremiah 38:14–18)

FRIDAY
Jerusalem Will Fall
(Jeremiah 21:1–7)

SATURDAY
Jerusalem Defeated and Zedekiah Exiled
(2 Kings 24:20–25:7)

SUNDAY
Choose the Life of Justice
(Jeremiah 21:8–14)

Teaching Tips

Words You Should Know

A. Stranger (v. 3) *ger* (Heb.)—A person who has journeyed to Israel from another country, living there with the purpose of becoming an Israelite in culture and religion

B. Nations (v. 8) *goyim* (Heb.)—Foreign powers, non-Israelites, those who do not follow God

Teacher Preparation

Unifying Principle—Do the Right Thing. Society often ignores and even condones the oppression of the vulnerable. Will righteousness be rewarded, and will evil face retribution? Through the prophet Jeremiah, God exhorts the people to either repent of injustice and deliver those who are oppressed or face destruction.

A. Read the Bible Background and Devotional Reading.

B. Pray for your students and lesson clarity.

C. Read the lesson Scripture in multiple translations.

O—Open the Lesson

A. Begin the class with prayer.

B. Ask the class: "Should an entire nation incur God's wrath for the sins of their leaders?"

C. Have the students read the Aim for Change and the In Focus story.

D. Ask students how events like those in the story weigh on their hearts and how they can view these events from a faith perspective.

P—Present the Scriptures

A. Read the Focal Verses.

B. Have the class share what Scriptures stand out for them and why, with particular emphasis on today's context.

C. Discuss the Background and The People, Places, and Times sections.

E—Explore the Meaning

A. Use In Depth or More Light on the Text to facilitate a deeper discussion of the lesson text.

B. Pose the questions in Search the Scriptures and Discuss the Meaning.

C. Discuss the Liberating Lesson and Application for Activation sections.

N—Next Steps for Application

A. Summarize the value of following God's way, knowing that the alternative leads to a nation's moral decline.

B. End class with a commitment to pray for the strength to act with justice and righteousness in imitation of God's character.

Worship Guide

For the Superintendent or Teacher
Theme: Repent of Injustice
Song: "O God, You Call for Justice"
Devotional Reading: Psalm 72:1–17

Repent of Injustice

Bible Background • JEREMIAH 22
Printed Text • JEREMIAH 22:1–10 | Devotional Reading • PSALM 72:1–17

Aim for Change

By the end of the lesson, we will: RECOGNIZE that the covenant relationship between God and His people requires justice, REPENT for injustice and seek to deliver the oppressed, and BECOME active agents of deliverance for the oppressed.

In Focus

The Quency Farm was a beautiful place. There were horses to ride, chickens to feed, and a wonderful petting zoo with a few exotic animals. The groundskeeper and the farm manager were excellent to work for, and the staff was friendly and fun. Schoolchildren and tourists would visit the farm. People enjoyed the sweet corn grown on the Quency Farm, and everyone purchased some before they left the farm.

Mr. Quency loved his farm more than anything. His family would try to have him slow down and just enjoy the farm, but he would not. If he wasn't walking, talking, or coming up with a new plan for the visitors to enjoy the farm, then things weren't going right. His best friends warned him that one day it could be taken away, and he needed to relax and thank the Lord for his blessings. Mr. Quency told them to stop talking such foolishness. God would never take his farm away. Even after he died, he knew the family would maintain the farm just fine.

One day, strong winds and heavy rains came and the forecast looked bad. Mr. Quency knew he could keep the farm afloat for about three days, but if it lasted longer than that, he would lose the farm. After a week of torrential downpours, Mr. Quency's beloved farm was ruined. Mrs. Quency saw her husband shed a tear as he looked up to the sky.

What do you hold onto so dearly? How would you react if you lost something you deeply cherished?

Keep in Mind

"Thus saith the LORD; Execute ye judgment and righteousness, and deliver the spoiled out of the hand of the oppressor: and do no wrong, do no violence to the stranger, the fatherless, nor the widow, neither shed innocent blood in this place" (Jeremiah 22:3, KJV).

"This is what the LORD says: Be fair-minded and just. Do what is right! Help those who have been robbed; rescue them from their oppressors. Quit your evil deeds! Do not mistreat foreigners, orphans, and widows. Stop murdering the innocent!" (Jeremiah 22:3, NLT).

Focal Verses

KJV **Jeremiah 22:1** Thus saith the LORD; Go down to the house of the king of Judah, and speak there this word,

2 And say, Hear the word of the LORD, O king of Judah, that sittest upon the throne of David, thou, and thy servants, and thy people that enter in by these gates:

3 Thus saith the LORD; Execute ye judgment and righteousness, and deliver the spoiled out of the hand of the oppressor: and do no wrong, do no violence to the stranger, the fatherless, nor the widow, neither shed innocent blood in this place.

4 For if ye do this thing indeed, then shall there enter in by the gates of this house kings sitting upon the throne of David, riding in chariots and on horses, he, and his servants, and his people.

5 But if ye will not hear these words, I swear by myself, saith the LORD, that this house shall become a desolation.

6 For thus saith the LORD unto the king's house of Judah; Thou art Gilead unto me, and the head of Lebanon: yet surely I will make thee a wilderness, and cities which are not inhabited.

7 And I will prepare destroyers against thee, every one with his weapons: and they shall cut down thy choice cedars, and cast them into the fire.

8 And many nations shall pass by this city, and they shall say every man to his neighbour, Wherefore hath the Lord done thus unto this great city?

9 Then they shall answer, Because they have forsaken the covenant of the LORD their God, and worshipped other gods, and served them.

10 Weep ye not for the dead, neither bemoan him: but weep sore for him that goeth away: for he shall return no more, nor see his native country.

NLT **Jeremiah 22:1** This is what the LORD said to me: "Go over and speak directly to the king of Judah. Say to him,

2 'Listen to this message from the LORD, you king of Judah, sitting on David's throne. Let your attendants and your people listen, too.

3 This is what the LORD says: Be fair-minded and just. Do what is right! Help those who have been robbed; rescue them from their oppressors. Quit your evil deeds! Do not mistreat foreigners, orphans, and widows. Stop murdering the innocent!

4 If you obey me, there will always be a descendant of David sitting on the throne here in Jerusalem. The king will ride through the palace gates in chariots and on horses, with his parade of attendants and subjects.

5 But if you refuse to pay attention to this warning, I swear by my own name, says the LORD, that this palace will become a pile of rubble.'"

6 Now this is what the LORD says concerning Judah's royal palace: "I love you as much as fruitful Gilead and the green forests of Lebanon. But I will turn you into a desert, with no one living within your walls.

7 I will call for wreckers, who will bring out their tools to dismantle you. They will tear out all your fine cedar beams and throw them on the fire.

8 People from many nations will pass by the ruins of this city and say to one another, 'Why did the LORD destroy such a great city?'

9 And the answer will be, 'Because they violated their covenant with the LORD their God by worshiping other gods.'"

10 Do not weep for the dead king or mourn his loss. Instead, weep for the captive king being led away! For he will never return to see his native land again.

The People, Places, and Times

Throne of David. When David offered to build the Temple for God in Jerusalem, the prophet Samuel delivered God's response that David would not build God a house, but that God would build David a house, a line of kings to reign forever, as long as they remained faithful to the Lord (2 Samuel 7:12). In His covenant with David, God promised that a descendant from David's family line would be the eternal king who would rule over God's people and all nations of the world (Isaiah 9:6–37; Micah 5:2, 4). Such stability in the royal line would have allowed the nation to prosper in peace, without infighting among princes vying for the throne. Unfortunately, since not even David's son managed to remain faithful to God throughout his reign, God allowed the kingdom to split, and the throne of David was not as powerful. When His people and their kings continued in sin, God allowed Babylonia to conquer them and overthrow the king on David's throne. The Lord would not fail in keeping His covenant, though. Through the royal line of David, the King of kings was born, and He will reign forever.

Background

This passage is particularly powerful because this chapter is nestled between two chapters that express that the destruction and exile of Judah are inevitable. This chapter finds the prophet Jeremiah expressing the grounds for the Babylonians leading the people of Judah away from their land, and those grounds are the people of Judah's blatant disregard for the covenant. However, their dismissal is not permanent. God always provides an opportunity to return home. No matter how far away they go and even if they cannot immediately return physically, they can return to the "hometown" values, which are epitomized by the covenant.

From what places is God calling us? What are the values that God is calling us to return to?

> ## At-A-Glance
>
> 1. Responding to God's Call to the Powerful (22:1–5)
> 2. Remembering God's Covenant with God's People (vv. 6–10)

In Depth

1. Responding to God's Call to the Powerful (22:1–5)

The message that God has the prophet speak to the king of Judah and his entourage is a simple set of imperatives. These instructions are not difficult to understand: Make decisions based on fairness; look out for those who have not been given an adequate opportunity because an individual or institution has robbed them; do not add any extra burden to people who already have a hard time whether they are immigrants, children, or disenfranchised women; don't harm people just because you can. These capture what God wants from the government of Judah.

The message is addressed to the leadership, because if they respond to God's call, then the people whom they lead will be affected by their decisions. It is important to note that people suffer because of bad leadership at a national level. We should not swiftly move past the addressees in the passage and apply this message to everyone. Although these are values that all of God's people should espouse, it is important that those with power use their power appropriately and model justice. Any government that shows favoritism to certain groups of people or further pushes down the downtrodden or increases obstacles for the already dispossessed is a government that has chosen to refuse to heed the call of God. Instead of siding with consolation, they choose to side with desolation.

In what ways do our nation and its leaders refuse to answer God's call?

2. Remembering God's Covenant with God's People (vv. 6–10)

The prophet imagines the nation in ruins. When people from other places inquire about how Jerusalem arrived at this point of despair, their answer will contain three actions that were committed: (1) abandoning the covenant, (2) worshiping other gods, and (3) serving other gods. From the earlier passage, it would seem that the cause of the destruction is rooted in not properly valuing humans, but the charge of idolatry is about incorrectly prioritizing God. The leadership's and the people's actions toward other humans are fundamentally connected to an improper view of God. If the people of Judah believed that they could be in good standing with God and God's covenant while being in bad standing with vulnerable people, then they neither understood the terms of the covenant nor the divine party with whom they were in the covenant. They should not expect God to execute the covenant while they exploit those created in God's image.

Furthermore, not understanding how a person or nation's actions are related to their relationship with God leads that person or nation to actually worship a god that is not the true God. Such a mistake in thinking can lead people to overestimate their value in God's eyes. Verse 6 gives a glimpse into this. Although the house of the king of Judah is precious to God as prime real estate, God will leave it vacant and dilapidated if they use their privilege for pushing others down rather than helping them up. Lebanon was known for its valuable cedars, which could represent the value of God's chosen people to God. However, God does not mind destroying what we consider important if our importance is rooted in the marginalization of other people.

Not only has the house of Judah improperly valued God and worshiped an idol, they actually serve or enslave themselves to this image. This is a god with whom they did not make a covenant, and this is a god who allows for the people to mistreat others without consequence. This is the god to whom the house of Judah enslaves itself. They choose to serve this non-god and become participants in a non-covenant, abandoning God and God's covenant. This in one way leaves them in a position worse than death (v. 10). However, in another way this puts into relief the gravity of the consequences of injustice and reminds the audience that they should return, repent, and go home before they are in a place of no return. Rather than forsake the covenant, they should forsake their pursuit of a god of greed, self-centeredness, pride, and lust that leads to destruction.

What are some things that we consider more important than God considers them? What have we sold ourselves to that contributes to the growth of injustice?

Search the Scriptures

1. Why is it important that the prophet mentions David in his utterance against the house of David (Jeremiah 22:2)? What does David represent?

2. Whom does Jeremiah directly address in this prophecy? Who all can hear his words (v. 2)? Why is it important that more hear that are addressed?

Discuss the Meaning

God calls His people to respond to His simple call to execute justice in their lives and in the lives of the people over whom they have decision-making authority. These are the values that the leadership and people of Judah have left behind. God is calling for them to repent and return to Him. With Him, their covenant a relationship is intact. With Him, the God of justice reigns and not the god of self-centeredness. With Him, treating people right is a prerequisite to being in relationship with God. These calls to respond and remember are urgent, because the further away one goes, the longer and more difficult it is to return.

In what ways do we and our nation need to return to God? What have we forgotten about God and our covenant that allows us to mistreat others?

Liberating Lesson

Some Americans consistently have difficulty recognizing the humanity of immigrants, especially those who are Black and brown. Atrocities have happened at our borders where we mistreat children. Many people have to hide under the radar and become invisible for their own survival. The way we treat these people is how God determines our faithfulness to the covenant. God wants us to remind them that He sees them, even though their safety may be in jeopardy if certain government officials see them. Although people ignore the hateful words of politicians that make whole populations feel forsaken, the Lord wants us to fully integrate those populations into the family of God. This should compel us not only to sympathize with our brothers and sisters but also to repent for when we did not prioritize their safety, salvation, and vindication.

Application for Activation

In our prayer life, it is important to have a correct image of the God to whom we are praying. We indeed do pray to a gracious God, but it is also needful to remember that we are praying to a God who loves justice. Let that guide what we pray for and whom we pray for. Let us not only pray for but actively seek people whom we come across that need to be covered with justice and salvation. Whether it is providing money or volunteering or organizing, let us be moved to help set people free. We should remember our covenant values and remember people's humanity, act with justice, and not add any extra obstacle to people who

are already burdened. We should actually work to alleviate those very burdens.

Follow the Spirit

What God wants me to do:

_____

_____

_____

_____

Remember Your Thoughts

Special insights I have learned:

_____

_____

_____

_____

More Light on the Text

Jeremiah 22:1–10

1 Thus saith the LORD; Go down to the house of the king of Judah, and speak there this word, 2 And say, Hear the word of the LORD, O king of Judah, that sittest upon the throne of David, thou, and thy servants, and thy people that enter in by these gates:

Jeremiah 22:1–10 continues a series of messages from the Lord to the kings of Judah. In general, these messages "indict" or criticize them for their sins and then declare God's judgment against them for their wrongdoing. The first message in Jeremiah 21:11–14 had commanded the kings to practice justice or else they would meet God's fiery wrath—not only the king but all of Jerusalem with them.

Now Jeremiah addresses a specific king of Judah, though he is not named here and his identity is unknown. We are told that this king "sits on the throne of David." This reminds us of the covenant that God had made with David four hundred years earlier, as described in 2 Samuel 7. God had promised that his descendants would maintain his throne and that he would have an everlasting kingdom. However, this did not mean that the Davidic king could do whatever he pleased without consequences. This long-term commitment to David did not mean that individual kings would not receive God's discipline for their actions (Psalm 89:30–33). After Babylonia destroyed Jerusalem in the days of Jeremiah, there was to be no Davidic king reigning over Israel for hundreds of years to follow. But with the coming of Jesus Christ, God fulfilled His promises to David. The Son of David will now reign over the kingdom of David and the kingdom of God for all eternity.

The present message is primarily for the king as the ruler and representative of the people, but His servants and all inhabitants of the city of Jerusalem are addressed here as well.

3 Thus saith the LORD; Execute ye judgment and righteousness, and deliver the spoiled out of the hand of the oppressor: and do no wrong, do no violence to the stranger, the fatherless, nor the widow, neither shed innocent blood in this place.

In the initial message to the kings, they were commanded to "execute judgment" (see Jeremiah 21:12). Now this unnamed king and his people are told to "execute judgment and righteousness." The Hebrew word for "judgment" is *mishpat* (**meesh-POT**), usually translated "justice" in modern English versions. The word for "righteousness," *tsedaqah* (Heb. **tse-daw-KAW**), is used in a number of ways in the Bible. Although we often think of the righteous person as someone who is morally

upright and to be contrasted with the wicked person, in this case, it refers specifically to treating others rightly and fairly according to God's holy standards. Justice and righteousness, then, are not two completely different ideas, but two words that together express one concept, something similar to what we mean today by "social justice."

The rest of the third verse makes it very clear what kind of justice God has in mind. First, as in Jeremiah 21:12, this means to come to the defense of those who have been robbed by "delivering" them from those who have oppressed them. He then lists three categories of people in society who tend to be marginalized, forgotten, or in need of special care: the stranger, the fatherless, and the widow. The first word, *ger* (Heb. **GAIR**), refers to foreigners, or non-Israelites, who have come to join the people of God. Today it would include immigrants, expatriates, and refugees living in foreign lands. The second term, *yatom* (Heb. **ya-TOME**), often translated "orphan," refers to a child who has lost their father, though not necessarily their mother. Such individuals lack the basic provision that a father was meant to provide. The third term, *'almanah* (Heb. **al-ma-NAH**), refers to widows, women who have lost their husbands, and thus, like orphans, have lost their primary provider. To do justice and righteousness means to maintain God's laws for all and treat everyone rightly in society, but it especially means to care for those who cannot care for themselves.

There are three ways in which the king and his people must not treat such people. First, they must not wrong, oppress, or cheat them. Second, they must not act violently toward them, which may even include physical violence. Third, they must not shed their "innocent blood," which indicates that such people have done no wrong but are simply being abused since they are defenseless. This may be a figure of speech referring to extreme abuse and does not necessarily mean that they are literally killing them, but in some cases such abuse may lead to death.

Elsewhere it is clear that not only were they not to abuse the foreigner, orphan, and widow, but they were to actively care for them (Deuteronomy 15:4, 7–8). It is also the responsibility of all of the people to extend justice to the poor. James reminds Christians, "Pure religion and undefiled before God and the Father is this, to visit the fatherless and widows in their affliction" (from James 1:27).

The situation is not much different in our own day. Around the world, many, especially those of African descent, find themselves among the foreigners, the refugees, the poor, and the oppressed. Sometimes the leaders are responsible for this oppression and abuse, and sometimes the general population is equally responsible. Regardless, it is clear from the beginning to the end of the Bible that one of the most basic ways in which God's people should "love their neighbor as themselves" is to care for those who lack care and defend the defenseless.

Although few of us may be in a position to care for and defend thousands, we can all look for opportunities to help some who are around us. As Christians, we should strive to see justice done for others, but we must also adopt an eternal perspective. In the present fallen world, we do not expect justice to be done at all times, but we are promised that in the end, the Judge of the world will ensure that all wrongs will be made right.

4 For if ye do this thing indeed, then shall there enter in by the gates of this house kings sitting upon the throne of David, riding in chariots and on horses, he, and his servants, and his people. 5 But if ye will not hear these words, I swear by myself, saith the LORD, that this house shall become a desolation.

If the king and the people turn from their wicked oppression of the defenseless, God will respond by extending grace toward them. He will withhold his just punishment and allow the king, his servants, and the people of the city to remain in their homes. He will ensure political stability, and they will continue to thrive.

But there is, of course, another option. The king and the people could decide to ignore God's messenger Jeremiah and continue to live the way they have been living, overpowering the helpless for the sake of their own gain. If they choose this path, God swears emphatically that He will bring judgment. Specifically, "this house," probably a reference to the royal palace, will become a ruinous waste. If they obey, kings will continue to live in the palace. But if they disobey, the palace will be empty, which is representative of broader destruction across the city as well.

Although the word is not used here, it is clear that God is looking for repentance. Repentance in the Bible is more than simply admitting that we have sinned or just feeling bad for our sin. Repentance includes turning from our sin and acting differently. Consistently throughout the Bible God delights in responding to repentance with mercy, compassion, grace, and forgiveness of sin. This is true under the old covenant that God had with Israel, and it is true under the new covenant today. When we turn from our sins and turn to Christ in faith, we receive an abundance of grace, mercy, and the forgiveness of sins through Christ.

6 For thus saith the LORD unto the king's house of Judah; Thou art Gilead unto me, and the head of Lebanon: yet surely I will make thee a wilderness, and cities which are not inhabited. 7 And I will prepare destroyers against thee, every one with his weapons: and they shall cut down thy choice cedars, and cast them into the fire.

Jeremiah continues to describe the coming judgment if the people will not repent of their wickedness. Here he addresses the king more directly. He first compares the king's house to Gilead and to the "head" or summit of Lebanon. Gilead is a hilly region within the territory of Israel, belonging to the tribes of Gad, Reuben, and Manasseh. It is east of the Jordan River in what is today northwest Jordan. Lebanon is a mountainous area to the north of Israel and famous for its tall cedars. Both are fertile regions that represent strength, beauty, stability, and prosperity. Comparing these places to the palace reminds us that for centuries God has brought blessing and prosperity to David, his family, and his people.

But no more. What was once fertile and forested God will now make like a desert. What was once richly inhabited will now be like empty, forgotten cities. God himself will send warriors against them to destroy them. They will cut down their best cedars, and they will not even be put to good use. They will simply be burned. "Cedars" reminds us of Lebanon, but this is probably also a reference to the palace in particular. When Solomon built the palace of the king centuries earlier, he made use of the famous cedars of Lebanon. As a result, "one of Solomon's buildings was called the Palace of the Forest of Lebanon … There were four rows of cedar pillars, and great cedar beams rested on the pillars" (1 Kings 7:2, NLT). These powerful images of cutting down these pillars indicate that nothing of the former glory will remain. All will be destroyed.

8 And many nations shall pass by this city, and they shall say every man to his neighbour, Wherefore hath the LORD done thus unto this great city? 9 Then they shall answer, Because they have forsaken the covenant of the LORD their God, and worshipped other gods, and served them.

These verses further explain why God is planning to destroy them. The prophet envisions travelers along the road near Jerusalem turning to the side and catching a glimpse of the ruins of the empty city. As they remember Jerusalem's former days of glory, one traveler turns to another in amazement and can't help but ask how this could have happened. Yet the traveler does not assume that this was random misfortune or chance. He rightly recognizes that Israel's God, Yahweh, is directly responsible for destroying His own city, the city that once contained His own Temple.

One traveler has a divinely inspired answer to his friend's question: God destroyed His own people because they abandoned their covenant with Him and worshiped and served other gods. This refers to the covenant relationship the nation had agreed to at Mount Sinai. God had graciously freed Israel from their bondage in Egypt, given them the land of Canaan, and showered them with blessings within the land. In light of these incredible gifts from God, Israel was to respond with absolute loyalty and allegiance to God. This loyalty to God included following many laws that reflect God's own holy character, but above all, it meant following the first two of the "Ten Commandments": they must not worship other gods or create idols. The Israelites of Jeremiah's day, like the many generations before them, had broken the very heart of the covenant agreement.

It had been clear that the cause of the coming destruction was their oppression of the helpless (v. 3), but now it appears that quite a different reason is given. But there is certainly no contradiction here. The causes for their punishment were many and interrelated (see 2 Kings 17:6–20). Jesus Himself tells us that the two greatest commands are to love God and to love your neighbor as yourself (Mark 12:28–31). Verse three highlights their failure to love their neighbor, and verse nine emphasizes that they have also failed to love God. As John teaches, the two cannot be separated: "If a man say, I love God, and hateth his brother, he is a liar: for he that loveth not his brother whom he hath seen, how can he love God whom he hath not seen?" (1 John 4:20, NLT).

It is both shocking and shameful that "many nations" will witness this destruction. The Hebrew word, *goyim* (**go-YEEM**), is the word typically used to refer to nations other than Israel, later referred to as Gentiles. God's design for Abraham's descendants, the Israelites, was that "all nations will be blessed through you" (Genesis 12:3, NLT). After God had delivered His people from slavery in Egypt and brought them to Mount Sinai to create a covenant agreement with them, He tells them that it is their responsibility to be a "kingdom of priests" (Exodus 19:6). In other words, like a priest, all Israelites had a responsibility to mediate knowledge of God to the surrounding nations so that they might come to acknowledge Him as the one true God and join Israel in worshiping Him alone. There were some small success stories like Ruth and Rahab, but in general Israel failed in this mission throughout her history. Instead of living holy lives distinct from the nations in order to be a light and witness to them, they both despised those nations and lived just like them. Now travelers from these same nations they were meant to reach with blessing shake their heads as they see how Israel has been cursed by her own God.

10 Weep ye not for the dead, neither bemoan him: but weep sore for him that goeth away: for he shall return no more, nor see his native country.

The final verse of this message from Jeremiah appears to be a reflection on how one ought to respond to this message of judgment from the Lord. The judgment will be so severe that it is better to be dead than to be alive in exile as a refugee. As in most cultures today, it was customary to weep and mourn for the dead at a funeral, but it makes more sense to save one's tears for the living who will never see their home again and will be buried in a foreign land.

Some believe that this verse is the beginning of the next message concerning Shallum, another name for King Jehoahaz. If so, "the dead" would refer specifically to King Josiah, and "him that goes away" would refer to his son and successor, Jehoahaz, who was carried off to Egypt, where he died (2 Kings 23:29–34). Since we see this same theme in verses 11–12 this may be the case, but it would be just as fitting to apply verse 10 to all of the dead and the exiled in light of the prior judgment (vv. 5–9).

Sources:
Adeyemo, Tokunboh, gen. ed. *Africa Bible Commentary*. Grand Rapids, MI: Zondervan, 2006. 876.
Craigie, Peter C., Page H. Kelley, and Joel F. Drinkard, Jr. Jeremiah 1–25. WBC. Dallas, TX: Word, 1991. 298, 300–301, 303–304.

Say It Correctly

Shallum. sha-**LOOM**.
Jehoahaz. jeh-**HOE**-ah-**HAZZ**.

Daily Bible Readings

MONDAY
Justice for Aliens, Orphans, and Widows
(Deuteronomy 24:17–22)

TUESDAY
God Requires Godly Rule by Kings
(Deuteronomy 17:18–20)

WEDNESDAY
Who May Enter God's Holy Presence?
(Psalm 15)

THURSDAY
God's Justice for the Unjust King
(Jeremiah 22:11–19)

FRIDAY
The City Suffers for Its Disobedience
(Jeremiah 22:20–23)

SATURDAY
Injustice Ends the Line of David
(Jeremiah 22:24–30)

SUNDAY
Repent of Misdeeds and Unjust Actions
(Jeremiah 22:1–10)

Notes

_____

_____

_____

_____

Teaching Tips

Words You Should Know

A. Backsliding (11:7) *meshuvah* (Heb.)—Back-turning, apostasy

B. Turn (12:6) *shuv* (Heb.)—To turn back, retreat, to change course or direction

Teacher Preparation

Unifying Principle—Measure Up! People often equate prosperity with righteousness. Is prosperity the standard by which people and society should be judged? Hosea reminds us that love and justice are God's standards.

A. Read the Bible Background and Devotional Reading.

B. Pray for your students and lesson clarity.

C. Read the lesson Scripture in multiple translations.

O—Open the Lesson

A. Begin the class with prayer.

B. As a class, compare and contrast concepts like love, justice, repentance, prosperity, righteousness, and faithfulness in terms of secular versus Christian views.

C. Have the students read the Aim for Change and the In Focus story.

D. Ask students how events like those in the story weigh on their hearts and how they can view these events from a faith perspective.

P—Present the Scriptures

A. Read the Focal Verses.

B. Have the class share what Scriptures stand out for them and why, with particular emphasis on today's context.

C. Discuss the Background and The People, Places, and Times sections.

E—Explore the Meaning

A. Use In Depth or More Light on the Text to facilitate a deeper discussion of the lesson text.

B. Pose the questions in Search the Scriptures and Discuss the Meaning.

C. Discuss the Liberating Lesson and Application for Activation sections.

N—Next Steps for Application

A. Summarize the value of God's many undeserved blessings.

B. End class with a commitment to pray to rely on and relate to God as a loving Father.

Worship Guide

For the Superintendent or Teacher
Theme: Return to Love and Justice
Song: "Trust and Obey"
Devotional Reading: Deuteronomy 8:11–20

Return to Love and Justice

Bible Background • HOSEA 11–12 | Printed Text • HOSEA 11:1–2, 7–10; 12:1–2, 6–14
Devotional Reading • DEUTERONOMY 8:11-20

Aim for Change

By the end of the lesson, we will: COMPARE prosperity as a worldly goal with the godly virtues of love and justice; REGRET the occasions where we have made material prosperity a greedy, covetous goal; and PRACTICE love and justice as key virtues.

In Focus

Sixteen-year-old twins Briana and Jackson and their family just wanted some warm food. Their father had lost his job, and their mom was sick. They wanted to eat and would volunteer to clean up in exchange for food. The twins left their two-bedroom apartment and their two siblings to find the family food.

They stopped at a church a few blocks away and asked if the church was still serving meals. The church said they were but the kitchen closed in 20 minutes. Jackson ran back to tell everyone, but their mother was too weak to go inside. Their father stayed with her and told the other kids to go. The children thought they would ask to take food for their parents.

To their surprise, they were told they could not take extras. Briana and Jackson managed to sneak bread and fruit in their pockets. The church's sign read, "We Are A Caring Church." Briana said, "They sure don't represent the care of God too well. Maybe the church down the street with the broken sign that simply read "All Are Welcome" might mean it."

Have you ever met or experienced rejection from people who claim to love the Lord? How are churches and believers guilty of saying they love the Lord, but not always displaying their love in genuine and meaningful ways?

Keep in Mind

"Therefore turn thou to thy God: keep mercy and judgment and wait on thy God continually" (Hosea 12:6, KJV).

"So now, come back to your God. Act with love and justice, and always depend on him" (Hosea 12:6, NLT).

Focal Verses

KJV 11:1 When Israel was a child, then I loved him, and called my son out of Egypt.

2 As they called them, so they went from them: they sacrificed unto Baalim, and burned incense to graven images.

7 And my people are bent to backsliding from me: though they called them to the most High, none at all would exalt him.

8 How shall I give thee up, Ephraim? how shall I deliver thee, Israel? how shall I make thee as Admah? how shall I set thee as Zeboim? mine heart is turned within me, my repentings are kindled together.

9 I will not execute the fierceness of mine anger, I will not return to destroy Ephraim: for I am God, and not man; the Holy One in the midst of thee: and I will not enter into the city.

10 They shall walk after the LORD: he shall roar like a lion: when he shall roar, then the children shall tremble from the west.

12:1 Ephraim feedeth on wind, and followeth after the east wind: he daily increaseth lies and desolation; and they do make a covenant with the Assyrians, and oil is carried into Egypt.

2 The LORD hath also a controversy with Judah, and will punish Jacob according to his ways; according to his doings will he recompense him.

6 Therefore turn thou to thy God: keep mercy and judgment and wait on thy God continually.

7 He is a merchant, the balances of deceit are in his hand: he loveth to oppress.

8 And Ephraim said, Yet I am become rich, I have found me out substance: in all my labours they shall find none iniquity in me that were sin.

9 And I that am the LORD thy God from the land of Egypt will yet make thee to dwell in tabernacles, as in the days of the solemn feast.

NLT 11:1 "When Israel was a child, I loved him, and I called my son out of Egypt.

2 But the more I called to him, the farther he moved from me, offering sacrifices to the images of Baal and burning incense to idols.

7 For my people are determined to desert me. They call me the Most High, but they don't truly honor me.

8 "Oh, how can I give you up, Israel? How can I let you go? How can I destroy you like Admah or demolish you like Zeboiim? My heart is torn within me, and my compassion overflows.

9 No, I will not unleash my fierce anger. I will not completely destroy Israel, for I am God and not a mere mortal. I am the Holy One living among you, and I will not come to destroy.

10 For someday the people will follow me. I, the LORD, will roar like a lion. And when I roar, my people will return trembling from the west.

12:1 The people of Israel feed on the wind; they chase after the east wind all day long. They pile up lies and violence; they are making an alliance with Assyria while sending olive oil to buy support from Egypt.

2 Now the LORD is bringing charges against Judah. He is about to punish Jacob for all his deceitful ways, and pay him back for all he has done.

6 So now, come back to your God. Act with love and justice, and always depend on him.

7 But no, the people are like crafty merchants selling from dishonest scales—they love to cheat.

8 Israel boasts, "I am rich! I've made a fortune all by myself! No one has caught me cheating! My record is spotless!"

9 But I am the LORD your God, who rescued you from slavery in Egypt. And I will make you live in tents again, as you do each year at the Festival of Shelters.

10 I have also spoken by the prophets, and I have multiplied visions, and used similitudes, by the ministry of the prophets.

11 Is there iniquity in Gilead? surely they are vanity: they sacrifice bullocks in Gilgal; yea, their altars are as heaps in the furrows of the fields.

12 And Jacob fled into the country of Syria, and Israel served for a wife, and for a wife he kept sheep.

13 And by a prophet the LORD brought Israel out of Egypt, and by a prophet was he preserved.

14 Ephraim provoked him to anger most bitterly: therefore shall he leave his blood upon him, and his reproach shall his LORD return unto him.

10 I sent my prophets to warn you with many visions and parables."

11 But the people of Gilead are worthless because of their idol worship. And in Gilgal, too, they sacrifice bulls; their altars are lined up like the heaps of stone along the edges of a plowed field.

12 Jacob fled to the land of Aram, and there he earned a wife by tending sheep.

13 Then by a prophet the LORD brought Jacob's descendants out of Egypt; and by that prophet they were protected.

14 But the people of Israel have bitterly provoked the LORD, so their LORD will now sentence them to death in payment for their sins.

The People, Places, and Times

Hosea. One of the minor prophets. He was an Old Testament prophet of the eighth century BC, called by God from the northern kingdom. He prophesied about the last forty years before the fall of the northern kingdom, warning the Israelites to return to God before it was too late. He was an older contemporary of Isaiah and Micah and began His ministry at a time when Israel was prosperous and powerful under King Jeroboam II (790–749 BC).

Background

The book of Hosea illustrates a time when the people of Israel had been unfaithful to God through worship. They sought out relationships with Assyria and Egypt that were not approved by God, all in pursuit of military gain, and subjected themselves to improper worship of Baal. Throughout the story of Hosea, God has shown His commitment to the people of Israel, and yet they continue to both reject His love and disobey His commands. The northern kingdom managed only two centuries remaining vibrant and alive, in large part because its leaders failed to teach the people of Israel how to seek and follow after God. Hosea predicted the downfall of Israel when Shalmaneser of Assyria conquered it and shortly after Judah went into captivity. In many ways, today's passages show how God is lamenting the frustrations of a people who continued to defile the meaning of worship. In chapter 12, Jacob, who later was renamed Israel, practiced deceit and yet was the common ancestor of all the twelve tribes of Israel. Jacob, however, diligent in his desire to seek God, wrestled with the angel to receive his blessings. Jacob's ancestors named in this text remained under the belief that their benefits would be a direct result of their success, without help from God. Jacob attempted to cleanse his home of idol worship (Genesis 35:2); however, his decedents remained steadfast in their worshiping of idols. As result, dishonesty, as noted by Jacob's past, became the norm in how people attained their wealth.

At-A-Glance

1. Israel's Deliverance (Hosea 11:1–2)
2. God's Reaffirming Love (vv. 7–10)
3. The Punishment of Israel (12:1–2)
4. Seek God's Love and Justice (vv. 6–14)

In Depth

1. Israel's Deliverance (Hosea 11:1–2)

God has in many ways envisioned the relationship that He maintained with Israel as similar to that of a parent and a stubborn child. God reemphasizes the love He possesses for His children despite the many times that the children of Israel continuously disobeyed God even after being brought out of Egypt (vv. 1–2). God continued to restore the people of Israel, and in many ways, this sets up the narrative for the Messiah that would come and offer reconciliation and hope.

What does the hope of a Messiah (Jesus) offer to the future of the people of Israel?

2. God's Reaffirming Love (vv. 7–10)

God reminds the Israelites what happened to Admah and Zeboim (NLT: Zeboiim), who both perished with Sodom and Gomorrah, yet God refuses to allow that to happen to the people of Israel. God remains adamant in His refusal to destroy Israel by reaffirming love and not anger. Instead of God's wrath (which would have been justified), God states that His "compassion is aroused." This is a reminder to the people of Israel of God's divine position. We cannot place our definitions of human characteristics onto how we understand God's behavior. God is infinitely larger than we could imagine, so when we note God's love despite our disobedience, we cannot attempt to rationalize it with our human understanding. God believed in the return of faithful people (vv. 10–11).

How do we come to understand God's divine love through His relationship with the people of Israel?

3. The Punishment of Israel (12:1–2)

At different times, Assyria and Egypt each conquered Israel and held their people captive, yet Israel still tries to make alliances and trade deals with them. Israel continues to use all forms of deceit and violence in pursuit of power. In many ways, these actions remain in direct conflict to the bondage that they were set free from as a people. Pursuit of their wishes and desires caused the people of Israel to fall. God at this moment is calling out Jacob and the people of Israel for their deceit and the deceit of his descendants who believed that their successes came from their works. God is now calling to bring a charge against the people of Israel; however, this charge is coming from His continued love for them.

Do you think that it would have been better to have the people of Israel destroyed to understand the seriousness of their actions?

4. Seek God's Love and Justice (vv. 6–14)

God urges the people of Israel once again to return to the ways of love and justice. They must put away the deceit and harm they have displayed since their release from Egypt. The boasting of riches and wealth is not rooted in justice or love, nor does it carry weight in God's kingdom. God reminds the Israelites of the Festival of Booths, a time when they spend a week living in tents to honor God's protection when they wandered the wilderness for forty years. However, God warns the people of Israel that if they continue to live in such a way that glorifies material success and idol worship, they would be sent back to the tents and placed in bondage.

How can one obtain wealth in a way that is still affirming of God's love and justice?

457

Search the Scriptures

1. How does Israel try to establish their own prosperity apart from God (Hosea 12:1)?

2. Usually, people run from the roar of a lion. What will hearers do when they hear God's lion-like roar (Hosea 11:10)?

Discuss the Meaning

1. Note the times in your life where you found yourself disobeying God and idolizing other things. How did God extend His love and mercy to you even at that time?

2. How do you understand success in any area of your life as it relates to your relationship with God?

3. Do you find yourself seeking love and justice even if the people and communities you love initially reject you?

Liberating Lesson

There are individuals and corporations in this country who continue to profit from deceit and improper business practices. These individuals and corporations find themselves hoping to obtain worldly wealth and prosperity. Meanwhile, they continue to widen the wealth gap globally. Their desire to achieve power, status, and wealth by human means has allowed them to lose sight of the destruction that they are causing to working class and poor people. In many ways, God is still calling out to them, both in love and strong rebuke. God desires all His children, even those that operate in deceit and material wealth, to bring justice and restore good order. We can often find ourselves seeking to obtain the material wealth of millionaires, meanwhile forgetting the reasons God blesses us with wealth in the first place. We have been given wealth so that we may extend back the same love God has shown us and share it among the least of these and work toward restorative economic justice.

Application for Activation

Always seek God daily in every aspect of your life. Ensure that you are keeping God at the head of your life (Matthew 6:33). Ask yourself, what are you faithful to? What do you find yourself idolizing? You can also examine if the blessings that God has provided you should be redistributed to those around you in need. Lastly, seek to trust God to continue being a provider in your life and not to trust in your own ability to provide.

Follow the Spirit

What God wants me to do:

_____

_____

_____

_____

Remember Your Thoughts

Special insights I have learned:

_____

_____

_____

_____

More Light on the Text
Hosea 11:1–2, 7–10; 12:1–2, 6–14

Prophet Hosea lived during the tragic final days of Israel, the Northern Kingdom before their exile to Assyria. The book uses a number of symbols to depict Israel's unfaithfulness on the one hand, and God's gracious, merciful, and persistently loving character on the other. It uses marriage and parenting metaphors—Israel as a promiscuous wife and an ungrateful or stubborn child—to show the people's unfaithfulness. Nonetheless, Israel's (or humanity's) unfaithfulness and stubbornness are not enough to exhaust God's redeeming grace, love, and mercy toward His people. While the imagery of the married, unfaithful, and wayward prostitute is used in the opening chapters of the book (chapters 1–3), the metaphor of a rebellious child is used in the eleventh chapter to depict Israel's disloyalty toward God. In spite of Israel's waywardness and rebellion, God's unparalleled character of love, mercy, justice, and grace is constantly displayed (11:1–11).

1 When Israel was a child, then I loved him, and called my son out of Egypt. 2 As they called them, so they went from them: they sacrificed unto Baalim, and burned incense to graven images.

Chapter 11 begins with the imagery of a court of law where God as His own witness seems to state His case, as it were, against His people, Israel. Indeed, this sounds more like a lament of a father who is disappointed over his son's behavior than a charge against his own son. The Lord calls to mind His fatherly dealings with Israel and their stubbornness and rebellion against Him. Here we have a picture of a father's tender love for his child—the Lord as the father and Israel the child—a picture He often employs to describe His relationship with Israel (Exodus 4:22–23; Isaiah 1:2–4). The phrase "When Israel was a child, then I loved him" refers to the formative years of Israel as a nation in Egypt during and after the time of Joseph and his generation. The Hebrew verb translated "love" here is 'ahav (**aw-HAHV**), which means "to have affection," with the idea to like or to have a close and intimate relationship. The effect of God's loving affection for Israel is both implicitly and explicitly stated. Firstly,

implicitly stated, "then I loved him" implies the Lord blessed Israel economically and numerically multiplied them after the death of Joseph and his generation (Exodus 1:6–10). The Egyptians' envious response resulted in the imposition of hard labor, torture, and bondage of Israel under the Egyptians. Secondly, explicitly expressed, God demonstrated His love for Israel by redeeming them from their bondage in Egypt—known as the Exodus. This is captured in the phrase "out of Egypt." Egypt is geographically, spiritually, and symbolically used here. Egypt was the geographical land from where Israel is physically liberated; it also symbolized idolatry, the worship of many gods and idols from which the Lord delivered Israel. In addition, Egypt represented bondage, torture, and suffering. The phrase, therefore, speaks of complete deliverance from bondage to new life in the Promised Land. The phrase is quoted concerning Jesus (Matthew 2:15). The love that led Him to deliver Israel from Egypt is the same that made Him bring His Son from Egypt to do the work of redemption among His people.

However, Israel did not appreciate or reciprocate God's love for them. Rather the more He loved and called them, the further they wandered away from God and worshiped the images of Baal (vv. 2–4). The translation of verse 2 appears problematic. KJV renders it "As they called them, so they went from them: they sacrificed unto Baalim and burned incense to graven images." The plural pronouns "they" or "them" probably refer to the prophets whom God used to call His "son," Israel, to return to Him. Other translations including NLT translate it "… the more I called to him, the farther he moved from me, offering sacrifices to the images of Baal and burning incense to idols." The singular pronoun "I" tends to point to God as the one speaking. Whether spoken by God or His prophets, the main issue here is Israel's obstinacy and waywardness.

As noted above, God called or delivered Israel both spiritually and physically out of Egypt (v. 2). God's main purpose for the Exodus was to separate Israel from the worship of idols and to establish an intimate relationship with them. Several times, God instructs Moses to go and tell Pharaoh to "Let my people go, so that they may worship me" (Exodus 5:1, 8:1, 9:1, 10:1). God recalls how the Israelites constantly rejected Him and followed other gods throughout their journey to the Promised Land. Instead of worshiping the Lord who showed them, love, they wandered farther from Him; they followed Baal by sacrificing to it and "burning incense to graven images."

7 And my people are bent to backsliding from me: though they called them to the most High, none at all would exalt him.

In spite of God's tender love and care for Israel (vv. 3–4), and warning of exile to Assyrian for refusing to repent (vv. 5–6), Israel (Ephraim) continues to rebel and reject God. The phrase "And my people are bent to backsliding from me" is a statement of disappointment by a father who loved his children. It points back to the efforts God made to keep the relationship between Him and His people alive. But the more He tried to make it work, the more they are habitually determined ("bent," KJV) to walk away from Him. The word "backsliding" comes from the Hebrew noun *meshuvah* (**meh-shoo-VAW**), which means back-turning or apostasy. This word comes from the root *shuv* (Heb. **SHOOV**), which will be used positively in Hosea's next prophecy (see 12:6 below). God wants them to turn back to Him, but they are turning away from Him instead. The clause "though they called them to the most High" refers to the effort made (by the prophets) to turn Israel back to the most High, but they remain adamant. None of them would extol or honor Him.

8 How shall I give thee up, Ephraim? how shall I deliver thee, Israel? how shall I make thee as Admah? how shall I set thee as Zeboim? mine heart is turned within me, my repentings are kindled together. 9 I will not execute the fierceness of mine anger, I will not return to destroy Ephraim: for I am God, and not man; the Holy One in the midst of thee: and I will not enter into the city.

Like a spoiled child, Israel habitually turned away from God, deliberately dishonoring the Lord their God. Israel justifiably deserved the severest punishment possible, and God was obligated to fulfill that part of the covenant (Deuteronomy 8:19–20). Like a stubborn son who would not listen to his parents, Israel was totally rebellious toward God, their Father. According to Jewish law, a defiant son was supposed to be turned over to the elders of the city and stoned to death (Deuteronomy 21:18–21). An earthly father could give up his son. However, since God is infinitely just and infinitely merciful, the two attributes are seemingly in conflict. Here mercy wins!

Rhetorically, as a father filled with love, compassion, and mercy, the Lord questions Israel. Here are two sets of parallelism, a feature common in Hebrew poetry. The first is "give thee up, Ephraim" with "deliver thee, Israel," and the second is "make thee as Admah" with "set thee as Zeboim." Each refers to one action. "Ephraim" was the second son of Joseph, one of the northern tribes of Israel. Ephraim and Israel here represent the Northern Kingdom; it means that all the inhabitants of the northern tribes were guilty. There was a breakdown of the discipline of the northern tribes; therefore, all deserved to be disciplined. To give them up or deliver them is tantamount to doing to them as was done to Admah and Zeboim—total destruction of the land and the people. Admah and Zeboim were among the five cities in the plain that included Sodom and Gomorrah

(Genesis 14:2), which were totally destroyed (Genesis 18:16–19:20; Deuteronomy 29:22–23).

Israel rightly deserved similar punishment. However, as He agonizes on this and envisioned what the outcome would be, God's heart of compassion takes over. He says His heart has "turned" (Heb. hafak, **haw-FAWK**, to change or transform), meaning He has changed His mind. The phrase "my repentings are kindled together" expresses the intensity of His compassion. The word for "repentings" is elsewhere translated "comfort" and refers to mercy or compassion. The idea of being "kindled together" is also used to describe times of great emotional distress (Genesis 43:30; 1 Kings 3:26).

The questions He poses in verse 8 are answered in verse 9. The Lord affirms, "I will not execute the fierceness of mine anger, I will not return to destroy Ephraim" (from v. 9). Here the Lord displays His characteristics of mercy and constancy. What seems like a change in God's action is in accordance with His eternal purpose of love and mercy for His people. In addition to deep compassion, faithfulness to His unconditional covenant with Abraham (Genesis 12:1–3) motivated the Lord to spare Israel from total destruction. However, His covenant with Israel at Sinai was conditional. If they failed to meet those conditions, God was obligated to withhold His blessings. Israel's possession of land with its blessings was based on the Abrahamic Covenant, but their enjoyment was based on the Mosaic Covenant. God was faithful to both covenants: He preserved the nation, but He disciplined them for their sins. The phrase "the Holy One in the midst of thee" confirms His faithfulness and constant presence to protect and preserve them in keeping with His covenant. The phrase "I will not enter into the city" means that He would not enter the city as He did to Admah and Zeboim and destroy them in anger.

10 They shall walk after the LORD: he shall roar like a lion: when he shall roar, then the children shall tremble from the west.

In the Scriptures, God's pronouncement of judgment is often immediately followed with a promise of hope. So is the case here. Here Hosea prophesies a better relationship between Israel and their God. They "shall walk after the Lord" means they will follow the ways of the Lord, in contrast to their former life of rebellion and obstinacy. Then the Lord "shall roar like a lion," not in the sense of hostility for destruction (5:14; 13:7), but as a signal and a call of return from captivity: both physically from exile and spiritually from sin. They would come from the west including the islands and coastlands of the Mediterranean Sea and Egypt. God calls people from everywhere to repentance.

12:1 Ephraim feedeth on wind, and followeth after the east wind: he daily increaseth lies and desolation; and they do make a covenant with the Assyrians, and oil is carried into Egypt. 2 The LORD hath also a controversy with Judah, and will punish Jacob according to his ways; according to his doings will he recompense him.

Hosea continues God's charge against Ephraim (i.e., Israel) for their waywardness. Using the figure of speech of wind, Hosea describes Israel's pursuit of vain things and their false reliance on humans rather than their God. The phrase "Ephraim feedeth on wind" means to eagerly strive after empty or worthless things. The "wind" is *ruakh* (**ROO-akh**), generally associated with air or breath and synonymous with emptiness. Not only do they purse vain things, but they also followed "after the east wind." The east wind, used figuratively here, is particularly destructive to this area since it blows in from the desert bringing searing heat with it. It represents not only the pursuit of the vain things but the ruin Israel is bringing upon itself (cf. Job 27:21). How does Israel do this? They increase daily in "lies and desolation"— continually deepening in faslehood and violence (see 4:1–2). Furthermore, they sought an alliance with worldly powers—Assyria and Egypt—hoping to secure help (5:13). Also, King Hoshea of Israel rebelled against Assyria by covenanting with Egypt. But this backfired. This led to the destruction of Israel and its capture by Assyria (2 Kings 17:3–6).

Verse 2 focuses on the sin of Judah, the Southern Kingdom. Although their sin seemed lighter (11:12), Judah was equally guilty and deserved discipline. The clause "The LORD hath also a controversy with Judah" means that the Lord has a charge against Judah. He "will punish Jacob according to his ways." Jacob, who was later named Israel, was the ancestor of all twelve tribes of Israel. Thus, the two kingdoms, here being represented by "Jacob" will be punished according to their deeds; none will go unpunished. Verses 3–5 give a brief history of Jacob. Like his descendants, Jacob practiced deceit. But in contrast to Israel and Judah, Jacob sought God. Jacob rid his house of idols (Genesis 35:2), but his descendants could not give up their idol worship.

6 Therefore turn thou to thy God: keep mercy and judgment and wait on thy God continually.

After laying the charge against Judah and Israel, Hosea calls on them for a change of heart and direction. "Therefore," he says "turn thou to thy God." The word "turn" is the Hebrew *shuv* (**SHOOV**), which means to turn back or retreat. It has the idea of changing a course or direction one was taking and turning to another. They have consistently wandered away from the God of their forefather Jacob, and now He wants them to turn back to Yahweh. To do that would mean to "keep mercy and judgment." Mercy and justice are the very foundation of God's principles. They

are fundamentally required of all followers of God; they define a proper relationship with the Almighty (6:6; Micah 6:8). Jesus refers to these as "the weightier matters of the law" (Matthew 23:23). To do these, they must "wait on thy God continually." This is a call to total surrender, hope, and reliance on God for strength. "Continually" has the idea of a consistent relationship with the Lord by keeping the precepts as children of the living God.

7 He is a merchant, the balances of deceit are in his hand: he loveth to oppress. 8 And Ephraim said, Yet I am become rich, I have found me out substance: in all my labours they shall find none iniquity in me that were sin.'

Here Hosea mentions some of the sins that the people of Israel had committed: using dishonesty in business (12:7), defrauding people to make more money, and oppressing the people, expressed here as "in his hand is the scale of cheating." Historically, Israel economically and materially prospered, and this led to their pride. They were so self-sufficient and delusional that they would say, "We don't need God." They thought that because of their wealth, they were righteous and sinless. This attitude that was common both in the eighth century BC and first century AD is still common today—not only in the world but also in the Christian churches.

9 And I that am the LORD thy God from the land of Egypt will yet make thee to dwell in tabernacles, as in the days of the solemn feast. 10 I have also spoken by the prophets, and I have multiplied visions, and used similitudes, by the ministry of the prophets.

But their pride and self-delusion will be debunked. The Lord would humble them. Here the Lord evokes His attribute of immutability with "the LORD thy God from the land of

Egypt." He recalls the history of the Exodus journey in the wilderness where they dwelt in tents. Instead of enjoying their houses, they would live in tents as their fathers did during their wilderness journey (13:4; Exodus 20:2). After the Assyrians were done with them, Israel would be grateful even for the booths they lived in for a week during the Feast of Tabernacles (Leviticus 23:33–43). Customarily, once a year the Israelites would spend a week living in tents during the Feast of Tabernacles to commemorate God's protection as they wandered in the wilderness for forty years (Deuteronomy 1:19–2:1). In verse 10, the Lord warns that He has spoken through the prophets and with different methods, all types of visions and parables to communicate to them (6:5; Amos 2:11; Ezekiel 3:14). Therefore, they cannot plead ignorance as a defense. Israel refused the admonitions but continued in their sin; therefore, the consequence of their sin will not be withheld.

11 Is there iniquity in Gilead? surely they are vanity: they sacrifice bullocks in Gilgal; yea, their altars are as heaps in the furrows of the fields.

Verse 11 seems to confirm the degree and gravity of their sin of idolatry and abject rejection of the Lord. As an affirmation of their utter depravity, the prophet poses a rhetorical question: "Is there iniquity in Gilead?" He answers his question: "surely they are vanity." Gilead was a region east of the Jordan known for its iniquity, vanity, idolatry, and wickedness. Gilgal, a major city just across the Jordan from Gilead in Canaan, is referred to as a place of false worship (4:15). Therefore, these places will be destroyed and their altars left as a heap of stones in the hollow of a plowed field.

12 And Jacob fled into the country of Syria, and Israel served for a wife, and for a

wife he kept sheep. 13 And by a prophet the LORD brought Israel out of Egypt, and by a prophet was he preserved.

With reference to Jacob's plight, Hosea tells Israel to remember their humble beginnings: their prosperity was not by their personal effort, but because God was gracious to them. "Jacob fled into the country of Syria," when he escaped from Esau to Padanaram (Genesis 28:2, 5). There he worked hard for His wealth. He served fourteen years (seven years for each of his two wives, Genesis 29:20–28), plus six more years to earn some of his father-in-law Laban's sheep (Genesis 30:31; 31:41). Hosea also reminded them how the Lord delivered Israel by the hand of a prophet, Moses, out of Egypt and preserved them. As Jacob tended Laban's flock, so the Lord cared for Israel in the wilderness, wandering. Unlike during Moses' leadership when he led the children and were preserved, present Israel has no regard for the prophets (4:5, 6:5, 9:7).

14 Ephraim provoked him to anger most bitterly: therefore shall he leave his blood upon him, and his reproach shall his LORD return unto him.

Despite warnings from the prophets, Israel was disobedient. They continued in their sin thereby aggravating the Lord's "anger most bitterly." Therefore the Lord will leave them with their guilt of bloodshed (1:4, 4:2, 5:2, 6:8). This also refers to violence they committed against others, including human sacrifices (3:2). The Lord gives up on them and will evoke justice. The clause "and his reproach shall his Lord return unto him" means the Lord will pay them with a taste of their own medicine. As in the Law of Moses, "their blood will be on their head" (Leviticus 20:11, 13, 16, 27). Here is a contrast between past divine preservation and present divine anger that would bring punishment (Isaiah 65:7). Although God is merciful and compassionate, He is also a just God, and every sin has its consequences and must be atoned. Graciously, God does not deal with us according to our sins. Thanks be to God for sending His Son to atone for us through grace.

Sources:

Biblesoft's New Exhaustive Strong's Numbers and Concordance with Expanded Greek-Hebrew Dictionary. 2006. Biblesoft, Inc.

Jamieson, Fausset, and Brown Commentary, Electronic Database. 2006, Biblesoft, Inc.

Life Application Study Bible NIV, Tyndale House Publishers, Inc. Carol Stream, Illinois.

Wiersbe, Warren W. *The Bible Exposition Commentary: Old Testament* 2004.

Zondervan NIV Study Bible, 2008 by Zondervan, Grand Rapids, Michigan.

Say It Correctly

Ephraim. **EEF**-ram.
Assyria. ah-**SEE**-ree-ah.
Admah. awd-**MAH**.
Zeboim. zeh-boe-**EEM**.

Daily Bible Readings

MONDAY
Receiving a New Vision of God
(Genesis 28:10–17)

TUESDAY
Justice for Gentile Believers
(Acts 15:10–17)

WEDNESDAY
The Up or Down Choice
(Deuteronomy 28:1–6, 15–19)

THURSDAY
Jesus, a Migrant from Egypt
(Matthew 2:13–15)

FRIDAY
Ephraim Spurns God's Love and Suffers
(Hosea 11:3–6)

SATURDAY
Once a Slave; Now a Brother
(Philemon 8–21)

SUNDAY
Respond with Love and Justice Daily
(Hosea 11:1–2, 7–10, 12:1–2, 6–14)

Notes

Wisdom

People experience God's wisdom in both the Hebrew Scriptures and the New Testament. During this quarter, we explore the many facets of wisdom as recorded in the book of Proverbs, in the Gospels, and in the letter written by James.

UNIT 1 • Wisdom in Proverbs

This unit explores the nature of God's wisdom as found in the book of Proverbs. These lessons describe how wisdom calls to us, the value of wisdom and the gifts she offers, and finally the metaphor of the feast of wisdom.

Lesson 1: June 7, 2020
The Call of Wisdom
Proverbs 1:1–4, 7–8, 10, 20–22, 32–33

People feel compelled by something greater than themselves to act wisely when confronting feelings of inadequacy to complete a task. How can they overcome these feelings of inadequacy and move forward? The wisdom of God instructs us to discern the direction we should go and gives us the insight we need to understand life.

Lesson 2: June 14, 2020
The Value of Wisdom
Proverbs 2:1–11

People search for life's meaning through wealth, wisdom, or other worldly things. What is the best method to search for meaning in life? Wisdom's treasure is more valuable than riches because it can center a person's heart, will, and thought toward a knowledge of God.

Lesson 3: June 21, 2020
The Gifts of Wisdom
Proverbs 8:8–14, 17–21

People desire wisdom and hope to be rewarded when they search for it. Why is wisdom so desirable? Wisdom's value is more than tangible gain; it gives knowledge and courage and leads toward God's path of justice and righteousness.

Lesson 4: June 28, 2020
Wisdom's Feast
Proverbs 9:1–6, 8–10, 13–18

Two competing voices call to us on life's journey: wisdom and folly. Why should we heed the call of wisdom? Wisdom gives instruction to the wise, yet the foolish suffer their own downfall.

UNIT 2 • Wisdom in the Gospels

This unit offers four lessons, one lesson from each of the four Gospels, that examines the wisdom of God seen in the teachings and life of Jesus.

Lesson 5: July 5, 2020
Wisdom's Vindication
Matthew 11:7–19

People often label unusual or unexpected behavior as eccentric, foolish, or even wrong; and the persons who act in such unusual ways are vilified. What should be our assessment when someone's behavior is unexpected? In Matthew, Jesus says his behavior and John's, while unusual in their day, will eventually be proven wise by their subsequent deeds.

Lesson 6: July 12, 2020
The Boy Jesus
Ecclesiastes 3:1, 7; Luke 2:39–52

Some young people amaze us with a wisdom that seems beyond their years. How should we respond to precocious wisdom? Luke records that the teachers in the Temple were awed by the wisdom of twelve-year-old Jesus, but Mary and Joseph were confused and exasperated.

Lesson 7: July 19, 2020
The Wisdom of Jesus
Mark 6:1–6

Some people amaze us by displaying unexpected wisdom. What happens when people show such extraordinary wisdom? Mark tells us that the people in Jesus' hometown were both astounded and offended by Jesus' wise teachings, and the religious leaders were incensed when Jesus' wisdom challenged their traditions.

Lesson 8: July 26, 2020
Wisdom: The Way, Truth, and Life
John 14:1–14

Some people say there are many ways to salvation and that everyone attains it by following his or her own way. What are we to make of such claims? Just as Proverbs contrasted the way of wisdom with false ways, Jesus proclaimed that He is the way, the truth, and the life through whom His disciples would come to know and understand God the Father.

UNIT 3 • Faith and Wisdom in James

This unit offers a five-lesson study of wisdom as seen in the letter of James. These lessons explore the interaction of faith and wisdom, including practical advice regarding faith in action and taming the tongue. The study ends by contrasting two kinds of wisdom.

Lesson 9: August 2, 2020
Faith and Wisdom
James 1:1–11

People desire to be seen as wise. What is the source of wisdom? The letter of James affirms that God gives wisdom generously and ungrudgingly to those who ask in faith.

Lesson 10: August 9, 2020
Hearing and Doing the Word
James 1:19–27

People read and talk about doing good, but find it difficult to help the most vulnerable in society. How is righteousness accomplished? According to James, righteousness is achieved by hearing and doing the Word of God.

Lesson 11: August 16, 2020
Faith Without Works Is Dead
James 2:14–26

Some people make bold claims about the standards by which they live, but their actions deny those claims. How can we tell when someone is genuine? James says the one who has faith will demonstrate that faith by his or her works, as did Abraham and Rahab.

Lesson 12: August 23, 2020
Taming the Tongue
James 3:1–12

The spoken word can be either an affirming or destructive force in the lives of vulnerable humans. How can the affirming force prevail in human interactions? James informs believers that only through the discipline required in taming the tongue can the fruits of godly wisdom be made visible in the lives of others.

Lesson 13: August 30, 2020
Two Kinds of Wisdom
James 3:13–18; 5:7–12

Throughout history, many have risked their lives by resisting oppressive regimes, thus saving the lives of others. What motivates a person to defy evil and choose to act for the good of strangers? James compares and contrasts the consequences of using wisdom for righteousness or for evil.

A Few Words About Wisdom

by Marvin A. McMickle, PhD

There are several ways in which a biblical commentary can talk about the word wisdom. One approach would be to seek a definition of the word: "wisdom is …." If that path is taken, then one would turn at once to the Hebrew word *khokmah* (**KHOKE-mah**), which carries the sense of sagacity or the ability to make prudent and productive choices that are rooted not in facts but in insight. This is the word that is most associated with Solomon and his actions and decisions. In 2 Chronicles, as Solomon is about to begin his reign as king of Israel, he asks God to "give me now wisdom and knowledge, that I may go out and come in before this people" (from 2 Chronicles 3:10). God was pleased with this request and granted it so that "Solomon's wisdom excelled the wisdom of all the children of the east country, and all the wisdom of Egypt" (1 Kings 4:30).

One would also consider the Greek word *sophia* (**sow-FEE-uh**), which carries the sense of cleverness or skill in reasoning, or *phronesis* (**FRO-nay-seese**), which suggests intelligence or understanding. The apostle Paul exhorts the Philippian church to "have this mind (*phroneo*) in you that was also in Christ Jesus" (Philippians 2:5). The word *sophia* is consistently associated with Jesus. Early in His earthly life Luke says, "And Jesus increased in wisdom (*sophia*) and in stature, and in favor with God and man" (Luke 2:52). Paul prays that the Colossians will know Christ,

"in whom are hidden all the measures of wisdom (*sophia*) and knowledge" (Colossians 2:3).

The language of Paul in Colossians 2:3 points to a second way to approach the concept of wisdom, which is to compare and contrast wisdom with other terms that may or may not be synonymous with the word. Paul talks about "wisdom and knowledge," or about matters of reasoning and matters of revelation. There is much that is available to everyone in terms of information. However, one must respect the difference between basic knowledge and true wisdom.

After a word study, another approach would be to identify those people who seem to possess or embody the word. In this sense, wisdom is not just to be possessed. The possession of wisdom should then result in certain actions. That is what is at the heart of James when he shows us what wisdom looks like in action: "But the wisdom that is from above is first pure, then peaceable, gentle, and easy to be intreated, full of mercy and good fruits, without partiality, and without hypocrisy" (James 3:17).

Yet another approach would be to look at those people who seem to belong to a professional class called "wise men" or "wise persons." The Hebrew word in this instance is *khakam* (**khaw-KAWM**), which is a variation of the aforementioned word for wisdom (**khokmah**). This group of people is most often associated with the priestly, learned class of other nations when they enter into the biblical story. This group appears after Aaron has laid down the staff of Moses in the royal court of Pharaoh (Exodus 7:11). In the book of Daniel we hear a great deal about this group (e.g., Daniel 2:2).

We also encounter this professional class of "wise men"—magicians—astrologers—sorcerers as part of the birth narrative of Jesus (Matthew 2). The Greek word in this text is *magos* (**MAW-goce**), which implies a mix between a magician and an astronomer. These magi clearly state that their journey from the east began when they had "seen his star in the east" (Matthew 2:2). Thus, the idea that they were astrologers makes sense. (The actual language offers several challenges to the popular Christmas carol "We Three Kings." The text does not say there were monarchs. The text says there were magi. The number three is probably associated with the three gifts offered to Mary and Joseph in homage to Jesus: gold frankincense, and myrrh.) How appropriate that the wise men of the east come to Bethlehem to pay homage to the baby of Bethlehem who is God's wisdom in human flesh.

In every instance, what we learn is that the wisdom of the *khakam*, the wise ones or sorcerers or astrologers of the east, was no match for the *khokmah*, or the true wisdom of God. Paul makes one of his greatest pronouncements on precisely this point when he says:

For it is written: "I will destroy the wisdom of the wise; the intelligence of the intelligent I will frustrate." Where is the wise person? Where is the teacher of the law? Where is the philosopher of this age? Has God not made foolish the wisdom of the world? For since in the wisdom of God the world through its wisdom did not know him, God was pleased through the foolishness of what was preached to save those who believe. Jews demand signs and Greeks look for wisdom, but we preach Christ crucified: a stumbling block to Jews and foolishness to Gentiles, but to those whom God has called, both Jews and Greeks, Christ the power of God and the wisdom of God. For the foolishness of God is wiser than human wisdom, and the weakness of God is stronger than human strength (1 Corinthians 1:19–25).

This discussion calls into question the beliefs and behaviors of many Christians today who seem to place as much faith in their horoscope as they do in the Bible and in the message of Jesus. What is to be made of those persons who believe that their being a Leo has any bearing on their daily lives or their eternal salvation? Fortune cookies are neither nutritious nor a source of human knowledge. Palm readings, fortune tellers, crystal balls, rabbits' feet, good luck charms, talismans, and other reliance on magic and manipulation are widely employed in modern American society.

I knew a church member who professed faith in Christ. However, he also wore a Star of David around his neck (espousing Judaism) and a ring with a star and crescent on his finger (espousing Islam). He also kept a rabbit's foot in his back pocket. He said he just wanted to be sure he had all his bases covered. It is a reminder of the life of no less a notable person than the 19th century abolitionist and former slave, Frederick Douglass, who wrote about how he used a magic talisman given to him by a "conjurer" to protect him when he was being beaten in an attempt to break his spirit and turn him into a compliant and submissive slave.

A final approach to understanding wisdom for this essay is to think about it as associated with a body of written materials or as part of an oral tradition of folklore. There seems to be no end to those who speak about "an old Chinese proverb" that says one thing or another. Many of us grew up hearing stories and seeing cartoons based upon Aesop's Fables. Joel Chandler Harris created a group of characters such as Uncle Remus, Br'er Fox, and Br'er Rabbit in stories that served as a kind of folklore among African Americans that taught various lessons about survival during slave era of the 19th century. Those stories are part of a much larger body of what Lawrence Levine calls "Afro-American folk" thought. People may remember that the story of Alex Haley in the book Roots involved an oral tradition passed down through seven generations of that family. However, that oral tradition was finally confirmed by Alex Haley when he traveled back to the ancestral village of Kunta Kinte in Juffureh, Gambia, and listened to a person called a griot who had memorized the history of events in that certain village and was able to recount that information at great length and with great detail.

This last approach allows us to think about the Wisdom Literature of the Old Testament that would entail the books of Proverbs, Job, and Ecclesiastes. It should be remembered that the Bible is not simply a book. Rather, it should be thought of as a library that houses sixty-six books of various literary types or genres. Those who study the Bible should always seek to do so with an awareness of which kind of literature one is considering. The Bible includes books that involve legal materials, history, prophecy, psalms or hymnology, poetry, and biographies. In the New Testament one can add books that are gospels and epistles as well. Most important to this discussion, though, is wisdom literature.

What is important to remember about wisdom literature is that, like other literary types or genres, the books are not all the same in form, content, or branch of theology. For instance, Proverbs is a collection of sayings or teachings built upon a simple premise that if a person behaves in a certain way, something good or bad will follow because of that action. An example of that would be Proverbs 22:6 that says, "Train up a child in the way he should go, and when he is old, he will not depart from it." This sounds like good advice, and it suggests a promised outcome for those parents who do what the proverb sets forth. The Book of Proverbs is full of such presumed promises.

The fact is, however, that a great many parents did precisely what the proverb suggested, but they did not receive the promised outcome. They did train up their child in the way the child should go, but much to the parent's grievous disappointment, their child did depart from the way in which the child had been trained. Many a family knows the heartache of seeing a beloved child turn their back on the faith and values that parents thought had been instilled in their children. It may seem to some parents that Proverbs does not work.

The problem of Proverbs is exposed by Job, because that book wrestles with the notion that being good and doing good does not always result in having good things come your way. Job is an impeccable example of godliness and devotion, yet his life is filled with one tragedy after another involving his family, his financial resources, his health, and his reputation. The book of Job is not simply about bearing up under suffering. The book of Job is also an antidote to the cheery optimism of Proverbs, because Job is a constant reminder that good things do not always come to people who do good things or who live good lives or who do everything God requires. As Rabbi Harold Kushner reminds us as he dealt with the reality that his son had been diagnosed with a degenerative disease that would claim his life during his teen years, bad things do happen to good people. Thus, Proverbs and Job are two books that must always be considered together; it should always be our aspiration to do what God asks and requires of us. However, there is always the possibility that something tragic can intrude upon your life no matter how good you are as a person. This observation is central to the wisdom tradition of the Old Testament.

Finally, we come to Ecclesiastes. This book openly rejects any notion that there is any pattern, rhyme, or reason to human existence. The notion that if you behave in a certain way you can expect a certain response from God or from other people is simply dismissed as folly or meaninglessness. The message of this book is clear when it says, "Meaningless! Meaningless, says the teacher.

Utterly meaningless! Everything is meaningless" (Ecclesiastes 1:1–2). There is no pattern that can be discerned. There is no single path that will inevitably lead to a better life. There is no guarantee or certainty concerning anything. Life is a series of random events. Thus, the best course of action for a man is to "eat and drink, and that he should make his soul enjoy good in his labour" (from 2:24).

By the end of Ecclesiastes there seems to be a slight turning in the original direction of Proverbs when it says, "Remember your Creator in the days of your youth, before the days of trouble come" (12:1). The book ends with this admonition: "Let us hear the conclusion of the whole matter: Fear God, and keep his commandments: for this is the whole duty of man" (12:13). Notice that this admonition does not include any assurance of what God will do on behalf of those who follow this advice, as one would expect in the book of Proverbs. Perhaps this is the clearest expression of wisdom; just do what the Lord commands as an end in itself!

Marvin A. McMickle, PhD, is the President of Colgate Rochester Crozer Divinity School. There he is also the director of the Doctor of Ministry Program and Professor of African American Religious Studies. He has authored seventeen books.

Sources:
Douglass, Frederick. *Narrative of the Life of Frederick Douglass.* Boston: Bedford Books, 1993. 77–80.
Haley, Alex. *ROOTS.* Garden City, NY: Doubleday, 1974. 574–578.
Hopkins, John. "We Three Kings of Orient Are." Chicago: GIA Publications, 2001. 218.
Kushner, Harold. *When Bad Things Happen to God People.* New York: Anchor Books, 2007.
Levine, Lawrence. *Black Culture and Black Consciousness: Afro-American Folk Thought from Slavery to Freedom.* New York: Oxford, 1977.
Richardson, Alan. *A Theological Word Book of the Bible.* New York: Collier Books, 1950. 282.
Roosevelt, Eleanor. in goodreads.com, #146841.

Wisdom for All People!

As we survey some of the wisdom literature found in the Old Testament, there is so much we can learn to positively influence our everyday living for our just God. As we focus on human wisdom—lessons transmitted from generation to generation through parents and teachers—let us, too, learn directly from the experience and tradition found in God's inerrant Word. In our study of the Gospel of Matthew in the New Testament, we will explore how Jesus teaches wisdom in His Sermon on the Mount and its relationship to the traditional teaching of the Mosaic Law. Let us also see what principles we can draw from the discussion to enhance our daily walk with God. From this quarter's study, we will learn about living, forgiving, loving, and praying for each other. These lessons can help us in our daily living—our daily interaction with others. They can help us live an ordered life, even to face life without worry. To whet your appetite, look at what Proverbs, in the New Living Translation, tells us of everyday wisdom that all people should embrace and practice.

"Hatred stirs up quarrels, but love makes up for all offenses" (Proverbs 10:12).

"If you search for good, you will find favor; but if you search for evil, it will find you!" (Proverbs 11:27)

"Worry weighs a person down; an encouraging word cheers a person up" (Proverbs 12:25).

"Hope deferred makes the heart sick, but a dream fulfilled is a tree of life" (Proverbs 13:12).

"Without oxen a stable stays clean, but you need a strong ox for a large harvest" (Proverbs 14:4).

"A bowl of vegetables with someone you love is better than steak with someone you hate" (Proverbs 15:17).

"Gray hair is a crown of glory; it is gained by living a godly life" (Proverbs 16:31).

"Wrongdoers eagerly listen to gossip; liars pay close attention to slander" (Proverbs 17:4).

"An offended friend is harder to win back than a fortified city. Arguments separate friends like a gate locked with bars" (Proverbs 18:19).

"Discipline your children while there is hope. Otherwise you will ruin their lives" (Proverbs 19:18).

"Wine produces mockers; alcohol leads to brawls. Those led astray by drink cannot be wise" (Proverbs 20:1).

Examining and Developing Wise Choices

by Cheryl Price, PhD

Preparing to teach requires a commitment to study, plan, pray, listen, encourage, and much more. Students are able to benefit in many ways from teachers who are prepared and excited to share God's Word. Providing various activities and experiences allows participants to strengthen and deepen their desires to build a relationship with God and to live God's Word.

During this quarter, share ways participants can become excited about God's Word and make better choices that are in God's will. Connecting God's Word to decisions and life choices has a powerful and strong basis for believers to draw upon.

Life is a struggle, and in many ways, teachers can assist people with developing a reservoir within themselves of God's love through God's Words and actions to face and handle the complexities and the mundanities them confront.

Trust God's Word. Proverbs 1:7 states, "The fear of the LORD is the beginning of knowledge ..." One way to encourage students to believe this to ask them to share life moments where they did not trust God and the results of that distrust. Have them create a journal where they rewrite (or type on any of their mobile devices) Proverbs 1:7 and then write how they trust God. Participants can be divided into groups and then share among themselves with the groups what they wrote and why.

Create a debate of two sides to support or oppose how believers can say no or avoid sinful invitations from "sinners" (Proverbs 1:10).

Making choices that are pleasing before God is often easier said than done. Although Christians sing, pray, and preach about God's wisdom in their lives, we often choose to follow others who make us feel better with less work. God's way may require more responsibility, energy, and time than believers are willing to give. God's always gives us the best, but our best for God can range from mediocre to excellent. Why such a range? Where is our consistency?

Lead a discussion regarding why it is easier or more convenient to do the opposite of what God would have us to do.

Have the class brainstorm how to stand firm in their choices for God when others are opposed to them.

Our lessons in wisdom are individually and collectively transmitted in our experiences and traditions. These pearl of wisdom lessons can be passed from parent to child, teacher to student, or from one generation to the next. Jesus taught His disciples then and now how wisdom is shown in our loving, living, forgiving, and praying for one another and us.

Ask the class to share their favorite proverbs from the Bible and other sources, including African proverbs. Have participants create proverbs individually or in small groups to share with the class.

Provide a time for participants to compare the benefits of wisdom and warnings in Proverb 1:8–19 and Proverbs 3:1–12.

Wisdom is a gift we have from God. Let us teach and learn from the gift of wisdom so that we can be blessings to God's creation in healthy and productive ways.

Cheryl Price, PhD, is Vice President of Content at UMI. She has co-authored and edited many books.

ELIZABETH FREEMAN

1742–1829
Abolitionist

A slave named Bet also know as "Mumbet" was born around 1742 as a slave in Claverack, New York. At some point in her life, she was sold to the Ashley family in Sheffield, Massachusetts. Then during her years in the Ashley household, she married and had a daughter, Betsy called "Little Bet." Her husband fought in the Revolutionary War and died. She was a strong woman, so when John's wife, Hannah Ashley tried to strike Bet's friend with a heated shovel, Bet put up her arm to prevent the blow. As Bet's wound healed, she refused to roll down her sleeve as a reminder to all of the cruel treatment that Hannah gave to her slaves.

In 1780, Massachusetts ratified their state constitution, which read in part: "All men are born free and equal, and have certain natural, essential, and unalienable rights; among which may be reckoned the right of enjoying and defending their lives and liberties; that of acquiring, possessing, and protecting property; in fine, that of seeking and obtaining their safety and happiness." Hearing this, Bet went to see Theodore Sedgwick, a lawyer who believed in the abolition of slavery. He defended both Bet and Brom, another Ashley household slave. The lawyer argued that "all men are born free and equal" meant that no one should be enslaved. The court in Great Barrington, Massachusetts agreed, thus setting a precedent that would abolish slavery in the state of Massachusetts. John Ashley was ordered to pay Bet and Brom for their labor and to pay damages as well.

Mumbet, as she was called, became the first African American woman to be freed under the Massachusetts constitution, which helped lead Massachusetts to be the first state in the union to abolish slavery. Slaves had no last names, so Bet changed her name to Elizabeth Freeman. She was probably eighty-five when she died in 1829.

Sources:

Africans in America/Part 2/Elizabeth Freeman (Mum Bett). http://www.pbs.org/wgbh/aia/part2/2p39.html (accessed 7/26/10).

"Elizabeth Freeman." Elizabeth Freeman Center. https://www.elizabethfreemancenter.org/who-we-are/elizabeth-freeman/ (access 3/26/19).

Teaching Tips

June 7
Bible Study Guide 1

Words You Should Know

A. Proverb (v. 1) *mashal* (Heb.)—A concise wise saying (or longer discourse) designed to teach one how to live

B. Simple (v. 4) *peti* (Heb.)—Naïve, untaught, inexperienced and therefore gullible

Teacher Preparation

Unifying Principle—Listen Up! People feel compelled by something greater than themselves to act wisely when confronting feelings of inadequacy to complete a task. How can they overcome these feelings of inadequacy and move forward? The wisdom of God instructs us to discern the direction we should go and gives us the insight we need to understand life.

A. Read the Bible Background and Devotional Reading.

B. Pray for your students and lesson clarity.

C. Read the lesson Scripture in multiple translations.

O—Open the Lesson

A. Begin the class with prayer.

B. Ask volunteers to describe the best advice they ever received. How was it helpful? In what circumstances have they successfully applied it?

C. Have the students read the Aim for Change and the In Focus story.

D. Ask students how events like those in the story weigh on their hearts and how they can view these events from a faith perspective.

P—Present the Scriptures

A. Read the Focal Verses and discuss the Background and The People, Places, and Times sections.

B. Have the class share what Scriptures stand out for them and why, with particular emphasis on today's context.

E—Explore the Meaning

A. Use In Depth or More Light on the Text to facilitate a deeper discussion of the lesson text.

B. Pose the questions in Search the Scriptures and Discuss the Meaning.

C. Discuss the Liberating Lesson and Application for Activation sections.

N—Next Steps for Application

A. Summarize the value of wisdom as a gift from God.

B. End class with a commitment to pray for godly wisdom for discerning life's direction.

Worship Guide

For the Superintendent or Teacher
Theme: The Call of Wisdom
Song: "Softly and Tenderly (Jesus is Calling)"
Devotional Reading: Psalm 34:11-18

The Call of Wisdom

Bible Background • PROVERBS 1
Printed Text • PROVERBS 1:1–4, 7-8, 10, 20-22, 32-33 | Devotional Reading • PSALM 34:11-18

—————————— **Aim for Change** ——————————

By the end of the lesson we will: RECOGNIZE the value of godly wisdom and direction, VALUE godly wisdom in our choices, and APPLY the standards of wisdom to a specific choice that needs to be made.

—————————————— **In Focus** ——————————————

Mae kept clicking back and forth between the websites for her top college picks. Her grandmother Daisy could see Mae was getting frustrated. "What's the matter, sweetie?"

"I still can't decide which college I want to go to." Mae showed her grandmother the pictures of both colleges, with their sunny campuses, happy graduates, and winning athletes. "They're both offering substantial financial aid. Both have active on-campus ministries. Both have the program I want. I can't decide; they both look so good."

Daisy never had to make this decision herself, but always wished she had gotten the opportunity. She often volunteered at a local Christian charity that offered tutoring and college admission guidance. "I'm glad to know you've already considered the finances, and how you'll stay plugged in at church. What did you think of the campuses?"

Mae sighed. "I haven't gotten to visit either of them. They're out of state, and we could hardly afford the hotels, much less the airfare."

"Well, you can't trust the college's website to show you what the school is really like. Contact a student who goes there now. Have you asked the colleges if they can help pay for you to come visit them? Some colleges do that, you know. Some charities too. I might even have some pull at a certain local charity…" Daisy said, winking at Mae.

Why is it important to seek wise counsel before making major decisions?

—————————————— **Keep in Mind** ——————————————

"The fear of the LORD is the beginning of knowledge: but fools despise wisdom and instruction" (Proverbs 1:7, KJV).

"Fear of the LORD is the foundation of true knowledge, but fools despise wisdom and discipline" (Proverbs 1:7, NLT).

Focal Verses

KJV **Proverbs 1:1** The proverbs of Solomon the son of David, king of Israel;

2 To know wisdom and instruction; to perceive the words of understanding;

3 To receive the instruction of wisdom, justice, and judgment, and equity;

4 To give subtilty to the simple, to the young man knowledge and discretion

7 The fear of the LORD is the beginning of knowledge: but fools despise wisdom and instruction.

8 My son, hear the instruction of thy father, and forsake not the law of thy mother:

10 My son, if sinners entice thee, consent thou not.

20 Wisdom crieth without; she uttereth her voice in the streets:

21 She crieth in the chief place of concourse, in the openings of the gates: in the city she uttereth her words, saying,

22 How long, ye simple ones, will ye love simplicity? and the scorners delight in their scorning, and fools hate knowledge?

32 For the turning away of the simple shall slay them, and the prosperity of fools shall destroy them.

33 But whoso hearkeneth unto me shall dwell safely, and shall be quiet from fear of evil.

NLT **Proverbs 1:1** These are the proverbs of Solomon, David's son, king of Israel.

2 Their purpose is to teach people wisdom and discipline, to help them understand the insights of the wise.

3 Their purpose is to teach people to live disciplined and successful lives, to help them do what is right, just, and fair.

4 These proverbs will give insight to the simple, knowledge and discernment to the young.

7 Fear of the LORD is the foundation of true knowledge, but fools despise wisdom and discipline.

8 My child, listen when your father corrects you. Don't neglect your mother's instruction.

10 My child, if sinners entice you, turn your back on them!

20 Wisdom shouts in the streets. She cries out in the public square.

21 She calls to the crowds along the main street, to those gathered in front of the city gate:

22 "How long, you simpletons, will you insist on being simpleminded? How long will you. mockers relish your mocking? How long will you fools hate knowledge?

32 For simpletons turn away from me—to death. Fools are destroyed by their own complacency.

33 But all who listen to me will live in peace, untroubled by fear of harm."

The People, Places, and Times

Wisdom Literature. The books of the Bible that are considered wisdom literature are Proverbs, Job, and Ecclesiastes. Sometimes some of the Psalms, Song of Solomon, and Lamentations receive this label too. This is a modern way to describe a genre of literature from the ancient Near East, which was plentiful in Egypt and Mesopotamian cultures as well. Sometimes wisdom literature directly presents adages or wise sayings (like Proverbs). Other pieces in the genre ponder a deep question over the course of many conversations and situations (like Job). These books present challenges in understanding them, as they ask questions, yet seem to contradict themselves, and voice doubts quite unlike the prophetic and narrative books. From this, however, we can learn that God is not afraid of our questions. He welcomes our honesty. Biblical wisdom literature asks questions but also assures us that God has the answers. We just need to trust Him.

Background

The purpose of the book of Proverbs is summed up in chapter 1:2. "To know wisdom and instruction; to perceive the words of understanding." In other words, the purpose of Proverbs is to teach the readers wisdom so that they will allow wisdom to govern their lives. Applying wisdom to one's life means approaching all of life's situations and challenges from God's point of view, thinking and living according to His will and truth. That is why "the fear of the LORD is the beginning of knowledge" (v. 7). Therefore, possessing wisdom is related to one's relationship with God. Reverence and awe toward God is the essential prelude to all wisdom and successful living. Wisdom is one of God's divine attributes. God in His grace must reveal it if we are to truly grasp it. Wisdom takes insights gained from our knowledge of God's truth and applies them to our daily lives.

If we have wisdom, it will lead to godly living. God wants us to be fair, just, and righteous. The foolish do not act in accordance with God's Word and reject all instruction. They are self-reliant and prideful. Their only hope is to answer wisdom's call to listen and obey, which will result in safety and peace. The alternative is to be destroyed by acting wayward and self-righteous (1:32–33). The results of seeking wisdom present a clear contrast with living a life of foolishness.

The Book of Proverbs, which is classified among the Wisdom Books of the Old Testament, is a collection of proverbial sayings. It is actually a collection of collections of proverbs composed by different authors over a period of time and finally collected into a single

book. Solomon wrote many of the proverbs, but he also collected 3,000 proverbs (1 Kings 4:29–34). Some proverbs in this book were written by Agur and Lemuel, who are otherwise unknown. Many scholars agree that the book is an anthology comprised of seven discrete units (1—9; 10:1–22:16; 22:17—24:22; 24:23—24:34; 25—29; 30; 31). Chapters 1 through 9, from which our first unit is taken, are considered wisdom for young people. But all people can learn from the wisdom shared.

How did Solomon use godly wisdom as king?

At-A-Glance

1. Wisdom for Godly Living
(Proverbs 1:1–4, 7–8, 10)
2. Wisdom Personified (vv. 20–22, 32–33)

In Depth

1. Wisdom for Godly Living (Proverbs 1:1–4, 7–8, 10)

Solomon is identified as the author. The student (son) is addressed by a teacher (father) (vv. 2–3). He is being told how to get wisdom for godly living, which will lead to appropriate actions. God wants us to be righteous, just, and fair. The teacher is the one who provides the student with the guidance and good advice necessary because they may lack proper judgment (v. 4).

The theme of the book of Proverbs is contained in verse 7. We are wise if we have a "fear of the LORD," which is awe, reverence, and respect of God. True wisdom comes from God. We need to have a relationship with God and obey God's Word. The Word gives us a revelation about who God is and His requirements for living as faithful believers.

Those who will not pursue wisdom are called "fools" who "despise wisdom and instruction" because they think they know everything and do not need God. Fools cannot distinguish between good and bad or right and wrong. People who are arrogant and self-sufficient will reject the need to depend on God or anyone else. It is very hard to convince them otherwise. They do not understand that God is the source of all wisdom and has given them the ability to attain success.

Families are the foundation where children should learn about loving and honoring God. Parents have to set an example. The instructions are a warning from the father to his son about listening to instructions given by his parents and not being enticed by sin (vv. 8–10). Sin often looks and feels good. However, it is only a temporary feeling that will leave us empty.

How can parents instruct and demonstrate to their children a "fear of the Lord"?

2. Wisdom Personified (vv. 20–22, 32–33)

Wisdom is personified and given a human voice (v. 20–33). Wisdom is shouting in the streets, on the corners, and the entrance of the cities to the "simple ones." They are questioned about how long they will continue to act foolish (v. 22). It is in these areas that many wayward people gather and commit sinful acts. Why continue down the same path you have seen others go down and be destroyed (v. 32)? Wisdom is not hidden; God is calling for the foolish to change course and live.

If we listen to God's wisdom, we can live in safety and peace no matter what the future holds (v. 33). We know God promised not to leave or forsake us. He will guide us as we face challenges if we ask for wisdom to make the right choices.

What foolish acts have you witnessed others do that godly wisdom has helped you avoid?

Search the Scriptures

1. What is the purpose of the Proverbs (Proverbs 1:2–3)?

2. What is "the beginning of knowledge" (v. 7)?

3. How can one avoid calamity in their life and have peace (vv. 32–33)?

Discuss the Meaning

1. Discuss the difference between knowledge and wisdom. Are both important?

2. When we have to make major decisions, it is good to seek wise counseling. Whom do you trust to give you wise counsel? How has their advice impacted your life?

3. How does one know when contemplating an important decision whether the choice is God's will versus your flesh?

Liberating Lesson

Life is full of choices. Every day we make choices about whether to go to work, what to do at work, what to eat, how to comb our hair, what clothes to put on, when to go to bed, and so on. Hundreds of choices are made with little thought. But life often gives us difficult decisions that need to be made.

When we witness injustices in our communities, we can either turn the other way or stop and intervene. If we intervene, there may be consequences that affect not only us but our family too. How can we use godly wisdom while trying to help others be treated fairly? It is not an easy answer. Perhaps join or organize protest groups, march, create online petitions, and learn other nonviolent techniques. We can no longer sit in the churches and ignore the social, religious, and civil injustices that are manifesting themselves in our communities. It is time to make a firm decision about how to help our neighbors no matter their race, religion, or nationality. What is God calling you to do? Seek wise counseling before acting and trust God for the outcome.

Application for Activation

When we have to make life-altering decisions, the burden can have us feeling inadequate trying to understand what to do. We need to seek to evaluate life situations in light of God's character and purposes and make decisions based on divine wisdom. We cannot rely on foolish people to help us. They will lead us astray, and our situation will end in calamity.

Whatever choices need to be made, we can rely on God for help. We are to make a conscious effort to apply godly standards of wisdom to the choice that needs to be made. We need to read the Word, pray, talk to other Christians who have shared experiences, pray some more, and then act in accordance with what the Holy Spirit guides us to do. If we obey the Spirit, we will have the benefit of peace.

Follow the Spirit

What God wants me to do:

_____

_____

_____

_____

Remember Your Thoughts

Special insights I have learned:

_____

_____

_____

_____

More Light on the Text

Proverbs 1:1–4, 7–8, 10, 20–22, 32–33

1 The proverbs of Solomon the son of David, king of Israel;

"Proverbs" is not only the title of the book, but it also designates the specific type of Wisdom Literature that comprises this book. "Proverb" in Hebrew is *mashal* (**maw-SHAWL**). Although a *mashal* is usually a brief, concise saying, it can also refer to longer discourses. Therefore a proverb refers to various forms of wise and insightful pronouncements that are designed to teach us how to live godly lives.

Solomon, the third King of Israel, reigned from 971–931 BC. A prolific writer, he wrote 3,000 proverbs; 1,005 songs (1 Kings 4:32), and at least two Psalms (72 and 127), as well as three of the five Wisdom Books in the Bible—Proverbs, Ecclesiastes, and the Song of Solomon (also known as the Song of Songs). Job and Psalms comprise the remainder of the Wisdom Literature that in general deals with our human struggles and real-life experiences. They emphasize the things that are necessary to gain moral excellence, and in so doing live a godly life that finds favor with God. Although most of the proverbs were written by Solomon (1:1, 10:1, 25:1), there were other authors as well such as "the sayings of the wise" (22:17–24:34), Agur and Lemuel (chapters 30 and 31 respectively).

Solomon qualifies to write the majority of this collection of wise sayings because of his own cry for wisdom. Although he was not the eldest son of David, Solomon was given the honor to succeed his father David and ascended the throne at only twenty years old. Nevertheless, when told by God that he could request anything he desired, a youthful Solomon wisely asked, "Give me now wisdom and knowledge, that I may go out and come in before this people: for who can judge this thy people, that is so great" (2 Chronicles 1:10).

481

God granted his request and Solomon's wisdom was so legendary even kings (1 Kings 4:34) and queens (1 Kings 10:1–13) came from near and far to sit and learn at the feet of Solomon. Solomon's request for wisdom to faithfully carry out his assignment as judge over the people of Israel is an example we can all follow. Each person has been given a divine purpose. Your assignment can only be faithfully executed through the wisdom that comes from God. James tells us that wisdom is available upon request (James 1:5).

2 To know wisdom and instruction; to perceive the words of understanding; 3 To receive the instruction of wisdom, justice, and judgment, and equity; 4 To give subtlety to the simple, to the young man knowledge and discretion.

After identifying himself as the principal author of the book of Proverbs, Solomon immediately sets forth the purpose of the book through a series of infinitive clauses (vv. 2–3)—to know, to perceive, to receive—and then explains who his intended audience is—the simple and the young man (v. 4).

The first stated purpose and the primary goal of the proverbs, these pithy sayings is "to know wisdom and instruction." Instruction (Heb. *musar*, **moo-SAR**) means doctrine or discipline. Wisdom (*khokmah*, **khoke-MAW**) is the skillful use of that knowledge by putting it into practice so that one can live a godly life, pleasing to the Lord. In the Old Testament *khokmah* often refers to the mental and physical skills of craftsmen, sailors, singers, and so on. Such was the case in the building of the tabernacle in the wilderness when God selected Bezaleel who was "filled with the spirit of God, in wisdom... and in knowledge, and in all manner of workmanship" (Exodus 31:2–3). But later on, as in Proverbs, *khokmah* focused on the skillful application of moral and ethical principles that resulted in godly living. Consequently, a person with wisdom had "expertise" or "skill" in godly living, and the proverb was the vehicle to help the simple and the young to know wisdom and instruction and to follow its precepts.

Along with knowing wisdom and instruction, the second stated purpose of Proverbs is "to perceive the words of understanding." *Bin* (**BEEN**), the Hebrew word for perceive is to have insight and discernment. Such things allow one to distinguish between right and wrong, as well as to gain mental acumen. Not only must we seek wisdom, but we must also perceive it when we find it.

Finally, the third delineated purpose of Proverbs is "to receive the instruction of wisdom, justice, and judgment, and equity" (v. 3). Receive (Heb. *laqakh*, **law-KAKH**) means to take in hand, to take possession of, or to accept. So the idea here is that the proverbs are to be grasped, to be taken hold of as a valuable possession. When received in such a manner, the proverbs will teach (1) wisdom, so the simple and the young can live wisely; (2) justice, that which is right or just; (3) judgment, how to decide a case; and (4) equity, evenness, uprightness, and straightness.

After giving the purpose for the proverbs, the writer now explains who his intended audience is. It is "to give subtilty to the simple, to the young man knowledge and discretion." Even though the proverbs are intended for the simple and the young man, their impact is so far-reaching that it also extends to the person who is wise. If the person who is already wise will pay attention to know, perceive, and receive these words of instruction, then they will become even wiser (1:5). The word simple (Heb. *peti*, **peh-TEE**) refers to someone who is naive and untaught. It is a person whose exposure to life and wisdom has been limited. Because of inexperience, they are gullible and easily influenced, especially in a negative direction.

7 The fear of the LORD is the beginning of knowledge: but fools despise wisdom and instruction. 8 My son, hear the instruction of thy father, and forsake not the law of thy mother: 10 My son, if sinners entice thee, consent thou not.

The initial six introductory verses climax in this theological expression, "the fear of the LORD is the beginning of knowledge." One cannot obtain knowledge of spiritual things if he or she begins at the wrong point, refusing to reverence God. The "fear the LORD" is to recognize who God is—holy, mighty, just, and worthy—and then to recognize who we are to God—flawed, ignorant, weak, but loved. This should make us respond by reverencing, worshiping, obeying, and serving Him. Even though the word "fear" (Heb. *yir'ah*, **year-AH**) is often used to describe situations that cause terror or anxiety, it is also commonly used to describe situations of reverence and respect to God or man. The essence of *yir'ah* is a recognition that you are under someone's or something else's power, plus a recognition of your relationship with that power. If you have a positive relationship, you can hope for mercy or favor. If not, you tremble for the worst.

The essence of true knowledge is fearing God. In fact, this phrase, "the fear of the LORD" is so central to the wisdom that it occurs 30 times in the Bible, and of that number, it occurs 14 times in Proverbs alone. Proverbs delineates these benefits of fearing the Lord: (1) it prolongs your life (10:27), (2) it provides confidence (14:26), (3) it helps in resisting evil (16:6), and (4) it produces riches and honor (22:4). These benefits result from hearing and heeding Proverbs 23:17: "be thou in the fear of the LORD all the day long."

Having contrasted the stark differences between the wise person who fears the Lord and the fool who despises wisdom, the sage now calls for the son to hear and then to heed the instruction of his parents. The word "hear" (Heb. *shama'*, **shaw-MAH**) does not only means to hear with the ear but also to heed and obey the instructions that were given. The instructions given are critical to living a good life with honor and integrity—do not pay attention to sinners who entice you with doing evil.

20 Wisdom crieth without; she uttereth her voice in the streets: 21 She crieth in the chief place of concourse, in the openings of the gates: in the city she uttereth her words, saying, 22 How long, ye simple ones, will ye love simplicity? and the scorners delight in their scorning, and fools hate knowledge?

Wisdom is a feminine noun, and here Solomon personifies wisdom as a woman calling out, a woman urgent in her pleas to spread wisdom. What she has to say is so important that she has to make sure that it is heard. So wisdom hits the streets to call out to all who have an ear to hear. In the streets, she raises her voice so that she can be heard above the noise of complacency and contempt. She does not limit her call to wisdom to the neighborhood side streets. She also goes to "the chief place of concourse," the main street, to make her speech. Unwilling to limit the scope of her message, she moves to the city gates, which was the seat of government. She doggedly takes her message wherever people are and poses her searing question to three groups of people. How long will the simple and the scorners continue to be set in their ways, and how long will fools actively eschew knowledge? If they only respond to wisdom's rebuke and take her counsel, a foolish person can become wise (1:23).

32 For the turning away of the simple shall slay them, and the prosperity of fools shall destroy them. 33 But whoso hearkeneth unto me shall dwell safely, and shall be quiet from fear of evil.

These final two verses in chapter 1 summarize clearly the two choices that are available, and the consequences of the choice that is made. The first choice is made by the simple, the naïve, and those who turn away and reject Lady Wisdom's call. They hate knowledge (1:22) and refuse to fear the Lord (1:7). Therefore fools suffer the consequences of their actions. Even what they consider "prosperity" will destroy them. The folly of the simple and the fool will ultimately result in death. By contrast, heeding the way of wisdom gives safety and peace. These contrasts between the consequences of folly (1:32) and of wisdom (1:33) set the tone for the rest of the book. These stark contrasts also set the tone for our lives as well. Regardless of where you are—the simple, or a fool—you can make a decision right now to change, heed the call of wisdom, and set the course of your life on a path of wise, skillful living that will bless your life and the lives of those around you.

Sources:
Douglas, J. D., editor. *New Bible Dictionary (Second Edition).* Downers Grove, IL: InterVarsity Press, 1982. 988–990.
Estes, Daniel. *Handbook on the Wisdom Books.* Grand Rapids, MI: Baker Books, 2005.
Henry, Matthew. *Matthew Henry Commentary on the Whole Bible.* Peabody, MA: Hendrickson Publishers, Inc., 1991.
Kidner, Derek. *The Proverbs: An Introduction and Commentary.* Downers Grove, IL: InterVarsity Press, 2003.
Life Application Study Bible, New Revised Standard Version. Wheaton, IL: Tyndale House Publishers, Inc., 1989. 1038–1042.
The NIV Study Bible (Tenth Anniversary Edition). Grand Rapids, MI: Zondervan Publishing House, 1995. 935–940.
Unger, Merril F. *The New Unger's Bible Handbook.* Chicago, IL: Moody Press, 1984. 229–230.
Walvoord, J.F., and Zuck, R.B. *The Bible Knowledge Commentary: Old Testament.* Wheaton, IL: Victor Books, 1985.

Say It Correctly

Proverbial. pro-**VERB**-ee-al.
Subtilty. **SUH**-till-tee.
Naïve. nie-**EVE**.

Daily Bible Readings

MONDAY
Faith Community Discerns Path of Wisdom
(Acts 6:1–7)

TUESDAY
Parents Joyfully Pass on the Faith
(2 Timothy 1:3-9)

WEDNESDAY
Learning the Fear of the Lord
(Psalm 34:11-18)

THURSDAY
Violence Not a Wise Choice
(Matthew 26:47-52)

FRIDAY
Vast Scope of Solomon's Wisdom
(1 Kings 4:29-34)

SATURDAY
Prize Wisdom and Insight
(Proverbs 4:1-9)

SUNDAY
Godly Wisdom for Life's Decisions
(Proverbs 1:1-4, 7-8, 10, 20-22, 32-33)

Teaching Tips

Words You Should Know

A. Buckler (v. 7) *magen* (Heb.)—A small shield

B. Preserve (v. 11) *shamar* (Heb.)—To watch or guard

Teacher Preparation

Unifying Principle—Seeking Meaning. People search for life's meaning through wealth, wisdom, or other worldly things. What is the best method to search for meaning in life? Wisdom's treasure is more valuable than riches because it can center a person's heart, will, and thought toward a knowledge of God.

A. Read the Bible Background and Devotional Reading.

B. Pray for your students and lesson clarity.

C. Read the lesson Scripture in multiple translations.

O—Open the Lesson

A. Begin the class with prayer.

B. Ask the class: "How can foolish choices influence your ability to make wise choices?"

C. Have the students read the Aim for Change and the In Focus story.

D. Ask students how events like those in the story weigh on their hearts and how they can view these events from a faith perspective.

P—Present the Scriptures

A. Read the Focal Verses and discuss the Background and The People, Places, and Times sections.

B. Have the class share what Scriptures stand out for them and why, with particular emphasis on today's themes.

E—Explore the Meaning

A. Use In Depth or More Light on the Text to facilitate a deeper discussion of the lesson text.

B. Pose the questions in Search the Scriptures and Discuss the Meaning.

C. Discuss the Liberating Lesson and Application for Activation sections.

N—Next Steps for Application

A. Summarize the value of accepting wise counsel.

B. End class with a commitment to pray for learning how to make wise choices.

Worship Guide

For the Superintendent or Teacher
Theme: The Value of Wisdom
Song: "The Riches of God's Word"
Devotional Reading: Proverbs 2:12–22

The Value of Wisdom

Bible Background • GENESIS 39; PROVERBS 2
Printed Text • PROVERBS 2:1–11 | Devotional Reading • PROVERBS 2:12–22

Aim for Change

By the end of this lesson, we will: UNDERSTAND the search for the wisdom that comes from God is most important; YEARN for the wisdom that comes from God; and CENTER our hearts, wills, and thoughts in the wisdom that comes from God.

In Focus

Caleb loved his father, Don, and trusted him. He often tried to imitate his father in pursuing the same things he did. He asked his dad several times to let him take karate. Don had taken karate as a child. Don finally agreed to let Caleb take karate lessons.

Caleb did not understand why his dad insisted on his watching the movie *Karate Kid* repeatedly. "Caleb, I know Bruce Lee is your hero, but there is a different reason I wanted you to watch *Karate Kid* so many times. The first reason is you should understand the importance of listening to the instructions of the teacher and do exactly as he instructs you. Second, just like you have followed my instructions without a clear understanding, you must also be willing to trust your instructors and follow their instructions."

Unassured, but willing to obey, Caleb did what his father asked and followed the teachings of his instructors. It was hard work, but Caleb made a decision to obey. He was diligent in his pursuit to develop his karate skills. Although he didn't have class every day, he took it upon himself to practice as though he did. In doing so, Caleb became top in his class and represented his class in the most challenging competitions. He, his father, and his instructors were very pleased with his accomplishments. Caleb was able to appreciate his father's wisdom even more.

People of faith grow in their recognition and appreciation of the role of divine wisdom in their lives. How do you allow wisdom to center your heart, your will, and your thoughts in God's will?

Keep in Mind

"For the LORD giveth wisdom: out of his mouth cometh knowledge and understanding" (Proverbs 2:6, KJV).

"For the LORD grants wisdom! From his mouth come knowledge and understanding"
(Proverbs 2:6, NLT).

Focal Verses

KJV **Proverbs 2:1** My son, if thou wilt receive my words, and hide my commandments with thee;

2 So that thou incline thine ear unto wisdom, and apply thine heart to understanding;

3 Yea, if thou criest after knowledge, and liftest up thy voice for understanding;

4 If thou seekest her as silver, and searchest for her as for hid treasures;

5 Then shalt thou understand the fear of the LORD, and find the knowledge of God.

6 For the LORD giveth wisdom: out of his mouth cometh knowledge and understanding.

7 He layeth up sound wisdom for the righteous: he is a buckler to them that walk uprightly.

8 He keepeth the paths of judgment, and preserveth the way of his saints.

9 Then shalt thou understand righteousness, and judgment, and equity; yea, every good path.

10 When wisdom entereth into thine heart, and knowledge is pleasant unto thy soul;

11 Discretion shall preserve thee, understanding shall keep thee.

NLT **Proverbs 2:1** My child, listen to what I say, and treasure my commands.

2 Tune your ears to wisdom, and concentrate on understanding.

3 Cry out for insight, and ask for understanding.

4 Search for them as you would for silver; seek them like hidden treasures.

5 Then you will understand what it means to fear the LORD, and you will gain knowledge of God.

6 For the LORD grants wisdom! From his mouth come knowledge and understanding.

7 He grants a treasure of common sense to the honest. He is a shield to those who walk with integrity.

8 He guards the paths of the just and protects those who are faithful to him.

9 Then you will understand what is right, just, and fair, and you will find the right way to go.

10 For wisdom will enter your heart, and knowledge will fill you with joy.

11 Wise choices will watch over you. Understanding will keep you safe.

The People, Places, and Times

The Book of Proverbs. Known as a book of wisdom, Proverbs is like a father sitting down with a young son to pass on valuable lessons learned after a lifetime of trials and errors. It is a collection of wise sayings primarily written by King Solomon referred to as having wisdom that "excelled the wisdom of all the children of the east country, and all the wisdom of Egypt" (1 Kings 4:30). Other contributors are Agur (chapter 30) and Lemuel (31:1–9). Although somewhat sporadic in its arrangement of topics, the clear purpose and theme of Proverbs are provided in the first seven verses: to provide teaching on wisdom, and prepare its readers for living godly lives in the fear of the Lord. Life is unpredictable, and at any given moment one may need advice about anything from family life to business decisions. Proverbs provides wisdom for these and more, particularly as it pertains to one's relationship with God and others.

Background

Proverbs was written in the tenth century BC and included in the Wisdom Literature or Writings section of the Old Testament. Solomon wrote most of the proverbs in the book. A few were also written by Agur and Lemuel, who are otherwise unknown. However, parts of the book of Proverbs also seem to have been borrowed from Egypt (e.g., from the Instruction of Amenemopet). Much of Proverbs' content is deeply spiritual, though not all. Overall, the book declares that wisdom is the task of mastering the art of living and is better than folly.

A proverb is a short teaching governing conduct and life, often similar to a parable. The reason is that many proverbs are condensed parables. Proverbs are spiritual instructions to ensure a godly, happy life here, and reward in the life to come. Because proverbs were not generally written, memorization was an effective way of teaching and learning. The short, concise phrases that comprise Proverbs lend themselves to the best method to reveal and remember a divine truth so that they are easy to pass on to the next generation.

The theme of the book, "The fear of the LORD is the beginning of knowledge: but fools despise wisdom and instruction" (1:7), immediately challenges the reader to evaluate which category they fall into. The writer then pleads with the reader, called "my son," to heed the coming instruction (1:8). This plea occurs throughout the book as though the writer knows his readers will need to be reminded repeatedly to listen and obey. The rest of the chapter and the next set the stage for the remainder of the book with the call of wisdom (1:20–33) and the value of wisdom (chapter 2).

What is a valuable piece of wisdom you have received from your elders?

At-A-Glance

1. The Pursuit of Wisdom (Proverbs 2:1–5)
2. The Provider of Wisdom (vv. 6–8)
3. The Purpose of Wisdom (vv. 9–11)

In Depth

1. The Pursuit of Wisdom (Proverbs 2:1–5)

These first five verses can be viewed as a series of conditions—a list of actions that, if obeyed, will lead to a reward. Within these five short verses are eight verbs used to urge the listener to take action: listen, treasure, tune your ear, concentrate, cry out, ask, search, and seek. Such active language indicates that the pursuit of wisdom is not to be passive but passionate. Wisdom is not attained from desire alone, but because one listens intently and purposefully to the wisdom of others. One who desires to be wise asks for insight, crying out with a sense of urgency, understanding that wisdom's value is like that of silver, popular as currency in ancient Israel (Genesis 37:28; Matthew 26:15). Wisdom is a treasure, readily recognizable, but not easily or abundantly accessible to all. Gaining wisdom is not a simple or static task, but requires constant effort in order to be uncovered. The reward for pursuing it is that it leads to one knowing God and understanding what it means to revere Him.

Where are some ways to pursue godly wisdom?

2. The Provider of Wisdom (vv. 6–8)

Proverbs 1:7 says that "the fear of the LORD is the beginning of knowledge." Although wisdom is to be actively sought, it must be understood that God is the one who gives godly wisdom. Mere human effort alone will not produce the wisdom needed to live a godly life and prevent unnecessary failures and pitfalls. Interestingly, God's involvement in providing wisdom is active as well. He grants abiding success or victory, common sense, wisdom, knowledge, and understanding, but also He shields, guards, and protects those who follow the path that wisdom laid out that leads to Him.

What is the difference between godly wisdom and other wisdom?

3. The Purpose of Wisdom (vv. 9–11)

One purpose of attaining wisdom is to provide discernment. The closer one grows to the Lord—honoring, respecting, and knowing Him—the more wisdom one gains. Wisdom allows a person to understand what is right, just, fair, and act accordingly. Knowing what is right, but not doing it, is simply knowledge. In verse 10, wisdom entering one's heart means it is internalized and familiar. Wisdom should become a part of a person's nature—giving insight that is practical and executable. As a result, there is a sense of joy from wisdom and the safety that it provides from heeding it, but also because it is birthed out of a relationship with the Lord, the source of joy.

Putting it simply, fearing the Lord leads to wisdom and understanding, which leads to one living with integrity, justice, and faithfulness, which inevitably leads to growing more in one's relationship with the Lord, which in turn results in more wisdom. The cycle continues, and in the midst of it all, joy is found.

Why is it sometimes difficult to move from simply knowing what is wise to actually doing what is wise?

Search the Scriptures

1. Why is the listener referred to as "my child" (Proverbs 2:1)?

2. To what is wisdom compared (v. 4)? What significance lies in those comparisons?

Discuss the Meaning

1. The overall theme of Proverbs is wisdom; however, it is important to note that the writers are specifically talking about godly wisdom. Read the following passages: Proverbs 3:7; 26:12, 16; 28:11. What does God's Word say about those who are wise in their own eyes?

2. While this passage indicates that wisdom is to be actively pursued, it is important to remember that receiving it is a gift from God.

Read 1 Kings 3:9–13. What can be learned from both Solomon's request and God's response?

Liberating Lesson

There is a saying that "Common sense isn't common." It accurately applies to wisdom as well. As seen above, there are many who mistakenly believe themselves to be "wise in their own eyes." While it is true that people can make good choices on their own, only respect and reverence for the Lord leads to a life characterized by godly wisdom. Unfortunately, our society is marked by people, both inside the church and out, making what they believe are "wise" choices but are rooted in self-preservation and selfish ambition, the antithesis of godliness. Any decisions—from how to care for the homeless in our own communities to immigrants from other countries—can be made to seem "wise" from a human perspective. However, this passage makes it abundantly clear that godly wisdom leads a person to not only understand what is right, just, and fair but to do it. In doing so, preservation of the just becomes the responsibility of the Lord, who is far more capable than any human.

Application for Activation

This week, seek out a more seasoned Christian and spend time in conversation with them. Prepare a few questions to ask about their faith and the lessons they have learned in their walk with the Lord, for example, "If there is one overall lesson that you could pass on to another, what would it be?"

James 1:5 tells us, "If any of you lack wisdom, let him ask of God, that giveth to all men liberally, and upbraideth not; and it shall be given him." What situations you are currently facing that require wisdom from God? Have you asked Him? If you have not, why? Identify those areas, seek God, and pray for clarity. As you consider options, remember to ask yourself if the course of action would be right, just, and fair, especially if it impacts others.

Then, James 1:6 continues, "But let him ask in faith, nothing wavering. For he that wavereth is like a wave of the sea driven with the wind and tossed." Now confront the temptation to trust in other things as you wait for clarity—money, education, friends, family, yourself. What often causes you to "waver" when seeking wisdom from God? How is your loyalty divided?

Follow the Spirit

What God wants me to do:

_____

_____

_____

_____

Remember Your Thoughts

Special insights I have learned:

_____

_____

_____

_____

More Light on the Text
Proverbs 2:1–11

Let's consider the relationship between a father and his son: the child is totally dependent on his father, relying on and trusting the father without any thought of his failing. Think about a child standing on a step with the father below. The father reaches out his arms and says, "Come on and jump; I'll catch you." The child, without hesitation or asking questions, leaps, putting their entire hope in knowing his father will not fail to catch them.

In this passage, Solomon is giving instruction to a son as to how to obtain the wisdom of the Lord. He is clear and detailed, and he tells the son how to search for wisdom, what to listen for, and what to do with the wisdom once he obtains it.

1 My son, if thou wilt receive my words, and hide my commandments with thee; 2 So that thou incline thine ear unto wisdom, and apply thine heart to understanding;

The father is giving instruction to the son, who is willing to obey. The ways of instruction are clear and precise. If the son is willing to listen and follow these instructions, the results are clear. Although the results of receiving the father's words are clear, the full payoff of doing so will not be explained for several verses (v. 5).

The father calls the son not just to hear him, but to "receive" it and "hide" the commandments away inside himself. When he does this, the result is that he wants to listen to wisdom and understanding. He will "incline [his] ear" and his heart willingly. We must listen to the Word of God very closely, not just hearing with an ear but hearing with the heart. The son gives his undivided attention, listening with ear and heart, to the wisdom of his father's instruction.

3 Yea, if thou criest after knowledge, and liftest up thy voice for understanding;

In searching for knowledge, there must be an urgency and desperation for it. When a baby cries because of hunger, it bellows as though nothing else matters, and its only focus is to soothe the hunger pangs. The baby can't be comforted with anything other than the nourishment that food will give. Just as we must do when searching for knowledge, we must see the value in knowledge and cry out for it, realizing its worth. The piercing cries for the milk may seem extreme to those observing from the outside because the need for the milk is coming from a hole, a place of emptiness. Our focus should be just as intense seeking the Lord's knowledge. We shouldn't be interested in how it appears to others around us, but we should pursue knowledge that will fill the void or hole in our souls.

Even as babies, we make our requests known. As children of God, we too are instructed to make our requests known before the Lord (Philippians 4:6). We lift our voice for understanding, causing us to ask specifically from the Lord. God is the One who can and will grant understanding. We cannot obtain understanding isolated from God. We need God to open our eyes to understanding (Psalm 119:18), so we ask Him by lifting our voice to Him for understanding.

4 If thou seekest her as silver, and searchest for her as for hid treasures;

The monetary value and simple beauty of silver have been recognized since antiquity. Here, Solomon is explaining that if you search for wisdom, like a person who wants to be rich would search for silver or treasure, you will be willing to work and enthusiastically determined to reach your goal. Like silver or hidden treasure, wisdom will not be easy to find. Silver must be mined from deep underground; treasure will be hidden away. As you search for silver or money, you know when you find what you are looking for, you will be satisfied and more than wealthy.

The goal here is to search for wisdom, which is from God, and we find it in His Word. So, we work diligently searching the Scriptures (2 Timothy 2:15), not becoming easily distracted or giving up soon, looking for wisdom in God's Word. We set aside structured time to study and consistently pursue the Lord in His Word.

5 Then shalt thou understand the fear of the LORD, and find the knowledge of God. 6 For

the LORD giveth wisdom: out of his mouth cometh knowledge and understanding.

Here we finally hear the payoff for listening to the father and enjoying our pursuit of wisdom. The result of searching for wisdom is finding the knowledge of God. That is, in pursuit of wisdom, we find God.

It is important to know His character and attributes in order to understand the vastness of who He is. We cannot contain the knowledge of who God is in His fullness, but we can come to appreciate Him in His holiness. Our time and experiences with Him build a more solid relationship with Him as we have evidence of and gain a deeper understanding of His absolute trustworthiness. He continues to prove His worthiness over and over. The parallel structure of this verse suggests knowledge of the Lord is the same as the fear of the Lord. To know Him is to stand in respectful awe of Him. Developing a personal relationship with the Lord is essential to understanding the fear of the Lord.

Through Scripture, we find how God wants us to live, to love, and to give. We can only know what God wants from us through studying His Word. He teaches us who He is and what He expects from those who love Him, His children. Consequently, we gain from Him His attributes and can put into practice His leadership and guidance in our lives.

God has wisdom and can distribute it as He chooses. God instructs us to ask Him if we desire wisdom (James 1:5). God is the one to give knowledge and understanding. Studying and searching the Scriptures outside of the Lord is just information. Knowledge and understanding come from God.

7 He layeth up sound wisdom for the righteous: he is a buckler to them that walk uprightly. 8 He keepeth the paths of judgment, and preserveth the way of his saints. 9 Then

shalt thou understand righteousness, and judgment, and equity; yea, every good path.

The Lord "layeth up" (Heb. *tsafan*, **tsaw-FON**, hide) wisdom for those who are righteous. He hides wisdom for the righteous, and he also hides the righteous from harm. For those who walk uprightly, the righteous, God is a buckler. The word "buckler" (referring to a small shield worn at the waist) here is the Hebrew *magen* (**maw-GAIN**), which means a shield. It is the same word God used when establishing His covenant with Abraham, saying, "I am thy shield" (Genesis 15:1). This helps the reader understand that to walk uprightly is to follow the covenant.

We must understand: Things will still happen to God's people; we are not able to escape life situations. However, the difference is, God will protect His people. The prophet Isaiah confirms situations may arise and things will happen, but this will not be the end of it all (Isaiah 54:17). We have a reason to be determined as we walk the path of righteousness. God promised to keep us. He "keepeth" (Heb. *natsar*, **not-SAR**) and "preserveth" (Heb. *shamar*, **shaw-MAR**) us because God is love, and that is what love does (1 Corinthians 13:7). Both verbs mean to watch, guard, and keep. He shows this love to those who show His love, his "saints" (Heb. *khasid*, **khaw-SEED**), that is "those who show *khesed*" (Heb. **KHEH-sed**), divine loving-kindness. When God keeps our way, we follow only the good paths, those that lead to understanding righteousness, justice (Heb. *mishpat*, **meesh-POT**; KJV: judgment), and fairness.

10 When wisdom entereth into thine heart, and knowledge is pleasant unto thy soul; 11 Discretion shall preserve thee, understanding shall keep thee:

Once wisdom truly becomes a part of us, believers think differently, therefore causing us to act differently. When wisdom is unmistakably in our hearts and not just in our heads, we can have joy in doing what is right. After wisdom enters the heart, righteousness is not enforced but actually pleasant or desirable. Believers want to do what is right. Wisdom causes a believer to take joy in pursuing a deeper relationship with the Lord.

As a conclusion, we get again the promise of protection. God and the wisdom He ordained to guide the universe will "preserve" and "keep," just as in verse 8 above. Again, this does not mean that nothing tragic will ever happen to the righteous. However, with wisdom in our hearts, we know to use caution in dealing and interacting with others. Our love for God as we diligently study His word causes a desire to do what is right and consequently steers the believer away from unnecessary, dangerous, and avoidable situations.

Sources:
Lane, Eric. *Proverbs: Everyday Wisdom for Everyone.* Focus on the Bible Commentary. Fearn, UK: Christian Focus Publications, 2007.
Henry, Matthew. *Matthew Henry's Commentary on the Whole Bible.* WORDsearch CROSS e-book.
Peterson, Eugene H., trans. *The Message: The Bible in Contemporary Language.* Colorado Springs, CO: NavPress, 2002.
The Preacher's Outline & Sermon Bible: 1 Samuel. Chattanooga, TN: Leadership Ministries Worldwide, 1996.
Richards, Lawrence O. *The Teacher's Commentary.* Wheaton, IL: Victor Books, 1987.
Severance, W. Murray. *That's Easy for You to Say: Your Quick Guide to Pronouncing Bible Names.* Nashville, TN: Broadman & Holman, 1997.
Strong, James. *Strong's Talking Greek & Hebrew Dictionary.* Austin, TX: WORDsearch Corp., 2007.

Say It Correctly

Agur. ah-**GUR**.
Lemuel. **LEH**-moo-ell.
Amenemopet. ah-**MEH**-no-**MOE**-pet.

Daily Bible Readings

MONDAY
Work for the Good of All
(Galatians 6:1–10)

TUESDAY
Live Together in Harmony
(Romans 15:1-6)

WEDNESDAY
Wisdom is Walking Together in Love
(2 John 4-11)

THURSDAY
Joseph Resists Temptation
(Genesis 39:6-18)

FRIDAY
Wisdom Saves from Temptation
(Proverbs 2:12-19)

SATURDAY
Walk on Just and Good Paths
(Proverbs 2:20-22; 4:24-27)

SUNDAY
Following Godly Wisdom Pays
(Proverbs 2:1-11)

Notes

_____

_____

_____

_____

Teaching Tips

Words You Should Know

A. Froward (v. 8) *patal* (Heb.)—Twisted

B. Wisdom (v. 11) *khokmah* (Heb.)—The knowledge and determination to make choices based on principles of right living according to God's law

Teacher Preparation

Unifying Principle—Wisdom's Reward. People desire wisdom and hope to be rewarded when they search for it. Why is wisdom so desirable? Wisdom's value is more than tangible gain; it gives knowledge and courage and leads toward God's path of justice and righteousness.

A. Read the Bible Background and Devotional Reading.

B. Pray for your students and lesson clarity.

C. Read the lesson Scripture in multiple translations.

O—Open the Lesson

A. Begin the class with prayer.

B. As a class, identify and discuss ways or circumstances where wisdom is more valuable than money. Be sure to include Proverbs 8:18 in your discussion.

C. Have the students read the Aim for Change and the In Focus story.

D. Ask students how events like those in the story weigh on their hearts and how they can view these events from a faith perspective.

P—Present the Scriptures

A. Read the Focal Verses and discuss the Background and The People, Places, and Times sections.

B. Have the class share what Scriptures stand out for them and why, with particular emphasis on today's themes.

E—Explore the Meaning

A. Use In Depth or More Light on the Text to facilitate a deeper discussion of the lesson text.

B. Pose the questions in Search the Scriptures and Discuss the Meaning.

C. Discuss the Liberating Lesson and Application for Activation sections.

N—Next Steps for Application

A. Summarize the value of asking for wisdom in all aspects of our lives.

B. End class with a commitment to pray for practicing and modeling wisdom within your family and future generations.

Worship Guide

For the Superintendent or Teacher
Theme: The Gifts of Wisdom
Song: "How Majestic Is Your Name"
Devotional Reading: Job 28:12–28

The Gifts of Wisdom

Bible Background • JOB 1; 42; PROVERBS 8
Printed Text • PROVERBS 8:8–14, 17–21 | Devotional Reading • JOB 28:12–28

Aim for Change

By the end of the lesson we will: RECOGNIZE the incomparable value of wisdom, APPRECIATE the difference between the rewards of wisdom and the rewards of mere wealth, and PURSUE godly wisdom rather than a substitute.

In Focus

Today's lesson at the fire academy was the blackout drill. The class of twenty cadets, dressed in full turnout gear with air bottles and breathing masks, stood before a training structure. They were ordered inside and found themselves in a room full of simulated smoke that was as dark as a moonless midnight.

"Masks off!" their instructor ordered.

The cadets all removed their air masks, frightened and confused in the dark as long seconds ticked by. It seemed like forever before the door opened and they stumbled out.

One cadet, Arnie, slumped onto the ground and complained to his buddy Melvin, "I just want to be an EMT! Why do I have to do this?"

"I've been doing this longer than you've been alive, son," the instructor told him, quietly. "In this business, seconds count, and lives are at stake—including yours. That's what I'm here for—to get you through your training so you can get the experience."

Melvin told Arnie, "Twenty years ago, there was a five-alarm in the old piano factory on 28th Street. Nobody knew there were squatters inside, but he found them in the dark and single-handedly pulled three people out. He's the best instructor in the academy."

Arnie realized there was too much he needed to learn.

Wisdom is more than just information. How can we take in what God has to teach us and find wisdom?

Keep in Mind

"Receive my instruction, and not silver; and knowledge rather than choice gold. For wisdom is better than rubies; and all the things that may be desired are not to be compared to it" (Proverbs 8:10–11, KJV).

"Choose my instruction rather than silver, and knowledge rather than pure gold. For wisdom is far more valuable than rubies. Nothing you desire can compare with it" (Proverbs 8:10–11, NLT).

Focal Verses

KJV **Proverbs 8:8** All the words of my mouth are in righteousness; there is nothing froward or perverse in them.

9 They are all plain to him that understandeth, and right to them that find knowledge.

10 Receive my instruction, and not silver; and knowledge rather than choice gold.

11 For wisdom is better than rubies; and all the things that may be desired are not to be compared to it.

12 I wisdom dwell with prudence, and find out knowledge of witty inventions.

13 The fear of the LORD is to hate evil: pride, and arrogancy, and the evil way, and the froward mouth, do I hate.

14 Counsel is mine, and sound wisdom: I am understanding; I have strength.

17 I love them that love me; and those that seek me early shall find me.

18 Riches and honour are with me; yea, durable riches and righteousness.

19 My fruit is better than gold, yea, than fine gold; and my revenue than choice silver.

20 I lead in the way of righteousness, in the midst of the paths of judgment:

21 That I may cause those that love me to inherit substance; and I will fill their treasures.

NLT **Proverbs 8:8** My advice is wholesome. There is nothing devious or crooked in it.

9 My words are plain to anyone with understanding, clear to those with knowledge.

10 Choose my instruction rather than silver, and knowledge rather than pure gold.

11 For wisdom is far more valuable than rubies. Nothing you desire can compare with it.

12 "I, Wisdom, live together with good judgment. I know where to discover knowledge and discernment.

13 All who fear the LORD will hate evil. Therefore, I hate pride and arrogance, corruption and perverse speech.

14 Common sense and success belong to me. Insight and strength are mine.

17 I love all who love me. Those who search will surely find me.

18 I have riches and honor, as well as enduring wealth and justice.

19 My gifts are better than gold, even the purest gold, my wages better than sterling silver!

20 I walk in righteousness, in paths of justice.

21 Those who love me inherit wealth. I will fill their treasuries."

The People, Places, and Times

Lady Wisdom. Her image is consistently positive. She is the one universal element without which everything else fails. Wisdom is not the shadowy female who frequents dark alleys in search of sexual gratification like the adulteress of Proverbs 7. She positions herself publicly beside the city gates where she can expect to attract a large audience. She affirms her integrity by stressing the truth, nobility, and righteousness of her words. Lady Wisdom boldly proclaims that her rewards are far more valuable than gold, silver, and jewels.

Background

Wisdom is first personified (pictured as having human personality) in Proverbs 3:15–18. Chapters 8 and 9 pick up on this personification, picturing wisdom as a woman—a woman who speaks, witnesses her existence before all humanity, and offers wealth and prosperity to all who find her. Lady Wisdom helps us better understand God by taking one of His attributes and giving it personality and consciousness. Thus, we can better comprehend how wisdom is integrated into our everyday lives.

The proverbs in Proverbs 3 through 9 warn the youth against temptations such as violent crimes (1:10–19; 4:14–19); rash pledges (6:1–5); laziness (6:6–11); deceit (6:12–15); and sexual impurity (2:16–19; 5:3–20; 6:23–35; 7:4–27; 9:13–18). Temptations may seem easy to avoid, but they can creep in when we are caught off guard and cause us to fall into sin.

When we are tempted, what can we do to resist?

At-A-Glance

1. The Pursuit of Wisdom (Proverbs 8:8–14)
2. The Promise of Wisdom (vv. 17–21)

In Depth

1. The Pursuit of Wisdom (Proverbs 8:8–14)

Many of the proverbs are addressed to youth to warn against the many pitfalls in life. If you apply the practical messages of God's wisdom, your life will be rich. If you forsake them and follow your own wisdom and understanding, you will be on a path of destruction. Wisdom here is affirming that her teaching is honorable and trustworthy. Her teaching is easy to understand for all who desire to do what is right. Her truth is hidden only to those who are willfully ignorant. The plea to acquire wisdom and knowledge rather than silver and gold is a testament to wisdom's value. Prosperity, power, prestige, and possessions are paltry when compared to the worth of wisdom. The wealth of the world is temporary, but the rewards of

wisdom are eternal. A principle here is that wisdom is of greater value than any material wealth and is actually the way to acquire true wealth spiritually and naturally. Furthermore, when we pursue wisdom, we receive the benefits of discernment and good judgment. We are able to detect helpful or harmful motives and navigate complex situations to honor God. Verse 13 calls back to the first chapter of Proverbs, saying those who fear the Lord hate evil. To be wise in chapter one is to fear the Lord; therefore wise people hate evil. Evil is defined here as pride, arrogance, corruption, and lying. Wise people will resist and challenge those who show these characteristics. Wisdom will empower us instead to show evidence of common sense, insight, and strength that bring true lasting success.

2. The Promise of Wisdom (vv. 17–21)

Those who truly love and seek wisdom will surely find it. In the New Testament James reaffirms that those who ask for wisdom from God will receive it, but they must be willing to follow it once they have it (James 1:5). Wisdom is tied to prosperity and also justice. It is the effect of wisdom to receive both. This may seem contradictory looking at the world around us, but it is made clear from the law, history, and the prophets in the Old Testament. The king who has great wealth also needs to rule justly, or he is seen as a bad king. The one who has material prosperity is commanded to use it to care for the poor and vulnerable (Deuteronomy 15:7–8). This reality of great power coming with great responsibility to care for the poor and defend the vulnerable is one of the distinguishing characteristics of Israel against the other nations that surround it. Solomon himself embodies this well; the wealthiest man in the world is also the wisest and rules with justice. He asks God for wisdom rather than wealth, which is why God blesses him with wealth and power, knowing he would use it righteously. It is our responsibility as believers to follow Jesus' example. He did not have material riches, but He had all the power of the Kingdom of God, which He used to heal the sick, cast out demons, confront the oppressive religious authorities, and care for those in need. We would be wise to seek wisdom to do the same works, recognizing that God can allow us to prosper with that same wisdom if we use it for His glory.

Search the Scriptures

1. How does wisdom describe her advice? (Proverbs 8:8)

2. What does wisdom compare her worth to? (vv. 10–11)

Discuss the Meaning

1. How have you seen wisdom benefit yourself or someone you know?

2. How is wisdom more profitable than silver or gold?

3. How does one get wisdom?

Liberating Lesson

Wisdom is a scarce commodity in today's world. Everywhere we look, people are making bad choices, trying to live life by their own rules. Some things we see so much in our politics, business, and culture are called evil here in Proverbs. Pride, arrogance, corruption, and lying are all evil, yet many Christians do not identify them as such. Wisdom walks with justice and good judgment, yet we often allow injustice to reign for the sake of our comfort and convenience. God's Word calls us to a very different life—a life of godly wisdom. Wisdom involves knowing God's will and His Word, then having the ability to apply this knowledge. God is able to give us the wisdom to pursue both personal and collective prosperity. We can all flourish while also pursuing justice. All of the people had their needs met in Solomon's

kingdom, and wisdom led to great wealth. Jesus shows us a Kingdom that is far greater, where God's power can supply our needs and challenge anyone who oppresses their neighbor. If we love God and love wisdom, we can find solutions to meet the pressing challenges and needs of our communities. We can have both justice and wealth if we have the wisdom and willingness to pursue them God's way.

Application for Activation

All in all, "wisdom is the principal thing; … with all thy getting get understanding" (from Proverbs 4:7). Many of us are taught and encouraged to seek material things—the economy depends on it. However, we do well to seek wisdom because our life depends on it. Many people have education, knowledge, and information—but they have no understanding. Instead of selfishly seeking wealth, we should seek wisdom. When we are humble enough to know that we need God's wisdom daily, God is faithful enough to give it. Wisdom is often demonstrated by the daily choices we make. This week keep a diary of all the major decisions you make. At the end of the week review your decisions to see if your choices demonstrated godly wisdom or foolishness. Determine if godly wisdom is a part of your life by the choices you made. Godly wisdom can cause us to have the success that is lasting and be a blessing to ourselves and others.

Follow the Spirit

What God wants me to do:

_____

_____

_____

_____

Remember Your Thoughts

Special insights I have learned:

_____

_____

_____

_____

More Light on the Text

Proverbs 8:8–14, 17–21

Proverbs 8 develops the idea of a personified Lady Wisdom, first mentioned in Proverbs 3. Here, she calls out—standing on the street corner, asking for any who are foolish or simple to listen and reap great rewards. After this overview of the worth, goodness, and richness of wisdom, she goes on to describe how she was the first thing God created and how she rejoiced as He formed the rest of the universe. Lady Wisdom shares a close relationship with God and desires a close relationship with any who will listen to her too.

8 All the words of my mouth are in righteousness; there is nothing froward or perverse in them. 9 They are all plain to him that understandeth, and right to them that find knowledge.

Wisdom begins her call to the simple by assuring them she is trustworthy. The words of wisdom are true and pure. The Hebrew of v. 8 emphasizes righteousness by placing that phrase at the beginning of the sentence: "In righteousness are all the words of my mouth." "Froward" means twisted, and perverse has a similar meaning of turning or distorting. The image left by these two words is of a physically gnarled and snarled mess. Wisdom has none of that. Instead, her words are "plain" (Heb. *nakoakh*, **naw-KOE-akh**), meaning upright and straight, making an image of the exact opposite of "froward or perverse." Lady

Wisdom will lead you on straight paths, with no twists or turns. Wisdom will communicate with you clearly. Even though we often stress about choices we make, if we take the time to listen to wisdom—whether from a trusted mentor or directly from the Word of God—the best course of action is clear.

10 Receive my instruction, and not silver; and knowledge rather than choice gold. 11 For wisdom is better than rubies; and all the things that may be desired are not to be compared to it.

A common refrain in Proverbs is that wisdom is better than wealth. This is easy for Solomon, the richest man in the world, to say. However, it is true that once you have enough money to physically sustain your household, no extra wealth will make you significantly happier. Proverbs often records that wisdom is better than gold, silver, or rubies. Rubies (Heb. *paninim*, **pah-nee-NEEM**) might refer to the precious gem that we call a ruby today, which would have been very expensive after trading it from where they are found in southeastern Asia. It could also refer to pearls or red corals, which could have come from the nearby Mediterranean Sea, though they were still rare beauties and difficult to obtain. No matter the exact kind of costly artifact, the Bible tells us that of "all the things that may be desired," wisdom is the most important. Wealth is not needed to live a life of blessing, peace, and joy. For that, wisdom is needed.

12 I wisdom dwell with prudence, and find out knowledge of witty inventions. 13 The fear of the LORD is to hate evil: pride, and arrogancy, and the evil way, and the froward mouth, do I hate. 14 Counsel is mine, and sound wisdom: I am understanding; I have strength.

Hebrew poetry often makes use of parallel structures, making a statement in one line, and then basically repeating that statement with close synonyms in the next line. This makes it hard to distinguish nuances between words since the point of using them together is to emphasize their similarity. Knowing this literary structure, note how these verses use every other word there is to describe wisdom. Lady Wisdom is associated with prudence, knowledge, "witty inventions" (Heb. *mezimmah*, **meh-zeem-MAH**, elsewhere translated discretion or planning), counsel, "sound wisdom" (Heb. *tushiyah*, **too-shee-YAH**, elsewhere translated counsel or aid), understanding, and even strength. All these many associations are meant to give the reader the feeling that wisdom has no end. It is broad, touching all aspects of life. She has thought of everything and has everything covered.

Of these associations, strength is the outlier. Each of the other synonyms for wisdom deal with the intellect, but "strength" here refers to physical power. Two kinds of strength might be in mind here as being in wisdom's possession. The verses immediately following this pertain to kings, princes, and judges all ruling with wisdom. Wisdom could be claiming to have the strength of these political figures behind her. However, the word for "strength" (Heb. *geburah*, **geh-boo-RAH**) can also refer specifically to God's mighty works. Later in Lady Wisdom's address, she tells how she was the first thing God created and how she witnessed His mighty deeds of Creation. God even delighted to use Wisdom as He built the universe. Therefore the strength wisdom claims here might refer to divine power. We only need to follow wisdom ourselves to have access to all kinds of intellectual rigor, but also to the power behind God's mighty works.

To fear the Lord is to realize you are under His power. If you are not obedient to His commandments, this "fear" is an actual terror. However, if you have a loving relationship with Him, He will use His power to bless you, and your "fear" is more akin to awe and respect.

"The fear of the LORD" is equated with many ideas in Proverbs. It is the beginning of wisdom (9:10), beginning of knowledge (1:7), knowledge of God (2:5), knowledge of the holy (9:10), and instruction of wisdom (15:33). It is also a fountain of life (14:27) that prolongs days (10:27) and turns away evil (19:23). This is the only example in Proverbs of the fear of the Lord being defined by what it is not. It is not evil.

It hates evil in all its various forms: pride, arrogance, evil paths, and froward (i.e., lying) mouths. "Hate" (Heb. *sane'*, **saw-NAY**) is associated with being someone's enemy. Evil is the enemy of those who honors the Lord. If we are to follow in the paths of wisdom, we too must hate evil. When you hate something, you jump at every chance you get to work against its spread, fueled by a fire to see right prevail. Wisdom is seen not only positively enforcing her counsel, but also fiercely defending her adherents from deceit that might try to pull them away from her. This ought to be the way we react to evil too. We must hate it and allow Christ's love to show the wisest paths to rebuild and reconcile after evil is punished.

17 I love them that love me; and those that seek me early shall find me. 18 Riches and honour are with me; yea, durable riches and righteousness. 19 My fruit is better than gold, yea, than fine gold; and my revenue than choice silver.

Although Wisdom hates her evil enemies, she loves those who seek her out. "Seek me early" (Heb. *shakhar*, **shaw-KHAR**) attempts to translate the poetic intensity and eager searching the word connotes. Wisdom is not trying to hide. The beginning of the chapter showed that she is calling publicly for any who will listen. Anyone who seeks for her will find her (cf. Jeremiah 29:13).

For the second time in this one speech (cf. v. 11), Lady Wisdom says she is more valuable than silver and gold, repeating herself so that even the simple will remember and understand. Not only is wisdom more valuable than gold, silver, and rubies, but wisdom has those same things in her possession. She has material wealth and riches to benefit us economically, plus she has "honour" (Heb. *kabod*, **kah-BODE**, usually translated glory) and righteousness to benefit us spiritually. "Durable" or lasting riches are found only with wisdom, as the Bible asserts often that wealth is transient. "Revenue" (Heb. *tebu'ah*, **teh-boo-AH**) refers to one's agricultural income, whether fruit, grain, or cattle. In an agrarian society as Solomon's, fruit, grain, and cattle were signs of wealth just as much as silver and gold. Wisdom tells us what her fruit and revenue are in the following verses.

20 I lead in the way of righteousness, in the midst of the paths of judgment: 21 That I may cause those that love me to inherit substance; and I will fill their treasures.

Instead of directly leading to gold and silver, Lady Wisdom leads those who love her down the ways and paths of righteousness and judgment (Heb. *mishpat*, **meesh-POT**, also translated justice). The purpose of walking these paths is so that those who love wisdom will inherit "substance," and be filled up with "treasures."

Wisdom leads us righteously and justly, not simply only because those are the best ways from a purely spiritual lens, but also because going those routes allows wisdom to grant us what is materially best too. The word translated here "substance" is difficult in the Hebrew, *Yesh* (**YESH**). It is usually translated "there is" or "there are," but that would not work with the rest of the sentence. One can supply another noun and say "There is [an inheritance] that I will cause those who love me to inherit." Or one can understand *yesh* as referring to something that simply is there, that exists, a "substance." From this much, we cannot tell if the "substance" is substantial, but the latter half of the verse clarifies that wisdom will "fill" her followers' treasures. "Treasures" here may refer to valuables themselves or to the place where they are stored. Wisdom will fill these treasure houses up with good things so that we have enough and more than enough. In this way, Lady Wisdom reflects God to us, showing us the best paths—paths of righteousness and justice—for our own benefit, and showering us with further blessings along the way. This is the extravagantly loving and wise God we serve.

Sources:
Elwell, Walter A. editor. *Evangelical Commentary on the Bible*. Grand Rapids, MI: Baker Book House, 1989. 415–416.

Say It Correctly

Froward. **FROE**-ward.
Agrarian. uh-**GRAIR**-ee-an.

Daily Bible Readings

MONDAY
Christ, the Wisdom of God
(1 Corinthians 1:18-25)

TUESDAY
God Abundantly Rewards Job's Faithfulness
(Job 1:1-5)

WEDNESDAY
God Restores Job's Family and Wealth
(Job 42:10-17)

THURSDAY
Wisdom Calls the People to Respond
(Proverbs 8:1-7)

FRIDAY
Wisdom Present and Active During Creation
(Proverbs 8:22-31)

SATURDAY
Choose Wisdom and Live
(Proverbs 8:32-36)

SUNDAY
Wisdom Affects All of Life
(Proverbs 8:8-14, 17-21)

Notes

Teaching Tips

June 28
Bible Study Guide 4

Words You Should Know

A. Foolish (v. 13) *kesilot* (Heb.)—Silly, stupid, pursuing folly.

B. Simple (v. 16) *peti* (Heb.)—Those who lack judgment, maturity, and experience; foolish.

Teacher Preparation

Unifying Principle—Invitation to Wisdom. Two competing voices call to us on life's journey: Wisdom and Lady Folly. Why should we heed the call of wisdom? Wisdom gives instruction to the wise, yet the foolish suffer their own downfall.

A. Read the Bible Background and Devotional Reading.

B. Pray for your students and lesson clarity.

C. Read the lesson Scripture in multiple translations.

O—Open the Lesson

A. Begin the class with prayer.

B. As a class, compare and contrast the call and promise of wisdom with that of folly. How are their methods and benefits different?

C. Have the students read the Aim for Change and the In Focus story.

D. Ask students how events like those in the story weigh on their hearts and how they can view these events from a faith perspective.

P—Present the Scriptures

A. Read the Focal Verses and discuss the Background and The People, Places, and Times sections.

B. Have the class share what Scriptures stand out for them and why, with particular emphasis on today's themes.

E—Explore the Meaning

A. Use In Depth or More Light on the Text to facilitate a deeper discussion of the lesson text.

B. Pose the questions in Search the Scriptures and Discuss the Meaning.

C. Discuss the Liberating Lesson and Application for Activation sections.

N—Next Steps for Application

A. Summarize the value of sharing wisdom with others.

B. End class with a commitment to pray for their commitment to pursuing godly wisdom.

Worship Guide

For the Superintendent or Teacher
Theme: Wisdom's Feast
Song: "God Has a Table"
Devotional Reading: Psalm 119:97–104

Wisdom's Feast

Bible Background • PROVERBS 9
Printed Text • PROVERBS 9:1–6, 8–10, 13–18 | Devotional Reading • PSALM 119:97–104

Aim for Change

By the end of the lesson, we will: COMPARE and contrast the call and promise of wisdom with that of folly, DESIRE to walk the path of wisdom and receive its benefits, avoiding the peril of foolishness, and GROW in the fear and knowledge of the Lord as the first step in walking the way of wisdom.

In Focus

James' wife died from complications of Parkinson's disease. He was feeling lonely and having a hard time adjusting to living alone, and his son Greg started to worry about him. Greg asked his daughter Carol if she would stay with her Grandpa for a few weeks in the summer, since she would be between semesters.

Carol would often find James dabbing his eyes, then pretending it was just allergies. "Grandpa, it will take time to recover from Grandma's death. I'm glad I'm here."

"Oh, you're sweet. I hope you'll get to go enjoy yourself some this summer too, instead of just hanging around with a sad old man," James said. "Now, tell me about this move I heard about from your father."

"OK! I met my new boyfriend Quinton online. He lives in LA and has come to visit me three times. He wants me to come live with him after I finish college. Grandpa, I think he might be the one!" Carol said, getting more and more excited.

"Carol, I love you. That's why I want you to listen to me. I do not think this is a wise decision. You do not know him. He could be trying to take advantage of you. Please, don't give your heart away just yet. Pray and ask God for wisdom about your relationship with this man."

Why should we take into consideration the godly counsel of older adults?

Keep in Mind

"Forsake the foolish, and live; and go in the way of understanding" (Proverbs 9:6, KJV).

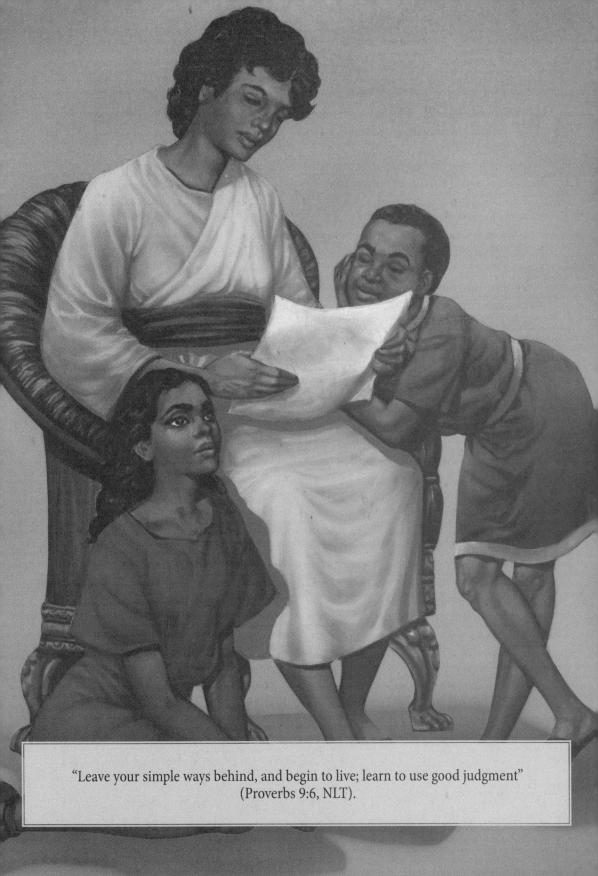

"Leave your simple ways behind, and begin to live; learn to use good judgment" (Proverbs 9:6, NLT).

Focal Verses

KJV **Proverbs 9:1** Wisdom hath builded her house, she hath hewn out her seven pillars:

2 She hath killed her beasts; she hath mingled her wine; she hath also furnished her table.

3 She hath sent forth her maidens: she crieth upon the highest places of the city,

4 Whoso is simple, let him turn in hither: as for him that wanteth understanding, she saith to him,

5 Come, eat of my bread, and drink of the wine which I have mingled.

6 Forsake the foolish, and live; and go in the way of understanding.

8 Reprove not a scorner, lest he hate thee: rebuke a wise man, and he will love thee.

9 Give instruction to a wise man, and he will be yet wiser: teach a just man, and he will increase in learning.

10 The fear of the LORD is the beginning of wisdom: and the knowledge of the holy is understanding.

13 A foolish woman is clamorous: she is simple, and knoweth nothing.

14 For she sitteth at the door of her house, on a seat in the high places of the city,

15 To call passengers who go right on their ways:

16 Whoso is simple, let him turn in hither: and as for him that wanteth understanding, she saith to him,

17 Stolen waters are sweet, and bread eaten in secret is pleasant.

18 But he knoweth not that the dead are there; and that her guests are in the depths of hell.

NLT **Proverbs 9: 1** Wisdom has built her house; she has carved its seven columns.

2 She has prepared a great banquet, mixed the wines, and set the table.

3 She has sent her servants to invite everyone to come. She calls out from the heights overlooking the city.

4 "Come in with me," she urges the simple. To those who lack good judgment, she says,

5 "Come, eat my food, and drink the wine I have mixed.

6 Leave your simple ways behind, and begin to live; learn to use good judgment."

8 So don't bother correcting mockers; they will only hate you. But correct the wise, and they will love you.

9 Instruct the wise, and they will be even wiser. Teach the righteous, and they will learn even more.

10 Fear of the LORD is the foundation of wisdom. Knowledge of the Holy One results in good judgment.

13 The woman named Folly is brash. She is ignorant and doesn't know it.

14 She sits in her doorway on the heights overlooking the city.

15 She calls out to men going by who are minding their own business.

16 "Come in with me," she urges the simple. To those who lack good judgment, she says,

17 "Stolen water is refreshing; food eaten in secret tastes the best!"

18 But little do they know that the dead are there. Her guests are in the depths of the grave.

The People, Places, and Times

Lady Folly. In opposition to Lady Wisdom, Lady Folly also calls for followers throughout the city, but she is heavily associated with adultery, her loudness, and her offerings of stolen water and bread. Lady Folly promises all manner of earthly pleasures, but these are all fleeting. Associating with her leads to death, just as surely as associating with Lady Wisdom brings life.

Background

The book of Proverbs reveals two major themes: wisdom and folly. Wisdom is knowledge, understanding, discretion, obedience, and instruction based on God's Word and reverence of God. Folly is everything that contradicts wisdom. The Old Testament provides God's truth through the Law, which was given by the priest; the wise men or sages gave the Word, which was given by God and wise counsel. Solomon is the sage that provided insight on the perplexities of life (Proverbs 1:1, 6).

This lesson's focus on chapter 9 concludes the entire collection of instructions and admonitions contained in Proverbs 1–9. Here, the writer makes explicit something only hinted at before: Lady Wisdom has an evil opponent in Lady Folly, and brings the two of them to a side-by-side showdown. Both women host lavish banquets, but the outcomes for the invitees are different. This portrait of the two women, each eager to attract her guests, reaffirms the benefits and gains to be won from paying attention to wisdom's teaching. Together, they show the vital importance of the choices that have to be made and the ultimate consequences that they carry.

Wisdom leads to life and prosperity. Why do you think her way is usually unpopular?

At-A-Glance

1. Wisdom's Invitation to the Banquet (Proverbs 9:1–6)
2. The Fear of the Lord Is the Beginning of Wisdom (vv. 8–10)
3. Folly's Invitation to the Banquet (vv. 13–18)

In Depth

1. Wisdom's Invitation to the Banquet (Proverbs 9:1–6)

Wisdom and foolishness are personified as rival young women who give out invitations for banquets at their houses. Lady Wisdom builds a house. It is supported by the seven stone pillars. The number seven in the Bible often represents completeness and perfection. Wisdom's house is also elegant and spacious.

Wisdom has prepared a feast with "slaughtered animals and mixed wine" as well as set her table for the guests (v. 2). The wine was mixed with water to decrease the likelihood of drunkenness (and to make the wine last longer). After this, she sends out her maidens to bid "the simple" to come to the banquet. "The simple" refers to those who lack judgment, maturity, and experience. They are subject to seduction by the foolish woman. When we do not know right from wrong, we can be easily fooled. So it is important to accept the invitation of wisdom to come to the feast she prepares which leads to maturity, insight, and life (vv.5–6).

Wisdom has done her work, and now she cries out from the place in the city; it is the people's response that makes the party possible. She is calling out for the simple who lack understanding. She is looking for those who are hungry for wisdom (those who know their hunger and are humble enough to seek wisdom). She is calling out for them so she can feed them. Her food and wine will give them wisdom. It is for their good that she invites them—but again, this invitation benefits those who know their need and are willing to do whatever it takes to meet it.

How will you stay hungry for wisdom and humbly seek it out even when you look successful?

2. The Fear of the Lord Is the Beginning of Wisdom (vv. 8–10)

Wisdom reflects on the behavior of a scoffer versus the wise. A scoffer is very arrogant and self-centered. They do not like for anyone to criticize them, so they only respond with hate towards others (v. 8). However, a wise person will appreciate the reprimand given and love the giver. The wise enjoy instruction because they want to become wiser and learn more (v. 9).

Of course, wisdom begins with "fear of the Lord" and "knowledge of the Holy One is insight." This is where life begins—the fear of the Lord. Back then and even today, wisdom begins when we choose to live our lives with an awareness that God sees how we treat one another and the earth that He gave us to steward. Wisdom happens when we realize that the way we deal with life, in general, reveals whether we revere God or not. And, of course, reverence is worship that enables us to hear wise sayings of the spirit. Submission to God is the first step toward a wise life.

How do you react toward someone who gets angry after you try to give them constructive criticism?

3. Folly's Invitation to the Banquet (vv. 13-18)

The foolish woman's invitation to her banquet is in direct contrast to the wise woman's invitation. The woman's "loudness" is symbolic of an adulterous person (cf. Proverbs 7:11). She lacks good judgment and is ignorant. The foolish woman does not even try to hide what her intentions are. She "sits right at the door of her house" to call people in who are passing by.

She intends to grab the attention of those who are gullible and convince them to come to her banquet. Lady Folly does not even work. Instead, she steals whatever she gives to her guests. In contrast to the wise woman's feast, the foolish woman offers "stolen water" and "bread eaten in secret." These are references to illicit sex (see Proverbs 5:15). She claims that "stolen water is sweet" and that "bread eaten in secret is pleasant," and entices young men to her secret rendezvous. However, after momentary joys, she lets them realize that there is no life where they are. The people who come to her banquet do not realize enjoying her feast will lead to them to the place of the dead (v.18).

It is very important to stop and think about the consequences of sin before yielding to temptation. We often make our decisions based on what looks great to us today, even though it may lead us to destruction. That is what folly does: it wants to deceive us to do what feels good today at the expense of what will be helpful in the future.

How do you think you would recognize if folly tried to entice you into doing something that may lead you down the path to destruction?

Search the Scriptures

1. What does the wise woman offer to those who come to partake of the feast (Proverbs 9:6)?

2. Compare and contrast the reaction of the scoffer and the wise when rebuked (v. 8).

3. What happens to the people who enjoy the feast offered by the foolish woman (v. 18)?

Discuss the Meaning

1. Explore what the fear of the Lord means. What does it look like in our day-to-day life to live in the fear of the Lord? How does one grow in the fear and knowledge of God to gain more wisdom?

2. The wise woman's banquet seems similar to the banquet Jesus described in a parable.

Read Luke 14:15–24 and then compare it to the wise woman's banquet. What similarities and differences can you identify?

Liberating Lesson

In today's society, it seems as though there are more foolish people than wise. Just listen to the news, and we can identify people who are not making good choices. Moreover, they frequently commit hateful acts toward others. Why do people behave this way?

The fear and knowledge of the Lord guide us down the path of wise living. We must seek after godly wisdom that will bring life-giving results. As we grow in wisdom, share with others what you have learned. We lose much as a society by not passing down the wisdom we have learned and by not taking the time to value our elders enough to listen to their wisdom. If you are tempted and make the wrong choice, repent and learn from it. But do not go back to living foolishly because that life will only lead to destruction. Wisdom is calling; will you answer?

Application for Activation

Whether you have the wisdom to share with others or are in need of wisdom yourself, a meal is a perfect setting to engage others in the wise discussion. Prepare a special meal and invite those whose wisdom you desire or those who you think need to hear your words.

Follow the Spirit

What God wants me to do:

_____

_____

_____

_____

Remember Your Thoughts

Special insights I have learned:

_____

_____

_____

_____

More Light on the Text
Proverbs 9:1–6, 8–10, 13–18

Proverbs 9 is a fitting conclusion to the introductory section of the book (Proverbs 1–8) where wisdom has taken the center stage. There are several lessons in the passage. First, it makes clear that wisdom and folly continually vie for human allegiance. Second, the ultimate choice lies with us and which call we answer, to whose invitation we respond, and with whom we choose to eat. Third, scoffers can be so hardened in their ways and choice that they do harm to teachers who challenge them (cf. 2 Timothy 4:3–4). Fourth, the wise are so open to wisdom's message that even her rebuke will spark their affection (cf. Psalm 141:5). Fifth, behind wisdom's invitation is God. To say yes to wisdom is to respond in reverent obedience to God. Last, to heed the call of folly is to forsake the land of the living and join the company of the dead.

1 Wisdom hath builded her house, she hath hewn out her seven pillars: 2 She hath killed her beasts; she hath mingled her wine; she hath also furnished her table. 3 She hath sent forth her maidens: she crieth upon the highest places of the city.

Wisdom is a woman of generous hospitality who invites all to a lavish banquet that she hosts. The house described here is one Wisdom herself has built. It represents an image of luxury and is a complete, ideal, or perfect building—understood from the use of seven as a perfect, complete number. It is certainly large enough to entertain everyone. In verses 1–2 Wisdom is pictured as an industrious, active woman (vv. 1–2), in contrast to the foolish woman (vv. 13–14). Wisdom has built a comfortable and permanent place for herself to live, in contrast to Folly's house, which is associated with the dead and Sheol in verse 18.

Wisdom sends forth her maidens (servants) to call people to the feast. In keeping with the dignity ascribed to her, Wisdom has "maidservants" to convey her invitations. Thus, she is a woman of wealth and influence. As in 8:2 (cf. 1:21) the summons is issued from on high, presumably at the city gates (cf. 8:3), so as to reach the invited. It is important to note that no qualifications are required for the invitees. They do not have to attain a certain level of knowledge to attend the banquet.

4 Whoso is simple, let him turn in hither: as for him that wanteth understanding, she saith to him, 5 Come, eat of my bread, and drink of the wine which I have mingled. 6 Forsake the foolish, and live; and go in the way of understanding.

Verses 4 to 6 offer her invitation to the banquet. In Proverbs 8, Wisdom cried out, first to all people (v. 4) and then to the simple and the foolish (v. 5). Now she calls out to the "simple," those who are naïve, imprudent, and inexperienced. Wisdom does not mean to insult her by calling her invitees "simple," and they are not portrayed harshly in these verses. She invites them to come to eat her bread and drink her wine, implying that wisdom is that which sustains the soul. To eat and drink at Wisdom's table is to begin travel on the path that leads to life and understanding. It is walking on the straight path of understanding. Wisdom has much to offer and is eager to do so. For those

who listen to Wisdom, to live in her house or to partake of her food and wine are different ways of envisioning a lifetime of learning.

There is a deliberate use of the imperative in this verse, which is echoed in the less coercive but subtle invitation issued in practically the same words by Lady Folly in verse 16 and Proverbs 4:17. The bread and wine are the counterparts to the stolen water and bread of verse 17.

8 Reprove not a scorner, lest he hate thee: rebuke a wise man, and he will love thee. 9 Give instruction to a wise man, and he will be yet wiser: teach a just man, and he will increase in learning. 10 The fear of the LORD is the beginning of wisdom: and the knowledge of the holy is understanding.

These verses enjoin us to choose our pupils wisely. Later, Jesus would teach in His Sermon on the Mount that we must not give "that which is holy unto the dogs, neither cast ye your pearls before swine, lest they trample them under their feet, and turn again and rend you" (Matthew 7:6). Rebuking scorners is a waste of time and energy; they will only hate you and your advice. The scoffer is proud and hardened beyond reproof. They mock Wisdom. A fool hears reproof and only hardens in exasperation. If one is to teach, it is better to teach the wise who will love the truth and wisdom you give them. Thus, one should not waste time and energy with scoffers or the wicked, but rather, with the wise and the righteous. The wise person is characterized by a willingness to endure rebuke. One who seeks wisdom is very receptive to any kind of instruction. Whenever such a person is rebuked, the response is very different from a scoffer's. That student loves rather than hates the teacher. A person who wants to be wise and is aware of the benefits of instruction is very open to any kind of guidance that increases learning.

A person's character is revealed by his or her response to correction and teaching. Scoffers will despise rebuke while wise people will welcome correction. The reader is, thus, invited into the story, not as one who teaches wisdom, but as one who could potentially be taught. Would the reader be a scoffer or a wise student? It is impossible to teach wisdom to the unreceptive, and therefore, wise students are warned against indifference and inattention.

Fear—or reverential awe as it implies in this verse—is the proper human response to Yahweh, the Holy One. "Fear" (Heb. *yir'ah*, **year-RAW**) is to realize you are under another's power. If you have a positive relationship with that authority figure, recognition of power becomes awe; if not, it becomes terror. Rather than a slavish tormenting fear that causes a person to cower and hide, the fear of God inspires one to grow in wisdom and reach out to others. The fear of God overcomes the twin evils of pride and cynicism, core traits of a foolish person. This is because God, rather than the self, is at the focus of a person's identity. Devotion to God lifts a person's life above the mundane, unsettled character of all things earthly. Yahweh is identified as the Holy One. Holiness is God's very essence. In other words, holiness is Yahweh's defining quality. All others described as holy have that quality solely because they are either in God's presence or are dedicated to God. No person or object ever becomes intrinsically holy. God's holy presence in a person's life empowers a person to live righteously.

13 A foolish woman is clamorous: she is simple, and knoweth nothing.

Here, we get to learn more about the other woman, Lady Folly. She calls the vulnerable to her own feast of stolen water and hidden bread, but her feast precedes the fool's descent into the place of the dead (v. 18). Folly is probably copying the acts of Wisdom (as Wisdom warns her hearers about Folly who seduces young men). It is rather ironic that someone so similar to Lady Wisdom can be so deadly.

Folly is unable to control herself—she is loud, ignorant, and knows nothing. These characteristics are antithetical to wisdom. A foolish woman or literally translated as "the woman of folly" depicts a contrast to Lady Wisdom between whom the virtuous man has to make a choice. She is characterized as animated by passion and is "clamorous" as the adulteress in 7:11. Her ignorance is far more than intellectual inadequacy; she is infecting all who listen to her with her own folly. She is the opposite of her dignified rival. She is simple in a bad sense; she has no preservative against evil, no moral fiber to resist temptation. She gives the impression of a shrewish person raucously making her pitch, in contrast to the dignified messengers Wisdom commissioned in verse 3.

14 For she sitteth at the door of her house, on a seat in the high places of the city, 15 To call passengers who go right on their ways:

Folly, like Wisdom, has a house of her own and invites guests to enter. She does not send forth her maidens; she does not stand in the streets and proclaim her mission. Lady Folly has an easier task; all she has to do is sit, beckon, and use a few seductive words. Her house is not supported by seven pillars, built on the grace of God, or upheld by the gifts of the Holy Spirit, like that of Wisdom (v. 1); it is an ordinary habitation of no stately proportions, but her own charms cause her victims to disregard her environment. Her house is in the highest and most conspicuous part of the city, and she sits before her door in reckless immodesty, plying her shameful trade (cf. Genesis 38:14; Jeremiah 3:2). The mimicry of her rival appears, for Wisdom "crieth upon the highest places of the city" (v. 3).

With shameless boldness, she cries to all that pass by; she addresses her solicitations to people who are going straight on their way, thinking nothing of her, having no idea of deviating from their pursued object. As they walk in the path of right and duty, she tries to turn them aside.

16 Whoso is simple, let him turn in hither: and as for him that wanteth understanding, she saith to him, 17 Stolen waters are sweet, and bread eaten in secret is pleasant.

The foolish woman, the personification of folly, uses the very same words that Wisdom utters (v. 4). Wisdom addressed the simple because they were inexperienced and undecided, and might be guided rightly; Folly now speaks to them because they have not yet made their final choice, can still be swayed by lower considerations, and may be led astray. Such people find it hard to distinguish between the good and the evil, the false and the true, especially when their sensual appetite is aroused and sides with the temptress. Such fools are easily deceived. This is the other class addressed by wisdom, and which Folly now solicits, urging them to follow her on the path of pleasure, promising sensual enjoyment and security. She brags about sin, for it is because a relationship with her is secretive that makes it so appealing.

Unstable and senseless, she furnishes her guests with stolen bread and water—to their detriment. Stolen water, she suggests, is sweeter than "drinking from your own well" (cf. 5:15). The metaphor of "stolen waters" refers primarily to adulterous intercourse, as to "drink waters out of one's own cistern" (Proverbs 5:15) signifies the chaste connection of lawful wedlock. Wisdom offers meat and wine to her guests; Folly offers bread and water. Wisdom invites openly to a well-furnished table; Folly calls to a secret meal of simple food. What the former offers are rich, satisfying, and comforting; what folly gives is poor, mean, and insipid. Yet this latter has the charm of being forbidden; it is attractive because it is unlawful. Things easily attained, the possession of which is gotten without effort or danger or breach of restraint, soon cease to charm. To some minds, the cleverness and secrecy required for success have an irresistible attraction.

Young men enter into Folly's house not knowing that the dead are there; there are none in the house that can be considered to be living. Wisdom's banquet leads to life, while Folly's banquet leads to death. The wise hear what the spirit is saying.

18 But he knoweth not that the dead are there; and that her guests are in the depths of hell.

The deluded youth is persuaded by the seductions of Folly and enters her house. The writer, then, in a few weighty words, shows the terrible result of this evil compliance. Once entangled in the toils of the tempter or temptress, the victim may pass through many stages, but he or she ends finally in the lowest depth—the destruction of body and soul. The terrible warning may be profitably repeated more than once.

Sources:

Dell, Katharine. *The Book of Proverbs in Social and Theological Context.* Cambridge, MA: Cambridge University Press, 2006.

Douglas, J. D., editor. *New Bible Dictionary (Second Edition).* Downers Grove, IL: InterVarsity Press. 1982, 988–990.

Fox, Michael V. *Proverbs 1–9: A New Translation.* New York: Doubleday, 2000.

Garrett, Duane. A. *Proverbs, Ecclesiastes, Song of Songs.* Vol. 14. The New American Commentary. Nashville, TN: Broadman & Holman Publishers, 1993.

Hartley, John E. *Proverbs: A Commentary in the Wesleyan Tradition.* Editors Alex Varughese, Roger Hahn, and George Lyons. New Beacon Bible Commentary. Kansas City, MO: Beacon Hill Press of Kansas City, 2016.

Horne, Milton P. *Proverbs and Ecclesiastes.* Smyth and Helwys Bible Commentary. Mason, GA: Smyth and Helwys Publishing, 2003.

Kidner, Derek. *Proverbs: An Introduction and Commentary.* Vol. 17. Tyndale Old Testament Commentaries. Downers Grove, IL: InterVarsity Press, 1964.

Life Application Study Bible. New Revised Standard Version. Wheaton, IL: Tyndale House Publishers, Inc., 1989. 1054.

McKane, William. *Proverbs: A New Approach.* London: SCM Press, 1970.

Murphy, Rowland E. *Proverbs*. Vol. 22, Word Biblical Commentary. Dallas, TX: Word Incorporated, 1998.

The NIV Study Bible (Tenth Anniversary Edition). Grand Rapids, MI: Zondervan Publishing House ,1995. 950.

Reyburn, William David and Euan McG. Fry. *A Handbook on Proverbs*. UBS Handbook Series. New York: United Bible Societies, 2000.

Spence-Jones H. D. M., ed. *Proverbs*. The Pulpit Commentary. New York: Funk & Wagnalls Company, 1909.

Unger, Merril F. *The New Unger's Bible Handbook*. Chicago, IL: Moody Press, 1984, 231.

Waltke, Bruce. *The Book of Proverbs: Chapters 1—15*. Grand Rapids, MI: Eerdmans, 2004.

Say It Correctly

Sheol. **SHEE**-ol.

Daily Bible Readings

MONDAY
Law Provides the Edge
(Psalm 119:97–104)

TUESDAY
Wise and Foolish Bridesmaids
(Matthew 25:1–13)

WEDNESDAY
Church Proclaims the Wisdom of God
(Ephesians 3:7–13)

THURSDAY
No Wise Person Among You?
(1 Corinthians 6:1–6)

FRIDAY
Wise and Foolish Builders
(Matthew 7:24–27)

SATURDAY
Benefits of Making the Wise Choice
(Psalm 1)

SUNDAY
Wisdom Delivers Many Benefits
(Proverbs 9:1–6, 8–10, 13–18)

Notes

_____

_____

_____

_____

Teaching Tips

Words You Should Know

A. Eschatological—Occurring in the end times, after the Final Judgment.

B. Soteriological—Relating to the doctrine of salvation through Jesus Christ.

Teacher Preparation

Unifying Principle—Wisdom in Action. People often label unusual or unexpected behavior as eccentric, foolish, or even wrong, and the people who act in such unusual ways are vilified. What should our assessment be when someone's behavior is unexpected? In Matthew, Jesus says His behavior and John's, while unusual in their day, will eventually be proven wise by their subsequent deeds.

A. Read the Bible Background and Devotional Readings.

B. Pray for your students and lesson clarity.

C. Read the lesson Scripture in multiple translations.

O—Open the Lesson

A. Begin the class with prayer.

B. Have the class discuss examples of people who behaved in unusual or unexpected ways, who were really displaying true Christian character. What do these findings suggest about living a Christian life?

C. Have the students read the Aim for Change and the In Focus story.

D. Ask students how events like those in the story weigh on their hearts and how they can view these events from a faith perspective.

P—Present the Scriptures

A. Read the Focal Verses.

B. Have the class share what Scriptures stand out for them and why, with particular emphasis on today's context.

C. Discuss the Background and The People, Places, and Times sections.

E—Explore the Meaning

A. Use In Depth or More Light on the Text to facilitate a deeper discussion of the lesson text.

B. Pose the questions in Search the Scriptures and Discuss the Meaning.

C. Discuss the Liberating Lesson and Application for Activation sections.

N—Next Steps for Application

A. Summarize the value of asking God for wisdom and applying wisdom.

B. End class with a commitment to pray for learning how wisdom is a strong defense.

Worship Guide

For the Superintendent or Teacher
Theme: Wisdom's Vindication
Song: "Soft and Tenderly Jesus Is Calling"
Devotional Reading: Matthew 10:1-14

Wisdom's Vindication

Bible Background • MATTHEW 11:1–19
Printed Text • MATTHEW 11:7–19 | Devotional Reading • MATTHEW 10:1–14

——————— Aim for Change ———————

By the end of the lesson, we will: EXPLAIN how the different actions of Jesus and John the Baptist both displayed divine wisdom, FEEL encouraged to behave in ways that follow Jesus even when they are contrary to people's expectations, and REVIEW our own behavior to determine whether it reflects godly wisdom.

——————— In Focus ———————

When Janice entered the employees' lounge, she found Dian, Holly, and Anitra already there. She went to the staff lounge and poured herself a cup, as the other three discussed Rachel, the new supervisor. Rachel joined only six months ago after Kathleen left.

Janice tried to stay out of office gossip, so she sat down, sipped her coffee, and opened her Bible to do a bit of study. But she couldn't help but overhear her coworkers making one put down after another about Rachel's demeanor and competence. She decided to speak up. "What's so bad about Rachel?"

Dian said, "She comes here acting like she's our friend. But when I asked her for last Friday off, she gave me nothing but static."

"Come on, Dian," Janice said, "you know the last Friday of the month is crunch time. You've been here long enough to know no one was going to get that day off, especially after Kathleen let Holly and Anitra out on the same day last quarter."

"It's not like Kathleen was any prize," Holly chimed in. "She didn't know how to speak to people, calling me by name like she's my girlfriend. Exasperated, Janice said, "Wait a minute—just what do you want? Somebody to be mean and boss us around and yell at us? Rachel's our supervisor and we should respect that." Then Janice went back to work.

Spreading gossip reflects poorly on the people who spread it. How do we close our ears and heart to it when it is spread? When should we speak up?

——————— Keep in Mind ———————

"The Son of man came eating and drinking, and they say, Behold a man gluttonous, and a winebibber, a friend of publicans and sinners. But wisdom is justified of her children" (Matthew 11:19, KJV).

"The Son of Man, on the other hand, feasts and drinks, and you say, 'He's a glutton and a drunkard, and a friend of tax collectors and other sinners!' But wisdom is shown to be right by its results" (Matthew 11:19, NLT).

Focal Verses

KJV **Matthew 11:7** And as they departed, Jesus began to say unto the multitudes concerning John, What went ye out into the wilderness to see? A reed shaken with the wind?

8 But what went ye out for to see? A man clothed in soft raiment? behold, they that wear soft clothing are in kings' houses.

9 But what went ye out for to see? A prophet? yea, I say unto you, and more than a prophet.

10 For this is he, of whom it is written, Behold, I send my messenger before thy face, which shall prepare thy way before thee.

11 Verily I say unto you, Among them that are born of women there hath not risen a greater than John the Baptist: notwithstanding he that is least in the kingdom of heaven is greater than he.

12 And from the days of John the Baptist until now the kingdom of heaven suffereth violence, and the violent take it by force.

13 For all the prophets and the law prophesied until John.

14 And if ye will receive it, this is Elias, which was for to come.

15 He that hath ears to hear, let him hear.

16 But whereunto shall I liken this generation? It is like unto children sitting in the markets, and calling unto their fellows,

17 And saying, We have piped unto you, and ye have not danced; we have mourned unto you, and ye have not lamented.

18 For John came neither eating nor drinking, and they say, He hath a devil.

19 The Son of man came eating and drinking, and they say, Behold a man gluttonous, and a winebibber, a friend of publicans and sinners. But wisdom is justified of her children.

NLT **Matthew 11:7** As John's disciples were leaving, Jesus began talking about him to the crowds. "What kind of man did you go into the wilderness to see? Was he a weak reed, swayed by every breath of wind?

8 Or were you expecting to see a man dressed in expensive clothes? No, people with expensive clothes live in palaces.

9 Were you looking for a prophet? Yes, and he is more than a prophet.

10 John is the man to whom the Scriptures refer when they say, 'Look, I am sending my messenger ahead of you, and he will prepare your way before you.'

11 I tell you the truth, of all who have ever lived, none is greater than John the Baptist. Yet even the least person in the Kingdom of Heaven is greater than he is!

12 And from the time John the Baptist began preaching until now, the Kingdom of Heaven has been forcefully advancing, and violent people are attacking it.

13 For before John came, all the prophets and the law of Moses looked forward to this present time.

14 And if you are willing to accept what I say, he is Elijah, the one the prophets said would come.

15 Anyone with ears to hear should listen and understand!

16 To what can I compare this generation? It is like children playing a game in the public square. They complain to their friends,

17 'We played wedding songs, and you didn't dance, so we played funeral songs, and you didn't mourn.'

18 For John didn't spend his time eating and drinking, and you say, 'He's possessed by a demon.'

19 The Son of Man, on the other hand, feasts and drinks, and you say, 'He's a glutton and a drunkard, and a friend of tax collectors and other sinners!' But wisdom is shown to be right by its results."

The People, Places, and Times

John the Baptist. Jesus' cousin, John the Baptist, preached a message of repentance. John was called to be a spokesman for God's truth. By living in the wilderness, he kept himself apart from the daily distractions of others and devoted himself to prayer and meditation. When he came out among the crowds to deliver his message, those who heard him were mesmerized by his words. John was careful not to draw attention to himself, a temptation that would compromise lesser men. He kept his attention focused on his mission—to announce the coming of the Messiah.

Background

By the time we reach Matthew 11, Jesus has just told his disciples to go first among the Jewish people, preaching the coming of the kingdom of heaven. One recurring theme in the Gospels, however, is the hardness of heart of the people who hear the good news of Christ's coming, an outcome similar to what Isaiah experienced in his prophetic ministry. When Jesus utters the words of Matthew 11:7–19 to the crowd, He does so immediately after responding to John's inquiry about His identity. At this point, John the Baptist is in prison, and he sends a disciple to ask Christ whether He is the Messiah. Jesus responds by saying that He is the fulfillment of Isaiah 35:5–6, which is as close to an affirmative response as John is going to get. Jesus then proceeds to discuss the relationship between his and John the Baptist's ministry, explaining John's role as the forerunner of the Messiah.

All of this takes place to reshape the people's view of what kind of Messiah they ought to expect. Many, especially those associated with the Zealot political party, expected the Messiah to be a military hero, ready and willing to violently free God's people from oppression. Jesus in His ministry continually subverts such expectations.

At-A-Glance

1. What Did You Expect? (Matthew 11:7–11)
2. Rebellion Breeds Foolishness (vv. 12–19)

In Depth

1. What Did You Expect? (Matthew 11:7–11)

In John the Baptist, the crowd might have been looking for a physically imposing, well-dressed man. After all, he was said to be a prophet of God, even Elijah, the one who would herald the coming Messiah. But such is not the way of the biblical prophets. Whether one thinks of Isaiah, Ezekiel, Jeremiah, Amos, Hosea, or any of the other biblical prophets, they did not come with luxury but with lives of difficulty. Jesus reminds the people that John the Baptist is no different. Instead, John is the last of the long line of biblical prophets upon whom the Spirit rested, but only for a time. The astonishing turn is the second half of verse 11, when Jesus says, "the one who is least in the kingdom of heaven is greater than [John]." The Christian believer is greater than the last of the great biblical prophets. Indeed, we are because the Holy Spirit does not rest upon the one who is united to Christ for only a short time. By the instrument of faith, the Holy Spirit indwells that believer, inaugurating a relationship with God, the likes of which had never been seen before.

When have you met someone and been surprised when you found out their occupation? When have you met someone and been surprised that they were a fellow believer?

2. Rebellion Breeds Foolishness (vv. 12–19)

Here, Jesus reveals that John indeed came in the spirit of the foretold Elijah predicted by the prophets, but Jesus also chides the people for not giving Him the respect that he deserves as a messenger of God's word. The final two verses bring this critique to a head. The people critiqued John for his fasting, both from normal food and from alcohol, saying that he was possessed by a demon. John's call for austerity and repentance rubbed them the wrong way. But when Jesus came welcoming sinners and eating and drinking with them, He was critiqued for the company He kept. In short, there are some people who will criticize you no matter what you do. What is most important is that you are faithful to the Lord in the midst of your situation. Both John and Jesus were messengers of the Word who were not discouraged by the rebellion of their hearers.

Have you ever been frustrated by someone not understanding you? How did you address that frustration?

Search the Scriptures

1. Why is Jesus so careful about quoting the Old Testament so much in His assessment of His hearers?

2. What does Jesus do that His hearers do not expect? (Matthew 11:19)

Discuss the Meaning

1. Where do we look for God's wisdom?

2. Have you ever encountered His wisdom in an unexpected space?

Liberating Lesson

Christ's declaration that the least in the kingdom of heaven is greater than John the Baptist ought to fill us with hope and confidence. If John was the greatest of those born of women (as we all are born), how much greater are we with the indwelling Holy Spirit! With this in mind, the battle against sin becomes one that we are readily equipped for. When despair and frustration attack us in the journey of this Christian life, we must remember these words of

Jesus and the fact that even He had discouraging moments in His ministry. But as in His case, wisdom is justified by her deeds and so also your vindication will come. Continue to fight on.

Application for Activation

Remind yourself and your fellow believers of the privileges you enjoy as believers in Christ.

Remember the cohesiveness of Scripture. The entirety of Scripture points to Christ, including the Law and the Prophets. Reading in this way yields amazing insights!

Follow the Spirit

What God wants me to do:

_____

_____

_____

_____

Remember Your Thoughts

Special insights I have learned:

_____

_____

_____

_____

More Light on the Text
Matthew 11:7–19

John the Baptist was incarcerated for six months. Doubtlessly he wondered why the Messiah—his cousin—had not rescued him. His disciples, who saw him as the priestly Messiah—given the two Messiah concept that originated during the intertestamental

521

period—had created doubt in his mind since their messianic expectations were not being met by Jesus whom John had announced as Messiah. To verify the truth, John sent two disciples to Jesus. Rather than answering them, Jesus performed miracles fulfilling Isaiah 61:1 then sent them to tell John what they had seen and heard. As John's disciples were leaving, the events of our passage begin.

7 And as they departed, Jesus began to say unto the multitudes concerning John, What went ye out into the wilderness to see? A reed shaken with the wind? 8 But what went ye out for to see? A man clothed in soft raiment? behold, they that wear soft clothing are in kings' houses.

As John's disciples were leaving, Jesus began this so-called eulogy of John the Baptist for the multitude. The two events occurred at the same time, so John's disciples did not hear this beautiful acclaiming oration. Jesus asked them, "What went ye out into the wilderness to see?" This references the action of the people who had flocked to John to hear him preach. During the intertestamental period, God sent no prophets. This made the appearance of John noticeable, and thus people flocked to him to hear the renewed voice of God. Yet, since many did not accept him and Herod had not incarcerated him, Jesus asked they went to see. "A reed shaken by the wind?"

In the region of the Jordan where John preached grew reeds—tall slender cane grass. The imagery of them shaking and bending in the wind was common and became proverbial for a weak vacillator who was easily swayed. The question sought whether they went to the desert to attentively view such a scene or such a person. It required them to reflect on and analyze their reactions to John. Jesus implied that if that was their expectation, they would have been disappointed, for John wasn't such a

character. He was made of sterner, sturdier and steady stuff and stood for truth and right.

Verse 8 shows Jesus following up from another perspective. If that wasn't your outlook, did you anticipate seeing a character clothed in soft luxurious attire? Only in the king's court would such characters be found and John neither wore nor promised material wealth. Our motives for following God or His representatives are important. We ought to seek God because He is good and right, not because His messenger puts on a flashy show, or because we hope to get something out of it.

9 But what went ye out for to see? A prophet? yea, I say unto you, and more than a prophet. 10 For this is he, of whom it is written, Behold, I send my messenger before thy face, which shall prepare thy way before thee.

Jesus follows up asking if they went to see a "prophet." In Greek *prophetes* (**pro-FAY-tace**) is a compound from the words pro "before" and *phemi* (**fay-ME**) "to say." Though some stress the predictive aspect of the prophetic role and others the proclamation, the prophet's work actually consisted of three elements—foretelling (predictions), for-telling (speaking for God) and forth-telling (proclamation). Primarily then, a prophet was a fearless spokesperson for God and, by that very nature, will not always meet human expectations, as was the case with John. They can only speak for and say what God wants them to say.

Jesus then identified John as a prophet yet more than a prophet. He was more than a prophet for he was unique. He was the last of the Old Testament prophets, while at the same time the first of the New Testament prophets. He was more than a prophet because he alone was the forerunner of the Messiah as the quote from Malachi authenticates (v. 10; Malachi 3:1). His was the unique privilege of preparing the world for the Messiah and introducing Him to the world. In this, he followed the ancient custom of being the herald of a new king who would assist residents in clearing and cleaning the roads for the advent of a new king.

Yet there are two other distinguishing characteristics captured here. First, the Jews expected Elijah to return to proclaim Messiah's advent (Malachi 4:5). It is within this tradition that Jesus spoke of John and presented him as the coming Elijah—Messiah's herald (v. 14). Second, John is unique among prophets in that he is the one prophet to have been prophesied by prophets.

11 Verily I say unto you, Among them that are born of women there hath not risen a greater than John the Baptist: notwithstanding he that is least in the kingdom of heaven is greater than he. 12 And from the days of John the Baptist until now the kingdom of heaven suffereth violence, and the violent take it by force. 13 For all the prophets and the law prophesied until John. 14 And if ye will receive it, this is Elias, which was for to come. 15 He that hath ears to hear, let him hear.

Starting here is Jesus' own evaluation of John. John was the greatest of the prophets. We have already seen some reasons for this avowal but there's more. His character, conviction, and faithfulness were impeccable. Also, he was made great by the privilege of being the only person to have been possessed by the Holy Spirit prenatally (Luke 1:41). He had the awesome opportunity, too, of being the personal proclaimer of Jesus the Messiah. John's role was great due to the greatness of the One he announced.

Yet, as great as John was, Jesus said, "The least important in the kingdom of heaven is more important than" John. Jesus spoke of the kingdom as future (Matthew 6:10; Luke 13:29), as eschatological (Matthew 25:34), and as present (Matthew 16:28; Luke 11:20; 17:20). The reference here is to the kingdom as present. What Jesus was saying is that the least of those experiencing the soteriological aspect (i.e., the salvation aspect) of the kingdom were greater than John, for while they were in it experiencing the blessings, John heralded it but didn't enter or experience it. In this sense, he is like Moses who led the children of Israel to the Promised Land but did not have the privilege of entering it himself. Both John and Moses led others to the door and were at the door but were not privileged to enter.

The next words of Jesus have caused problems for scholars. The Greek word *biazo* (bee-ODD-zo, "suffereth violence") means to use or apply force. The form of the verb that appears here can be either passive voice (where the subject of the sentence receives the action of the verb) or a voice not used in English, called the middle voice (in which the subject participates in the result of the action, or prefers the action on themselves). Either meaning could be compatible in the context. The middle voice would suggest that the kingdom is experiencing violence as it forces its way forward; that is, the violence occurs partially from the kingdom's own actions. The passive voice would imply that the kingdom is being stormed as people of violence "take it by force."

How can the kingdom of God suffer violence from humans? Some see a reference to the same kind of sentiment that incited the crowd's attempt following the feeding of the 5,000 to take Jesus by force and make Him king over the nation in keeping with their idea of a Messiah. The kingdom has certainly been persecuted in its time, but it does not make sense for Jesus to mention this as He praises John and his ministry.

We can look at the one other New Testament passage that uses this word to help us understand this use. Luke records a parallel statement of Jesus as, "since that time [the time of John] the kingdom of God is preached, and every man presseth (*biazo*) into it" (16:16). Implied in this statement are two truths that should not be missed. First is the success of the mission of the kingdom. It has been unstoppable. Under both Jesus and John, it has been successfully making its way forward despite opposition as many embraced it. Second, this embracing has been enthusiastic and overwhelming in a good sense. The word for "suffereth violence" and "presseth into" is *biazetai* (**bee-ODD-zeh-tie**) while the word for the violent entrants *biastai* (**bee-oss-TIE**) is from the same root. This is a play on words, the implication being that the forceful progress of the kingdom elicits a similar response from the entrants, both being positive. The kingdom is surging forward more rapidly than any expected.

When Jesus refers to "all the prophets and the law," He means the entire Old Testament. The Jewish scriptures are divided into three sections: Law, Prophets, and Writings. Sometimes Jews would use any two to reference all—law and prophets or law and writings. Here it is referenced as "the prophets and the law." The implication is that the Old Testament scriptures pointed to John who culminated the last of the Old Testament prophets while at the same time inaugurating the new dispensation. He was the Elijah to come and so fulfilled the last Old Testament prophecy. Jesus further confirmed this notion (v. 14).

What Jesus was saying here is that John was indeed the fulfillment of Malachi's prophecy. He was indeed the Elijah to come. If we look at John the Baptist himself, this was his own self-understanding. He dressed like the first Elijah; he doggedly and fearlessly represented the truth just as the first Elijah had and he defended the truth as the first Elijah. Yet, he was neither a reincarnated Elijah nor a return from heaven of the first Elijah. Rather, John the Baptist came in the spirit and power of the first Elijah. He called people to repentance and obedience just

as the first Elijah and thus unmistakably was the fulfillment of the last Old Testament prophecy.

Jesus followed this up with one of His favorite sayings, "He that hath ears to hear; let him hear." While all of us have ears and should be able to hear, many who are not impaired still do not hear. Some people listen but do not truly hear. They are preoccupied with their own thoughts or with what they want to say next so they do not hear what is said. Others hear and understand what is said but do not what to do it. They want to do their own thing. After enunciating significant truths Jesus uttered this statement as an exhortation not only to hear but to do the right thing. That command is still relevant for Christians today, many of whom experience a disconnect between their walk and their talk, between their desire and their performance.

16 But whereunto shall I liken this generation? It is like unto children sitting in the markets, and calling unto their fellows, 17 And saying, We have piped unto you, and ye have not danced; we have mourned unto you, and ye have not lamented.

In this section, Jesus turned from the people's thinking of and reaction to John's person and mission to their reaction to Him and His own mission. The generation can be compared to children playing in the streets. They are divided into two groups—the performers and the complainers. Nothing the performers do is acceptable to the other side. They neither dance to wedding music that is piped nor lament at funeral dirges. They fall somewhere on a continuum between being hard to please and wanting to have their own way. Jesus ties this analogy back to John's ministry in the following verses.

18 For John came neither eating nor drinking, and they say, He hath a devil. 19 The Son of man came eating and drinking, and they say, Behold a man gluttonous, and a

winebibber, a friend of publicans and sinners. But wisdom is justified of her children.

With the parable of the children in the marketplace, Jesus compares the reception given to John's mission and His own. Just as the complaining children in street playing cannot be pleased with either festive wedding songs or funeral dirges, even so, his contemporary generation is not pleased whether the prophets are celebratory or solemn. They rejected John the Baptist who came as a recluse living in the wilderness, preaching repentance and without social interactions. But they also rejected Jesus who lived among them and had social interactions with everyone. They said John had a devil, while Jesus was a glutton and a drunk (KJV: "winebibber") who ate with publicans and sinners. Criticizing one for one action and criticizing the other for the opposite action reflects a lack of wisdom.

Instructively then, the problem was neither with Jesus nor John. It was with the generation and its leaders—the scribes and Pharisees. They received neither John nor Jesus and like perverse children refused to be satisfied with any proposition offered them. They, like us, need to realize that God uses various messengers to accomplish varied missions. It is not ours to question why but rather to accept them all to fulfill God's purposes.

Sources:

Arndt, William and F. Wilbur Gingrich. *A Greek-English Lexicon of the New Testament.* Chicago: The University of Chicago Press, 1959.

Barclay, William. *The Gospel of Matthew.* Vol. 2, Rev. Ed. The Daily Bible Study Series. Philadelphia, PA: The Westminster Press, 1975.

Blunt, Brian K., gen. ed. *True to Our Native Land: An African American New Testament Commentary.* Minneapolis: Fortress Press, 2007.

Freeman, James. *The New Bible Manners and Customs of the Bible.* Gainesville, FL: Bridge-Logos Publishers, 1973.

Jeremias, Joachim. *The Parables of Jesus.* 2nd Rev. Ed. New York: Charles Scribner's Sons, 1972.

Spence-Jones, D. M., ed. *The Pulpit Commentary, St. Matthew.* New York: Funk & Wagnalls Company, 1978.

Keener, Craig S. *A Commentary on the Gospel of Matthew.* Grand Rapids, MI: Wm. B. Eerdmans Publishing Co., 1999.

Lange, John Peter. *The Gospel According to Matthew.* St. Albans, UK: Wentworth Publishing, 2016.

Lenski, R. C. H. *The Interpretation of St. Matthew's Gospel.* Minneapolis, MN: Augsburg Publishing House, 1943.

Nicholl, Francis D. *The SDA Bible Commentary.* Vol. 5. Hagerstown, MD: Review and Herald Publishing Association, 1980.

Robertson, A.T. *Word Pictures in the New Testament.* Nashville, TN: Broadman Press, 1930.

Daily Bible Readings

MONDAY
Wise Counsel for Defending Your Faith
(Matthew 10:16-23)

TUESDAY
Wise Deeds of the Coming Messiah
(Isaiah 35:3-10)

WEDNESDAY
John the Baptist, God's Messenger
(Luke 7:24-28)

THURSDAY
The Messiah's Wise Deeds
(Matthew 11:1-6)

FRIDAY
Woes on Unwise Cities
(Matthew 11:20-24)

SATURDAY
Wisdom's Invitation to Come and Rest
(Matthew 11:25-30)

SUNDAY
Wisdom Is Vindicated by Her Deeds
(Matthew 11:7-19)

Say It Correctly

Intertestamental. in-ter-**TESS**-ta-**MEN**-tal.
Eschatological. ess-ka-toe-**LAH**-gi-cal.
Soteriological. so-**TEIR**-ee-oh-**LAH**-gi-cal.

Teaching Tips

Words You Should Know

A. Asking (v. 46) *eperotao* (Gk.)—To demand, inquire or desire

B. Subject (v. 51) *hupotasso* (Gk.)—To submit oneself to; to obey or make oneself a subordinate

Teacher Preparation

Unifying Principle—Wisdom that Amazes. Some young people amaze us with a wisdom that seems beyond their years. How should we respond to precocious wisdom? Ecclesiastes affirms that there is a time to speak and a time to be quiet, and Luke records that the teachers in the Temple were awed by the wisdom of twelve-year-old Jesus, but Mary and Joseph were confused and exasperated.

A. Read the Bible Background and Devotional Readings.

B. Pray for your students and lesson clarity.

C. Read the lesson Scripture in multiple translations.

O—Open the Lesson

A. Begin the class with prayer.

B. Have the class discuss the wisdom in children.

C. Have the students read the Aim for Change and the In Focus story.

D. Ask students how events like those in the story weigh on their hearts and how they can view these events from a faith perspective.

P—Present the Scriptures

A. Read the Focal Verses.

B. Have the class share what Scriptures stand out for them and why, with particular emphasis on today's context.

C. Discuss the Background and The People, Places, and Times sections.

E—Explore the Meaning

A. Use In Depth or More Light on the Text to facilitate a deeper discussion of the lesson text.

B. Pose the questions in Search the Scriptures and Discuss the Meaning.

C. Discuss the Liberating Lesson and Application for Activation sections.

N—Next Steps for Application

A. Summarize the value of the opportunity to know the wisdom of God through Jesus.

B. End class with a commitment to pray to wait on the Holy Spirit to guide them in their speech and actions.

Worship Guide

For the Superintendent or Teacher
Theme: The Boy Jesus
Song: "Mary Had a Baby"
Devotional Reading: Leviticus 12:1–8;
Numbers 3:11–13

The Boy Jesus

Bible Background • ECCLESIASTES 3:1–15; LUKE 2:39–52
Printed Text • ECCLESIASTES 3:1, 7; LUKE 2:39–52 | Devotional Reading • LEVITICUS 12:1–8; NUMBERS 3:11–13

—————— Aim for Change ——————

By the end of the lesson, we will: EXPLORE the account of Jesus' experience in the Temple at the age of twelve, SENSE the awe experienced by all those who witnessed Jesus' wisdom as well as Mary and Joseph's angst, and REJOICE in the opportunity to know the wisdom of God.

————————— In Focus —————————

Arthur and Dot couldn't help but be proud of their daughter, Regina. She was a precocious child who would graduate high school at sixteen, and then to college.

Of course, Arthur and Dot were concerned about Regina being around older children all the time. They prayed that their daughter would be among kids who were good influences on her, and they made sure she stayed active in her church. Things turned out very well for Regina, who was accepted at her top pick: the Massachusetts Institute of Technology.

Regina found college somewhat more challenging than high school but still took on double majors in engineering and in marketing. After she finished, Regina established her own engineering firm that quickly grew and obtained a large regional clientele.

"I don't understand all that you do, Regina," Arthur said when he visited her for a lunch date. "But I'm always glad to support you. Your mom and I are excited for you."

"Thanks, Dad," Regina said. "I am very happy that you and mom always prayed and supported me. I truly thank God for being with me and listening to me."

"God is always listening, Regina," Dot said. "And we are too."

The wisdom of God brings blessings to all who are open to receiving it, young or old. Can we appreciate it when someone does better work whether they are young or old?

——————— Keep in Mind ———————

"And the child grew, and waxed strong in spirit, filled with wisdom: and the grace of God was upon him" (Luke 2:40, KJV).

"There the child grew up healthy and strong. He was filled with wisdom, and God's favor was on him" (Luke 2:40, NLT).

Focal Verses

KJV **Ecclesiastes 3:1** To every thing there is a season, and a time to every purpose under the heaven:

7 A time to rend, and a time to sew; a time to keep silence, and a time to speak;

Luke 2:39 And when they had performed all things according to the law of the Lord, they returned into Galilee, to their own city Nazareth.

40 And the child grew, and waxed strong in spirit, filled with wisdom: and the grace of God was upon him.

41 Now his parents went to Jerusalem every year at the feast of the passover.

42 And when he was twelve years old, they went up to Jerusalem after the custom of the feast.

43 And when they had fulfilled the days, as they returned, the child Jesus tarried behind in Jerusalem; and Joseph and his mother knew not of it.

44 But they, supposing him to have been in the company, went a day's journey; and they sought him among their kinsfolk and acquaintance.

45 And when they found him not, they turned back again to Jerusalem, seeking him.

46 And it came to pass, that after three days they found him in the temple, sitting in the midst of the doctors, both hearing them, and asking them questions.

47 And all that heard him were astonished at his understanding and answers.

48 And when they saw him, they were amazed: and his mother said unto him, Son, why hast thou thus dealt with us? behold, thy father and I have sought thee sorrowing.

49 And he said unto them, How is it that ye sought me? wist ye not that I must be about my Father's business?

50 And they understood not the saying which he spake unto them.

NLT **Ecclesiastes 3:1** For everything there is a season, a time for every activity under heaven.

7 A time to tear and a time to mend. A time to be quiet and a time to speak.

Luke 2:39 When Jesus' parents had fulfilled all the requirements of the law of the Lord, they returned home to Nazareth in Galilee.

40 There the child grew up healthy and strong. He was filled with wisdom, and God's favor was on him.

41 Every year Jesus' parents went to Jerusalem for the Passover festival.

42 When Jesus was twelve years old, they attended the festival as usual.

43 After the celebration was over, they started home to Nazareth, but Jesus stayed behind in Jerusalem. His parents didn't miss him at first,

44 because they assumed he was among the other travelers. But when he didn't show up that evening, they started looking for him among their relatives and friends.

45 When they couldn't find him, they went back to Jerusalem to search for him there.

46 Three days later they finally discovered him in the Temple, sitting among the religious teachers, listening to them and asking questions.

47 All who heard him were amazed at his understanding and his answers.

48 His parents didn't know what to think. "Son," his mother said to him, "why have you done this to us? Your father and I have been frantic, searching for you everywhere."

49 "But why did you need to search?" he asked. "Didn't you know that I must be in my Father's house?"

50 But they didn't understand what he meant.

529

51 And he went down with them, and came to Nazareth, and was subject unto them: but his mother kept all these sayings in her heart.

52 And Jesus increased in wisdom and stature, and in favour with God and man.

51 Then he returned to Nazareth with them and was obedient to them. And his mother stored all these things in her heart.

52 Jesus grew in wisdom and in stature and in favor with God and all the people.

The People, Places, and Times

Feast of Passover. The Feast of Passover celebrates the Jews' passage from slavery to freedom and commemorates the occasion in which the death angel passed over the Hebrew households in Egypt (see Exodus 12–13). Jews are commanded to remember the night of their liberation by partaking of the Seder, a traditional meal with each item of food representing part of the liberation story. During biblical times, the seven-day celebration was held in Jerusalem and attendance by the entire family was required (see Exodus 23:14–17).

Why is it important to gather with family during an important religious celebration?

Background

The Gospel of Luke provides the most comprehensive picture of Jesus' ministry of all four of the Gospels, with about one-third of the material included only appearing in this account. Luke focuses on Jesus as the Son of Man, the promised Messiah.

Beginning with the birth announcements of John the Baptist and Jesus, Luke provides multiple indicators of Jesus' divine nature, while revealing his true humanity.

When Mary and Joseph went to present Jesus in the Temple, the elderly Simeon was led there by the Spirit. He saw Jesus, took Him up in his arms, blessed God, and prophesied. At that same time, Anna, a widowed prophetess who served in the Temple, entered, and she too thanked God for the Redemption in Jerusalem.

Mary and Joseph could not begin to fathom the magnitude of what it would mean to raise the boy Messiah, but 2:19 says that Mary pondered these things she witnessed in her heart.

How do events at our birth affect our upbringing?

At-A-Glance

1. A Time for Everything (Ecclesiastes 3:1, 7)
2. The Family Returns Home (Luke 2:39–40)
3. Boy Jesus in the Temple (vv. 41–52)

In Depth

1. A Time for Everything (Ecclesiastes 3:1, 7)

It is believed that Solomon wrote Ecclesiastes near the end of his life. As the wealthiest and wisest king of his time (1 Kings 3:10–13), his experiences were vast. Unlike his father David, he failed to remain wholeheartedly committed to the Lord, led astray to worship idols because of his multiple relationships with Gentile women. His thesis after surveying life was that "everything was meaningless," but that in the end it was best to "fear God and keep his commandments" (12:13–14).

The "Time for Everything" poem (3:1–8), compares opposite occurrences, and Solomon surmises that every activity has an appropriate point in time and duration, and that in the end He acknowledges God is sovereign over all.

Verse 7 may reference mourning, as ancient Jews would tear clothes and be silent but would mend and speak when the season of mourning was over. However, the latter portion could also refer to the truth that there is wisdom in knowing when to hold onto words, and when to share them.

In Luke 2, we see the time has come for prophecy to be fulfilled, and Jesus' true nature to be publicly revealed.

2. The Family Returns Home (Luke 2:39–40)

Mary and Joseph prove to be devout Jews. From Mary's response to the angel Gabriel (1:38), to her song magnifying God for what He had done (1:46–53), to Joseph's obedience in not divorcing Mary (Matthew 1:18–24), they consistently demonstrate faith and obedience.

They continue to follow the Law after Jesus' birth. Circumcising Him on the eighth day, they name Him "Jesus" as instructed by the angel. After the forty days of purification, Mary and Joseph travel from Bethlehem to the temple in Jerusalem, to present Jesus to God, as required for the firstborn son. The ceremony required a sacrifice—either a lamb or two pigeons. The couple's two pigeons indicate that they were poor, but that was not a hindrance to their faithfulness. And once it was complete, they go home.

Afterward, the boy Jesus grows and becomes strong, as any child could typically be expected to do. However, His divinity is revealed as the grace of God filled Him with supernatural wisdom.

3. Boy Jesus in the Temple (vv. 41–52)

As required each year, Mary and Joseph make the pilgrimage to Jerusalem for the Passover, the feast that commemorated the death angel "passing over" the firstborn in Israel when God delivered the Israelites from Egypt. At twelve years old, this would possibly have been a year of preparation for Jesus, as according to Jewish custom, Jewish boys were considered and presented as men at thirteen.

After the week-long festival, the entire family starts the journey back to Jerusalem. They are twenty miles away before Mary and Joseph realized that Jesus had not joined them. After three days, they located him in the temple.

Since conception, there had been glimpses that the "grace of God was upon Jesus." However, Mary and Joseph are still not prepared to find Him deeply engaged in theological discussions with well-respected rabbis. He is not merely listening, but understanding, eagerly inquiring and answering questions, which astonished all.

As any mother would, Mary questions Jesus. His response, well beyond his years, indicates that while they had not yet come to fully understand, He already definitively knew He had been commissioned by God for a specific purpose.

Jesus, being fully divine, yet a fully human boy, then willingly submits to their authority, returning home to Nazareth, where He would continue to grow—physically and spiritually. There would be no mention of his life again until it was time for Him to go public in ministry, eighteen years later.

Search the Scriptures

1. Where do Mary and Joseph find Jesus? What does Jesus call the place?

2. Where do we see both Mary and Jesus knowing there is "a time to speak and a time to stay silent"?

Discuss the Meaning

Solomon talks about a time for everything and comes to understand that God sovereignly controls all. Read Isaiah 7:14, Isaiah 9:6–7 and Luke 2:25–32. What does this reveal to you about time, prophecy and God?

Liberating Lesson

Much attention is given to Jesus' ministry as an adult. His conception and birth is the focus every Christmas; His death, burial, and resurrection on Resurrection Sunday. However, little attention is given to the subtle ways God intentionally showed Jesus' parents in childhood, who he was destined to be. It appears that they knew it cognitively, but not experientially. In contrast to Anna, Simeon, and the shepherds who worshiped the Messiah, Mary and Joseph saw a child—their child. As a result, they seemed to underestimate and even get frustrated, when God's power and leading were evident in His life.

We often do the same. Not only do we underestimate God's power in our own lives but in the lives of others. We put parameters on how God can use someone—he is too young or too old, her personality is too quirky, his past too checkered. We sit in awe of a child who seems wiser than his age dictates but do not encourage his spiritual growth, neglecting to recognize that God works through and in children as well. We put God in a box, and when He does not "fit," instead of adjusting our expectations, we get frustrated. In doing so, we miss the opportunity to marvel in God's greatness and worship Him in response.

Application for Activation

Mary and Joseph were living their lives when one day, God sent an angel and changed everything. While we will not have such a drastic experience as that, there has probably been some redirection in life. Spend time this week reflecting on how God has redirected your life. Consider your response to the change. Was it one of joy, worship, and obedience? In hindsight, what clarity do you now have?

There may be ways that God is prompting your heart now. Journal, pray and discuss it with someone with godly wisdom who will encourage and counsel you. Then, choose obedience.

Follow the Spirit

What God wants me to do:

_____

_____

_____

_____

Remember Your Thoughts

Special insights I have learned:

_____

_____

_____

_____

More Light on the Text

Ecclesiastes 3:1 To every thing there is a season, and a time to every purpose under the heaven:

7 A time to rend, and a time to sew; a time to keep silence, and a time to speak;

Children go to school on weekdays. Many believers go to church on Sunday mornings. Most people sleep at night. There is a time for every activity. Time passing can be just a meaningless clock ticking away, or we can see it as having a "purpose" as God intended it.

Verse 7 seems tinged with sorrow, for typically a Jew would "rend" his garments to express sorrow over death (Genesis 37:34; Joshua 7:6; 2 Samuel 3:31; Job 1:20). Its companion phrase (a time to keep silence) may also signify silent sorrow (see Job 2:12–13; John 11:20). If we could only master the last part of verse 7—"a time to keep silence, and a time to speak." Sometimes our silence causes problems or does not intervene to prevent them out of fear. Other times we need to be silent and instead speak and spark conflict and hurt. Truly our voices can be great tools for both good and evil. In the case of young Jesus, He spoke before it was socially acceptable, but His words were the words of wisdom and truth that needed to be heard by those in the Temple.

Luke 2:39 When Jesus' parents had fulfilled all the requirements of the law of the Lord, they returned home to Nazareth in Galilee. 40 There the child grew up healthy and strong. He was filled with wisdom, and God's favor was on him.

The requirements of the Law of the Lord is referred to were Jesus' circumcision and dedication as the firstborn male in the Temple in Jerusalem. During that trip to keep the covenant God made with Israel, Simeon, an elder, and Anna, a prophetess, both prophesied over Jesus that He was the Messiah that had been long awaited in Israel. With that revelation in mind, Joseph and Mary return to Galilee, their hometown. Verse 40 first states the expected pattern of the child Jesus growing up in good health and strength. It is the desire of every loving parent that their child grow up healthy, and Jesus is no exception as fully human. But the second part of the verse gives another glimpse into Jesus' anointing and divinity: He was filled with wisdom and God's favor was on Him in a way that was recognizable even at a young age. Jesus was again affirmed as special from birth to childhood.

41 Now his parents went to Jerusalem every year at the feast of the Passover.

The feasts were part of the Jewish customs and practices. Celebrating the feasts was in fulfillment of the covenant God had with them. The Passover feast mentioned in this verse was the first of the three major annual festivals of the Jews; it was celebrated in Jerusalem in the month of Nisan (March–April), from the 14th to the 21st. The first day, the 14th, was the actual Passover feast, while the remaining days were called Feast of Unleavened Bread. The Passover commemorated the miraculous deliverance of the Israelites from Egyptian bondage and the sparing of their firstborn when the destroying angel smote the firstborn of the Egyptians. The Greek word translated "Passover," *pascha* (**PAS-khah**) in this verse, is used to refer to the meal, the day, the festival, or the special sacrifices connected with the Passover feast. But specifically, it refers to the paschal supper eaten on the first day of the feast, the 14th of Nisan. The Hebrew word translated "Passover" is *pasakh* (**PEH-sakh**); it means "to pass over, skip over or to spare."

Later observances of the Passover differ in certain respects from the first and original celebrated in Egypt on the night before the deliverance. The Passover lamb was slain in the Temple, rather than at home (Deuteronomy 16:5–6); the blood was sprinkled on the altar instead of the door posts; and apart from the family sacrifice for the Passover meal, there were public and national sacrifices offered each of the seven days of the Feast of Unleavened Bread. Each year the people recited the meaning of the Passover; they later started singing the Hallel (Psalms 113–118) during the meal. These changes made to the Passover, and it became a perpetual ordinance that made it last through generations, even to the time of Jesus. In keeping with the yearly observance, every devout Jew, including Jesus' parents, was expected to go to Jerusalem, to the Temple for the Passover.

42 And when he was twelve years old, they went up to Jerusalem after the custom of the feast. 43 And when they had fulfilled the days, as they returned, the child Jesus

tarried behind in Jerusalem; and Joseph and his mother knew not of it.

Jesus' parents observed the Passover from year to year. In the course of time, as indicated by the stage of Jesus' growth, He became twelve years old. At this time, He went to Jerusalem for the Passover according to the custom of the feast. The Greek word translated "custom" is *ethos* (**EH-thoce**); it signifies "usage prescribed by law; a manner, habit; a rite or ceremony." The word translated "feast" is *heorte* (**heh-or-TAY**); it means a "holy day." Making the journey to Jerusalem, performing the special sacrifices, eating the Passover meal, and all that is done in observing the Passover had become a habit or rite prescribed by Law for the Jews. All these acts were performed during holy days—specific seasons or days set apart unto the Lord. The feast lasted over a period of eight days. The first and the last days were Sabbath days in which no one was required to do any servile work other than making preparations for the meal. Those who traveled to Jerusalem from other towns, like Jesus and His parents, had to stay in Jerusalem during the period of the feast. This is what is meant by "they ... fulfilled the days."

After they had observed the days of the feast, the boy Jesus waited behind in Jerusalem while His parents headed back home. As someone who had a divine mission to accomplish and a purpose to fulfill on earth, His waiting behind in Jerusalem immediately after Passover was certainly in accordance with His mission. Consequently, the Passover of Jesus' twelfth year on Earth occasioned His first purposeful interaction with the Jewish public. As the Son of God who came to fulfill God's will, Jesus' tarrying wasn't an act of His own will but of God's. There was a heavenly outpouring of spiritual virtue upon the boy Jesus at the age of twelve to reveal His divine nature.

In the meantime, His parents didn't realize they left Him behind as they journeyed home.

44 But they, supposing him to have been in the company, went a day's journey; and they sought him among their kinsfolk and acquaintance. 45 And when they found him not, they turned back again to Jerusalem, seeking him.

In the course of the journey, assumption gave way to awareness. Mary and Joseph became aware that Jesus was not in the group after traveling an entire day. The Greek word for "company" (*sunodia*, **soo-no-DEE-ah**) denotes "companions on a journey" or a "company of travelers." When they discovered that He was not in their group, they started searching for Him among their relatives. The Greek word translated "sought" (*anazeteo*, **ah-nah-dzay-TEH-oh**) denotes "to seek carefully," that is, to search out someone while having some difficulty in the process. This means it was quite an effort trying to search for Jesus through the group of travelers.

We see hints here of how Mary and Joseph traveled. It was a significant distance between Nazareth and Jerusalem, and travel is safer in numbers. Since all Jews are expected to come to Jerusalem for the Passover, there must have been many families on the road. The holy family must have been traveling with a large "company" of "kinsfolk and acquaintance" and assumed Jesus was with someone else in their caravan as they set out.

46 And it came to pass, that after three days they found him in the temple, sitting in the midst of the doctors, both hearing them, and asking them questions. 47 And all that heard him were astonished at his understanding and answers.

After three days of searching for Jesus, His parents eventually found Him in the Temple in discussion with the doctors. The Greek word translated "doctors" (*didaskalos*, **dee-DAS-kah-loce**) signifies "instructor, teacher, or master." These doctors were teachers of the Law who taught the Jewish religion; they were also called scribes, professional expositors of the laws of Judaism. The scribes underwent special training and had to pass rigid examinations before being officially recognized. They were highly respected within the Jewish community. These were the caliber of people with whom the boy Jesus was having an intellectual discussion at age twelve.

He was listening and "asking them" questions. The Greek word translated "asking" (*eperotao*, **eh-peh-row-TAH-oh**) signifies "to demand, inquire or desire" and suggests asking with some eagerness. Jesus seemed to demand answers from the doctors based on what He desired to know. An impartation by the Holy Spirit certainly inspired Him at that age to make intelligent inquiries that astonished these learned doctors. He exhibited profound understanding; He gave them amazing answers. To them, He was a sort of prodigy. They didn't know He had a divine nature, which was actually manifesting. He did not only inquire of them, He also gave them answers. The Greek word translated "answers" (*apokrisis*, **ah-POE-kree-sees**), meaning "a response," tells us that Jesus was also asked questions to which He gave responses. His answers, He revealed an understanding that astonished the doctors in the Temple.

It is of great spiritual benefit to be inquisitive about spiritual matters. This will cause us to make inquiries about God, His Word, and the life we possess in Him. An inquisitive disposition is sure to bring inspiration, and by inspiration we get illuminating knowledge that leads to growth and spiritual maturity. Within the community of faith, it is therefore advisable to dialogue with others and to make inquiries of those whom the Lord has ordained to teach us His Word. This might require us to voice our convictions about certain issues of the faith and to accept correction when we are wrong. In this way, we will grow in faith and wisdom. This is why we have to commit ourselves to lifelong learning in the community of faith.

48 And when they saw him, they were amazed: and his mother said unto him, Son, why hast thou thus dealt with us? behold, thy father and I have sought thee sorrowing.

The Greek word translated "amazed" (*ekplesso*, **ek-PLACE-so**) means "to be struck with astonishment." This was how Jesus' parents felt upon discovering Him in the temple. They didn't expect to see Him in the temple with the teachers of the Law.

The fact that He was unperturbed and feeling comfortable with these learned men inflamed their amazement and was in sharp contrast to their feelings of anxiety that had mounted over the period of a three-day search for Him. Anxiety made Jesus' mother upset about His actions. In an outburst of emotions typical of mothers, she inquired why He had done this to them. The Greek word translated "dealt" (*poieo*, **poy-EH-oh**) simply means "to do" so that phrase denotes "hath done to us." Though she knew that her son was the Messiah, the Son of God, she was still puzzled as to what the reason could be for His unusual behavior.

49 And he said unto them, How it is that ye sought me? Wist ye not that I must be about my Father's business? 50 And they understood not the saying which he spake unto them.

It was customary for a Jewish teacher to instruct his students by asking probing and leading questions. Jesus seems to already use this technique when He replies to His mother with a question that offers an explanation: a question that justifies His presence in the temple, and explains His absence from the caravan of travelers. The Greek word translated "wist" (*eido*, **AY-do**) means "to know, to be aware," hence "Wist ye not" can be translated, "Don't you know?" or "Are you not aware?" Jesus' response appears to admonish His parents that they should have known He would be somewhere on assignment for His Heavenly Father. His reply reveals His willingness and commitment to his Father's business while making them aware of its importance.

In His question, He speaks of an inner compulsion. He says, "I must …." The Greek word for "must" (*dei*, **DAY**) denotes "it is necessary"; it is used to indicate a necessity brought about by certain circumstances. In this case, Jesus is saying, by reason of His Father's will, He had to do His Father's business. It was necessary for a divine purpose to be fulfilled, which made every other thing less significant— even traveling back home with His parents.

51 And he went down with them, and came to Nazareth, and was subject unto them: but his mother kept all these sayings in her heart.

The arrival of Jesus' parents seemed to mark the end of His three-day mission in the Temple. In his reply to His mother in verse 49, He questioned her with His spiritual authority as the Christ, the Son of God, who came from heaven to fulfill God's work on earth. But His full awareness of the fact that He was human, a boy of twelve, and still under parental care, made Him conduct Himself in the most appropriate manner: He went back to Nazareth with His parents and became subject to them. The Greek word translated "subject" (*hupotasso*, **hoo-poe-TASS-so**) means "to submit oneself to, to obey or make oneself a subordinate." He was still a child, Jesus complied with natural order by submitting Himself to the authority

and protection of His parents. His mother became a repository of His sayings. The Greek word translated "kept" (*diatereo*, **dee-ah-tay-REH-oh**) signifies "to keep carefully, to observe strictly." This gives us the idea of Jesus' mother meticulously collecting every saying of Jesus and storing them in her heart.

52 And Jesus increased in wisdom and stature, and in favour with God and man.

Every child is expected to grow into adulthood. Growth in children is characterized by physical, mental, and spiritual development. As Jesus grew up, He increased in wisdom. The Greek word for "wisdom" (*sophia*, **so-FEE-ah**) is used in a broad sense to mean "human and spiritual wisdom." Increasing in wisdom is an indication of spiritual development and growing in the Holy Spirit, for the wisdom of God is one of the principal manifestations of the Spirit in one's life.

Other attributes accompanied wisdom to bring about Jesus' spiritual development. Jesus increased in stature. The Greek word for "stature" (*helikia*, **hay-lee-KEE-ah**) signifies "age, maturity in years or size." Jesus grew normally physically, denoting His human aspect alongside His divine aspects. He also increased in favor. The word translated "favor" (Gk. *charis*, **KHA-reece**) denotes "graciousness or grace." It speaks of the divine influence of blessings upon the heart, and its reflection in the life of a person. This graciousness or divine influence in Jesus' life continuously attracted benefits, gifts, pleasure, and acceptability from God and people.

Sources:

Bock, Darrell L. *Baker Exegetical Commentary on the New Testament: Luke 1–9:50.* Grand Rapids, MI: Baker Books, 1994.

Packer, J. I. and M. C. Tenney eds. *Illustrated Manners and Customs of the Bible.* Nashville, TN: Thomas Nelson Publishers, 1980.

Global Study Bible, English Standard Version. Wheaton, IL: Crossway Publishers, 2012. 1420–1422.

Keener, Craig S. *The IVP Bible Background Commentary: New Testament.* Downers Grove, IL: Intervarsity Press, 1993. 191–196.

Radmacher, Earl D., ed. *Nelson Study Bible, New King James Version.* Nashville, TN: Thomas Nelson Publishers, 1997. 1078–1079, 1083–1084, 1689–1692.

Ryrie, Charles C. *Ryrie Study Bible, New International Version.* Chicago, IL: Moody Press. 1986. 1404–1406.

Walvoord, John F., and Roy B. Zuck, eds. *The Bible Knowledge Commentary: Old Testament.* Wheaton, IL: Victor Books, SP Publications, Inc., 1983.983-984.

—. *The Bible Knowledge Commentary: New Testament.* Wheaton, IL: Victor Books, SP Publications, Inc., 1983. 208–210.

Zondervan Study Bible, New International Version. Grand Rapids, MI: Zondervan Publishers, 2002. 1570–1572.

Say It Correctly

Seder. **SAY**-dur.
Nisan. **NEE**-san.
Hallel. ha-**LELL**.

Daily Bible Readings

MONDAY
Everything Has Its Time and Season
(Ecclesiastes 3:2–8)

TUESDAY
Perform Your God-Given Task
(Ecclesiastes 3:9–15)

WEDNESDAY
The Firstborn Belong to God
(Numbers 3:11–13)

THURSDAY
Jesus Presented to the Lord
(Luke 2:21–24)

FRIDAY
Simeon Praises God for the Child
(Luke 2:25–35)

SATURDAY
Anna Speaks about the Christ Child
(Luke 2:36–38)

SUNDAY
The Wise Boy Jesus Amazes Teachers
(Ecclesiastes 3:1,7; Luke 2:39–52)

Notes

Teaching Tips

Words You Should Know

A. Offended (v. 3) *skandalizo* (Gk.)—Trip up; cause to stumble, or to cause displeasure

B. Unbelief (v. 6) *apistis* (Gk.)—Faithlessness, disbelief, unfaithfulness, or disobedience

Teacher Preparation

Unifying Principle—Wisdom That Astounds and Offends. Some people amaze us by displaying unexpected wisdom. What happens when people show such extraordinary wisdom? Mark tells us that the people in Jesus' hometown were both astounded and offended by Jesus' wise teachings, and the religious leaders were incensed when Jesus' wisdom challenged their traditions.

A. Read the Bible Background and Devotional Reading.

B. Pray for your students and lesson clarity.

C. Read the lesson Scripture in multiple translations.

O—Open the Lesson

A. Begin the class with prayer.

B. Ask the class: "When did someone you know display surprising insights and knowledge? What was the reaction of others? Was anyone surprised? Did anyone express disbelief or reject the person? What was your personal response?"

C. Have the students read the Aim for Change and the In Focus story.

D. Ask students how events like those in the story weigh on their hearts and how they can view these events from a faith perspective.

P—Present the Scriptures

A. Read the Focal Verses.

B. Have the class share what Scriptures stand out for them and why, with particular emphasis on today's context.

C. Discuss the Background and The People, Places, and Times sections.

E—Explore the Meaning

A. Use In Depth or More Light on the Text to facilitate a deeper discussion of the lesson text.

B. Pose the questions in Search the Scriptures and Discuss the Meaning.

C. Discuss the Liberating Lesson and Application for Activation sections.

N—Next Steps for Application

A. Summarize the value of learning and living in the wisdom of Jesus.

B. End class with a commitment to pray for God's wisdom over personal or community beliefs.

Worship Guide

For the Superintendent or Teacher
Theme: The Wisdom of Jesus
Song: "To Us the Voice of Wisdom Cries"
Devotional Reading: Mark 7:14–23

The Wisdom of Jesus

Bible Background • MARK 6:1–6; 7:1–23
Printed Text • MARK 6:1–6 | Devotional Reading • MARK 7:14–23

Aim for Change

By the end of the lesson, we will: IDENTIFY the reason or reasons the people in Nazareth could not accept the wisdom of Jesus, REPENT of the occasions when Jesus' words made us feel offended instead of accepting them as wisdom, and COMMIT to accepting the words of Jesus even when they challenge us.

In Focus

Hassan gathered his things, thanked Mrs. Jenkins for her time, and got up to leave. She walked with him to the door and said, "Be sure to tell your mama we're praying for her. See you on Sunday at church."

As he walked down the steps toward his car, Hassan wondered if Mrs. Jenkins had heard a word he said. He was volunteering as a community organizer trying to encourage people to vote. Mrs. Jenkins was on the board of trustees of the biggest church in his territory, and he hoped she would see her way clear to having a meeting there.

Hassan was as personable and charming as he knew how to be, but Mrs. Jenkins, he knew, always looked down on his family. They were considered outsiders; they were renters, not homeowners, and his parents hadn't gone to the same high school as the longtime neighborhood fixtures. People wouldn't see him as anything other than "Foster Edwards' boy." His years away at college and abroad, and his work to show people how to get the most out of their government services didn't count with them.

Hassan sat behind the steering wheel of his car and sighed. He offered a quick prayer that he might find a more open heart and listening ear before his next appointment. *Even if people can't see you for who you have become, God knows what is in your heart. Do we understand that it is more important to please Him than to please others?*

Keep in Mind

"And when the sabbath day was come, he began to teach in the synagogue: and many hearing him were astonished, saying, From whence hath this man these things? and what wisdom is this which is given unto him…? And they were offended at him" (from Mark 6:2–3, KJV).

"The next Sabbath he began teaching in the synagogue, and many who heard him were amazed. They asked, 'Where did he get all this wisdom and the power to perform such miracles?' ... They were deeply offended and refused to believe in him" (from Mark 6:2–3, NLT).

Focal Verses

KJV **Mark 6:1** And he went out from thence, and came into his own country; and his disciples follow him.

2 And when the sabbath day was come, he began to teach in the synagogue: and many hearing him were astonished, saying, From whence hath this man these things? and what wisdom is this which is given unto him, that even such mighty works are wrought by his hands?

3 Is not this the carpenter, the son of Mary, the brother of James, and Joses, and of Juda, and Simon? and are not his sisters here with us? And they were offended at him.

4 But Jesus, said unto them, A prophet is not without honour, but in his own country, and among his own kin, and in his own house.

5 And he could there do no mighty work, save that he laid his hands upon a few sick folk, and healed them.

6 And he marvelled because of their unbelief. And he went round about the villages, teaching.

NLT **Mark 6:1** Jesus left that part of the country and returned with his disciples to Nazareth, his hometown.

2 The next Sabbath he began teaching in the synagogue, and many who heard him were amazed. They asked, "Where did he get all this wisdom and the power to perform such miracles?"

3 Then they scoffed, "He's just a carpenter, the son of Mary and the brother of James, Joseph, Judas, and Simon. And his sisters live right here among us." They were deeply offended and refused to believe in him.

4 Then Jesus told them, "A prophet is honored everywhere except in his own hometown and among his relatives and his own family."

5 And because of their unbelief, he couldn't do any miracles among them except to place his hands on a few sick people and heal them.

6 And he was amazed at their unbelief. Then Jesus went from village to village, teaching the people.

The People, Places, and Times

Nazareth. The name of this city means "branch." Nazareth only gained prominence after the life of Jesus. Located in lower Galilee, it lies halfway between the Sea of Galilee and the Mediterranean Sea. In Jesus' day, Nazareth was a small village, having only one spring to supply fresh water to residents. Today that spring is known as Mary's well. Nazareth did not have a good reputation in Jesus' day, as reflected in Nathanael's question, "Can there any good thing come out of Nazareth?" (John 1:46). Jesus was rejected by His townspeople and was thrown out of the synagogue there (Luke 4:16–30; Matthew 13:54–58; Mark 6:1–6). The early church was also looked upon with disdain, being referred to as a sect of the Nazarenes (Acts 24:5). Modern Nazareth has about 20,000 residents, most of whom are Muslims and Christians.

Background

Mark, the shortest of the Gospels, emphasizes Jesus' actions more than His teachings, recording eighteen of His miracles, but only one major sermon and four parables. He does not present a biography of Jesus detailing his Jewish family history. In fact, Mark does not quote the Old Testament or reference Jewish culture extensively, leading scholars to believe that he wrote primarily so that Gentile Christians would know Jesus as the Son of Man and Savior-King who conquers everything from storms to demons to death.

Mark 5 begins with Jesus and His disciples arriving on the east side of the Sea of Galilee in the region of Gerasenes and immediately being met by a man possessed with many demons. This demon-possessed man kneeled in His presence. The demons within him recognized Jesus and begged Him to be merciful. Jesus cast the demons out of the man and sent them into a herd of two thousand pigs that drowned themselves. Those who witnessed the deliverance and heard about it from the man as he shared his story throughout Decapolis, marveled at Jesus' power.

After crossing back over to the other side, Jairus, a leader of the synagogue confronted Jesus. Falling to Jesus' feet, Jairus asked that He would heal his daughter, who was on the brink of death. On the way to heal the girl, a woman who had been suffering from bleeding for twelve years, in desperation, thought, "If I could touch His garments, I will be made well." She touched them and was healed. When Jesus asked who touched Him, she fell to her knees and confessed that it was she. Before Jesus and His disciples could get to Jairus' daughter, she died. Jesus reassured those present that the girl was only sleeping. Many mocked Him. Unmoved, Jesus took her parents, Peter, James, and John inside. There, He resurrected her.

These are the events directly leading up to Mark 6:1–6.

What commonalities are found in these three accounts from Mark 5?

At-A-Glance

1. A People Offended (Mark 6:1–3)
2. A Prophet Dishonored (vv. 4–6)

In Depth

1. A People Offended (Mark 6:1–3)

Upon healing Jairus' daughter, Jesus and his disciples traveled about twenty miles southwest back to Nazareth, the area where he grew up. On the Sabbath, Jesus did as He would have for years living in the area: He went to the synagogue. However, instead of sitting to learn with others from the community, He returned on this second trip back to Nazareth as a teacher—a rabbi, traveling with His students. Jews were used to educated rabbis speaking with wisdom and authority, but Jesus amazed them.

Their amazement did not lead to honor and respect, however. Instead, they were skeptical and offended. They questioned Him, stumbling over the fact that someone so common and familiar to them could teach with such power.

There was disbelief that a mere carpenter could be so wise and perform miracles, implying that such gifts could not come from God, and thus must be from Satan. They insulted His heritage, calling Him "Mary's son" instead of following the tradition of identifying children by their father.

Finally, they point out that his family is no more special than their own—his four brothers and at least two sisters lived among them. It is worth noting that although His brothers did not believe in Him before the crucifixion (John 7:5), James would go on to become a leader in the church and the author of the book of James. And Jude would write the New Testament book titled after him.

Have you ever encountered a situation where people most familiar with someone are the most unsupportive of that person?

2. A Prophet Dishonored (vv. 4–6)

Then Jesus told them, "A prophet is honored everywhere except in his own hometown and among his relatives and his own family." Simply reflecting on the events immediately prior to this visit proves the accuracy of this statement. A woman had faith that she would be healed if she could just touch his clothes. A leader in the synagogue had faith that his daughter would be healed if Jesus touched her. A man with many demons worshiped him, and even the demons recognized his authority. Yet, in His own hometown, among His own people, Jesus only found a few willing to have enough faith to even come to Him for healing. His inability to work was not because He was limited in power, but because He performed miracles in the presence of faith. There was such a void that even He was astonished by their lack of faith. Sadly, this was a foreshadowing of how others would respond to him in the future.

This experience also served as a teaching moment for the disciples, who witnessed all of these events. This occurred prior to His commissioning of the twelve to go out two by two to teach and perform miracles. His instructions was "If any place will not welcome you or listen to you, shake the dust off your feet, when you leave, as a testimony against them." (6:11, NLT) He modeled what He taught, even though it was a verdict against His own people.

Why is it sometimes difficult to accept godly wisdom from people we know well?

Search the Scriptures

1. Regarding the saying "a prophet has no honor in his own hometown", read 2 Chronicles 36:16 and Jeremiah 1:1–2 and 11:18–23. Consider a prophet's calling. Why might they be met with such hostility, especially among their own people?

2. Mark 6:5 notes that even in spite of the lack of faith in the town, a few people who were sick still sought Jesus and were healed. What does this teach us about Jesus? What does this teach us about godly wisdom?

Discuss the Meaning

1. "Familiarity breeds contempt." Mark 6:1–6 is a perfect illustration of this quotation. In a

Gospel written for Gentile Christians, who did not have the perfect Jewish lineage or prior knowledge of Judaism, why might this account be included? What would be an advantage of their lack of familiarity about who the Messiah is (or should be)?

2. How does this passage serve as a warning to those who are followers of Christ, especially those who have followed Him for a number of years?

Liberating Lesson

It is tempting to read Mark 6:1–6 and judge the actions of those in Jesus' hometown. How can they reject the Savior, having heard of His miracles and witnessed His wisdom and teaching? How could they be so offended by Jesus that they would not even go to Him?

In reality, we have a tendency to do the same. We have access to God's Word. We read it. Yet, we can get offended when His words convict our hearts and reveal our sin. But because we realize that we should not be offended by the message (His Word), we sometimes lash out at the messenger—the pastor who preaches a convicting message, the spouse who lovingly confronts, the friend who challenges or holds us accountable. We may not ask aloud "Who do you think you are?" But our actions reveal our attitude.

We stop praying and stop seeking Him. As a result, our faith falters and we neglect our relationship with the Lord. Mark reveals that in the end, we are the ones who suffer. We would do well to remember the line from the old hymn, *What a Friend We Have in Jesus*, "Oh what peace we often forfeit, oh what needless pain we bear, all because we do not carry, everything to God in prayer"

Application for Activation

Sometimes we are so familiar with a passage that we forget to marvel at who God really is.

Ask God to give you fresh eyes as you read. Perhaps imagine you are one of the people in a story or one of the first recipients of the Gospel.

Consider a recent message, either one received while reading God's word, or hearing it, in which you have been offended. Consider why you were offended. Pray and, if necessary, repent.

Follow the Spirit

What God wants me to do:

_____

_____

_____

_____

Remember Your Thoughts

Special insights I have learned:

_____

_____

_____

_____

More Light on the Text

Mark 6:1–6

Jesus has returned to Capernaum on the west side of the Sea of Galilee (5:21) after His teaching and miraculous works on the east side (4:35ff), including the region of Gadarenes (5:1ff). In His return to Capernaum, a great multitude gathers at the seashore to hear Him teach. He heals a woman who has been sick for twelve years and raises a girl from death (5:21ff).

6:1 And he went out from thence, and came into his own country; and his disciples follow him.

Having had a successful ministry in Capernaum and other regions, Jesus returns to His hometown of Nazareth with His disciples. This seems to be His second trip back home and His second mission in the synagogue (Luke 4:16; cf. Matthew 13:53ff). "Country" here is the Greek *patris* (**pah-TREECE**), which means a fatherland, native town, or city. Although Jesus was born in Bethlehem (Matthew 2:1), he grew up in Nazareth (Matthew 2:23) from which Joseph and Mary went to Bethlehem to register (Luke 2:4ff).

2 And when the Sabbath day was come, he began to teach in the synagogue: and many hearing him were astonished, saying, From whence hath this man these things? and what wisdom is this which is given unto him, that even such mighty works are wrought by his hands?

On the Sabbath day, He goes into the synagogue, a habit He has formed from childhood (cf. Luke 2:41–50). Since He grew up in the town, He was therefore a familiar face to the worshipers and rulers of the synagogue. He was also familiar with the worship rituals and was no stranger. According to Jewish customs in synagogue service, which include Scripture reading (cf. Luke 4:17), Jesus reads from the Scriptures and then begins to expound the Word of God. The nature of His teaching is so profound that His audience and worshipers in the synagogue are amazed and dumbfounded at the wisdom with which He is teaching. They begin to question among themselves, "From whence hath this man these things?" Probably many of the people have not heard Him speak before, and so this is their first experience. They are amazed. However, there is an undercurrent of skepticism among some of them regarding the source of His authority and power, as implied in the questions "Where does this man get all this?" and "What sort of wisdom does He possess that all these miracles are wrought through Him?" Many probably thought it was disrespectful for a young man such as Jesus to teach with more authority than the local elders who had more life experience.

3 Is not this the carpenter, the son of Mary, the brother of James, and Joses, and of Juda, and Simon? and are not his sisters here with us? And they were offended at him.

The people's hostile and negative attitudes toward Jesus become more apparent in the following rhetorical and derogatory questions. "Is not this the carpenter?" In Matthew He is referred to as the carpenter's son; Joseph was a carpenter by trade. Growing up Jesus must have learned carpentry from His adoptive father, Joseph. Before going into His public ministry at age thirty, Jesus must have worked in that trade. Carpenters were regarded as common peasants, unlearned, at least not educated to the degree of the rabbis and scribes. Therefore Jesus, to them, is just an ordinary man who worked with His hands as other common people did. The next question is both derogatory and demeaning: "Isn't this the son of Mary?" In the Jewish culture, men are not usually described or identified as sons of their mother, even if their fathers were dead. Describing Jesus as the "son of Mary" here is probably intended as a put-down, and perpetuates the rumor being circulated at that time that He was an illegitimate child because of the nature of His birth (John 9:29, 34). Equally contemptuous are the next questions: "Is not this ... the brother of James, and Joses, and of Juda, and Simon?" And "Are not his sisters here with us?" All this implies that He is an ordinary person that they know

very well and probably grew up with Him. Why does He parade Himself as a rabbi and miracle-worker?

With such knowledge and familiarity of His background, the people became "offended at Him." "Offended" is the Greek verb *skandalizo* (**skan-dah-LEED-zoh**) from which the English "scandalize" is derived. It literally means "trip up," i.e., stumble or to cause displeasure. It is to be offended by someone—that is, to see in another what I disapprove of and what hinders me from acknowledging his authority; it is to cause a person to begin to distrust and desert one whom he ought to trust and obey. The mention of Jesus' siblings substantiates the fact that subsequent to the birth of Jesus, other biological children were born to Mary and Joseph. James is the one at the council at the Jerusalem church (Acts 12:17; 15:13; 21:18; 1 Corinthians 15:7; Galatians 1:19; 2:9, 12) and the author of the epistle of James (James 1:1). Juda (Jude) is the author of the book of Jude, but little is known about the rest of His brothers and sisters. The people, therefore, upbraid him with the meanness of His relations and upbringing. Although astonished at His doctrine (v. 2), they are offended at His person (v. 3). Prejudiced against Him, they look at Him with contempt and for that reason reject His teaching.

4 But Jesus said unto them, A prophet is not without honour, but in his own country, and among his own kin, and in his own house. 5 And he could there do no mighty work, save that he laid his hands upon a few sick folk, and healed them. 6 And he marvelled because of their unbelief. And he went round about the villages, teaching.

Jesus acknowledges their unbelief and reproves them with what is phrased like common proverbial saying: that a prophet is not recognized in his own country, among his people, and in his own family. Unlike other places and regions where we see Jesus perform miracles of stilling the storm (4:35ff), casting out demons (5:1ff), and healing the sick (5:21ff), He could not do such miracles in His own homeland because of their obstinate unbelief. However, He is able to lay hands on a few sick people, and they are healed. "Unbelief" is from the Greek *apistia* (**ah-peese-TEE-ah**). It means faithlessness, i.e., disbelief, unfaithfulness, or disobedience. Their unbelief cost them the privilege of experiencing miracles and healing as other regions had. The wording that Jesus "could there do no mighty work" could be to contradict an Almighty God. However, we read nowhere in the Scriptures that Jesus failed to heal anyone or any case that is brought to Him, nor did unbelief of anyone present prevent Him from healing anyone who came to Him. Indeed, we read repeatedly in the Bible phrases stating that He "healed them all" or "everyone." Rather, their unbelief and their contempt of His person kept them from bringing their sick to Christ to be healed. Astonished at their unbelief, Jesus goes "round about the villages, teaching," seeking out those who will hear the Word, even if His own town will not.

Sources:
Butler, Trent, gen. ed. *Holman Bible Dictionary.* Nashville, TN: Broadman & Holman Publishers, 1991. 1010–1011.

Daily Bible Readings

MONDAY
Jesus Restores Leader's Daughter to Life
(Mark 5:35–43)

TUESDAY
Samaritans Testify to Wisdom of Jesus
(John 4:27–29, 39–42)

WEDNESDAY
All Wisdom Dwells in Christ
(Colossians 2:1–5)

THURSDAY
Jesus Denounces Human Traditions
(Mark 7:1–8)

FRIDAY
God's Wisdom Trumps Human Commands
(Mark 7:9–15)

SATURDAY
The Heart Not the Stomach Defiles
(Mark 7:17–23)

SUNDAY
Jesus' Wisdom Astonishes His Hometown
People
(Mark 6:1–6)

Say It Correctly

Joses. **JOE**-sess.
Gerasenes. **GEH**-rah-**SEENS**.
Jairus. **JAY**-rus.
Gadarenes. **GAH**-dah-**REENS**.
Capernaum. cah-**PURR**-nay-um.

Teaching Tips

Words You Should Know

A. Way (v. 6) *hodos* (Gk.)—A traveler's way or to a way of thinking, feeling, and deciding

B. Truth (v. 6) *aletheia* (Gk.)—Not falsehood, whether pertaining to God or earthly matters; personal excellence

C. Life (v. 6) *zoe* (Gk.)—State of living, every living soul, and the absolute fullness of life

Teacher Preparation

Unifying Principle—Finding One's Way. Some people say there are many ways to salvation and that everyone attains it by following his or her own way. What are we to make of such claims? Just as Proverbs contrasted the way of wisdom with false ways, Jesus proclaimed that He is the way, the truth, and the life through whom His disciples would come to know and understand God the Father.

A. Read the Bible Background and Devotional Readings.

B. Pray for your students and lesson clarity.

C. Read the lesson Scripture in multiple translations.

O—Open the Lesson

A. Begin the class with prayer.

B. As a class, have participants role-play the discussion Jesus has with His disciples in the upper room and their questions of Him and the answers He gives.

C. Have the students read the Aim for Change and the In Focus story.

D. Ask students how events like those in the story weigh on their hearts and how they can view these events from a faith perspective.

P—Present the Scriptures

A. Read the Focal Verses.

B. Have the class share what Scriptures stand out for them and why, with particular emphasis on today's context.

C. Discuss the Background and The People, Places, and Times sections.

E—Explore the Meaning

A. Use In Depth or More Light on the Text to facilitate a deeper discussion of the lesson text.

B. Pose the questions in Search the Scriptures and Discuss the Meaning.

C. Discuss the Liberating Lesson and Application for Activation sections.

N—Next Steps for Application

A. Summarize the value of trusting the wisdom which comes from Christ.

B. End class with a commitment to pray for loving Jesus as He loves us.

Worship Guide

For the Superintendent or Teacher
Theme: Wisdom: The Way, Truth, and Life
Song: "More Precious than Silver"
Devotional Reading: Proverbs 3:13–18

Wisdom:
The Way, Truth, and Life

Bible Background • PROVERBS 3:17; 8:32–36; JOHN 14:1–14
Printed Text • JOHN 14:1–14 | Devotional Reading • PROVERBS 3:13–18

―――――――――― **Aim for Change** ――――――――――

By the end of the lesson, we will: EXPLORE the encounter between Jesus the disciples in the upper room, APPRECIATE the difficulty the disciples had in understanding Jesus, and CELEBRATE the promise of Jesus to prepare a place for His followers and hear and respond to their prayers.

―――――――――― **In Focus** ――――――――――

Lester stood before his crew at the loading dock, preparing to give them their final instructions before the trucks were loaded and they all set out for their long-haul run across the country. Foremost, of course, was the safety check of the vehicles. They also had to check the bill of lading and ensure that each tractor-trailer was loaded with the correct goods.

Lester had succeeded the legendary Big Dave as team leader because he was more experienced than the other drivers. Because of that, the company owner asked Lester to go on another run to make a pickup that required a fast turnaround. Lester told his crew they would have to go ahead without him and he would join the caravan in a day or so.

"How are we supposed to manage without you?" Herb asked. "We haven't been that way before. At least if we had Big Dave, we would feel better."

"You get there the same way you navigated every other trip. You haven't forgotten how to read a map, have you?" Lester said.

"Guys," Lester said, "have you not been paying attention? I taught you everything I know, and I learned from the best, Big Dave. I didn't hold anything back. So, really, you learned from Big Dave, too. I believe you can do this," Lester said. "You should have the confidence you can do this, too."

How do we cultivate the faith that God will see us through the things outside of our experience?

―――――――――― **Keep in Mind** ――――――――――

"Jesus saith unto him, I am the way, the truth, and the life: no man cometh unto the Father, but by me" (John 14:6, KJV)

"Jesus told him, "I am the way, the truth, and the life. No one can come to the Father except through me" (John 14:6, NLT).

Focal Verses

KJV John 14:1 Let not your heart be troubled: ye believe in God, believe also in me.

2 In my Father's house are many mansions: if it were not so, I would have told you. I go to prepare a place for you.

3 And if I go and prepare a place for you, I will come again, and receive you unto myself; that where I am, there ye may be also.

4 And whither I go ye know, and the way ye know.

5 Thomas saith unto him, Lord, we know not whither thou goest; and how can we know the way?

6 Jesus saith unto him, I am the way, the truth, and the life: no man cometh unto the Father, but by me.

7 If ye had known me, ye should have known my Father also: and from henceforth ye know him, and have seen him.

8 Philip saith unto him, Lord, show us the Father, and it sufficeth us.

9 Jesus saith unto him, Have I been so long time with you, and yet hast thou not known me, Philip? he that hath seen me hath seen the Father; and how sayest thou then, Show us the Father?

10 Believest thou not that I am in the Father, and the Father in me? the words that I speak unto you I speak not of myself: but the Father that dwelleth in me, he doeth the works.

11 Believe me that I am in the Father, and the Father in me: or else believe me for the very works' sake.

12 Verily, verily, I say unto you, He that believeth on me, the works that I do shall he do also; and greater works than these shall he do; because I go unto my Father.

13 And whatsoever ye shall ask in my name, that will I do, that the Father may be glorified in the Son.

14 If ye shall ask any thing in my name, I will do it.

NLT John 14:1 "Don't let your hearts be troubled. Trust in God, and trust also in me.

2 There is more than enough room in my Father's home. If this were not so, would I have told you that I am going to prepare a place for you?

3 When everything is ready, I will come and get you, so that you will always be with me where I am.

4 And you know the way to where I am going."

5 "No, we don't know, Lord," Thomas said. "We have no idea where you are going, so how can we know the way?"

6 Jesus told him, "I am the way, the truth, and the life. No one can come to the Father except through me.

7 If you had really known me, you would know who my Father is. From now on, you do know him and have seen him!"

8 Philip said, "Lord, show us the Father, and we will be satisfied."

9 Jesus replied, "Have I been with you all this time, Philip, and yet you still don't know who I am? Anyone who has seen me has seen the Father! So why are you asking me to show him to you?

10 Don't you believe that I am in the Father and the Father is in me? The words I speak are not my own, but my Father who lives in me does his work through me.

11 Just believe that I am in the Father and the Father is in me. Or at least believe because of the work you have seen me do.

12 I tell you the truth, anyone who believes in me will do the same works I have done, and even greater works, because I am going to be with the Father.

13 You can ask for anything in my name, and I will do it, so that the Son can bring glory to the Father.

14 Yes, ask me for anything in my name, and I will do it!"

The People, Places, and Times

Philip. He was one of the Twelve Disciples whom Jesus called directly. Philip, along with Peter and Andrew, was from Bethsaida of Galilee (John 1:44).

Thomas. Also called Didymus, or "the twin," Thomas was one of Jesus' twelve disciples. He is the one who said that he would not believe that Jesus was resurrected from the dead unless he could touch the nail prints in Jesus' hands and the wound from the spear in His side.

Background

During His ministry, Jesus repeatedly prepared the disciples for His approaching suffering and death. Jesus tells the disciples that one of them would betray Him (John 13:21). At the same time, He also informs the disciples that He will soon be leaving them and that they could not follow Him (v. 33). Undoubtedly, these things disturbed the disciples. When Peter asks Jesus where He was going, Jesus responds that Peter cannot follow Him now but will follow Him afterward. It is not difficult to see why the disciples would have been troubled. They were coming to grips with the fact that the One they had given up everything to follow was now telling them that He was about to leave them to go to a place where they could not follow. It must have seemed as if they were losing the very reason for which they had existed for the past three years.

At-A-Glance

1. Jesus, the Way to Comfort (John 14:1–4)
2. Jesus, the Way to the Father (vv. 5–11)
3. Jesus, the Way to Powerful Living
   (vv. 12–14)

In Depth

1. Jesus, the Way to Comfort (John 14:1–4)

Jesus had told His disciples of His approaching suffering and departure (John 13). Now, He aims to calm the turmoil raging in their hearts. Jesus encourages them by telling them not to let their hearts be troubled. Jesus' news apparently threw the disciples' minds into disarray and sends them into a spiritual tailspin, but Jesus provides the key that will lead them out of their mental anguish. He points to Himself as the basis for sustaining peace in the midst of the storm of difficult circumstances by telling them if they believe in God to believe in Him as well. Even though He will no longer be present with the disciples physically, He assures them that where He is going, He is preparing a place for them. This is a wisdom that would leave us deeply conflicted if it were not for the one speaking it. It is wisdom that requires faith to apply. Jesus challenges us continually to see that the best wisdom is not a matter of analysis or principle, but flows directly from God. This provides great comfort, not only for the disciples but also for us. Jesus was reinforcing that His words were trustworthy; we can place our faith in His words because He is faithful to keep them.

How do you find comfort in difficult situations?

2. Jesus, the Way to the Father (vv. 5–11)

Thomas is looking for Jesus to give a location where they can meet Him. As Jewish men, they were taught the presence of God was at the Temple in Jerusalem. Philip is looking for a private meeting with God, so He can know God. They had heard the prophets had such marvelous encounters. Jesus rejects both requests. He instead makes a radical statement about how to know God. Jesus does not point His followers to a path but to a person, namely, Himself: "I am the way."

Jesus is not claiming to have uncovered some hidden truth the disciples can understand to know God. He is not telling His disciples to practice profound principles to reach God. He is not even telling them they can encounter God at a certain physical location. He is claiming something much stronger than that. We cannot work our way to God at all. Instead, God has come to us in Jesus Christ. Jesus declares anyone who has seen Him has seen the Father (v. 9). If they could not believe it from His words, they could certainly know it by looking at what Jesus had done. Jesus reveals the character and personality of God to us (cf. John 1:18). We are to place faith in Christ as the way to the Father because it is only through Him that we can know the Father as He truly is.

How have you tried to make following Jesus harder than the simple Way He showed us?

3. Jesus, the Way to Powerful Living (vv. 12–14)

Christ then notifies His disciples that placing their faith in Him will cause them to lead lives that exhibit the power of God (vv. 12–14). We will do greater works than those Christ did in His earthly ministry because He is with the Father. It is important to note that Jesus says that the works testified of His relationship with the Father. These were not gratuitous or pointless displays of power, but a demonstration of His authenticity as the Son of God. Furthermore, Jesus lets us know that it is the Father who is at work through Him. This reveals the unity of Jesus and the Father.

Placing all our trust in Jesus produces two results. First, faith in Christ yields fruitful lives that both demonstrate our relationship with Him and glorify the Father (John 15:8). Christ comes to give us "abundant life," promising to do anything we ask in His name, to the glory of the Father. Of course, this is not a blank check given to us with which we can expect

to receive all of our wildest desires. When we ask for things in Jesus' name, we are to ask for things that are consistent with His character and purpose. Putting all our trust in Christ guarantees that we will experience power-filled lives because He aims to glorify His Father's name.

Second, placing faith in Christ gives us the power we need to live out the Christian life. Before ascending into heaven, Jesus delivers a parting promise to His disciples: the Holy Spirit will come to them. The only way we can live powerful lives that reflect Christ's presence is by the Holy Spirit dwelling in us. The Holy Spirit gives us power, desire, and knowledge to live the Christian life, and the Spirit is only accessible through faith in Christ.

What is the biggest request you've ever asked for in Jesus' name? How has He responded?

Search the Scriptures

1. How did Jesus tell the disciples to deal with anxiety in their hearts (John 14:1)?

2. According to Jesus, how can we know the Father (vv. 6–7)?

3. What does it mean to "ask in Jesus' name" (vv. 13–14; 15:7)?

Discuss the Meaning

1. How does Jesus challenge the way we typically think about religions as ways to get to God?

2. How is the wisdom that Jesus shares in John 14 different from other types of wisdom?

Liberating Lesson

We live in a society where many consider it arrogant to claim that there is only one way to the truth. Accordingly, a popular view is that all religions are the same. This is not the view expressed in Christian Scripture. Anyone who studies religion beyond the surface knows that the truth claims or theologies are different across religious traditions. It is a great irony that it is in Western secular societies that used to be most Christian that claims of sameness are most often made. These claims can disregard the ways diverse peoples around the world articulate their own faith traditions. It is a different sort of arrogance to dismiss the distinct faiths of millions of people in order to impose on them convenient uniformity and false tolerance. To water all religions down to being "all the same" is to not take them seriously for what they profess. That does not mean different faiths do not have similarities; they do. Many faiths agree on some aspects of ethics or prescribed actions. Many of them have similar values and behaviors: for instance, the desire to pursue peace, the condemnation of violence, the importance of care for others, and the value of all life. Yet the truth claims remain distinct. Jesus declares there is only one way to God, though Him, Jesus. As Christians we must embrace the claim of Jesus, recognizing that we are claiming something different than other religions.

In a world where people try to suppress religious differences, we would be wise to advocate for freedom to choose our faith. Christians should be advocates for true tolerance and religious freedom.

Application for Activation

We cannot get to God, but God has come to us. Our God loved us enough to come to us in the flesh. As Christians, we can boldly claim that our way, our truth, our life is not a principle, place, or pursuit but a person, Jesus Christ. Jesus invites us to seek Him for wisdom and guidance. For us, His way is always the best way. Take time this week to pray, read Scripture, and seek God for His wisdom concerning your day or more important decisions. He is faithful to give wisdom if we posture our hearts to obey His directions.

Follow the Spirit

What God wants me to do:

_____

_____

_____

_____

Remember Your Thoughts

Special insights I have learned:

_____

_____

_____

_____

More Light on the Text
John 14:1–14

1 Let not your heart be troubled: ye believe in God, believe also in me.

Here, Jesus tells the disciples not to be troubled in their hearts. Jesus emphasizes this truth by pointing to faith in Him as the relief or antidote for worry or anxiety. In Greek, the word "troubled" is *tarasso* (**tah-RAH-so**), which means "agitated, disquieted, or stirred up." In the context of this passage, Jesus ushers in faith as a comfort to relieve the anxious disciples, much like a welcome medicine for a nagging illness or parental reassurance about a child's nightmare. In this scenario, the disciples' concern was well -founded, since they had just learned that one would betray Jesus, that one would deny Him, and that they couldn't go with Him wherever it was He was going (John 13). Jesus' own spirit was "troubled" when He announced that one would betray Him (13:21). It is remarkable that Jesus ministered to them with compassion in spite of the fact that His much more serious anguish was now only hours away. Peter must have been the most visibly shocked to learn he would deny Jesus, since Jesus immediately responded to his concern with His declaration that Peter would be disloyal (John 13:38). Jesus immediately follows this with His words of comfort. When our hearts are troubled, when things look their worst, our best response is faith or belief in our Lord; nothing less will open the door to His peace and comfort (Psalm 42:5). Nothing is more important than guarding our hearts (Proverbs 4:23; 1 Corinthians 16:13–14; 2 Peter 3:17), but at the same time, we as believers have good reason to take courage, unlike those without hope in God.

2 In my Father's house are many mansions: if it were not so, I would have told you. I go to prepare a place for you.

The hope of eternity with Him was given as a source of comfort, not only for the disciples but also for countless believers through the ages, confronting all the multiple anxieties they as individuals and the church as a whole would face. Jesus' intent was to minister comfort in the face of potentially overwhelming distress; His response (begun in v. 1) was thorough and multifaceted. Added to faith in God and Himself was the reminder of the disciples' (and our) final reward. Our reward will not be to live in luxury, either here or in the afterlife. The word translated "mansion" is simply "dwelling place" in Greek (*mone*, **moe-NAY**). Jesus reassures them that He would not deceive them by promising them something that was so grand but wasn't the truth. Along with having our name written in the book of life (Isaiah 62:2; Revelation 2:17; 3:12; 21:27), everything becomes new in Christ (2 Corinthians 5:17), including our coming new home in God's kingdom.

3 And if I go and prepare a place for you, I will come again, and receive you unto myself; that where I am, there ye may be also.

This isn't an impersonal second coming to which Jesus refers; He won't be sending a butler, an angel, or anyone else to escort us to our heavenly home. He will come Himself and receive us personally (1 Thessalonians 4:17). In John 14:3, the phrase "I will come" is a common, single word in Greek (*erchomai*, **ER-khoe-my**) and refers to individuals arriving or returning, appearing or making an appearance. The emphasis is on "again," just as being born is common but being born "again" is noteworthy (John 3:3). Heaven would be sufficient joy if we just got to be with Him. Wherever He is should be where we want to be; wherever He is not should be the place to avoid at all costs. Nonetheless, it is to His Father's house that we will be going, the home of the King of kings and Lord of lords, the Creator of the universe— being ushered by Christ at His Second Coming to God's eternal home will be glorious beyond words (Luke 22:30; Revelation 21).

4 And whither I go ye know, and the way ye know.

Jesus is trying to tell or remind His disciples that they already know in their hearts where He is going and how to get there. This would be one of the things of which the coming Comforter would continue to remind them after Jesus' departure, and about which He would continue to teach them (cf. John 14:26).

5 Thomas saith unto him, Lord, we know not whither thou goest; and how can we know the way?

With childlike innocence, Thomas asks about what Jesus just told them that they already knew. Perhaps Thomas' response is an illustration of our own level of spiritual awareness, in reality knowing more than we think we do and being less in the dark than we believe we are at times. The disciples had received a full load of bad news, and perhaps, had they had more time to digest Jesus' discourse, they might have been less reactive. In any case, Jesus doesn't entrust the matter to their faulty memories and previous knowledge but continues to explain in order to be certain they do in fact know what they need to know.

6 Jesus saith unto him, I am the way, the truth, and the life: no man cometh unto the Father, but by me.

It is easy to put the emphasis on this verses' key words "way" (Gk. *hodos*, **hoe-DOS**), "truth" (Gk. *aletheia*, **ah-LAY-thay-ah**), and "life" (Gk. *zoe*, **dzo-AY**). Yet this statement was in response to Thomas' question—what is the way to where He is going? The emphasis is on the words "I am" at the beginning of the sentence. Either one of these words could have been understood and left out by Greek grammar rules, but Jesus emphatically uses both the personal pronoun (*ego*, **eh-GO**, "I") and a simple present form of the verb "to be" (*eimi*, **ay-ME**, "am"). These words are further emphasized by their placement at the beginning of the sentence. Jesus would not have failed to get His disciples' attention with this allusion to the divine name, with so much grammatical emphasis.

In Greek, the word "way" is *hodos* and refers to a traveler's way or to a way of thinking, feeling, and deciding. John clearly establishes that the Word is God (1:1), the Word became flesh (1:14), and the Word is truth (17:17). "Thy word is true from the beginning" (Psalm 119:160). Jesus completes the circle by stating that He is the truth and is one with God (John 10:30); Paul echoes the same sentiment in his letters. It is the truth that sets us free (John 8:32) and that leads us to salvation (Ephesians 1:13). Even His critics know that, as truth, Jesus would never deceive anyone (Luke 20:21). As the embodiment of truth, Jesus stands in perfect contrast to the devil, in whom there is no truth (John 8:44).

In Greek, the word "truth" is *aletheia* and is used in a variety of contexts, including references to personal excellence and to truth pertaining to God. Again, it is a common word that is used in these ways over 100 times in the New Testament—until Jesus says He is the truth. No one can ever accuse Jesus of having made mediocre claims. Just in John's Gospel alone, preceding His ultimate statement in 14:6, Jesus similarly stated that He was the Bread of Life (6:35); that He came to give life, and life more abundantly (10:10); that He gives eternal life to His sheep (10:28); and that He is the Resurrection and the Life (11:25).

In the Greek, the word "life" in this context is *zoe*, the meaning of which includes the state of living, every living soul, and the absolute fullness of life. Like the words "way" and "truth," "life" is a common word used well over 100 times in the New Testament—until Jesus says He is the life. The latter part of 14:6 is what is known as an "exceptive statement," meaning "all and only." All may come to the Father through Jesus, and only those coming through Jesus may come to the Father. No matter how politically incorrect His statements may seem, Jesus was, is, and always will be the true and only way to God the Father.

7 If ye had known me, ye should have known my Father also: and from henceforth ye know him, and have seen him.

Jesus' words are a not-so-subtle rebuke of the disciples for their lack of awareness of just who had been with them for so long. Regardless of the disciples' shortsightedness, Jesus patiently continues to explain that in seeing and knowing Him, they have already seen and known the Father. Almost before they can realize they have been rebuked for their lack of awareness, Jesus immediately extends comfort in His reassurance that, at least from this point forward, they no longer need to be unaware of the Father. As Jesus stated (John 10:30), He and the Father are one. Jesus is God and reveals God to us. The disciples had a common awakening experience, which came soon enough and was similar in essence for all of them. God does this by sending the Holy Spirit after Jesus ascended to heaven.

8 Philip saith unto him, Lord, show us the Father, and it sufficeth us. 9 Jesus saith unto him, Have I been so long time with you, and yet hast thou not known me, Philip? He that hath seen me hath seen the Father; and how sayest thou then, Show us the Father? 10 Believest thou not that I am in the Father, and the Father in me? the words that I speak unto you I speak not of myself: but the Father that dwelleth in me, he doeth the works.

Philip wanted a sign. One cannot help but empathize with Philip, since he sounds like so many today who, no matter how much they know or are told, insist on saying, "If I could just see God once, that would settle it for me. If just once I could witness a real miracle, then I'd become a believer. Why can't God just show His face for one split second?" Just like Philip, modern skeptics ignore what is right in front of them. In Philip's case, it was the living Jesus, God in the flesh, worker of miracles, forgiver of sins, standing before him and talking to him. Yet he didn't understand what he was hearing. In this light, Jesus' response (v. 9) is both understandable and appropriate. Jesus' exasperation is showing as He peppers Philip with a series of questions, quoting his own question back to him. Jesus stresses His unity with the Father once again. When we read these passages consecutively, we see the patient Teacher gently guiding His future apostles, who soon will faithfully carry out His Great Commission to the four corners of the world— that is, once they get it straight who He is.

11 Believe me that I am in the Father, and the Father in me: or else believe me for the very works' sake.

Although Jesus' conversation is in response to questions from Thomas and Philip, all the disciples are present and Jesus is addressing all of them in His typical teaching fashion. What was stated as a question in verse 10 is now affirmed indicatively. There should be no more disbelief: Jesus is in fact in the Father and the Father in Him. The full implications of this, however, are hard to grasp. It is no wonder that the early church continued to struggle with the essence of Jesus' words. One can hardly imagine how He could have communicated His deity any more clearly than He did. At first, it was hard for even the disciples to grasp that Jesus was a deity; then, after He ascended, whether or not He had really been human became the prime issue of the Gnostics (thus the emphasis on Jesus' human birth and physical crucifixion in the Apostles' Creed). There were many struggles about Jesus' divinity and humanity through the fifth century when the Council of Chalcedon finally set the boundaries for orthodox doctrine about the union of divine and human natures in Christ. Today, there are still people who have no problem with Jesus' humanity but struggle greatly with His divinity. Likewise, some accept His divinity but diminish His humanity (cf. 1 John 4:2).

12 Verily, verily, I say unto you, He that believeth on me, the works that I do shall he do also; and greater works than these shall he do; because I go unto my Father.

At this point, Jesus moves on to a different subject, one of many He would address on that auspicious night. The "greater works" to which Jesus refers (v. 12) would not be possible if He stayed with them, but were only possible because He was leaving them. Jesus' words are not only about the fantastic advances in ministry that they were going to accomplish when the Holy Spirit came. He also offered them another facet of His multi-layered message of comfort and courage regarding His impending death and subsequent departure. His message was entirely about comfort, assurances, and taking heart for the great things that awaited them. These eleven men—the original pillars of the faith and the architects of the New Testament church—needed at that moment to hear some words of encouragement, reassurance, and hope from their departing Master.

13 And whatsoever ye shall ask in my name, that will I do, that the Father may be glorified in the Son.

Jesus would deny these particular men nothing. He left in their charge the greatest task ever given to any human, and He knew what they would need in order to accomplish the work He had given them. Many people have heard some preacher at some time try to interpret this as some kind of mysterious combination or formula by implying or claiming that all you have to do is say all the right words and include all the potential caveats and specific disclaimers, and God is almost obliged to accommodate you. Unfortunately, many in the church have a gross misconception of what it means to abide in Christ, which impairs their understanding of how things work in God's kingdom. When we abide in Christ, His power flows through us to accomplish His purposes in the world. The Holy Spirit is the agent, sent by the resurrected Christ, and we are the vehicles through which He flows. It is not our confession or religious invocation that garners the forces of heaven to do our bidding. It is only when our hearts are surrendered, when we are living

in and for God, when our will is attuned to His, and when our prayers are for His purposes, in His name, and for His glory that He will answer, even beyond all we ask or think (Ephesians 3:20).

14 If ye shall ask any thing in my name, I will do it.

It is here that we find some of the most poignant parting words known to humankind. Jesus, the Savior, is preparing for His death, burial, and resurrection. He is equipping His disciples with the most important things they will need to know as they carry out His work without His physical presence. The reiteration of John 14:13 must be heard in the context of the whole passage. This kind of repetitive reassurance is the type one gives a loved one who needs comfort. We tend to say things more than once when we want someone to believe us, especially if there is an impending separation. Yes, when our hearts become one heart like that of the disciples (v. 1), when our faith is sure and steady, when our will is surrendered to Christ, and when our purpose is completely for God's glory, most certainly we, too, can believe like the disciples that our prayers will be answered.

Sources:

Henry, Matthew. *Commentary on the Whole Bible.* Christian Classics Ethereal Library.org. http://www.ccel.org/h/henry/mhc5John.xv.html

New Testament Greek Lexicon. Bible Study Tools.com. http://www.biblestudytools.com/lexicons/greek

Passage Lookup. Bible Gateway.com. http://www.biblegateway.com/passage.

Smith, Huston. *The World's Religions.* San Francisco, CA: Harper, 1991. 56.

Tenney, Merrill C. *The Expositor's Bible Commentary.* Edited by Frank E. Gaebelein. Grand Rapids, MI: Zondervan Publishing House, 1981.

Say It Correctly

Gnostics. **NOSS**-tix.
Chalcedon. **KAL**-ceh-don.
Bethsaida. beth-**SAY**-duh.
Didymus. **DIH**-dih-mus.

Daily Bible Readings

MONDAY
Wisdom, Source of Abundant Life
(Proverbs 3:13–18)

TUESDAY
Jesus Does What the Father Does
(John 5:19–24)

WEDNESDAY
Love as I Loved You
(John 13:31–35)

THURSDAY
Spirit of Truth Dwells in You
(John 14:15–17)

FRIDAY
Love Binds Believers to God
(John 14:18–24)

SATURDAY
Spirit of Wisdom Promised to All
(John 14:25–31)

SUNDAY
Jesus, the Way to the Father
(John 14:1–14)

Notes

Teaching Tips

Words You Should Know

A. Temptations (v. 2) *peirasmos* (Gk.)—Trials that have a goal in mind

B. Entire (v. 4) *holokleros* (Gk.)—An animal that can be used for sacrifice or a priest who can represent the people

Teacher Preparation

Unifying Principle—The Pursuit of Truth. People desire to be seen as wise. What is the source of wisdom? The letter of James affirms that God gives wisdom generously and ungrudgingly to those who ask in faith.

A. Read the Bible Background and Devotional Reading.

B. Pray for your students and lesson clarity.

C. Read the lesson Scripture in multiple translations.

O—Open the Lesson

A. Begin the class with prayer.

B. Ask the class to share stories of past experiences with trials and hardships. Then ask how those have made them wiser and more productive in their discipleship.

C. Have the students read the Aim for Change and the In Focus story.

D. Ask students how events like those in the story weigh on their hearts and how they can view these events from a faith perspective.

P—Present the Scriptures

A. Read the Focal Verses.

B. Have the class share what Scriptures stand out for them and why, with particular emphasis on today's context.

C. Discuss the Background and The People, Places, and Times sections.

E—Explore the Meaning

A. Use In Depth or More Light on the Text to facilitate a deeper discussion of the lesson text.

B. Pose the questions in Search the Scriptures and Discuss the Meaning.

C. Discuss the Liberating Lesson and Application for Activation sections.

N—Next Steps for Application

A. Summarize the value of having faith as we persevere through challenges.

B. End class with a commitment to pray for God's guidance in our decision making.

Worship Guide

For the Superintendent or Teacher
Theme: Faith and Wisdom
Song: "Comfort, Comfort Now My People"
Devotional Reading: Isaiah 40:1–8

Faith and Wisdom

Bible Background • JAMES 1:1–11
Printed Text • JAMES 1:1–11 | Devotional Reading • ISAIAH 40:1–8

———————— Aim for Change ————————

By the end of the lesson, we will: CONSIDER the relationship between wisdom and perseverance through trials, AFFIRM the value of trials and hardships in making us more wise and productive disciples, and PRAY for godly wisdom by which to endure life's trials and temptations.

———————— In Focus ————————

Cornelius' ancestors were careful keepers of their family history. His great-grandmother inscribed their family tree onto the pages of a large Bible, and his grandfather continued to add to it. Cornelius was amazed to see his name written on a family tree that stretched back to the 1840s.

The African Diaspora consists of millions of people like Cornelius whose ancestors were stolen from the Motherland for the Mid-Atlantic Slave Trade. Their faith gave them strength and their experiences gave them wisdom to pass on to successive generations.

The first name on Cornelius' family was a man named John who was born a slave in the 1840s. John became a Christian after he was freed from slavery. The church operated a school that taught John to read and write. Eventually, John became a preacher, and the church paid for his college education. John organized schools so that other people could attain college educations. Cornelius is a member of his ancestor John's church and attended a historically black college that his ancestor helped support. Cornelius learned that faith and wisdom can help believers overcome life's trials.

What wisdom was passed down to you through the experiences of your ancestors? What wisdom have you learned through your own experiences? What role did faith in God have in your ancestors' experiences and your own experiences?

———————— Keep in Mind ————————

"If any of you lack wisdom, let him ask of God, that giveth to all men liberally, and upbraideth not; and it shall be given him" (James 1:5, KJV).

"If you need wisdom, ask our generous God, and he will give it to you. He will not rebuke you for asking" (James 1:5, NLT).

Focal Verses

KJV **James 1:1** James, a servant of God and of the Lord Jesus Christ, to the twelve tribes which are scattered abroad, greeting.

2 My brethren, count it all joy when ye fall into divers temptations;

3 Knowing this, that the trying of your faith worketh patience.

4 But let patience have her perfect work, that ye may be perfect and entire, wanting nothing.

5 If any of you lack wisdom, let him ask of God, that giveth to all men liberally, and upbraideth not; and it shall be given him.

6 But let him ask in faith, nothing wavering. For he that wavereth is like a wave of the sea driven with the wind and tossed.

7 For let not that man think that he shall receive any thing of the Lord.

8 A double minded man is unstable in all his ways.

9 Let the brother of low degree rejoice in that he is exalted:

10 But the rich, in that he is made low: because as the flower of the grass he shall pass away.

11 For the sun is no sooner risen with a burning heat, but it withereth the grass, and the flower thereof falleth, and the grace of the fashion of it perisheth: so also shall the rich man fade away in his ways.

NLT **James 1:1** This letter is from James, a slave of God and of the Lord Jesus Christ. I am writing to the "twelve tribes"— Jewish believers scattered abroad. Greetings!

2 Dear brothers and sisters, when troubles of any kind come your way, consider it an opportunity for great joy.

3 For you know that when your faith is tested, your endurance has a chance to grow.

4 So let it grow, for when your endurance is fully developed, you will be perfect and complete, needing nothing.

5 If you need wisdom, ask our generous God, and he will give it to you. He will not rebuke you for asking.

6 But when you ask him, be sure that your faith is in God alone. Do not waver, for a person with divided loyalty is as unsettled as a wave of the sea that is blown and tossed by the wind.

7 Such people should not expect to receive anything from the Lord.

8 Their loyalty is divided between God and the world, and they are unstable in everything they do.

9 Believers who are poor have something to boast about, for God has honored them.

10 And those who are rich should boast that God has humbled them. They will fade away like a little flower in the field.

11 The hot sun rises and the grass withers; the little flower droops and falls, and its beauty fades away. In the same way, the rich will fade away with all of their achievements.

The People, Places, and Times

Diaspora. This term is used in biblical writing to refer to the Jews who were scattered abroad and living outside of Israel. Owing to the Assyrian invasion of Israel and the Babylonian exile from Judah, the twelve tribes of Jews were dispersed and settled in the civilized countries of the world at that time yet remained connected to the mother country.

Compare and contrast the Jewish Diaspora with the African Diaspora.

Background

The epistle of James teaches its readers that behavior should reflect belief. It is composed of short sayings that are reminiscent of those found in the Wisdom Literature of Proverbs and Ecclesiastes. According to some scholars, the sayings are organized by "minor association of thought or language," which contrasts with much of Paul's writings that are intentionally sequenced to build one unifying argument. Thus, the structure of the epistle of James does not allow us to easily define the main idea of the text. However, James 1:22 seems to aptly describe the aim of the epistle when it instructs its readers to "be ye doers of the word, and not hearers only, deceiving your own selves."

Many scholars believe that the epistle's writer is James, the half-brother of Jesus. The epistle itself does not include any biographical information that directly identifies its writer as the half-brother of Jesus. However, the writer's chosen title may offer an indirect connection. The writer identifies himself as "James, a servant of God and the Lord Jesus Christ." The title is unique in the Bible insofar as it is the only time that two very common titles are coupled together. The Old Testament includes several people who are described as "servants of God." New Testament personages are often described as "servants of the Lord Jesus Christ" or some variation of the title. The unique title employed in the epistle's salutation may reflect the ministry of James to the Jewish Christian community.

What does it tell you about Christian leadership that the most influential apostles call themselves servants?

At-A-Glance

1. To the Diaspora, Rejoice! (James 1:1)
2. Joy In The Midst of Trial and Difficulty (vv. 2–4)
3. The Way to Wisdom: Prayer (vv. 5–8)
4. The Poor Shall be Raised (vv. 9–11)

In Depth

1. To the Diaspora, Rejoice! (James 1:1)

The epistle is addressed to the Christian Jewish Diaspora. The "twelve tribes which are scattered" is a reference to the children of Israel who live outside of Palestine. By the first century AD, there were many Jewish communities outside of Palestine. Many of the oldest communities were comprised of the descendants of slaves who were dislocated from their homeland during the Assyrian conquest and Babylonian captivity. The youngest communities were comprised of Jews who used Roman roads to settle in centers of commerce made possible by the Pax Romana peace. The diaspora is a diverse array of people separated by empire and experience but united by race and religion.

The verse concludes with the usual salutation of the time which most translations render as "greetings." However, it is worth noting that this word literally means "rejoice, be glad."

2. Joy In The Midst of Trial and Difficulty (vv. 2–4)

James addresses his readers as "brothers" (or "brothers and sisters"). Many Bible commentaries note that he is the brother of Jesus, but he chooses to emphasize that he is the brother of all believers. James demonstrates that the spiritual closeness of those in Christ can conquer the vast geographical distances that separate the scattered diaspora.

He returns to the idea of joy in verse two. However, this time he complicates the idea of joy by adding in sorrow. He adds the troubles of life, but he does not detract the imperative to be glad. From the standpoint of Jewish Wisdom Literature, experiencing the good and the bad of life are occasions when people learn more about God and self. James articulates this viewpoint when he says that trials are testing of faith, an exercise that strengthens faith over time, like a muscle. James' perspective on trials' producing character is also reminiscent of Paul (Romans 5:3) and of Peter (1 Peter 1:6).

3. The Way to Wisdom: Prayer (vv. 5–8)

James now turns his attention to wisdom. In the previous section, we can already see that he is influenced by Jewish Wisdom Literature. In this passage, we see the strong connection between wisdom and faith. James writes that wisdom is attainable from God through prayer to anyone who asks in faith. He issues a stark admonition to the doubter, whom he calls "double minded." This term is unique in the New Testament and ancient Greek literature. Some biblical scholars believe that James coined the term. The meaning is clear enough, though, referring to people who cannot choose between two mutually exclusive choices.

4. The Poor Shall be Raised (vv. 9–11)

James makes a third turn in the text. He now turns to the subject of poverty and riches. Most of his readers would have identified with the former social location. James assures them that God will not only raise the oppressed, but He will also bring down the oppressor. It is a complete reversal of fortunes, and God stands on the side of His people, especially the oppressed.

Search the Scriptures

1. How does James' understanding of endurance in this passage compare or contrast with Paul's understanding in Romans 5:3–4?

2. Where does James advise looking for wisdom?

Discuss the Meaning

1. Discuss the meaning of wisdom. How does wisdom in the epistle of James compare to the Wisdom Literature of the Old Testament such as Proverbs, Ecclesiastes, or Job?

2. The epistle of James has a focus on connecting belief to behavior. Are there any teachings that you believe, but find it difficult to practice?

3. James teaches that whenever you face trials of any kind, consider it nothing but joy. Is it truly possible to remain joyful in any trial? What are the most difficult trials that you have had in your life, and what can you do in those situations to be joyful? Does James offer any hint on how to remain joyful?

Liberating Lesson

The African Diaspora is like the Jewish Diaspora in several ways. First, God is a liberator. Both diasporas experienced the bondage of slavery but were freed. Nevertheless, as James notes in his passages on poverty and persecution, the diasporas are not free from oppression.

The epistle of James is refreshingly practical in its advice to Christians, particularly those who feel the bitter pangs of oppression. God our Liberator remains on the side of His oppressed people, and God is still speaking to them.

The epistle of James, though addressed to a different diaspora, speaks to the descendants of Africa and tells us to rejoice, have patience, and endure because the oppressor will wither away.

Application for Activation

Many people do not create time in their day to reflect on their life experiences, nor do they pray for wisdom from it. Over the next week, please try to reflect on your life and your community.

Take time every day this week to reflect on your experiences the past day and pray that God will grant you wisdom. Additionally, take time each night to reflect on the collective experiences of a group that you belong to and pray that God will grant you wisdom. Remember, while reflection is important, wisdom is an exercise of faith!

Follow the Spirit

What God wants me to do:

_____

_____

_____

_____

Remember Your Thoughts

Special insights I have learned:

_____

_____

_____

_____

More Light on the Text

James 1:1–11

1 James, a servant of God and of the Lord Jesus Christ, to the twelve tribes which are scattered abroad, greeting.

Many Bible scholars agree that this James is the half-brother of our Lord Jesus Christ. When Jesus was here on earth, James was not a believer. However, here he calls himself a servant (Gk. *doulos*, **DOO-loce**) not only of God but also of Jesus Christ. It is significant to note that he calls himself just a servant. Paul also calls himself both a servant and apostle of Jesus Christ (see Romans 1:1; Philippians 1:1). A servant or bond slave had no right or wish of his own. He only wished to do his master's bidding. James writes to Jews who believe in Jesus Christ and are "scattered" or in different parts of the Roman Empire. Today the recipients of this letter also include Christians around the world.

2 My brethren, count it all joy when ye fall into divers temptations;

James calls the recipients of the letter "brethren" (Gk. *adelphoi*, **ah-dell-FOY**). The use of this word here shows that there is intimacy between James and the readers. The closeness is made stronger by the use of the personal pronoun "my" (Gk. *mou*, **MOO**), which could have been left out. They all belonged to the same family. James says, "Count [reckon, calculate, or consider] it all joy." To count indicates a conscious decision of the mind to understand the situation. James is not saying that temptations are pleasurable. Instead, he says the readers should see them as beneficial. This requires an act of the mind. The Greek word translated "fall into" (*peripipto*, **peh-ree-PEEP-toe**) is more literally rendered "surrounded by." Temptations (Gk. *peirasmos*, **pay-rass-MOCE**) actually means trials that have a goal in mind. Thus, to "fall into divers temptations" means to be surrounded by trials or tests that are intended to strengthen rather than trip us up and cause us to fail. It is in light of this understanding that James says these trials should be welcome—"count it all joy." The nature of the temptations is not described, but the word "divers" suggests they could include all kinds of things.

3 Knowing this, that the trying of your faith worketh patience.

The word "knowing" introduces another instruction for using the mind. Know in your mind, not experientially, that the "trying [testing] of your faith" will result in finding it to be genuine. By using "knowing," James teaches that we are not to respond to our sufferings with our body, but with our mind. Likewise, when we respond to trials emotionally, the outcome may not be God-glorifying.

The word for "trying" is *dokimion* (**doh-KEE-me-own**) in Greek. It is also used to describe the process of qualifying gold as a standard (cf. Proverbs 27:21). It refers to something that has been tried and found to be authentic or of solid character. A faith that is tested and found genuine results in patience. Patience here is not a passive attitude. Instead, it is active endurance, which suggests that if one bears suffering well, one will become stronger.

4 But let patience have her perfect work, that ye may be perfect and entire, wanting nothing.

The full working of patience leads to three things: (1) perfection, (2) wholeness, and (3) wanting nothing or not lacking anything. Becoming perfect (Gk. *teleios*, **TEH-lay-oce**) involves a particular goal. Thus, if borne well, trials will make the bearer of them perfect. This is not sinless perfection; it means maturity and the ability to take on honorable tasks for God because the person has proven to be of solid character. The word "entire" (Gk. *holokleros*, **hoe-LOW-klay-roce**) is used to describe an animal that can be used for sacrifice or a priest who can represent the people. It conveys the idea of a thing complete in all its parts. Thus, it refers to the Christian who has overcome those things that may disqualify him or her from ministry. The phrase "wanting nothing"—not one thing left behind or lacking—is another description of maturity. These three things are not to be seen

as three levels of maturity but different pictures given to capture the same truth.

5 If any of you lack wisdom, let him ask of God, that giveth to all men liberally, and upbraideth not; and it shall be given him.

Those who have not yet attained perfect patience may still lack (Gk. *leipo*) wisdom. The word "wisdom" (Gk. *sophia*, **sow-FEE-uh**) is not merely knowledge. It is the ability to apply knowledge. Wisdom gives a believer a sense of direction that will help him or her know how to respond to trials in a way that will lead to maturity. Wisdom comes from God (cf. Proverbs 2:6). Similar to Jesus' promise, "Ask, and it shall be given you" (from Matthew 7:7), God gives wisdom to all "liberally" (Gk. *haplos*, **hah-PLOCE**). This word refers to a simplicity and singleness of mind, thereby suggesting that God gives wisdom generously, willingly, and wholeheartedly. He does not give conditionally, recalling our past sins, nor does He constantly remind us how indebted we are to Him for such a great gift. The phrase "upbraideth not" indicates that God will not deride us for our need, but that He delights to give and gives with no strings attached.

6 But let him ask in faith, nothing wavering. For he that wavereth is like a wave of the sea driven with the wind and tossed.

James now talks about how we are to ask God for this gift of wisdom. This verse can also serve as a guide to help us to pray properly. The word for "wavering" or "doubt" in Greek conveys the idea of a person debating with himself. His mind is not made up. This is a clear contrast to God, who is single-minded (cf. *haplos*, v. 5). The wavering person is like a wave of the sea driven with the wind and tossed. The wave does not have constancy. It is at the mercy of the wind. So is the person who doubts. He or she is unstable, without conviction or a sense of direction. Even though this person prays to God, he or she does not have confidence in God. Wavering and doubting here is not due to weakness, ignorance, or immaturity. It is a choice to doubt God because of the attraction of other things, the desire for immediate gratification, or other reasons.

7 For let not that man think that he shall receive any thing of the Lord. 8 A double minded man is unstable in all his ways.

A person who prays and then wavers or doubts should not deceive himself by thinking that he is going to receive a response from the Lord. The word "think" in this verse plays into the same rational or correct mindset that James appealed to earlier (vv. 2–3). In other words, any thinking person ought to know the end of such wavering is no answer from the Lord. The term "double minded" (Gk. *dipsuchos*, **DEEP-soo-koce**) referring to man literally means double-souled and is analogous to a dual personality. The unstable man is the believer who wants to enjoy God's blessings of joy and inner peace (v. 2), but also enjoy the sinful pleasures of this world. This condition of "double-mindedness" is serious because it carries over into other areas of a person's life. In contrast, the pursuit of God must become the sole goal of every believer.

9 Let the brother of low degree rejoice in that he is exalted: 10 But the rich, in that he is made low: because as the flower of the grass he shall pass away. 11 For the sun is no sooner risen with a burning heat, but it withereth the grass, and the flower thereof falleth, and the grace of the fashion of it perisheth: so also shall the rich man fade away in his ways.

This piece of wisdom seems to echo the teachings of Jesus (Matthew 6:19–21; Luke 6:20–25) and Paul (2 Corinthians 8:9); indeed the poor are the recipients of the Kingdom of God (Matthew 5:3), much more valuable than the earthly riches that can be accumulated in this life. Earthly wealth is not bad or evil itself, but it is unwise to trust in earthly riches. Earthly riches are temporary, and those who gain them by unjust means will see them lost just as easily. It is difficult for the rich who trust in riches to enter the Kingdom of God as Jesus says (Mark 10:24). Wealth can easily become an idol, but the poor in spirit recognize God alone should be worshiped and served. There is also an embedded assumption here that the rich people that James is speaking about are gaining or maintain their riches by injustice whether actively or passively. Participating in unjust systems for personal gain is just as much sin as committing personal injustice. Flowers are only beautiful for a season, depending on the weather and environment they are in. In the same way, being rich in the world's view looks good for a season and depends on the environment, and their wealth and their status will pass away.

Say It Correctly

Diaspora. dee-ASS-purr-uh.
Pax Romana. POX roe-MAH-na.

Daily Bible Readings

MONDAY
Suffering on Behalf of the Church
(Colossians 1:24–29)

TUESDAY
Saved by God's Mercy
(Titus 3:3–7)

WEDNESDAY
Ask: God Will Supply Your Needs
(Luke 11:9–13)

THURSDAY
Rejoice in Your Sufferings
(Romans 5:1–5)

FRIDAY
God's Loving Actions Toward Sinners
(Romans 5:6–11)

SATURDAY
Grass Withers But God's Word Stands
(Isaiah 40:1–8)

SUNDAY
Wisdom Overcomes Trials and Temptations
(James 1:1–11)

Notes

Teaching Tips

Words You Should Know

A. Naughtiness (v. 21) *kakia* (Gk.)— Malignity, malice, ill will, desire to injure

B. Undefiled (v. 27) *amiantos* (Gk.)—Free from deformity and debasement, having full force and vigor

Teacher Preparation

Unifying Principle—Talk is Cheap. People read and talk about doing good but find it difficult to help the most vulnerable in society. How is righteousness accomplished? According to James, righteousness is achieved by hearing and doing the word of God.

A. Read the Bible Background and Devotional Reading.

B. Pray for your students and lesson clarity.

C. Read the lesson Scripture in multiple translations.

O—Open the Lesson

A. Begin the class with prayer.

B. Display a variety of mirrors and discuss the purpose and value of a mirror. Discuss how ridiculous it would be for one to look into the mirror and then ignore what he or she saw. Relate that to James 1:22–23.

C. Have the students read the Aim for Change and the In Focus story.

D. Ask students how events like those in the story weigh on their hearts and how they can view these events from a faith perspective.

P—Present the Scriptures

A. Read the Focal Verses.

B. Have the class share what Scriptures stand out for them and why, with particular emphasis on today's context.

C. Discuss the Background and The People, Places, and Times sections.

E—Explore the Meaning

A. Use In Depth or More Light on the Text to facilitate a deeper discussion of the lesson text.

B. Pose the questions in Search the Scriptures and Discuss the Meaning.

C. Discuss the Liberating Lesson and Application for Activation sections.

N—Next Steps for Application

A. Summarize the value of self-control.

B. Make plans to visit a nursing home, hospice center, or a homebound member of the congregation for the purpose of sharing comfort and encouragement.

Worship Guide

For the Superintendent or Teacher
Theme: Hearing and Doing the Word
Song: "Lord Christ, We Praise Your Sacrifice"
Devotional Reading: 1 Corinthians 1:26–31

Hearing and Doing the Word

Bible Background • JAMES 1:19–27
Printed Text • JAMES 1:19–27 | Devotional Reading • 1 CORINTHIANS 1:26–31

Aim for Change

By the end of the lesson, we will: REALIZE the proof of wisdom is not just in what we say, but what we do, EXPRESS compassion for those who are most vulnerable and desire to act on their behalf, and ENGAGE in ministry that demonstrates the religion that James describes.

In Focus

Julian looked out the window as the car pulled away from the police station. He turned and stared at the back of his father's head. He started to say, "Dad …?"—but caught a glimpse of his father's face in the rear-view mirror: stern and angry. He thought better of it. His father always kept silent when he was really angry.

Julian slumped in the back seat. He and his buddies Trent, Conrad, and Vinny had gone out carousing at a bar in the neighborhood where they met Norris, an upperclassman from a rival fraternity. What began as friendly trash-talking turned into not-so-friendly insults, with Julian making the worst of them. Trent told him to back down, but Julian wouldn't listen. Soon, the argument turned into a fight.

Julian knew how lucky he was that the worst this run-in with the police got him was a court date. He hated to think how his mom reacted when she heard he had been arrested. Julian was almost too embarrassed to breathe when he made phone call to his father to bail him out. Dad always told him to keep a cool head and to think before he spoke. "Son, people will remember you by what you say, but they will know you by what you do," his father always said.

Julian knew what he first had to say. "Dad?" he said. "I'm sorry."

Anger shuts down conversation and gets in the way of relationships. How do we put anger in its proper place?

Keep in Mind

"But be ye doers of the word, and not hearers only, deceiving your own selves" (James 1:22, KJV).

"But don't just listen to God's word. You must do what it says. Otherwise, you are only fooling yourselves" (James 1:22, NLT).

Focal Verses

KJV **James 1:19** Wherefore, my beloved brethren, let every man be swift to hear, slow to speak, slow to wrath:

20 For the wrath of man worketh not the righteousness of God.

21 Wherefore lay apart all filthiness and superfluity of naughtiness, and receive with meekness the engrafted word, which is able to save your souls.

22 But be ye doers of the word, and not hearers only, deceiving your own selves.

23 For if any be a hearer of the word, and not a doer, he is like unto a man beholding his natural face in a glass:

24 For he beholdeth himself, and goeth his way, and straightway forgetteth what manner of man he was.

25 But whoso looketh into the perfect law of liberty, and continueth therein, he being not a forgetful hearer, but a doer of the work, this man shall be blessed in his deed.

26 If any man among you seem to be religious, and bridleth not his tongue, but deceiveth his own heart, this man's religion is vain.

27 Pure religion and undefiled before God and the Father is this, To visit the fatherless and widows in their affliction, and to keep himself unspotted from the world.

NLT **James 1:19** Understand this, my dear brothers and sisters: You must all be quick to listen, slow to speak, and slow to get angry.

20 Human anger does not produce the righteousness God desires.

21 So get rid of all the filth and evil in your lives, and humbly accept the word God has planted in your hearts, for it has the power to save your souls.

22 But don't just listen to God's word. You must do what it says. Otherwise, you are only fooling yourselves.

23 For if you listen to the word and don't obey, it is like glancing at your face in a mirror.

24 You see yourself, walk away, and forget what you look like.

25 But if you look carefully into the perfect law that sets you free, and if you do what it says and don't forget what you heard, then God will bless you for doing it.

26 If you claim to be religious but don't control your tongue, you are fooling yourself, and your religion is worthless.

27 Pure and genuine religion in the sight of God the Father means caring for orphans and widows in their distress and refusing to let the world corrupt you.

The People, Places, and Times

Widows and Orphans. In the Mosaic Law, special regard was given to widows and orphans. They were partly dependent on family, especially the eldest son, who received a double portion of the inheritance. They also participated in the third type of tithe, which occurred every three years (Deuteronomy 26:12–13); in gleaning produce left in the field (24:19–21); and in religious feasts (16:14). God proclaimed Himself "married" to the widow and orphan (Psalm 68:5) and condemned those who oppressed them (Malachi 3:5). The New Testament church continued to support widows, though Paul instructed that the younger ones try to remarry.

Do widows and orphans still require the church's special care today? If so, how do we best help them?

Background

James, the half-brother of Jesus, was among the early leaders of the church and was based in Jerusalem. Although the epistle of James is placed toward the end of the New Testament, it is actually the first letter of instruction written to the church—thus the first book of the New Testament written. The primary audience for this epistle was the Christian Jews spread across the world due to persecution in Jerusalem and Rome because of their faith in Christ. The major theme of James' letter is to offer instruction for godly living in the midst of a self-indulgent world. This letter is viewed as a book of wisdom and instruction for Jewish believers. James appealed for his fellow believers to join outward actions with their inward faith. Scholars believe that James wrote this epistle in the mid-40s AD around the time of the council in Jerusalem (Acts 15). He was one of the first martyrs of the church, executed in AD 62.

At-A-Glance

1. Behaving the Word (James 1:19–20)
2. Living by the Word (vv. 21–25)
3. Representing the Word (vv. 26–27)

In Depth

1. Behaving the Word (James 1:19–20)

In proverb fashion, James instructs believers to "be swift to hear, slow to speak, slow to wrath" (v. 19). This letter is written early in the church's life. The believers are facing persecution for their faith in Jesus Christ. As James offers up his instruction, he most likely bases it on a combination of wisdom Scriptures such as Proverbs 10:19, 4:17, 19, and Ecclesiastes 5:2. Wisdom literature was captured by scribes and passed down orally as Jews met in the synagogues and talked in their homes. James takes the practicality of the proverbs and

relates them to his audience, who also would have heard such lessons as they were growing up. The purpose of reviving such language and instruction in the culture of his day is to usher in a new era (the reign of the kingdom of God) with wisdom from the old. He takes the time to remind them in the midst of persecution and rejection to be patient, seek God for His wisdom, trust God in the midst of trial, and act honorably to best represent their faith in Christ. Also, because his audience is scattered abroad and this letter is most likely written in Greek, James suspects that these believers might be influenced away from their Jewish roots.

He reminds them of those teachings that should influence their behavior, as well as incorporates Jesus' teachings on how to handle mistreatment and anger (Matthew 5:38–41, 47). James reminds readers that anger does not produce the righteous living that God desires from His people (James 1:20). It does not work in our favor or God's when we are unable to control our emotions. God is patient and longsuffering with us; therefore, we must do the same for others. Jesus Himself said that offense will come (Matthew 18:7), but it takes the wisdom of God to remain Spirit-led in the midst of adversity and trials. When we act on the principles James outlines—being quick to hear, slow to speak, slow to wrath, limiting anger—then we can make good decisions, keep our relationships intact, and glorify God.

In your adult life have you remembered or been reminded of a lesson you learned from when you were a child?

2. Living by the Word (vv. 21–25)

James continues his discourse by providing additional instruction on managing one's emotions. He appeals to readers to put away worldly lifestyles and behaviors to welcome humility and gladness the Word of God that had planted inside them by the Holy Spirit. He emphasizes that it is by receiving the truth as revealed through Jesus Christ that souls are saved. As the Word of God is planted into hearts, it brings about transformation into the true kingdom living and God's ways of doing and being. Similarly, Paul wrote that Christians are not to be influenced or live by the patterns and dictates of the world's system but to be transformed by the renewing of our minds (Romans 12:1–2). Only then can we know what is the good, acceptable, and perfect will of God. Likewise, James, whose letter is a forerunner to Paul's writings, instructs believers to live above reproach. It is important to the early church leaders that Christians live counter to their culture so as to best represent the power of God on earth. Key to the successful reflection of God's love and grace is to bear the fruit of the Spirit (Galatians 5:22–23). To be doers of the word and not hearers only (v. 22) means to put the engrafted Word of God into practical application. James said that if we are hearers of the Word and not doers, we only deceive ourselves.

James uses an illustration to further drive home his point of how one can engage in self-deception about righteous living (vv. 23–24). When a person looks in a mirror, he or she sees an image for a moment, but when away from the mirror, the image is forgotten. The Word of God is our mirror to remind us that without Christ, our image is out of focus. Only when we look in the mirror of the Word and see the righteousness of Christ are we reminded what we are supposed to look like. The Word of God reminds us that we are in Christ but still growing into the knowledge of Him—which requires us to be diligent in study, fervent in prayer, and quick to obey. James went on to say that those who look into the perfect law of liberty, which is freedom in Christ, will live by the Word and be blessed.

How have you seen or heard of people blaming Christians for not living out their faith?

3. Representing the Word (vv. 26–27)

James defines what real religion looks like for his audience by providing two contrasting images. He says that those who proclaim to be devout in their beliefs and actions but are unable to control their mouths only deceive themselves. James emphasizes that religion that does not reflect God's heart is in vain. In other words, it is not enough to give outward expressions of devotion to God when one's lifestyle does not reflect one's words. Attending church every Sunday, paying tithes, and serving in ministry should be done out of loving obedience to God and in gratitude for salvation through Jesus Christ, but it is all for nothing if there is no true transformation of the heart. Our works should express our love and reverence and not be a mere duty. God does not want us to pay lip service to love Him; He wants our love to be genuine and thus expressed in how we live and what we do.

James further explains that "pure religion and undefiled before God and the Father is this, To visit the fatherless and widows in their affliction" (from James 1:27). God is always intentional in wanting His people to live selflessly by caring for the needs of others. Showing mercy to those who are marginalized is true religion—devotion to God—in practice. In the culture of the early church, those who had no one to care for them had no means to move out of their social station. The love of God is so great that He made provision for them through those called by His name. God always commanded His people to care for the least, and Jesus was intentional to bring His ministry to the poorest of the population.

James closes this part of the discourse by stressing that believers should keep themselves "unspotted" from the world, not allowing the world's way of living to be their marker. Only through active participation with the Holy Spirit can one live a life that is unspotted, unstained from the world. As Christians, we are not to live according to the world's standards, which run contrary to the Word of God; instead, we are to reflect the living Word, Jesus Christ, who came to do the will of Him who sent Him (John 5:30).

Examine yourself to see if your participation in church is done in love or obligation. What do you need to change to perform your ministries out of love again?

Search the Scriptures

1. How does James advise believers to behave (James 1:19)?

2. How does James recommend believers use the Word of God (v. 22)?

Discuss the Meaning

1. Discuss what true religion looks like in today's context. How would James evaluate the body of Christ today? What would he say about how we treat widows and orphans?

2. How does one remain unspotted from the world in today's culture? Is it possible?

Liberating Lesson

At one time or another, we are all guilty of only talking a good game when it comes to living according to godly principles, representing the best of Christ in our sphere of influence, being concerned about the world around us and having great intentions on being more helpful to those in need. In today's lesson, James calls us to not just be hearers of the Word but also to carry it out in our everyday lives in our thoughts and deeds. Often, we can get stuck because there is so much to be done; it can be an overwhelming task to change the world—let alone ourselves! When we embrace change in baby steps, taking one action at a time and doing it consistently, transformation takes place.

Application for Activation

Really listen for God's instruction through the preached Word and in your time of personal devotion and Bible study. Take time to be quiet before the Lord and write down what He is speaking to you through the Holy Spirit. As you listen, take steps to move in God's direction. Make a conscious effort to assess habits, behaviors, and actions that do not line up with the Word of God. Repent, and ask the Holy Spirit to help you act differently. Be patient with yourself. Trust that God has heard you and that His Word will change your heart if you yield to His way.

Follow the Spirit

What God wants me to do:

_____

_____

_____

Remember Your Thoughts

Special insights I have learned:

_____

_____

_____

_____

More Light on the Text
James 1:19–27

19 Wherefore, my beloved brethren, let every man be swift to hear, slow to speak, slow to wrath: 20 For the wrath of man worketh not the righteousness of God.

James began by acknowledging that the ones to whom he is writing were also children of God the Father and righteous Judge. Therefore, there exists a bond of love between Him and them. It is from that sense of love that James admonishes the believers to remember, to hear the Word of God that had already been entrusted to them so that they would not fall under His judgment. James knows that a zealot-like fervor for rebellion is sweeping throughout the region, and many are being influenced by its call for violence against Rome. He does not want those who follow Christ to be caught up in the hostility and anger in the same manner as those who do not belong to the risen Lord. God's Word is powerful. It has the ability to change hearts and affect the character, but it should not be shared hastily with others until its work in the hearer is evident. James also admonished believers to be slow to wrath (Gk. *orge*, **or-GAY**; any violent emotion, especially anger), so that, by their lives and actions, they would demonstrate that a different message is at work in their hearts. James understands that people's anger inhibits the development of God's righteous work within him.

21 Wherefore lay apart all filthiness and superfluity of naughtiness, and receive with meekness the engrafted word, which is able to save your souls.

Evil flows from within us and expresses itself in our actions toward others. James instructs the believers to put off all "filthiness" (Gk. *rhuparia*, **roo-pah-REE-ah**; defilement or dishonor) as though it were a dirty, useless garment. The work of righteousness would then begin to show

itself and help to empower the believers to hold in check their abundance (KJV: "superfluity") of "naughtiness" (Gk. *kakia*, **kah-KEE-ah**; malignity, malice, ill will, desire to injure). Such a state can only be accomplished in believers when they welcome the Word of God with true humility. God's Word then attaches itself to the very core fabric of our being and begins the work of transforming our evil nature into one pleasing to our righteous God and Savior.

22 But be ye doers of the word, and not hearers only, deceiving your own selves. 23 For if any be a hearer of the word, and not a doer, he is like unto a man beholding his natural face in a glass: 24 For he beholdeth himself, and goeth his way, and straightway forgetteth what manner of man he was.

James' admonition for believers is to demonstrate to others how the Word of God is at work within them. They are to do this by the way they live before others and by making a habit of doing the Word. Living out the Word of God in this fashion also provides evidence for the believers that they are not pretending or playing at being righteous, thereby deluding themselves. James offers the analogy of one looking at his face in a mirror (KJV: "glass"). The best mirrors of the day were made out of Corinthian brass, but the image reflected back was often distorted. It would have been easy, then, for the individual to look at the reflection of the face he has had since birth (Gk. *genesis*, **GHEH-neh-sees**, "natural") but then turn away and forget what he looks like or what he had become.

25 But whoso looketh into the perfect law of liberty, and continueth therein, he being not a forgetful hearer, but a doer of the work, this man shall be blessed in his deed.

James contrasts the natural man with the spiritual man (see John 3:6). The Word of God, which produces the spiritual man, perfects the law and sets man free from his sinful nature or natural self. But in order for the Word of God to have its desired effect, believers need to "continueth" (Gk. *parameno*, **pah-rah-MEH-no**; to always be near) in that Word. The act of gazing intently into the Word of God enables believers to retain the image of what the Holy Spirit is producing within them. The blessing for the believer is founded upon the actions that flow from the changed life that is the product of the Holy Spirit's work. This blessing manifests itself in the deeds of the believer that are a result of having built inwardly upon the solid ground of the Word of God.

26 If any man among you seem to be religious, and bridleth not his tongue, but deceiveth his own heart, this man's religion is vain.

For James, true religion is evidenced by the fruit that religion produces in the individual. A true believer, one who has permitted the Word of God to take root within themselves, will not be like the zealots who made uncontrolled and impassioned speeches against Roman occupation. Instead, that person will "bridleth" (Gk. *chalinagogeo*, **khah-LEE-nah-go-GEH-oh**; to hold in check or restrain) his tongue. The word that James uses for "religious" (Gk. *threskos*, **thrace-KOCE**) refers to giving scrupulous attention to the details of worship. This would include being careful of one's actions and one's speech when involved in religious activities. However, if one does not control his tongue when not engaging in religious activities, then

that individual is only deceiving his own "heart" (Gk. *kardia*, **kar-DEE-ah**; the center and seat of spiritual life). For that individual, religion is in "vain" (Gk. *mataios*, **MAH-tie-oce**), which means his religion is useless and of no purpose.

27 Pure religion and undefiled before God and the Father is this, To visit the fatherless and widows in their affliction, and to keep himself unspotted from the world.

James closes his counsel by explaining to believers that the type of religion that pleases God is both "pure" (Gk. *katharos*, **kah-thah-ROCE**; free from corrupt desire, sin, and guilt) and "undefiled" (Gk. *amiantos*, **ah-MEE-an-toce**; free from deformity and debasement, having full force and vigor). The evidence that one possesses a religion that merits God's favor is found through the actions of caring for (KJV: "visiting") the fatherless and widows in times of distress, actions that reflect the work of the Holy Spirit on one's character. By encouraging believers to show concern for widows and the fatherless, James is reminding them that their heavenly Father identified Himself as the God of the fatherless and the widow (Psalm 68:5).

Sources:
Dunn, James D. G. and John W. Rogerson. *Commentary on the Bible.* Grand Rapids, MI: Wm. B. Eerdmans Publishing Company, 2003.
HarperCollins Study Bible (NRSV). New York: Harper Collins Publishers, 2006. 2052–2054.
Hebrew Greek Key Word Study Bible (KJV), 2nd ed. Chattanooga, TN: AMG Publishers, 1991. 1528, 1743, 1751.
Keener, Craig S. *The IVP Bible Background Commentary: New Testament.* Downers Grove, IL: IVP Academic, 1994.
Tasker, R. V. G. *The General Epistle of James: An Introduction and Commentary.* Grand Rapids, MI: Wm. B. Eerdmans Publishing Company, 1982.
Unger, Merrill. *Unger's Bible Handbook.* Chicago: Moody Press, 1967. 785–786.

Say It Correctly

Engrafted. en-GRAFT-ed.

Daily Bible Readings

MONDAY
Impartial Relationships with One Another
(Leviticus 19:13–18)

TUESDAY
Praised for Steadfast Faith in Persecution
(2 Thessalonians 1:3–5, 11–12)

WEDNESDAY
The Poor Blessed; the Rich Criticized
(Luke 6:20–26)

THURSDAY
Suffering for Doing the Right Thing
(1 Peter 3:13–19)

FRIDAY
God's Choice—the Foolish, Weak, Lowly
(1 Corinthians 1:26–31)

SATURDAY
Treat the Rich and Poor Impartially
(James 2:1–7)

SUNDAY
The Wise Hear and Do Good.
(James 1:19–27)

Notes

Teaching Tips

Words You Should Know

A. Naked (v. 15) *gumnos* (Gk.)—Having little or no clothing.

B. Dead (v. 17) *nekros* (Gk.)—No longer living, deceased.

Teacher Preparation

Unifying Principle—Just Do It. Some people make bold claims about the standards by which they live, but their actions deny those claims. How can we tell when someone is genuine? James says the one who has faith will demonstrate that faith by his or her works, as did Abraham and Rahab.

A. Read the Bible Background and Devotional Reading.

B. Pray for your students and lesson clarity.

C. Read the lesson Scripture in multiple translations.

O—Open the Lesson

A. Begin the class with prayer.

B. As a class, role-play a believer's interaction with a person who is without enough to eat or wear. Have some students play the role of a believer who has "faith" but not works; others will show how faith is put into action. Debrief afterward.

C. Have the students read the Aim for Change and the In Focus story.

D. Ask students how events like those in the story weigh on their hearts and how they can view these events from a faith perspective.

P—Present the Scriptures

A. Read the Focal Verses.

B. Have the class share what Scriptures stand out for them and why, with particular emphasis on today's context.

C. Discuss the Background and The People, Places, and Times sections.

E—Explore the Meaning

A. Use In Depth or More Light on the Text to facilitate a deeper discussion of the lesson text.

B. Pose the questions in Search the Scriptures and Discuss the Meaning.

C. Discuss the Liberating Lesson and Application for Activation sections.

N—Next Steps for Application

A. Summarize the value of how faith and works must be interwoven in our lives.

B. End class with a commitment to pray for doing faith.

Worship Guide

For the Superintendent or Teacher
Theme: Faith Without Works Is Dead
Song: "I Love the Lord; He Heard My Cry"
Devotional Reading: Matthew 18:23–35

Faith Without Works Is Dead

Bible Background • JAMES 2:14–26
Printed Text • JAMES 2:14–26 | Devotional Reading • MATTHEW 18:23–35

———————— Aim for Change ————————

By the end of the lesson, we will: COMPARE and contrast faith that is no more than empty talk with a faith that is proved by actions, REFLECT on the power of Abraham's and Rahab's examples of faith in action, and DECIDE to demonstrate faith with tangible works.

———————— In Focus ————————

Barnabas plopped the morning newspaper down on his desk. Leading the business section was an article about a protest against his company over its record on diversity.

"No outsider has any business telling me who I should hire or who I should promote," Barnabas complained. He added, "We absolutely believe in diversity."

"That's not reflected in your numbers," said Stanley, Barnabas' best friend, and spiritual adviser. "And it's not what people see when they look at your company." Stanley and Barnabas were members of the men's group at their church. Stanley was the man who always told Barnabas what he needed to hear, whether or not he wanted to hear it.

"But we are always looking for good candidates," Barnabas said. "We send representatives to all the career days at the local high schools and to the regional job fairs in our field."

"Sure," Stanley said. "But so does everyone else. You don't get extra credit for doing the minimum. Do you actually make any hires from those contacts?" Barnabas sat in uncomfortable silence. "I'll take that as a no," Stanley said. "It doesn't help if you don't live up to what you claim. Saying you're committed doesn't count if you don't do it."

How much more can be accomplished for the glory of God if we put faith into action with works as well as with words?

———————— Keep in Mind ————————

"For as the body without the spirit is dead, so faith without works is dead also"
(James 2:26, KJV).

"Just as the body is dead without breath, so also faith is dead without good works" (James 2:26, NLT).

Focal Verses

KJV **James 2:14** What doth it profit, my brethren, though a man say he hath faith, and have not works? can faith save him?

15 If a brother or sister be naked, and destitute of daily food,

16 And one of you say unto them, Depart in peace, be ye warmed and filled; notwithstanding ye give them not those things which are needful to the body; what doth it profit?

17 Even so faith, if it hath not works, is dead, being alone.

18 Yea, a man may say, Thou hast faith, and I have works: shew me thy faith without thy works, and I will shew thee my faith by my works.

19 Thou believest that there is one God; thou doest well: the devils also believe, and tremble.

20 But wilt thou know, O vain man, that faith without works is dead?

21 Was not Abraham our father justified by works, when he had offered Isaac his son upon the altar?

22 Seest thou how faith wrought with his works, and by works was faith made perfect?

23 And the scripture was fulfilled which saith, Abraham believed God, and it was imputed unto him for righteousness: and he was called the Friend of God.

24 Ye see then how that by works a man is justified, and not by faith only.

25 Likewise also was not Rahab the harlot justified by works, when she had received the messengers, and had sent them out another way?

26 For as the body without the spirit is dead, so faith without works is dead also.

NLT **James 2:14** What good is it, dear brothers and sisters, if you say you have faith but don't show it by your actions? Can that kind of faith save anyone?

15 Suppose you see a brother or sister who has no food or clothing,

16 and you say, "Good-bye and have a good day; stay warm and eat well"—but then you don't give that person any food or clothing. What good does that do?

17 So you see, faith by itself isn't enough. Unless it produces good deeds, it is dead and useless.

18 Now someone may argue, "Some people have faith; others have good deeds." But I say, "How can you show me your faith if you don't have good deeds? I will show you my faith by my good deeds."

19 You say you have faith, for you believe that there is one God. Good for you! Even the demons believe this, and they tremble in terror.

20 How foolish! Can't you see that faith without good deeds is useless?

21 Don't you remember that our ancestor Abraham was shown to be right with God by his actions when he offered his son Isaac on the altar?

22 You see, his faith and his actions worked together. His actions made his faith complete.

23 And so it happened just as the Scriptures say: "Abraham believed God, and God counted him as righteous because of his faith." He was even called the friend of God.

24 So you see, we are shown to be right with God by what we do, not by faith alone.

25 Rahab the prostitute is another example. She was shown to be right with God by her actions when she hid those messengers and sent them safely away by a different road.

26 Just as the body is dead without breath, so also faith is dead without good works.

582

The People, Places, and Times

Rahab. When the Israelites sent spies to get a feel of Jericho and the surrounding land of Canaan, Rahab hid the two Israelite spies from local authorities. She recognized the God of Israel as the one true God (Joshua 2:11) and begged the spies to spare the lives of her and her family. The spies instructed Rahab to hang a scarlet rope from her window and then their lives would be spared. This happened, and everyone under Rahab's roof was saved. Later, Rahab became the mother of Boaz, whom we read about in the book of Ruth.

Background

James, the brother of Jesus Christ, is popularly agreed as the author of this epistle. The date of James is difficult to ascertain, but the epistle must have been written before AD 62 when James was martyred, with AD 44–48 being the most probable date of writing.

James' audience was the Jewish-Christians who he described as "the twelve tribes scattered among the nations" (1:1). They were scattered as a result of the persecution that ensued after the death of Stephen (Acts 7:54–58). The emerging attitudes of these Jewish-Christians necessitated the writing of this letter. These attitudes included oppression of the poor (5:1–6), religious superficiality (1:22–27), discrimination (2:1–13) and bitterness (3:1–12, 4:1–3).

The passage for today seems to contradict Paul's teaching that salvation is by faith alone. It was a stumbling block to Martin Luther, who could not reconcile Paul and James on the issue of faith and works. James' letter is not about salvation, however, but argues against a faith that is alone—a faith stripped of practical responses of gratitude to God for salvation. While Paul's argument is that justification is by faith alone, it is clear from the rest of his teaching that this faith is not alone. It needs to be "worked out with fear and trembling" (Philippians 2:12).

At-A-Glance

1. Work: Evidence of Faith (James 2:14–19)
2. Those Who Accompanied Their Faith with Works (vv. 20–26)

In Depth

1. Work: Evidence of Faith (James 2:14–19)

Some people believe James seems to be in sharp contradiction with Paul on the issue of justification by faith in these verses. However, both authors agree with each other. The words "faith" and "works" are used differently by Paul in Romans 3–4 and James in James 2:14, 17, and 26. In Romans "faith" means "a living trust in God," but in James, it is a mere belief, uninspired by the Spirit of God. The "works" for Paul are deeds to fulfill the law, by rote legalism; for James "works" are done out of love. Putting it differently the works Paul speaks about are those that precede faith, while the works of James are those done in faith. James teaches that "faith without work is dead," inwardly and outwardly. Such faith bears no fruit and never will because it is dead.

The little parable (vv. 15–17) about sending a needy brother or sister away without assistance parallels John's question: "But whoso hath this world's good, and seeth his brother have need, and shutteth up his bowels of compassion from him, how dwelleth the love of God in him?" (1 John 3:17). Evidence of authentic faith is seen in the work of obedience accompanying it.

"A man may say" (James 2:18) indicates that James understands the well-known argument present in his time. He does not argue for the superiority of works over faith; rather, he argues that there is no authentic Christian faith without works of righteousness. Such faith is worthless, like that of demons that believe in

God and shudder (v. 19) but fail to back it up with obedience to God.

How can believers demonstrate their faith in a society where a tight budget governs spending?

2. Those Who Accompanied Their Faith with Works (vv. 20–26)

James in this section proves his point by alluding to their ancestors Abraham and Rahab the prostitute as examples of those who backed their faith with work. Abraham "being justified by works" seems to be a contradiction to Paul's statement that "Abraham believed God, and it was counted unto him for righteousness" (Romans 4:3; Galatians 3:6). Both Paul and James support their position with Genesis 15:6 but in different events and context. Paul's reference to Abraham's faith was at a time between when Abraham had been promised a child and when Isaac finally arrived. James, on the other hand, refers to Abraham's faith when he offered Isaac, his son, upon the altar (Genesis 22:1–19). This kind of faith was accompanied by action—offering his son on the altar for sacrifice. Abraham was not justified by this action but by the faith that produced it.

Rahab, the second proof, was also mentioned in Hebrews as a heroine of the faith (11:31). According to James, her actions were proof of her faith. By faith, she risked her life to save the lives of the Israelite spies (Joshua 2:1–21). James concludes his argument with a human body as an illustration: "As the body without the Spirit is dead, so faith is dead without work" (James 2:26). To put it differently, just like death and decay ensue when the body is separated from the spirit, faith will decay without righteous works to sustain it.

How would you reconcile Paul and James on this issue of faith and works? Would you share a situation where you accompanied your faith with action?

Search the Scriptures

1. Why might some believers think there can be a divide where some have faith and some have works (James 2:18)? What happens with a congregation tries to have faith without works or works without faith?

2. If the demons do believe in one God and fear Him, why are they condemned (v. 19)?

3. What actions proved Abraham's faith (vv. 21–23)? What actions proved Rahab's (v. 25)?

Discuss the Meaning

1. Discuss how James 2:18 is not in contradiction with Romans 3:28.

2. When a person does nothing for the physical needs of another because they are unable to help, is the person's faith a dead faith?

Liberating Lesson

We are in a society where people are taught to spend strictly according to their budget; things outside the budget are not prioritized. This sometimes makes it challenging to help believers who approach us for help (when we can). Nevertheless, failure to do so is an expression of lacking faith. Some people want to be told earlier about a need so they can factor it into their expenses, but there are certain cases that do not work that way. For example, the case in James, where a believer just approaches you and asks for your help. Speaking words of encouragement and not attending to that need is inauthentic faith. Further, personal faith in Christ for salvation without social justice is dead. Helping the homeless find shelter, clothing the naked on the street, visiting prisoners and the sick, and speaking for the oppressed or persecuted are ways of authenticating our faith. We are called to demonstrate our faith by action.

Application for Activation

Consider visiting prisoners or shelters this week to provide nice clothes, nonperishables, words of encouragement, and other personal items.

Participating in the projects of your church is another way of demonstrating your faith. Identify one or more projects in the church and become active!

Follow the Spirit

What God wants me to do:

_____

_____

_____

_____

Remember Your Thoughts

Special insights I have learned:

_____

_____

_____

_____

More Light on the Text

James 2:14–26

Do Paul and James disagree on the subject of faith and works (cf. Ephesians 2:8–10; James 2:24)? Is Scripture inconsistent or, worse, contradictory? Are we justified by faith alone, or are works involved? Christians have wrestled with these questions ever since the first century.

14 What doth it profit, my brethren, though a man say he hath faith, and have not works? can faith save him?

The literary construction of this part of James is one of a proposition supported by arguments and then summarized with conclusions. The proposition opens with a pair of rhetorical questions, the first of which basically says, "Suppose a man says he has faith." This is quite different from "Suppose a man has faith." To actually have faith versus *saying* you have faith are two entirely different things. The second rhetorical question today would be worded, "Claimed faith without works can't save him, can it?" Of course, the correct answer is no, as James will demonstrate.

15 If a brother or sister be naked, and destitute of daily food, 16 And one of you say unto them, Depart in peace, be ye warmed and filled; notwithstanding ye give them not those things which are needful to the body; what doth it profit? 17 Even so faith, if it hath not works, is dead, being alone.

The proposition continues with a hypothetical example, employing hyperbole indicating someone in dire straits or desperate need, with a "naked" (Gk. *gumnos*, **goom-NOCE**) brother or sister who is also "destitute of daily food." The common phrase "Depart in peace" means, in essence, "Go get what you need from someone else—but know that I care." Another similar response might be "You'll be in my thoughts and prayers." Such words come from a faith that is useless and dead (Gk. *nekros*, **neh-KROCE**), which is the plain sense of the word; James is not pulling punches. "What good is a dead faith?" James asks. Salvation or justification, it can be said, is comprised of both hearing and doing; the same can be said of faith and works (cf. Matthew 7:24; 1 Thessalonians 1:3). Genuine faith is a gift that comes from God (Ephesians 2:8), and works are a natural expression of such faith. Faith and works are two sides of the same coin. For many, Paul and James have put faith and works at odds—and too often the argument has been framed as if one must make an either-or choice. In reality, they were talking about two types of faith—only one of which is alive, while the other is dead, incapable of saving anyone (cf. Galatians 5:6, 6:15; 1 Corinthians 7:19).

18 Yea, a man may say, Thou hast faith, and I have works: shew me thy faith without thy works, and I will shew thee my faith by my works. 19 Thou believest that there is one God; thou doest well: the devils also believe, and tremble. 20 But wilt thou know, O vain man, that faith without works is dead?

Having stated his proposition with rhetorical and hypothetical questions that beg an obvious answer, James next argues his case via a fictional debater. Person A has faith without deeds; Person B has faith with deeds. From Person A, James asks for evidence of the faith he claimed to possess, reminding him that even demons can make such claims. For Person B, the evidence of faith speaks for itself—the deeds are the evidence.

21 Was not Abraham our father justified by works, when he had offered Isaac his son upon the altar? 22 Seest thou how faith wrought with his works, and by works was faith made perfect? 23 And the scripture was fulfilled which saith, Abraham believed God, and it was imputed unto him for righteousness: and he was called the Friend of God.

It would be both normal and expected for any Jew talking about faith to mention Abraham. Both Paul (Romans 4:9) and James describe God calling Abraham righteous because of his faith. James here revisits the familiar details of Abraham's "works"—offering Isaac on the

altar by faith—actively trusting God, even if it meant cooperating with God while He went against His own promise. James is saying that Abraham's obedient "work"—a tangible act of faith in putting Isaac on the altar and being willing to sacrifice even the son of promise—was a fulfillment of Scripture. James refers to Genesis 15:6 when God reckoned Abraham's faith as righteousness—a faith in the seemingly impossible covenant promise of countless generations born to an elderly couple. Abraham had faith, and God made a covenant with him. Then Abraham proved his faith with the "work" of obeying God and being willing to sacrifice Isaac.

24 Ye see then how that by works a man is justified, and not by faith only.

Having made his proposition with questions, illustrations, and an example, plus having presented an argument from the Old Testament, James makes an early conclusion prior to making yet another argument from the Old Testament. It is this statement, which too many have pulled out of the context of his carefully constructed presentation, that has caused problems and confusion through the centuries. Such approaches to interpreting Scripture are simply poor hermeneutics.

Earlier, James made a parallel argument, which also must remain within the context of his epistle, regarding being a hearer of the Word versus being a doer (1:22–25).

25 Likewise also was not Rahab the harlot justified by works, when she had received the messengers, and had sent them out another way?

James next appeals to an opposite type of character from the Old Testament for "Exhibit 2" of the argument part of his presentation. Some might feel as if they cannot relate to the head of the Jewish nation, the national shining star, Abraham. What about an example from the opposite side of society— would that be closer to home or at least more relatable? Rahab was a prostitute, yet both she and Abraham were examples of faith and works. This unlikely pair shared both differences and similarities. One was Hebrew, the other Gentile; one was called by God, the other originally destined for destruction; one was a man, the other a woman; one was the father of faith, the other a lowly prostitute; one went through a long-term process of interacting with God and proving his faith; the other only had hearsay to guide her quick thinking. For similarities, both were foreigners, both showed hospitality to strangers (Genesis 18:1–5; Joshua 2:1), and both became ancestors of Jesus (Matthew 1:2, 5). Rahab took her place in history next to Abraham because she had faith in God and acted on her faith—a simple but profound lesson that is completely transcultural for all believers.

26 For as the body without the spirit is dead, so faith without works is dead also.

James makes his second parallel conclusion, creating a second passage that many after him would neatly clip from its clear context and use to make claims that do not square with either James' complete argument or the whole counsel of God from both testaments. The concept of faith without works is so easy that even demons can do it. No lifestyle change is needed, nor are sacrifices required. No compassion is necessary, and no giving of time, treasure, or talent will be expected. Most Americans claim to be "Christian," but how many live Christian lives? Many attend church occasionally, but what are they doing during the week? A modern adage holds that standing in a donut shop doesn't make one a donut, and walking into a garage doesn't turn someone into a car, so going to a church doesn't make you a Christian. Christians would do well to cease and desist from justifying their absence or lack of compassion, and instead begin at once to incarnate the hands and feet and heart of Jesus in a cold, lonely, and desperate world.

Sources:
Adeyemo, T., I. Coulibaly, Francis I. Andersen, S. Ngewa, and H. Tewoldemedhin. *Africa Bible Commentary.* Nairobi, Kenya: Word Alive Publishers, 2006.
Blue Letter Bible. BlueLetterBible.org.
Burdick, Donald W. "James." *The Expositor's Bible Commentary with the New International Version: Hebrews, James, 1, 2 Peter, 1, 2, 3 John, Jude, Revelation, Vol. 12.* Edited by Frank E. Gaebelein. Grand Rapids, MI: Zondervan, 1981. 181–185.
Draper, Charles W., Chad Brand, and Archie England, eds. *Holman Illustrated Bible Dictionary.* Grand Rapids, MI: Holman Reference, 2003.
Earle, R., & Purkiser, W. T., eds. *Beacon Bible Commentary.* Kansas City, MO: Beacon Hill Press, 1964.
Howley, George C. D., F. F. Bruce, and Ellison, Henry L. Ellison, eds. *The New Layman's Bible Commentary in One.* Grand Rapids, MI: Zondervan, 1979.
Kistemaker, Simon J. *James and I–III John.* New Testament Commentary. Grand Rapids, MI: Baker Publishing Group, 1986. 87–102.
Martin, R. A. and John H. Elliott. *James, 1–2 Peter, Jude.* Augsburg Commentary on the New Testament. Minneapolis, MN: Fortress Press, 1982. 28–36.
Myers, Allen C., John W. Simpson, Philip A. Frank, Timothy P. Jenney, and Ralph W. Vunderink, eds. *The Eerdmans Bible Dictionary.* Grand Rapids, MI: Wm. B. Eerdmans Publishing Company, 1996.
Radmacher, Earl D., Ronald B. Allen, and H. W. House, eds. *Nelson Study Bible (NKJV).* Nashville, TN: Thomas Nelson Publishers, 2001.
Today's Parallel Bible (KJV/NIV/NASB/NLT). Grand Rapids, MI: Zondervan, 2000.

Say It Correctly

Hermeneutics. HER-meh-NOO-tix.
Imputed. im-PYUT-ed.
Rahab. RAY-hab.

Daily Bible Readings

MONDAY
Abraham Blessed for Fearing God
(Genesis 22:9–19)

TUESDAY
Spies Saved by Rahab's Quick Actions
(Joshua 2:1–7)

WEDNESDAY
Forgive Others Like God Forgave You
(Matthew 18:23–35)

THURSDAY
Devoted to Good Works, Avoiding
Distractions
(Titus 3:1–2, 8–11)

FRIDAY
Works Guided by Loyalty to God
(Deuteronomy 6:4–9)

SATURDAY
Receive God's Mercy by Showing Mercy
(James 2:8–13)

SUNDAY
Faith and Works Must Go Together
(James 2:14–26)

Notes

Teaching Tips

August 23
Bible Study Guide 12

Words You Should Know

A. Perfect (v. 2) *teleios* (Gk.)—Complete, having attained a particular virtue

B. Turn around (v. 3) *metago* (Gk.)—To guide, direct, or lead over

Teacher Preparation

Unifying Principle—Bite Your Tongue. The spoken word can be either an affirming or destructive force in the lives of vulnerable humans. How can the affirming force prevail in human interactions? James informs believers that only through the discipline required in taming the tongue can the fruits of godly wisdom be made visible in the lives of others.

A. Read the Bible Background and Devotional Reading.

B. Pray for your students and lesson clarity.

C. Read the lesson Scripture in multiple translations.

O—Open the Lesson

A. Begin the class with prayer.

B. As a class, recall the childhood chant, "Sticks and stones may break my bones, but words will never hurt me." Have students tell why they agree or disagree with the sentiment. Given what James says about the destructive power of the tongue (thus, of words), why would a parent teach a child such a slogan?

C. Have the students read the Aim for Change and the In Focus story.

D. Ask students how events like those in the story weigh on their hearts and how they can view these events from a faith perspective.

P—Present the Scriptures

A. Read the Focal Verses.

B. Have the class share what Scriptures stand out for them and why, with particular emphasis on today's context.

C. Discuss the Background and The People, Places, and Times sections.

E—Explore the Meaning

A. Use In Depth or More Light on the Text to facilitate a deeper discussion of the lesson text.

B. Pose the questions in Search the Scriptures and Discuss the Meaning.

C. Discuss the Liberating Lesson and Application for Activation sections.

N—Next Steps for Application

A. Summarize the value of using their tongues to bring healing and refreshment to others.

B. End class with a commitment to pray for consistency in speech.

Worship Guide

For the Superintendent or Teacher
Theme: Taming the Tongue
Song: "Pass It On (It Only Takes a Spark)"
Devotional Reading: Isaiah 50:4–11

Taming the Tongue

Bible Background • JAMES 3:1–12
Printed Text • JAMES 3:1–12 | Devotional Reading • ISAIAH 50:4–11

Aim for Change

By the end of the lesson, we will: EXPLAIN how James' illustrations demonstrate the power of the tongue, REPENT of times when the use of our tongues has ignited a destructive fire, and PRACTICE controlling the tongue so it becomes a consistent source of refreshment to others.

In Focus

Eugene wondered how Jerry made it through the day with everyone always angry at him over the things he said. Eugene and Jerry hung out all the time and were as tight as brothers. They had even been the best man for each other when they both got married. They lived in the same neighborhood, went to the same church, and each of them had three kids who went to the same schools and participated in Sunday school and youth activities.

However, while Eugene was well-liked and had lots of friends, that wasn't the case with Jerry. Jerry always came off as mean. He had a way of phrasing every comment like an insult. Worse, Jerry always got defensive when people told him to tone it down, or he would claim, "It was a joke; you're too sensitive!"

Eventually, people avoided talking to Jerry unless they absolutely had to. More and more, Eugene found himself making excuses for his friend—excuses his other friends didn't want to accept. Eugene was frustrated because he knew Jerry to be a good and loyal friend, but everyone they knew was put off by him. Eugene prayed that Jerry would learn to understand the effect he was having on people and to see things from the view of those who got hurt by his comments.

How can we learn to step outside of ourselves and truly be as good to others the way God wants us to be, and not just as we think we are?

Keep in Mind

"Even so the tongue is a little member, and boasteth great things. Behold, how great a matter a little fire kindleth!" (James 3:5, KJV).

"In the same way, the tongue is a small thing that makes grand speeches. But a tiny spark can set a great forest on fire" (James 3:5, NLT).

Focal Verses

KJV **James 3:1** My brethren, be not many masters, knowing that we shall receive the greater condemnation.

2 For in many things we offend all. If any man offend not in word, the same is a perfect man, and able also to bridle the whole body.

3 Behold, we put bits in the horses' mouths, that they may obey us; and we turn about their whole body.

4 Behold also the ships, which though they be so great, and are driven of fierce winds, yet are they turned about with a very small helm, whithersoever the governor listeth.

5 Even so the tongue is a little member, and boasteth great things. Behold, how great a matter a little fire kindleth!

6 And the tongue is a fire, a world of iniquity: so is the tongue among our members, that it defileth the whole body, and setteth on fire the course of nature; and it is set on fire of hell.

7 For every kind of beasts, and of birds, and of serpents, and of things in the sea, is tamed, and hath been tamed of mankind:

8 But the tongue can no man tame; it is an unruly evil, full of deadly poison.

9 Therewith bless we God, even the Father; and therewith curse we men, which are made after the similitude of God.

10 Out of the same mouth proceedeth blessing and cursing. My brethren, these things ought not so to be.

11 Doth a fountain send forth at the same place sweet water and bitter?

12 Can the fig tree, my brethren, bear olive berries? either a vine, figs? so can no fountain both yield salt water and fresh.

NLT **James 3:1** Dear brothers and sisters, not many of you should become teachers in the church, for we who teach will be judged more strictly.

2 Indeed, we all make many mistakes. For if we could control our tongues, we would be perfect and could also control ourselves in every other way.

3 We can make a large horse go wherever we want by means of a small bit in its mouth.

4 And a small rudder makes a huge ship turn wherever the pilot chooses to go, even though the winds are strong.

5 In the same way, the tongue is a small thing that makes grand speeches. But a tiny spark can set a great forest on fire.

6 And among all the parts of the body, the tongue is a flame of fire. It is a whole world of wickedness, corrupting your entire body. It can set your whole life on fire, for it is set on fire by hell itself.

7 People can tame all kinds of animals, birds, reptiles, and fish,

8 but no one can tame the tongue. It is restless and evil, full of deadly poison.

9 Sometimes it praises our Lord and Father, and sometimes it curses those who have been made in the image of God.

10 And so blessing and cursing come pouring out of the same mouth. Surely, my brothers and sisters, this is not right!

11 Does a spring of water bubble out with both fresh water and bitter water?

12 Does a fig tree produce olives, or a grapevine produce figs? No, and you can't draw fresh water from a salty spring.

The People, Places, and Times

James. The New Testament identifies several men named James, not surprising as it is derived from the Hebrew name Jacob, one of the patriarchs of Judaism. James, the son of Zebedee, had a brother John, was a fisherman by trade, and was one of Jesus' closest disciples. James, the son of Alphaeus, was another of Jesus' disciples. James is also the name of the father of Judas (not Iscariot, but another of Jesus' disciples). James, the son of Joseph and Mary, grew up with Jesus but did not believe He was the Messiah until after the Resurrection. Although there is still debate among scholars, the author of this letter is believed to be James, the younger half-brother of Jesus. James became a leader in the church at Jerusalem at a time when persecution of Jewish believers was increasing, thus scattering Christians throughout the Roman Empire. This forced many of the displaced Jewish Christians to settle in nations of unbelievers.

Background

During the time of this writing, religious leaders were no longer ignoring the new Christian church. Although they were still a part of Judaism, Christians were now being singled out, and the persecution of Christians had begun in earnest. Two other men named James mentioned in the New Testament (the apostle identified as the son of Zebedee and the brother of John, and the apostle identified as the son of Alphaeus) had been martyred. Similarly, Stephen had been stoned to death for his faith. In this increasingly hostile and dangerous atmosphere, it is not surprising that many Christians were abandoning the faith.

Internal strife was also taking place within the church. Christians were dealing with doctrinal arguments, false teachers, power struggles, gossip, and slander. The Christians were being encouraged to pursue self-fulfillment. During this time, many philosophers believed and taught the importance of knowledge for the sake of knowledge. Very little importance was placed on putting knowledge into practice. They mistakenly taught that the way to spiritual

enlightenment was through knowledge. James wrote to combat this mindset. Faith, not knowledge, is key. Our faith is rooted in our hearts; it is this faith that transforms us into "doers." James insisted Christians must seek to attain the will of God. Only then can we bring about a change in our life, and in the life of the church. The remaining apostles, as they had been instructed to do, were off on missionary efforts. It was left to James, as leader of the Jerusalem church, to encourage the Christians and to provide much-needed instruction to sustain them during this period of persecution. Like the excellent pastor he was, James taught the believers to keep their eyes on Christ, not their situation, and to continue to live lives that reflected Jesus Christ and His teachings.

At-A-Glance

1. Wisdom for Teachers (James 3:1–3)
2. Wisdom from Environment (vv. 4–6)
3. Wisdom for the Tongue (vv. 7–8)
4. Wisdom for the Double-Minded (vv. 9–12)

In Depth

1. Wisdom for Teachers (James 3:1–3)

This word of wisdom is aimed at those who would teach the Word of the Lord. Teachers are in a position to inform and misinform others. James cautions that this highly valued and respected position should not be taken lightly. James warns those who aspire to teach, informing them they would receive harsher judgment and greater condemnation. James is certainly aware of the power teachers hold in shaping the spiritual lives of others. He warns teachers to examine their motives and not be self-serving. Teachers are tasked with stronger speech ethics as a way of achieving the maturity needed to keep the "whole body" in check.

Why do teachers need to select their words carefully and weigh the effect of their words on those they lead?

2. Wisdom from Environment (vv. 4–6)

James demonstrates the challenges of taming the tongue using images of things that affect daily life and survival. Horses are a common form of land transportation, but wild horses had to be tamed in order to be useful. James describes the tongue similarly. Using a bit, a skillful rider can control the horse's every move. An experienced captain will successfully guide a ship of any size by controlling the rudder. Particularly if a ship is experiencing severe sea conditions, mastery of the rudder makes the difference between death and deliverance. James challenges believers to control their speech to avoid self-destruction. Describing the tongue as a fire, James cautions against allowing Satan to use the tongue to "setteth on fire the course of nature." The tongue has the power to ignite the fire of hell.

How can we learn to control and modify the words that come out of our mouths?

3. Wisdom for the Tongue (vv. 7–8)

James issues another startling revelation. Animals can be tamed, but the tongue cannot. Trained animals were known to be an amazing sight in the first century Greco-Roman culture. However, James says the skills do not exist that can tame the tongue. His shocking comparisons continue. Since the Fall of humanity, snakes have been considered repulsive and deadly. James similarly characterizes the untamed tongue. James' description recalls David's prayer to be delivered from evil men who "have sharpened their tongues like a serpent; adders' poison is under their lips" (Psalm 140:3). James issues this sobering reality—words kill. Without God,

James warns, believers would not only destroy other Christians but also be consumed by the deadly poison that resides within the power of the tongue.

What are some examples of how your words can produce negative impacts on someone's life?

4. Wisdom for the Double-Minded (vv. 9–12)

The contradictions James describes are reflective of our human nature. James addresses these double-minded, double-talking contradictions by using the example of believers who speak out of both sides of their mouths—blessing God, yet cursing people. God is consistent, and Christian speech must consistently reflect the heart of God. Words from the mouth speak the content of the heart (cf. Luke 6:45). James says blessings can neither come from a heart filled with venom nor can curses come from a heart of love. In much the same way that olives cannot come from a fig tree nor can a spring produce both fresh and salt water, James punctuates the need for believers to think, say, and do those things that reflect who they are in Christ. The reality of the heart will flow through the consistency of ethical speech. We can choose to listen to the voice of God and do His will, or we can choose to put ourselves first and the care, concern, and love of others last.

When people irritate you, how difficult is it to stop and pray before speaking?

Search the Scriptures

1. How does James tell us that teachers will be judged (James 3:1)?

2. In what ways does James say our lives are controlled by what we say (vv. 3–5)?

3. How does James describe the tongue (vv. 6–8)?

Discuss the Meaning

In these verses, James points out the dangers of an unbridled tongue. How have you seen the wisdom of restraining one's speech in a difficult situation make a difference in the outcome?

Liberating Lesson

What a wonderful gift speech is. Christians have the ability to exhort, coach, and build up other believers through our speech. Similarly, our words provide the vehicle to lovingly counsel the lost and to soothe and console the suffering and bereaved. This gift of speech is most perfectly employed when we speak words of truth and witness to others of God's saving plan. We must be very careful not to abuse this wonderful gift. Many Christians would never imagine causing someone physical harm. Yet this is exactly what we do when we say thoughtless, careless, and unkind things to or about others. Especially if the person or people-group we are talking about has historically not been allowed space and attention to speak for themselves, we must be careful that our words about them are loving and truthful. Each day offers us a challenge to not only walk in the will and the way of our Lord but also to speak in ways that glorify Him.

Application for Activation

It's never easy to listen to someone say unfair, incorrect, or mean-spirited things to us. Yet as Christians, we are never allowed to respond in the same matter. Our obligation is always to show a dying world that we are the children of a living God. We can only do this when our walk and our talk mirror those of our Savior. What comes out of our mouths must be loving. This means that our motivation to speak must be godly and intended to comfort, heal, and teach godly principles to others. Pray, and ask God to use your speech today as a vehicle for aid, comfort, and reconciliation.

Follow the Spirit

What God wants me to do:

_____

_____

_____

_____

Remember Your Thoughts

Special insights I have learned:

_____

_____

_____

_____

More Light on the Text

James 3:1–12

1 My brethren, be not many masters, knowing that we shall receive the greater condemnation.

The Greek word *didaskaloi* (**dee-DASS-kah-loy**), translated in the King James Version as "masters," also means "teachers." The teachers in this context were Jewish males, including the author, with expert training in the Scriptures. As such, they were authority figures held in high esteem. Some people wanted to become teachers to attain higher social status. However, those trained in the Scriptures were also charged with imparting to the community how to live according to God's will. Therefore, they were held to a higher standard. If they led the believers astray, they would be judged and suffer condemnation (Gk. *krima*, **KREE-mah**) more harshly than others. Technically, *krima* could be any sentence passed by a judge in a court, but it is almost always used to describe a negative judgment, making condemnation an appropriate translation.

2 For in many things we offend all. If any man offend not in word, the same is a perfect man, and able also to bridle the whole body.

The Greek word for "offend" is *ptaio* (**PTAH-yo**) and means to stumble. James acknowledged that as human beings we too often get tripped up and do or say things unintentionally. But the person who has the ability to guard his speech achieves perfection in disciplining his entire body. The Greek word for "perfect" (*teleios*, **TEH-lay-oce**), when referring to human beings, does not mean without sin. Rather, it symbolizes completion, the attainment of virtue in a moral sense. For example, the person who is able to deal with young children without complaining or anger is considered perfect in patience. A "bridle" (Gk. *chalinos*, **khah-lee-NOCE**) is literally a harness that fits over a horse's head. It has a bit that fits into the horse's mouth and reins that guide the animal in the direction it should go. Figuratively, to "bridle" one's speech means to show restraint.

3 Behold, we put bits in the horses' mouths, that they may obey us; and we turn about their whole body.

Horses were a common mode of transportation in the first century. Soldiers also used them in battles whether as cavalry mounts or as chariot teams. People who ride horses use a bridle to control or guide the horse's movement. The horse responds to the tugging on the bit in its mouth by turning its whole body in the direction its rider wants it to go. Likewise, when we demonstrate the ability to control our speech, we display the discipline to govern other parts of our body and guide them in the direction they should go.

4 Behold also the ships, which though they be so great, and are driven of fierce winds, yet are they turned about with a very small helm, whithersoever the governor listeth.

James furthers his argument on the importance of selecting teachers who have mastered the ability to guard their speech (and therefore their whole bodies) by using the example of a ship at sea being steered by something as small as a rudder. The Greek verb *metago* (**meh-TAH-go**) means to guide, direct, or lead over. Similar to the horse, a large ship, which needs the power of strong winds in order to move it, is able to be steered this way or that by a relatively small rudder.

5 Even so the tongue is a little member, and boasteth great things. Behold, how great a matter a little fire kindleth!

James finally gets to the heart of his sermon: that something as small as the tongue can wield great power for good or evil. The forest fire metaphor is a good example of how a single spark can start a fire that can quickly burn out of control. If the right person is in control of speech, then he or she can guide others in the right way to go. Likewise, a single word by a person with no self-control can do damage that can take months or even years to repair.

6 And the tongue is a fire, a world of iniquity: so is the tongue among our members, that it defileth the whole body, and setteth on fire the course of nature; and it is set on fire of hell. 7 For every kind of beasts, and of birds, and of serpents, and of things in the sea, is tamed, and hath been tamed of mankind.

James returns again to the metaphor of the tongue represented by the teacher within the community whose speech could bring good or evil to bear. This verse is obscure, and many scholars have found it difficult to interpret. The world of first-century Rome was far removed from our contemporary society, and many of the metaphors and images used in ancient writings such as the Bible are unfamiliar to today's readers. The Greek word for "iniquity," elsewhere translated unrighteousness, is *adikia* (**ah-dee-KEE-ah**) and means a deed violating law and justice, as in an unfair judge. A biased judge who hands down an unjust ruling negatively impacts the individual, his or her family, and the whole community. Or the tongue, with its potential for sin, represents a smaller version of the potential for all of humanity to sin. James likened the tongue to a living being. However, in contrast to all the creatures of the land and sea which human beings are capable of restraining and taming (Gk. *damazo*, **dah-MOD-zo**), humans appear to be incapable of taming the tongue.

8 But the tongue can no man tame; it is an unruly evil, full of deadly poison.

We might believe that James exaggerated the power of the tongue by comparing it to fires raging out of control. However, he takes very seriously the power of someone in the authority position of a teacher to do great harm if he does not have the ability to control his speech. James refers to the tongue as "an unruly evil" (Gk. *kakon*, **kak-ON**). In the Greco-Roman context of the first century, the word "evil" meant to be foul or rotten down to the bone. It was an inward decay, somewhat like cancer developing and spreading through one's body. Anyone who has ever been the victim of slander knows how lies left unchallenged can destroy careers and lives.

9 Therewith bless we God, even the Father; and therewith curse we men, which are made after the similitude of God.

It is ironic that the very same tongue we use to bless God is also used to curse others.

To bless (*eulogeo*, **yew-low-GEH-oh**) someone is to speak well of them or to praise them. In contrast, "to curse" (Gk. *kataraomai*, **kah-tah-RAH-oh-my**) someone means to doom or call down evil upon him or her. As creatures made in the image and likeness (Gk. *homoiosis*, **hoe-MOY-oh-sees**) of God, we should have only good words for one another.

10 Out of the same mouth proceedeth blessing and cursing. My brethren, these things ought not so to be.

The Greek word for "mouth," *stoma* (**STOW-ma**), refers both to the physical facial feature and to speech, especially eloquent speech. It also means the point on a sword. Metaphorically, the tongue can be a sharp sword cutting down people with insults and imprecations. Or it can offer words of praise that lift up people. The notion that both virtuous and vile speech can come from the same source is anathema to James.

11 Doth a fountain send forth at the same place sweet water and bitter?

Fresh or living (Gk. *glukus*, **gloo-KOOS**, literally "sweet") water is from a new or previously unused source. Bitter or brackish (Gk. *pikros*, **peek-ROCE**) water is fresh water mixed with salt water, such as in river estuaries. Living water is uncontaminated and refreshing; you wouldn't want to drink from brackish water that has not been treated to remove the salty taste. Those of us who grew up in urban areas have probably never encountered brackish water. However, those from rural areas likely learned as children not to drink such water. James rhetorically asks whether fresh and brackish water can come from the same source, knowing that his audience, who had come in contact with both types of water, would answer no.

12 Can the fig tree, my brethren, bear olive berries? either a vine, figs? so can no fountain both yield salt water and fresh.

Being an effective preacher requires delivering a message using illustrations your audience is familiar with. James does a commendable job demonstrating his point using metaphors, images, and illustrations from the world around his audience, such as the modes of travel to the methods of agriculture. Anyone who has ever cultivated or produced crops for food knows that a fig tree cannot yield olives any more than a grapevine can produce figs. This would be an aberration of nature. The fig tree can only produce figs and the olive tree only olives, as is their nature. Likewise, salt (Gk. *halukos*, **hah-loo-KOCE**) water cannot yield sweet (fresh) water. James is making the point that a person with an evil disposition is not likely to be virtuous, as it is not in them to do so.

Sources:

Bauer, Walter, William F. Arndt, F. Wilbur Gingrich, and Frederick W. Danker. *A Greek-English Lexicon of the New Testament and Other Early Christian Literature, Second Edition*. Chicago: University of Chicago Press, 1979.

Bible Study Tools. www.BibleStudyTools.com. *Bakers Evangelical Dictionary*. "James." http://www.biblestudytools.com/dictionaries/bakers-evangelical-dictionary/James-theology

Davids, Peter H. *The Epistle of James*. The New International Greek Testament Commentary. Grand Rapids, MI: Wm. B. Eerdmans Publishing Company, 1982.

Got Questions Ministries. "Book of James." http://www.gotquestions.org/Book-of-James.html

HarperCollins Study Bible (NRSV). New York: Harper Collins Publishers, 2006. 2052–2058.

Daily Bible Readings

MONDAY
Unwise Not to Listen to Teachers
(Proverbs 5:7–14)

TUESDAY
Testimony of a Wise Teacher
(Isaiah 50:4–11)

WEDNESDAY
Slander and Abusive Language Not Allowed
(Colossians 3:1–11)

THURSDAY
Use Tongue to Speak God's Praise
(Psalm 119:169–176)

FRIDAY
Believers Anointed with Fire and Tongues
(Acts 2:1–12)

SATURDAY
Tongues and Teachers Are God's Gifts
(1 Corinthians 12:27–31)

SUNDAY
Speech Is for Healing and Refreshment
(James 3:1–12)

Say It Correctly

Alphaeus. **AL**-fee-us.
Zebedee. **ZEH**-buh-dee.

Teaching Tips

Words You Should Know

A. Glory (v. 14) *katakauchaomai* (Gk.)—Arrogant boasting above someone; vaunting one's self; assuming superiority over another

B. Sensual (v. 15) *psuchikos* (Gk.)—Belonging to the material rather than the spiritual world, stimulating only the body

Teacher Preparation

Unifying Principle—Wise Up! Throughout history, many have risked their lives by resisting oppressive regimes, thus saving the lives of others. What motivates a person to defy evil and choose to act for the good of strangers? James compares and contrasts the consequences of using wisdom for righteousness or for evil.

A. Read the Bible Background and Devotional Reading.

B. Pray for your students and lesson clarity.

C. Read the lesson Scripture in multiple translations.

O—Open the Lesson

A. Begin the class with prayer.

B. Invite participants to a time of reflection on whether they have been using godly or earthly wisdom to make recent decisions. Encourage repentance from the latter.

C. Have the students read the Aim for Change and the In Focus story.

D. Ask students how events like those in the story weigh on their hearts and how they can view these events from a faith perspective.

P—Present the Scriptures

A. Read the Focal Verses.

B. Have the class share what Scriptures stand out for them and why, with particular emphasis on today's context.

C. Discuss the Background and The People, Places, and Times sections.

E—Explore the Meaning

A. Use In Depth or More Light on the Text to facilitate a deeper discussion of the lesson text.

B. Pose the questions in Search the Scriptures and Discuss the Meaning.

C. Discuss the Liberating Lesson and Application for Activation sections.

N—Next Steps for Application

A. Summarize the value of acting with patience and in godly wisdom.

B. End class with a commitment to pray for accepting God's wisdom as a way of life.

Worship Guide

For the Superintendent or Teacher
Theme: Two Kinds of Wisdom
Song: "Jesus, Lover of My Soul"
Devotional Reading: Psalm 32:1–11

Two Kinds of Wisdom

Bible Background • JAMES 3:13–18; 5:7–12
Printed Text • JAMES 3:13–18; 5:7–12 | Devotional Reading • PSALM 32:1–11

—————— Aim for Change ——————

By the end of the lesson, we will: DESCRIBE the value of acting with wisdom from above and patience in the midst of trials, TURN from actions that have been done out of earthly wisdom and lack of patience, and EMBRACE wisdom from God and seek to demonstrate it.

—————— In Focus ——————

"Why does everybody act like Mr. Morris is so great?" Delilah asked. "He's not all that."

"Mr. Morris?" Serena replied. "Mr. Morris is great. I've been buying from him for years. He never brags about anything; he just gets the job done."

Mr. Morris ran the corner store and pharmacy. The store had been in the neighborhood and his family for three generations. Delilah was starting to patronize a new store in the area because she had some complaints about Mr. Morris. "The steps and the sidewalk outside are always dirty, and there are always people hanging by the door asking for money and prices are too high. Yet, Mr. Morris does nothing about it."

"The prices are what they are," Serena pointed out. "And as for how Mr. Morris runs his place, it's what he doesn't do that's more important. Mr. Morris doesn't hassle people for being broke. The other place does." Serena went on, "And Mr. Morris knows his customers because he's built up relationships over the years. It isn't like that at the chain, and you know it. Didn't you tell me last week that every time you go in, there's always a new team of workers?"

With her hands on her hips, Serena finished, "Mr. Morris runs a good place. You would see that if you weren't so cranky. It's God's role to judge, not ours."

Could we measure up if God judged us the way we judge other people?

—————— Keep in Mind ——————

"But the wisdom that is from above is first pure, then peaceable, gentle, and easy to be intreated, full of mercy and good fruits, without partiality, and without hypocrisy" (James 3:17, KJV).

"But the wisdom from above is first of all pure. It is also peace loving, gentle at all times, and willing to yield to others. It is full of mercy and the fruit of good deeds. It shows no favoritism and is always sincere" (James 3:17, NLT).

Focal Verses

KJV James 3:13 Who is a wise man and endued with knowledge among you? let him shew out of a good conversation his works with meekness of wisdom.

14 But if ye have bitter envying and strife in your hearts, glory not, and lie not against the truth.

15 This wisdom descendeth not from above, but is earthly, sensual, devilish.

16 For where envying and strife is, there is confusion and every evil work.

17 But the wisdom that is from above is first pure, then peaceable, gentle, and easy to be intreated, full of mercy and good fruits, without partiality, and without hypocrisy.

18 And the fruit of righteousness is sown in peace of them that make peace.

James 5:7 Be patient therefore, brethren, unto the coming of the Lord. Behold, the husbandman waiteth for the precious fruit of the earth, and hath long patience for it, until he receive the early and latter rain.

8 Be ye also patient; stablish your hearts: for the coming of the Lord draweth nigh.

9 Grudge not one against another, brethren, lest ye be condemned: behold, the judge standeth before the door.

10 Take, my brethren, the prophets, who have spoken in the name of the Lord, for an example of suffering affliction, and of patience.

11 Behold, we count them happy which endure. Ye have heard of the patience of Job, and have seen the end of the Lord; that the Lord is very pitiful, and of tender mercy.

12 But above all things, my brethren, swear not, neither by heaven, neither by the earth, neither by any other oath: but let your yea be yea; and your nay, nay; lest ye fall into condemnation.

NLT James 3:13 If you are wise and understand God's ways, prove it by living an honorable life, doing good works with the humility that comes from wisdom.

14 But if you are bitterly jealous and there is selfish ambition in your heart, don't cover up the truth with boasting and lying.

15 For jealousy and selfishness are not God's kind of wisdom. Such things are earthly, unspiritual, and demonic.

16 For wherever there is jealousy and selfish ambition, there you will find disorder and evil of every kind.

17 But the wisdom from above is first of all pure. It is also peace loving, gentle at all times, and willing to yield to others. It is full of mercy and the fruit of good deeds. It shows no favoritism and is always sincere.

18 And those who are peacemakers will plant seeds of peace and reap a harvest of righteousness.

James 5:7 Dear brothers and sisters, be patient as you wait for the Lord's return. Consider the farmers who patiently wait for the rains in the fall and in the spring. They eagerly look for the valuable harvest to ripen.

8 You, too, must be patient. Take courage, for the coming of the Lord is near.

9 Don't grumble about each other, brothers and sisters, or you will be judged. For look—the Judge is standing at the door!

10 For examples of patience in suffering, dear brothers and sisters, look at the prophets who spoke in the name of the Lord.

11 We give great honor to those who endure under suffering. For instance, you know about Job, a man of great endurance. You can see how the Lord was kind to him at the end, for the Lord is full of tenderness and mercy.

12 But most of all, my brothers and sisters, never take an oath, by heaven or earth or anything else. Just say a simple yes or no, so that you will not sin and be condemned.

The People, Places, and Times

Oath. Covenants were always confirmed or accompanied by an oath (cf. Genesis 26:28; Ezekiel 17:18). The oath by which allegiance to the covenant was sworn involved a self-cursing formula to guard against disobedience. A person who enters a covenant places himself in the position where curses will fall upon him if he violates the covenant obligations. The Mosaic Law commands that Israelites swear by God's name (Deuteronomy 10:20). Taking a sworn oath in the Lord's name declared acceptance of God as their highest authority. Jesus cautions, however, not to make oaths at all, but to be known as so faithful to your word that you do not need to swear (Matthew 5:33–37).

Background

The thesis of the book of James, Jesus' half-brother, can be found in James 2:17: that faith alone without works is dead. This is not contradictory to Paul's treatment of faith or the claim central to the Reformation that justification is by faith alone. Like John Calvin, the Reformation theologian, said, "We dream neither of a faith devoid of good works nor of a justification that stands without them." Instead, we know that true faith is always accompanied by good works, and the book of James reminds us of what those good works look like. This does not mean that as Christians, we work to earn God's approval, as such work will never yield the result we want, which is perfection. Instead, faith links us to Christ, who justifies us and sanctifies us. As we look to the wisdom that James teaches us, let us remember the right relationship between faith and works: that in the life of the Christian, they are distinct but inseparable.

The book itself is referred to by some as the New Testament book of Proverbs. Such a characterization is not unfounded. Here, proper patterns of Christian behavior are set with an emphasis on the commitment that the Christian is to have to the poor, the widow

and the orphan, those whom the LORD has expressed a special care for.

In Depth

1. Two Types of Wisdom (James 3:13–18)

According to James, there is false wisdom that stems from bitter jealousy and self-interest. In fact, these are demonic impulses because they run counter to the values imparted by the Gospel. Jealousy and bitterness suggest discontentment, which runs counter to the message throughout the Scriptures that in Christ, we have all that we need. Self-interest and a mind constantly curved in on itself suggest a self-absorption that does not readily lead to a love of God and love of neighbor, the two great commandments. According to James, it is these impulses that undergird all types of sin. Alternatively, we are to be peacemakers, sowing seeds of purity, peace, and gentleness. By showing mercy because Christ has been merciful to us, impartiality because Christ's grace was extended to us without bias, and sincerity because of the full commitment that Christ exhibited on the cross, we exhibit the wisdom from above.

When have envy and covetousness blinded you to your love of neighbor?

2. Endure! (James 5:7–12)

In the midst of trials, perhaps the last thing we want to hear is the encouragement to endure. Often while suffering, we just want the suffering to stop. Unfortunately, life in a fallen world is full of suffering, so James' advice is appropriate throughout our lives: Be patient for the coming of the Lord. We are not to grumble as the people of Israel did at the brink of the Red Sea crossing and in the wilderness, for such a response reveals a lack of gratefulness for the gracious deliverance that the Lord has given us. Instead, James encourages us to look to the prophets and to Job as models. At first glance, even this seems difficult, as the prophets were, for the most part, reluctant, and Job's suffering was compounded by friends who were not understanding. But each of those stories end with the Lord's vindication, and so also will our stories end.

Relate a time when the Lord alleviated your suffering, whether through a friend or other means.

Search the Scriptures

1. James says seeds of peace sprout into what plant?

2. What actions lead to judgment and condemnation (James 5:9, 12)?

Discuss the Meaning

1. Is the Christian life of wisdom easier or more difficult than life without it?

2. What is the best remedy for envy?

Liberating Lesson

The book of James lends itself to application quite easily, as application is the theme of the entire book. Like the book of Proverbs, the book points us to wisdom, the right use of knowledge. This is the stem from which good works flower and the root of that plant is the Holy Spirit. This is a plant that merits daily watering through immersion in the Word and prayer, as we seek the Lord for daily wisdom. When you work, submit each conversation to the test: Am I seeking and encouraging the wisdom from above or so-called wisdom from below? Are my conversations pure? Do they flow with mercy? Do they yield good fruit? Or do they yield bitterness and anxiety? Asking these questions of ourselves can guide us as we seek the sanctification that only the Holy Spirit can truly offer.

Application for Activation

When you suffer misfortune, immediately run to the Lord in prayer and ask for endurance. Sometimes it is best not to pray that the trial will end, but that God will make you strong enough to go through it.

Pray daily for the coming of the Lord. Orient your heart toward that day when all suffering shall cease.

Follow the Spirit

What God wants me to do:

_____

_____

_____

_____

Remember Your Thoughts

Special insights I have learned:

_____

_____

_____

_____

More Light on the Text
James 3:13–18; 5:7–12

James 3:1–12 cautions would-be teachers to exercise proper stewardship of the tongue especially since more will be required of them. Improper use of the tongue seemed to have been a big issue in James' community, for he repeatedly revisits it. This time he commends those who control their tongues calling them perfect (vv. 1–2); he illustrates the power of the tongue—it is like a bridle to a horse and a rudder to a ship (vv. 3–5); he likens it to a small spark that can ignite a fire to consume a forest and to a fire that can cause a world of iniquity—it can cause havoc to its owner and be destructive in the community (v. 6).

To exhibit the unruliness of the tongue, he notes that while it is possible to train savage creatures, people find it impossible to train the tongue. He climaxes the section by showing the paradox of how we use the tongue—to hallow God, the Father, and to curse people who are made in God's image. He shows that just as it is impossible to have the same fountain produce bitter and sweet water simultaneously and for a fig tree to bear olives, even so, we cannot have blessings and cursing coming from the same tongue. This week's lesson is set directly following these arguments.

13 Who is a wise man and endued with knowledge among you? Let him shew out of a good conversation his works with meekness of wisdom.

James begins with a rhetorical challenge, asking who is wise among his audience. The question implies that then as now, there were those who opined that they are wiser and more understanding than others and could perform actions better. Rather than condemning or refuting their claim, James challenges them to prove it through their conduct. This directive is aimed at the would-be teachers addressed earlier (3:1). Here James is inquiring whether or not they have the wisdom to match their claim—to be practical teachers. Note his question, asking for someone both "wise" (Gk. *sophos*, **sow-FOCE**, a practical teacher) and understanding (Gk. *epistemon*, **eh-pee-STAY-mohn**, an expert,

skilled, and scientific person). If such persons are present, James challenges them to show it by their "conversation" (Gk. *anastrophe*, **ah-na-strow-FEE**)—their conduct, walk, and excellent manner of life. Such people would especially show meekness, or a gentle manner. Mere intellectual acumen does not make a great teacher—comportment is a great contributor.

14 But if ye have bitter envying and strife in your hearts, glory not, and lie not against the truth. 15 This wisdom descendeth not from above, but is earthly, sensual, devilish. 16 For where envying and strife is, there is confusion and every evil work.

James now sets forth two possible paths for the way forward—a negative and a positive. The first is a path to shun. Envy (Gk. *zelos*, **ZAY-loce**), by itself, is not necessarily negative. *Pikros* (Gk. **pee-KROCE**) is added to denote its negative implication. Bitter envy can best be characterized as jealousy, which will lead to strife. Implicit in the statement is the notion that the hearts of some would-be teachers were bitter with envy, jealousy, self-seeking, dissension, and pride. This naturally led to feelings of superiority on their part and inferiority on that of others. James strongly warns them not to take pride in that state. He employs the word *katakauchaomai* (**ka-ta-kow-KHA-oh-my**), which connotes vaunting one's self or assuming superiority over another. This says any who call themselves Christian who display such attitudes are misrepresenting Jesus. This calls for recognition of the fact that, as the name implies, a Christian is an imitator of Jesus Christ whom we must be careful not to misrepresent.

Verse 15 informs us that this kind of wisdom—that which allows talk that is inconsistent with the life—doesn't have its roots in the divine realm. This is significant, for he had already shown that all true wisdom or gifts come from God (James 1:5, 17). Such wisdom, he says, is earthly (Gk. *epigeios*, **eh-PEE-gay-oce**; literally "upon the earth"), meaning it has its genesis on earth and would thus be subject to earthly limitations; and sensual (*psuchikos*, **puh-soo-khee–KOCE**), meaning it belongs to the material rather than the spiritual life, stimulating only the body. Finally, he says it is devilish—demonic or demon-like.

Sadly found in some church and organizations, envious and self-seeking actions cause a factious rivalry. They often have their source in the same outlook that produced the first sin—the desire for personal gain. Often, it is cleverly hidden from unsuspecting adherents until too late.

The first sin was rooted in self, and it is still at the base of every sin. Not only are selfish ambition and factiousness rooted in selfishness, so are divisive and destructive behavior. One feels no jealousy or envy of another unless one compares oneself with another and determines she or he is ahead. Envy and self-seeking also produce "confusion," that is, a disorder that comes from instability. We must decide not to follow the devil's footsteps but to guard against his wiles. This requires self-control and constant connection with our source of help—Jesus.

17 But the wisdom that is from above is first pure, then peaceable, gentle, and easy to be intreated, full of mercy and good fruits, without partiality, and without hypocrisy. 18 And the fruit of righteousness is sown in peace of them that make peace.

The second path is the direct opposite of the first. It comes from God—it is from above. Christians need to saturate their environment with prayer and the Word. They need to cast down the world's wisdom so Christ can enter and God's wisdom can take residence. The characteristics James outlines set heavenly wisdom apart from the earthly. The traits listed are those that would be in demand in any organization and desirable for any good teacher.

Possessors would thrive in a church setting or a school environment. It is evident that those possessing them are gifted by the Holy Spirit and are in union with divine agencies. Looking at some of the qualities listed will prove helpful for disciples and teachers.

James says those who possess heavenly wisdom will be pure. This means it is devoid of ulterior motives and self-interest. The next characteristic is peaceable. The root word is peace, which implies that this wisdom or its owner promotes peace. Contrary to popular belief, peace is not necessarily the absence of strife. It has the Hebrew *shalom* in purview and references a well-being that emanates from knowing all is well with God, and He is our friend. Such vertical connections naturally have horizontal dimensions that enrich and empower the possessor's interpersonal relationships.

James further lists the characteristics of gentleness (equitableness), charitable giving, mercy, fruitfulness in the faith, fairness, and sincerity. These are wonderful traits to possess and practice for eternity preparation and kingdom building. Those who follow us want us to be genuine and sincere. God expects us to be genuine and sincere.

The chapter climaxes with a very profound statement. It states that the outcomes of justice emanate from peace and are found in those who cultivate peace. Some people appear to thrive on conflict or contention. They seem to hate peace. James says, on the contrary, there are those who cultivate peace and sow seeds that bear fruit in righteousness. Love and peace should lubricate every Christian's actions and interactions.

James 5:7–12

James 5:1–6 outlines unjust practices for Christians generally and employers particularly, especially the selfish rich. It invites them not to mistreat employees but to pay honest wages, refrain from wanton luxurious living at the expense of workers, and refrain from condemning and murdering innocent people. James advises the selfish rich that their greed stores up for them the fires of hell and that the cries of their mistreated workers have not gone unnoticed by the Lord of Hosts. Our passage follows this section. Yet, it is important to note that James was not scolding, castigating, ostracizing, or berating the wealthy for being rich. Rather, he was advising them on what riches could do to them and of the impending judgment that was certain to accompany their choice. While we are moral agents free to make our own decisions, there are consequences that accompany the choices we make. James lays out some of these consequences here for all to see.

7 Be patient therefore, brethren, unto the coming of the Lord. Behold, the husbandman waiteth for the precious fruit of the earth, and hath long patience for it, until he receive the early and latter rain. 8 Be ye also patient; stablish your hearts: for the coming of the Lord draweth nigh.

The "therefore" shows a tie with what precedes it, but the context is a change of both addresses and subject. His talk to the selfish rich about the judgment brings him to address the saints who are oppressed. It marks a shift from censure of the rich to the exhortation of the saints. This is visible by his return to the endearing word "brethren" (Gk. *adelphos*, **ah-del-FOCE**). He begins with a call to patience. Patience here is not the usual word but comes from a compound word implying being of a long spirit and not losing heart.

They must be patient for the coming (Gk. *parousia*, **pah-roo-SEE-ah**) of the Lord, that is, the Second Advent. Apparently, then, like now there were those who were restless about an apparent delay in the Advent, especially in the face of the unjust practices of the rich. These rich are prospering despite their unjust

behaviors, unholy actions, and murderous practices. But verse 5 predicts their impending judgment. Christians should thus be patient, for the reign of terror by the rich and their instigator—Satan—might be long but won't be forever. The wicked shall not reign forever over God's people. Their demise is coming. In the meantime, we must be patient.

James' exhortation gives overt expression and responds to an implied question his readers may have had. This question, given all the injustices of the rich, or why are they still prospering and for how long will they continue to reign over God's people, was not new. David had grappled with it (Psalms 73:2–3), as did the prophet Habakkuk (Habakkuk 1:1–4).

Many of us may still be grappling with this question. We too need to take heart, learn from James' response, and continue to set our timers and remember the Second Coming of Christ. It is much nearer now than then. It is later than we think. Therefore, look beyond the problems or difficulties of the present to the goal ahead. Set your gazes on it, get your motivation from it, and let it brighten any dark spots in life.

To strengthen his point, James used an illustration from nature/agriculture. Biblical society was agrarian; hence, much of its imagery reflect that setting. Here James says after planting seeds a farmer must wait for the harvest since nothing he does can control the process. Palestine is very dry and arid between June and September. The autumn (early) rains came in mid-October to November to soften and water the ground to allow the farmer to plow and plant seeds. The December/January rainfall penetrated the soil deeply thus allowing the crops to grow. Without this rain, the seeds would not germinate. The spring (latter) rain coming in March/April was eagerly anticipated, for it was needed to ready and promote the maturing and ripening of the grain for harvest. Without it there would be no crop to harvest.

James used this geographical phenomenon for spiritual and theological significance as the Old Testament prophets had done. Jesus sowed the seeds. Just as the farmer need the patience to wait for nature to do its work to ensure a good harvest, so Christians must be patient to allow Christ's agent—the Holy Spirit—to attain a good work in and through them. In light of this, Christians are exhorted to be patient and to make their heart stable.

9 Grudge not one against another, brethren, lest ye be condemned: behold, the judge standeth before the door.

The brethren were groaning against each other regarding the problems. A common human propensity in stressful times is to turn on each other. James implores them to stop and gives them the purpose for his call—so they are not condemned. This call is reminiscent of Jesus' warning not to judge because we would be judged by the same measurement (Matthew 7:1–2). James gives another reason for his call—the judge is at the door—another reminder that Jesus is coming soon.

10 Take, my brethren, the prophets, who have spoken in the name of the Lord, for an example of suffering affliction, and of patience. 11 Behold, we count them happy which endure. Ye have heard of the patience of Job and have seen the end of the Lord; that the Lord is very pitiful, and of tender mercy.

To ensure he reached the hearts of his readers with his urgent and vital appeal, James went from "brethren" (*adelphos*, v. 9), to "my brethren" (*adelphos mou*, v. 10). This builds affection and grabs attention. To further reinforce the need for patience, he cites the prophets, who spoke in the Lord's name, as examples of suffering and patience. One would think that to speak on behalf of God would have granted the prophets respect and

shielded them from the people's venom, but sadly their position rarely commanded respect and was often at odds with the powerful. Some were mistreated, others were executed, some were killed, but all faced intense opposition. Their perseverance and steadfast courage despite these odds can serve to uplift the discouraged as they model how to patiently endure suffering.

James follows up with the universal truth that those who endure are considered happy. He then cites the patience of Job, who neither complained nor renounced his faith under severe pressures and who was richly rewarded thereafter by God. God can be depended upon, for God has pity and is full of mercy (cf. Psalm 136).

12 But above all things, my brethren, swear not, neither by heaven, neither by the earth, neither by any other oath: but let your yea be yea; and your nay, nay; lest ye fall into condemnation.

This verse is somewhat problematic in that it seems not to connect with either what precedes it or what follows. While the prior verses deal with patience and the succeeding verses with prayer, one must recall that the original was not separated by punctuation. That said, we must note that the section begins with a command not to grumble against each other. A climax that calls for Christians to be circumspect in their speech is fitting and poignant. To provide this climax, Jesus' words in the Sermon on the Mount seem to have influenced James. Swearing here does not refer to the use of expletives or curse words. It is a prohibition against oaths, a call to take our words seriously. Too many are content with the idea that a word is wind forgetting that it is irretrievable once released. A call to let our "Yes" be "Yes," and your "No" be "No" is an appeal for our words to show integrity.

Sources:

Arndt, William and F. Wilbur Gingrich. *A Greek-English Lexicon of the New Testament*. Chicago: The University of Chicago Press, 1959.

Barclay, William. *The Letters of James and Peter, Rev. Ed.* The Daily Bible Study Series. Philadelphia, PA: The Westminster Press, 1976.

Blunt, Brian K., gen. ed. *True to Our Native Land: An African American New Testament Commentary*. Minneapolis, MN: Fortress Press, 2007.

Keener, Craig S. *The IVP Bible Background Commentary: New Testament, James*. Downers Grove, IL: InterVarsity Academic Press, 1993.

Loh, I-Jin and Howard A. Hatton, *A Translator's Handbook on the Letter From James, Online edition*. New York: United Bible Societies, 1997), 11–12.

Melbourne, Bertram L. *The Practical Christian: Money, Mouth, Mind and More*. Hagerstown, MD: Review and Herald Publishing Association, 2014.

Nicholl, Francis D. *The SDA Bible Commentary, Vol. 7*. Hagerstown, MD: Review and Herald Publishing Association, 1980.

Robertson, A.T. *Word Pictures in the New Testament*. Nashville,TN: Broadman Press, 1930.

Spence-Jones, D. M. ed. *The Pulpit Commentary, The Epistle of James*. New York: Funk & Wagnalls Company, 1978.

Wiersby, Warren W. *The Bible Expository Commentary*. Wheaton, IL: Victory Books, 1989.

Say It Correctly

Stablish. **STAB**-lish.
Fastiousness. fuh-**SEE**-shuss-ness.

Daily Bible Readings

MONDAY
Wisdom About End Time Signs
(Matthew 24:3–14)

TUESDAY
Wisdom for Speaking a Prophetic Message
(Jeremiah 38:1–6)

WEDNESDAY
Wisdom in Knowing Hearts Without Blame
(1 Thessalonians 3:6–13)

THURSDAY
Wisdom in Speaking Clearly
(Matthew 5:33–37)

FRIDAY
Living Gracefully with One Another
(1 Peter 4:7–11)

SATURDAY
Wisdom in the Prayer of Faith
(James 5:13–20)

SUNDAY
Acting Wisely with Patience and Love
(James 3:13–18; 5:7–12)

Notes

A

Abomination: A foul and detestable thing

Affliction: Anguish, burden, persecution, tribulation, or trouble

Angel: A messenger of God, not eternal or all-knowing; specific types include cherubim and seraphim

Ascension: Raising up in authority or physical place. Can especially refer to the event forty days after Jesus' death, burial, and Resurrection, when He returned to heaven to sit at the right hand of the Father (Acts 1:9–11)

Atone: To propitiate, satisfy the demands of an offended holy God; or reconcile to a holy God after sin

B

Baptize: To dip, immerse, or submerge

Blameless: Irreproachable, faultless, flawless

Blessedness: Happiness, joy, or prosperity, to be well spoken of by God or others

Bless the Lord: To bend the knee in praise to God

Blood of the Lamb: The blood that Jesus shed on the Cross that redeems humanity

Bowels: To ancient Middle Easterners, the place of emotion, distress, or love

C

Called by God: Appointed or commissioned to fulfill a task

Charge: Admonish, order, command

Chosen: To be approved and selected by God

Christ: The Anointed One, the expected Messiah the Jews hoped for and whom Christians believe came as Jesus of Nazareth

Commandments: God's mandates; the entire body of Laws issued by God through Moses for Israel

Conduct: Manner of living

Confess: To acknowledge or fully agree

Consider: To determine or make out

Covenant: An agreement or promise between God and humanity based on God's character, strength, and grace

Crucifixion: A method of Roman execution in which a criminal was hung on a cross

D

Decalogue: From "ten words" in Greek; the Ten Commandments

Desolation: The state of being deserted or uninhabited

Disciples: Learners, students, followers

Dominion: Rule or reign

Dwelling place: A person's refuge or home

E

El: The Hebrew word for "god" or "mighty one"

Evil: Bad, unpleasant, or displeasing things

Evil doer: A malefactor, wrongdoer, criminal, troublemaker

Evil spirits: Messengers and ministers of the devil

Exalt: To raise up to the highest degree possible

Exhortation: Giving someone motivation to change his or her behavior either by rebuke or encouragement

F

Faithfulness: Steadfastness, steadiness

Fear of the Lord: Reverence or awe of who God is, resulting in obedience to Him and abstaining from evil

G

Glory: Splendor, unparalleled honor, dignity, or distinction; praise and worship

God's bride: The church

God's own hand: God's strength, power

Gospel: The Good News of Jesus the Messiah's arrival and presence of His kingdom

Graven image: An idol cut (often from stone, wood, or metal) and worshiped as a god

Great Tribulation: A time of great suffering that has not been experienced since the world began (Matthew 24:21, Revelation 7:14)

H

Hallowed: Consecrated, dedicated, or set apart

Hear: Listen to, yield to, or obey

Hearken: Pay attention to, give attention to

Heart: The figurative place of emotion and passion

Heathens: The Gentiles, all those who are not a part of the people of God

Holy: Anything consecrated and set aside for sacred use; set apart from sin

Honor: To revere or value

Host: An army or vast number

I

Idolatry: The worship of anything other than God

Infidel: One who is unfaithful, unbelieving, and not to be trusted

Iniquity: Perversity, depravity, guilt, sin

J

Just: Righteous, that which is right and fair

Justice: Righteousness in government

K

Kingdom of Christ: The rule and reign of Christ as King both now and in the age to come

L

Law: Either the Mosiac Law or any human law; synonyms include commandments, ordinances, statutes, legal regulations, authoritative instructions, and teachings

Logos (LOW-gos): (Gk.) Word; the Word of God, either the Bible or Jesus

M

Manna: Food from heaven baked into a kind of bread, which God miraculously gave to the Israelites in the wilderness

Messiah: The Anointed One

Minister: A servant, an attendant, one who executes the commands of another

Mosiac Law: The law passed down by Moses from God to the Hebrew people at Mt. Sinai

O

Omnipotent: All powerful

Omnipresent: All present, being everywhere

Omniscient: All knowing

Ordained: Established and founded by God; founded, fixed, or appointed

P

Parousia (par-oo-SEE-ah): (Gk.) presence, appearing; Christ's Second Coming

Peace: Wholeness, quietness, contentment, health, prosperity; more than an absence of conflict or problems, but every part of life being blessed

Pentateuch: The first five books of the Old Testament

Power: Boldness, might, or strength, especially God's

Prophets: People filled with the Spirit of God and under the authority and command of God, who pleaded His cause and urged humanity to be saved

Profit: To gain or benefit to succeed, especially in Spiritual things; to move forward or succeed in one's efforts

Prosper: Examined, tested, tried

Psalm: A piece of music or a melody, especially one dedicated to God or a god

Purity: Sinlessness, without blemish spiritually

R

Ransom: To buy back or pay a price for a person, buying their freedom

Redeem: To ransom or purchase

Refuge: A shelter from rain, storm, or danger; stronghold or fortress; a place to run to and be secure when the enemy threatens

Repent: To turn back from sin and turn to God in faith

Righteous: To be declared not guilty

Righteousness: Justness, rightness, especially God's, which He works as a gift in His people; the right way to live as opposed to a lifestyle that treats others unfairly or unjustly

S

Sabbath: From "ceasing (from work)" in Hebrew; the day set aside to worship God

Sanctuary: The holy place, either in the Tabernacle or the Temple

Salvation: Rescue, safety, or deliverance, especially from eternal punishment

Satan: A fallen angel who is opposed to God and His people

Savior: Defender, rescuer, or deliverer; a term applied to Christ as the rescuer of those who are in bondage to sin and death

Scribes: Secretaries, recorders, men skilled in the Law during Jesus' day

Selah (SEH-lah): (Heb.) A pause in singing to allow for an instrumental musical interlude or silent meditation

Septuagint: "Seventy" in Latin; the Greek translation of the Hebrew Old Testament made by 70 Jewish scholars beginning in the third century BC

Servant: A slave, subject, or worshiper

Shalom (sha-LOME): (Heb.) Peace, prosperity, blessing

Shekinah Glory: The awesome presence of the Lord; His honor, fame, and reputation

Shofar (sho-FAR): (Heb.) A ram's horn; commonly used in celebration, as well as in signaling armies or large groups of people in civil assembly

Soul: The immaterial part of a person (what leaves the body after death), or the whole being, the self, one's life

Stiffnecked: Obstinate and difficult

Strengthen: To secure, make firm

Strive: To struggle, to exert oneself

Supplication: Seeking, asking, entreating, pleading, imploring, or petitioning

T

Tabernacle: A tent; the name of the portable temple constructed by Moses and the people of Israel

Tetragrammaton: YHWH; the four consonants of God's name, as the Jews would often write it

Torah: (Heb.) Law, instrument, or direction; the first five books of the Old Testament

Transfiguration: A change or transformation. Often refers to Jesus' transformation while on the Mount of Olives with His disciples Peter, James, and John, when His face shone like the sun and His clothing was white as snow (Matthew 17:2; Mark 9:2; Luke 9:29)

Transgression: Sin, rebellion, breaking God's Law

Try: In the sense of a test: refined or purified

Trumpet: A ram's horn or simple metal tube used in celebration as well as in signaling armies or large groups of people in civil assembly

V

Vanity (vain): A waste, a worthless thing, or simply emptiness

W

Wisdom: Prudence, an understanding of ethics

Woe: Grief or sorrow

Worship: Bow down deeply, show obedience and reverence

Wrath: Burning anger, rage

Y

Yahweh: God's name, often spelled with consonants only (see Tetragrammaton)

Notes

Notes

Notes

Notes